KOREA: THE LIMITED WAR

David Rees was born in 1928, and graduated from University College, Swansea, in 1952. He is a free-lance writer and a frequent contributor to the *Guardian* and *The Spectator*. He lives in Kensington, England, and is also the author of *Age of Containment: The Cold War*.

President Truman and General MacArthur during the Wake Island meeting, 15 October 1950, the only occasion on which the two men me

BY DAVID REES

KOREA:
The Limited War

PENGUIN BOOKS INC
BALTIMORE, MARYLAND

Penguin Books Inc., 7110 Ambassador Road,
Baltimore, Maryland 21207

First published by St. Martin's Press, Inc., 1964
Published in Pelican Books 1970

SBN 14 021192 6
Copyright © David Rees, 1964

Printed in the United States of America by
Kingsport Press, Inc.

To Margie and Goronwy Rees

CONTENTS

CHAP.   PAGE

Introduction: The Age of Limited War   x

PART I

THE NORTH KOREAN WAR
25 June 1950 – 25 November 1950

1	The Beginnings	3
2	The Toughest Decision	21
3	The Pusan Perimeter	36
4	Formosa and Korea: The Republicans Look West	55
5	Inchon: The Impossible Victory	77
6	Crossing the Parallel: Farewell to Containment	98
7	Meeting at Wake	115
8	The Drive to the Yalu	123

PART II

FROM VICTORY TO STALEMATE
25 November 1950 – 8 July 1951

9	An Entirely New War	155
10	The War of Containment	178
11	The Great Debate	196
12	The Recall	214
13	Bevan and British Rearmament	230
14	The Communist Spring Offensives	243
15	The MacArthur Hearings	264

PART III

WAR FOR PEACE
8 July 1951 – 27 July 1953

CHAP.		PAGE
16	Relaxing the Pressure	289
17	Deadlock at Panmunjom	310
18	The Cauldron of Rebirth	328
19	Peking: Bacteria for Peace	347
20	Tokyo: Blockade and Interdiction	364
21	The Fall of the Democrats	385
22	The Atomic Threat	402
23	The Truce of the Bear	421
	Postscript: Is Time on our Side?	435
	Appendices	455
	Acknowledgments	501
	Glossary of abbreviations	502
	Index	503

ILLUSTRATIONS

Plates

President Truman with General MacArthur during the Wake Island meeting, 15 October 1950   *Frontispiece*
US Army

The Pusan Perimeter   *US Marine Corps*   *facing page* 112

The Naktong River   *US Marine Corps*   113

Aerial View of Inchon   *US Air Force*   113

Inchon: RED beach assault, 15 September 1950   128
US Marine Corps

The Frontier of Containment   *US Army*   128

The First Iron Curtain capital   *US Army*   129

The Frontier of Liberation, Hyesanjin, 21 November 1950   *US Army*   240

The Meat Grinder   *Imperial War Museum*   240

The Chinese Tide Turns (*caption, read 25th for 2nd Div.*)   *US Army*   241

The Joint Chiefs of Staff, 1949-53   *US Army*   256

The Restoration of the ROK Government to President Syngman Rhee, Capitol Building, Seoul, 29 September 1950   *US Army*   256

The United Nations delegation to the armistice talks outside 'the United Nations house' at Kaesong, 17 July 1951   *US Army*   257

The Communist delegation to the armistice talks at Kaesong, 16 July 1951   *US Army*   257

The power house at the Supung Dam, Suiho Reservoir   368
US Navy

F-86 Sabrejets over Korea   *US Air Force*   368

The Hunters: MIG-15s   *US Navy*   368

The Bridges at Sinanju, linking Pyongyang with Sinuiju and Manchuria   *US Air Force*   369

Low level attack. An F.80 Shooting Star jet of the Fifth Air Force   *US Air Force*   369

Panmunjom, looking towards the north-west   *US Navy*   384

Pork Chop Hill   *US Army*   384

Panmunjom, 27 July 1953   *US Navy*   385

vii

General Mark Clark signs the armistice agreement at
the UNC base camp at Munsan, Korea *US Navy* 385
General James Van Fleet, CG, EUSAK, 1951-53 432
US Army
Vice Admiral R. P. Briscoe, COMNAVFE, 1952-54 432
US Navy
General O. P. Weyland, CG, FEAF, 1951-54 432
US Air Force
Lt.-Gen. George E. Stratemeyer, CG, FEAF, 1949-51 432
US Air Force
Lt.-Gen. Maxwell D. Taylor, CG, EUSAK, 1953-54
with Mark Clark and Col. Commanakous, 6 March
1953 *US Army* 433
Kim Il Sung *China Pictorial* 433
General Peng Teh-huai *China Pictorial* 433

Maps

The North Korean Invasion *page* 5
Retreat of the Naktong *facing page* 40
The Pusan Perimeter *page* 47
The Inchon landing 87
Capture of Seoul by X Corps 92
MacArthur's Divided Command 126
Military Situation South of the Yalu, Nov. 1950 149
Battle of the Chongchon 158
Retreat from Chosin 163
Communist New Year Offensive 179
UNC Advance to Line Kansas 192
First Communist Spring Offensive 246
Second Communist Spring Offensive 253
UNC Advance to the Iron Triangle 258
Panmunjom Area 295
The Main Line of Resistance 304
Main POW camps in North Korea 331
Sea and air war against North Korea *facing page* 370
Operation Strangle *page* 376
The MLR in the Pork Chop Area 412

Maps by H. C. Waddams and B. P. Elkins

Supposing a war to have commenced upon a just motive; the next thing to be considered is, when a Prince ought in prudence to receive the overtures of a peace. Which I take to be, either when the enemy is ready to yield the point originally contended for, or when the point is found impossible to be ever obtained; or when contending any longer, though with probability of gaining that point at last, would put such a Prince and his people in a worse condition than before.

The Conduct of the Allies.

INTRODUCTION

When foreign affairs were ruled by autocracies or oligarchies the danger of war was in sinister purpose. When foreign affairs are ruled by democracies the danger of war will be in mistaken beliefs.

ELIHU ROOT

There is . . . but one response possible from us: Force, Force to the utmost, Force without stint or limit, the righteous and triumphant Force which shall make Right the law of the world. . . .

WOODROW WILSON

The objective of war was conceived to be victory, that of diplomacy, peace. Neither could reinforce the other, and each began where the other left off.

HENRY KISSINGER

. . . the United States is neither omnipotent nor omniscient . . . we cannot always impose our will . . . we cannot right every wrong or reverse every adversity . . . there cannot be an American solution for every world problem. . . .

JOHN F. KENNEDY

In the autumn of 1915 the US Acting Secretary of War, Henry Breckinridge, was summoned to the presence of Woodrow Wilson. The President was trembling and white with rage and pointed to a newspaper report that the General Staff was preparing plans for the possibility of war with Germany. Was this true? Breckinridge replied that he did not know. Whereupon Wilson directed him to find out, and if the report were true, to relieve every officer on the General Staff and order him out of Washington.

Wilson's anger on this occasion would have been shared by most of his fellow-countrymen, and at any time since in most Western democracies a similar such revelation of military planning would arouse the wrath of many liberal-minded people. The story therefore not only illustrates the point that from the Revolution to the present day liberalism is the dominant American political philosophy, but that liberalism is invariably hostile to the Hobbesian view of man and society which permeates military thought in all countries. It is therefore against this background of the liberal attitude to foreign policy and war that the Truman Administration's decision to wage limited war in Korea, and the extremely hostile response to that decision by American public opinion, must be considered. The essence of the problem can be briefly stated; the Korean War was the first important war in American history that was not a crusade.

All Western nations are heavily influenced by the humane ideals of Christianity, the Enlightenment, the scientific revolution, and from these and other influences the liberal tradition has been distilled. As far as foreign policy is concerned the most important result of liberalism has been the dissociation of power and policy. Liberalism assumes that all states are equally interested in peace, that force and 'power politics' are always to be deprecated in international relations, and that the conflicting policies of countries and power groups can usually be harmonised by the same means that govern internal domestic differences — due process, reason, common sense, elementary morality and institutions such as the United Nations. War on the other hand is a completely different state of existence to peace, an aberration, and it can only be justified when fought as a crusade against tyrants in a mood of righteous indignation. Then, maximum force must be used to end the conflict as quickly as possible, and so total wars fought by democracies quickly take on an ideological character as witness the two great wars of the present century.

Moreover war must be divorced from 'political' considerations such as the balance of power, for in the liberal view Von Clausewitz's dictum that war is a continuation of politics by other means is immoral. A distinguished example of this all-or-nothing outlook may be seen in Bertrand Russell's consideration of preventive war against the USSR when Russia did not possess nuclear weapons, and his later advocacy of policies which would inevitably result in the submission of the West. Democratic public opinion therefore makes it immensely difficult for Western governments to use force as a rational instrument of foreign policy for the liberal assumes that *Realpolitik* is a dirty word rather than an indispensable ingredient of any foreign policy.

No Western nation adheres more to this liberal-puritan tradition than the United States. In addition to the limitless revolutionary goals of the Declaration of Independence, America enjoyed a century of invulnerable isolation before 1914 — thanks to British sea power — and the country was able to escape recognition of the relationship between force and diplomacy which European governments and peoples could not ignore. Both the total wars of our time ended in a spectacular victory, especially the second world war. Thus as late as March 1945, so little was the forthcoming struggle with the USSR and its allies foreseen that in the spirit of the Fourteen Points and the Atlantic Charter Roosevelt was able to tell a joint session of Congress that the system of alliances and the balance of power which had plagued international relations for centuries had ended with the successful Crimea Conference: 'I am sure that — under the agreement reached at Yalta — there will be a more stable political Europe than ever before. . . .' Indeed, Roosevelt's insistence on the complete primacy of military objectives during his war-time disputations with Churchill is an excellent example of the liberal attitude in action. MacArthur's ringing challenge to Truman in 1951 that there was no substitute for victory might well have been uttered by FDR eight or nine years previously.

Yet within two years of the end of the second war the Truman Administration had promulgated a containment policy against the USSR which was not meant to destroy Communism but to halt its expansion. Thus even before the Korean War there was widespread dissatisfaction in the United States at a policy which could not be projected in the traditional utopian terms. Then, in June 1950, came the North Korean invasion. Following MacArthur's great victory over the Communist armies as a result of his landing at Inchon it seemed to many in the US and also in the UN that within a Far Eastern context a total solution could be found for the Korean problem resulting in the unification of the country which had first been promised by the Allies in 1943.

But this was not to be. With the full Chinese Communist intervention in Korea during November 1950 the Truman Administration decided that the price of an united Korea would be, if not a general war, at least a wrong war with the wrong enemy, Communist China. It was therefore decided to limit the

American commitment to a defence of South Korea in an action which would give the North Atlantic powers time to build up what Secretary Acheson called 'situations of strength'. Moreover, further predatory moves by the Communist bloc would be deterred and a third world war averted by a policy of negotiating from strength, of which Acheson was the foremost western advocate.

Although the American constitution and many other statutes enshrine the principle of civilian supremacy over the military so great was the public and Congressional support given to the MacArthur plan for carrying the war to China that Truman could only retain control over his foreign policy by dismissing the General. As a result the President was quite unable to appear as a popular war leader over Korea, and hence the tragedy of the fall of the Democrats in November 1952 because those in office had been unable to reconcile what they thought a sound foreign policy with public opinion. Even if MacArthur had not existed there would have been some such challenge over a limited war, so great was the influence of the absolutist tradition at this time. The dilemma of reconciling foreign policy with public opinion thus remains, and the challenge exists for all great presidents.

In spite of its nominal adherence to containment the pre-Korean War defence policy of the Truman Administration was in fact largely based on air-atomic striking power. In improvising a containment policy in the Far East by meeting the Communist challenge by conventional forces the Administration through its military advisers, the Joint Chiefs of Staff, limited not only military action to the area of Korea, but, as noted, limited its objectives after the Chinese intervention to a restoration of the *status quo ante bellum*. In emphasising their North Atlantic foreign policy Truman and Acheson were also attempting to limit popular participation in the Korean War. Resources that could be spared for Korea were also limited, as well as the weapons systems and target systems which were used inside the peninsula. Not only were atomic weapons not used, but the important North Korean port of Rashin, for example, near the sensitive Soviet border, was partly restricted to UNC air attack.

In drastically limiting such military aspects of the war in Korea the Administration was only following Von Clausewitz's view of the political nature of war; since all relationships between states are dynamic ones, without this political direction war becomes uncontrolled violence. We read in *On War*:

> That the political point of view should end completely when war begins would only be conceivable if wars were struggles of life or death, from pure hatred. As wars are in reality, they are . . . only the manifestations of policy itself. The subordination of the political point of view to the military would be unreasonable, for policy has created the war; policy is the intelligent faculty, war only the instrument, and not the reverse. The subordination of the military point of view to the political is, therefore, the only thing which is possible.[1]

How far the absolutist opponents of Truman, Acheson and the Joint Chiefs disagreed with this view may be seen in MacArthur's testimony to the Senate Committees investigating his recall and the military situation in the Far East. MacArthur emphasised his utter abhorrence of war which he regarded in the nuclear age as a 'fantastic' solution to international tensions and a form of 'mutual suicide'. The entire efforts of society should concentrate on an attempt to outlaw war. But, the General went on, if the United States were inescapably involved in war — as in Korea — then all political considerations which restricted the military should be abolished and the war fought (as in the past) to a clear-cut solution as quickly as possible. The Truman Administration, complained MacArthur, had introduced a new and reprehensible concept into military operations: '. . . the concept that when you use force, you can limit that force . . .' It would be better to lose the war in Korea than to fight a limited war. . . .

MacArthur himself, as the President's chief opponent, did not completely sever policy from power for as will be seen his chief concern was that time was not on the side of the West and that the traditional approach to war which he believed in anyway should be emphasised to maximise support for his own policy. But testimony before the Jenner Sub-committee in 1954-55 by senior US commanders in the Far East during the Korean War showed how absolutist ideas commanded wide support

[1] p. 598 (translated by D. J. Matthijis Jolles).

among the generals. Thus Generals Mark Clark, James Van Fleet, George Stratemeyer, Edward Almond and Admiral Turner Joy all proclaimed their belief that war was a non-political instrument with which politicians should not meddle. And the Sub-committee's report recommended 'that methods should be explored to eliminate political interference in the conduct of hostilities and the negotiation of a military armistice.' Apart from Generals Matthew Ridgway and Maxwell Taylor it appears that every single senior American commander involved in the Korean War disagreed with the policy of limited hostilities. MacArthur of course with his charismatic personality was unique in personifying the liberal attitude to war; that so many of the other Korean commanders departed from the professional military ethic can probably be traced back to the civilian exaltation of victory over all other considerations in the second world war, as Samuel Huntington has pointed out.

Yet the practitioners of containment in Korea did not always succeed in effectively combining power and policy. Once the truce negotiations opened, ground operations against the Chinese armies were curtailed so that there was little incentive for the Communists to make peace. Not until after Eisenhower's victory in the 1952 presidential election with a mandate to end the war was the impasse at Panmunjom broken. Then at last the American atomic threat to the Chinese mainland combined with the post-Stalin thaw induced Peking to liquidate its Korean adventure. Yet this final phase of the Korean War, 'the talking war', in which the Communists so cleverly used integrated military action, propaganda and political manœuvring is a classic example of how they fuse power and policy. For the Communist belief in the absolute supremacy of political considerations in war, combined with their surgical skill in using force to advance their long-term aim of world domination, is the complete antithesis of the liberal approach to peace and war.

This leads us to one last consideration. What should be the ends of limited war in an age when total war means annihilation? Recent history suggests that limited wars have occurred more often than the debate over the great limited war in Korea suggests. The Greek civil war, the Malayan insurrection, the Arab-Israeli wars, Indochina, Suez, Hungary, the protracted Quemoy affairs, and the guerilla wars in Laos and South

Vietnam are all examples of limited war of one kind or another. Even the simmering Berlin crisis from the airlift to the early 1960s contains the elements of limited war. In all these clashes the schoolmen of limited war have differentiated carefully between wars fought between the satellites of great powers and those involving secondary powers only. It seems impossible to definite limited war in such a way that it can be applied to all clashes but perhaps Henry Kissinger's attempt in *Nuclear Weapons and Foreign Policy* is the best:

> A limited war . . . is fought for specific political objectives which, by their very existence, tend to establish a relationship between the force employed and the goal to be attained. It reflects an attempt to *affect* the opponent's will, not to *crush* it, to make the conditions to be imposed seem more attractive than continued resistance, to strive for specific goals and not for complete annihilation (italics quoted).[1]

Limited war is thus political war *par excellence*, in that 'purely military' considerations are excluded. Given the expansionist aims of the international Communist movement and the simultaneous existence of nuclear weapons, a strategy of limited forces for limited ends, whether it be called containment or negotiating from strength, is the only one which can conceivably fulfil any rational purpose if some sort of *modus vivendi* is ever to be reached with the Communists — or even, as is quite likely, if no *détente* is agreed in our time. President Kennedy's brilliant handling of the Cuban crisis in October 1962 has shown just how effective such a strategy can be. It may well be that a limited conflict on the Korean scale will never happen again. But the lessons of Korea and the actions of the two blocs in that Far Eastern war are relevant to every phase of the cold war, whether it be the Communist guerilla campaigns in South East Asia, the Geneva disarmament talks of such supreme trouble spots as Berlin and Cuba. Only when the West fully appreciates that power and policy, like idealism and *Realpolitik*, can never be separated and that limited war is the fusion of both will we ever meet the Communist challenge decisively on the most important battleground — our own minds.

[1] p. 140.

PART I

THE NORTH KOREAN WAR
25 June 1950–25 November 1950

CHAPTER ONE

THE BEGINNINGS

> We see, therefore, that war is not merely a political act
> but a real political instrument, a continuation of political
> intercourse, a carrying out of the same by other means.
>
> Von Clausewitz

> Communists do not in the least idealise acts of violence.
> They would be very pleased to drop violent methods if
> the ruling classes agreed to give way to the working classes.
>
> Joseph Stalin

THE INVASION

W AR came to Korea at dawn on a Sunday morning. At 0400 hours local time[1] on 25 June 1950 the Korean People's Army launched its offensive against the Republic of Korea. After a co-ordinated artillery and mortar barrage at many points seven infantry divisions, an armoured brigade, and other independent units moved south across the Parallel on a 150-mile front from the Yellow Sea to the Sea of Japan. The invasion force included 150 Russian-built T-34 tanks. Opposing the North Korean forces which numbered about 90,000 men were elements of four South Korean divisions and a brigade. They lacked any heavy equipment and were stationed in defensive positions below the 38th Parallel.

The offensive progressed from west to east and the Ongjin peninsula was soon sealed off with Kaesong occupied by about 0930. Meanwhile the main North Korean effort, launched by two infantry divisions and supported by most of the tank brigade, struck down the Uijongbu corridor, the historic invasion route

[1] Dates and times of events in Korea and Japan are given throughout in Far Eastern time which is 14 hours ahead of Washington (EST) and 9 hours ahead of London (GMT). Thus 0400 25 June in Korea would be 1400 EST, 1500 EDT 24 June, in New York and Washington; and 1900 GMT, 2000 BST 24 June, in London.

taken by the Mongols and the Manchus which leads to the ROK capital of Seoul. Chunchon in the central mountain chain was threatened by another two Communist divisions, while supporting a thrust down the east coast were amphibious landings at Kangnung and Samchok, the last over forty miles south of the Parallel. Later in the day railway stations, airfields and petrol storage tanks in the Seoul district were attacked by North Korean Yak fighters. At 1100 Radio Pyongyang in the northern capital announced that the North Korean Government had declared war against South Korea because of an invasion of the North launched by 'the bandit traitor Syngman Rhee'. Rhee, the broadcast went on, would be arrested and executed. Just over two hours later at 1335 the North Korean Premier, Kim Il Sung, claimed over the radio that as North Korean territory in the Haeju area had been attacked by South Korean forces that morning, South Korea would have to take the consequences of North Korean counteraction. By 1500 the North Koreans were claiming that their forces were ten to fifteen miles south of the 38th Parallel along the entire front.

The first news of the invasion had reached the American military advisory group in Seoul around 0600 when five US advisers with the ROK Seventeenth Regiment in the Ongjin peninsula reported that the unit was about to be overrun. These men were then flown out by two liaison aircraft sent from Seoul. Not for another three hours did the news reach the US Far East Command headquarters in Tokyo when it received a copy of an emergency message sent by the American Embassy military attaché in Seoul at 0925 to the Pentagon. Washington had first heard the news of the invasion from an unofficial source when shortly after 8 p.m., Saturday, 24 June, the United Press office in the capital was cabled by its Korean correspondent that a large-scale North Korean attack was under way. The State Department knew nothing and as it was early Sunday morning in the Far East the telephone circuits to Korea were closed.

At last at 9.26 p.m. the State Department received a cable from Ambassador John Muccio in Seoul which ended: '. . . It would appear from the nature of the attack and the manner in which it was launched that it constitutes an all-out offensive against the Republic of Korea.' The surprise in Seoul, Tokyo and Washington was equally great, for although it was known

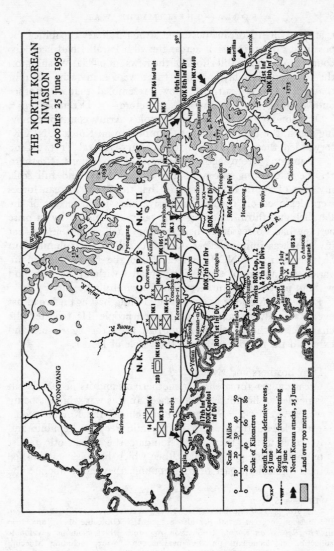

THE NORTH KOREAN
INVASION
0400 hrs 25 June 1950

that the North Koreans possessed strong military capability the possibility of an invasion across the 38th Parallel had been discounted. When the full shock of the news hit official Washington the following Sunday morning there were many who thought that the complete surprise shown resembled that of another Sunday morning not nine years before—7 December 1941.

On Monday, 26 June, as the People's Army continued moving south, the United Nations Commission on Korea (UNCOK) forwarded these conclusions to Secretary-General Trygve Lie: '. . . judging from actual progress of operations Northern regime is carrying out well planned, concerted and full scale invasion of South Korea, second, that the South Korean forces were deployed on a wholly defensive basis in all sectors of the Parallel, and third, that they were taken completely by surprise as they had no reason to believe from intelligence sources that invasion was imminent.'[1] Later in its full report submitted in September 1950 UNCOK characterised the North Korean invasion as 'an act of aggression initiated without warning and without provocation, in execution of a carefully prepared plan'.[2]

Earlier on Monday at 0930 Kim Il Sung had again broadcast over Radio Pyongyang to the Korean people. He repeated the charge that the South Koreans had been the aggressors and exhorted his troops to liberate the whole of Korea:

Dear brothers and sisters!
Great danger threatens our motherland and its people. What is needed to liquidate this menace? In this war which is being waged against the Syngman Rhee clique, the Korean people must defend the Korean Democratic People's Republic and its constitution, they must liquidate the unpatriotic fascist puppet regime of Syngman Rhee which has been established in the southern part of the republic; they must liberate the

[1] UN doc. S/1507.
[2] A/1350, p. 32, para. 202. This UNCOK report covers the background to the invasion in great detail. See also S/1496, UNCOK cable of 25 June, 1960 in *The Record on Korean Unification 1943-1960* which contains a valuable collection of documents on the invasion, pp. 86-105, including Muccio's message and S/1507. The standard work on military operations for the first five months of the war is Appleman, *South to the Naktong, North to the Yalu*, which makes great use of interviews on all aspects of operations. It has never been verified that the NK Government declared war.

southern part of our motherland from the domination of the Syngman Rhee clique; and they must restore the people's committees there — the real organs of power. Under the banner of the Korean Democratic People's Republic we must complete the unification of the motherland and create a single, independent, democratic state. The war which we are forced to wage is a just war for the unification and independence of the motherland and for freedom and democracy. . . .[1]

Within a few hours of this speech North Korean tanks were approaching the outer suburbs of Seoul.

THE TWO KOREAS

The Asian peninsula which would become the scene of the first military effort by a world organisation's multi-national army, as well as of the fourth most costly, yet undeclared, war in blood and money in the history of the United States, was little known in the West.

Korea is a mountainous country about 600 miles long from north-east to south-west and about 150 miles wide, but between Pyongyang and Wonsan the peninsula narrows to a 'waist' of under 100 miles, an area that was to achieve great strategic significance during the Korean War. In the north, the Yalu and the Tumen rivers separate it from Manchuria; there is an eleven mile boundary with the USSR at the mouth of the Tumen. Not only does the climate with its extremes of temperature ranging from 105° F. to −40° F. render the country unsuitable for the operations of a Western mechanised army, but an even greater handicap is the extremely rugged terrain. The main mountain chain runs down the east coast from the Yalu to Pusan, with a spur branching off to Mokpo. Proceeding inland and northwards, the mountains reach 9,000 feet, and although on the western agricultural side of the peninsula there are places where the going is good for armour, the characteristic scenery is one of twisting, narrow valleys covered with rice paddies and terraces out of which climb jagged peaks, the hills of Korea.

The earliest name for the country was Chosun (The Land of

[1] *Pravda*, 27 June, 1950, quoted in Berger, *The Korean Knot*, p. 101.

the Morning Calm), an indigenous tribal name. The medieval Koryo dynasty with its capital at Kaesong gave the country the name by which it is known now, but from 1392 until its annexation by Japan in 1910, Korea was ruled by the Yi dynasty which moved the capital to Seoul, although maintaining the country's tributary status inside the Chinese Confucian system. After the Manchu invasions of the seventeenth century a self-imposed period of isolation lasted until 1876 when Japan, only twenty-three years after Perry's expedition, herself forced a trade treaty on the hermit kingdom. This event, coupled with Korea's strategic position between the declining imperialism of China, the rising imperialism of Japan, and the permanent imperialism of Muscovy, precipitated the modern history of Korea. From Korea any one of the powers could menace the other two; in adjacent seas hovered western men-of-war, their captains ever eager to assist in carving out lucrative spheres of influence for their countries. By 1894 rival Japanese and Russian intrigues in Korea had gone far enough for the Celestial Empire to attempt to restore its suzerainty. The Japanese response astonished the world. Landing at Inchon the invaders swept through Pyongyang to the Yalu, which they then crossed to take Port Arthur. As a result China was ejected from Korea, which became completely independent, and events built up for the final showdown between Japan and Russia.

The British and Americans supported Japan as an opponent of Czarist expansionism and when the Russian fleet at Port Arthur was attacked without the courtesy of a declaration of war during 1904, Western countries insisted on their neutrality. Once again a landing at Inchon was followed by an advance to the Yalu. The utter destruction of the Czar's Far Eastern army at Mukden followed. Japanese paramountcy in Korea was established and moreover recognised by Theodore Roosevelt's Administration despite the protests of Korean nationalists among whose leaders was the young patriot Syngman Rhee. In 1910 Korea was annexed by Japan and became the Chosen Government-General; a generation of colonial rule followed during which national sentiment was stifled and the country modernised, with a certain degree of industrialisation.

The recent history of Korea begins with the Cairo Declaration of 1 December 1943 by Roosevelt, Churchill and Chiang

Kai-shek when a promise of the eventual unity and independence of the country was given: '. . . The aforesaid three great powers, mindful of the enslavement of the people of Korea, are determined that in due course Korea shall become free and independent.' The qualification reflected Roosevelt's opinion that the Koreans should be educated in democracy by a trustee-ship of the great powers. According to the Yalta papers the President at that conference proposed to Stalin that the wards of Korean democracy should be the US, the USSR, and China, and that it was not necessary for Britain, presumably as the only imperialist power on the allied side, to take part. Stalin, however, remarked to Roosevelt that if left out the Prime Minister might 'kill us', and this part of the conference ended with informal agreement for a four-power trusteeship. There matters remained until Potsdam, when the military of the three participating powers agreed that following Russia's entry into the Pacific War there should be some demarcation line in Korea between American and Soviet operations. Without consulting the Russians, US Army planners decided that as at least two major ports would be required to sustain any American occupation forces in Korea the line should be drawn north of Seoul to include Inchon as well as Pusan. This line, which was approved by General Marshall, then US Army Chief of Staff, ran near, but not on, the 38th Parallel.

On 26 July the Potsdam Declaration reaffirmed the Cairo provisions and when the USSR adhered to the Declaration on entering the war against Japan on 8 August all four powers were committed to Korean independence 'in due course'. The next development was precipitated by the impending surrender of Japan after the atomic bombing of Hiroshima (6 August) and Nagasaki (9 August). Immediately following the Japanese offer of surrender on 10 August all senior agencies of the US Government discussed the draft of General Order No. 1 which General MacArthur, as Supreme Commander for the Allied Powers, would issue as the directive under which all Japanese forces would surrender. As regards Korea the order provided that all Japanese forces north of the 38th Parallel would sur-render to the Soviet commander, while those south of the line would capitulate to the American commander. After approval by the State Department, and the Joint Chiefs of Staff, President

Truman also approved the order on 15 August, and it was subsequently cleared with the British and Soviet Governments. MacArthur then issued the directive on 2 September, the day of the Japanese surrender aboard the *Missouri* in Tokyo Bay.

American forces were spread all over the Western Pacific and not until 8 September did a regiment of the XXIV Corps land at Inchon; the next day Lt.-Gen J. R. Hodge, Corps Commander, and Vice-Admiral Kinkaid, Seventh Fleet, received the surrender of the Government-General at Seoul. The Russians had entered Korea on 12 August and their forces already had reached the 38th Parallel.

The Parallel, so soon to become the Korean iron curtain, had no topographic or economic basis. It cut through provinces, counties and towns, dividing the relatively industrialised north of the country from the agricultural south, so that any long-term benefits to be gained from the Japanese industrialisation of Korea were completely nullified, as of course the resources of one zone were complementary to the other. The census in 1949 showed that of Korea's thirty million people about twenty one million lived south of the 38th Parallel, but besides the new ideological hostility between the rulers of the two occupation zones there was already a historic division between north and south. Agrarian reform had made some progress in the north, while the more conservative south lagged behind. But there was too a certain strategic reality about the 38th Parallel as a dividing line. It had been proposed as a demarcation line between the Japanese and Russian spheres of influence in 1904-5, and after 1950 it would be again recognised by the contestants in Korea as reflecting a natural strategic division as the fighting see-sawed up and down the peninsula.

Politically, the destinies of the north and the south had been polarised long before the joint occupation of 1945. The leading South Korean politician, Dr Syngman Rhee, had established the exiled Korean Provisional Government in Shanghai as long ago as 1919. He had attended Princeton, had known Woodrow Wilson, and had lobbied tirelessly for his cause in the US between the wars. A nineteenth-century liberal with autocratic tendencies, Rhee had increasingly become identified with the conservatives. In 1945, at the age of sixty-nine, he was unquestionably the best known of all Korean leaders.

In the north, the emerging leader was Kim Il Sung, né Kim Sung Chu, who had taken the name of a dead Korean resistance hero. A member of the Communist underground in Korea which had been active against the Japanese as early as 1935, Kim had fled to the Soviet Union in 1938, and is reputed to have fought at Stalingrad with the Red Army, returning to Korea in 1945 as a thirty-five-year-old major in the Soviet occupation forces. Another focus of Korean nationalism existed in Yenan, far from the influences of Wilsonian idealism, where escaped guerillas and bandits formed the Korean Volunteer Corps to fight the Japanese and the Kuomintang alongside the Chinese People's Liberation Army.

Within the first few months of military government it became obvious to the American occupying forces that the trusteeship plan was fanatically resented. Immediate independence was wanted. Nevertheless at the Moscow foreign ministers conference in December James Byrnes and Molotov agreed that a Joint Commission representing the two occupying powers be convened in Korea to work out trusteeship proposals for a period of up to five years. The Joint Commission met in Seoul in March, 1946, but soon became deadlocked. South Korean political parties, demanding immediate independence, demonstrated violently against the trusteeship proposals and as the Russians refused to hear representatives of parties opposing the Joint Commission, this left the Communists as the only group they would welcome. On grounds of both expediency and principle the Americans could not tolerate the exclusion of the Rightist groups and the Commission adjourned *sine die* in May.

Moves were now made by both sides to create Korean states in their respective occupation zones. An Interim Legislative Assembly, half its members appointed, half elected, met in Seoul at the end of 1946, and in May 1947 the Korean elements of the military government were designated the South Korean Interim Government. The Americans remained as advisors with financial control; SKIG was dominated by a Rightist Rhee-led coalition. Events in the north were equally predictable. Early in 1946 a national Provisional People's Committee, with Kim Il Sung as chairman, easily took over control of the Soviet zone, for the Russians had never run their zone through military government as such, retaining the people's committees of the coalition

'People's Republic' set up immediately after the liberation and which had been suppressed in the south. In the summer of 1946 all North Korean political parties were streamlined into the Korean National Democratic Front which in November obtained 97% of the votes in an election for new people's committees. A convention of the committees created the Korean People's Assembly and in February, 1947, 'provisional' was dropped from the title of the national People's Committee. An embryonic Korean People's Republic had been smoothly created.

One more attempt was made to solve the insoluble problem on a bilateral basis when the Joint Commission met again in May 1947. Once again violent demonstrations eventually stalled the Commission. An American proposal for all-Korean free elections was rejected by the Russians; a counter proposal for an assembly composed of *equal* representation from north and south was rejected by the Americans. Most suggestions for a peaceful unification of Korea ever since have been based on one or another of these mutually unacceptable proposals which would lead to either an anti-Communist assembly dominated by the South-North population ratio, or one which could be wrecked by Communist parliamentary obstructionism and extra-parliamentary *agitprop*. And with the collapse of the Joint Commission, the Korean hot potato was now presented to the United Nations.

In September, 1947, Byrnes's successor in the State Department, George Marshall, because of the 'inability of the two powers to reach agreement', asked the world organisation to unite Korea.[1] On 14 November Korean unification formally became a United Nations responsibility with the creation of the Temporary Commission on Korea (UNTCOK) to supervise elections. The Eastern bloc boycotted the voting on the grounds that Korea was a four-power matter and the Russians refused access to North Korea when the Commission arrived in Seoul. When the UN Interim Committee authorised elections in South Korea, this was characterised as another illegality, for the operations of that body itself was regarded by the USSR as an illegal attempt to bypass the Security Council.

On 10 May 1948 South Korean elections were held, later described by the chairman of UNTCOK as 'a valid expression

[1] Goodrich, *A Study of US Policy in the United Nations*, p. 29.

of the free will of the electorate in those parts of Korea which were accessible to the Commission'; UNTCOK also favoured immediate unification of Korea under a regime developed from the South Korean government.[1] Three months after the elections, on 15 August 1948, the Republic of Korea was formally proclaimed with Syngman Rhee as its president. Parallel developments were also taking place in the north to match the victory of the conservatives in the South Korean polls and the subsequent ending of the occupation regime. On September 3rd a new Supreme People's Democratic Assembly ratified a new constitution and on the 10th Kim Il Sung assumed office as Premier of the Democratic People's Republic of Korea, the day following the proclamation of the new satellite state.

Three months later on 12 December 1948 the UN General Assembly recognised that the South Korean Government was the only one based on 'the free will of the electorate' in Korea and a permanent UN Commission on Korea was created. The US, the UK, France and Canada recognised the ROK, but neither Korea state became a UN member, due to the activities of the opposite bloc. At the end of 1948 two antagonistic Korean regimes founded on opposed ideologies and interests, and each claiming jurisdiction over the whole of Korea, faced each other over the 38th Parallel.

THE DEFENCE PERIMETER

The North Korean invasion, as noted, came as a complete surprise to the United States Government. Korea had been written off in the formulation of US defence policy at the end of the 1940s. As early as May 1947, the then Secretary of War, Robert Patterson, had urged the State Department to consider withdrawal of the two US divisions, 45,000 men, from Korea for budgetary reasons. In September that year General Albert Wedemeyer reported to President Truman that only by a massive commitment of ground troops could Chiang be saved from the

---

[1] McCune, *Korea Today*, p. 230-1. McCune's book has a useful survey of the US and Soviet policies in their respective zones, as well as the moves leading to the creation of the ROK and the DPRK.

Communists; as far as Korea was concerned Wedemeyer recommended the withdrawal of the occupying troops from both zones and that a South Korean defence force be built up to meet the threat from the North. The JCS, Eisenhower, Nimitz, Spaatz, then submitted a memorandum to Secretary Marshall, 'The Joint Chiefs of Staff consider that, from the standpoint of military security, the United States has little interest in maintaining the present troops and bases in Korea. . . .'[1]

Any US forces in Korea, the memo went on, were a liability as any offensive operation the US might undertake in Asia would by-pass that peninsula. Enemy occupation of Korea could be neutralised by air action. Furthermore, nationalist disorders in Korea could make the position of the occupation forces untenable. There was also the consideration of 'the present severe shortage of military manpower'. This was getting near to the heart of the matter for the economy minded Republican 80th Congress had cut defence appropriations to the bone. The war had ended at the beginning of fiscal year 1946, ending in June that year; defence expenditure for that year had been cut to $45 billion. For fiscal 1948, defence appropriations were only $11.25 billion, and following Truman's electoral victory over Dewey in November 1948, defence spending was pegged to a figure of $15 billion, the maximum which the economy — or rather the taxpayer — was supposed to be able to carry. The army was the chief victim of the axe; when the Korean War broke out there were only one and one third divisions in the continental US. It was a classic case of mortgaging security to economy of which even the British public could have been proud.

The strategic corollary of this economy drive was the emergence with the fiscal '48 budget of the USAF as the dominant element in defence strategy. Aircraft were assumed to be the most economic manifestation of military power and thus doubly popular electorally, for as the late Elmer Davies once remarked, it was understood in Washington that only ground troops have mothers. The report of the Finletter Commission on air policy in January 1948 further emphasised the dominant role of the air-atomic policy when it stated that the Russians would not

[1] Truman, *Memoirs II*, 343.

possess nuclear weapons until the end of 1952. This encouraged the belief that the Communists would not use force until they had a large nuclear stockpile and the means to deliver it. If war came at any time it would be total war with a major Soviet invasion of Western Europe, and in that case the USAF's role would cease to be that of a deterrent, and become the one instrument capable of bringing victory. The belief in total war and SAC's strategy of annihilation meant that such outposts as Korea were only too dispensable.

In due course withdrawal of the two divisions was approved by the JCS and MacArthur, but shortly after the evacuation started disturbances led to the ROK Assembly asking in September 1948 for the withdrawal to be halted. In February 1949 the Far East Commander was in favour of 'prompt withdrawal' of troops from Korea, and in the following month he publicly excluded Korea (and Formosa) from the American defence perimeter and reported to Washington at the same time that the ROK forces were strong enough to justify withdrawal.[1] Meanwhile Moscow had withdrawn its forces from North Korea by December 1948.

Besides the political reasons for the withdrawal, there was strong professional reluctance in the US Army to fight on the mainland of Asia; in case of all-out war Korea could become another Bataan. The last units of the occupation force therefore left on 29 June 1949, and with them went MacArthur's responsibilities in Korea. For since independence, it was the State Department which dealt with the ROK.

Although it was suggested in Congress by Representative Judd of Minnesota — an old China hand — that the Communists would take over in a year, the Administration and many others saw the threat to the ROK as a matter of internal security. From the very inception of the ROK Communist subversion had seemed a major threat. A Communist uprising at Yosu, in south west Korea during October-November 1948 had been ruthlessly suppressed, and at one time one quarter of the country was

---

[1] Truman, *Memoirs II*, p. 347; *New York Times*, 2 March 1949. In May 1951 MacArthur said that he had 'concurred' in what he now thought to be 'a very grave mistake.' 'There was nothing peculiarly threatening at that time in Korea when the decision was made to get out,' the General went on. Senate *MacArthur Hearings*, pp. 242-3.

under martial law. In 1949 Pyongyang was claiming there were 77,000 Communist partisans in the field, and border raids were another problem, carried out by forces — on both sides — up to battalion strength, although these increased in intensity from the north as artillery was used against Ongjin twice in the summer of 1949. Added to terrorism and propaganda was economic discontent which produced serious inflation. Rhee's inherent authoritarianism, greatly accentuated by these difficulties, alienated many supporters inside and outside the government as his police used arbitrary methods against all opponents. But there was a direct connection between the paramilitary methods used by the Communists and absence of many civil liberties in the South.

There had been generous US economic aid in an attempt to shore up this precarious dependency; the US army had provided $250 million during the occupation, and during fiscal '50, $120 million ECA funds had been granted by Congress, with another $100 million voted for fiscal '51. Military assistance was difficult. The US Army had once again helped with about $110 million worth of equipment on their departure from Korea, but Rhee's bellicosity had limited military aid. During February 1949, the President had predicted that his army 'could defeat North Korea within two weeks', and in October he was 'sure we could take Pyongyang in three days'. In February 1950 he stated that the hour of unification was approaching. Eventually a $10.9 million military aid programme was arranged in January 1950, but only a few hundred dollars worth of signal equipment had actually arrived in Korea by the time of the invasion. With about 98,000 men organised in eight divisions, the ROK army was little more than a constabulary force. Only 65,000 men had received unit training. They lacked heavy artillery, tanks and aircraft, and hardly merited the description given them by General Roberts, head of the US Korean Military Advisory Group (KMAG), 'the best doggoned shooting army outside the United States'.

There seemed to be little appreciation of the real capability of the Korean People's Army which was undergoing a swift build-up in early 1950. Activated in February 1948 with the amalgamation of sections of the Korean Volunteer Corps with resistance groups from the Soviet zone, the KPA was a formidable force. KVC elements from Yenan had been edged out of power by the Soviet faction, for there was a bitter struggle between those who preached Maoist tactical doctrine based on a refinement of the large scale guerilla methods which had defeated Chiang Kai-shek and those adherents of more orthodox Red Army doctrine in which armour and artillery were regarded as necessary in any attempted large scale military action. By 1950 most of the key positions in the KPA were held by the Soviet faction, a victory concurrently reflected politically in the defeat of the Yenan Korean Communists, formerly the Korean Independent Alliance, inside the Korean CP, or, as it was known, the Korean Labour Party.

In June 1950 the KPA possessed seven divisions ready for combat, three other newly-activated divisions, two independent regiments, and an armoured brigade, the 105th, which was raised to the status of division a few days after the outbreak of war. Each infantry division was triangular in organisation, and possessed organic artillery and self-propelled gun battalions. In training and equipment it was an extremely well prepared force, particularly strong in artillery, and possessing in the T-34 tank a powerful weapon by any military standards. There were also five brigades of the paramilitary Border Constabulary to bring up the front-line strength of the North Korean ground forces at the outbreak of war to about 135,000 men. There was a small Korean People's Armed Forces Air Corps of 150-200 aircraft, mostly Yak-9 fighters and Ilyushin-10 ground attack bombers. A torpedo boat navy was insignificant.[1]

It was the intention and not the threat of the KPA that was misunderstood in Tokyo and Washington. The possible capability of this force to invade the ROK was acknowledged, but a series of reports from the Intelligence Section of the Far East Command (FECOM) insisted that guerilla activities and psychological warfare were most to be feared. In March 1950, for example, G-2 of the Far East Command reported that 'it is believed that there will be no civil war in Korea this spring or

---

[1] Due to the many thousands of NK POWs taken after Inchon more is known about the political and military background of the PPRK than of any other Communist satellite state in the post-war period. See particularly Appleman, pp. 7-13; and Montross and Canzona; US Marine Operations in Korea, 1950-53, Vol. I, The Pusan Perimeter, pp. 19-36.

summer,' an opinion often seen in these offerings from October 1949 onwards.

In the Senate Hearings after MacArthur's dismissal, Louis Johnson, Defence Secretary at the time of the North Korean invasion, said that 'Wolf' had been cried so often in Intelligence reports, it was difficult to know what to believe. Acheson summed up on this problem: 'all these agencies (FECOM, State, Department of the Army, CIA) were in agreement that the possibility for an attack on the Korean Republic existed at that time, but they were all in agreement that its launching in the summer of 1950 did not appear imminent'.[1] Thus when the Secretary of State told the National Press Club on 12 January 1950 that the US defence perimeter in the Pacific extended from the Aleutians to Japan through Okinawa to the Philippines, and that areas outside the line, such as Korea and Formosa, would have to rely on self-defence and the UN, he was expressing perfectly the result of the total-war policies of the Administration which had excluded such a challenge as that which arose on 25 June 1950.

Speculation as to Communist motives for launching the June invasion must still remain largely conjectural. Why was invasion chosen so unsportingly in Korea to destroy the ROK? With Soviet expansionist adventures in Europe and the Near East precluded by NATO and the Truman Doctrine, it may be relevant to remember that in 1949 with the Japanese Peace Treaty in sight a re-armed Japan might have been drawn into a Pacific pact, Far Eastern NATO. The Japanese C.P. reached its post-war peak in 1949 with only 9.5% of the vote, so little help from that quarter would be forthcoming to offset such a move.

In December 1949 Mao Tse-tung arrived in Moscow for his first known trip abroad to negotiate the Sino-Soviet treaty, announced on 15 February 1950, which was specifically aimed at 'Japanese imperialism' or 'any state that may collaborate in any way with Japan in acts of aggression'. Military invasion and conquest of the ROK would not only be an opportunist exploitation of a promising local situation, but it would show the Japanese that Rhee, like Chiang, was a defenceless puppet

---

[1] For Acheson's review of the large amount of Intelligence material on North Korean preparations see *Hearings*, pp. 1990-92. Also Willoughby, *MacArthur 1941-51*, pp. 330-34.

of the Americans. The forces of Japanese neutralism might then be won over to the CP in that country. (In the event, of course, both Rhee and Chiang were saved by the June invasion.) But even if Japan remained in the American defence orbit, the Communist planners could easily have argued that the acquisition of South Korea, with Pusan only a hundred miles from Kyushu, would be a valuable strategic gain to their own defence perimeter running through Sakhalin or the Kuriles across Korea to Port Arthur.

Acheson's Press Club speech only reflected a military weakness which the Communists knew already, that the US did not have the men to garrison South Korea, and that a mere UN commitment in Korea *might* mean that an indigenous Communist attack in an Asian country would be tolerated by the West out of weakness and miscalculation. This reasoning of course would influence the Chinese to acquiesce in the Soviet plans for the invasion, for a successful take-over in South Korea would help to implement Chinese ambitions everywhere throughout South East Asia: even in spite of past differences Stalin must surely have told Mao of his grand Korean design during the Chinese leader's ten weeks in Moscow which ended in March 1950. That no major diversionary move occurred on the Eurasian frontier between East and West when the Korean war started indicates that the war took place inside an Asian rather than a global orientation as far as the Sino-Soviet bloc were concerned. This supposition may be supported by the fact that Communist propaganda throughout the war was angled to represent the US and the UN war effort as Western imperialist aggression aimed at eventually destroying the revolt of colonial nations all over the world, but particularly in Asia.

Lastly, the planning of the invasion. It was a Soviet war plan, reportedly worked out by the Russian General Antonov, and during the winter of 1949-50, the remainder of the KVC crossed into Korea, Sino-Korean relations, long strained, were patched up, and large scale Russian deliveries of tanks, artillery and heavy equipment were made to North Korea. Furthermore, later interrogation of captured Chinese Communist POWs in Korea revealed that there was a ' somewhat ambiguous ' major strategic redeployment of the Chinese Communist Fourth Field Army from south China to Manchuria beginning as early as April 1950

— a prescient precautionary move in case the KPA overreached itself.[1]

With this well-trained and heavily-armed Soviet satellite army now fully ready for action, and with the current political confusion and strategic weaknesses of American Far Eastern policy, together with the political and economic chaos in the ROK, there could hardly have been a better moment to launch a North Korean invasion across the 38th Parallel than in June 1950. Even the return of the moderates in the May 1950 elections for the ROK assembly and the slight improvement in the guerilla position in the South would indicate that this was the moment to strike before Korean unification by armed invasion became too risky. Throughout June Radio Pyongyang broadcast new proposals for the peaceful unification of Korea, appealing to the people over the heads of the ROK Government, stigmatised as a clique of traitors. The last and most impressive of these proposals was issued on 19 June when the People's Army was taking up its position just north of the Parallel. 'The soundest strategy in war is to postpone operations until the moral disintegration of the enemy renders the mortal blow both possible and easy.'

---

[1] Whiting, *China Crosses the Yalu*, p. 23. On relationships between the DPRK and the USSR and the PRC during 1948-50 see Chaps. 2 and 3. Of Peking's troop moves to the north-east in the spring of 1950 Whiting comments: 'It placed Peking's best troops in a position to backstop Pyongyang, in the event North Korean plans went awry.' The detailed account here of the Chinese build up in Manchuria during the summer and the autumn and the movement into Korea is based on the *Chinese Communist Forces (CCF) Army Histories* compiled by the US Eighth Army's G-2 from intelligence estimates and checked against prisoner interrogation in Korea.

CHAPTER TWO

THE TOUGHEST DECISION

This was the toughest decision I had to make as President.
TRUMAN, *Memoirs*.

THE PRESIDENT AND HIS ADVISERS

SHORTLY after Muccio's telegram reporting the 'all out offensive' arrived in the State Department, Dean Rusk, Assistant Secretary, telephoned Acheson at his farm at Sandy Spring, Maryland. Acheson in turn telephoned Truman at Independence, Missouri, where the President had gone home for the weekend to attend to family business. 'Mr. President,' the Secretary said, 'I have very serious news. The North Koreans have invaded South Korea.'

Truman and Acheson decided to alert the United Nations and a call went to Trygve Lie, the Secretary-General. There was still a chance the fighting might be merely a raid. At 2 a.m., after further telegrams from Muccio and MacArthur left no doubt that this was the real thing, Acheson again spoke to Truman; they agreed to alert the Security Council and to bring the invasion before it as a threat to world peace. Under the Charter economic sanctions, a blockade or collective military action could be authorised.

The Council assembled at 2.20 p.m., Sunday 25 June. The second dawn of the war was coming up over Korea. Jacob Malik had boycotted the Security Council since January 1950 as a protest against its refusal to seat the Peking regime instead of the Chinese Nationalists. Malik's own absence in the Soviet view could only add to the illegality of the proceedings. But there were still eleven members around the horseshoe table; John Chang, the ROK's observer, had been asked to the proceedings.

By 6 p.m. the US resolution which called for a cease-fire and a North Korean withdrawal to the Parallel had been passed

9—0—1, with Yugoslavia abstaining. It also called for all members 'to render every assistance to the United Nations in the execution of this resolution'.[1]

Acheson had again telephoned Truman at about 11.30 a.m. Sunday. He had predicted that the resolution would be passed but that the North Koreans would ignore it. Truman immediately decided to return to Washington and at 2 p.m. the *Independence* roared off towards the east from Kansas City Municipal Airport. The President kept to himself for the flight and landed at Washington at 7.15 EDT. After a hurried dinner at Blair House, just across Pennsylvania Avenue from the White House which was being reconstructed, the first crucial conference began. Besides Truman and Acheson, there were present the Defence Secretary, Louis Johnson; Army Secretary, Frank Pace; Air Secretary, Thomas Finletter; Navy Secretary, Francis Matthews; Chairman of the JCS, General of the Army Omar Bradley; Army Chief of Staff, General Collins; Air Force Chief of Staff, General Vandenberg; and the Chief of Naval Operations, Admiral Sherman. Also from the State Department there were Under Secretary Webb, Assistant Secretaries Rusk and Hickerson, and Ambassador-at-large Philip Jessup.

Truman has written in his *Memoirs* that there was 'complete, almost unspoken acceptance on the part of everyone that whatever had to be done to meet this aggression had to be done. There was no suggestion from anyone that the United Nations or the United States could back away from it.'[2] The President was certain that an uncontested invasion of South Korea could start a chain reaction of aggression which would eventually start a world war in the way that fascist aggression before 1939 had ended in war. This was the American 'Rhineland'—which this time would be disputed by force. It would also mean the end of the United Nations unless this challenge could be met.

Three preliminary moves were ordered. Arms and equipment were to be sent to the ROK from Japan; MacArthur was given wide discretion to use his air and naval forces to evacuate US nationals—there were 500 KMAG personnel and 1,500 civilians

---

[1] The complete text of all relevant UN resolutions on Korea may be seen in *The Record on Korean Unification 1943-60.*

[2] See Truman, *Memoirs II*, Chap. 22 for the Blair and White House story, Also Goldman, *The Crucial Decade*, Chap. 8.

in Korea; and the Seventh Fleet, placed under MacArthur's operational control, was ordered north from the Philippines to Sasebo, Japan. (But as MacArthur's GHQ considered the outbreak of general war a possibility, the ships were in fact diverted to Okinawa away from Soviet and Chinese air bases.) As yet no action was taken on a State-Defence recommendation that the Fleet neutralise Formosa by preventing if necessary both a Chinese Communist invasion of the island and Nationalist forays towards the mainland.

Both Sherman and Vandenberg thought that the North Koreans could be stopped by air and naval action, but Collins thought that if the South Koreans were broken, then US ground forces would be necessary. Bradley remarked that the US would have to draw the line somewhere, and while he thought Russia was not ready for a general war over Korea, they were testing the United States, 'and the line ought to be drawn now'. As the meeting adjourned Acheson showed the President a message from John Foster Dulles, the US special ambassador negotiating the Japanese Peace Treaty, who had just returned to Tokyo from Korea when the fighting started; '. . . to sit by while Korea is overrun by unprovoked armed attack would probably start a disastrous chain of events leading most probably to world war. We suggest that the Security Council might call for action. . . .'

Throughout Monday the news from Korea got worse. President Rhee appealed for more US aid. Later in the day MacArthur signalled that 'a complete collapse' was imminent and at 9 p.m. there was another conference at Blair House.[1] The decision was quickly taken by the President. Louis Johnson was ordered to call MacArthur on the scrambler phone and to tell him Truman's instructions. The General was to use his air and naval forces to help the ROK south of the Parallel. With his vesting of command in Korea, MacArthur was also ordered to send the Seventh Fleet to the Formosa Straits to prevent Communist action 'that might enlarge the area of conflict'.

[1] The first North Korean aircraft to be destroyed by the USAF, a Yak fighter, had been downed by an F-82 Twin Mustang on a covering mission for evacuation aircraft in the Seoul area about 1150, K.T., 27 June. This was about the time of the second Blair House meeting in Washington on Monday night when the initial decision to intervene was taken. See Gurney, *Five Down and Glory*, p. 239.

The next morning, Tuesday 27 June, Truman saw Congressional Leaders who approved of his action, and the same day, Thomas Dewey, titular Republican leader, also supported the President. For the first time for many months there was domestic agreement on Far Eastern policy, occasioned not only by the support given to South Korea, but by the placing of the Fleet in the Formosa Straits, which in effect protected the Nationalists.

At 12.30 an official 'Statement by the President' announced to the world the decisions taken the previous evening: '. . . I have ordered United States air and sea forces to give the Korean Government troops cover and support. The attack upon Korea makes it plain beyond all doubt that Communism has passed beyond the use of subversion to conquer independent nations and will now use armed invasion and war. It has defied the orders of the Security Council. . . . Accordingly I have ordered the Seventh Fleet to prevent any attack on Formosa . . . I am calling on the Chinese Government on Formosa to cease all air and sea operations against the mainland . . . A return to the rule of force in international affairs would have far reaching effects. The United States will continue to uphold the rule of law. . . .'

Later the same day, the Security Council met again. The US delegate was pressing for a resolution which would endorse US action and provide for an international military effort to aid South Korea. Its authority for intervention under the existing resolution was imprecise. At 10.20 the vote was taken on the new American resolution which included the recommendation that the members of the United Nations 'furnish such assistance to the Republic of Korea as may be necessary to repel the armed attack and to restore the international peace and security in the area'.

The resolution was passed 7-1-2 with Britain, France, Nationalist China, Cuba, Ecuador and Norway voting for the resolution. Egypt and India abstaining, and Yugoslavia, after tabling an alternative cease-fire proposal, voting against. For the first time in history an international body had voted force to meet force. And the next day, Wednesday the 28th, the US National Security Council was told that the British Government had already responded to the resolution by placing its naval forces in Japanese waters under MacArthur's control.

Thursday, 29 June, saw the climax of the crisis. Seoul had fallen on 28 June and at 7 a.m. 29 June MacArthur signalled the Pentagon that ROK casualties were approaching 50%. The best doggoned shooting army outside the US was falling apart. There was doubt whether the Han River line just south of Seoul could be held, announced Tokyo over the telecon.[1] Mac-Arthur himself had gone to Korea on 29 June, flying to Suwon in dirty weather in his Constellation, the *Bataan*. The airfield was under attack by North Korean YAKs, and his Constellation returned to Japan with orders to pick him up at 5 p.m. Suwon was the temporary home of KMAG and the Advanced Command Group, a survey team sent to Korea from Tokyo on the 27th; and although President Rhee's Government had already moved to Taejon, he himself was there to meet MacArthur, who then motored to the banks of the Han. There the shambles of the ROK army was in full flight from the tanks and aircraft of the North Koreans. Without US ground troops the ROK seemed lost. But MacArthur himself was still confident that he could hold the line of the Han if Washington could let him have two of the four divisions of the Eighth Army in Japan. Moreover, within an hour MacArthur had conceived a plan not only to save South Korea, but to defeat utterly the North Korean Army as well.

Anticipating his directives, during the flight to Suwon, Mac-Arthur had already ordered Lt-Gen. Stratemeyer, Commanding General, Far East Air Forces, to bomb North Korean targets above the 38th Parallel. MacArthur's authority was 'permissive, not restrictive', Maj.-Gen. Courtney Whitney, MacArthur's confidant, has written; 'Here was no timid delay while authorisation was received from Washington; here was the capacity for command decision and the readiness to assume responsibilities which had always been MacArthur's forte.'[2]

But readiness to assume responsibility was found not only in Suwon and Tokyo that Thursday. At 4 p.m. — it was now 5 a.m. Friday in Tokyo — Truman gave his first press con-

---

[1] Abbreviation for teletypewriter conference. Incoming messages were projected on a screen in the respective operations rooms.
[2] Whitney, *MacArthur: His Rendezvous with History*, p. 326.

ference since the beginning of the crisis. 'We are not at war,' he told a reporter, and also allowed quotation of his agreement that the United States was supporting a United Nations police action in Korea. It was an exchange the President would later regret when the decision not to ask for a declaration of war from Congress, because of the need for immediate action and to emphasise the collective nature of the UN intervention, would be heavily attacked by the Opposition. Moreover, too, political opponents could place sole responsibility on the President for the exercise of his war powers in sending American forces to Korea.

From his press conference Truman went to a meeting of the National Security Council in the White House at 5 p.m. Besides those present at the earlier conferences were Dulles and Averell Harriman, head of ECA activities in Europe. It was obvious to all that sea and air forces were unable to stop the North Koreans. State and Defence now recommended that air and naval forces be used above the 38th Parallel, that small units of US service troops be used to help the ROK Army throughout South Korea, and that for the purpose of defending Pusan port and airfield, American combat troops should be used. This would safeguard the one port in Korea through which a later build-up of forces could take place.

The President was uneasy about committing troops. But Acheson produced a Soviet reply to an American note sent on the 27th in effect asking the Soviet to call off the North Koreans. The reply suggested that Moscow, although unwilling to do anything about halting its Korean satellite, would not intervene in Korea against the US forces. This ambiguous note stated that events in Korea were an internal affair of that country, that intervention was illegal, but little more.

The note opened up the way for the sending of American ground forces, for it now seemed less likely that a general war — with Korea as a preliminary diversion — was imminent. 'I wanted to take every step necessary to push the North Koreans back behind the 38th Parallel,' Truman has written. 'But I wanted to be sure that we would not become so deeply committed in Korea that we could not take care of such other situations as might develop.' The new orders lifting the restrictions on the 38th Parallel and authorising the despatch of the service and combat troops to Pusan went out from Washington at 5.40

p.m. on Thursday as the conference ended. Full intervention had been carried one stage further as the risks of general war became slightly less obvious.

Later that evening Acheson was back at the White House with an offer from Chiang of 33,000 men for the Korean fighting. Truman was at first sympathetic to the idea, but the Secretary argued that their dispatch to Korea would weaken Formosa itself, and that their re-equipping would be necessary. Full discussion was left to the morning when the final act of the drama of the toughest decision was played out. At 3 a.m. Friday, 30 June a message from Tokyo reached the Pentagon. MacArthur was asking for permission to send a Regimental Combat Team[1] to Korea. Unless the North Koreans were held, the whole country would be overrun. The General also asked if he could use two of his divisions from Japan to build up for a counter offensive. Collins then had a telecon 'conversation' with MacArthur. Weren't the service and combat units already ordered to Pusan sufficient until the President had consulted his advisers? MacArthur repeated that Korea was lost unless ground troops were sent in.

Collins contacted Frank Pace, the Secretary of the Army, who telephoned Truman at 5 a.m. The President immediately authorised MacArthur to send in the RCT. A White House conference was called for 8.30 to discuss the sending of the two divisions. At the meeting the subject of Chiang's offer came up first. To Acheson's further objection that Nationalist troops in Korea might mean the Chinese Communists entering, the Joint Chiefs of Staff added their objections that these Formosan troops would be as helpless as Rhee's army without tanks and heavy equipment. 'I then decided,' writes Truman, 'that General MacArthur should be given full authority to use the ground forces under his command.' This meant that all four divisions of the Eighth Army in Japan, or whatever forces MacArthur could spare, were to be sent to Korea. Finally, at Admiral Sherman's suggestion, a naval blockade of the entire Korean coast was ordered. These orders which completed the military commitment of the United States to South Korea went out from the Pentagon at 1.22 p.m. on Friday afternoon, 30 June, 0222 hours, 1 July in Tokyo. The first two companies of the 24th Infantry Division

[1] Equivalent to a British Brigade Group.

arrived in Pusan by air on 1 July from Japan and pushed off towards the north to engage the North Koreans. Aircraft, ships, survey teams and service troops could all be withdrawn, but with the infantry moving north through the monsoon rains went their country's prestige and an irrevocable commitment to great national and international ends. The ground forces would have to stay in Korea until they were destroyed or driven out. Without declaration the Korean incident had become the Korean War. For Truman the decision to intervene was 'the toughest decision' of his entire presidency.

CRUSADE FOR CONTAINMENT

Many strands of idealism and calculation went into the making of the Korean decision, in reality the series of decisions taken in Washington between 25 and 30 June, 1950. First of all it represented a heroic and deliberate attempt to uphold the rule of law in international life, to see that aggression was repelled and collective security upheld. As such it was overwhelmingly welcomed in the US as it was in Western Europe by non-Communists. Compared with the occupation of the Rhineland, Austria, and Czechoslovakia by the Third Reich, the occupation of South Korea would represent no such similar dramatic access of strength to the Communist bloc, but the President and his advisers thought that here was a challenge of wills between West and East that had to be met. Acceptance of a Korean *anschluss* would lead to other Communist advances that would eventually result in another world war which the West would have to fight with fewer resources. The historic analogy with the Nazi aggression of the 1930s was present in all minds; the 38th Parallel had to be defended if the whole cycle of Twentieth Century wars was to be broken — 'these damnable wars', General Collins was to call them in the MacArthur Hearings. Rarely in history has a great power sacrificed so much for so little material gain as the United States would do in defending the barren hills of Korea. For the Korean decision was primarily a political decision in the Jeffersonian tradition of American idealism.

But the decision also represented a strategic answer to the question posed by the North Korea attack: Where and how does a world power maintain its position without risking anni-

hilation? For in defending South Korea the Administration was
applying its own policy of *containment*, lately discounted in
practice by the air-power policies of SAC. Containment had
been formulated by George Kennan, head of the State Department's Policy Planning Staff in 1947. Instead of accepting Communism's post-war advances until a general war started, Kennan
argued that the United States should contain its opponent's
moves by a series of interlocking political-economic-military
alliances. Communism was a vast historic force:

> Its main concern is to make sure that it has filled every nook
> and cranny available to it in the basin of world power. But
> if it finds unassailable barriers in its path, it accepts these philo-
> sophically and accommodates itself to them. The main thing
> is that there should be pressure, increasing constant pressure,
> towards the desired goal. There is no trace of any feeling in
> Soviet psychology that that goal must be reached at any given
> time. . . .
>
> In these circumstances it is clear that the main element of any
> United States policy towards the Soviet Union must be that of
> a long-term, patient but firm and vigilant containment of
> Russian expansive tendencies. It is important to note, however,
> that such a policy has nothing to do with outward histrionics:
> with threats or blustering or superfluous gestures of outward
> 'toughness'. . . .
>
> It is rather a question of the degree to which the United States
> can create among the peoples of the world generally the im-
> pression of a country which knows what it wants, which is
> coping successfully with the problems of its internal life and
> with the responsibilities of a World Power, and which has a
> spiritual vitality capable of holding its own among the major
> ideological currents of the time. . . .
>
> . . . the United States has it in its power to increase enor-
> mously the strains under which Soviet policy must operate, to
> force upon the Kremlin a far greater degree of moderation
> and circumspection than it has had to observe in recent years,
> and in this way to promote tendencies which must eventually
> find their outlet in either the break-up or the gradual mellow-
> ing of Soviet power. . . .[1]

[1] Kennan, *American Diplomacy 1900-1950*, pp. 118, 119, 126-7.

This was a radical departure from the absolutist traditions of previous American foreign policy which had veered between isolationism in peace time and crusades for total victory in war time. As Communism was a major threat for the foreseeable future, the reply would take many forms, depending on the circumstances — a Hamiltonian expression of American calculation and self-interest, arrived at after close concert with the nation's allies. Essentially containment was a policy of pragmatic *Realpolitik*, a fusion of idealism, economic aid, diplomacy, and force. It was historically analogous to the balance-of-power strategies, based ultimately on the 'far-distant, storm beaten ships' of the Royal Navy, which Great Britain had manipulated so successfully for several centuries against continental tyrants. Two total wars meant that Britain's world supremacy was at an end. The United States would now have to take up the sceptre, and during the first few months of 1947 when containment was promulgated in Washington, Truman, Marshall, Forrestal and Acheson were all extremely conscious of living through a supreme period in their country's history.

The Truman Doctrine which had helped to save Greece and Turkey in 1947 was a form of containment, as was the victory won under American supervision over the Greek Communist insurgents two years later. The strategy of the Berlin Airlift was another example, but above all containment's most impressive and successful monument was the interlocking system of alliances and arrangements which linked the US to Western Europe through the Marshall Plan, NATO and a development brought on by the Korean War, SHAPE. Here was the creation of a new balance of power which might halt the Soviets without the holocaust.

But reliance on SAC alone to win or deter total war meant that the Administration had ignored the necessary military basis of containment, preparation for limited war. Containment had never been applied to the Far East, as the planners considered that here neither the institutions, nor the potential moral and material strength existed on which to build. A greater mistake was that until well after the defeat of the Kuomintang, Mao Tse-tung was not thought to be a 'real' Communist. Now, by an act of strategic improvisation in Korea, the United States would contain this Communist adventure, but would insist on limiting its commitment as much as possible. Western Europe was the main preoccupation of the Administration which for a year after the North Korean invasion regarded it as a diversion to mask a possible Soviet move against the NATO area. For it was in Western Europe that the main threat to North America lay. If the USSR could dominate the second largest concentration of industrial power on earth for which the US had already fought the Third Reich, and where alone lay the bases from which SAC could either deter a Russian invasion of West Europe or deliver a knock-out nuclear blow if the worst happened, then the whole balance of world power would swing against the Western Hemisphere. It followed then that the defence of South Korea would reassure NATO allies that the US would defend the alliance at all costs; and Washington would also emphasise that it would not allow too many resources to be diverted to the Far East. In this way Truman's decision protected Western Europe's security: 'We let it be known that we considered the Korean situation vital as a symbol of the strength and determination of the West.'[1]

Complex 'Pacific' considerations also influenced the Administration. Japan was another heavily industrialised area with strategic bases which must be kept in American hands for the defence of the Pacific. The fall of South Korea would menace this vital link in the defence perimeter. That much was simple. But the decision to neutralise Formosa was influenced by, and would influence, domestic political forces quite apart from its military importance on the flank of any fighting in Korea. Before 25 June, Formosa's occupation by the Chinese Communists had been considered inevitable by the Administration, a position that had been savagely attacked by the Republicans. The island's neutralisation was welcomed by the China Lobby, but not by America's allies, especially the British who regarded it as a unilateral US action. Thus the decision on Formosa meant that the Administration's freedom to manœuvre between the British and the Republicans was limited from the very outset of the Korean War, and would continue to decrease as the war went on.

Nowhere was the combination of idealism and self-interest in the Korean decision more evident than in the way UN

[1] Truman, *Memoirs II*, p. 358.

approval was sought for the American intervention. In the Security Council resolution of 27 June, calling for assistance to repel the armed attack, there was both retroactive approval for American action to help ROK and authorisation to create an international force to fight in Korea. The idealist Utopian, moral demands of American policy were met by the call from the world body to fight for collective security: the use of force in defence of containment was thereby sanctified by the authority of the United Nations. Confusion between these elements by the public would in future embarrass the Administration, for at first the emphasis was on the crusading idealistic aspects of intervention rather than the calculations of containment. American spokesmen in the UN emphasised that the South Korean regime had been supported by the US, and brought into being by UN supervised elections, so there was a moral commitment from both the UN and its most powerful member to protect South Korea. The US, as Truman and Acheson would time and time again emphasise, also believed in the long term aims of the UN, and in supporting to the limit UN collective action, the United States was rationalising its idealistic objectives of replacing — wherever possible — multilateral security treaties by the authority of the UN.

American global political objectives were therefore vastly helped by the UN association, but in a moral rather than a material way. Eventually fifty-three out of fifty-nine UN members in June 1950 approved the Second Security Council resolution; forty countries offered aid in one form or another and fifteen members besides the US sent armed forces while another five sent medical units. But the predominantly Western nature of the enterprise was shown by the fact that most of the non-Korean ground troops were from NATO or Commonwealth countries, although Latin America sent token supply contributions. Apart from India's medical unit — the Nehru government had 'accepted' the second Security Council resolution — there was little support from the Afro-Asian bloc which did not want to be involved in the clash between West and East.

The relatively small UN contribution, always excepting that of the US, was shown by the figures at the end of 1951 when the UN Command had stabilised the lines. Over half of the total forces under the UN command in Korea were American,

out of a total of nearly 600,000. In January 1953 as the war drew
to its close and the ROK army provided an ever-increasing manpower contribution which eventually reached about 400,000 out
of the 768,000 men under the Eighth Army, the two American
companies which had landed in Korea on 1st July 1950 had
grown to 350,000 men, including about 100,000 USAF and service
personnel. And although the detachments from the other Allied
countries totalled only 44,000 men they were disproportionately
valuable in emphasising the collective, coalition nature of the
Korean war effort.

From the very beginning of the war the Communists claimed
that intervention by the US and the UN was illegal. In the
Soviet view the fighting was an internal affair, and therefore the
Security Council was precluded by the Charter from any consideration of the matter. American intervention, initially taken
before the resolution of 27 June, was illegal not only because it had
ex post facto authorisation, but because both China and the USSR
were not represented on the Security Council and major issues
had to be decided by not less than seven members including
the five permanent members. A 'Kuomintangite' held China's
seat and the USSR had boycotted the agencies of the UN since
January 1950 as a protest against Peking's non-admission. Gromyko's long note of 4 July went on to compare United States
support of the ROK to British support of the Confederacy (sic),
and mentioned the Anglo-American intervention against the
Bolsheviks in 1919: 'It is universally known how this inter-
ventionist adventure ended.'

These important legalisms were refuted at length by Attlee on
5 July moving a motion of support in the House of Commons
for the British Government's action in backing the resolution
of 27 June. (The motion was carried without a division, only
two members speaking against it.) The Prime Minister
said that the ROK was a fully constituted and recognised
government, resulting from elections supervised by the United
Nations. And time was of the essence if the aggressor were to be
defeated. Characteristically, he discussed Rhee's bad political
reputation:

I am not concerned to defend the [ROK] Government, or to
estimate whether it is a good or a bad Government, but I never

knew that an excuse for assaulting someone peacefully pursuing his way was that his character was not very good. . . .

Dealing with the accusations of illegal intervention, Attlee went on:

The ordinary principles of international law recognise that any State which is attacked has a right to defend itself, and that any other State has a right to assist the state which is the subject of aggression. The Charter of the United Nations has not taken away this inherent right. On the contrary, it expressly states in Article 51 that 'nothing in the present charter shall impair the inherent right of individual or collective self-defence if an armed attack occurs against a member of the United Nations, until the Security Council has taken the measures necessary to maintain international peace and security.' It is true that Article 51 only mentions in this connection an armed attack against a member of the United Nations, and the Korean Republic is not a member. But the purpose of Article 51 is not to create a new right but merely to make it clear that an inherent right vested in every state is not prejudiced. . . . The broad principle is that all states may be endangered if the aggressor is allowed to get away with the fruits of aggression in any part of the world.[1]

It was obvious that if the Soviet Union *had* vetoed the Korean proposals in the Security Council, the Allies would have invoked Article 51 and demanded approval of their action from the General Assembly, a contingency which gave rise to the 'Uniting for Peace' resolution passed in November 1950 which specifically provided for emergency meetings of the Assembly to bypass a Security Council made impotent by the Soviet veto.

As for the absence of Communist China, the Nationalist delegate could only be replaced by the action of the Security Council — and this had not been done. Moreover, Attlee said, a practice had grown up in the Council that if a permanent member abstained or absented itself this did not invalidate the resolution. The Soviet Union itself had accepted this custom,

[1] House of Commons Debates, 5th series, Vol. 477, Coll. 485-95 for Attlee's speech.

which the Secretary-General had ruled did not amount to a veto. For although the UN Charter did demand in Security Council decisions 'the affirmative vote of seven members, including the concurring vote of permanent members,' it also required that the Council 'should be able to function continuously.' The Charter never intended that absence by a permanent member should impose what Attlee called 'a blanket veto' on all proceedings. He concluded therefore that the absence of the Soviet delegate 'did not invalidate these resolutions.'

Two days after Attlee's speech, on 7 July, the Security Council passed another resolution on Korea, one which provided the complete identification of American military power there with the aims of the United Nations. The creation of an 'unified command' was recommended and the United States was asked 'to designate the commander of such forces' supplied to the command by UN members. 'In the course of operations against North Korean forces', the resolution went on, the Command could use the UN flag as well as the flags of its various national contingents. The American stand for a new containment policy in Korea was thus almost formally declared a crusade for collective security by the world body.

Following this resolution, on 8 July President Truman designated General of the Army Douglas MacArthur as the Commander-in-Chief of the Unified Command, the United Nations Command. CINCFE put on a new hat as CINCUNC; and the General Headquarters, Far Eastern Command (GHQ FEC) then became the principal part of General Headquarters, United Nations Command (GHQ UNC). The new Command was formally established by MacArthur on 24 July; he continued to regard himself acting primarily as CINCFE responsible to the President, who was, of course, the agent of the United Nations.

The problems and responsibilities facing the General were immense. Even the thought of failure in his mission, he confided to Averell Harriman in August, 'makes me feel sick in my stomach'. Could MacArthur's forces stop the headlong advance of the People's Army towards Pusan?

CHAPTER THREE

THE PUSAN PERIMETER

There is never a convenient place to fight a war when
the other man starts it.

Adm. ARLEIGH BURKE, in 1958

I realised that on the highest levels there was, for a
little while at least, a feeling that only the Air and Navy
forces would be required to contain this thing.

MATTHEW RIDGWAY, *Soldier*

DELAYING ACTION

'ALL great enterprises have to be launched on sacrifices',
Philip Deane has written of the Eighth Army's holding
action during the first weeks of the war which alone made
possible future operations in Korea. At first, the Korean People's
Army seemed irresistible. 'When it struck, it struck like a
cobra', MacArthur later remarked in the Senate Hearings after
his recall. According to a captured North Korean intelligence
report, it was expected that South Korea would be conquered
within two months of the invasion; it appears that Kim Il Sung
had set 15 August as the date for the total liberation of Korea,
the fifth anniversary of V-J Day.[1]

There were good grounds for the Communists' high expectations. By the end of June over half the ROK Army had been
destroyed and in Japan the four infantry divisions of the
Eighth Army had been stripped to 70% of their established
strength by defence economies. There were only ninety-two
medium tanks in the whole of MacArthur's command and these
were mothballed because they were too heavy for Japanese roads.
The first Americans into Korea were two rifle companies from
the 21st Infantry Regiment, 24th Infantry Division. These men
were airlifted into Pusan on 1 July with understrengthed

---

[1] Montross and Canzona, I, p. 18; Appleman, p. 345.

mortar, recoilless rifle and rocket launcher (bazooka) platoons. In command was Lt.-Col. Charles B. Smith of the Regiment's 1st Battalion. Next day Task Force Smith arrived in Taejon by train, and after a reconnaissance Smith later ordered a defensive position to be set up about three miles north of Osan, about twenty-five miles south of the Han River. By 4 July, the task force was assembling at Pyongtaek about ten miles south of Osan; it had been joined by a battery of 105mm. howitzers.

On that same Independence Day the Advanced Command Group was absorbed by the headquarters of the US Army Forces in Korea (USAFIK), activated at 0001 4 July under the command of Maj.-Gen. William F. Dean, CG, 24th Division, who had arrived in the Taejon the previous day. As Task Force Smith prepared to meet the North Koreans, apparently thought to be a musket-armed rabble who would quickly be sent packing back to the 38th Parallel, other UN operations were taking place against the invaders. On 2 July the Small North Korean Navy of torpedo boats which had supported the east coast landings were quickly sunk or run aground near Chumunjin by a small Anglo-American task group. Two days later detailed instructions were sent from Tokyo for the implementation of the blockade of Korea which had already been ordered.

The 2 July also saw a B-29 Superfortress strike from Okinawa against Yonpo airfield near Hungnam in North Korea where most of the NKAF's Ilyushin light bombers were based. During the next two days, 3-4 July, a series of strikes was launched against airfields and other installations in the Pyongyang-Chinnampo west coast area by aircraft operating from the USS *Valley Forge* and HMS *Triumph* in the Yellow Sea. Over thirty NK aircraft were claimed destroyed on the ground. This phase of the war at any rate was soon over for by the end of July with its Yaks shot out of the sky and its Ilyushins destroyed on the ground, the NKAF no longer existed as a fighting force. Command of the air having been established over enemy territory, henceforward UN aircraft were engaged on close support to the ground troops and on bombing targets north of the firing line.

It was left to the ill-prepared US and South Korean infantry to bear the brunt of the North Korean offensive. In the early hours of 5 July, Task Force Smith, 540 men including the gunners, took up their positions north of Osan. Shortly after

0700 an NK tank column was seen approaching from Suwon and 0816 the first shots were fired between American and Communist ground forces in Korea. The T-34s sailed through Smith's position and carried on clanking down the road to Osan after four had been knocked out; 2.36" bazooka and howitzer shells tended to bounce off the thirty-five ton Soviet tank which mounted an 85mm. gun. . . . Later in the morning the American position across the highway was enveloped by NK infantry, supported by more T-34s, and at 1430, after having held off the Communists as long as possible, Smith ordered a withdrawal to avoid being overrun. The Americans scattered over the hills to Ansong and points south having lost all their equipment. Following this action, the North Koreans continued south and on the 6th forced an American withdrawal from the next blocking position at Pyongtaek, held by men of the 34th Regiment of Dean's division. Dean was so disappointed at this withdrawal that the regimental commander was relieved. The 34th Regiment now guarded Chonan while the 21st took up positions in front of Chochiwon, south on the easterly road to the Kum River. Both regiments now suffered heavily as they fought two NK divisions with armour, but the initial momentum of the Communist advance was delayed appreciably. Not until a week after the fall of Osan were the invaders lined up on the Kum, forty miles to the south, where the bridges were blown in 24th Division's sector on 12/13 July.

While the defences of the Kum in front of Taejon were being prepared a new command structure had been created as more American reinforcements arrived. In Japan the Eighth Army had been commanded by Lt.-Gen. Walton H. Walker, one of Patton's Corps commanders in Europe, and on the afternoon of 13 July he took over control of his army in Korea, Eighth US Army in Korea (EUSAK). Walker's headquarters were in a school in Taegu—there was a relay station in the town on the old Tokyo-Mukden cable—and also on the 13th the ROK Army moved its HQ to Taegu from Taejon. The Army was soon followed by the ROK Government. On the 14th, command relationships were formalised when President Rhee wrote to MacArthur placing under the Unified Command all the ROK armed forces. Thus under what was known as 'the Taejon Agreement' Walker directed the ROK Army through its Chief of Staff, at this time Lt.-Gen. Chung Il Kwon, although of course the ROKA was never part of EUSAK. This arrangement continued throughout the war and still forms the basis of the UNC in Korea.

Following the commitment of the 24th Division, the 25th Infantry Division (Maj.-Gen. William B. Kean) landed in Korea between 10 and 15 July, and on the 18th the 1st Cavalry Division (infantry) under Maj.-Gen. Hobart R. Gay went ashore in an amphibious landing at Pohang-dong on the east coast. These forces were then sent into blocking positions south and east of Taejon. While the 24th Division sought to delay the main Communist thrust down the Seoul-Taejon axis, the North Koreans were also advancing on a wide front across the entire Korean peninsula. To the east of Chonan, five NK divisions and an armoured regiment were in action in the central mountains where Chungju was the key road centre. From here these forces were in a position to force the two important passes through the Sobaek Mountains at Mungyong and Tanyang which crossed the watershed between the upper valleys of the Han and the Naktong and thus led from central Korea to the far south. On the east coast the NK 5th Division had swung inland at Kangnung and after rampaging through the Taebaeks to Yongwol had emerged again on the east coast at Ulchin. By 17 July this NK division was in Yongdok, only ninety miles north of Pusan; although the position was critical the ROK 3rd Division managed to hold the Communist advance in a series of bloody battles. Then, as the North Koreans to the west of Yongdok pushed through the Han-Naktong watershed, all attention was concentrated on the 24th Division's delaying action at Taejon.

Standing behind the moat of the Kum River, Taejon commands the main road south to the Naktong and Pusan; and from the city radiates a network of routes into south and west Korea. Walker hoped that a delaying action here would give him enough time to deploy his other two divisions in Korea and so slow the retreat to the Naktong; once behind the river barrier he was convinced he could hold on in Korea. But while at this time many US detachments fought with suicidal heroism, Philip Deane, who covered these few weeks of the war for the London *Observer*, later recorded that others were baffled by the reasons for intervention. Consequently morale suffered: 'What is this police action?' Others, according to Marguerite Higgins in *War in Korea*, 'threw down their arms cursing their government for what they thought was embroilment in a hopeless cause'. Now, at Taejon, further sacrifices were demanded.

On 13-14 July the NK 4th and 3rd Divisions crossed the Kum at Kongju and Taepyong-ni, held by the exhausted 34th and 19th Regiments respectively. The tactics used here and at Taejon a few days later by these NK formations were a classic illustration of the tactics that carried the People's Army from the Parallel to within thirty miles of Pusan. First, the North Koreans would develop frontal pressure by infantry assault groups, using tanks wherever possible; then, while the defenders were pinned down, flanking forces would move to the rear, establish roadblocks and complete the envelopment. Success was facilitated at first because US units tended to deploy near the embanked roads, or bunds. These invariably ran above the paddy fields which, stinking with their fertiliser of human excrement, covered all the space between the hills so easily taken by the Communist infantry working to the American rear.

Following the debacle on the Kum the two regiments fell back to near Taejon City and dug in. To the east, Dean's 21st Regiment tried to keep the road to Okchon open. When the North Koreans opened their assault against the city on the morning of 19 July, Dean was in Taejon; the incoming artillery fire against the airstrip made him remark it was as intense as anything he had seen in Europe. That evening, unknown to the defenders, the Communists were already moving round to the east of Taejon, and next morning the battle came to its climax as the T-34s entered the city. New 3.5" bazookas had been flown from the US to Korea and were used for the first time at Taejon on the 20th when they accounted for eight tanks. Altogether at least fifteen T-34s were destroyed that day, but the odds were far too great for Dean to hold the city with 4,000 men. In the flaming exploding inferno of Taejon Philip Deane saw Dean, 'a gallant general . . . immaculate in battle dress directing bazooka fire against tanks not fifty yards away'. After personally supervising the perforation of a T-34, the general was at last overrun. His division's last reserve — himself — had been committed. For his defence of Taejon he was awarded the Medal of Honour. He escaped from the city but, like many of his men,

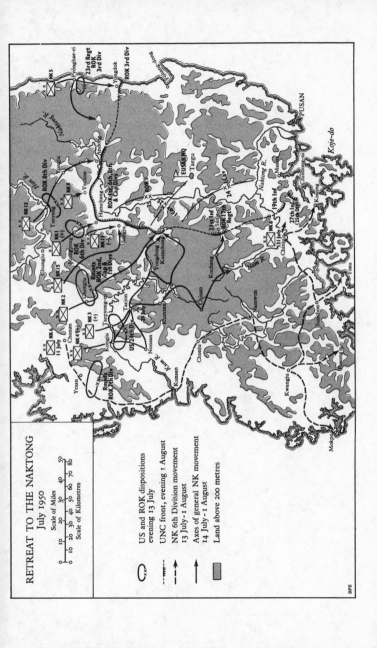

RETREAT TO THE NAKTONG
July 1950

Scale of Miles
0 10 20 30 40 50
Scale of Kilometres
0 10 20 30 40 50 60 70 80

US and ROK dispositions
evening 13 July

UNC front, evening 1 August

NK 6th Division movement
13 July–1 August

Axes of general NK movement
14 July–1 August

Land above 200 metres

BPE

was ambushed outside at a North Korean roadblock and posted missing. After wandering over the hills for over a month, Dean was at last captured by the Communists. Like his namesake, the gallant newspaperman was also captured after the fall of Taejon at Yongdong, and both men spent the rest of the war in North Korea resisting all indoctrination attempts. Both these men's books are two of the outstanding personal chronicles of the war.[1]

PUSAN STAKES

Now began the frantic race in space and time between the North Korean advance and the United Nations build-up for the prize of Pusan and with it all Korea. Although Taejon was a Communist victory, never again would American troops have to fight against such odds. During the last week of July, 1st Cavalry and 25th Division were falling back on the upper and middle Naktong along the Sangju-Kumchon front, and on 1 August EUSAK directed that all its forces make a planned withdrawal behind the Naktong to the defensive positions of the Pusan Perimeter. By 4 August all the bridges across the river had been blown, and the perimeter battles proper began.

But even before the retreat into the perimeter had been accomplished, a new threat to Pusan had emerged during the last few days of July. As the NK 4th and 3rd Divisions moved across the Kum in mid-July, the NK 6th Division turned west at Chonan, crossed the Kum estuary at Kunsan, and captured Chonju about the time Taejon fell. Its aim was to flank the entire UNC forces in Korea by moving on Pusan from the west. Advancing on the Chonju-Namwon-Kwangju-Sunchon axis, the division met hardly any resistance and elements occupied Mokpoo, Psang, and Yosu. When the full division reassembled at Sunchon on 24 July, Walker knew that a major threat had developed. Air reconnaissance indicated that the NK 6th Division was moving at an average speed of two miles per hour night and day.

[1] *General Dean's Story* and *Captive in Korea* have vivid descriptions of the events leading to Taejon.

Immediately 24th Division was sent south, but of course this division was in a bad way after Taejon. After ambushing an US force at Hadong, on the south coast road, during 27 July, elements of the NK division continued to advance and on the 31st this *schwerpunkt* of the People's Army stormed into Chinju and carried on eastwards towards Masan, only 30 miles from Pusan. This development, after one of the most brilliant manœuvres of the entire war, precipitated a supreme crisis. The next few days were crucial. On 1 August, Walker ordered 25th Division to the Masan sector. Most of 24th Division was now across the Naktong in the Changnyong area and in the nick of time one of the regiments of this division, now commanded by Maj.-Gen. John H. Church, managed to stop the North Koreans around a pass called 'the Notch' on the main road west of Masan. On the same day, 2 August, another regiment from 25th Division set up a blocking position on the coast road at Chindong-ni, barely five miles south of Masan. After a wild and confused encounter with the North Koreans here and the next day the enemy drive on Masan came to a halt. Both 25th Division, by now responsible for the entire Masan sector, and the NK 6th Division then started to regroup for the next round. Walker thought that had the Communists driven straight and hard for Pusan instead of occupying the south-western Korean ports, he could not have stopped them.[1]

Another danger at this time came from the refugees which clogged the roads, often providing a screen for North Korean infiltrators. By the end of July 25,000 a day were crossing into the UN lines. The reason for this exodus from Communist-held territory was panic at the terror sweeping those areas which the KPA had liberated. A notebook on a captured Communist guerilla tells of the fate that came to many thousands of South Koreans that summer as anti-Communists and leadership elements alike were liquidated. 'Apprehended twelve men; National Assembly members, police sergeants and [town of] Myon leaders. Killed four of them at the scene, and the remaining eight were shot after investigation by the People's court.'[2] Any doubts that many South Koreans had felt about their government were effectively dispersed as the killings by the NK Security

[1] Appleman, p. 247.
[2] *Ibid*, p. 211.

Police rallied support to Rhee, now proved right in his insistence that there could be no compromise with Pyongyang.

But the outcome of the struggle was still undecided as the Pusan Perimeter, the Korean Torres Vedras, was set up at the beginning of August. The perimeter was a rectangular area about eighty miles from north to south and fifty miles from west to east. On the west the Naktong River formed the boundary except for the sector south of the confluence of the Naktong and the Nam River where the line ran across the hills to the Korea Strait at Chindong-ni. To the north the limits of the perimeter at first stretched across the mountains north-eastwards from Waegwan, on the Naktong, to Yongdok on the Sea of Japan; but during August 1950 this line was pushed back to an irregular front running eastwards from Taegu (fifty-five miles north-eastwards of Pusan) to Pohang-dong (sixty miles north of Pusan).

South of Waegwan the perimeter was held by the US 1st Cavalry, 24th Infantry and 25th Infantry Divisions in that order. The ROK Army, reorganised during late July into two corps and five divisions, held the line east of Waegwan with its II Corps adjacent to the inter-army boundary, and I Corps manning the sector near the east coast. Opposite the ROKA stood the NK II Corps, while facing the Eighth Army along the Naktong-Nam front was the NK I Corps. The North Korean GHQ, with Kim Il Sung as Commander-in-Chief, was known as Supreme Head-quarters, but throughout the perimeter battles the North Korean forces in the south were controlled by the KPA Front Head-quarters at Kumchon where General Kim Chaek was in command. His Chief of Staff was Lt.-Gen. Kang Kon, later killed by a land mine at Andong on 8 September.

By 4 August American ground combat troops in Korea numbered 47,000 while those of the ROK were about 45,000. This meant that the numeral discrepancy between the two sides was not as great as was thought at the time, for it was later discovered that the KPA had suffered about 58,000 casualties on the way south to the Naktong and at the beginning of August numbered about 70,000 men deployed in ten infantry divisions and an armoured division. MacArthur's GHQ had estimated NK casualties at this time as about 31,000 but Tokyo, like all other observers, had failed to realise the tremendous losses inflicted on the KPA by the ROKA in its tenacious fighting withdrawal down the central mountains. Moreover, ending the numerical superiority which the Communists had enjoyed until the end of July, US reinforcements arrived at Pusan at this time, so giving Walker a powerful spurt in the race for the deep-water port alone through which his men could be supplied. These units began landing on the following dates:

29th Infantry Regiment, from Okinawa (sent to Masan and eventually incorporated in 25th Division)	24 July
5th Regimental Combat Team, from Hawaii (sent to Masan and eventually attached to 24th Division)	31 July
2nd Infantry Division, from Tacoma, the first ground troops to reach Korea from the US (one regiment in Army reserve, one regiment to 24th Division front)	31 July
1st Provisional Marine Brigade, from San Diego (in reserve at Masan)	2 August

Apart from replacements and the third regiment of 2nd Division, no other ground troops reached the perimeter until the arrival of nearly 2,000 men from the British 27th Infantry Brigade sent from Hong Kong and which landed at Pusan on 29 August. Also during the first weeks of August, five armoured battalions of about sixty-nine tanks each arrived in Pusan and by the end of the month there were over 500 M-26 Pershings and M-4 Shermans in the perimeter, outnumbering the T-34s by five to one. The single most valuable weapon the Communists possessed had been checkmated.

As soon as reinforcements started landing, Walker decided to attempt a counter-offensive on the Masan front with the intention of retaking Chinju and diverting NK resources from the north. Named after the commander of 25th Division, Task Force Kean, including the Marines and RCT-5 besides two regiments of the 25th, struck westwards on 7 August. In temperatures of over 100 degrees which felled more men than the North Koreans the offensive had mixed success. On the high road to Chinju elements of the 25th reached the Chinju pass on 12 August, but in the centre RCT-5 ran into serious trouble, losing two artillery battalions in a NK ambush, although its spearhead did reach the Masan-Chinju road. On the coastal road the Marines were luckier and by the 12th had almost reached Sachon, their tactical air force destroying a large NK motorised column on the way at Kosong. But the same day the Marines were ordered to withdraw back towards Masan as they were wanted on the Naktong where a new crisis had broken out. By the 14th, Task Force Kean was back where it started; Chinjun had not been taken, not a single enemy soldier had been diverted from other fronts, but at least the NK 6th Division had been fought to a standstill and for the rest of the month there was a stalemate on this sensitive front.

The situation to the north was everywhere critical when Kean was ordered to halt the drive to Chinju, but nowhere was it more serious than in 24th Division's sector on the Naktong Bulge, a large loop of the river just north of its juncture with the Nam. Ten miles east of the Naktong here lay Miryang on the main road-rail route from Pusan to Taegu. Its loss would slice the perimeter in two, so causing the entire defence to collapse. During the night of 5-6 August, the NK 4th Division started crossing the Naktong near Yongsan, from where the Communists could easily drive east to Miryang. The screening elements of the 24th Division which held the hills overlooking the river were swept aside and soon the North Koreans had occupied the Obong-ni Ridge — Cloverleaf Hill complex, the terrain key to the Bulge. Although the river was a quarter of a mile wide, underwater bridges of logs and sandbags meant that artillery and tanks could cross the Naktong; by the 11th, Yongsan was under fire and the North Koreans were infiltrating east of the town.

The situation demanded the strongest reserve force Walker possessed. On 15 August the Marines were attached to 24th Division, and a general assault against the North Korean bridgehead was ordered. This co-ordinated attack started on 17 August, and although a battalion of 24th Division took Cloverleaf without much difficulty, the frontal assault by the Marines against Obong-ni was stopped. During the day a T-34 column was destroyed in the pass between these two hills; and then, on 18

August, the Marines took Obong-ni Ridge. By the evening of the 18th, the Marines were on Hill 311 overlooking the Naktong and next day the NK 4th Division was finally driven back across the river with terrific casualties after losing most of its equipment in what was known as the First Battle of the Naktong Bulge. The operation 'ranks with the hardest fights in Marine Corps history', according to the official historian.[1]

While the North Koreans were being thrown back across the Naktong near Yongsan, to the north five of their divisions with armour were deployed in a great arc around Taegu, attacking in three directions with the main axis of the offensive down the corridor of the Naktong valley. Opposing the invaders were the 1st Cavalry Division and the ROK 1st Division. Crossing the upper Naktong between 5 and 8 August in the Sangju area, this NK thrust advanced twenty miles through the mountainous country above Taegu and by 18 August the Communists were in the Tabu-dong area about fifteen air miles north of the town. North Korean artillery shelled Taegu that day, and the ROK Government went on its travels once again in a final move to Pusan. Below Waegwan on the Naktong front near Taegu, North Korean attempts to cross the river at Nochon and Yongpo were beaten back with heavy losses. But the situation north of Taegu remained serious and Walker switched to the area from the south a regiment of 25th Division. A corridor on the Taegu-Sangu road near Tabu-dong, known as 'the Bowling Alley' became the scene of a series of tank battles, and between 18 and 25 August, thirteen T-34s and five self-propelled guns were knocked out by American tanks and bazookas while the ROK infantry fought to hold the hilltops. By this time the position on the Taegu front was stabilised.

It was during the fighting around Taegu that reports of enemy concentrations across the Naktong from Waegwan led to 'an extraordinary bombing mission' (Appleman) which followed a request from MacArthur to Stratemeyer to lay on a saturation bombing attack on these assembly areas. Accordingly on 16 August, ninety-eight B-29s dumped almost a thousand tons of bombs on the trans-Naktong sites in twenty-six minutes. But no evidence was ever produced that this mission had killed

[1] Montross and Canzona, I, p. 239.

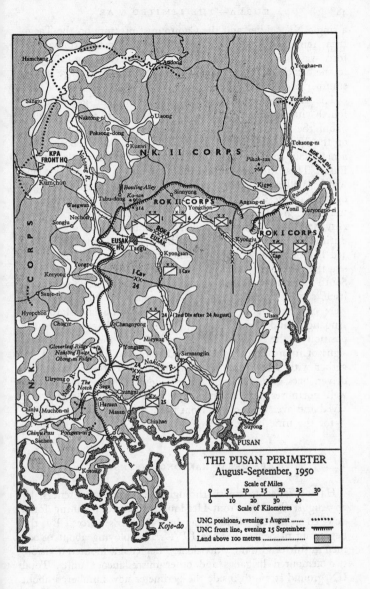

THE PUSAN PERIMETER
August–September, 1950

Scale of Miles
0   5   10   15   20   25   30

Scale of Kilometres
0   10   20   30   40

UNC positions, evening 1 August ....
UNC front line, evening 15 September ⌐⌐⌐⌐⌐
Land above 100 metres ....

Hamchang
Sangju
Andong
Yonghac-ri
Yongdok
Naktong-ni
Uisong
Paksong-dong
Kunwi
Toksong-ni
ROK 3rd Div
17 August
KPA FRONT HQ
N.K. II CORPS
Pilsak-san
766
Kumchon
Naktong R.
Bowling Alley
Ka-san
902
Tabu-dong
314
Sinnyong
Kigye
Waegwan
Nochon
ROK II CORPS
Yongchon
Angang-ni
Pohang-dong
Songju
ROK EUSAK
1
8
7
Kyongju
ROK I CORPS
Yonil
Kuryongpo-ri
EUSAK HQ
Taegu
Kyongsan
Cap
5
3
Yongpo
I Cav
Kenyong
24
I Cav
Suie-ri
Hyopchon
24
(2nd Div after 24 August)
Chogye
Changnyong
Cloverleaf Ridge
Naktong Bulge
Obong-ni Ridge
Yongsan
Miryang
Samnangjin
Uiryong
24
Naktong R.
15
The Notch
Saga
Chungni
Chinju
Muchon-ni
Hanan
Masan
25
Chinhae
Chinju Pass
Sachon
Pongam-ni
Suyong
PUSAN
Kosong
Ulsan
Koje-do

RPB

a single NK soldier and the Communist pressure on the Taegu front remained unaltered. Carpet bombing by the strategic air force was as little use to the defenders of the Naktong in 1950 as to the attackers bogged down in the Normandy *bocage* in the summer of 1944.

The North Koreans had also made dramatic gains on the fourth vital sector of the Pusan Perimeter during early August. From the Angang-ni area, twelve miles west of Pohang-dong on the Taegu lateral road, the invaders could drive south down a mountain corridor which ran through Kyongju all the way to Pusan. This threat to the northern avenue to his base was one which Walker always worried about and some of the bitterest fighting of the war occurred here after the KPA at last evicted the ROK 3rd Division from the Yongdok area on 5 August. Advancing to Pohang-dong which Communist patrols entered during 10-11 August, the NK 5th Division trapped the ROK 3rd Division against the coast and so the only way out was by sea, the evacuation not being completed until 17 August. These South Koreans were then landed at Kuryongpo-ri. Pohang-dong itself soon became a no-man's-land, and the North Koreans were checked in the hills before reaching the lateral road at Angang-ni and Yongchon to the east. By 20 August, when the position on the Naktong Bulge and at Taegu were also showing signs of improvement, the ROK Capitol and 3rd Divisions, together with Task Force Bradley and Task Force Pohang, had driven back two shattered NK divisions to the Pihak-san area well north-west of Pohang-dong. The Kyongju corridor was saved and over most of the front there was a lull in the fighting — for the time being.

KPA GREAT NAKTONG OFFENSIVE

Having failed to smash through the perimeter defences, by 20 August the NK Front Headquarter started planning for a new co-ordinated offensive against Walker's forces. By the beginning of September the KPA was deploying about 98,000 men in thirteen infantry divisions, a depleted armoured division, two armoured brigades and other miscellaneous units. Total UN ground strength inside the perimeter now numbered about

180,000 men, but a large proportion of the ROK Army strength of 92,000 was in labour units. The aggregate of American ground combat strength, not counting service troops, was about at this time 67,000, including the Marines and the British Brigade. But fast as Walker's build-up in manpower and especially firepower had been, this was not the only disadvantage facing the KPA as the supreme trial of strength for Pusan approached. In July the North Koreans had been able to wage a war of manœuvre, but after the beginning of August, there was only one way in which they could reach Pusan, and that was the most expensive; head-on assault against the perimeter defences with rapid exploitation of any break-throughs. Thus, inevitably, Kim Chaek's plan for the new offensive envisaged simultaneous attacks on the Masan sector, in the Naktong Bulge, at Taegu, and in the Kyongju corridor area, the same strategy as in early August but with greater co-ordination. The KPA while suffering heavy casualties was still a powerful fighting force. Its food supply was bad, but ammunition and motor fuel still managed to reach the perimeter despite heavy air attacks on its line of communications. Impressment, too, partly made up the drain of casualties.

This great achievement of the North Korean high command in maintaining their armies on the perimeter front when open to unchallenged air attack merits some brief discussion, as it looks forward to problems which remained throughout the war in one form or another. As soon as the NKAF was destroyed, FEAF Bomber Command, composed of the four B-29 groups sent from the US to augment the one group already in the Far East, started a campaign against such 'strategic' targets as existed in North Korea. However, so desperate at first was the position of the ground forces that this strategic bombing was interrupted for a carefully planned interdiction campaign against important road and rail routes leading south from North Korea, and the heavies were even used for close support as on the Naktong. While Bomber Command worked north of the Han on interdiction, Fifth Air Force, its basic pre-war mission the air defence of Japan, took out targets south of this river. But, powerful as it was, the interdiction campaign did not stop NK re-supply.

Even more important again at this time was close support.

E

Soon the only important airfield open in Korea was K2 at Taegu. Only Dakotas and Mustangs could be used here, although a Mustang squadron of the ROKAF flew from an airstrip at Chinhae throughout the perimeter fighting. Flying from the nearest air bases on Kyushu, Itazuke and Ashiya, F-80 Shooting Star jets could not spend more than twenty minutes over the battlefield, but efficiency was greatly increased when a FAF/ Army Joint Operations Centre was set up at Taegu on 14 July. Also at Taegu an advance HQ of the FAF was operational by 24 July, as well as a tactical air control centre with TAC parties down to each US regiment and ROK division. While great havoc was inflicted on the People's Army by close support attacks, precise evaluation was impossible as immobilised enemy equipment was not always destroyed.

Another — intramural — difficulty was that the Air Force in general favoured interdiction attacks on rear areas as the best way of halting the NK offensive, for according to theory, 'effects accrue geometrically as the force is increased arithmetically'.[1] But the demand for close support — endorsed by GHQ — was intensified with the obvious successes of the Navy-Marine system, which with aircraft operating from carriers off the Korean south coast, and with controllers in the firing line, could bring down pulverising fire as little as fifty yards ahead of the troops. The Army-Air Force system on the other hand with TAC parties and L-6 Mosquito spotter aircraft ranged as far ahead as ten miles in front of the firing line. A commander of TF 77 has estimated that less than 30% of the fleet's strike potential controlled by airborne spotters was used effectively.[2] Thus rival claims between interdiction and close support initiated a controversy over the best use of air power in Korea which was to last for the duration. Tactical aircraft 'had done superbly against the mechanised forces of the Axis in Europe', James Gavin has summed up, 'and they were expected to do even better against the primitive Asiatic armies. The contrary was the case'.[3] With its thousands of human carriers the KPA was in fact not dependent on mechanical transport.

[1] Stewart, *Airpower: The Decisive Force in Korea*, p. 28. The phrase is O. P. Weyland's, Stratemeyer's successor at FEAF.

[2] Cagle and Manson, *The Sea War in Korea*, p. 58.

[3] Gavin, *War and Peace in the Space Age*, p. 130.

But whatever these nascent differences on the application of air power in Korea, there can be little doubt that the air forces probably exercised greater influence on the outcome of the war during the perimeter period than at any time between 1950 and 1953. Walker was the first to recognise this: '. . . if it had not been for the air support that we received from the Fifth Air Force, we should not have been able to stay in Korea'.[1]

The importance Walker attached to his air support was amply justified when the great North Korean offensive against the Pusan Perimeter opened on the night of 31 August/1 September with a massive assault against the 25th Division's sector west of Masan. Large numbers of enemy infantry broke into Kean's rear areas. Haman, only ten miles west of Masan, was occupied, while Masan itself at this time was infested with the Communist fifth column. Simultaneously to the north in the Naktong Bulge sector where 2nd Division had relieved 24th Division on 24 August, strong forces from two NK divisions with tanks crossed the river and were in Yongsan by the evening of 1 September. By also reaching the Yongsan-Changnyon road the North Koreans had cut the 2nd Division in two. Both in the Masan and the Bulge sectors the perimeter had thus been broken by 2 September. By 6 September Waegwan had been abandoned by 1st Cavalry, and the North Koreans to the east were on Hill 902, the walled city of Ka-san which gave observation into Taegu ten miles away. On 5 September the British 27th Brigade, composed of a battalion from both the Middlesex Regiment and the Argyll and Sutherland Highlanders, was committed on the Naktong below Waegwan. The fighting then see-sawed in the hills eight miles north of Taegu with Hill 314 marking the limit of the NK penetration. On the eastern front, Pohang-dong fell again on 6 September; the North Koreans had already crossed the lateral Taegu road at Angang-ni although Kyongju remained in South Korean hands. Fifteen miles to the west the North Koreans had also achieved an initial breakthrough and Yongchon was briefly occupied on 6 September. Thus the lateral Taegu road had been cut at two points. Everywhere the crisis was almost as grave as that of late July.

[3] Appleman, p. 477.

Walker's response was instantaneous. The Marines were sent to the Yongsan area and between 3 and 5 September the combined US forces there drove back the North Koreans to the Obong-ni area in the Second Battle of the Naktong Bulge. The NK 4th Division suffered extremely heavily and to the north in 2nd Division's sector the NK forces in the Changnyon sector were also repelled. The Marines were then released on the reserve on 5 September; for the rest of the perimeter fighting the North Koreans were on the defensive in the Naktong Bulge area. Similarly, after a week's heavy fighting all over the perimeter it became obvious that the North Koreans were unable to exploit their breakthroughs, so skilful was Walker in concentrating his reserves and his firepower at the threatened points. In the 25th Division Nam River sector, where the crisis was over by 7 September, Appleman records that the NK dead were so numerous that a regimental commander thought the carnage exceeded that in the Trun area of the Falaise gap in 1944 when the German Seventh Army was torn apart after the Battle of Normandy.

This was perhaps Walker's greatest moment. Moving swiftly all around the perimeter by liaison plane and armoured jeep, the bulldog Texan general invariably carried a repeating shot-gun, because, as he told a fellow officer, 'I don't mind being shot at, but these —— are not going to ambush me.' At the most critical moment about 5 September when at Taegu, Pohang and in the south, the perimeter looked like falling apart, Walker had orders drafted which would have initiated a retreat to 'the Davidson Line'. Previously surveyed by one of his staff, this extended from north of Ulsan to near Miryang and then south across the Naktong to near Masan. However, while deciding to stand firm, Walker ordered EUSAK HQ moved to Pusan from Taegu as the elaborate teleprinter equipment which connected him with the Dai-Ichi was the only such installation in the Far East and irreplaceable if destroyed or captured by the North Koreans. Walker himself stayed behind in charge of a tactical command post; on 6 September EUSAK and ROKA headquarters opened at Pusan where rich Koreans were already leaving for the Tsu-shima islands in the Korea straits.

As the fighting came to its final climax at this time, the knowledge seeped through the perimeter that MacArthur was

EXAMINATION COPY QUESTIONNAIRE

Here is an examination copy of a Penguin book FOR COURSE ADOPTION CONSIDERATION. We shall greatly appreciate receiving from you the following information. Thank you for your cooperation.

Book Title:_____

Course Description:_____

_____ Is the level of this book appropriate for your students?
        Too elementary?_____Too advanced?_____

_____As a text, this book will serve well as
        Basic____Supplementary____Suggested Reading____

_____I am planning to use this book and will be ordering approximately_____copies.*

_____I am not planning to use this book because_____

_____

For any additional comments or criticisms please use the space below or write directly to Penguin Books (see reverse side).

Name_____ Position _____

School Address_____

_____ Zip_____

*Advance information on the probable size of an order is very helpful to a publisher in estimating stock requirements.

PENGUIN BOOKS INC
72 FIFTH AVENUE
NEW YORK, NEW YORK 10011
ATT: COLLEGE DEPARTMENT

planning an amphibious landing deep in the Communist rear, and in anticipation of its coming offensive EUSAK organised two corps whose headquarters had been formed in the US during August. On 13 September Maj.-Gen. Frank W. Milburn's I Corps became operational and to it were attached the 1st Cavalry, 24th, and ROK 1st Divisions together with the British Brigade; while on 23 September when Maj.-Gen. John B. Coulter's IX Corps was activated it included 2nd and 25th Infantry Divisions. By then it had become obvious that Walker had won the perimeter battles; and the performance of this master of defensive strategy is an excellent contemporary illustration of the thesis recently advanced by B. H. Liddell Hart in *Deterrent or Defence* that the power of the defence on modern war is ever increasing. The four US divisions which had defended the Naktong had at different times held fantastic frontages varying from between twenty to forty miles, while the British Brigade, south of Waegwan with under 2,000 men, was holding an 'immense'[1] front of 18,000 yards, over ten miles.

Including convolutions of the ground and remembering the high proportion of service troops, each US division was lucky if it had a force/distance ratio of 400 men to the mile, but of course this was a *strategic* ratio. By skilfully using his reserves and interior lines, Walker was able to increase his *tactical* ratios to much more at such threatened spots as Masan, the Naktong Bulge, Taegu and Pohang-dong, so that the initial numerical advantage which the North Koreans were able to organise was soon nullified. In exploiting these different ratios Walker knew, as Liddell Hart says, that 'the crucial factor in the defence of any wide front is the *time* factor'.[2]

But the corollary of these considerations was that a break-out from the perimeter would be prohibitively expensive. Therefore MacArthur meant to end the Naktong deadlock and destroy the People's Army by an amphibious landing at Inchon, the port of Seoul. The Communist army would then be caught between the hammer of the Eighth Army and the anvil of the newly-formed X Corps. While the last desperate fighting was going on all around the perimeter, the first convoys had left Japan for Inchon. The two months allowed by the North Korean

[1] Barclay, *The First Commonwealth Division*, p. 19.
[2] Liddell Hart, *Deterrent or Defence*, p. 174.

Supreme Headquarters for the conquest of South Korea had run out. Time was up for the Korean People's Army. Simultaneously the domestic political scene in the United States had been powerfully influenced by MacArthur's activities during the perimeter fighting.

CHAPTER FOUR

FORMOSA AND KOREA: THE REPUBLICANS LOOK WEST

> 'Europe is a dying system. It is worn down and will
> become an economic and industrial hegemony of Soviet
> Russia. . . . The lands bordering the Pacific with their
> billions of inhabitants will determine the course of his-
> tory for the next ten thousand years. . . .'
>
> DOUGLAS MACARTHUR, on Leyte, in 1944

THE GREAT CONSPIRACY

FROM its very outset the Korean War was deeply involved in domestic politics. Ever since the autumn of 1949 a great revulsion against the Administration's foreign policy had swept the country, skilfully exploited by the Republican opposition. The origins of this profound dissent from the policies of Truman and Acheson were complex; the emotions raised were unprecedented in American history since the Civil War.

The basis of this schism which developed after 1949 was the frustration felt at the world position of the United States at the end of the 1940s. America had crushed its Axis enemies in its righteous anger, but there was no new Jazz Age, no new period of 'normalcy'. Instead, the alarming stain of Stalinist Communism spreading across Europe meant that after liberating Western Europe from Hitler, the United States had now to embark on a costly aid programme to save it from the other great twentieth-century tyrant. But containment and its manifestations in the Truman Doctrine and the Marshall Plan were not designed to destroy Communism in the great tradition of American total crusades against foreign despots. On the contrary as a true response to the great historic challenge of Communism — Arnold Toynbee was on the cover of *Time* during March 1947 — containment was a long-term programme operating over decades and designed not to end in war, but to bring the Soviets to the conference table. Communism had to be lived with; but there was not going to be an American one world. As early as June 1946 Acheson, then Under Secretary of State, was saying that 'We have got to understand that all our lives, danger, the uncertainty, the need for alertness, for effort, for discipline will be upon us. This is new to us. It will be hard for us.'

Internationalist Republicans such as Senator Arthur Vandenberg and John Foster Dulles supported the Administration's move to shore up Western Europe, and thus the bi-partisan foreign policy was born, chiefly through Vandenberg's chairmanship of the Senate Foreign Relations Committee in the Republican-controlled eightieth Congress. But the frustrations and limited objectives of containment were accepted only so long as the policy succeeded, as it did, of course, in Europe. In the Far East, the collapse of the Nationalist regime in China came as a traumatic shock to most Americans. A century of American missionary effort and commercial enterprise had been repudiated by a movement which not only rejected Western democracy, but in particular regarded the United States as the paper tiger world centre of imperialism, decadence and reaction. All the valid justifications of State Department's China White Paper issued in August 1949 could not explain away the downfall of Chiang Kai-shek. For behind this bulky 1,000-page valediction to the Kuomintang lay the reality that the Communists had won a victory of historic proportions in China. *Who was to blame?* Here was the Achilles heel of the Truman Administration.

Moreover, within a few weeks of the China White Paper, there was another unpleasant shock. A primitive detection device in Alaska recorded a slight increase in stratospheric radio-activity: the Russians had the bomb—three years before the schedule assigned them by the Finletter Commission. The news was announced by the President on 23 September, 1949 when on the domestic scene too public attention was focused on Communist activities—but with far greater human interest value than Mao's victory. The Hiss affair in all its complexities was now moving into its second year of accusation, counter accusation. Eventually in January 1950 the second trial came to an end. The verdict: Hiss was guilty on both counts of perjury. But for the Statute of Limitations, the scion of Baltimore, Harvard Law School, class of 1929, and sometime adviser to FDR at Yalta would have been punished for espionage.

In September 1949 Senator Vandenberg was writing in his journal, 'The whole country is in a state of nerves. Everybody is under tension. Nothing is right. The whole tenor of senatorial correspondence has changed. Everybody is mad about something. . . .'[1] What was a matter of regret to the champion of bi-partisanship was to the leading Republican senator, Robert A. Taft, an opportunity to rally his party after eighteen years in the political wilderness. Son of one Republican president, strongly influenced by another when he served from 1917 to 1920 in Herbert Hoover's relief administration, Taft, like Roosevelt, was a true son of American privilege. By his orthodoxy, integrity and parliamentary brilliance, he had come to dominate the Republicans in Congress; he was chairman of the Senate Republican Policy Committee in the late 1940s. As a Mid-westerner from Ohio, Taft regarded the Eastern ' me—too ' internationalist wing of his party with almost as much distaste as the Democrats. This was the section of the GOP which had dominated each national convention since 1940; in each election its candidate had been defeated. After Truman's surprise victory in 1948, Taft, according to his biographer, William S. White, 'was at times almost literally besides himself'.[2] He honestly believed the Democrats were destroying America.

With the absence of Vandenberg from the Senate because of illness after the end of 1949, and the consequent decline of influence in the party of the internationalist faction, Congressional control of the Republicans passed into the hands of the orthodox right wingers. In the Senate, Wherry of Nebraska, Republican floor-leader, Knowland of California, 'the Senator from Formosa', and Styles Bridges of New Hampshire were in the ascendant, representing the Midwest conservative bloc which made up their party's strength on the Hill. Inspired by Taft, they rejected all ' me — too ' advice and determined to fight the coming 1950 mid-term elections on a platform of all-out opposition to the Democrats. In the light of the loss of China, the Soviet atomic bomb and the conviction of Hiss, traditional Republican beliefs were re-formulated; one of the most powerful of American political myths emerged, that of the great conspiracy.

[1] The Vandenberg Papers, p. 515-16.
[2] The Taft Story, p. 83.

The pre-war isolationism which Taft had once supported was manifestly absurd in 1949. Isolationism in the nineteenth and early twentieth centuries was based on the assumption of American omnipotence resting on a basis of American virtue in avoiding 'entangling alliances'. The reality was that the Monroe Doctrine was underwritten by the British Navy. Yet still in the later 1940s, ignoring the challenge of international Communism, the neo-isolationism of Taft and the right-wing Republicans was predicated on the threat to America from within, not without, for they believed that since 1933 the Democrats had been preparing for a socialist America in a Communist-dominated world. For Taft, the supreme danger came from what MacArthur was to describe in his Boston speech of July 1951 after his recall as the 'insidious forces working from within which have already so drastically altered the character of our free institutions'. The New Deal, Fair Deal, deficit budgeting, high taxes, emphasis on executive action, the increasing influence of the military in government were all evidence of a crypto-totalitarian threat to the legislature and the traditional American values. Even many non-Taftites were worried by the spectre of the garrison state as the cold war increased in intensity. 'Keep America solvent and sensible,' Taft had said in 1947, 'and she has nothing to fear from any foreign country.'

Given this promise of the new isolationalism, it followed that the New Dealers had condoned the infiltration of the civil service by Communist agents, conspired with Stalin at Yalta to sell Chiang down the river, while all the time ceaselessly intriguing in all spheres of American life to destroy the principles of the Founding Fathers. Containment was only another aspect of the great betrayal in that it had ignored the threat of Communism in the Far East. Dislike of high taxation, awareness of alleged subversion, and the necessity for all-out support for Chiang were the main planks of the new Republicanism. With its sinister explanation of all that happened in America since 1933, the theory of the great conspiracy was one which could not be underbid. This conspiratorial interpretation of modern history reconciled what D. W. Brogan has called 'the illusion of American omnipotence' with the fact of limited American world power in 1949. Yet the Communist subversion net was inevitable once Lenin was in power, the cold war inescapable since Stalingrad; the irreconcilable conflict between the Soviet and the West, which the Communists expect history to solve in their favour, had started in 1917, not 1933 or 1947. In its classical form, the outlines of the great conspiracy were established by McCarthy. 'How can we account for our present situation,' the Senator would ask in his famous philippic against General Marshall on 14 June 1951,[1] 'unless we believe that men high in this government are concerting to deliver us to disaster. This must be the product of a great conspiracy, a conspiracy on a scale so immense as to dwarf any previous such venture in the history of man. . . . To what end? To the end that we shall be contained, frustrated, and finally fall victim to Soviet intrigue from within and Russian military might from without.'

But they were not only orthodox Republicans who accepted the dogmas of the new isolationalism. In the Midwest, the farmers and progressive populist forces which had generally supported Truman as late as 1948 had always been anti-Eastern, anti-British, and strongly nationalist. The reverse side of La Folletteian populism was xenophobically suspicious of the internationalism implicit in the Truman-Acheson policies, and always ready to see Communism in American urban Leftism. Immigrant groups all over the United States would hardly care to identify themselves with a party being called un-American by the Opposition. And the Catholics, who had supported the Democrats during the bad days of the 1930s, like the immigrant groups, had discovered that the Hierarchy had been extremely anti-Communist and anti-liberal long before the events of 1949.

The indications were, then, that in the winter of 1949-1950, the Roosevelt-Truman electoral coalition which had been nationally in the ascendant since 1933 — with the exception of the 1946 mid-term elections — was beginning to break up. The Midwest and the urban masses were responsible to the demagogy of the Republican revival, the South had already broken with the Democratic leadership in 1948 when it bolted the election platform over Civil Rights, and there was widespread exasperation with containment which as a policy could not be projected in traditional terms to maximise electoral support.

[1] *Congressional Record*, 82nd Congress, 1st Session, pp. 6556-6603, 'The History of George Catlett Marshall'. Cf. Rovere, *Senator Joe McCarthy*, pp. 137-43.

Even more alarming than these shifts in the ground swell of public opinion was their effect on Congress, through which the Administration had to get its foreign and domestic programmes if it was to regain lost ground in the country. There were constitutional as well as electoral considerations in Congressional opposition which was concentrated in the Senate. Not only did Senators reflect voters' opinions, but the very structure of the American government with its separation of powers meant that Congress with its investigating committees had always interfered with the executive's function of directing foreign policy. For its own reasons the Senate would give added leverage to the popular outcry against the Administration. The chief target of the Opposition in the Senate was Dean Acheson. 'The Secretary of State,' wrote Henry Adams in 1906, 'has always stood as much alone as the historian. Required to look far ahead and around him, he measures forces unknown to party managers, and has found Congress more or less hostile ever since Congress first sat. The Secretary of State exists only to recognise the existence of a world which Congress would rather ignore. . . . Since the first day the Senate existed, it has always intrigued against the Secretary of State whenever the Secretary has been obliged to extend his function beyond the appointment of consuls. . . .'[1]

The Senate as a whole resented Truman as a 'strong' president, and in particular it disliked Acheson's China policy which it saw as executive appeasement of Communism. Furthermore Truman and Acheson had not consulted Congress over the Far East as they had over Europe. Such consultation, of course, might well have forestalled future criticism, as no one in Congress wished to support the collapsing Kuomintang with troops; bi-partisanship on China need not have meant, if properly handled, a different policy. But this was not to be. William S. White has estimated that at least 70% of the Democrats in the 82nd Congress did not fully support Truman, whom they distrusted. Acheson, moreover, was actively disliked, if not hated by the Senate; his political strength came from his closeness to Truman and the high regard in which he was held by the State and Defence Departments. With his brilliance, his aloofness, his apparent Anglophilia and his inability to tolerate Congressional fools gladly, the greatest Secretary of State of modern times was

[1] Quoted in Goldman, p. 124.

barely listened to by the Senate, dominated ultimately at this time by Taft, that innermost member of the Senate's inner hierarchy, 'the Club'.

Indeed, relations between the Republican senators and Acheson were so bad in 1950 that after some particularly offensive questioning by Senator Wherry in a closed Appropriations Committee hearing Acheson exploded. 'Don't you dare shake your dirty finger in my face,' he shouted, half-guying his opponents as he took a swing at Wherry across the table. This 'inexpertly aimed and executed' blow was intercepted by, appropriately enough, a nearby State Department legal aide. 'Curiously enough,' Acheson records, 'my relations with Senator Wherry became much easier.'[1] More revealing than the egregious Wherry was Senator Hugh Butler of Nebraska, another Republican senator, who in a tirade against Acheson said, 'I watch his smart aleck manner and his British clothes and that New Dealism, everlasting New Dealism in everything he says and does, and I want to shout, "Get out! Get out! You stand for everything that has been wrong with the United States for years." '[2] The remark not only reflected the personal dislike of Acheson on the Hill, but expressed Midwestern populist hostility to the East, the Senate's resentment of the State Department, Taft's traditionalism against Truman's instinctive liberalism, pre-1929 America's dislike of post-1933 America, in short that fundamental schism in American society and culture between innocence and sophistication expressed by its novelists from Mark Twain and Henry James to Scott Fitzgerald and J. D. Salinger.

COLLAPSE OF THE KMT

Chairman Mao who can be compared to the sun in the east,
Which shines over the world so brightly,
so brightly,
Heigh-ai-yo-, heigh-heigh-heigh-yo.
Without Chairman Mao, how can there be peace?
Heigh-ai-yo.

Transcending all other issues thrown up by devotees of the great conspiracy was the fall of Chiang which by the end of

[1] Acheson, *Sketches from Life*, p. 129-30.
[2] Goldman, p. 125

1949 had become a debate on the future of Formosa as well as
on the reasons for his fall and consequent flight to that salub-
rious island one hundred miles off the Chinese mainland. The
Asia-first elements among the Republicans were about to make
the retention of the island by the Nationalist rump the chief,
almost the only plank, in their foreign policy. For throughout
America there was a sense of profound shock over the speed of
the Communist takeover. It had all happened so quickly.

Towards the end of 1947, after the end of General Marshall's
futile mission to reconcile the Kuomintang and the Communists,
Mao's armies began to expand their guerilla operations into a
formal offensive strategy. The Red leader knew that after twenty
years he had won his war, and by March 1948, the US Embassy
in Nanking was reporting on the 'criminally inept and wasteful'
Nationalist strategy. In August the same year, Secretary of
State Marshall was advising Nanking that there were no 'rigid
plans for our future policy in China'. Washington had written
off Chiang and was cutting its losses — over $2 billion since
V-J day. The Gimo in future would have to go it alone. In
September came the first large scale defection of Nationalist
troops at Tsinan in the north, followed by the disastrous fall of
Mukden later in the year, the result of the notorious 'wall
psychology' which tied up Chiang's soldiers in isolated fortress-
cities. It was the beginning of the end. After these defeats the
Chinese People's Liberation Army possessed more American
equipment than the Kuomintang armies.

Chiang had resigned the presidency of the Republic of China
in January 1949; retaining control of the Nationalist $500 million
specie reserve, the air force, and China's art treasures for the
last four millennia, he fled to Formosa. Shanghai fell in May; on
1 October the Central People's Government of the People's
Republic of China was proclaimed from the great Tien An Men
Gate in Peking. And in December the last remnants of the
Nationalist Government raised their standard at Taipeh: Sun
Yat-sen's revolution was reduced to an exiled plutocratic family
clique awaiting invasion and further flight. The whole Chinese
mainland with its 500 million inhabitants was under Communist
control. Their chief weapon in the civil war, Mao Tse-tung had
just written, was not the machine gun, but Marxism-Leninism.
All mankind would have to go through 'the process of eliminat-

ing classes, state power, and parties' before 'universal harmony' would be achieved.

In Acheson's view, expressed in the State Department's China White Paper, 'The Nationalist armies did not have to be defeated; they disintegrated. . . . Nothing that this country did or could have done within the reasonable limits of its capabilities could have changed the result; nothing that was left undone by this country contributed to it. It was the product of internal Chinese forces, forces which this country tried to influence, but could not. . . .' Even the loss of Formosa was foreseen in Washington. The Joint Chiefs decided in August that the island should not be held by American troops, and in October there was an unanimous agreement between the three services and the State Department that the island would fall before the end of 1950. However, in December the Joint Chiefs changed their mind and recommended a small military aid programme. The President sided with the State Department in opposing the recommendation on political grounds because American prestige would be further damaged by backing Chiang. This decision was publicly announced on 5 January 1950 by Truman. Unfortunately for the Administration, a current classified State Department briefing bulletin for its PROs, which denied Formosa any strategic value, was skilfully leaked by MacArthur's GHQ in Tokyo. This meant that Washington's last goodbye to Chiang would be heatedly debated in Congress.

Taft and Knowland stated forcibly the basic Republican attitudes on Formosa: Chiang should be supported and under no circumstances was Peking to be recognised. They attacked Truman and Acheson for not applying the containment policy to China: 'The only reason so much heat has been engendered about the Formosa situation,' said Taft, 'is the bitter resentment of the State Department and its pro-Communist allies against any interference with its policy of liquidating the Nationalist Government.' Not only were Roosevelt, Truman, Marshall and Acheson guilty of planning that great historical cataclysm, according to the demonology of the China Lobby, but also among the guilty were the specialists of the Far Eastern Department of the State Department, Owen Lattimore, John Stewart Service, John Carter Vincent, Philip Jessup, most of whom in the early and middle 1940s had considered that the Yenan Communists were also nationalist agrarian reformers.

Replying to these attacks in his 'defence perimeter' speech on 12 January, Acheson dwelt on his Far East policy. He dismissed the conspiracy theory of Chiang's fall. 'Now what I ask you to do is to stop looking, for a moment, under the bed and under the chair and under the rug to find these reasons, but rather to look at the broad picture.' The broad picture showed there was political conflict between China and Russia, and that the United States hoped this would develop into a 'Titoist' situation. If the new Chinese government went along with the Russians it would lose the support of the Chinese masses. Whether by friction between Moscow and Peking, or by popular revulsion against Mao, the United States stood to gain. If the United States were not to be identified with colonialism in Asia — and that force now included Chiang — American recognition of Peking and Mao's acquisition of Formosa was inevitable. 'We must not undertake to deflect from the Russians to ourselves the righteous anger and the wrath, and the hatred of the Chinese people which must develop.'[1] Abandoned eventually after the Chinese intervention in Korea, the Administration's theory of Mao Tse-tito was cherished longingly and long in Britain, despite the anger, wrath and hatred turned by China towards the West in Korea. The British were not altogether wrong. A Communist doctrinal deviation did emerge in Peking eventually, but one more virulent than even Moscow's 'revisionist' orthodoxy.

But events were moving so quickly in the early months of 1950 that Acheson was unable to implement his China policy of bringing Washington into line with the British in recognising Peking. The Administration needed Republican support in Congress for their European policies, and for this the price was non-recognition of Peking. Small amounts of economic aid were still supplied to Formosa, so Chiang, who had resumed the presidency of the Nationalist regime in March 1950, was not completely abandoned. Other events strengthened the opposition's hand. Hiss was found guilty on 21 January; ten days later, the President announced that work would begin on the 'so-called hydrogen or super-bomb'. On 3 February Fuchs appeared at

[1] For the text of the 'defence perimeter' speech see *Documents on International Affairs*, 1949-1950 (R.I.I.A.), pp. 96-108.

Bow Street; Truman had known from London before his directive on the H-bomb that the Harwell scientist had passed on information not only on atomic, but thermo-nuclear weapons. Finally, in these hectic few weeks which saw the birth of the momentous domestic anti-Communist campaign, the junior Senator from Wisconsin made his play for power on 9 February in a talk to the Women's Republican Club of Wheeling, West Virginia. There were, McCarthy said, 205 — or 81 or 57 — Communists in the State Department. It was a speech which shook the world; the Republicans had let the genie out of the bottle. McCarthy should 'keep talking and if one case doesn't work out he should proceed with another,' Taft commented; his attitude 'was pragmatism run wild', White apologetically remarks. Yet McCarthy's denunciations consistently expressed in demagogic form Taft's ideas. By May 1950 McCarthy had clinched a deal with the political archæologists of the China Lobby and discovered the Pacific. Acheson and Ambassador Jessup were the 'pied pipers of the Politbureau'; the 'Acheson-Lattimore axis' wanted to 'push the vast Pacific into the Kremlin's arms', and turn it into a 'Red Lake'. Nonsensical as this was, from now on Acheson would have to spend much time explaining that he was not a Communist and did not employ traitors.

With the North Korean invasion and the Seventh Fleet in the Formosa Straits, Acheson's China Policy was doomed. At first the Republicans hailed the neutralisation decision; containment at last was applied to Formosa. However, Taft in his Senate speech on 28 June alleged that the Administration was responsible for the North Korean invasion. They had agreed to the partition of Korea on the 38th Parallel in the first place, had failed to arm South Korea adequately, and the Democrats' China policy had encouraged the North Korean invasion by not standing by the Nationalists. Furthermore, Taft alleged that the 'defence perimeter' speech had given the North Koreans the final green light. Thus within the first few days of the outbreak of the Korean War the myth of the great conspiracy was invoked by the leading Republican to explain its origin. But on the whole Taft thought that Truman's Korean decision was right; while he doubted the constitutional legality of the President's action, he would have voted for a joint Congressional resolution approving intervention. Taft's tortuous, circuitous approval meant there

F

was, for the time being, domestic political unity over Far East policy.

This was a precarious truce. The Administration regarded their defence of Formosa as a temporary expedient because the Communists had attacked South Korea, and not Formosa itself, the fall of which had been expected. America's allies wanted no part of the 'neutralisation' policy, which they regarded as a unilateral US action. Washington still hoped that in the future a complete dissociation from Chiang could be effected. But for the Republicans an alliance with Chiang was a basic nationalist dogma of their foreign policy for that Republican ocean, the Pacific. That this truce, born of the June crisis and the early fighting in Korea, broke down so soon was largely due to the remarkable personality and activities of that most Republican of Generals, Douglas MacArthur.

THE MACARTHUR PROBLEM

MacArthur's extraordinary career raises many a historical speculation on the problems of civil-military relationships. The Founding Fathers with their classical learning and the example of Cromwell, James II and George III behind them, were rightly fearful of 'the man on horseback'. But MacArthur was no Boulanger, Schleicher or Franco, although he spoke sometimes with the tones of St. Cyr and Potsdam rather than of West Point. He did not represent 'the Army', as no such force in the continental European sense exists in the United States, and he was actively hostile to the Naval establishment during the second war. But MacArthur was a 'political general', surrounded by controversy throughout his career and prepared to alter civilian policy through the association of his military prestige with one of the two major parties in the state.

Roosevelt had known this and the startling differences between Truman and MacArthur which were to develop soon after the outbreak of war in Korea were less a manifestation of civil-military clash — the Pentagon undeviatingly supported the Administration throughout the crisis — than of a major domestic conflict on foreign policy, and indeed on the nature of war itself. In alliance with the opposition, a field commander with an uniquely strong personality and distinguished record would advocate an essentially political programme completely unacceptable to his superiors, often using military reasons underlined by his own prestige to strengthen his case. McLellan and Lincoln provide a possible comparison, for the immense importance of the personalities involved was decisive. There seems no exact British analogy. The alliance between Bonar Law, F. E. Smith and Henry Wilson over Ulster has elements, as Mr. Robert Blake has pointed out, of a threat to the integrity of the state that recall 1641 rather than 1914. Here a military faction was directly interfering on an issue of domestic policy. Possibly as the issue was that of the conduct of the war itself, the way in which the Asquithian opposition was able to exploit Lloyd George's difficulties with the generals in 1918 culminating with the Maurice affair is a much closer British illustration of the Truman — MacArthur — Taft relationship. There can be no doubt however that the great debate between the Democrats and the Republicans over Korea would not have taken its form but for the immense exacerbation of the situation by MacArthur's personality — this in no way discounts Truman's character as a worthy opponent of the General in the personality stakes. But controversy between MacArthur and Washington was not new. It had happened before during World War II. Then James Forrestal, Roosevelt's last Secretary of the Navy and Truman's first Secretary of Defence, had called it 'the MacArthur problem'.

In July 1950 MacArthur held more imposing titles, and the power that went with them than any other American officer had held before. Not only was he Commanding General US Army, Far East, but also Commander-in-Chief, Far East. His unified command, with air, land and sea forces, included Japan, the Philippines, the Ryukus (Okinawa), the Marianas and other western Pacific islands. As CINCFE the chain of command ran directly from JCS to the Secretary of Defence to the President, through which channel UN resolutions were transmitted to MacArthur in his capacity as CINCUNC (the least of his worries). But the best hat with the most braid that Douglas MacArthur wore was that of Supreme Commander for the Allied Powers (SCAP); the abbreviation stood for MacArthur's GHQ staff as well as himself. He was the sole executant *for* the Allies, and thus exercised the functions of head of state from the earth-quake proof Dai-Ichi building in Tokyo, named after the famous Japanese insurance company. These viceregal powers were unique in the United States history. If MacArthur's military achievements meant that his staff compared him with Napoleon and Alexander, his position as SCAP and the reforms he initiated recalled, not without justice, the great British proconsuls ruling African and Asian peoples in the tradition of the despotic liberalism of the imperial idea . . . Milner, Cromer, Curzon, perhaps Warren Hastings.

The vice-regal analogy is not only a political one, but a personal one as well. The best-known American generals in Europe in their different ways were personifications of the egalitarian image of American life, the smiling Eisenhower, the steel-spectacled Omar Bradley ('the GI's general'). Even Patton, who postured with pearl-handled pistols and sometimes shot chandeliers with them, was acting out the tough-guy part, not showing off his professional authority, but craving affection and crying when moved. MacArthur's autocratic behaviour and patrician aloofness which reminded Sir Alan Brooke of the manner of a *grand seigneur,* when he visited Tokyo in 1945[1] was also apart from another American military tradition, that of the professional officer's reserve and implicit obedience to civilian authority as exemplified in George Marshall and Matthew Ridgway.

Yet MacArthur was brought up in a conventional American military background. Born in 1880 in Little Rock, Arkansas, he was the son of Arthur MacArthur, who had won the Congressional Medal of Honour leading the charge of Sheridan's cavalry at Missionary Ridge during the battle of Chickamauga in 1863. Arthur MacArthur became a national hero for his pacification of the Philippines after 1898, but he was sacked by the first Roosevelt after clashes with the civil authority. So Douglas MacArthur's distrust of politicians was well in the family tradition. MacArthur graduated in 1903 from West Point, with, it has been said, the highest scholastic record of anyone leaving the academy. In 1918 he was the youngest brigadier general in the US Army in France, and commanded the famous Rainbow Division drawn from all over the States; immediately after the

[1] Bryant, *Triumph in the West,* p. 508 ff.

war, he was made superintendent of West Point, again the youngest ever appointed.

Out of place in the Jazz Age, MacArthur became President Hoover's Chief of Staff in 1930, and this led to the most famous incident in his life between the wars, the rout by regular troops of the unemployed veterans, the bonus marchers, from the Capitol in Washington in July 1932. It was a serio-comic moment. MacArthur, wearing full uniform with medals, sitting on a white charger, and accompanied by his aide, Major Dwight Eisenhower, watched the troops — the cavalry were commanded by Major George Patton — drive the bonus marchers down Pennsylvania Avenue and from their shanty town on the Anacostia Flats. But the leftish thirties were as uncongenial to MacArthur as the roaring twenties. After serving for five years as Chief of Staff — longer than anyone else — he left for the Philippines to command the Commonwealth's new army, taking the rank of Field Marshal.

The Japanese invasion of the islands in December 1941 meant that the American forces were trapped on the Bataan peninsula and MacArthur marooned on Corregidor in Manila Bay. Two decisions then taken by Roosevelt were to have a profound effect on MacArthur's career and personality. He resented FDR's refusal to reinforce the islands — it was impossible at that time — and his anger at first burst out in sympathy for a suggestion that Washington neutralise the islands. Roosevelt instantly rejected this possible appeasement of the Japanese; probably from the Philippines debacle grew MacArthur's distrust of politicians of the Democratic variety who had condemned him to defeat in the Far East because of the Europe-first strategy of the Roosevelt-Churchill grand design. Secondly, Roosevelt ordered him to leave Corregidor — if he could — and escape to Australia. Fleeing Corregidor by PT boat and B-17, MacArthur and a small group reached Melbourne; he was appointed South West Pacific Supreme Commander. Before the Australian Parliament, the American Ambassador conferred on him the Congressional Medal of Honour for his defence of the Philippines. The Road to Tokyo lay ahead.

October, 1944 and MacArthur *had* returned to the Philippines. Shortly after the Leyte landing he was speculating on the postwar world: 'Europe is a dying system. It is worn down and will

become an industrial and economic hegemony of Soviet Russia
. . . The lands touching the Pacific with their billions of inhabitants will determine the course of history for the next ten
thousand years.' He resented that the Pacific War had been
starved in the interests of Europe; Roosevelt had made the
same old mistake of intervening in European quarrels, which,
'we can't hope to solve because they are insoluble'.[1]

There was also a great inter-service conflict between Mac-
Arthur and the US Navy which originated over the Navy's
dislike of MacArthur's publicity methods, manipulated by his
sinister PRO, Brig.-Gen. Le Grande Diller. Florid communi-
ques emanating from GHQ invariably excluded the Navy and
Marine Corps, bloody battles still raging were presented as victories, and no news except that presenting MacArthur as in-
fallible was allowed through a draconian censorship. Underlying
these techniques was the calculation that propaganda exploitation of success might result in greater resources being sent to the
theatre; possibly too, this policy was a compensation for the
major decisive battles the Navy and Marines had won at Coral
Sea, Midway, Leyte Gulf, Iwojima and Okinawa. There was the
hubristic, complex, perfectionist character of MacArthur at the
bottom of it all. George Kenney, his South West Pacific Air
Chief of Staff and no sycophant, has also written of the public
relations build-up:

> They never seemed to realise that they didn't have to sell
> Douglas MacArthur. The General was a brilliant, colourful,
> likeable personality who could sell himself much better with-
> out any help. He was not a demi-god, he was human.[2]

Forrestal was exercised by MacArthur's personality; in
March, 1945 he made the perceptive comment that 'he had a
high degree of professional ability, mortgaged, however, to his
sensitiveness and vanity.' MacArthur was a great general in
spite of and not because of the propaganda build-up. The flaw
of pride was, however, ever present. Yet it was only fitting that
his long journey from Melbourne to Tokyo should end on the
decks of the *Missouri* when he took the Japanese surrender.

[1] Millis (Ed.), *The Forrestal Diaries*, pp. 17-18.
[2] Quoted from Kenney's *The MacArthur I Know*, in Spanier, *The Truman-
MacArthur Controversy*, p. 147.

The famous general was about to become the first American pro-consul.

The increasing seclusion in which MacArthur had lived after Leyte meant that to the Japanese he was a remote, inaccessible figure, almost like someone out of the Oriental rather than the Occidental political tradition. In the Philippines and Japan some thought that he was indeed a God. In late 1945, the visiting Sir Alan Brooke was impressed and considered MacArthur the war's 'greatest general and best strategist', a genius, although the CIGS also thought that he didn't appreciate fully 'the situation in Europe'.[1] During these years, the Supreme Commander initiated through his staff the notable reforms of post-war Japan, imposing a liberal revolution, incorporating many New Deal features from above. MacArthur has said that he prefers to be remembered for the SCAP years than as a general; he regards it as 'the humanist capstone of his achievement' according to Willoughby. The sword had been turned into a ploughshare, the victory communiqué into a law code, and in these SCAP years MacArthur had become increasingly given to historical speculation. Reported *Life* magazine in the crucial spring of 1951, 'Greece, Rome, the Middle Ages, the Renaissance, the age of Britain's greatness — all the splendid and tragic meanings of the drama of these countries are the constant prompters of his mind and spirit.'[2]

It was now that a MacArthur cult was created, by his staff, which far surpassed the admiration in which the General was encapsulated during the South West Pacific years. 'He's too enormous,' one of the high priests told John Gunther, 'too unpredictable. I don't really understand him. No one could.' Others thought he was the greatest man alive, the greatest man who had ever lived. There were several factions in the Court of the Dai-Ichi. Close to MacArthur were his aides, Colonels 'Larry' Bunker and 'old Sid' Huff; and Maj.-Gen. Marquat, head of SCAP's economic and scientific section. Of major importance was Maj.-Gen. Charles Willoughby (né Tscheppe-Weidenbach), former lecturer in military history. He had been MacArthur's Intelligence Officer since 1941 and still spoke with a strong German accent. After 1945 he had edited for the

---

[1] Bryant, *loc. cit.*

[2] Rovere and Schlesinger, *The General and the President*, p. 92.

Department of the Army, the 'MacArthur Histories', the authorised version of the Pacific War and the principate in Japan. Willoughby, Huff and Marquat were known by correspondents as 'the Bataan gang' as they escaped with MacArthur in the torpedo boat from Corregidor.

Closest of all to the king was Brig-Gen. Courtney Whitney, a former Manila corporation lawyer, organiser of MacArthur's secret service in the Philippines during the occupation, chief draughtsman of the new Japanese constitution, and generally regarded as MacArthur's *eminence gris* and 'Secretary of State'. A deadly rivalry, characteristic of all MacArthur's staffs, existed between the two senior advisers; both Willoughby and Whitney have written MacArthur biographies, but Whitney's is generally regarded as the authoritative one.

On a lower level stood the military commanders of FECOM, Vice-Admiral Joy, Lt.-Gen. Stratemeyer, FEAF; Lt.-Gen. Walker, Eighth Army, and Maj.-Gen. Edward Almond, GHQ Chief of Staff. Of this group, the most in MacArthur's confidence was Almond. He was known as 'the man who hates correspondents'. because of his efforts in protecting SCAP from heretics. There were other personal retainers: Lt.-Col. Story, pilot of MacArthur's Constellation, *Bataan*, and Mrs. Phyllis Gibbons, English governess of MacArthur's son, Arthur MacArthur. . . .

In the summer of 1950, an Augustan calm reigned in the Dai-Ichi and throughout SCAP's *imperium*. With the signing of the Japanese Peace Treaty it was expected that MacArthur would at last retire to take his place in history, long foreseen by his chroniclers. The war on the 38th Parallel came as a complete surprise, as did the President's decision to intervene on 26 June. For MacArthur it was 'Mars' last gift to an old warrior.'

AUGUST CRISIS: CINCUNC AT TAIPEH

MacArthur had long disapproved of the Administration's China policy and thought that, as Whitney puts it, 'the military fortunes of America lay in the hands of those who understood little of the Pacific and practically nothing about Korea.'.[1] Just

[1] Whitney, p. 319.

before the fighting in Korea started, MacArthur had emphasised in Tokyo the importance of Formosa to Louis Johnson, a Cabinet opponent of Acheson, and Omar Bradley. They had agreed with him. But the Administration still hoped at some future time to retrieve its China policy. 'The present military neutralisation of Formosa,' the President said in a message to Congress on 19 July, 'is without prejudice to the political questions affecting that island . . . With peace re-established, even the most complex political questions are susceptible of solution.' When Collins and Vandenberg visited Tokyo in July, MacArthur had suggested that he go to Formosa to explain to Chiang the reasons why his offer of troops for Korea had been turned down. On 27 July, the National Security Council decided that military aid and a survey team should be sent to Formosa, for JCS had been expressing great concern about the military situation on the island. Replying to MacArthur's suggestion that he visit Taipeh, JCS suggested that he send a senior officer and go later himself as apparently the State Department was worried about the political problems raised by the neutralisation of the island. In any case, the decision was up to him as the responsible commander, and on 31 July, MacArthur, Almond, Whitney, Willoughby and Stratemeyer flew down from Tokyo to discuss defence problems with the Gimo.

The talks with Chiang and Madame Chiang, conducted in an atmosphere of cordiality, caused consternation in Washington and in Allied capitals where they were seen as possibly precipitating Nationalist action against the mainland in violation of the neutralisation order, action of which MacArthur approved. Chiang issued a statement on 1 August announcing that the meeting had taken place at a 'most difficult time' for his cause, but that 'the foundations were thus laid for a joint defence of Formosa and for Sino-American military co-operation'. The communique looked forward to collaboration with 'our old comrade in arms, General MacArthur', who was much admired on Formosa 'for the determination with which he has carried on the common struggle against totalitarianism in Asia, and for the depth of his understanding of the menace of Communism'. The admiration was mutual, for on returning to Tokyo, the General praised Chiang for his 'indomitable determination to resist Communist domination'.

A Truman intimate, Averell Harriman, was despatched hurriedly to Tokyo to keep MacArthur in line—and to insist that the war in Korea was a collective effort and that American action on Formosa was temporary, indicating no change of policy. Harriman arrived on 6 August and expounded official policy to MacArthur in several long conclaves. But back in Washington, he reported to Truman that, 'For reasons which are difficult to explain, I did not feel that we had come to a full agreement on the way things should be handled on Formosa ... He accepted the President's position and will act accordingly but without full conviction. He has a strange idea that we should back anybody who will fight Communism ...' MacArthur also felt that the US had not improved its position by 'kicking Chiang around' and he was 'prepared to deal with the political problems' of Formosa. SCAP was letting it be known that he was used to policy making: but yet the basis of his dealing with Formosa was his military *expertise*.[1]

As MacArthur had privately promised to be good, Truman publicly stated that they 'saw eye to eye on Formosa policy'. By this time a military survey team under Maj.-Gen. Fox had arrived in Taipeh on 4 August. But on 10 August, back came a blast from Tokyo. The Formosa visit had been 'maliciously misrepresented to the public by those who have invariably in the past propagandised a policy of defeatism and appeasement in the Pacific ...' This was countered by a directive from the Secretary of Defence on 14 August[2] that 'no one other than the President as Commander-in-Chief has the authority to order or authorise preventative action against concentrations on the mainland ...' The cravens were obviously in the White House, State and the Pentagon. ...

But an even bigger uproar between Truman and MacArthur was to follow. Deeply immersed in supervising the fighting on the perimeter, and even more in the planning for the Inchon landing, MacArthur was asked on 17 August to send a message for the annual convention of the ex-service organisation, Veterans of Foreign Wars. 'This was an excellent opportunity,' writes Whitney, not apparently being ironical, 'to place him-

[1] Truman, *Memoirs II*, 368-79, and Whitney, pp. 368-83 cover the viewpoints of the protagonists in this August crisis.

[2] Truman gives the date of this directive as the 14th. Whitney, the 5th.

self on record as being squarely behind the President.' In Washington it was interpreted differently. The message stated that, with Formosa, United States air power could dominate 'every Asiatic port from Vladivostok to Singapore', Its fall to a potential enemy would push back the defence perimeter to the Pacific coast of the United States, for the island was an unsinkable aircraft carrier and submarine tender. If Formosa fell, war was 'inevitable'. There was also an extremely powerful refutation of the State Department policy of avoiding action that would antagonise anti-colonialist sentiment in Asia:

Nothing could be more fallacious than the threadbare argument by those who advocate appeasement and defeatism in the Pacific that if we do not defend Formosa we alienate continental Asia. Those who speak thus do not understand the Orient. They do not grasp that it is in the pattern of the Oriental psychology to respect and to follow aggressive, resolute and dynamic leadership — to quickly turn from a leadership characterised by timidity or vacillation — and they underestimate the Oriental mentality. . . .

This pro-Formosan manifesto was embargoed for the 28th but on 26 August, Acheson, Johnson and Bradley were summoned to the White House; Harriman had been told by a newspaperman about the message. It was too late to suppress it, as it was set up, and it was eventually printed in the *US News and World Report*, and read into the Congressional Record. Truman was furious; the onslaught on his Far East policy had even been sent over the Army's teleprinter network from Tokyo, and he gave 'serious thought' to dismissing the General. MacArthur was ordered to withdraw — at least officially — his message; according to Whitney this was his 'first clear illustration of the devious workings of the Washington-London team' who wanted to hand over Formosa to the Communists.

There were other serious internal political problems at hand in Washington; on 25 August, Navy Secretary Matthews had openly called for a preventive war, 'instituting a war to compel co-operation for peace'. Fortunately, as far as the allies were concerned in the UN, Warren Austin, the US ambassador had sent a long letter to Trygve Lie on that same day repeating the official policy on Formosa, but there also were signs that a new Sino-Soviet policy was emerging. Chou En-lai had cabled the Secretary-General on 20 August demanding participation in UN discussions on Korea; '. . . The Chinese people cannot but be concerned about solution of the Korean question . . .' Two days later Malik unleashed a new tirade against US Korean policy, threatening a 'widening of the conflict' if the war continued. Although Chou again cabled Lake Success on the 24th, this time belatedly protesting against Truman's neutralisation order to the Seventh Fleet, on 27 and 30 August the emphasis in two new messages was again on Korea, protesting this time against alleged American air attacks north of the Sino-Korean Yalu frontier line in the Antung region. As August passed without Communist military victory in Korea, the Chinese may have as early as this seen a future threat to their whole position in Asia. MacArthur's activities and possibly Matthews' speech, further meant that the Paper Tiger was becoming a 'mad dog' in Peking's propaganda.

But on both sides the diplomatic and propaganda emphasis was returning to the Korean crucible at the beginning of September, away from Formosa. Inside the Administration, Louis Johnson was forced to resign on 12 September, to be succeeded by Truman's 'greatest living American', George Marshall, who strongly supported the Truman-Acheson line. Johnson was discredited not only because of his association with the drastic budgetary cuts in the defence programme before Korea, but because of his hostility to Acheson and his suspected private advocacy of preventive war.[1]

By Marshall's accession to the Administration, Truman's position had been politically strengthened; military developments also were about to bring a dramatic change in the whole nature of the Korean War: the X Corps landed at Inchon on 15 September.

---

[1] In Johnson's words there was a 'really violent discussion' between Acheson and himself on the subject of Formosa during the Blair House conference of 25 June, *Hearings*, p. 2580. According to Hanson Baldwin in the *New York Times*, 1 September 1950, Matthews' speech was a trial balloon endorsed by Johnson who had been 'selling the same doctrine of preventive war in private conversation around Washington.' Whiting, p. 188. Johnson had also quarrelled with Truman over the appointment of Thomas Finletter as Air Secretary.

CHAPTER FIVE

INCHON: THE IMPOSSIBLE VICTORY

> Some operations if carried out to their logical end may
> change the entire aspect of war. . . . The entire movable
> army strikes at the enemy in the heart of his own country.
> Such resolutions by great generals are stamped with the
> mark of true genius.
>
> DENNIS HART MAHAN

> A swift and vigorous transition to attack — the flashing
> sword of vengeance — is the most brilliant point of the
> defensive.
>
> VON CLAUSEWITZ

OPERATION CHROMITE

MacARTHUR first thought of an amphibious landing at
Inchon during his visit to the front near Suwon on 29 June,
before American troops were sent to Korea. Watching the
remnants of the South Korean Army falling back across the
Han, he knew that, if the Communist advance continued, their
supply-lines would become over-extended. A landing deep in the
rear at Inchon, would not only confront the invaders with a
two-front war, but disrupt these supply lines completely for
the Inchon-Seoul area was the most important road and rail hub
in Korea. An amphibious landing here would combine the
tactical surprise of his landing on the Admiralty islands in
February, 1944, which had shortened the Pacific War by a
month with the massive strategic envelopment of Hollandia
two months later when his forces leapfrogged 500 miles along
the New Guinea coast to outflank an entire Japanese army.
Inchon would be a vast turning movement in the classical tradition. And if his forces were heavily engaged in the South, he
must still go ahead. Jackson had struck in the Valley when
McClellan was only five miles from Richmond on the Chicka-
hominy.

There were added political attractions in that the capital of South Korea was only eighteen miles east of Inchon, and its recapture would provide one of those psychological warfare gestures that so attracted MacArthur. On the international level he conceived a victory here as reversing the whole shameful tide of 'defeatism and appeasement' in the Far East. Inchon would not merely be a military victory. In the Dai-Ichi world view, 'MacArthur courageously set his eyes on a greater goal; to salvage the reputation of Allied arms, to bring into sharper focus the colossal threat of imperialist Mongoloid pan-Slavism under the guise of Communism, and to smash its current challenge in one great blow.'[1]

Planning immediately started in Tokyo on Operation BLUE-HEARTS to put the 1st Cavalry Division ashore at Inchon as early as 20 July. But the rapid North Korean advance meant that the division had to be sent in at Pohang-dong and BLUE-HEARTS was abandoned on 10 July. On the same day, however, Lt.-Gen. Shepherd, Commander, Fleet Marine Force, Pacific, told MacArthur in Tokyo that if the JCS approved, it would be possible to get the whole of the 1st Marine Division to Korea in six weeks and in action by 15 September. MacArthur then asked the Pentagon for the remaining two regiments of the division—the 5th Marine Regiment, sailing between 12 and 14 July from San Diego, was about to leave for the Pusan Perimeter where it would be temporarily designated the 1st Provisional Marine Brigade. After mobilisation of the Division's reserves was ordered, on 25 July JCS approved the despatch of only the 1st Marines, but changing their minds, decided to send 7th Marines as well on 10 August. MacArthur would thus have the full division for his venture, but only two Marine regiments for D-Day, 15 September.

The division's base at Camp Pendleton, California, was frantic with activity during the last days of July as reservists arrived for their hasty training and as tanks, trucks and aircraft were demothballed. The first transports for Japan left San Diego on 13-14 August and the division's commanding general, Maj.-Gen. O. P. Smith, left by air for Tokyo on 18 August. Seven thousand miles away a battalion of the 7th Regiment, training with the Sixth Fleet at Suda Bay, Crete, was ordered east via Suez and Ceylon

[1] Willoughby, *MacArthur 1941-51*, pp. 347-8.

and left for Japan on 16 August. It was D-Day minus thirty.

As the Stateside effort got under way, planning for the landing, known as Operation CHROMITE, proceeded. This was the responsibility of the Joint Strategic Plans and Operations Group, an inter-service planning group under the control of the Operations Division of the Far East Command. (This group was the chief planning agency for the UNC during the war.) From JSPOG emerged the 'Special Planning Staff', the nucleus of the future staff of the X Corps which would go ashore at Inchon on 15 September and which Almond was assigned to command on 26 August when the Corps was activated. The new Corps was a GHQ reserve quite separate from EUSAK. MacArthur also intended that Almond would retain his position as Chief of Staff, FEC, as he hoped the war would end soon after the landing, and thus FEC would 'lend' its chief of staff and other planners to X Corps for the operation.[1] Besides the Marines, the Corps' second division was created by building up with all available reinforcements and even South Koreans, the 7th Infantry Division (Maj.-Gen. David G. Barr), the one division of the Eighth Army not sent to Korea from Japan.

The successive objectives of the operation called for the neutralisation of Wolmi-do, the island controlling Inchon harbour, a landing in the city, seizure of Kimpo Airfield, and the capture of Seoul. The main drive would be carried out by the Marine Division while 7th Division would cover the right flank and move south towards Suwon. Both divisions would then form a blocking position as Eighth Army advanced north from the Pusan Perimeter. This was the plan once the X Corps was ashore. In charge of getting the men ashore was Rear Admiral James H. Doyle, the Pacific Fleet's Amphibious Group Commander, who would lead the Attack Force, Task Force 90. All the work of co-ordination with the Landing Force (Marines) was done aboard Doyle's flagship, *Mount McKinley*, tied up at Tokyo docks. Doyle was responsible to Vice-Admiral Struble, Seventh Fleet, who was in over-all command of the invasion armada,

---

[1] Almond never returned to the Dai-Ichi as COS, FEC, after leaving for Inchon on 12 September 1950. The Acting COS, Maj.-Gen. Doyle Hickey, was confirmed in the post on 16 April 1951, only, it should be noted, after MacArthur's dismissal. Hickey then remained COS until 27 March 1953. (OCMH to author, 14 June 1962.)

and who in his turn reported to Vice-Admiral Joy, COM-NAVFE.

From the beginning, there was strong, almost violent opposition to CHROMITE. The Eighth Army staff objected to weakening the perimeter by taking away the Marine Brigade, and held that if the forces earmarked for Inchon could be sent to Pusan, the North Koreans could be beaten without what they regarded as a dangerous grandstand play. Other officers suggested alternative sites for the landing. But Chinnampo, the port of Pyongyang was too far north, at Kunsan the envelopment would be too shallow, and Posung-Myon, on the west coast near Osan, had an inadequate road net behind the beach. The most relentless opposition came from the Navy and Marines, 'We drew up a list of every conceivable and natural handicap and Inchon had 'em all,' said Doyle's gunfire support officer, Lt.-Commander Arlie Capps.

For the port was unique in its disadvantages. The sea approach to the harbour was through the narrow Flying Fish channel, which not only had a five-knot current, but was studded with rocks, shoals, reefs and islands which piled up the tides into a bore. The tidal range was immense for the Far East, ranging from twenty-three average spring tides to thirty-three feet maximum spring tides. On the ebb, the harbour became a vast mudflat stretching out three miles to sea. Most landing craft drew twenty-three feet, but the vital LSTs drew twenty-nine feet, and thus only on 15 September and 11 October — give a day or so — would the springs be high enough to take them into Inchon — and even then they could enter or leave port only for three hours on each tide. There were other difficulties about the inadequacy of Inchon harbour, which, at the best, could handle only 6,000 tons a day, 10% of Pusan's capacity. Pier space was restricted, cargo-handling facilities were few, and the off-loading spaces were separated by the causeway to Wolmido, which meant that cargo planning was further complicated. The Marines had never landed in the centre of a city before, so the 'beaches' at Inchon would be the twelve-foot high sea-walls which would have to be climbed by ladders from the assault craft. Even the geography, as well as the hydrography, favoured the defence. Not only Wolmi, but the steep hills of the town looked down on the 'beaches', and as the bad conditions in the channel precluded a night assembly of the fleet, the main landing would have to take place in the evening, allowing two hours of daylight for the two Marine regiments to get a toehold in a seaport city of 250,000 inhabitants, about the size of Norfolk, Virginia, or Cardiff. Everything about Inchon violated all the precise Navy-Marine doctrine carefully evolved during the Pacific War.

It was with these facts that Smith was briefed by Doyle after he arrived in Tokyo from Pendleton on 22 August, and preliminary conferences with Almond and MacArthur produced no results. But bigger brass than Smith were opposed to CHROMITE. The operation was a matter of 'great concern'[1] to JCS, and Collins and Sherman were in town determined to make MacArthur call the whole thing off. Omar Bradley himself had stated less than a year before, during the B-36 hearings, the 'Revolt of the Admirals', that in the atomic age large-scale amphibious operations would never again occur, and in spite of all the strategic and tactical objections to Inchon, what impression had MacArthur given to Smith? 'It was more than confidence which upheld him; it was supreme and almost mystical faith that he could not fail.'[2]

Six weeks of debate on Operation CHROMITE came to a climax when the whole plan was debated on 23 August. The conference opened at 5.30 p.m. on the sixth floor of the Dai-Ichi. As well as MacArthur and his commanders, Stratemeyer, Joy and Almond, there were the two Chiefs of Staff and a strong Navy-Marine contingent, Radford, CINCPAC, Struble, Shepherd and Doyle, whose experts waited in Almond's office. Doyle opened the meeting by listing the Navy's objections. He introduced to the meeting his experts who detailed all the hydrographic and navigational dangers at Inchon. Surprise was said to be vital, yet the enemy too, knew the dates of the high tides that were necessary for a landing. Doyle summed up: 'The best I can say is that Inchon is not impossible.'

General Collins then voiced the Army's strategic misgivings. He was worried about weakening the perimeter by the withdrawal of the Marine brigade for Inchon, and wondered whether, once the X Corps was ashore, it could not be pinned down. The Army Chief of Staff probably had Anzio in mind; many Army

[1] *Hearings*, p. 1295.
[2] Montross and Canzona, Vol. II, *The Inchon-Seoul Operation*, p. 39.

opponents of Inchon had pointed out that it violated a basic strategic precept, that of dividing one's forces in face of a superior enemy. Collins, supported by Sherman, went on to suggest a landing at Kunsan, where X Corps would be nearer the perimeter if anything went wrong, and where the tides and beaches were better. The discussion raged back and forth until MacArthur presented his case, speaking for forty-five minutes, puffing at his corn-cob pipe.

He passionately defended his plan, demonstrating to his audience that it was not logic but intuition which had guided his choice of Inchon. 'The very arguments you have made as to the impracticabilities involved will tend to ensure for me the element of surprise. For the enemy commander will reason that no one would be so brash as to make such an attempt.' If experienced American amphibious specialists thought Inchon was almost out of the question, then so would the Communists. MacArthur recalled Wolfe's victory at Quebec. He, too, had been opposed by his staff, who like Montcalm had regarded an assault up the cliffs to the south of the city as impossible. So the French had left the heights unguarded and Canada had been won on the Plains of Abraham. Like Wolfe, MacArthur would take the enemy by surprise, and like Quebec, Inchon would be an impossible victory. The Navy had not let him down and, although he considered it a 5,000 to 1 risk, the assault would succeed.

As far as Collins' suggestion for Kunsan was concerned, Mac-Arthur went on, it would merely outflank and not envelop the enemy. It would not cut the Communist supply route and the Eighth Army would still be condemned to a bloody war of attrition in the perimeter. The amphibious weapon was the most powerful weapon his command possessed, and to be employed properly it should strike deep and hard. . . .

MacArthur outlined the political importance of Korea in the world struggle. 'It is plainly apparent that here in Asia is where the Communist conspirators have elected to make their play for global conquest. The test is not in Berlin or Vienna, in London, Paris or Washington. It is here and now—it is along the Naktong River in South Korea. . . .' If the war in Korea were lost, the fate of Europe would be jeopardised. In Europe the war was being fought with words, in Korea with arms, and the prestige

of the Western world hung in the balance. Concluded Mac-
Arthur, 'I can almost hear the ticking of the second hand of
destiny. We must act now or we will die.' Inchon would succeed, and it would save 100,000 lives. 'We shall land at Inchon
and I shall crush them. . . .' he ended, his voice sinking to a
whisper.

The conference then broke up with MacArthur neither asking
for, nor receiving, the approval of the Joint Chiefs present. Most
of those present had been convinced by MacArthur's case.[1]
Shepherd and Sherman however privately pleaded with him the
next morning to land at Posung-Myon where some Navy frog-
men had secretly landed and found beach conditions suitable.
MacArthur was insistent on Inchon; 'I wish I had that man's
confidence', Sherman remarked before he left for Washington
with Collins. Both Smith and Doyle were told to go ahead with
the detailed planning for CHROMITE — and on 28 August,
JCS approved. Moreover, the more the Tokyo planners thought
about Inchon, the more they came to see that their objections
justified it, and they became fascinated by the illogical choice
of the port for a landing.

The final plan for the assault was ready by 4 September. On
D-Day, 15 September, the tides at Inchon were 0659 and 1919,
with a maximum of thirty-one feet of water in the evening. On
the morning tide, a Battalion Landing Team (BLT-3) of 5th
Marines would land at GREEN beach on Wolmi-do at 0630.
The remaining two battalions of the regiment with ancillary
forces making up Regimental Combat Team-5 would land at
RED beach, Inchon's sea front, at H-hour 1730. All three battalions of RCT-1 would simultaneously go ashore at BLUE beach
three miles south-east of RED where it could command the road
and rail routes into Inchon from Seoul. At H-hour, when there
were twenty-five feet of water on the flow tide, eight LSTs would
set out from the Task Force to land at RED almost immediately
behind the assault force, bringing tanks, bulldozers, engineers
and shore party port control teams to get Inchon working to its
maximum capacity.

[1] Whitney, Willoughby, Montross and Canzona, II, and Karig, *Battle Report,
The War in Korea* are the best sources for this conference and the planning of
CHROMITE. But see also Appleman, Chap. 25, and Cagle and Manson, Chap.
3, for excellent general surveys from their respective service viewpoints.

As this masterpiece of amphibious ingenuity depended on surprise and minimum opposition, so great were the hazards, intelligence was a major problem. A Joint Special Operations group from Far East Command's G-2 had sent over 200 agents into the area, and from all estimates it was eventually decided that there were about 500 North Koreans on Wolmi-do, another 500 at Kimpo, and about 1,500 in Inchon. But last-minute reinforcements could alter these figures and a series of deception measures were organised. Chinnampo was bombarded by a British task force as D-Day approached and at Kunsan the British frigate *Whitesand Bay* put a raiding party ashore to coincide with air strikes and psywar leaflet drops in the area. A bombardment of Samchok on the east coast was laid on for D-Day, as well as an ROK landing near Yongdok (which was abortive on the day). A particularly daring project was the landing of a naval officer, Lt. Eugene Clark on Yonghung-do, fifteen miles south of Inchon to inspect beach conditions in the landing zone. One night he rowed to the harbour wall, discovering that the mud was waist-deep; the Marines, as planned, would have to enter Inchon on ladders. Clark was also supposed to land on nearby Palmi-do and restore the Inchon harbour entrance beacon in Flying Fish channel.

In early September a new crisis broke out with the great North Korean offensive against the Pusan Perimeter. Walker was particularly reluctant to part with the Marine Brigade. Weakening the perimeter now might mean that, as the X Corps took Inchon, the People's Army might be entering Pusan. The 1st Marines had now arrived in Japan and on 13 September the Marine Brigade reverted to its old designation of 5th Marines prior to joining the rest of the Division at Inchon. Smith insisted that CHROMITE could not be carried out without the two Marine regiments and Struble worked out an ingenious compromise. A regiment of the 7th Division was held in Pusan harbour aboard the transports as a literally floating reserve for the perimeter before leaving for Inchon at the last moment. Such were the margins the planners were working on.

The first slow convoy had already left Japan when the JSC suddenly queried the operation again on 7 September. Not only had all reserves in Japan, but most of those in the US had now been committed to Korea. There was nothing left if any-

thing went wrong at Inchon. MacArthur replied that the landing was the only way out of a hopeless war of attrition, and on
8 September Inchon was re-approved by the Joint Chiefs, who
had obtained the unnecessary endorsement of the President.
They, at least, would have it in writing if disaster occurred;
nevertheless Washington expected the destruction of the North
Koreans south of the 38th Parallel. This new query was dismissed by MacArthur as 'pessimism at its worst', yet never
before had he shown so much last minute hesitancy about a
landing, the largest amphibious force he had ever commanded.
'No, there was no doubt about the risk. It was a tremendous
gamble.'[1]

THE LANDING: D-DAY AT INCHON

The complicated machinery of CHROMITE had started
when the slow Pontoon Movement Group left Yokohama on
5 September. Struble's armada of 260 ships, carrying nearly
70,000 men, including vessels from Australia, Canada, New
Zealand, France, Holland, as well as the British escort carrier,
Triumph. Included in the fleet were thirty-seven Japanese-
manned LSTs produced by SCAP. The Marine Division was to
outload at Kobe, the 5th Marines from Pusan, and 7th Division
from Yokohama. Most of the escorting vessels assembled at
Sasebo. A series of assembly points were arranged in the East
China Sea. At IOWA, for example, the Yokohama convoy would
meet its components from Sasebo, while a transport movement
from Kobe would meet the Pusan supply vessels at ARKANSAS.
The end of the open sea navigational phase and the beginning
of the approach to Flying Fish channel indicated CALIFORNIA
had been reached.

All movements were on schedule on 11 September when
typhoon KEZIA loomed in from the Pacific with winds of 125
m.p.h. At sea, bound for Sasebo, Doyle remarked on the bridge
of *Mount McKinley* that it was one of the worst storms he had
ever encountered. The transports were ordered to hold their
course otherwise the entire operation would be dislocated and
soon KEZIA wandered away from the invasion force. On the

[1] Whitney, p. 358.

evening of 12 September, MacArthur, Almond, Whitney and other V.I.Ps flew from Tokyo to Itazuke in CINCUNC's new Constellation, *SCAP*, and then boarded the *McKinley* at Sasebo. The flagship cast off in the small hours of 13 September bound for Inchon. It was the anniversary of Quebec.

By the night of the 14th the fleet was closing in on CALIFORNIA and just before dawn on D-Day, helped by the glimmer of the beacon Clark had managed to light on Palmi-do, the *McKinley* steamed into the Inchon narrows, Wolmi-do had been bombed, rocketed, napalmed and shelled for five days and now the pre-landing bombardment from Struble's cruisers started at 0545. It was followed by an air strike from the carriers and then three rocket ships headed for the island just ahead of the landing craft (LCVPs) to dump their deadly load on Wolmi's defenders. At 0633 the first troops of 5th Marines were ashore on GREEN to meet only scattered shots. The flag was raised on Radio Hill, dominating Inchon harbour, at 0655, and the whole of this 105-metre high feature which had caused the planners so much worry was taken by 0800. The watching commanders on the bridge of the *Mount McKinley* had already seen the flag; with the Marines in control of Wolmi. MacArthur sent a message to Struble aboard his flagship *Rochester*:

THE NAVY AND THE MARINES HAVE NEVER SHONE MORE BRIGHTLY
THAN THIS MORNING MACARTHUR.

Wolmi-do had been taken without a single fatality, as well as the attached islet of Sowolmi-do where the defenders, although dazed from the air strike and the bombardment, made a fight for it. By noon the whole Wolmi complex was occupied and the first part of CHROMITE had succeeded. The tide rolled back and by early afternoon the Marines on Wolmi were marooned by a vast sheet of Yellow Sea mud — the mud where so many ships could go aground and be at the mercy of the North Korean artillery. There was little activity in Inchon a few hundred yards away over the causeway, but how many North Koreans were hidden in the waterfront buildings? Once again at 1430 the cruisers started firing, this time at targets in Inchon itself, preparing for the main landing at 1730. The tide came flowing in and at 1645 the amphibious tractors pushed off from the transports for the beaches. A huge pall of smoke from burning buildings covered the city.

On RED beach, although the tide was racing in, the top of the sea wall was still four feet above the ramps of RCT-5's landing craft, mostly LCVPs, as they touched ground at 1731. The men clambered ashore on their ladders under a rain of grenades from their comrades behind. On the right of the beach the important objective of the British Consulate was soon taken and a platoon established on the base of the commanding Observatory Hill. Above the sea wall on the left of RED a North Korean bunker pinned down the Marines, and there was a fight for Cemetery Hill, another dominating feature where a Communist mortar company eventually surrendered, as dazed by the invaders' fire-power as the defenders of Wolmi-do. By midnight the regiment held a firm line across Observatory Hill which controlled RED beach; everything had gone almost according to plan, although there had been some confusion over company objectives in the mêlée. Equally important, the LSTs had been run ashore and were disgorging their equipment while still under North Korean fire. 'Of all the calculated risks taken at Inchon, perhaps the most daring was the decision to ground eight LSTs abreast on

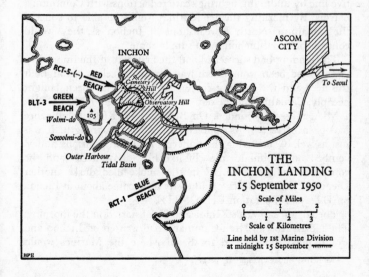

THE
INCHON LANDING
15 September 1950

RED beach immediately after the assault troops landed.'[1] The success of the Red beach assault had meant that within six hours the Marines were firmly lodged inside Inchon City.

Over on BLUE beach where RCT-1 landed south of the city, and where the assault craft were mostly the slower LVT amphibious tracked vehicles, smoke from the fires in Inchon and rain clouds obscured the beach from the task forces as H-hour approached. Behind the rocky sea wall on the right of the beach lay some industrial suburbs. There was also a big ditch in the middle of the landing zone. The first wave on the left was ashore at exactly 1730, but the amtracs trundled inland only to be halted by a collapsed road as the men got out and occupied the high ground overlooking the beach. Some craft from the second wave grounded on mud 300 yards offshore and the Marines had to wade ashore, while other amtrac drivers exchanged shots with North Koreans on the waterfront. Elements of the 1st Marines' reserve battalion went ashore on the Inchon tidal basin harbour wall, and were re-embarked just in time to prevent them stranding. With the sea wall dynamited on BLUE to let later waves through as some measure of beach control was established, this regiment too had reached its objective line by midnight, fighting scattered actions with Communist patrols. By morning the 1st Marines would be able to squeeze the remaining North Koreans out of Inchon as they would control the Seoul-Inchon main supply route.

The landing had succeeded and the first part of the impossible victory had been won. There was a general feeling throughout the fleet and the landing force that victory had been bought cheaply. Casualties for the day were only 196 — 20 KIA, 1 DOW, 1 MIA and 174 wounded. On BLUE as on RED, Intelligence had been correct in its appreciation of enemy strength. It was just as well. Considering the undermanned gun positions honeycombed on Wolmi-do, the cliff-like hills above RED and the confused landing at BLUE in the smoke-filled dusk, another Dieppe or Omaha Beach could easily have come about at Inchon on D-Day of Operation CHROMITE.

The advance towards Kimpo and Seoul started in the morning. The North Korean High Command had written off Inchon and would make their stand for Seoul where the Marines would

[1] Montross and Canzona, II, p. 125.

have their fire power neutralised by a built-up area, and face a capital turned into a fortress. Smith planned a two-pronged move to Seoul, 1st Marines would advance direct to Han and the industrial suburb of Yongdungpo, while 5th Marines would take Kimpo, cross the Han to the north and strike into Seoul from the north-west.

Civil government had been re-established in Inchon on the 17th, but there was still mopping up to be done by the 1st Regiment of the (South) Korean Marine Corps, under the direction of RCT-5. No one, friend or foe, was safe from the ROK Marines: as the US Marine historians comment in a throat-clearing manner, 'No fault could have been found with the thoroughness of these Korean allies who were perhaps inclined to be too zealous when they suspected subversion.' Other fighting took place on the main road to Seoul, where early on the morning of 17 September six T-34s and 200 NK infantry were ambushed by 5th Marines. No sooner was the action over when MacArthur, Struble, Almond, Shepherd and Smith, accompanied by a body of X Corps officers appeared on the scene. After the departure of CINCUNC and his entourage a suspicious noise was heard from the culvert on which his Jeep had been parked and seven North Koreans were flushed out, the only survivors of the tank column. The next morning, 7th Infantry Division started landing at Inchon; and on 21 September the Marine Division's third rifle regiment, 7th Marines, disembarked.

After a confused night action by the enemy, 1st Air Force Division — a composite force patched up from various shattered units — Kimpo fell on 18 September, offering up two undamaged Stormoviks and a YAK fighter. Little used by the North Koreans, it would become one of the busiest airports in the Far East within a week. By 20 September 5th Marines had crossed the Han as planned and in twenty-four hours were only 5,000 yards north-west of Syngman Rhee's Capitol. But brave and determined resistance slowed them at this point and at Yong-dungpo, too, the 1st Regiment had only reached the Han after heavy fighting on 22 September.

But there was a feeling that Seoul was about to fall. In the south the Eighth Army, opening its offensive on the 16th, had not crossed the Naktong in force until 19 September. This un-expected enemy resistance had given MacArthur on the 17th a moment of alarm that perhaps after all Inchon had been too deep a penetration and that the perimeter could be contained by the North Koreans; he had contemplated a second landing at Kunsan. But the first Naktong crossings soon turned into a pursuit when the People's Army in the south fell apart on the 23rd, and Inchon was spectacularly justified as Walker's forces started moving north. By 26 September 1st Cavalry from the south had linked with 7th Infantry at Osan and large numbers of North Koreans were surrounded. Meanwhile the Associated Press, Tokyo Office, had announced the fall of Seoul on 22 September, in the South West Pacific victory communique tradition. It was not so. The last, bloodiest and most spectacular phase of Operation CHROMITE would take another five days.

THE TERRIBLE LIBERATION

'Few people can have suffered so terrible a liberation,' commented R. W. Thompson on the fall of Seoul. Thompson, who covered the war during the autumn of 1950 for the London *Daily Telegraph*, and later wrote the fascinating *Cry Korea* about his experiences from Inchon to the Chongchon and the December retreat, already at this time found something 'profoundly disturbing' about the campaign. It was the immense results of American firepower that particularly depressed Thompson. 'The slightest resistance brought down a deluge of destruction blotting out the area', and with it hundreds, thousands of civilians. These close support tactics had been used in Europe; in poverty-stricken Korea their effects seemed all the more devastating. But the North Koreans would fight on occasion as savagely in defeat and retreat as on the offensive, although they lacked heavy equipment and possessed by then only a few T-34s. At the heart of the West's military thought lies the belief that machines must be used to save its men's lives; Korea would progressively become a horrific illustration of the effects of a limited war where one side possessed the firepower and the other the manpower.

The apocalyptic fall of Seoul which ended the first phase of the war was an illustration of some of these aspects of the fighting. The reasons for the frontal assault on the city were not entirely military. MacArthur and Almond were impatient to capture the ROK capital by 25 September, as then GHQ could issue a victory communique exactly three months after the North Korean invasion. On 23 September Almond made it clear to O. P. Smith, not for the first time, that the city must fall by the 25th. The X Corps commander was dissatisfied with the Marines' progress, while most Marine officers thought that they were being hurried too much. Almond now suggested that as 5th Marines were stalled north-west of the city, 1st Marines should be brought round to the south-east to attack Seoul from that direction. Smith opposed the plan as he understandably wanted to preserve the tactical integrity of his division. He insisted that no change be made in the plan for reducing the capital and that 1st Marines should continue to attack across the Han from Yong-dungpo while 7th Marines, now having arrived at Inchon, should be brought round to the north. The Marine Division could then advance into Seoul in a united front. Meanwhile, protecting the left flank of the Division on the Kimpo peninsula was the 187th Airborne Regimental Combat Team, flown into the airfield from Japan on 24 and 27 September. Elements of the KMC Regiment were also active in this area eliminating NK remnants.

Almond backed down and then decided instead to send the 32nd Infantry Regiment from 7th Division, with the ROK 17th Regiment attached, into Seoul from the south-east. On the 25th, 32nd Infantry crossed the river in Marine amtracs and seized South Mountain dominating Seoul, while the ROK regiment fanned out to the east after the crossing to control the main road and rail routes out of Seoul towards Chunchon and the central mountains. A completely new battle for Seoul had been cobbled together by Almond in his attempt to take the city on time — a gigantic psychological warfare stunt which could hardly succeed as it was later discovered that over 20,000 North Korean troops were making a last-ditch stand. Most of these Communist troops were destroyed.

During the 25-26th Seoul became an inferno as the Marines advanced into the city in a scything movement from south, north and west. They slowly ground forward under a hail of protecting artillery, mortar fire and close air support which levelled whole acres. The defenders fought with great tenacity to the end, firing from rooftops, trees and side streets. Intense

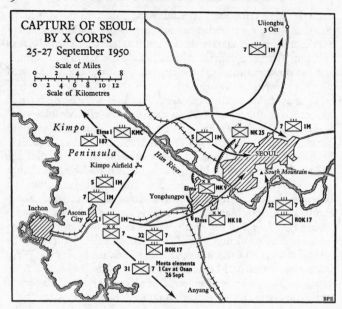

CAPTURE OF SEOUL
BY X CORPS
25-27 September 1950

heat from the burning buildings added to the nightmare, and suicide squads attacked American tanks. On the 26th, the 7th Division moving westwards from South Mountain after their crossing of the Han, joined hands with the Marines, but the fighting went on. Oblivious of the holocaust in central Seoul, Tokyo had gone ahead and announced the fall of the city on the 25th. Not until the afternoon of the 27th did the 5th Marines reach the Capitol of the ROK. Surrounded by hills blazing with napalm and huge benevolently smiling posters of Stalin and Kim Il Sung, the Stars and Stripes at last floated over the shattered fifth city of Asia.

Two days after the fall of Seoul, MacArthur restored the government of the Republic of Korea to Seoul in an emotionalistic ceremony with Rhee held in the Capitol. There was another of those historic parallels with the South West Pacific campaign which occur throughout the MacArthur period of the Korean War. In February, 1945, MacArthur had restored the government of the Philippines to Osmena in the Malacanan

Palace in Manila, understandably, like Rhee's elevation, a fitting climax to a great military achievement. But then, as in 1950, Washington had tried to deny MacArthur his moment. In 1945 it had been Harold Ickes, FDR's peppery Secretary of the Interior, who had tried unsuccessfully to introduce directly into the liberated islands what Willoughby quaintly calls 'many of the concepts then colloquially known in the United States as the New Deal'.[1] In September 1950 the Joint Chiefs had similarly tried unsuccessfully to stop the ceremony of Rhee's restoration — much to the Dai-Ichi's anger — because Washington wanted to get as little involved with Rhee as it did with Chiang. (There was no way of seeing the extent which the Administration would be involved with both in the near future.) The trouble sprang from the fact that in Korea the UN was committed to defend in the name of resisting aggression a regime of 'not very good character' which in the past had frequently denied the blessings of freedom and democracy to its own subjects.

The bad political habits of the Rhee regime have not only obscured recognition that UN action in Korea was in defence of the border rather than for the purpose of bringing complete democracy to the ROK, but that the behaviour of the North Korean regime towards its opponents was infinitely worse than anything perpetrated by the ROK Government. In the early months of the war civilian Communists and captured guerillas had sometimes been summarily shot by the South Korean authorities; the executions ceased after protests in the US and Western Europe. These incidents were disgraceful, but unlike the Berias of Pyongyang, the ROK Government was in many ways responsible to UN opinion. Only when the People's Army fell back after Inchon did the full extent of the atrocities under Communist occupation in South Korea become known. The terror, as noted above, had begun with the advance of the KPA, when not only anti-Communists, but all leadership elements wherever possible had been killed. With Inchon and the Naktong break-out, the North Korean Security Police had immediately stepped up their executions. Everywhere the advancing UNC columns found mass graves and in Taejon alone the bodies of between 5,000 and 7,000 South Korean civilians were found.

[1] Willoughby, p. 253.

The NK Security Police had proceeded with their work until the Americans were about to recapture the city. A provisional report by the UN Command charged that 26,000 non-combatant South Koreans had been liquidated by the Communists during their occupation of the south.[1]

In the days following the fall of Seoul it seemed indeed as if the war was over. The 'one great blow' had succeeded and the strategist's dream of complete annihilation had come about. The Korean People's Army had either been shattered on the Naktong, surrounded in the South when Walker's motorised task forces had slashed through after the breakout to Kunsan, Taejon and Osan, inflicting fearful casualties on the way, or destroyed in the battles at Inchon-Seoul. Of the invading army and all its reinforcements which had crossed the 38th Parallel since 25 June it appears that not more than 25,000 to 30,000 disorganised enemy soldiers reached North Korea. Many of those who had escaped death or capture in the south were later caught in the North, a shattered rabble destined for the POW cages. Large amounts of equipment were captured, including hundreds of artillery pieces and survey teams soon located 239 knocked-out T-34s south of the 38th Parallel and 74 destroyed self-propelled 76mm. guns. Those NK troops who did escape, including the commanding general and staff of the KPA Front Headquarters at Kumchon, assembled in the 'Iron Triangle' area twenty miles north of the Parallel on the central front from where NK guerilla activities were directed in the following months. In early November Tokyo would claim 135,000 NK prisoners in addition to 200,000 casualties inflicted, making a grand total of 335,000 North Korean losses. UN casualties during the Inchon-Seoul operation were only about 3,500.[2] The KPA had been virtually destroyed and never fought again above corps strength throughout the war. In 1953 it was estimated to number only about 50,000 men. MacArthur's strategy had been spectacularly vindicated.

That Inchon has become a forgotten victory and not a famous one is due not entirely to the subsequent course of the war in

[1] *Hearings*, p. 3428, a report from the UNC to the Security Council on 6 November 1950. Also Appleman, p. 587-8. See below, p. 316, n.1, for a final Communist war crimes estimate prepared by the US Army.

[2] State Department Bulletin, 13 Nov. 1950; Appleman, p. 541.

Korea, which swept away the dazzling prospects raised by Mac-Arthur's classic victory into a depressing military stalemate and a political partition of Korea. Although no account of Inchon fails to use the conventional glowing adjectives, a revisionist approach to the whole concept and execution of this twentieth-century Cannae has grown up in all three of the American armed services. Predictably the most extreme discounting of the operation has come from the USAF, for in total-war thinking it should never have happened. Thus we read that the landing meant virtually nothing. Stratemeyer's successor at FEAF, General Weyland, has written that 'its actual effects were quite secondary to the air attacks in the destruction of the NKPA. . . . But if the full effects of the air attacks had been recognised, the new forces might have been introduced to better advantage at Pusan. . . .'[1]

A rather more ambiguous Army attitude is expressed by an official historian from the Office of the Chief of Military History, Lt.-Col. Schnabel, which puts its point in its title, *The Inchon Landing, Perilous Gamble or Exemplary Boldness?* After Mac-Arthur decided early in the campaign to land at Inchon he

> let nothing prevent him from carrying out that plan at the earliest moment. He willingly accepted certain risks. To assemble the last of the assault force, he weakened further Walker's precarious defences in southern Korea. He over-rode the counsels of Navy and Marine officers expert in amphibious warfare who argued well against Inchon as a landing site. With little positive knowledge of the enemy's strength and fortifications in the target area, he risked a possible debacle by committing the bulk of his reserves when he had no source of immediate reinforcement.[2]

The North Korean army was so badly thrashed that it never properly recovered. Results are what count, and therefore Inchon was clearly justified. Or was it, considering what could have happened if anything had gone wrong?

The most detailed and searching criticism of CHROMITE has come from those whose star had never shone brighter as

[1] Stewart, *Airpower*, p. 18.
[2] *Army* magazine, May 1959.

on that heroic September morn in Flying Fish channel. The USMC historians are quite emphatic: 'Even success did not alter the conviction of Navy and Marine amphibious specialists that risks had been assumed in the Inchon landing which might have resulted in disaster.'[1] The naval history of the war has pointed out that the landing only beat a Communist mine-laying effort in Inchon by a photo-finish, and that security was almost completely lost. In Japan, where the landing was known as 'Operation Common Knowledge', a Communist spy ring had obtained full details a week before D-Day, but was unable to get through to Pyongyang. One of the naval historians, Commander M. C. Cagle, has suggested that Inchon, while a great vindication of amphibious sea power, by no means proves that *any* beach can be taken in such a landing. Meticulous planning is always necessary, and for the future the Navy should always have a veto on such operations. Reversing the usual laws of military planning, Inchon was 'arbitrarily' chosen by MacArthur, and then reasons were found to justify it:

5,000 to 1 is certainly the outer odds limit for an amphibious assault.[2]

Inchon, then, could not have happened under any other commander but MacArthur. It sprang from his overpowering personality and his self-confidence, and his plan was supported by no one else for it looked back to an age of warfare unencumbered by specialist objections and peripatetic Joint Chiefs. It remains an astonishing achievement precisely because it was a triumph not of military logic and science, but of imagination and intuition. It was justified on no other grounds, but the most overwhelming, most simple; it succeeded and remains a Twentieth Century Cannae ever to be studied.

Yet within the logics of the Korean War, Inchon appears as an ambiguous victory as far as its ultimate results are concerned. Its very success meant that the UN's war aims, shorn from political considerations, were raised from the 38th Parallel to the Yalu, and as Stalin's Korean satellite was vanquished so the new far more formidable enemy of Communist China was to

[1] Montross and Canzona, II, p. 198.

[2] See 'Inchon, Analysis of a Gamble' and 'Errors of the Korean War' by Cagle in *US Naval Institute Proceedings* for January 1954 and March 1958 respectively. Also Cagle and Manson, pp. 78-81.

take the place of North Korea. In his pursuit of the new post-Inchon objectives, MacArthur was unassailable, so great was his prestige, whatever misgivings the Pentagon possessed. After his impossible victory even MacArthur's self-confidence grew, and so, as a result of recommendations made by the United Nations, Inchon led to the Chongchon, a defeat as disastrous as any imagined by contemporary critics of Operations CHROMITE. MacArthur's greatest victory was his last victory.

CHAPTER SIX

CROSSING THE PARALLEL:
FAREWELL TO CONTAINMENT

One of the great realities of political life is the cumulative nature of all political change, the factor of momentum in all political affairs, the dynamic character of all alteration in political prestige. The Soviet leaders know this; and it explains why they are sensitive about yielding anything under pressure, even at the remotest ends of their empire.

GEORGE KENNAN

THE CHALLENGE:
'A UNIFIED, INDEPENDENT AND DEMOCRATIC KOREA'

ALTHOUGH it was not until Inchon that North Korea was defeated, the possibility that peace might be restored not on the basis of the *status quo ante bellum* but on the unification of Korea under UN auspices had been canvassed from the very beginning of the war. As early as 5 July during the House of Commons debate on Korea, Henry Hopkinson, the Conservative MP, had remarked that in repelling the North Korean invasion it would be strategically impossible to stop on the 38th Parallel: 'I suggest that the proper course will be for the democratic countries to proceed to occupy the whole of Korea including Northern Korea. . . .' Eden, on the Opposition front bench, seemed to agree with this view, in a rather ambiguous way, but for the next few weeks little was heard from the politicians as the chief problem then was whether Walker's men could stay in any part of Korea at all. In the Dai-Ichi there were no such doubts.

When Collins had visited Tokyo in mid-July, MacArthur had told him on the 13th that he intended to destroy the North Korean forces and not merely drive them back; and that it might be necessary to occupy all Korea. About the same time Rhee cabled Truman saying that, 'for anything less than re-unification to come out of these great sacrifices of Koreans and their powerful allies would be unthinkable', but it was not until 17 August that the Administration first showed that it was not thinking of stopping on the 38th Parallel if all went well — a demonstration of confidence, perhaps, in the defences of the Pusan perimeter. Speaking in the Security Council debates on Korea, Warren Austin, the American delegate, remarked that 'the United Nations must see that the people of Korea attain complete individual and political freedom. . . . Shall only a part of the country be assured of this freedom? I think not. . . . The General Assembly has decided that fair and free elections should be held throughout the whole of the Korean peninsula. . . . We are waiting, and while we wait, the strength of the United Nations increases.' And on 1 September in a broadcast, the President said the Koreans had a right to be 'free, independent, and united'.[1]

But Washington had not finally made up its mind in spite of these indications of which way the wind was blowing. The imminence of the landing at Inchon, however, soon made it imperative that some sort of military directive be issued to MacArthur — Collins and Sherman had agreed in August, during their stay in Tokyo, that as MacArthur's ultimate military objective was the destruction of the North Korean military forces, ground operations should be extended 'beyond the 38th Parallel as necessary to achieve that goal'.[2] After becoming an official JCS recommendation on 7 September, this Tokyo agreement was discussed by the National Security Council on 11 September. From this discussion emerged a further paper which the President approved that same day and which was sent to MacArthur in the form of a JCS directive on 15 September, D-Day at Inchon. In it, in Truman's paraphrase, 'MacArthur was to conduct the necessary military operations either to force the North Koreans behind the 38th Parallel or to destroy their forces. If there was no indication of threat of entry of Soviet or Chinese Communist elements in force . . . (he) was to extend his operations north of the Parallel and to make plans for the occupation of North Korea . . . no ground operations should take place north of the 38th Parallel in the event of Soviet or

[1] Higgins, *Korea and the Fall of MacArthur*, p. 51; Whiting, pp. 78-9; Truman, *Memoirs II*, pp. 379-80.
[2] Cagle and Manson, p. 112.

Chinese Communist entry.' This NSC recommendation and its succeeding directive faithfully reflected the confusion at the very top of the Government about risks entailed in moving across the Parallel, for 'only after MacArthur had been allowed fully to commit himself would there occur the intervention which was the condition on which the commitment was not to take place.'[1]

Inchon fell, and the advance into the suburbs of Seoul made it clear that the collapse of the North Korean Army was at hand. The fear of Chinese or Soviet intervention was outweighed by the desire to exploit the victory politically, to realise the hopes expressed during the Naktong fighting for the unification of Korea which had been an objective of the US since 1943, and of the UN since 1947. Even more pressing was the need to exploit the situation militarily, and to destroy completely the People's Army, even if it did mean moving across the Parallel — a development justified by the Security Council mandate of 27 June to 'restore international peace and security in the area'. There were also pressing domestic political reasons why Korean unification should be attempted. There were mid-term elections in November; and even before the end of September, Senator Knowland had announced that a failure to cross the Parallel would constitute appeasement of Russia. This was a conviction not confined to the Republicans. A total military victory demanded a total political settlement to justify the Korean sacrifices to the American people, satisfying the psychic need for a clear-cut, absolute solution for Korea in the pre-cold war tradition of American political thought.

Containment, therefore, predicated on a calculated return to the *status quo ante* in cold war and limited war engagements between East and West, was the chief policy casualty of Inchon. Almost two years before John Foster Dulles was to condemn containment as 'negative, futile and immoral', and to advocate the 'liberation' of Communist satellites, a Democratic Administration was embarking, without many doubts, on just such an adventure. The cautious Kennan opposed the new policy but was overruled. The next move was to get UN sanction for the move north.

The delegations to the new session of the General Assembly met at Lake Success on 19 September; the next day, Acheson

[1] Millis, *Arms and the State*, p. 274.

made it clear that he had abandoned his former views, expressed in June, that UN action in Korea was designed 'solely for the purpose of restoring the Republic of Korea to its status prior to the invasion from the north'.[1] Now Korea was to be returned to its own people under the guidance of the UN, according to the Secretary of State. But there was some confusion in finding suitable legal forms for the process of unification. The State Department thought that the resolution of 27 June would cover any action, but Truman wanted a new vote on a new resolution, so Acheson set about lining up the Allies to support a resolution to be introduced into the Assembly. (With Malik back in the Security Council, it would be pointless to ask that body for a new ruling.)

But what was the precise relationship between the military operations in North Korea and the proposed UN recommendation to unify the country? This tortuous boundary would be explored in the MacArthur Hearings and defined, hardly convincingly, by the Secretary of State in these terms:

> *Senator Cain:* If, Sir, the Red Chinese had not entered the war and our allied forces would have rounded up all of those who were party to the aggression in Korea, we would then have unified Korea by force; would we not?
> *Secretary Acheson:* Well, force would have been used to round up the people who were putting on the aggression . . . unifying . . . it would have been through elections and that sort of thing. . . .[2]

Thus force was never explicitly sanctioned by the eight-power resolution which would be passed by the Assembly. But in recommending that "all appropriate steps be taken to ensure conditions of stability' in Korea it was an authorisation of an advance to the Yalu, for how else could elections be held for a 'unified, independent and democratic' Korea? The vagueness was a concession to uncommitted countries, and left room for manœuvre if there was immediate external Communist intervention. It was also designed to meet the objections of those who thought the proposed settlement was taking on the appear-

[1] *State Department Bulletin*, 10 July 1950.
[2] *Hearings*, p. 2258.

ance of a victor's settlement, by no means mandatory under the UN Charter, which was primarily concerned with suppressing breaches of the peace.

The eight-power resolution, reportedly largely drafted by Acheson himself, but presented by Britain and seven others, also called for the creation of the new UN Commission for the Unification and Rehabilitation of Korea to bring about the new Korea after the shooting stopped. Ernest Bevin stated on the 26th that 'there could no longer be a North and South Korea', and just before he left New York for home, on 29 September, announced there should be 'no artificial perpetuation' of the division of Korea. The resolution moreover had the support of many, 'not only in Washington or among the Allied UN delegations, but in the general public who saw in the Korean issue a golden opportunity for establishing the moral authority and effective power of the United Nations. Merely to repel aggression would be a modest gain; but if the UN could show itself equal to dealing with the total situation, eliminating the division which was at the root of the trouble, and re-creating a free and united Korea as a viable unit in the international community, it would be an impressive proof of the moral leadership and practical strength of the international organisation. Many who had little sympathy with MacArthur's political views were to combine in abetting his conquest of North Korea.'[1]

Thus at Lake Success the only alternatives seemed to be either ruling North Korea as a virtual colony of the UN until elections were held, or abandoning it to the Communists and so presenting the UN with the very conditions which had started the war in the first place.

While these issues were debated in the corridors at Lake Success, the *real* decision to drive north to the Yalu had been taken in Washington about two weeks before the Allied resolution appeared before the General Assembly on 7 October. As X Corps blasted its way into the heart of Seoul, off went another directive to MacArthur from JCS on 27 September, which according to Richard Neustadt, a White House assistant at this time, was approved by the insiders 'on or about 24 September' after 'some amount of inter-allied consultation'. CINCFE was told that his military objective was 'the destruction of the North

[1] Millis, p. 276.

Korean Armed Forces' and in attaining this objective 'he was authorised to conduct military operations north of the 38th Parallel'. Such action was authorised provided at the time 'there had been no entry into North Korea by major Soviet or Chinese Communist forces, no announcement of an intended entry, and no threat by Russian or Chinese Communists to counter our operations militarily in North Korea'. Furthermore, no non-South Korean ground forces were to be used in the provinces bordering the USSR or Manchuria 'as a matter of policy'.[1] This sensitivity to the Korean borders had already resulted in Washington prohibiting the bombing of Rashin, seventeen miles from the Soviet border and 110 miles from Vladivostok after a B-29 strike against the port in August — the port was also excluded from the UNC blockade.

The fundamental confusion regarding Chinese intentions remained obscured even more by the intoxication of victory than it had been two weeks before when the crossing of the Parallel had first been planned. MacArthur, replying to this directive, immediately sent JCS his plan for the conquest of North Korea.

Eighth Army would advance to Pyongyang, and X Corps, still under the control of GHQ, would be withdrawn from the Inchon-Seoul area for another amphibious landing at Wonsan in north-east Korea from where it would advance westwards and join Walker's army. The plan was approved by JCS on 29 September, and MacArthur was also sent an encouraging message by the new Defence Secretary, George Marshall, the same day: 'We want you to feel unhampered strategically and tactically to proceed north of the 38th Parallel.'[2]

This was reasonably clear enough. On 30 September, Warren Austin spoke to the Political Committee of the UN:

Today the forces of the United Nations stand on the threshold of military victory. . . . The aggressor's forces should not be permitted to have refuge behind an imaginary line because

[1] See Truman, *Memoirs II*, 380-82 for the directives of 15 and 27 September. The much more detailed paraphrases of these messages in *Hearings* p. 718-20 show that on 15 September MacArthur was told that 'final decisions cannot be made at this time'. Also Neustadt, *Presidential Power*, p. 131.

[2] Montross and Canzona, Vol. III, *The Chosin Reservoir Campaign*, p. 6; *Hearings*, p. 1241.

that would recreate the threat to the peace of Korea and of the world. . . . The question of whether this artificial barrier shall remain removed and whether the country shall be united now must be determined by the United Nations.[1]

The next day, 1 October, the frontier of containment was passed when ROK troops pushed north over the Parallel on the east coast road heading towards Kosong. Washington wanted to avoid making too much fuss over the crossing, so MacArthur was stopped from making a 'dramatic announcement' (Truman). He was allowed instead to make an unconditional surrender demand to the North Koreans to 'forthwith lay down your arms and cease hostilities under such military supervision as I may direct'. The answer came not from Pyongyang, but from Peking and Moscow. Chou En-lai's warnings on the consequences of crossing the Parallel and new Soviet proposals on Korea presented by Vyshinsky at Lake Success were together a last co-ordinated Sino-Soviet diplomatic move to save their Korean satellite. The UN plan for the conquest of North Korea was a challenge to the Communist bloc, which was accepted with alacrity. The response to the challenge had been in the making for almost six months; when delivered, it determined the course of the Korean War until its end.

THE RESPONSE: RED CHINA CROSSES THE YALU

As noted in April 1950, a redeployment of the 4th Field Army (an army group) of the People's Liberation Army from South China to Manchuria was under way, and, by mid-July, three Chinese Communist armies had been moved to the north. Lacking an army corps organisation, each Chinese Communist army was made, usually of three, sometimes, four divisions of about 10,000 men each. So, in addition to regular troops numbering about 100,000 men in Manchuria, the reinforcements brought the total up to about 180,000 men. Other armies moved to Shantung, between Shanghai and Mukden, at the same time, where they could be moved to either Korea or Formosa.[2]

[1] Goodrich, 130-31.
[2] Whiting, p. 23, 64-67, 119-21.

Following these precautionary military moves, mobilisation of Chinese domestic opinion against the United States started soon after fighting broke out in Korea. With the invasion of Formosa necessarily postponed after June, the chief enemy now of the People's Republic of China was less the Kuomintangite bandit remnants on Taiwan than American imperialism in all its manifestations. The first development was the beginning of the Orwellian 'Hate-America' movement which went on throughout the Korean War, and during *Resist American invasion of Taiwan and Korea* week, 17-24 July, 1950, 'an accumulation of hate was produced that must have been a record even for a Communist country.'[1]

But this orgy of mass conditioning was not aimed to prepare Red China for immediate intervention in Korea. Throughout, the Chinese term *fan tuei* (resist) was used to denote non-violent opposition to the US; *k'ang yi*, connoting active opposition, as employed against the KMT and the Japanese, would gradually appear as the campaign increased in intensity. During this first phase, the hate campaign had other uses. It would justify stepping up measures against those unliquidated elements on the mainland who would be only too glad to welcome the American imperialists. Economic norms could be increased by the big stick of the foreign threat, and, even more important, the controlled hysteria provided an additional means of organising thousands of committees on the local level for future use. These had already started to proliferate during the Stockholm Peace Appeal agitation in May and June. The Hate-America campaign, using the threat of intervention, was now becoming the single most important stimulus in consolidating the regime.

By mid-August, the dangers of a Communist setback on the Pusan perimeter front coupled with MacArthur's visit to Taipeh, and Washington's new line about possibly unifying Korea had forced a change on Chinese Communist foreign policy. Following Chou's cable to Lake Success on 20 August that 'the Chinese people cannot but be concerned about solution of the Korean question' and the protests about the alleged Yalu air intrusions, a whole series of statements at the end of August

[1] Levi, *Modern China's Foreign Policy*, p. 296.

alerted the population to a new American threat. The paper
tiger of July had now become a mad dog, and the Americans
were now declared to be worse than the Nazis and the Japanese
imperialists. In the influential *World Culture*, an article on
26 August implied that China regarded the Korea situation with
great concern: 'North Korea's friends are our friends. North
Korea's enemy is our enemy. North Korea's defence is our
defence. North Korea's victory is our victory.' But in a broadcast to North America, the last three solidarity phrases were
omitted, so careful was Peking not to raise the external temperature of the crisis. But, most significantly, internally the term
k'ang yi, the exhortation to action, was being used in relation to
the supposed American threat. A massive home front mobilisation was beginning, to fight the United Nations action in Korea.[1]

The defeat in the Security Council at the beginning of September of Malik's Korean cease-fire proposals, which had also
asked for Peking's participation in these talks, meant that
neither Soviet or Chinese diplomacy had any chance of initiating a Korean solution before the beginning of the expected
Allied counter-offensive. With the success of Inchon, the whole
emphasis of Peking's messages to the West now changed from
propaganda accusation to statements of intent if the 38th
Parallel was crossed.

Just after the landing, MacArthur accused the Chinese of
releasing 'a vast pool of combat-seasoned troops of Korean
ethnic origin' (the KVC) to Pyongyang which had furnished
'substantial if not decisive' help to the North Koreans. As the
delegates at Flushing Meadows discussed the crossing of the
Parallel, the Foreign Affairs Ministry in Peking on 22 September
admitted the transfer, implying that more aid might be on the
way: 'We clearly reaffirm that we will always stand on the side
of the Korean people . . . and resolutely oppose the criminal
acts of American imperialist aggressors against Korea. . . .'
Three days later *People's Daily* published a detailed statement
of its grievances against the US, and the same day saw General
Nieh Jung-chen, acting Chief of Staff of the PLA, informing
K. M. Panikkar, the Indian ambassador to Peking, that the
Chinese Communists would not let the Americans come up to

[1] See Whiting, Chaps. 5 and 6 for evolution of Peking's Korean Policy at this
time.

the Yalu. 'They may even drop atom bombs on us. What then? They may kill a few million people. Without sacrifice a nation's independence cannot be upheld.'[1]

Time was now running out very quickly. The Allies were enthusiastically agreed to move north to the Yalu and Chou En-lai gave the strongest warning yet in an official speech in Peking on 30 September, when he said that the Chinese People 'will not tolerate foreign aggression, nor will they supinely tolerate seeing their neighbours being savagely invaded by the imperialists'. On 2 October, Sino-Soviet moves to preserve the North Koreans came to a head simultaneously. Vyshinsky presented a Soviet counter-proposal on Korea to the Political Committee. It called for an immediate withdrawal of foreign troops from the country after a cease-fire, equality for North and South Korea in a new commission to rule the country until all-Korean elections could be held, and creation of a UN commission to observe the elections with members from countries bordering Korea. At this stage of the war, it was too much to expect that North Korea could be given the opportunity to obstruct or manipulate all-Korean elections, or for Peking to be represented on the supervising commission. A cease-fire after Inchon was out of the question and unacceptable to the West. For by now, the almost casual decision in Washington to cross the Parallel after Inchon was becoming an official United Nations operation. At midnight the same day in Peking, Chou formally summoned K. M. Panikkar to a conference in the Ministry of Foreign Affairs. Dismissing the ROK advance over the Parallel as of no consequence, the Chinese Prime Minister declared that should American troops enter North Korea, China would enter the war.[2] Like the Russians in 1904, Communist China was now making the crossing of the 38th Parallel a *casus belli*.

Once the Political Committee — a committee of the whole of the Assembly — had passed the eight-power resolution while rejecting the Soviet proposals on 4 October the way was open for the resolution to be introduced into the General Assembly. This was done by Kenneth Younger, the UK Minister of

[1] Panikkar, *In Two Chinas*, p. 108.
[2] Panikkar, p. 110. 'He was emphatic: "The South Koreans did not matter, but American intrusion into North Korea would encounter Chinese resistance."'

State at the Foreign Office, on 7 October and passed by 47-5-7. Negative votes were cast by the USSR, Ukraine, Byelo-russia, Poland and Czechoslovakia. Egypt, Lebanon, Syria, Yemen, Saudi Arabia, Yugoslavia and India abstained. The heart of the resolution lay in these two clauses in which the Assembly recommended that:

1 (a) All appropriate steps be taken to ensure conditions of stability throughout Korea.

   (b) All constituent acts be taken, including the holding of elections, under the auspices of the United Nations, for the establishing of a united, independent and demo-cratic government in the sovereign state of Korea.

The Rubicon of the Korean War had been passed with the enthusiastic support of the Western Allies.

In Korea the first patrols of the Eighth Army, from 1st Cavalry, had moved over the 38th Parallel in the Kaesong area at 5.14 p.m., KT, on the day the crucial vote was taken, while a general Eighth Army advance across the Parallel began on the morning of the 9th in the same sector. But Chou's warning had not meant that the victory atmosphere in Washington was dispelled. On the contrary. The directive of 27 September which authorised the move north was predicated on the absence of any external Communist threat. Second thoughts prompted Truman and JCS to remove even this reservation on 9 October and to go ahead anyway. If Chinese intervention occurred, MacArthur was now told to go ahead as long as '*in your judgement, action by forces now under your control offers a reasonable chance of success*'.[1] It was in exercising his discretionary powers, and not, of course, in crossing the Parallel, that MacArthur would later be arraigned. For the only, vital, qualification which Washington had imposed on the drive to the Yalu was MacArthur's interpretation of *reasonable*.

A last unconditional surrender demand was issued by the General on 9 October in which MacArthur stated that unless there was a North Korean capitulation, he would proceed 'to

[1] This crucial directive is paraphrased in Truman, *Memoirs II*, p. 383 and *Hearings*, p. 720.

take such military action as may be necessary to enforce the decrees of the United Nations'. The General Assembly of course had no power to issue 'decrees', but emphasising that this was the current mood at the UN, the Interim Committee of the UN Commission for the Unification and Rehabilitation of Korea, created by the resolution of 7 October, advised the UN Command on 12 October to take over the civil government of North Korea pending elections. In practice this meant that American military government now ruled in the occupied part of North Korea. Meanwhile the advance north went on.

As 1st Cavalry and the 27th Commonwealth Brigade, now renamed after the arrival of an Australian battalion, pushed north towards Kumchon, Sariwon and the magic objective of Pyongyang, 'the first Iron Curtain capital', a last warning came from Peking's Foreign Ministry on 10 October. Attacking the General Assembly's resolution as 'against the will of the overwhelming majority of the world's population' the statement went on: 'The Chinese people cannot stand idly by with regard to such a serious situation created by the invasion of Korea. . . . The American war of invasion in Korea has been a serious menace to the security of China from its very start.' The same day, fast-moving ROK spearheads from the South Korean I Corps moving up the east coast from the perimeter reached the large port of Wonsan, over a hundred miles north of the Parallel. . . . The Chinese armies were ordered into Korea during the next day or so.

The new enemies of the United Nations Command were less publicity conscious and legalistically minded about their entry into Korea than their opponents. From mid-September onwards another massive redeployment of Chinese Communist Forces was under way which would put, in eight weeks, nine armies across the Yalu into Korea. Planning for this movement must have started in August and involved the 4th Field Army under Lin Piao as well as the 3rd Field Army under Chen Yi. That a major movement from the south to Manchuria was taking place at this time was known to American Intelligence, but the disposition of these forces after mid-October, and even more important, their intention, was not known. Only a few days after the Eighth Army moved across the Parallel, Peking accepted the challenge. Starting about 14 October, the first of around a third of a million men were entering Korea, undetected, over the great international bridges at Antung and Manpojin.[1]

Near Manpojin, in the last few days of the month, Philip Deane and his colleagues, including the British Vice-Consul in Seoul, George Blake, watched thousands of Chinese pouring south with artillery and Molotov trucks along roads signposted, 'Chinese People's Army'. The captives had thought that liberation was near. 'Those, perhaps, were our worst moments.'

After centuries of isolation and domination by the West, China was embarking on a forward policy that was to make her one of the greatest and most feared countries of the world.

EVERYBODY TURNED OUT TO BE WRONG

Over a decade after the UN passed the point of no return in its Korean policy with the resolution to unify the country, the State Department issued a detailed statement refuting any similarities between the Laos crisis of 1961 and the Korean situation in 1950. Commenting on this in April 1961 Max Freedman, the *Guardian* Washington correspondent remarked: 'It is clear now, though all was in doubt at the time, that the United States blundered into one of the supreme mistakes of its history when it discounted Mr Panikkar's warning about Chinese intervention in North Korea.'[2] What then was the reasoning which led the United States to discount serious Chinese intervention, and to make such a miscalculation in balancing aims against risks in marching into North Korea? What relevance has it to other limited war situations with the Communist bloc?

Firstly of course there was the strong domestic pressure inside the US to unite Korea. This feeling was shared by the Allies and the great majority of the UN. MacArthur again was a powerful force in his own right at any time, but most of all

---

[1] See Whiting, pp. 116-24, for further details of the Yalu crossing. 'The best available evidence to the author places the first crossing of the Yalu by Chinese Communist troops between October 14-16', p. 192. SLA Marshall, *The River and the Gauntlet*, p. 14, also places CCF entry into Korea on 14 October. According to X Corps intelligence, from two civilian employees of Pyongyang Railroad Bureau, 'there had been a continuous flow of CCF soldiers through Manpojin beginning on 12 October'. Appleman, p. 756.

[2] *The Guardian*, 4 April 1961.

after Inchon. Against these powerful pressures which made a drive to the Yalu almost, but not completely, certain, there were the warnings relayed via Panikkar, and also through other allied and neutral channels, and from American embassies in Moscow, Stockholm, New Delhi and London. But Panikkar in Truman's words 'had in the past played the game of the Chinese Communists fairly regularly so that his statement could not be taken as that of an impartial observer'.[1] The warning could be no more than a relay of Communist propaganda designed to twist the arm of the United Nations into turning down the eight-power resolution. Why should Chinese Communist bluster just before the voting in the Political Committee and the General Assembly be listened to? Why should it influence the voting? It was not unreasonable for Washington to think the Chinese were bluffing *at the time*.

Secondly, it was thought that as the Chinese had not intervened in August when merely a couple of extra divisions could have pushed the Eighth Army into the sea, why should they attempt military intervention in October. 'I don't think China wants to get chopped up,' a Washington official commented at this time. But this ignored the fact that the Naktong was not the 38th Parallel (or the Yalu), and that Peking's interests were not the same as Pyongyang's.

The communications problem was another factor. There was no direct link between Peking and Washington. Panikkar, while, therefore, a fellow-traveller to Washington, was a representative of a fellow-Asian country to the Chinese leaders. The Chinese revolution stood for the reassertion of Asian interests against the West. Panikkar, although from a country that was neutralist and not Communist, might be preferable to those traditional go-betweens, the Swiss and Scandinavians who, from a Communist viewpoint, were only technically neutral. Traditional channels of diplomatic communication were no longer valid.

But apart from objective political and military calculations by both sides, there were subjective differences between the two sides which meant that Peking and Washington were quite unable to understand each other's frame of reference. Washington still held in September 1950 what Acheson had implied in the 'defence perimeter' speech, that the Chinese Communist

[1] *Truman*, p. 383.

revolution was more Chinese than Communist. Once the Korean problem was solved, Formosa would be allowed to fall into Communist hands and then the traditional friendship between China and America would be resumed. Most of State's Far Eastern Experts for years now had believed that the motivation of Peking's foreign policy was purely nationalist. In an intra-mural conference held in October 1949, only one participant, Bernard Brodie, had emphatically opposed the majority view, stating that post-war experience in Eastern Europe showed that since Communism relied so heavily on coercive techniques, indigenous cultural patterns were destroyed, and that therefore as far as US interests were concerned, the alignment of the Peking regime 'remains very closely Russian and very definitely hostile'.[1]

But statements by Truman and Acheson just before Inchon show that they thought China could still be influenced by expressions of American good will, and that their basic policy towards China, although stalled after 25 June, could eventually be implemented. Truman had announced during his broadcast on 1 September that 'we hope in particular that the people of China will not be misled or forced into fighting against the United Nations and the American people who have always been and still are their friends.'[2]

A few days later, on 10 September, Acheson was still convinced that the Chinese were feuding with the Russians over the Chinese northern provinces: 'Now I give the people in Peking credit for being intelligent enough to see what is happening to them. Why should they want to further their own dismember-ment and destruction by getting at cross purposes with all the free nations of the world who are inherently their friends and have always been friends of the Chinese as against this im-perialism coming down from the north I cannot see. . . .'[3]

But Peking saw the situation very differently. With its Marxist-Maoist framework it seemed as if the US and its allies could menace China, if not its territorial integrity then its

---

[1] *Institute of Pacific Relations*, pp. 1551–1682. Transcript extracted by the McCarran Subcommittee of the Senate Judiciary Committee of a round table discussion inside the State Department on China policy, 6-8 October, 1949.

[2] Truman, *Memoirs*, II, p. 380.

[3] *Spanier*, p. 99.

The Pusan Perimeter, First Battle of the Naktong Bulge. Three knocked-out North Korean T34s on the road from the Naktong to Yongsan. Obong-ni ridge in the background, three dead Marines in the foreground. 18 August 1950

The Naktong River. A Marine patrol on Hill 311 at the western apex of the Naktong Bulge. 19 August 1950

Aerial view of Inchon. Note GREEN beach on Wolmi-do facing Flying Fish channel, and RED beach immediately to the left of where the causeway joins the mainland. Observatory Hill rises out of the centre of the city, with the Inner Tidal basin on the extreme right

internal stability and its position as a great Asian and a Communist power. Underlying American policy was this incomprehension that to Peking not merely MacArthur's activities over Formosa, but the whole of American policy, was an expression of a historic imperialist force which could easily attempt the destruction of the new China. Helping North Korea was not merely a defensive measure, an end in itself, but a necessary means to the end of upholding Communist power in Asia for further advances. A determined opponent in a position of strength in a unified, independent, non-Communist Korea could exploit many opportunities inside China. Thus, initial intervention in Korea, with no professed ends beyond keeping some part of Kim Il Sung's state in being, was partially defensive, but with offensive possibilities, depending on the developing situation, and with the ultimate end of advancing Peking's interests in Asia. Western goodwill was stupidity, naïveté, hypocrisy, for no such conception existed in Marxist calculations.[1]

These difficulties of mutual incomprehension were compounded by the structure of the pluralist and monolithic societies which faced each other across the Yalu. While professing good will, American policy had also to warn China not to intervene, as an act of domestic political reinsurance. The Administration had been attacked by the Republicans for not making their position clear to the South Koreans before June. When Truman, Acheson and Warren Austin warned Peking against any move into North Korea, they were speaking primarily to the domestic opposition, and to show the Allies that they were standing firm on collective security. Peking would see these warnings as direct threats, although they were not primarily directed to the Chinese. When Chou issued his counter-warning, he meant what he said. It was discounted in Washington, not only because Panikkar was a suspect source, but because the Administration believed that Peking really thought the same way as it did, and saw that a serious American threat to China did not exist. In the first few days of October, 1950, the Chinese thus exaggerated

[1] Even the State Department's China White Paper had failed to arouse Mao's gratitude. He commented, ' Disrupt, fail, disrupt again, fail again, till their doom—that is the logic of imperialism and all the reactionaries in the world. They will certainly not go beyond this logic. This is a Marxist law. We say: "Imperialism is very vicious. That means that its fundamental nature cannot be changed. . . ."' Whiting, p. 12.

the seriousness of the situation, while the Americans discounted its gravity, an incidental revelation of the respective pessimism and optimism of Communist and democratic ideologies.

The moment of truth would come on the Chongchon when Truman and Acheson would see that they had the same enemy in the East as they had contained in Europe. For the right motives, awareness of and sympathy to the Asian anti-colonial revolution, the assumptions of their China policy had been wrong. And on the issue of the strategic importance of Formosa and the nature of what he was to call 'this new Frankenstein that is being gradually congealed and coalesced in China'[1] Mac-Arthur was right. The motivations of the new China were not neutralist and nationalist, but imperialist and totalitarian.

'Everybody that had to do with it turned out to be wrong', complained Senator Brien McMahon in the MacArthur Hearings when told that all agencies of the government thought Chinese intervention improbable. 'They really fooled us when it comes right down to it, didn't they?' asked Senator Saltonstall of the Secretary of State. All criticism of Acheson must be muted because of the shattering honesty of his reply: 'Yes, Sir.'[2]

[1] *Hearings*, 251.
[2] *Hearings*, p. 1835.

CHAPTER SEVEN

MEETING AT WAKE

'. . . I've never had a more satisfactory conference since
I've been President.'
HARRY TRUMAN, at Wake Island, 15 October 1950

No sooner had the Eighth Army crossed the Parallel than
Truman announced on 10 October that he was meeting
MacArthur the coming weekend at Wake Island, the square-
mile speck of sand and coral between Tokyo and Honolulu. The
President would take advantage of the visit to express to Mac-
Arthur the nation's appreciation for 'the great service which he
is rendering world peace'. He would discuss with his commander
'the final phase of the United Nations action in Korea'. Hawaii
had also been suggested for the meeting by Secretary Marshall
— Roosevelt had received MacArthur at Pearl Harbour in 1944
— but the General, prestige high after Inchon, had chosen Wake
for the site of what would be the Korean victory conference.
Unknown to the participants, however, the Chinese had also
chosen that same weekend to start their move into Korea.

But the first and only meeting between these two Olympians
at Wake left not only the accord of victors, but accusations of
trickery between those who were soon to become open political
enemies. The President has accused MacArthur of misleading
him about Chinese intentions in Korea; while Whitney, on the
other hand, sees the meeting as a scheme by a Washington
politician to use MacArthur's prestige to get votes for the mid-
term elections, and also as a 'sly political ambush' to give the
Administration an excuse if anything went wrong in Korea.

Truman's motives for wishing the meeting, were, however,
simple. He wanted in the first place personally to contact his
Oriental pro-consul, whose realm of authority *The Times* respect-
fully remarked on 14 October, 'seems to belong more to Roman
times than to our own'. The President thought that all

MacArthur's thoughts 'were wrapped up in the East'. He had not visited America for thirteen years, and was out of touch with what 'home-folks' were thinking. In resorting to personal diplomacy, Truman would also show his Far East commander 'the world-wide picture as we saw it in Washington'.[1] This meant that MacArthur must acknowledge that Chinese Communism could not be overcome by force, and that Western Europe and not Korea was all-important in the Administration's policies. There were to be no more incidents such as that of the VFW letter or 'permissive' interpretations of his directives on the Chinese borders such as that which had led to the order to FEAF to bomb above the Parallel in June, before sanction from Washington. On 9 October two F-80 jets had 'beaten-up' a Soviet airfield sixty miles inside the USSR border near Vladivostok; all such incidents with Korea's northern neighbours must be rigorously avoided. In spite of Inchon and the triumph of American arms in Korea, there was little trust between the President and the General; but Truman hoped that an understanding, not any new dramatic decision, could be worked out on the West Pacific island between himself and his overmighty subject.

If Truman had taken the measure of his General after the VFW letter, even if he had done nothing after it, there seems little doubt that both before and after Wake, MacArthur seriously underestimated the President. Much of Truman's distinction lay in the differences with his predecessor. Samuel Huntington has written that while FDR embodied the popular will and acted as a tribune of the people, Truman exercised his prerogative as 'a Burkeian virtual representative of the nation',[2] often taking his great decisions without too much reference to Congress and public. If not a supreme political genius, he was nevertheless one of the great presidents: his personal qualities were sometimes hidden by his mild appearance. For if MacArthur was the patrician American personification of one of Mars' best friends, Truman, with his small-town Missouri background, his toughness, humanity, common sense, his experience of the Senate and his deep awareness of American history and

---

[1] For the Wake meeting in all its detail see Truman, *Memoirs II*, Chap. 23, and Whitney pp. 384-95, 'The Enigma of Wake Island'. Also Spanier, Chap. 6.
[2] Huntington, *The Soldier and the State*, p. 383.

civil-military relations, represented a vital part of the American consciousness almost outside the General's comprehension. Operating a liberal domestic policy with mostly New Deal personnel, the Administration's conservative containment foreign policy was operated by realistic lawyers, soldiers and diplomats, and much of Truman's strength came from his ability to run these two virtually separate administrations which only really met in his own person. With his characteristic single-mindedness he was now prepared to make an 18,000-mile journey to show the world that there were no divergences between the White House and the Dai-Ichi. He was prepared to go more than half way in the geographical sense, but not in the political sense, to make MacArthur's submission easier: 'I thought he might adjust more easily if he heard it from me directly.'

The *Independence* left Washington on 11 October for St. Louis where the President stayed overnight, and, after stops at the Fairfield-Suisun Air Force Base in California and at Pearl Harbour, arrived at Wake on 15 October. It was dawn, 6.30 a.m. MacArthur was waiting, 'his shirt was unbuttoned, and he was wearing a cap that had evidently seen a good deal of use' (Truman). The *New York Times* reported:

> As Mr. Truman's plane came to a stop, MacArthur strode to the foot of the launching ramp, and with hand outstretched, greeted the President with every appearance of warmth and friendliness.
>
> 'Mr. President,' General MacArthur began, seizing Mr. Truman's right arm while pumping his hand. President Truman smiled and said: 'How are you, General? I'm glad you are here. I've been a long time meeting you, General.'
>
> 'I hope it won't be so long next time, Mr. President,' General MacArthur replied.
>
> Observers noted that MacArthur did not salute his Commander-in-Chief.

The two men then drove in a 1948 Chevrolet to the Quonset Hut office of the airline manager for their private meeting. The surroundings were in complete contrast to the martial pageantry of the summit meeting between FDR and his ex-Chief of Staff in 1944, for the meeting at Wake, write Rovere and Schlesinger, 'suggested that two magistrates of mighty power were meeting in some war-scarred neutral zone to fashion a new truce and new alliance'. Even now the exact time as well as the full content of their conversation has not been established. In his biography Whitney suggests half an hour, while MacArthur in the Senate Hearings claimed they talked for three-quarters of an hour. Truman has written that they talked 'for more than an hour alone'.

MacArthur assured Truman that victory was won in Korea and that the Chinese Communists would not intervene. He apologised for any embarrassment caused by the VFW statement, and said that he was 'not in politics' in any way — the politicians had made a 'chump' of him in 1948. Truman goes on to write that the General thought it would be possible to send a division from Korea to Europe by January 1951, and again repeated that there was little possibility of Chinese intervention. MacArthur seems to have accepted the President's ruling on all points; 'Our conversation was very friendly — I might say much more so than I expected,' Truman comments, arousing the speculation as to just what did the President expect? According to Whitney they discussed at length 'of all things at this time, the fiscal and economic problems of the Philippines', during a 'relatively unimportant conversation'. With their meeting over, they went on to a second conference just after 7.30 in the administration building, where advisers of both men were gathered. MacArthur was accompanied only by a small group, Whitney, Colonel Bunker, his ADC, and Lt.-Col. Story, his pilot, while the delegation from Washington was considerably, almost absurdly, larger. Present were Harriman, as Special Adviser to the President, Ambassador Jessup, Dean Rusk, Admiral Radford, Frank Pace, Omar Bradley, Colonel Hamblen from the Pentagon and Colonel Mathews, Bradley's executive officer. Ambassador Muccio had flown with MacArthur from Tokyo. Others present according to Whitney were Charles Ross, Presidential press secretary, and 'numerous other Truman aides and aides' aides'. including Maj.-Gen. Harry Vaughan, the White House ADC of deep-freeze fame. It was an astonishing confrontation of some of the most powerful, conflicting and bizarre figures of the Truman era.

Unknown to the participants (so it was later said) Jessup's

secretary, Miss Vernice Anderson, was in the next room, and as the door was ajar took down shorthand notes of the conference. Her transcript when added to the notes also taken by Jessup, Rusk, Pace, Bradley and the two Pentagon colonels provided the record so craftily released by the Administration during the MacArthur Hearings, for therein was the General's unequivocal statement discounting Chinese intervention.[1] The transcript was angrily denounced by MacArthur in the Hearings as the result of 'some surreptitious eavesdropping, stenographic eavesdropping', and he never acknowledged the words attributed to him, presumably as he thought they were an inadequate record of his assumptions.

The transcript shows that many subjects were discussed in the conference, Korean elections and rehabilitation, possible war-crimes trials, the Japanese peace treaty, and a Truman Doctrine for the Pacific. Emphasising what he had already told the President, MacArthur affirmed that all formal resistance in Korea would be over by Thanksgiving. The Eighth Army would then be withdrawn to Japan, leaving two divisions of the X Corps to occupy North Korea until elections were held at the beginning of 1951. 'All occupations are failures', the General said, to which the President nodded agreement. Half way through the conference came the exchange that would not be forgotten or forgiven:

The President: What are the chances for Chinese or Soviet intervention?
General MacArthur: Very little. Had they interfered in the first or second months it would have been decisive. We are no longer fearful of their intervention. We no longer stand hat in hand. The Chinese have 300,000 men in Manchuria. Of these probably not more than 100/125,000 are distributed along the Yalu River. Only 50/60,000 could be gotten across the Yalu River. They have no air force. Now that we have bases for our Air Force in Korea, if the Chinese tried to get down to Pyongyang there would be the greatest slaughter. . . .

With the Russians, MacArthur went on, it was a little different.

[1] The transcript, 'Substance of Statements Made at Wake Island', is reprinted *in toto* in Rovere and Schlesinger, pp. 253-62.

Their strong Siberian air arm nevertheless was 'no match for our Air Force'. A combination of Chinese ground and Russian air was ruled out because their ground-air co-ordination would be flimsy and, 'I believe that the Russian air would bomb the Chinese as often as they would bomb us.'

As the general conference came to an end the President said that he and MacArthur had talked fully about Formosa. 'There is no need to cover that subject again. The General and I are in complete agreement.' But in the MacArthur Hearings the General maintained that it had only been agreed that it need not be discussed at the conference. The differences still remained. After lasting from 7.36 to 9.12 this main gathering now broke up and was followed by 'discussions on technical matters' (Truman) between members of the two groups. MacArthur met Bradley and Pace, while Muccio conferred with State Department officials. This last conference which lasted an hour and a half was thus the third meeting at Wake.

Obviously, despite MacArthur's temporary acceptance of Truman's ideas, the chief interest of the conference is in the further light it casts on the official reasoning on Chinese intervention. That Bradley shared MacArthur's optimism may be seen by his request in the general conference for an infantry division to be sent to Europe from Korea about January. Besides, on 12 October, CIA had concluded that Chinese full-scale intervention in Korea was 'not probable in 1950'. Both Tokyo and Washington had interpreted their intelligence — 90% of incoming Far East intelligence to the Pentagon came from MacArthur's command[1] — as indicating that while Peking had the *capability* to invade Korea, it did not have the *intention*, assessing their information on the assumption that the enemy 'would act in accord with an American conception of the rational.'[2]

But there was a further complexity in this political-military evaluation of intelligence. Some, possibly like MacArthur and Willoughby, believed that Chinese capability would be so attrited in getting across the Yalu — only 50/60,000 men — that they discounted Chinese intention. Others, possibly like Truman and Acheson, discounted intention for political reasons from the beginning of the crisis and would thus easily accept the

[1] *Hearings*, p. 1234.
[2] Higgins, p. 59.

low effective capability on the Yalu estimated by MacArthur. Both errors would discount Chinese intervention but for different reasons. One group would fundamentally doubt capability, the other intention, and both reinforce the other in their belief that the Chinese would really not intervene in Korea.[1]

As for the Soviet threat this may have been more real at the time than is yet known. Both John Spanier and I. F. Stone, writing from different viewpoints, have concluded that the timing of the meeting at Wake could easily have been contingent on a Russian ultimatum following the strafing of the Soviet airfield on 9 October. For originally the President had only planned to fly that weekend to St. Louis to get together with the home folks, as his sister was to be presented with the title of Worthy Grand Matron by the Grand Chapter of Missouri, Order of the Eastern Star. Certainly an apology was soon coming from the State Department to the USSR, together with an offer to make restitution for damages. For whatever risks were to be taken with the Chinese, any Soviet involvement in Korea was worth buying off with a trip to the Pacific and a personal warning to MacArthur about his trigger-happy pilots.

Possibly this maze of ambiguities, some resolved, some not, account for the good-bye scenes on the air-strip. MacArthur refused to stay at Wake, 'there are many pressing matters awaiting my return to Tokyo', as his duties were apparently more onerous than those of the President's. Observers noted that the General frequently consulted his watch while a communique was being prepared. Back on the apron the reporters got to work. 'Mr. President,' asked the late Anthony Leviero of the *New York Times*, 'How did things shape up?' 'Perfectly . . .

---

[1] Being only human, both Truman and Attlee have prevaricated on the responsibility of crossing the Parallel. Truman has complained that he was assured at Wake by MacArthur that 'there was no danger of Chinese intervention', although the initial recommendation to move across the Parallel was taken on 11 September by the NSC in Washington, over a month before Wake, and approved by him. Attlee's version is a complete misrepresentation of his government's enthusiasm for crossing the Parallel in September: 'It was MacArthur who insisted on going beyond [the Parallel]': *A Prime Minister Remembers*, p. 236. Bevin was much more honest. During the December debate in the Commons after the Chinese intervention, he defended the original aim of uniting Korea. On the resolution of 7 October he said: 'I offer no apology for that Resolution, to which I was party. . . .' H.C. Deb., Vol. 482, Col. 1459 (14 December 1950).

I've never had a more satisfactory conference since I've been president.' MacArthur was less forthcoming: 'All comments will have to come from the publicity man of the President,' although later he relented and said he had 'greatly enjoyed' the meeting. Leviero summed up the atmosphere when he wrote that Truman left Wake 'highly pleased with the results, like an insurance salesman who had at last signed up an important prospect while the latter appeared dubious about the extent of the coverage'. The last farewells were cordial. MacArthur was presented with a fourth oak-leaf-cluster to his D.S.M., and Whitney was promised a second General's star. Both men scrutinised the communique, which MacArthur initialled. The reporters heard the important prospect's last words: 'Goodbye, sir, and happy landings . . . It's been a real honour to talk to you. . . .' The *Independence* took off at 11.35, just five hours after arriving at Wake. Five minutes later the *SCAP* left for Tokyo. Back across the Date Line in Honolulu it was still the 14th.

Truman evidently believed that he had imposed an understanding at Wake. In his speech in the San Francisco Opera House on his return he was full of the meeting, 'Now I want Wake Island to be a symbol of our unity and purpose for world peace. . . .' In Washington he remarked that MacArthur was loyal to the government and to the President. 'He is loyal to the President in his foreign policy.' For the Wake conference was not an ambush, but a last attempt to reach an understanding between policies and personalities that were really irreconcilable. Truman's optimism was unfounded. MacArthur can hardly have changed his views after an hour's conversation, though no doubt he thought of himself as loyal. The drive to the Yalu, which was getting under way in Korea when they met at Wake, would precipitate a vast new crisis which would lead to the final break. The Korea-first policy of Tokyo and the Europe-first policy of Washington could not be reconciled, like other even greater conflicts, by such summit meetings as that between the President and pro-consul on Wake Island.

CHAPTER EIGHT

THE DRIVE TO THE YALU

The war is very definitely coming to an end shortly.
                    DOUGLAS MACARTHUR, 21 October 1950
Enemy advances, we retreat; enemy halts, we harass;
enemy tires, we attack; enemy retreats, we pursue.
                                    MAO TSE-TUNG
It is better to abandon a whole province than to divide
an army.
                                    VON SCHLIEFFEN

THE ROAD TO HYESANJIN

No sooner was MacArthur back from Wake Island than the Eighth Army took Pyongyang on 19 October. Elements of the 1st Cavalry Division were on the southern edge of the city by about 1100 after advancing up the main road from Sariwon. Almost simultaneously the ROK 1st Division was in the suburbs after slicing through the hills to the east on the road from Suan. By 1000 next morning the entire area of the oldest city of Korea had been occupied. While a special American task force searched the government buildings on the north side of the Taedong for intelligence material, the first Iron Curtain capital settled down to a wave of looting and witch-hunts enthusiastically carried out by 'United Nations North Koreans'. Everywhere at first were the same grinning posters of Stalin and Kim Il Sung that had adorned Seoul.

On the 20th MacArthur arrived at Pyongyang airfield — 'Any celebrities here to greet me? Where's Kim Buck Too?' — and witnessed later in the day a paratroop drop by the 187 Airborne RCT north of the capital in the Sukchon-Sunchon area. The drop failed in its objective of trapping high NK officials fleeing towards the Yalu, but CINCUNC was supremely optimistic on the outcome of the war, for the next day he stated in Tokyo that the fighting was very definitely coming to an end. That same day, 21 October, the Communist radio announced that the NK Government had moved to Sinuiju at the mouth of the Yalu opposite Antung in Manchuria, but the political and military remnants of North Korean power soon moved on to Kanggye. This was a much better centre for a delaying action, lying deep in the mountains on the main road south of Manpojin, and only twenty miles from Manchuria. But as if to emphasise that the final stages of the war were at hand, and that Korea would be united in a matter of weeks, Walker took up personal control of Eighth Army advance headquarters on 24 October. This new CP had been established two days previously in Kim Il Sung's own former headquarters at Pyongyang.

The plan for the conquest of North Korea had been conceived by MacArthur about the time of the fall of Seoul. Anticipating his unrestricted authority to cross the Parallel, on 26 September he directed JSPOG to prepare plans for operations in North Korea which would employ X Corps in an amphibious landing on the east coast, preferably at Wonsan. Although it seems that at one time MacArthur had intended to place X Corps under EUSAK once Seoul had fallen, he had by the 26th decided to retain control of X Corps as a separate GHQ force and therefore unity of command in the field during the advance into North Korea would be exercised solely through his own person as Commander-in-Chief. The bad news had been sent to Walker on 27 September, and on the same day an Operations plan was presented to MacArthur. It proposed that Eighth Army would move north to Pyongyang while X Corps after landing at Wonsan would advance west on the lateral road to the NK capital, thus trapping any remaining Communist forces to the south. The planners also suggested that both parts of the divided command should then move to the Chongju-Hungnam line across the 'waist' of Korea; only ROK forces would carry the advance to the Manchurian border in keeping with the JCS directive of the same day. As noted above the plan was sent to Washington for approval and soon became the official strategy for the conquest of the north. D-Day at Wonsan was provisionally fixed for 20 October: the town later became the site of Almond's command post.

Walker and his staff thought that an overland movement to Wonsan was best, and that X Corps should come under Eighth

Army and continue the advance towards Pyongyang as it was in such a favourable position to move north at the end of September. Walker also thought that X Corps should then continue to advance to the Yalu in the west, while Eighth Army moved eastwards towards Wonsan; in any case EUSAK staff were sure that Wonsan would fall to the ROK I Corps before the projected landing could take place. The separation of the two forces violated US Army unity-of-command doctrine, indeed of the principles of war, and could only be justified if there were no other solution to the problem of occupying North Korea. Morever the plan was opposed also by MacArthur's own GHQ staff. Maj.-Generals Doyle Hickey (Acting Chief of Staff), Edwin Wright (G-3, Operations), and George Eberle (G-4, Logistics) all agreed with Walker, but apparently their views were never brought to MacArthur. Almond, while insisting that it was 'cheaper to go to Wonsan by sea' because the roads were so bad, had also expected X Corps to come under EUSAK. Admiral Joy, the Far East Naval Commander, thought the Wonsan landing was unnecessary since X Corps could have 'marched overland to Wonsan in a much shorter time and with much less effort than it would take to get the Corps around' by sea. It was only 150 miles overland from Inchon to Wonsan, but 800 miles by sea. The Navy also knew that outloading X Corps through Inchon would tie up the inadequate facilities of that port when it was desperately needed to supply Eighth Army.

Furthermore, the 7th Division would have to go by road to Pusan for embarkation to north-east Korea, jamming up the supply routes to Seoul from the south.

MacArthur's reasons for the continued separation of the commands was that as the Taebaek range, the rugged spinal mountain divide of Korea, effectively split the North Korean east and west coasts, separation and advance on two axes was the only way to overcome this geographical difficulty. As he planned to turn X Corps into the Korean occupation force once the war was over, he could exercise closer control over a significant part of his command in this way. Besides, MacArthur's great belief in amphibious operations *per se*, his personal closeness to Almond, the rivalry and hostility between the X Corps commander and Walker—a characteristic manifestation of the Dai-Ichi atmosphere in the field—all bent him towards the divided

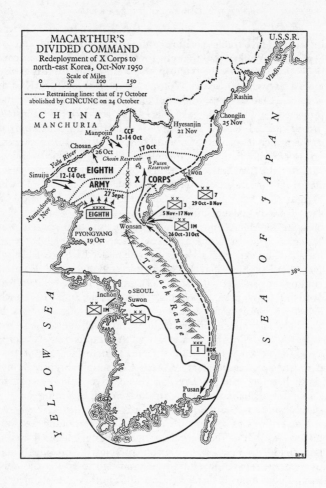

MACARTHUR'S
DIVIDED COMMAND
Redeployment of X Corps to
north-east Korea, Oct–Nov 1950

Scale of Miles
0   50   100   150

.... Restraining lines: that of 17 October
abolished by CINCUNC on 24 October

U.S.S.R.

Vladivostok

CHINA
MANCHURIA

Rashin

Manpojin

CCF
12–14 Oct

Hyesanjin
21 Nov

Chongjin
25 Nov

Chosan
26 Oct

17 Oct

Chosin Reservoir

Fusen
Reservoir

Yalu River

CCF
12–14 Oct

Sinuiju

EIGHTH
ARMY

X   CORPS

Iwon

xx 7
29 Oct–8 Nov

27 Sept

xxxx
EIGHTH

Namsi-dong
1 Nov

PYONGYANG
19 Oct

xx 3
5 Nov–17 Nov

Wonsan

xx 1M
26 Oct–31 Oct

SEA   OF   JAPAN

Taebaek Range

38°

Inchon

SEOUL
Suwon

xx 1M

xx 7

xxx I ROK

YELLOW   SEA

Pusan

BPE

command. Thus from the very beginning of the drive to the Yalu, dating really from the planning for Inchon in August, there was tension between Eighth Army and X Corps staffs with attendant logistic, operational, liaison and personal difficulties. For example, during the battle for Seoul Walker had requested X Corps, without success, to extend their 'anvil' eastwards to NK escape routes through Chunchon. Also, there was no physical contact between the two commands as they moved north after the end of October, apart from one meeting between patrols.[1]

Some of the objections to Operation TAILBOARD were soon proved correct. Arriving off Wonsan on 19 October, 9 days after the town fell to the ROK I Corps, which was also scheduled to come under Almond's command, the task forces, commanded as at Inchon by Doyle and Struble, found the harbour blocked by mines. To the disgust of the bored Marines, who had ceased to be operational on 7 October when the Eighth Army assumed responsibility for the Inchon-Seoul area, they were kept at sea until 26 October before they could begin an administrative landing. Three days later on the 29th, 7th Division started disembarking on the shore at Iwon, fifty miles up the coast from Hungnam, and began moving towards the Manchurian border eighty miles to the north. But by this time the first dash to the Yalu by the Eighth Army in the west was already coming to an end.

The reasonably swift advance to Pyongyang from the Parallel had exceeded the planners' expectations and, just before the Communist capital fell, MacArthur issued on the 17th a new restraining line running north of Chongju through Toksili to Songjin on the east coast, which was well above the Korean 'waist' between Sinanju and Hungnam, the only really defensible line north of the Parallel. On 24 October, MacArthur did away altogether with the restraining line for non-Korean UN forces and exhorted all commanders 'to drive forward with all speed and full utilisation of their forces'. The same day JCS

[1] For an exposition of these problems see especially Blumenson, 'MacArthur's Divided Command', *Army* Magazine, November 1956. Also Appleman, pp. 609-12. Both Whitney (pp. 409-14, 424-25) and Willoughby (pp. 366-68, 373-76) give the reasons for MacArthur's post-Inchon strategy, including the final offensive, in some detail. Almond's testimony in *Interlocking Subversion in Government Departments*, pp. 2101-03 is also useful. For the US Navy's viewpoint, Cagle and Manson, pp. 118-20.

informed MacArthur that this was 'not in consonance' with their directive on 27 September. MacArthur, in reply, invoked Marshall's message of 29 September 'to feel unhampered' in his operations and stated that his order was justified by 'military necessity'—his ROK forces were weak and badly led.[1] Nothing more was heard at the time, but in effect CINCUNC had disregarded a policy directive about keeping his Western forces clear of the Yalu and had got away with it.

This was the most triumphant moment of the war for the UNC as Walker's forward motorised columns swept north along the roads, disregarding guerillas in their rear, the responsibility of Coulter's IX Corps. Crossing the Chongchon at Sinanju 24th Division from I Corps turned westwards along the coast road to Sinuiju and the Yalu. There was little opposition. The chase apparently reminded 'Johnny' Walker, a big-game hunter, who had ranged the Gobi, of his quail-shooting days in Bell County, Texas. The 1st Cavalry were planning a big Tokyo victory parade, and FEAF Bomber Command having erased their 'strategic' targets in North Korea had stood down and sent back two B-29 groups to the US. By 1 November the 21st Regiment of the 24th Division had reached the village of Chonggo-dong, near Namsidong, and only eighteen air miles from Sinuiju. Behind the Americans, the Argylls and the Australians were at Chongju, while the Middlesex battalion at Taechon in the Kuryong valley were the northernmost British troops in Korea, about forty air miles south of the border. The British Brigadier, B. A. Coad, thought they 'had cracked the nut' and that the show was over.[2]

But at the very moment of triumph everything started to go wrong. To the east of I Corps the South Korean 6th Division of the ROK II Corps had made a lightning advance up the central mountains to the Chongchon valley. Continuing northeastwards towards Kanggye, the South Koreans were in Huichon on 23 October. The 7th Regiment of this division now swung west, passed through Onjong on 24/25 October and headed north for its objective of Chosan on the Yalu. On the morning of the 26th a reinforced reconnaissance platoon of the 7th Regiment was

---

[1] *Hearings*, p. 1240-41.
[2] Coad, 'The Land Campaign in Korea', *Journal of the R.U.S.I.*, February 1952.

Inchon: RED beach assault, 15 September 1950. Marines from the 5th Marine Regiment dig in above the harbour wall, while the LST hard on their heels prepares to disgorge supplies. The smaller assault transport is an LCM (Landing Craft, Mechanised)

The frontier of containment. Officers of the ROK 3rd Division and KMAG advisers on the Parallel in the east coast road sector near Chumunjin, 30 September 1950. This was the first UNC division to enter North Korea

The first Iron Curtain capital. U.S. troops from the 5th Cavalry Regiment, 1st Cavalry Division on the southern outskirts of Pyongyang, 19 October 1950

facing Manchuria at Chosan, the first (and only) forces under EUSAK command to reach the Yalu. But the day before, on 25 October, a battalion of the 2nd Regiment from the ROK 6th Division had headed out of Onjong for Pyoktong on the Yalu and found itself under fire south of Pukchin. The battalion was destroyed — but not by North Korean remnants but by Chinese Communist Forces. At the same time a CCF prisoner was taken near Onjong, and that town itself was overrun by the Chinese early on the morning of the 26th. In the next three days the remainder of the ROK 6th Division was heavily defeated in the Huichon-Onjong area, and the 7th Regiment to the north around Kojang was surrounded and forced to scatter over the hills. Survivors brought back a bottle of Yalu water for Syngman Rhee. Simultaneously the other division of II Corps, the 8th, retreated southwards after incurring some losses from the Chinese.

Walker now saw that his whole right flank was open with the collapse of II Corps, and ordered up the ROK 7th Division to the Chongchon, but by 1 November the Corps had been pushed back to the vicinity of Kunuri. Not only were the Chinese south of the Chongchon in this area, but they were also threatening the centre of the western front at Unsan. On 25 October, as part of the general advance, the ROK 1st Division was driving towards this town. That morning they captured the first Chinese POW in Korea and for the rest of the month Chinese troops fought the South Koreans to the north and east of Unsan. Walker then sent a regiment of the 1st Cavalry to help the Koreans, but this unit, the 8th Cavalry Regiment, was overwhelmed at Unsan between 1 and 3 November. As the Chinese at Unsan and Kunuri threatened the Chongchon crossing, 24th Division was recalled from Chonggo-dong which marked the limit of the advance in the north-west. Walker was now concerned to withdraw the army behind the Chongchon, holding bridgeheads in the Sinanju-Anju area for the purpose of resuming the offensive. The Kunuri position was stabilised, the Anju bridgehead held, and after a furious fight over the Taeryong crossing at Pakchon on 5 November, the Commonwealth Brigade withdrew to the first line of hills north of the Chongchon. During the next day Chinese operations in the west faded away; after stopping the apparently irresistible advance to the Yalu, the

K

Chinese First Phase Offensive was over. Coinciding with these developments MIG-15 jet fighters from Manchurian bases were in action over North Korea for the first time on 1 November when some US F-51 Mustangs were engaged south of Sinuiju.[1]

During this fighting in the West the Chinese had also been active on X Corps front. On 25 October elements of the ROK 3rd Division were advancing northwards from Hungnam towards the Chosin Reservoir when a Chinese prisoner was captured. The South Koreans pressed ahead against mounting resistance and on 28 October fought a very heavy action with the Chinese in the Sudong area. Next day sixteen Chinese prisoners were captured and later interrogated personally by Almond through an interpreter in Hamhung. The Chinese had crossed the Yalu at Manpojin on 14-16 October; a division blocked the way to Chosin. Going to the help of the South Koreans, the 7th Marine Regiment fought a pitched battle with the Chinese on the road north in the Sudong-Chinhung-ni area between 2 and 7 November. Then, as in the west, the enemy faded away, leaving behind a huge question mark. Were the Chinese entering Korea in force? Certainly, in view of later events, the date of 25 October when the Chinese entered action for the first time should be remembered.

MacArthur was cautious at first. On 4 November JCS were told that Chinese action probably constituted screening measures to protect a remnant of the North Korean state: 'A final appraisement should await a more complete accumulation of military facts.' Next day he issued a special report to the Security Council listing twelve incidents of UNC contact with the Chinese Communist forces ranging from Manchurian anti-aircraft fire to the prisoners: '. . . United Nation Forces are meeting a new foe. . . .' Then, on the 6th, in the same special communiqué from GHQ which claimed a grand total of 335,000 NK casualties, CINCUNC claimed that the Chinese intervention across the Yalu based on 'the privileged sanctuary of Manchuria' was 'one of the most offensive acts of international lawlessness of historic record. . . .' At the same time Stratemeyer was ordered to take out the twin 3,098-foot bridges which linked Antung with Sinuiju and over which supplies reached the

[1] The first jet air battle in history took place on 8 November 1950 when a Fifth Air Force F-80 shot down a MIG-15 over the Sinuiju area.

Chinese in Korea. When Washington heard of this order, it was cancelled, and all strikes within five miles of the frontier were prohibited; there was an agreement with the British not to take action which affected Manchuria. But MacArthur immediately protested so vigorously against this order, demanding that his reasons be brought to the President's attention that the prohibition was lifted. The movement over the bridge threatened the 'ultimate destruction of the forces under my command', so by using this threat MacArthur was really asking for the policy change which was effected; 79 B-29s and 300 fighter bombers destroyed much of the town on 8 November, although of course most of the Chinese Communist troops were already in Korea by this time. If anything, the strike was too late.

Having won this point, the General followed up with two messages on the 7th which told JCS he was proposing a new advance to take 'accurate measure . . . of the enemy strength' and demanding the right of hot pursuit over the border for his aircraft attacked from Manchuria. Although the Administration sympathised with this request the Allies without exception turned it down, so great was the fear of Chinese intervention by this time. Then, as the fighting died away on both the east and the west front, Radio Sinuiju announced on 7 November that 'volunteer units formed by the Chinese people' had taken part in operations under the command of the North Korean GHQ on 25 October. The first mention of the volunteers had been made in the Peking press five days before on the 2nd, and on 11 November the Chinese Ministry of Foreign Affairs replied to MacArthur's special report when it was admitted that Chinese People's Volunteers (CPV) were helping North Korea, following the example set by Lafayette in the American Revolution and the Anglo-American volunteers in the Spanish Civil War. By its disengagement and its 'volunteer' description for its forces Peking was thus limiting its initial intervention while preparing for further action, and waiting to see if there was any UN retreat or diplomatic response.

Time was now running out quickly when the National Security Council met on 9 November to discuss the new situation. Bradley thought that MacArthur could hold his position, but further interference from Manchuria might increase pressure to attack bases there; there could be no question of that without an UN decision. From the military point of view, a line further back in Korea would be more defensible but that would have political disadvantages, losing South Korean support. He was not so optimistic as MacArthur that bombing the Yalu bridges would stop the Chinese Communists moving into Korea; General Bedell Smith of CIA, which had just estimated that the Russians would not go to war themselves while tying down the West in Korea, pointed out that the Yalu would be frozen shortly anyway. Marshall was worried about the risky dispersion of X Corps and Bradley replied that this was so because MacArthur was carrying out his directive to occupy the whole of Korea and hold elections. Acheson suggested that a buffer zone in North Korea be established under the UN. He thought that primarily the Chinese were trying to keep the US involved; secondly they were interested in the border and the big Suiho hydro-electric plant on the Yalu upstream from Antung. An exploration of a demilitarised zone on the Yalu was worth trying, although the Communists would insist on all foreign troops leaving Korea.

The Secretary of State summed up: MacArthur's directive should not be changed, and that without bombing Manchuria, writes Truman, 'he should be free to do what he could in a military way'. State would meanwhile try and see if negotiations were possible with the Chinese. The Administration had decided to go ahead with the advance north, hoping for the best with MacArthur. And in doing so, recognising the military risks, yet making no firm orders to restrain MacArthur, 'policy' had become disastrously separated from the power available to carry it out. Truman and Acheson still thought the Chinese would not intervene in force; and there were other pressing domestic political reasons why nothing would be done to halt MacArthur. The Republicans had made significant gains in the Congressional mid-term elections a few days before the NSC meeting, strengthening the hostility to Peking on Capitol Hill.

Assurance after assurance was given to Peking that there was no hostile UN or US intent. On 8 November the Chinese were asked to send a delegate to Lake Success to discuss MacArthur's report; this was rejected by Chou, who proposed instead that the delegate invited on 29 September by the Security Council to discuss Formosa could also talk about 'the question of armed intervention in Korea by the United States Government'. A draft motion tabled by the Allies on the 10th asking Peking to withdraw its nationals from Korea declared it was the policy of the UN to hold the frontier with Manchuria 'inviolate' and to protect all Korean and Chinese interests in the frontier zone. Acheson emphasised that the UN and the US had no 'ulterior designs in Manchuria' and on the 16th the President stated that the US would take 'every honourable step to prevent any extension of the hostilities in the Far East'. Bevin followed with a soothing message to Peking on the 22nd from HMG, but as far as Tokyo, Washington and London were concerned it was now a case of the blind leading the blind, with the man in Tokyo thinking that he knew where he was going.

For when Eighth Army G-2, and therefore Willoughby at FECOM Intelligence, CIA and the White House made their last estimate of China's intentions it was based on a figure of about 60,000 Chinese in North Korea. Not only was the figure wildly wrong, with over 180,000 Chinese troops already in Korea by 1 November, but it was only appreciated in the forward areas how precarious were the means of gathering this vital intelligence. Air reconnaissance facilities in the Far East had not been built after the demobilisation at the end of the Pacific War, and the detailed maps of Korea needed to complement photocoverage hardly existed. An indigenous spy network in Korea had fallen apart when the American occupation ended in 1949 and another to take its place under Willoughby's auspices, the 'Korean Liaison Office' was hardly ready when the June invasion and the following Communist occupation smashed it — nothing more was heard from these agents. A third net was in process of being built in late 1950, but was not complete. Thus the Chinese Communist Army of over 300,000 men as described in S. L. A. Marshall's classic on the Chongchon, *The River and the Gauntlet*, was 'a phantom which cast no shadow. Its every secret — its strength, its position, and its intention — had been kept to perfection, and thereby it was doubly armed. . . .'

Both the movement and the concentration had gone undetected. The enemy columns moved only by night, preserved an absolute camouflage discipline during their daytime rests and remained hidden to view under village rooftops after reaching the chosen ground. Air observation saw nothing of this mass manœuvre. Civilian refugees brought no word of it. . . . Within that hill country, a primitive army, lacking in heavy equipment can be stowed away in less space than a hunt would use for the chasing of foxes. And Eighth Army did not have sufficient troop strength to probe and prowl every corner of the outland where hostiles might be hiding. . . .[1]

Immediately after the fighting at Unsan, Walker realised that the Sinuiju quail shoot was off, and that there could be no advance to the north without careful preparation, for by the end of October his Army had outrun its supply lines. His Intelligence thought that the Chinese wanted to bluff the Eighth Army away from the frontier, help the North Koreans, and to screen a further advance of their forces over the Yalu. But there was a great deal of unease at Eighth Army; after Unsan, according to Marshall, 'the operators took it as proof that China was in deadly earnest'. MacArthur wanted to push ahead to the Yalu as quickly as possible, but with so many logistical difficulties Walker in mid-November was strongly against a hasty advance to the frontier. With his two American corps totalling four divisions, the British brigade, and an ROK corps on the right flank, he wanted his Army lined along the Chongchon to be reasonably sure of its supply position before moving. After delays and misgivings the last offensive was planned to kick off on 24 November, the day after Thanksgiving.

It was much the same over on X Corps front, separated now from Eighth Army by a guerilla-bandit-filled gap of fifty miles.[2] By mid-November the Corps was seriously over-extended. At the extremities the US 3rd Division had begun landing at Wonsan on 5 November, and over a hundred miles north-eastwards up the coast the Capitol Division from ROK I Corps was moving towards the Soviet border with the South Korean 3rd

[1] Marshall, *The River and the Gauntlet*, pp. 1, 14.

[2] On 14 November patrols from the ROK 8th Division of II Corps, operating from Maengsan, near Tokchon, and from the 3rd Division of X Corps, met near the village of Songha-dong on the lateral road between Sunchon and Yonghung. This was just west of inter-command boundary, longitude 126° 45" East, and was the only contact after several other attempts had failed due to terrain and guerillas. Appleman, pp. 746-8.

Division on its inland, left flank. From Iwon 7th Division was moving through Pungsan towards the Yalu, while, in the centre of the Corp's front two regiments of the 1st Marine Division were pushing north from Hungnam along the single mountain road to the Chosin Reservoir, sixty miles south of the frontier. Reaching the mountain plateau at Koto-ri on 10 November, the Marines met a new enemy, General Winter: 'The doctors reported numerous cases where the men came down to the sickbay suffering from what appeared to be shock. Some of them would come in crying; some of them were extremely nervous; and the doctors said it was simply the sudden shock of the terrific cold when they were not ready for it.'[1] The march into the unknown continued.

Three important events occurred on 15 November. Elements of 7th Marines occupied Hagaru at the southern tip of the Reservoir; it was four degrees below zero. MacArthur directed Almond that the Marines in the coming offensive, instead of marching north as originally planned to the Yalu from the Reservoir, were to swing west and link with Eighth Army advancing north eastwards along the Sinanju-Kanggye-Man-pojin axis, so cutting in a co-ordinated movement the Communist main supply route. Thirdly, Smith, the Marine Divisional Commander, wrote from Hungnam to the Commandant of the Marine Corps, Gen. Gates, questioning the wisdom of a winter campaign in North Korea with his division strung out along the one road from Hungnam to the Yalu. Smith was also concerned about the gap between his division and Eighth Army. It appears that he deliberately restricted the advance of the division, for between 10 and 23 November the Marines, with virtually no enemy opposition, averaged one mile a day in the advance north while Hagaru was built up into a base. This caution in all probability saved the Division from annihilation in the next few weeks. As during the planning for Inchon the Marine command was finding itself at odds with MacArthur on both tactical and strategic grounds, for CINCUNC still manifestly possessed a 'supreme and almost mystical faith that he could not fail' on the Yalu any more than he could at Inchon. The rush to the frontier in fact was another tremendous gamble; one of the directives for the offensive published on the 20th

[1] Montross and Canzona, Vol. III, p. 121.

indicated that an occupation and not a battle was expected as the UN forces moved to the Yalu. Nevertheless, after the 15th, the Marines accepted the 'possibility of imminent and formidable' Chinese intervention.[1]

Nevertheless even the cautious Marines would have been amazed had they known the aggregate of Chinese strength in Korea by the middle of November. From innumerable prisoner interrogation reports it appears that four CCF armies crossed the Yalu between about 14 and 20 October; the 39th and 40th through Sinuiju, and the 38th and 42nd through Manpojin. While the 42nd Army marched to the Chosin Reservoir-Sudong area, the 39th was in front of Unsan, the 40th at Onjong and the 38th at Huichon. By the end of October two more armies, the 50th and 66th, had crossed over on the Antung-Sinuiju bridges and were deployed on the Chinese west flank. Had the 24th Division and the Commonwealth Brigade continued their advance, at the end of the month they would have encountered these forces; probably three Chinese who surrendered to the British at Taechon came from these armies. Thus by 1 November six Chinese armies, eighteen divisions, at least 180,000 men, were in Korea, these formations made up the XIII Army Group of the Fourth Field Army. By the middle of November three more armies, the 20th, 26th and 27th, each of four divisions, had moved to the Chosin area on X Corps front, and the 42nd Army had moved into the Eighth Army zone. These armies in the east comprised the IX Army group of the Third Field Army. Not counting ancillary units this meant that at least 300,000 Chinese infantry soldiers were across the Yalu by 15 November.

MacArthur's reasons for launching his final offensive were clarified in a message to Marshall after the strike against the Sinuiju bridges, reproduced by Whitney, and in another to JCS just as the advance started, a reply to their suggestion that he halt on the Yalu heights. MacArthur himself later discussed his reasoning with the Senate Committees[2] and Whitney and Willoughby have also elaborated in the references to his post-Inchon strategy noted above. CINCUNC had three alternatives. He could pull back to the waist; he could go on to the Yalu; or he could stay where he was. The last was absurd as it would possess

---

[1] Montross and Canzona, III, p. 133.
[2] *Hearings*, pp. 19-21.

the disadvantages of the first two courses without any of their advantages. MacArthur regarded a retreat to the waist as a political disaster, leaving as it would a large part of North Korea in Communist hands. It would be an act of appeasement, a Far Eastern Munich, a defeat for the West and a repudiation of the UN's Korean objectives. In disagreement with Bradley who thought that on military grounds at least the waist was a better line, a view that was also forwarded to Washington by the British Chiefs of Staffs at this time, MacArthur was convinced that his forces were insufficient even to hold the isthmus as the terrain was so mountainous. (It should be remembered that when the Eighth Army established its trans-peninsular line above the Parallel in 1951 it had been heavily reinforced.) Conversely, MacArthur held, advance to the Yalu would fulfil the aims of the UN for an united Korea without any qualification. It would present Peking with a barrier along the Yalu and would thus forestall any major Chinese attack, for MacArthur had always thought from the beginning of the war that Peking's actions in the Korean situation sprang solely from aggressive and not defensive motives. If there *was* a Chinese counter-offensive — so we are told — his forces would then retreat swiftly after springing the Red trap, a claim particularly disputed by his critics, as his disposition indicated that he expected immediate success. In retrospect it seems that these arguments and the calculations that underlay them are one of the great historic examples of human fallibility.

Yet the end seemed in sight even before the great 'end-the-war' offensive started. Elements of the 17th Infantry Regiment of the 7th Division from Pungsan reached the Yalu on 21 November at the wrecked town of Hyesanjin. A few hundred yards away were the ice-covered hills of Manchuria and a few Chinese sentries. A week later Task Force Kingston from the 32nd Infantry Regiment entered Singalpajin on the river, twenty miles west of Hyesanjin. A hundred and fifty miles to the south-west the Eighth Army was already falling before the Chinese. The watch on the Yalu was over as soon as it had begun. These were the only American troops to reach that frontier of liberation.

REVOLUTIONARY WAR: LURING IN DEEP

The tactics used against the UN Command by the Chinese People's Volunteers, or the Chinese Communist Forces (CCF) as they were known, differed little at first from those used against the KMT and the Japanese. Lightly-armed, highly-trained, and inured to tough living conditions, the Chinese invariably assembled and attacked at night, making full use of terrain. Assault groups broke off from parent units and approached enemy positions through valleys, stream beds or draws, or mountain defiles, synchronising their attack on the objective. Ambushes were favoured as the UN forces could then be broken up and reduced in detail.

The CCF were armed not only with Russian weapons but with American, Canadian and British arms captured from the Chinese Nationalists; US soldiers often mistook enemy fire for their own. Artillery and mortar support were well below Western levels, and fire was therefore usually concentrated on front-line targets to the neglect of the rear. It was only after the beginning of the stalemate in mid-1951 that CCF artillery and heavy equipment were built up by the Russians to rival that of the UNC. Logistics at first were also rudimentary; the Chinese soldier went into the offensive carrying enough rice, millet and soya bean for five to six days; withdrawal from the line for replenishment invariably precluded sustained offensives and time after time it was noticed that the momentum of Chinese attacks fell away in this period. Communications were primitive. The radio net only reached down to regimental level, with telephones down to company CPs. Below, whistles and flares were used. Each infantry division, triangular in organisation with three regiments, and possessing a nominal strength of 10,000 men, carried also an artillery battalion. The CCF army was made up of three, sometimes four of these divisions.

The largest Chinese military organisation encountered by the UNC in Korea was the army group, made up of from two to six armies, corresponding roughly to a Western army as the individual Chinese army was equivalent to a British or American corps. Chinese army groups were controlled by Field Army GHQ, which reported direct to Chu Teh's War Ministry in

Peking. During the initial Chinese intervention it appears that a joint KPA-CPV headquarters staff was set up in Mukden under the direction of General Peng Teh-huai, who as Vice-Chairman of the People's Revolutionary Military Council, the highest military planning body in China, was deputy commander of Peking's armed forces. Soon Peng was made sole commander of the CPV in Korea, nominally under Kim Il Sung's 'KPA-CPV Combined Headquarters' set up with the CCF intervention to preserve the fiction of Chinese 'volunteer' status. Yet with the crossing of the Yalu by the two army groups from Lin Piao's and Chen Yi's field armies, control of the Communist effort in Korea now passed to Peking, no matter how influential a pressure group were the North Koreans with their attendant task force of Soviet advisers and experts.

The strategic doctrines of the Chinese Communists are found in Mao's writings, which were and are extensively studied as military text books, and which have become a blueprint for all Communist anti-colonial guerilla campaigns. A general Maoist maxim useful to keep in mind when considering Chinese activities in Korea, whether on the battlefield or in the conference tent at Panmunjon, is the Red leader's neo-Leninist definition of war:

There are only two kinds of war in history, just and unjust. We support just wars and oppose unjust wars. All counter-revolutionary wars are unjust, all revolutionary wars are just. . . . A war which will be waged by the overwhelming majority of mankind and of the Chinese people will undoubtedly be a just war . . . and will form a bridge leading world history into a new era . . . an era of lasting peace for mankind. . . .[1]

Of particular significance therefore to Chinese strategy in Korea are Mao's two great studies on war distilled from his experiences fighting the KMT and the Japanese, *Strategic Problems of China's Revolutionary War* (1936) and *On the Protracted War* (1938). As war itself is a form of political activity, Mao says, and as the struggle must result in the final triumph of Communism, it follows that the Communists are not concerned with attempting to win a quick victory divorced from political ends. Time is

[1] *Selected Works of Mao Tse-tung*, I, p. 179.

on their side and they count upon the anxiety of their reactionary imperialist adversaries to end the war quickly, obsessed as they are with a mechanistic approach to war in which weapons are all-important, and besides being ruled by other subjective considerations. Objective factors favour our side, emphasises Mao, and therefore a long war ensures the total political mobilisation of the masses which will clinch the victory.[1]

Now, in the autumn of 1950, the motorised columns of Walker and Almond were sweeping forward towards the Manchurian border. *The Protracted War* outlines the three phases of Maoist strategy:

> The strategy should be that of employing our main forces in mobile warfare, over an extended, shifting and indefinite front: a strategy depending for success on a high degree of mobility, and featured by swift attack and withdrawal, swift concentration and dispersal. . . .
>
> Since the . . . war is a protracted one and the final victory will be China's, we can reasonably imagine that this protracted war will pass through the following three stages. The first stage is one of the enemy's strategic offensive . . . the second stage may be termed the stage of strategic stalemate. . . . We say that it is easy to attack an enemy on the move precisely because he is then not on the alert, that is, he is inadvertent. These two things — creating illusions for the enemy and springing surprise attacks on him — are used to make the enemy face the uncertainties of war while securing for ourselves the greatest possible certainty of gaining superiority, initiative, and victory. . . .
>
> We have always advocated the policy of 'luring the enemy to penetrate deep' precisely because this is the most effective military policy for a weak army in strategic defence against a strong army. . . .[2]

Yet even after the first check given to the UN forces at the end of October by the employment of these classic Maoist manœuvres, there were still many difficulties for Peking to surmount before moving into the third stage of its campaign, the strategic

---

[1] For the text of *Strategic Problems*, ibid., I, pp. 175-253; for that of *Protracted War*, ibid., II, pp. 157-243.

[2] *See Selected Works*, II, pp. 163-4, 183-5, 217, 224.

counter-offensive. Even if the Chinese armies south of the Yalu possessed a certain immunity with their base areas in Manchuria, the potentialities of UNC firepower and air power were immense. That the leadership recognised they were risking counter-action by the USAF, including perhaps nuclear strikes, is shown not only by General Nieh's statement to Ambassador Panikkar. Throughout the autumn of 1950 air-raid drill was carried on in north-east China and air-raid shelters were being built in Mukden. No doubt the appearance of the MIGs in Korean skies on 1 November were linked with an air defence programme against the threat of Stratemeyer's B-29s which had already caused so much havoc in North Korea. The Chinese were quite willing to risk atomic attack; as long ago as 1946 Mao had dismissed the bomb: 'The atomic bomb is a paper tiger with which the US reactionaries try to terrify the people. It looks terrible, but in fact is not . . . the outcome is decided by the people, not by one or two new weapons. . . .'[1] The Western emphasis on the bomb as the ultimate weapon was only further evidence of a mechanistic approach to war.

Besides, there were other advantages in the situation which Peking could exploit. The ROK forces which comprised half of the Eighth Army indicated that Walker's right flank was vulnerable; beyond the South Koreans yawned the gap between the two commands. Moreover, MacArthur's US divisions were strung out along totally inadequate roads in vulnerable mechanised columns all the way from Hyesanjin to Sinanju. Thus the three weeks disengagement in November by the CCF would give greater time for preparing the counter blow, in luring the enemy in even deeper where they could be engaged in a classic Maoist war of annihilation and finally for rallying the home front. Concurrently with the military preparation in Korea, the *Resist America, Aid Korea* campaign, formally initiated on 4 November, stepped up new heights of controlled hysteria. Resistance to the US and UN was justified less on ideological solidarity with North Korea than with the necessity for national defence, a safer emphasis for a regime so recently established, and embarking on a major foreign adventure. The term *k'ang yi* was now universally used to prepare for action against the Americans. Already on 26 October the Chinese People's

[1] Whiting, p. 135.

Committee in Defence of World Peace and Against American Aggression was formed to organise the campaign which lasted to the end of the war, and beyond. Taking time off from listening to the broadcast torture and execution of reactionaries and oppositional elements at this time, the public were forced to attend Hate America harangues such as this, extracted from one of the primers of the campaign:

[The United States] is the paradise of gangsters, swindlers, rascals, special agents, fascist germs, speculators, debauchers, and all the dregs of mankind. This is the world's manufactory and source of such crimes as reaction, darkness, cruelty, decadence, corruption, debauchery, oppression of man by man, and cannibalism. This is the exhibition ground of all the crimes which can possibly be committed by mankind. This is a living hell, ten times, one hundred times, one thousand times worse than can be possibly depicted by the most sanguinary of writers. Here the criminal phenomenon that issue forth defy the imagination of human brains. Conscientious persons can only wonder how the spiritual civilization of mankind can be depraved to such an extent.[1]

Yet although the possibility of general war was mentioned in internal Chinese press comment, a prolonged limited war in Korea was depicted as a victory for China as it would stop the US occupation of the entire country and drain away American resources. Defending North Korea was not an end in itself by any means, but a means of increasing Peking's power and prestige as well. However much the Chinese public was being conditioned to withstand total war if necessary, Peking was also planning for a protracted war with ends not precisely defined. How could they be when US counter-intentions were not known? Right up to the last minute, Mao and Chou were not sure what their massive intervention in Korea would bring in this, the Year of the Tiger in the Chinese calendar.

MOST IMPORTANT ALLY

The Hallowe'en fighting at Unsan and the identification of the

[1] Montross and Canzona, Vol. III, p. 91.

Chinese south of the Yalu had precipitated a particularly profound feeling of unease in Britain with the Korean situation. The decision to support South Korea in June had at first been as popular with the British as it had been with the Republicans. American intervention was welcomed, less for its Asian implications than for indicating that any Soviet military move in Europe would be met by force, a vindication of collective security. As Attlee had stated on 27 June, '. . . the salvation of all is dependent on prompt and effective measures to arrest aggression wherever it may occur.'

The House of Commons debate on 5 July, following the Prime Minister's motion of support for his government's action in backing United Nations action in Korea, evoked almost unparalleled pro-American speeches from all sides. From the Opposition front bench Eden mentioned the sense of confidence which he had and 'which I believe the government have, that General MacArthur is in command of operations'; that 'shrewd and competent general', as a Labour back-bencher, the Reverend George Lang, put it, 'with a great history behind him and the heart of a lion'. It could have been a GOP conclave on Capitol Hill. Tom Driberg, while supporting the motion, told the House that he had been alarmed to find that in his own constituency (Maldon, Essex) 'ordinary, non-political people' were taking the line that it was 'about time we had a smack at 'em anyway'.[1] Only S. O. Davies and Emrys Hughes opposed the motion. Attlee's refutation of the Communists' legal objections to intervention has been noted, but there were also echoes in his speech of the deliberations in Blair House over a week before; the line had to be drawn in Korea unless there was to be another world war.

Press and public thus on the whole strongly supported the decision to intervene. On the non-Communist left, *Tribune* strongly supported Truman's decision to intervene in Korea, but the *New Statesman*, conceding North Korean aggression, thought in its first leader on the war that the invasion had 'given American imperialism just the opportunity it desired'. Showing its fundamental suspicion of US policy, the magazine editorialised a week later that if the Russians were surprised that American

[1] A political person who wanted to take a smack was Tory MP Peter Roberts who asked for an atomic bomb to be dropped on 'the capital of North Korea'.

intervention in Korea had prevented forcible unification, the Communists had still committed the US to 'a costly colonial war'.

On Formosa of course there was general British agreement that the Government was right in deciding that the Royal Navy was to have nothing to do with the Seventh Fleet in the Formosa Straits. Sensitive to Indian and Asian neutralist opinion, the British believed even more strongly than Acheson that the Chinese Communists, often presented in the British press at this time as left-to-centre nationalist reformers, should not be forced into the Kremlin's arms by Western involvement with Formosa. There was still, it was generally believed, a strong prospect of detaching Peking from the Communist bloc. Thus quite consistently the British position over the 'neutralisation' order was that if there were any clash between the Chinese Communists and the Americans in the Formosa Straits, the UK would accept the verdict of the UN as to future action. The most important ally from the very beginning was not going along with the tortuous re-commitment of the Administration to Chiang.

Differences over Formosa were secondary, however. Speaking at Taunton at the end of July, Attlee described Communism as a 'damnable and sterile' creed; on 12 September, as the fighting in the Pusan Perimeter came to its climax and as the invasion fleet crept up the Korean coast towards Inchon the Government announced a new rearmament programme of £3,600 million over the next three years. The Korean crisis within three months had already forced a first change in the budgetary structure which was to become even further distorted by defence expenditure before the winter was over.[1]

Until the Chinese intervention there was no doubt at all that the Government supported Korean reunification. On 27 October Hugh Baillie, the president of the United Press, interviewed Attlee in 10 Downing Street. The first ROK troops had reached the Yalu, and, unknown to Attlee, were already falling back before the Chinese. 'Much as he approved the results of the Korean War, however,' writes Baillie, 'he didn't think much of the war itself. It was obvious that he had no enthusiasm for wars in

---

[1] Pre-Korean War UK defence appropriations for 1950-51 were an estimated £780 million; a £100 million increase announced on 26 July 1950 was part of the September figure.

Asia "where the white race could be poured into a bottomless pit".[1] Yet the debate on the King's speech at the opening of the new parliament a few days later on 31 October probably marked the high-water mark of MacArthur's popularity in Britain. Attlee spoke warmly of his 'masterly strategy' at Inchon, and remarked that the end of the campaign was in sight. Churchill praised the general's 'brilliant conduct and measurement of military events', sentiments which were written into the King's speech. 'The success of this historic act,' said the Monarch, '. . . marks a decisive moment in world affairs, and is arousing fresh hopes of achieving a united, free and independent Korea. . . .' There was thus no suggestion up to the initial Chinese intervention that MacArthur was 'going beyond' the Parallel without authorisation.

Within the next few days it became known that the Chinese were operating in some force up to seventy miles south of the Yalu. Having committed themselves to Korean unification and to giving MacArthur a *carte blanche* to achieve it there was now nothing Whitehall could do to influence a notoriously uncontrollable foreign general carrying out an UN resolution. The British Chiefs of Staff told Washington that they thought a halt on the waist was best for military reasons; and conferences between the State Department and the representatives of the UK, Canada and France discussed the possibility of a buffer zone in the area north of the waist but that was all. MacArthur would say at the end of November that he had received no suggestion from any authoritative sources that he halt the advance — and even if British suggestions had penetrated officially to the Dai-Ichi, would the General regard them as authoritative? As CINCUNC, his chain of command came from the General Assembly's recommendations to the President to the JCS. . . .

Public advocacy in Britain of stopping the advance was thus left to the opposition on the Right — and the Left. The motivations of the Labour Left in opposing the advance to the Yalu in Parliament and press were suspect for they distrusted Washington more than Peking, whether MacArthur existed or not. But Lord Salisbury's House of Lord's speech on 15 November criticising the advance on strategic rather than political grounds, and coming from a man who had opposed the initial British

[1] Baillie, *High Tension*, pp. 237-8.

recognition of Peking in January 1950, carried more weight: '. . . the danger of our present position is that we have, if anything, advanced too far. We have reached a point when the enemy's lines of communication are not in Korea at all, and cannot therefore be attacked without grave diplomatic risks'.[1] Here Salisbury was recognising a fundamental strategic reality of the war. Given a policy of limited war restricted to Korea's borders, there was an inverse ratio between the amount of territory controlled by one side, and the effectiveness of logistics and air power. In July at the gates of Pusan, Communist communications and supply lines overran themselves; in November, fifty miles south of the Yalu, it was the UN Command which faced supply difficulties as it reached a frontier beyond which its air power could not strike at a new enemy massing to meet it. Following Salisbury's warning, Churchill in the Commons the next day voiced concern of the Opposition at the dangers of too great a commitment to the Far East. The Allies must not get 'pinned down' in China, or the approaches to China, when the danger in Europe was paramount. This after all was a passionately held belief by both Government and Opposition at Westminster. America's most important ally thought Korea was essentially a diversion.

As the slow advance to the Yalu went on, the Government's attitude to MacArthur's authority — following Washington's lead — was given in a reply to Desmond Donnelly, the then Left Labour back bencher, on 20 November. Denying a suggestion that the General had been guilty of disobedience Ernest Davies, Foreign Under-Secretary, baldly stated that MacArthur had been entrusted by the UN with the conduct of operations in Korea, and that it was 'for him to decide how best to employ' his forces. Whatever the half-hearted attempts by the British to halt the advance at the waist and suggest a buffer zone, there was nothing more to be said publicly. From the forward positions on the Chongchon River to the Cabinet office in Whitehall, all were keeping their fingers crossed and hoping that the worst would not happen. In his message to Chou on 22 November, Bevin assured him that the UN had 'no hostile intent' towards the new China. The only objectives of the UN action were to create a 'free and independent' Korea — exactly what

[1] H. L. Deb., Vol. 169, Col. 281.

the Chinese were determined to prevent, and showing that the frame of reference of Communist intentions was the same in London as in Washington. Although in the mid-December debate on the Korea crisis Bevin stated that the Government were 'gravely concerned' about the final drive to the Yalu, this last message shows that, like Truman and Acheson, Attlee and Bevin did not think that the objective of an united Korea would really provoke a massive Chinese counteraction. In the last resort HMG was prepared to go along with MacArthur. After all with no direct control over him there was nothing else the British could do but to follow the lead of that lion-hearted commander in his last offensive.

HOME BY CHRISTMAS: YOU PICK YOUR MAN. . . .

Thanksgiving Day, 23 November, was celebrated all over the front. Highly-organised air drops supplied the troops with turkey and all the accessories, including coffee and mince tart. For many this was their last hot meal. The next morning Mac-Arthur, accompanied by Whitney and Willoughby, flew to Sin-anju to see the beginning of the offensive. According to Apple-man, 'Optimism and enthusiasm as to chances of the attack succeeding seemed to prevail.'[1] On Walker's west flank, 24th Division and the ROK 1st Division with the Commonwealth Brigade in reserve would advance to the Yalu in the Sinuiju-Suiho area. In the centre 25th and 2nd Divisions would advance north and north-eastwards respectively along the Kuryong and Chingchon valleys to the border; while on the right covering the mountains around Tokchon was the ROK II Corps, omin-ously described by Walker to correspondents as 'unpredictable'. The 1st Cavalry Division was in reserve at Sunchon.

On X Corps front two Marine regiments, 5th and 7th, had reached Yudam-ni at the eastern tip of the Chosin Reservoir. From here they were scheduled to start their advance on the 27th across the gap to link with the northward movement of the Eighth Army at Mupyong, and so on to Kanggye and Man-pojin on the border. Looking after the guerillas and guarding the west flank and rear was the responsibility of 3rd Division,

[1] p. 776.

while in the centre three battalions of 7th Division had been ordered to move due north to the frontier via the east side of the Reservoir; the rest of the division would expand its zone on the Yalu at Hyesanjin linking on its right with ROK 1st Corps moving towards Chongjin and so on to the Soviet border. The basis of the offensive was the envelopment between the right flank of the Eighth Army and the Marine movement west. GHQ's euphoria was not qualified by the strength of the enemy, which was given at about 100,000 front-line troops with 40,000 guerillas in the UNC rear; UN front-line strength was about 100,000 out of a Command numbering altogether about 377,000, 200,000 of which were South Koreans. Half the command were supply and service troops strung out from the Yalu and the Chongchon south to Pusan. Moreover, Tokyo's estimates of the Chinese forces in Manchuria, probably put out to make the Pentagon's flesh creep, ranged up to half a million men.

In spite of these figures — alarming enough without the knowledge of the full Chinese movement into Korea — there was no doubt of victory in MacArthur's message to the command published on 24 November, the last MacArthur victory communiqué:

'The United Nations massive compression envelopment in North Korea against the new Red armies operating there is now approaching its decisive effort. The isolating components of the pincer, our air forces of all types, have for the past three weeks, in a sustained attack of model co-ordination and effectiveness, successfully interdicted enemy lines of support from the North so that further reinforcements therefrom has been sharply curtailed and essential supplies markedly limited. The eastern sector of the pincer, with noteworthy and effective naval support, has steadily advanced in a brilliant tactical movement and has now reached a commanding envelopment position cutting in two the northern reaches of the enemy's geographical potential. This morning the western sector of the pincer moves forward in a general assault in an effort to complete the compression and close the vice. If successful this should for all practical purposes end the war, restore peace and unity to Korea, enable the prompt with-

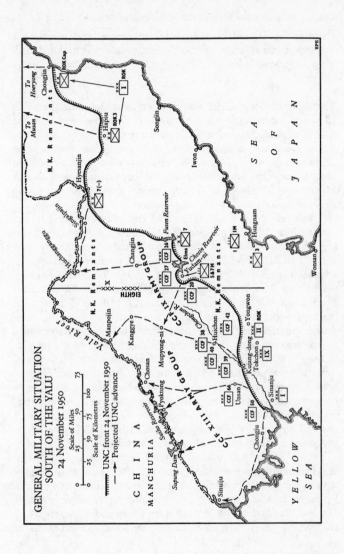

GENERAL MILITARY SITUATION
SOUTH OF THE YALU
24 November 1950

Scale of Miles
0   25   50   75

Scale of Kilometres
0   25   50   75   100

▬▬▬ UNC front 24 November 1950
– – – ➤ Projected UNC advance

drawal of United Nations military forces, and permit the complete assumption by the Korean people and nation of full sovereignty and international equality. It is that for which we fight.'[1]

The Commander-in-Chief was reported as saying to Coulter, CG, IX Corps, referring to his communiqué, 'Tell the boys from me that when they reach the Yalu, they are going home. I want to make good my statement that they are going to eat their Christmas dinner at home.'[2] After bravely flying over the Yalu wastes — and the Chinese armies — in his Constellation, *SCAP*, MacArthur returned to Tokyo where a message from JCS awaited him.

It was a worried distillation of all the heart-searching in the capital since the NSC meeting of 9 November. There was a growing concern in the UN, MacArthur was told, about involvement with Red China, and a general East-West conflict. Limiting the advance near the Yalu might avoid trouble. The Pentagon suggested that MacArthur therefore hold his forces on the Yalu heights dominating the river, principally with ROK troops. In the north-east, the advance should be stopped at Chongjin. MacArthur immediately replied that it would be 'utterly impossible' to stop his command short of the frontier because of the terrain. Besides, prompt implementation of his offensive plan would 'effectively appeal to the reason in the Chinese mind'. In the Senate Hearings, Collins insisted that the command could have been stopped short of the Yalu; as the offensive never got that far the point was academic.[3] But what was relevant and would not be forgotten by JCS was that MacArthur had ignored their suggestions now as well as those of 24 October.

Yet if Washington was so worried about the Chinese, why did Truman not *order* MacArthur to halt? There were reasons which went far beyond the traditional reluctance of the Pentagon not to supervise a field commander directly — and besides, MacArthur was no ordinary commander. Bradley had emphasised on 9 November that there were military risks in

---

[1] Montross and Canzona, Vol. III, p. 144.
[2] Whitney makes it conditional: 'If this operation is successful, I hope we can get the boys home by Christmas.' *MacArthur*, p. 416.
[3] *Hearings*, pp. 1229-30, 1300, 1312.

driving to the Yalu but they must be subordinated to policy. Therefore the Joint Chiefs deferred to State. Changing MacArthur's orders were a matter of 'policy'. If Truman were to be advised to halt the victory march, then Acheson would have to tell the President. But, as Richard Neustadt has written in superb study of why Truman did *not* take this decision, Acheson, 'already under fire from the Capitol, was treading warily between the Pentagon and that inveterate idealist about generals, Harry Truman.' And Marshall, who had been Chief of Staff when Bradley was a divisional commander, and who had preceded Acheson in State, was toppling over backwards not to meddle with his successors. Because of subjective factors operating with all the main participants in Tokyo and Washington, the drive to the Yalu had now become an end in itself divorced from political necessity. Reportedly in these last few days Acheson and Marshall and Bradley were intensely worried: starting from the planners' arcana deep in the Pentagon, the feeling was growing that the Chinese might be already south of the Yalu and ready to strike at both parts of the divided command. But no advice was given to the President to halt MacArthur. Years later Truman said:

What we should have done is stop at the neck of Korea right here [pointing to a globe]. . . . That's what the British wanted. . . . We knew the Chinese had close to a million men on the border and all that. . . . But [MacArthur] was commander in the field. You pick your man, you've got to back him up. That's the only way a military organisation can work. I got the best advice I could and the man on the spot said this was the thing to do. . . . So I agreed. That was my decision—no matter what hindsight shows.[1]

There was no possibility that MacArthur had provoked the Chinese counter-offensive. What would be held against him, and this is the heart of the MacArthur tragedy, was that he failed to make preparations to meet the attack, and that his judgment had been grievously wrong. Already caught in the

[1] Neustadt, *Presidential Power*, p. 128. See pp. 123-47 for an analysis of the Washington end of the drive to the Yalu and the shifting Korean objectives between Inchon and the Chongchon.

trap of its commander's personality, the United Nations offensive to end the war was itself the victim of a massive Chinese counter-offensive. Only the Chinese had known that two armies were on the move in the mountains of North Korea just south of the Yalu on the day after Thanksgiving.

PART II

FROM VICTORY TO STALEMATE

25 November 1950 – 8 July 1951

CHAPTER NINE

AN ENTIRELY NEW WAR

We have a claim on the output of the arsenals of London as well as of Hanyang, and, what is more, it is to be delivered to us by the enemy's own transport corps. This is the sober truth, not a joke.

MAO TSE-TUNG

DEFEAT ON THE CHONGCHON

DURING the first day of the offensive in the words of MacArthur's special communiqué to Lake Success, 'The gigantic UN pincers moved according to schedule. . . .' Virtually unopposed advances of up to eight miles were made all along the Western front as the Eighth Army moved ever closer to the Yalu. 'But, then,' Stratemeyer, still surprised, told the Jenner Subcommittee four years later, 'lo and behold, the whole mountainside turned out to be Chinese. . . .' On the second morning of the offensive, 25 November, Baker Company, 9th Infantry Regiment, 2nd Infantry Division (Maj.-Gen. L. B. Keiser) walked slowly up Hill 219 guarding the east bank of the Chongchon near the hamlet of Singhung-dong on the northern limit of the advance on the road to Kanggye. After a stiff climb, the men were within twenty-five yards of the first knob of the summit at 1030 when they were hit by a shower of grenades and a burst of rifle fire. Five Chinese broke away and ran along the ridgeline. The first shots of the 'new war' in Korea had been fired.

Inconclusive fighting went on for 219 all day and throughout the night, when the Americans still holding the slopes could see tracers flying across the Chongchon and hear artillery firing in the hills around them. But the broken nature of the ground, with its endless hills, valleys and ridges, and the difficulties in getting field telephones and portable radios to work, meant that in these opening stages of the battle operations were compart-

mented, so precluding any immediate intelligence appreciation
of the general situation. Two miles below Hill 219 a camp on
the flood plain of the Chongchon at Kujang-dong was overrun
by a wild Chinese charge across the river from the north-west,
and, after a moment of panic by one artillery unit, was beaten
back. More significantly, two companies on the west bank of
the river were routed, and 2nd Division's line breached in such
a way that it never recovered, so affecting the position of the
entire Army.

Everywhere the pattern of attack was the same. Usually
moving at night, the Chinese assault companies used feeder
valleys and draws leading into the Chongchon valley to move
against the rear of the Americans, first surprising and then
overrunning the defenders as the battle developed as a series
of isolated engagements. Attacks were accompanied by weird,
frightening noises from bugles, flutes, drums, rattles, whistles,
and shepherd's pipes which simulated the sound of a cock
crowing. There was no question of linear defence in this war of
infiltration, but those US units that were able to stand and
fight soon realised that Chinese tactics were mechanical and
repetitious, making their enemy extremely vulnerable once their
tricks were known. Illumination in particular demoralised the
Chinese: apparently they were then worried more by light
than by death.

By the evening of the 26th, 2nd Division had been forced back
two miles down the Chongchon. On the far right one of its
three regiments had been stalled near the South Korean sector;
on the left, in the Kuryong valley, 25th Division was coming
under mounting pressure. But already by this time the battle
had been lost. The entire ROK II Corps of three divisions on
Eighth Army's right flank around Tokchon had disintegrated
under a thunderbolt unleashed by the Chinese command from
its concentration area around Huichon.[1] From here the Chinese
had been able both to weaken decisively the two US divisions
on Walker's right and also to move across the Chongchon and
smash the entire UN front in Korea at its most 'unpredictable'
part.

[1] For the details of the Chinese break-through see Cameron, 'The Lost
Corps', *Military Review*, Vol. 33, No. 2. Cameron was KMAG adviser to the
8th Division which, with the 6th and 7th Divisions, made up the Corps.

Earlier on the 26th, the Turkish Brigade (Turkish Army Command Force) had been sent towards Tokchon from Kunuri to help the South Koreans. Air observers had noted that hundreds of men were working on the Huichon-Tokchon cart track turning it into a highway; the Turks soon met a Chinese road-block at Wawon, only a third of the way to Tokchon and well in the rear of IX Corps. Here was the decisive Communist manœuvre. With the whole front yawning from Kunuri to Hagaru as a result of the annihilation of II Corps and the dispositions of the divided command, a Chinese turning movement to the west could threaten a large part of the Eighth Army itself through its broken right flank. Six Chinese armies, the eighteen divisions from the CCF XIII Army Group, were in action against EUSAK.

Extrication of I Corps' two divisions from the west coast via Pakchon, Sinanju, and so down the western route to Sukchon and Pyongyang was soon under way, jamming the roads for fifty miles with transport. Keiser's division would therefore have to hold a hinge around Kunuri to cover the withdrawal across the Chongchon of I Corps and 25th Division, fortunately deployed in depth in the Kuryong valley and able to counter the Chinese with its artillery.

Due to the incredulity of the higher echelons that the end-the-offensive had not even got off the ground before the Chinese had struck, Keiser was not able to order a pull-back towards Kunuri until the morning of the 28th. By this time even GHQ in Tokyo had realised that the withdrawal had turned into a retreat, the retreat into a flight. In a special communiqué the same day MacArthur informed the UN that

> Enemy reactions developed in the course of our assault operations of the past four days disclose that a major segment of the Chinese continental forces in army, corps and divisional organisation of an aggregate strength of over 200,000 men is now arrayed against the United Nations forces in North Korea. . . . Consequently we face an entirely new war.[1]

Even at this high moment of crisis, on the 29th Walker's statement on the disaster contained the essence of MacArthur's new version of the offensive: 'The assault launched by the Eighth Army five days ago probably saved our forces from a trap

[1] *Hearings*, p. 1834.

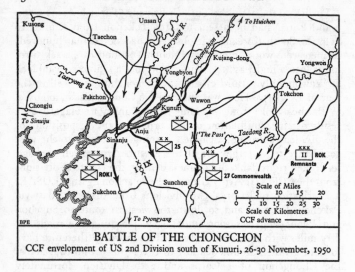

BATTLE OF THE CHONGCHON
CCF envelopment of US 2nd Division south of Kunuri, 26-30 November, 1950

which might well have destroyed them. . . . The timing of our attack to develop the situation was, indeed most fortunate.'[1]

Nothing could have been further from reality at this moment. At daybreak on the 29th a Turkish convoy driving north from Sunchon had been ambushed several times south of Kunuri; the Chinese were already across 2nd Division's withdrawal route in depth, but in the general confusion the threat was only thought to be a road-block. As the fatal decision was taken by 2nd Division to withdraw due south via the Kunuri-Sunchon road, so the Chinese build-up here went on. Early on the 29th IX Corps authorised Keiser's retreat to Sunchon: the route itself was left to Keiser. Later in the morning Keiser spoke on the radio to Milburn, CG, I Corps, who asked him: 'How are things going?' Keiser replied: 'Bad, right now. I'm getting hit in my CP.' Milburn then said, 'Well, come on out my way', meaning via Anju. But as Keiser wasn't under I Corps, and also thought that 25th Division hadn't yet cleared the Anju crossing, he was disinclined to withdraw to Sunchon the long way round. Flying back to his CP later from IX Corps in an L5 spotter plane, Keiser saw the road to the south jammed with refugees;

[1] Thompson, *Cry Korea*, pp. 252-53.

he felt that if these people were ahead of the enemy he still had time to get out on the Sunchon road. Later, he thought he had seen part of the Chinese movement into his own rear.[1]

The last phase of the retreat from the Chongchon started on the morning of the 30th. An ineffectual attempt to clear the ridges on the Kunuri-Sunchon road had failed to disperse the widely-held idea that there was only a shallow road-block to 'bash through'. Up until noon the alternatives remained of moving west or south; to remain at Kunuri meant annihilation by the Chinese advancing from east and north. But once the order was then given to move south there could be no reversal. What awaited 2nd Division after five days of fighting in zero temperatures was not a road-block, but a whole Chinese division dug in on both sides of the route for six miles to the pass at the highest point of the Kunuri-Sunchon road. The leading vehicles were soon picked off, jamming the road as the intensity of the enemy fire increased towards the south. There were between thirty and forty machine-guns and ten mortars firing onto the road. There was no place to hide as the storm of steel beat down on the Americans, for the knocked-out trucks, jeeps, tanks, and weapon carriers, enfiladed on both sides, offered no protection to the demoralised, tottering infantry.

The climax came at the pass beyond which the relieving Commonwealth 27th Brigade, transferred to IX Corps reserve, had been halted by the Chinese. Keiser walked through at about 1515 when this passageway was almost totally blocked by piles of American, Turkish and South Korean dead mixed up with shattered trucks. Napalm trickled down the hillside from the furious air strikes which had yet failed to stop the division's agony. The Chinese fire came down like tropical rain, while just above the road, bullets from the fighter-bombers hit the embankment, hailing the road with ·50-calibre machine-gun clips. 'The din,' S. L. A. Marshall observes, 'was terrific.' The last broken remnants of the division's artillery got through the pass in the early hours of the morning of 1 December; small groups of men found their own escape routes across the hills into the friendly lines of 27th Brigade and 1st Cavalry to the south. The lucky rearguard got out through Anju. The unnecessary march through the pass had cost the Division over 3,000 casual-

[1] Marshall, pp. 263-64.

ties and nearly all its equipment in one afternoon. The Eighth Army was saved by its speedy retreat; but North Korea was now lost to the United Nations. Inchon had been cancelled out by the Chongchon.

In the Pentagon the chief concern was now to co-ordinate the retreat of Eighth Army with that of X Corps. On 29 November JCS expressed their concern about the exposed position of Almond's command, but MacArthur's reply still maintained that terrain precluded a continuous line across the waist and that he could contract X Corps into the Hungnam-Wonsan area. Then on the 30th MacArthur was finally *ordered* to withdraw X Corps from north-east Korea and that the withdrawal of the two commands should be co-ordinated to prevent enemy forces from passing between or outflanking them. This meant that JCS were insisting on a regrouping of all forces under Walker's command in some defence line across the peninsula. Whatever the Chinese did the days of the divided command were now numbered.[1]

But as late as a command conference in Tokyo on 1 December attended by Walker, Almond, Hickey, Willoughby and Whitney, it was thought that Pyongyang could still be held and that X Corps could strike into the rear of the Chinese — a characteristic suggestion in the moment of disaster from the ever-sanguine Almond. However, as X Corps came under heavy fire and the Chinese took Songchon on the lateral Pyongyang-Wonsan road, MacArthur saw that only disengagement could save his forces, so outrunning the Communists and stretching their supply lines and making them vulnerable once again to his air power. This strategy, first outlined in the command conference, was now put into immediate effect, but presented to the Pentagon with political undertones which initiated the last and most momentous phase of the Truman-MacArthur controversy which was to drag on until the General's firing. For on 3 December MacArthur was not only telling JCS that he could not hold the Korean waist due to the familiar reasons of terrain, logistics, and inadequate forces. Instead, in a message that first indicated to JCS the new MacArthurian strategy for dealing with Red China's aggression, he announced that unless 'some positive and immediate action is taken . . . steady attrition leading to final

[1] *Hearings*, pp. 972-74, 1141-46.

destruction [of the command] can reasonably be contemplated. . . .'[1] Concurrently, according to Truman, 'within a matter of four days he found time to publicise in four different ways his views that the only reason for his troubles was the order from Washington to limit the hostilities to Korea. He talked about 'extraordinary inhibitions' . . . 'without precedent in military history' and made it plain that no blame whatsoever attached to him or his staff'. The situation in Korea was now so critical that JCS replied that they considered preservation of the command the primary consideration: '. . . Consolidation of forces into beach-heads is concurred in.' Simultaneously Truman ordered Collins to Tokyo to find out what the facts were.[2] Within a week of the launching of the end-the-war offensive, evacuation from Korea was a possibility, so great was the reversal.

In the early hours of 5 December the first (and still the last) Communist capital to be held by the West was evacuated by its British rearguard from the newly-arrived 29th Brigade. Huge amounts of supplies and petrol had been fired in the confusion and hysteria before the evacuation, and a mile-high pall of ochreous smoke towered over the wrecked city which awaited the entry of the Chinese armies and Kim Il Sung's return. Followed by a vast horde of refugees, the erstwhile liberators were fleeing south as fast as possible in bumper-to-bumper columns of transport to halt at a familiar line: the 38th Parallel. The way back to the frontier of containment was taking even less time than the autumn advance. There would be no return journey north.

RETREAT FROM CHOSIN

If the EUSAK's retreat from Pyongyang resembled a twentieth-century version of the flight from the Beresina, the march to safety of the 1st Marine Division trapped seventy-eight miles north of Hungnam at the Chosin Reservoir by the Chinese offensive arouses echoes of another ten thousand who hacked their way to safety through the hordes of Asia.

[1] Whitney, pp. 423-26, Willoughby, pp. 377-78.
[2] Truman, II, pp. 404-5, 417.

The two regiments of the Marine Division at Yudam-ni had started clearing the road westwards to Mupyong on the morning of the 27th: at the far north-east limit of X Corps' advance the South Koreans had entered Chongjin on 25 November. The first night of their offensive, 27/28 November, the Marines were attacked in strength by the Chinese not only in frontal assault, but along their main supply route south. The next morning the Division had been split into three isolated perimeters at Yudam-ni, Hagaru, and Koto-ri by Chinese attacks which had reached to Chinhung-ni, thirty-seven miles south of Yudam-ni. Operating against X Corps, but primarily against the Marine Division, were the twelve divisions of the CCF IX Army Group, three Chinese armies. Three Chinese divisions were in action at Yudam-ni and another five on the supply route to Chinhung-ni.

The Marine positions held against the Chinese after heavy fighting; the situation at Hagaru, with its base and vital airstrip was particularly serious for only a battalion from the Marine 1st Regiment and some US Army troops held the perimeter through which the regiments at Yudam-ni would have to withdraw. On 1 December about ten thousand Marines started the fourteen-mile march to Hagaru; their disengagement was fantastically difficult as contact with the enemy was so close that the ridges on both sides of the twisting, precarious road had to be cleared if the force was to survive. By the 3rd, the first stage of this epic of collective and individual heroism was over when the leading Marines reached Hagaru, from where Smith had directed the march of the 5th and 7th Regiments, although the rearguard was not inside the new perimeter until the next afternoon.

The worst was over at Hagaru for the time being. From Koto-ri on 29 November a relieving force of nearly 1,000 men composed of Marines, US Army personnel and British Marine Commandos from 41st Independent Commando attached to Smith's command had set out for Hagaru. Task Force Drysdale, named after the Royal Marine Lt.-Col. who commanded the unit, was ambushed at 'Hellfire Valley' above the Changjin River. But the serious situation at Hagaru forced Smith to order Drysdale to proceed at all costs. Only four hundred men reached their destination to reinforce the garrison, but the action was considered justified, so vital was it to hold Hagaru.

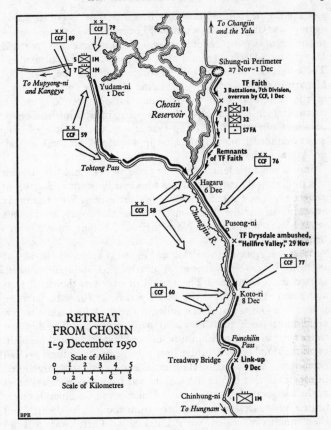

Meanwhile three battalions of the 7th Infantry Division (two infantry, one artillery) had almost been destroyed east of the Reservoir. On 27 November Almond had helicoptered in for a conference after these Army units' first fire-fight with the Chinese. Gesturing to the north, the X Corps commander said, 'We're still attacking and we're going all the way to the Yalu. Don't let a bunch of Chinese laundrymen stop you.'[1] That night

[1] Gugeler, *Combat Actions in Korea*, p. 69. See pp. 62-87 for the action fought by these 7th Division troops east of the Reservoir.

and for the next three days the three battalions were in action against the Chinese who eventually overwhelmed them. Out of the force of 2,500 men only 1,000 survivors managed to reach Hagaru by 2 December, and only 385 of these were able-bodied. These terrible losses had to be placed against the saving of Hagaru itself, and with it the Marine Division. The importance of the air cover given the Marines during their long march meant not only invaluable close support in fighting the omnipresent Chinese but that the evacuation was possible of over 4,500 wounded from Hagaru airstrip, mostly by Dakotas to Yonpo Airfield, Hungnam.

Smith, meanwhile, annoyed by press reports that his division was in flight told correspondents who had flown into Hagaru on 4 December, 'Gentlemen, we are not retreating. We are merely attacking in another direction.' As a morale-booster, his famous remark was magnificent. Nevertheless, the long march south had to go on.

After a regroupment at Hagaru, the next stage, the break-out to Koto-ri where a garrison of nearly 4,000 was surrounded, started on 6 December. The arrival of over ten thousand men and 1,000 vehicles filled the small perimeter there to bursting point: the journey of eleven miles in the snow had taken thirty-eight hours with the Chinese active everywhere. The last ten miles from Koto-ri to Chinhung-ni posed an additional problem to all the usual ones. A bridge over a gorge in Funchilin Pass had been blown and special prefabricated equipment was parachuted into Koto-ri. But before the withdrawal from this last perimeter to the sea got under way over 100 Marines and Commandos were buried in a mass grave dynamited from the iron-hard earth and then hurriedly sealed with bulldozers. There was a brief burial service:

> Out of dust thou art taken
> Unto dust shalt thou return
> Out of dust thou shalt rise again. . . .

On the afternoon of 8 December the first of 14,000 men started marching southwards as fighting went on for the ridges that dominated the road; twenty-four hours later men and vehicles began moving across the bridge carefully placed over

he next three days the three battalions were in action
ne Chinese who eventually overwhelmed them. Out of
of 2,500 men only 1,000 survivors managed to reach
y 2 December, and only 385 of these were able-bodied.
rible losses had to be placed against the saving of
tself, and with it the Marine Division. The importance
r cover given the Marines during their long march
ot only invaluable close support in fighting the omni-
Chinese but that the evacuation was possible of over
nded from Hagaru airstrip, mostly by Dakotas to Yon-
d, Hungnam.

meanwhile, annoyed by press reports that his division
ght told correspondents who had flown into Hagaru on
er, 'Gentlemen, we are not retreating. We are merely
in another direction.' As a morale-booster, his famous
vas magnificent. Nevertheless, the long march south
on.

regroupment at Hagaru, the next stage, the break-out
i where a garrison of nearly 4,000 was surrounded,
1 6 December. The arrival of over ten thousand men
vehicles filled the small perimeter there to bursting
e journey of eleven miles in the snow had taken thirty-
urs with the Chinese active everywhere. The last ten
n Koto-ri to Chinhung-ni posed an additional problem
usual ones. A bridge over a gorge in Funchilin Pass had
vn and special prefabricated equipment was parachuted
-ri. But before the withdrawal from this last perimeter
got under way over 100 Marines and Commandos were
a mass grave dynamited from the iron-hard earth and
riedly sealed with bulldozers. There was a brief
vice :

Out of dust thou art taken
Unto dust shalt thou return
Out of dust thou shalt rise again. . . .

e afternoon of 8 December the first of 14,000 men
arching southwards as fighting went on for the ridges
ninated the road; twenty-four hours later men and
egan moving across the bridge carefully placed over

---

destruction [of the command] can reasonably be contemplated. . . .'[1] Concurrently, according to Truman, 'within a
matter of four days he found time to publicise in four different
ways his views that the only reason for his troubles was the
order from Washington to limit the hostilities to Korea. He
talked about 'extraordinary inhibitions' . . . 'without precedent
in military history' and made it plain that no blame whatsoever
attached to him or his staff'. The situation in Korea was now so
critical that JCS replied that they considered preservation of the
command the primary consideration: '. . . Consolidation of
forces into beach-heads is concurred in.' Simultaneously Truman ordered Collins to Tokyo to find out what the facts were.[2]
Within a week of the launching of the end-the-war offensive,
evacuation from Korea was a possibility, so great was the
reversal.

In the early hours of 5 December the first (and still the last)
Communist capital to be held by the West was evacuated by its
British rearguard from the newly-arrived 29th Brigade. Huge
amounts of supplies and petrol had been fired in the confusion
and hysteria before the evacuation, and a mile-high pall of
ochreous smoke towered over the wrecked city which awaited
the entry of the Chinese armies and Kim Il Sung's return. Followed by a vast horde of refugees, the erstwhile liberators were
fleeing south as fast as possible in bumper-to-bumper columns of
transport to halt at a familiar line: the 38th Parallel. The
way back to the frontier of containment was taking even
less time than the autumn advance. There would be no return
journey north.

RETREAT FROM CHOSIN

If the EUSAK's retreat from Pyongyang resembled a
twentieth-century version of the flight from the Beresina, the
march to safety of the 1st Marine Division trapped seventy-eight
miles north of Hungnam at the Chosin Reservoir by the Chinese
offensive arouses echoes of another ten thousand who hacked
their way to safety through the hordes of Asia.

[1] Whitney, pp. 423-26, Willoughby, pp. 377-78.
[2] Truman, II, pp. 404-5, 417.

M

The two regiments of the Marine Division at Yudam-ni had started clearing the road westwards to Mupyong on the morning of the 27th: at the far north-east limit of X Corps' advance the South Koreans had entered Chongjin on 25 November. The first night of their offensive, 27/28 November, the Marines were attacked in strength by the Chinese not only in frontal assault, but along their main supply route south. The next morning the Division had been split into three isolated perimeters at Yudam-ni, Hagaru, and Koto-ri by Chinese attacks which had reached to Chinhung-ni, thirty-seven miles south of Yudam-ni. Operating against X Corps, but primarily against the Marine Division, were the twelve divisions of the CCF IX Army Group, three Chinese armies. Three Chinese divisions were in action at Yudam-ni and another five on the supply route to Chinhung-ni.

The Marine positions held against the Chinese after heavy fighting; the situation at Hagaru, with its base and vital airstrip was particularly serious for only a battalion from the Marine 1st Regiment and some US Army troops held the perimeter through which the regiments at Yudam-ni would have to withdraw. On 1 December about ten thousand Marines started the fourteen-mile march to Hagaru; their disengagement was fantastically difficult as contact with the enemy was so close that the ridges on both sides of the twisting, precarious road had to be cleared if the force was to survive. By the 3rd, the first stage of this epic of collective and individual heroism was over when the leading Marines reached Hagaru, from where Smith had directed the march of the 5th and 7th Regiments, although the rearguard was not inside the new perimeter until the next afternoon.

The worst was over at Hagaru for the time being. From Koto-ri on 29 November a relieving force of nearly 1,000 men composed of Marines, US Army personnel and British Marine Commandos from 41st Independent Commando attached to Smith's command had set out for Hagaru. Task Force Drysdale, named after the Royal Marine Lt.-Col. who commanded the unit, was ambushed at 'Hellfire Valley' above the Changjin River. But the serious situation at Hagaru forced Smith to order Drysdale to proceed at all costs. Only four hundred men reached their destination to reinforce the garrison, but the action was considered justified, so vital was it to hold Hagaru.

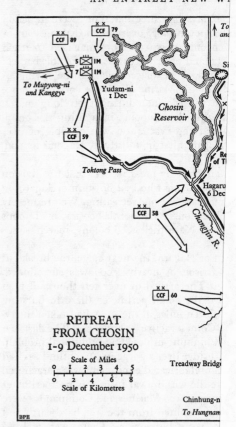

RETREAT
FROM CHOSIN
1-9 December 1950

Scale of Miles
0 1 2 3 4 5

Scale of Kilometres
0   2   4   6   8

Treadway Bridge

Chinhung-ni
To Hungnam

Meanwhile three battalions of the 7th I[nfantry] infantry, one artillery) had almost been Reservoir. On 27 November Almond ha[d] a conference after these Army units' fi[rst contact with the] Chinese. Gesturing to the north, the X C[orps commander said] 'We're still attacking and we're going all [the way to the Yalu.] Don't let a bunch of Chinese laundrymen [stop you.']

¹ Gugeler, *Combat Actions in Korea*, p. 69. Se[e for the actions] fought by these 7th Division troops east of the [Reservoir.]

AN ENTIRELY NEW WAR   165

the chasm by engineers. About the same time some Marines from the north had scrambled into the lines of the men from the 1st Regiment who had fought their way north from Chin-hung-ni. In the small hours of the 10th the van of the column from the north entered Chinhung-ni while the rear was still in Koto-ri; the break-out from Chosin was over. By late on 11 December all units were staged to the Hamhung-Hungnam area and started preparing for evacuation from North Korea as there was only one way out for X Corps now: by sea. The survival of the Marine Division had been a great achievement, not only of courage and endurance, but also of its traditional *esprit de corps*. The CCF IX Army Group had been so savaged by American firepower during the march from the Yudam-ni to the sea that it was unable to press home an attack on the Hungnam perimeter, and even disappeared from the Korean battlefield for three months. Marine casualties, however, were not light, for during the Division's ultimately pointless Chosin campaign it had suffered nearly 4,400 battle casualties, 718 of them fatal, and over 7,000 non-battle casualties, mostly frostbite cases who soon got well.

The evacuation, covered by the fleet's seven carriers, was already under way when the Marines arrived in Hungnam. Almond had been ordered by MacArthur on 9 December to redeploy to the Pusan area and report to Eighth Army: the meteoric history of the independent X Corps was almost over, although its commander still thought that the corps could have held the Hungnam perimeter for the winter. For Almond, as for the others in the Dai-Ichi, the divided command remained not a means of policy but an end in itself. When MacArthur flew into Yonpo on 11 December for his last visit to North Korea, the date of 27 December was set for X Corps to pass under Eighth Army, yet fate was still to cheat Walker of the overall command of all UN ground troops in Korea.

Wonsan was evacuated by the 10th, and on the 14th Marines completed their embarkation out of Hungnam for Pusan, to be followed by the body of the 7th Division which had safely made its way down from the Yalu. Last to go were the defenders of the perimeter, 3rd Division. It was decided to ship the ROK I Corps to Samchok where it could join the rest of the South Korean Army; the ROK 3rd Division went out through

Hung-nam, while most of the Capitol Division was evacuated from Songjin, a particularly exposed position. Altogether 105,000 military personnel were evacuated and 91,000 Korean refugees, many of whom had marched with the Marines from Chosin. All X Corps' equipment was also saved as a result of the evacuation by over 100 ships and supervised by the expert Doyle in sole charge as Commander, Task Force 90, aboard the *Mount McKinley*.

Tactically unaffected by Eighth Army's less leisurely retreat in the west, the strategic necessity for evacuating X Corps once the Chinese had smashed through on the Chongchon only emphasised the side-show nature of the campaign in the northeast. When Almond boarded the *McKinley* on 20 December, responsibility for the defence of Hungnam passed to Doyle until the evacuation was completed on Christmas Eve and the entire waterfront was blown to bits with hundreds of tons of explosives. It was only fitting that the master-planner of Inchon and Wonsan should preside over the liquidation of a campaign which he more than anyone had made possible. As the *McKinley* steamed south on Christmas Day, North Korea was once again under Communist control.

ATTLEE IN WASHINGTON

As the Chinese poured through the Tokchon gap for the third day, Washington knew at last that its North Korean adventure had failed, that the new situation was even more grave than the June crisis. On the morning of 28 November Truman spoke to his personal staff in his White House office. Moving to the centre of his desk the President fiddled around with his papers and said: 'General Bradley called me at 6.15 this morning. He told me a terrible message had come in from General MacArthur. . . . The Chinese have come in with both feet.' According to the Alsop Brothers on 1 December, Truman's first reaction was that the time had come for a final atomic showdown with Moscow. Later on the 28th a meeting of the National Security Council was held with Truman in the chair. Marshall and the Joint Chiefs were agreed of the necessity for avoiding war with China, and Acheson thought that if the US bombed the Manchurian airfields where there were at least 300 bombers which could threaten the airfields in Japan and Korea, the Russians would come into the war. Harriman said that a NATO supreme commander should be appointed, emphasising that the Administration was determined to retain its North Atlantic strategy while presenting an uncompromising front to the Chinese in Korea. Underlying the discussion was a belief that war with China would solve nothing; it was the USSR that was the chief enemy.[1]

However, next day Acheson in a public speech laid down the Administration's opinion in speaking of Peking's intervention as an 'act of brazen aggression . . . the second such act in five months. . . . This is not merely another phase of the Korean campaign. This is a fresh and unprovoked aggressive act, even more immoral than the first.'[2] On 30 November the crisis came to its head, when Truman was trapped into making a statement on the atomic bomb which caused consternation all over the West. Remarking in his press conference that the US would 'take whatever steps are necessary to meet the military situation', Truman was asked: 'Will that include the atomic bomb?' 'That includes every weapon we have.' 'Mr. President, you said, "every weapon we have". Does that mean that there is active consideration of the use of the atomic bomb?' 'There has always been active consideration of its use. . . .'[3] Although the JCS had already recommended against the use of the bomb in North Korea, the damage was done and a release later in the day emphasising that only the President had the authority to sanction its use failed to catch up with the original impact.

In London the message was received during the second day of a debate on foreign affairs in which great concern was expressed not only on the use of the bomb, but on the possibility of the West getting involved in war with China, a recurrent British nightmare. Bevin was off-form, and Churchill, after regretting that the UNC had not stopped at the Korean waist, went on to express his fears of a strategic diversion:

[1] Goldman, p. 178; Alsop, *The Reporter's Trade*, pp. 161-3; Truman, *Memoirs II*, pp. 408-11.
[2] *State Department Bulletin*, 18 December 1950.
[3] Truman, II, p. 419.

. . . the United Nations should avoid by every means in their power becoming entangled inextricably in a war with China . . . the sooner the Far Eastern diversion . . . can be brought into something like a static condition and stabilised, the better it will be. . . . For it is in Europe that the world cause will be decided . . . it is there that the mortal danger lies.

The underlying fear caused by the latest Korean developments was best expressed by R. A. Butler:

Of one thing I am certain, and it is that the British people as a whole wish to be sure, before their fate is decided in this respect, that they are helping to decide their own fate.

Attlee then terminated the debate by announcing that he was flying to Washington to meet Truman.[1]

Arriving on 4 December, Attlee and his staff — Bevin was not well enough to travel — disappointed the many photographers by not carrying a single umbrella. The talks which went on for four days covered every aspect of Anglo-American policy in the crisis; they are described at length in Truman's *Memoirs*, most disappointingly in Attlee's own account. On the strategic essentials, the two Governments were agreed that Western Europe was all important and that war with China was to be avoided. But after the events of the last ten days the Americans were in no mood to grant any concessions to Peking. Attlee suggested that Communist China be brought into the UN, for the British still thought as strongly as ever that not only was Peking ripe for Titoism, but that once in the world organisation, 'it would be possible to use the arguments of the Principles of the United Nations in dealing with them'. Attlee also advanced the proposal that, while perhaps leaving Chiang on Formosa, the Americans might recognise Peking's control of the mainland.

Speaking with all the fervour of a convert, Acheson rejected all concessions: he could hardly have done otherwise after the Chongchon. Truman had remarked that the Chinese were obviously Soviet satellites, but whether they were or not, the Secretary insisted, they would now probably act in much the

[1] For what is certainly one of the two or three most dramatic debates at Westminster since 1945 see H. C. Deb., Vol. 481, Coll. 1161-1440.

same way, and it was a mistake to count on their goodwill: Acheson's lesson had been learnt the hard way. The friendship of the Chinese could not be bought, and the Allies should not try to prove to them that they were more friendly than the Russians. The only policy towards Peking should be one of strength to stop further aggression in the future. Besides, any policy of concession would not be supported by the American people. It would be a 'very confusing thing' to try to get them to accept aggression in the East while resisting it in Europe. The people would be divided, the moral resolutions of the country would be lost and that was far more dangerous than alienating Asian opinion in the UN. . . .

Attlee, faced with this comprehensive statement of the new American position on Peking, which successive Administrations would follow well into the 1960s, 'seemed a little taken aback', saying, 'Perhaps we could limit our negotiations to the question of keeping the Communists on the 38th Parallel.' Here was the vital policy agreement of the Washington talks, the abandonment of the objective of uniting Korea by force as proposed by the UN resolution of 7 October, and a reversion to the original war aim of preserving South Korea. North Korea was thus written off. 'After a brief flirtation with the terrifying potentialities of a policy of liberation, a chastened, uncertain, but still stubborn Democratic Administration was returning to its true love — containment.'[1] On this there was a complete understanding. Truman had said the US would only get out of Korea if thrown out, to which Attlee had warmly responded: 'We are in it with you. We'll support you. We'll stand together on those bridgeheads. . . . Our whole purpose is to stand with you.' In fighting a limited war of containment there were, of course, great difficulties. Acheson favoured a cease-fire later rather than sooner, for then the Allies would perhaps not be negotiating from weakness. Thus military developments would now precede policy making, for Red China had to be contained on the 38th Parallel before talks could begin. Even then this would be difficult enough because the Administration, caught between its own public opinion and that of the Allies, could not manœuvre by granting any concessions to Peking. Peace could not be

<hr/>

[1] Higgins, p. 88.

bought in Korea by a UN seat or by US abandonment of Formosa.

The communiqué issued at the end of the talks on 8 December looked forward to these difficulties when it guardedly but unmistakably referred to achieving UN purposes in Korea 'by peaceful means'. There could be no thought of appeasement or rewarding aggression, but 'we are ready, as we have always been, to seek an end to the hostilities by means of negotiation'. Both countries pledged a large rearmament effort. On China's seat in the UN, the Governments differed, but it would not interfere 'with our united effort in support of our common objectives'. There was a brief reference to the atomic bomb which stated that the President hoped it would never be used, but 'that it was also his desire to keep the Prime Minister at all times informed of developments which might bring about a change in the situation'. Obviously there was no consideration of its use in Korea. Not only was 'Liberation' dead two years before its Dullesian promulgation, but the Truman-Attlee talks also showed that 'Massive Retaliation' was also impractical when only the US still possessed overwhelming air-atomic striking power.

The question of the bomb had been informally discussed between the two leaders in a stag dinner at the British Embassy the night before when they had talked, in Truman's words, 'as only two men can talk who have spent a lifetime in politics'. Truman complained of those Republican Senators who wanted to 'disrupt the nation's foreign policy . . . men who saw nothing wrong in plunging headlong into an Asian war but would raise no finger for the defence of Europe; who thought a British Prime Minister was never to be trusted, but Chiang Kai-shek could do no wrong'. Attlee, in turn, had spoken of the cross he had to bear, not from his official Opposition but from 'some of his own Labour Party leaders, especially Aneurin Bevan and his group, and the trouble they gave him'. In this last meeting between the two men while still in office their personal rapport was obvious, and both were suited by temperament and conviction to waging limited war. Yet the policies carried through after this conference were eventually fatal for both Administrations. To the Republicans, who, possibly rightly, suspected secret agreements, the decisions represented too many concessions to the British. To the Labour Left, any British concessions to the US were equally anathema and Bevan would shatter the second Attlee government by accusing his colleagues of being too eager to follow Truman's lead. The isolationisms of both countries would now increase in strength as the Korean War entered its decisive phase.

THE BIG BUG-OUT

While Truman and Attlee attempted to chart the future course of limited war, 'the big bug-out' went on in Korea. By 15 December the Eighth Army had retired to a position behind the lower Imjin in the West and thence along the 38th Parallel, after a withdrawal of 120 miles in just ten days. Apart from the Air Forces there had been virtually no contact with the Chinese on the move south. Their offensive had faded out after five days due to their weak supply system, but after a leisurely regrouping around Pyongyang what MacArthur called 'the bottomless well of Chinese manpower' moved towards the Parallel by foot, ox cart, pack horse, sledge, and the two-humped Bactrian camel.

Peace moves were being initiated in Lake Success. Following the Security Council's invitation to Peking to discuss Formosa, General Wu Hsui-Chuan, Lin Piao's chief of staff, addressed the Council on 28 November. In a Vyshinskyesque rant the General demanded that the Council itself condemn US aggression in Taiwan and intervention in Korea. Following this hardly conciliatory approach, the neutrals, led by India, sponsored a proposal to set up a negotiating group of three to approach the belligerents for a cease-fire; this was passed by the Assembly on 14 December, but opposed by the Soviet bloc. The Administration had succeeded in squaring the circle with its support, for it had insisted that a cease fire could not be conditional on a general political conference which would have to follow later. It thus preserved its position that there could be no concessions while its armies were in retreat. It was hardly a surprise to Washington therefore when Chou En-lai rejected the cease-fire approach which he refused to recognise.

Chou stated that it was only a manœuvre by the Americans to get a breathing space, and remarked that after Inchon the

US had not supported cease-fire proposals when the North
Koreans were in full retreat. Only by US withdrawal from
Korea and Formosa could a cease fire come about. He moreover
gave notice, in his reply of 22 December, that China would now
attempt the unification of Korea by force, for the UN crossing
of the Parallel in October had 'thoroughly destroyed, and hence
obliterated forever, this demarcation line of political geography'.
Thus the war aims of the two sides had been reversed by the
Chongchon and Chou's reply was the proclamation of a second
Communist attempt to conquer South Korea.

In the United States over 50% of the people thought that
World War III was imminent, according to the polesters. The
JCS thought the danger of war was 'greatly increased' and on
6 December sent a general war warning to all unified commanders: in the Mediterranean the Sixth Fleet put to sea.[1] On
Capitol Hill huge new defence appropriations were voted; by
January the original $13.5 billion defence budget for fiscal '51 had
been quadrupled to $52 billion. The Korean War economic boom
thus got under way, but in keeping with its general belief that
in spite of Korea the greatest danger would be around 1953, the
Administration decided against a general mobilization. The
rearmament drive was planned instead to create a production
base for extremely rapid expansion in the future, a decision
which governed all procurement policy henceforward. Nevertheless, the US Armed Forces which in June 1950 numbered 1½
million men, and which had been increased by a million since
that date, were now set a target of 3½ million, with twenty
trained divisions. And already, during the NATO Council meeting of September 1950, one of the most momentous Western
reactions to the North Korean invasion had been agreed upon —
that of West German rearmament.

Other important decisions were made. A state of emergency
was proclaimed on 16 December, after a broadcast speech on
the crisis by Truman the previous evening, and simultaneously
a total economic embargo was placed on trade with China.
Peking's assets in the US were frozen. It was announced on
19 December that not only was Eisenhower going to Europe as
NATO Supreme Commander but the US was sending more
ground troops to the continent. This was the beginning of the

[1] *Hearings*, p. 1630.

'Great Debate' which, merging with the crisis of MacArthur's recall, would go on for the next six months. The schism in political life had already been shown by the demand by House and Senate Republicans for the dismissal of Acheson; Senator Wherry moreover had accused Truman to his face during a briefing for Congressional leaders of manipulating his Intelligence reports to obtain more personal power. And in a dramatic radio address on 20 December Herbert Hoover called for a US retreat to Fortress America to preserve for the world the 'Gibraltar of Western Civilisation'. But whatever the demands for total withdrawal from Europe and war with China, the Administration was implacably determined to go ahead with its agreed NATO-aligned policies.

If there was hardening resolve to stick to a growingly unpopular course within the Administration, anger and frustration in Congress, confusion and fear among the general public, Tokyo, too was going through a traumatic experience occasioned not only by the defeat in the north. MacArthur for the first time in his career was getting a very bad press. Indignant, yet exaggerated, cables outwards from Tokyo presented the erstwhile Alexander of the Orient as the incompetent who had produced one of the greatest defeats in American military history. The retreat — or 'disengagement' — was being described as a shameful *sauve-qui-peut*, a simultaneous First Bull Run, Pearl Harbour and an Ardennes about to terminate in a new Dunkirk from another Bataan. An American mechanised army had been licked by Chinese peasant hordes; seldom has the praiseworthy American facility for self-examination been so exercised in our time.

The counts were few, but overwhelming in their simplicity. Already, in November, MacArthur had known of the Chinese massing in Manchuria. Why had he launched his offensive when he did? And how and why had his G-2 failed to discover the hundreds of thousands of Chinese already in Korea? Not only were the timing and the Intelligence behind the offensive under attack, but the dispositions. There was the deadly question of the divided command, the gap between Walker and Almond, the whole conception of X Corps' mission, and its corollary, the refusal to establish a line across the waist because of the 'rugged mountainous terrain', through which the Chinese had manœuvred with such ease. (Although in fairness to MacArthur it should be remembered that in destroying the ROK II Corps, the CCF rolled up Eighth Army's right flank rather than exploited the gap.) From this point the criticisms zeroed in to the rivalry between Walker and Almond and the hierarchic, unhealthy, un-American court politics of the Dai-Ichi. In short, the offensive according to Homer Bigart of the *New York Herald Tribune* was 'an invitation to disaster'. Even professional military historians such as T. N. and R. E. Dupuy have suggested that it would have been better to have held the northeast advance at Hungnam and only then, using X Corps as a screening force or a mobile reserve, have pushed to the Yalu in the north-west around Sinuiju.

But the disaster was more than just a defeat for MacArthur. Not only had the hopes of a unified Korea vanished, but China had overnight been raised to the rank of a world power as the People's Republic of China became the first Communist power to defeat a Western army in major battle. That it was an Asian Communist army that had defeated one of the greatest of all American generals only added to the impact. Quite correctly S. L. A. Marshall has called the Chongchon in *The River and the Gauntlet*, 'one of the major decisive battles of the present century'.

Only indirectly has MacArthur admitted that his offensive was a failure. Within weeks of the debacle, history was being rewritten in Tokyo as the offensive was now described not as an end-of-war *ratissage* but as a spoiling attack. In the Senate Hearings the General talked about 'a reconnaissance in force . . . the dispositions of those troops, in my opinion, could not have been improved upon, had I known the Chinese were going to attack . . .' The faithful Whitney has gone so far as to describe the offensive and its outcome as 'one of the most successful military manœuvres in modern military history', while to Willoughby, 'the withdrawal, as such, did not worry anybody'. But after 1953 the absurdity of this rationalisation has merged into the fundamental basis of MacArthur's criticism of the Democrats' Korean policy. MacArthur had always assumed that if the Chinese intervened in Korea, the United States would strike back across the Yalu (in spite of the warnings to the contrary in his directives after Inchon). Moreover, Whitney goes on, if such a clear warning had been given to Peking, the Chinese would never have risked their Korean involvement, an extremely doubtful supposition in view of what is now known about Peking's preparations. Indeed, we are told, the Chinese must have known through 'international poltroonery' [Whitney] that they would be immune. How? Through the British officials Burgess and Maclean, soon to defect to the USSR, an assumption particularly free from any risk of verification. Thus in spite of the Wake transcript, MacArthur claimed infallibility.[1]

The confusion is even apparent when MacArthur has talked of his strategy in terms of military analogy, for he avoids any forgivable admission of error and defeat. In 1956 he compared his strategy with its rapid advances and retreats to that of Wellington's in the Peninsula,[2] but in 1951 during the Hearings he was emphatic in his dislike of the war of attrition that he had been called upon to fight in Korea. He asked how long the US could afford to 'fight in this accordion fashion — up and down — which means your cumulative losses are going to be staggering'.[3] Obviously, then, an accordion war in 1951 was hardly worth fighting. All these explanations surround the central proposition of the MacArthur case: it was not he who was wrong, but Truman. For after their aggression in Korea, MacArthur insisted, the Chinese Communists should have been met instantly by counter measures carried to their homeland.

Furthermore, the alleged activities of what Willoughby calls in his monumental tirade, *Aid and Comfort to the Enemy*, the 'disaster school' of war correspondents, the 'ragpickers of modern literature' who helped the enemy at this critical time by their 'calculated treason and subversion' in defaming MacArthur, is a good indication of the Dai-Ichi's morbid sensitivity to press criticism. Yet the ultimate explanation of the Yalu defeat is simple. The last push was launched because MacArthur thought — intuitively — he could win another 'tremendous gamble', hence the strange symbiosis between Inchon and the Chongchon. In both operations, MacArthur relied on his judgement to the exclusion of all other considerations. One succeeded, one failed, and, a further penalty, the defeat, has

---

[1] *Hearings*, pp. 19-21, Whitney, pp. 393-4, 426, Willoughby, p. 378.
[2] Montross and Canzona, Vol. III, p. 346.
[3] *Hearings*, p. 30.

overshadowed the victory. Beyond all the strategic controversies, the great general's career between the June invasion and his dismissal resembles the course of a classical tragedy: the fall of the mighty brought about by the flaw of pride, the sin of *hubris*.

At the front throughout December the moral collapse of the Eighth Army was complete, as bug-out fever raged everywhere, and even GHQ succumbed to what the naval historian M. C. Cagle calls 'panic and inertia'.[1] Yet in the Chongchon battle the Eighth Army's US troops had fought well, with the exception of the rout of the artillerymen at Kujang-dong, before withdrawal became imperative. The army had been preserved and the 13,000 UNC casualties of the great retreat from North Korea were relatively light compared with some World War II operations.[2] But there was a crisis of leadership as the silence from the Dai-Ichi added to the confusion in the field, and the next giant Chinese offensive was awaited with fear. GHQ's estimate that there were over a million of the hordes about to move south, including those on the way in Manchuria, reflected the spirit of the month, although this hysteria was already producing a reaction.[3] At this darkest moment of the crisis with the Eighth Army above Seoul expecting the Chinese offensive at any hour, Walton Walker was killed on 23 December when his jeep was smashed off the bund into a paddy field by an ROK truck: the victor of the Naktong was posthumously awarded a fourth, general's, star.

Walker's successor, Lt.-Gen. Matthew Ridgway, until then Deputy Chief-of-Staff, immediately flew to Japan, conferred with MacArthur on Christmas Day, and stepped onto the frozen Korean ground at Taegu the next day still wearing his Pentagon battle blouse. Ridgway was appalled at the state of

---

[1] Cagle, *Errors of the Korean War*.

[2] Ardennes, 80,000: Okinawa, 65,000: Iwojima, 20,000. The figure of nearly 13,000 UNC casualties from 24 November to 12 December, including 'the Battle of Sinanju', is given by Willoughby in *Aid and Comfort to the Enemy*, p. 10. Cf. his *MacArthur*, pp. 382-4.

[3] Famous Eighth Army joke at this time: How many platoons make a horde? Also, a scale of Chinese manpower: three swarms equal a horde, two hordes equal a human flood, two floods equal 'a bottomless well of Chinese manpower'. Another view expressed to Rene Cutforth in Seoul by an American officer: 'You can't fight millions and millions of drugged fanatics, and it's not worth the waste of life to try. What are we here for, anyway? This is supposed to be a police action. Bug right out, I say.' *Korean Reporter*, p. 33.

patrolling, morale and Intelligence of his new command: 'All Intelligence could show me was a big red goose egg out in front of us with "174,000" scrawled in the middle of it.'[1] The army felt beaten, and did not know what it was fighting for or why: Ridgway immediately started touring the battlefield telling his troops that they were going to stay in Korea and fight.

But on New Year's Eve the Chinese started their attack, their shock troops moving forward, crying, *Kill G.I.* It was the first of three major offensives in the next six months aimed at China's conquest of the whole of Korea, and designed to bring 'universal harmony' to the Land of the Morning Calm. Peking announced that its intention was 'to liberate Korea . . . crush the imperialist aggression . . . drive warmonger MacArthur into the sea. . . .' *Pravda* exulted in the retreat of the 'Anglo-American interventionists' and looked forward to 'when the American aggressors will be totally defeated and annihilated'. Threatened with a Communist advance which could destroy his forces above the Han, Ridgway ordered a retreat to the Pyongtaek-Samchok line about seventy miles below the Parallel. The decision was made the more necessary by the Communist thrust along the Chunchon-Wonju axis which could outflank the Eighth Army once again by a break-through down the central mountains. From Chunchon east the ROK front had collapsed and no one knew exactly the extent of the enemy infiltration there, where reconstituted North Korean divisions were in action.

As the bug-out from Seoul went on, rats ran through the city crowded with fleeing refugees and looters. On the Han River flats, the BBC correspondent René Cutforth watched US MPs turn back the pathetic columns of refugees by gun-point and then order the ice across the river to be mortared, so great were the numbers jamming the Army's transport moving south to Suwon and Pyongtaek. No one saw the war as a crusade any longer, most thought that here was the enemy high tide. The pontoon bridges across the Han were blown on 4 January as the capital of South Korea changed hands for the third time. When the last rearguards crossed the river, the red flag of the Democratic People's Republic of Korea was already flying from the Capitol in Seoul. It was the lowest ebb of the entire war.

---

[1] Ridgway, *Soldier*, p. 205.

CHAPTER TEN

THE WAR OF CONTAINMENT

> We are not interested in real estate. We are interested only in inflicting maximum casualties on the enemy with minimum losses to ourselves. To do this we must wage a war of manœuvre, slashing at the enemy when he withdraws and fighting delaying actions when he attacks.
>
> MATTHEW RIDGWAY, after arrival in Korea

JCS AT FRONT: MACARTHUR PROGRAMME REJECTED

ALL Korean policy — and ultimately all American foreign policy — now turned on whether Ridgway could hold the line after the Eighth Army's 275-mile retreat, the longest in American military history. On the western front which was held by I and IX Corps the new general ordered aggressive patrolling and on 7 January an RCT from 25th Division which moved north from Pyongtaek found that there were only Chinese screening forces south of Suwon. But on the central front, where X Corps, integrated with the Eighth Army on Ridgway's assumption of command, had moved into the line on 2 January, there was heavy fighting for Wonju as the enemy, thrusting down the mountains from Chunchon gained momentum. Disintegration of two ROK divisions on the east-central front opened a gap between X Corps and the ROK III Corps on its right. North Korean forces reached to Yongwol, and when checked there, continued infiltrating over the roadless, snow-covered mountains to join the Communist guerillas in the far south. By the 16th the Wonju salient had been abandoned, but only after a most significant stand by 2nd Division which had checked this central Chinese thrust, and so prevented a turning movement round the flank of the two corps in the west. Unlike Walker, Ridgway strongly believed in using his American divisions in the mountainous centre of the front as well as on the easier tank country of the 'invasion route' to the west. Simultaneously the Chinese in the Suwon sector were completely on the defensive because of increasing supply difficulties.

178

As this fighting swayed to and fro, a series of messages between JCS and MacArthur over American policy in the Far East resulted in a visit to the front by Collins and Vandenberg which was far more than a mere routine tour of inspection. The latest crisis between Washington and Tokyo had originated with the Chongchon and MacArthur's subsequent programme for dealing with the new war and the new enemy. When Collins had visited Tokyo in early December, MacArthur had told him that unless the restrictions on the Yalu were removed, he could not hold in Korea and that evacuation was inevitable. He wanted the bombing and blockade of China, together with the maximum use of Chinese Nationalist forces based on Formosa. Throughout December inspired stories from Tokyo harped on the possibility of evacuation, a way round the presidential order of 6 December to all theatre commanders (meaning MacArthur)

COMMUNIST NEW YEAR OFFENSIVE
January 1951

to exercise 'extreme caution' in their public statements and to clear all speeches and press releases with the State or Defence Departments. As MacArthur's operational directives dated from September, after consultations between Truman, Acheson, Marshall and Bradley, a new directive was sent to him on 29 December. From 'estimates available' (viz: MacArthur's) JCS concluded that the Chinese Communists had the strength to force the US out of Korea. As MacArthur could expect no further reinforcements at present, and as the Administration did not consider Korea a place to fight a major war, he was told to defend his line in Korea in 'successive positions' subject to the 'primary consideration of the continued threat to Japan'. If he was forced back to the Kum, then evacuation would be necessary to preserve his command. But the directive emphasised that if it was at all possible without heavy losses he should stay on in Korea. 'A successful resistance to Chinese-North Korean aggression at some position in Korea and a deflation of the military and political prestige of the Chinese Communists would be of great importance to our national interest. . . .'[1]

The reply from Tokyo was 'probably MacArthur's most important single comment on the Korean War' (Whitney). The General thought that the Administration had lost the will to win in Korea with its emphasis that the country was not the place to fight a major war; he also thought that the responsibility for evacuation was being unfairly placed on him. His scorching reply to Washington on 30 December was in fact a policy counter-proposal which if adopted he thought would not only save Korea but 'inflict such a destructive blow upon Red China's capacity to wage aggressive war that it would remove her as a further threat to peace in Asia for generations to come' (Whitney):

1. Blockade the coast of China.
2. Destroy, through naval gunfire and air bombardment, China's industrial capacity to wage war.
3. Secure reinforcements from the Nationalist garrison in Formosa to strengthen our position in Korea, if we continue to fight for that peninsula.

[1] *Hearings*, pp. 2179-80, Whitney, pp. 429-30. These paraphrases differ slightly and Whitney's is quoted above.

4. Release existing restrictions upon the Formosan garrison for diversionary action (possibly leading to counter in-vasion) against vulnerable areas of the Chinese mainland.

If this programme was initiated the pressure against the UN Command would be released and then evacuation would not be necessary. As for the Russian reaction, that much-debated point when these proposals became public, they would be guided solely by their own interests, and would not be affected by what measures US launched against China.[1]

The message caused consternation in Washington. On 9 January a reply was sent in the form of another directive to Tokyo. The retaliatory programme against China was turned down all along the line. Blockade would require British consent, the Formosan troops were best employed where they were, and unless the Chinese attacked US forces outside Korea, there could be no air or naval measures against the mainland. Once again MacArthur was told to defend Korea in 'successive posi-tions' subject to his primary mission of defending Japan. Should it become evident, however, in MacArthur's judgement, 'that evacuation is essential to avoid severe losses of men and material', then he should evacuate.[2]

This was the climax of the crisis. MacArthur regarded this last suggestion as a 'booby trap' and sent back such a 'gloomy' reply (Bradley) that it brought about action which may well have deprived him of any real authority over his Korean army three months before his dismissal. He told JCS that morale was low because his troops were embittered by 'shameful propaganda which has falsely condemned their fighting qualities', and that subject to policy considerations, the Eighth Army should be evacuated. But — the devastating ending — although the posi-tion in Korea was untenable under the 'extraordinary limitations and conditions' imposed upon the command, 'it can hold, if overriding political considerations so dictate for any length of time up to its complete destruction'.[3] With this statement Mac-Arthur was trying to reverse policy by using the threat of the Eighth Army's engulfment as a lever to force Washington to

[1] *Hearings*, pp. 2180-81, Whitney, pp. 432-34.
[2] *Hearings*, pp. 331-33, Whitney, 434-35.
[3] *Hearings*, p. 906, Whitney, p. 435-36.

adopt his programme. As Walter Millis has written, such a threat of annihilation was the deadliest a military commander could raise against civilian superiors in a democratic society (and especially politicians as heavily engaged as the Democrats). In all eventualities — except one — MacArthur would be also free of responsibility, for if the war were carried to China it would be Washington's decision, and if evacuation were ordered, as he had offered to fight to destruction, then he could not be blamed for that, too. But, in any case, whether he was to be blamed or not, in manœuvring in this way so as to maximise his political support in the US, CINCFE was absolutely convinced national interest demanded the adoption of his programme. The effect of this message of 10 January on official Washington was inevitably dramatic. For the Pentagon it was 'our lowest point' (Marshall) a 'very difficult time' (Sherman). When Truman saw the message he was 'deeply disturbed. . . . He was saying that we would be driven off the peninsula or, at the very least, suffer terrible losses' and that policy 'approved by me was not feasible'.[1]

Counter action by Washington was drastic. Three new documents were issued, although probably no one now thought that any message could influence MacArthur. The first was yet another directive on 12 January, ordering MacArthur to stay in Korea if possible. On the same day JCS produced a contingency paper for the National Security Council which the planners had been working on since 28 November. This 16-point document detailed possible action against Communist China if the Eighth Army were driven out of Korea or confined in the Pusan Perimeter with no hope of break-out, or if the Chinese attacked UN forces outside the peninsula. It included among others the four points of the MacArthur message of 29 December and a copy was sent to the Dai-Ichi. Thirdly, on 13 January, Truman sent MacArthur a personal letter explaining in some length the advantages for the US and the Allies if the fight could continue in Korea. This brave message ended with the proposition that, if the worst came, MacArthur should withdraw to the Korean offshore islands, particularly Cheju-do, and fight on from there . . . 'if we must withdraw from Korea, [let] it be clear to the world that that course is forced upon us by military

[1] *Hearings*, pp. 329, 1600. Truman, *Memoirs II*, p. 461.

necessity and that we shall not accept the result militarily or politically until the aggression has been rectified'. The significance of the new war aim of rectifying aggression would not have been lost on MacArthur. [1]

Accompanying this barrage of orders and exhortations were Collins, Vandenberg and Bedell Smith (CIA)[2] who had left Washington on 12 January *en route* for Tokyo and Korea: what JCS desperately wanted to know was how far Ridgway and his Army were able to hold in Korea and so remain an instrument of policy irrespective of MacArthur. Whitney records that when Collins arrived in Tokyo on the 14th he thought evacuation was inevitable, but if so the Army Chief of Staff soon discovered that the situation, although bad, had been exaggerated. 'Now it happens that just about the time we arrived things began to look up,' he rather ambiguously said in the Senate Hearings. At EUSAK HQ in Taegu on the 15th, Collins told newsmen, 'As of now we are going to stay and fight', and while he toured the front at regimental level, Vandenberg went on a patrol twelve miles ahead of the lines. The Chiefs saw for themselves that Ridgway was curing the bug-out fever, that offensive preparations were under way as another RCT reconnaissance, Operation WOLFHOUND, struck through Osan to Suwon on the 15-16th, and that the CCF, halted at Wonju had been stopped all along the front for the present. On the 17th Collins reported this news back to Truman. Henceforward, MacArthur, who had now ceased to exercise close supervision over the Eighth Army, was increasingly bypassed by Truman and JCS in dealing with Ridgway. The new Army commander, less than a month out of the Pentagon, must have known what Truman wanted in Korea, fully agreed with that policy, and had his own ideas on how to fight for it which were soon to be spectacularly demonstrated.

Realising that at least at this juncture there was no sale for his programme of striking across the Yalu, MacArthur tentatively endorsed the Truman-JCS-Ridgway policy which now, as every

[1] *Hearings*, pp. 324-34, 737-8, 907. *Truman*, II, pp. 461-63.

[2] Just as the OSS had been excluded from MacArthur's theatre in World War II, so CIA had been virtually banished from Korea after Inchon until Smith's visit to Tokyo. This was a further irritant to the Pentagon. Although MacArthur denied that this was so in the *Hearings* ('tommyrot . . . bunkum . . .'), Secretary Marshall recalled 'in a hazy sort of way' Smith referring to 'some difficulty' with Willoughby. *Hearings*, pp. 86, 122-3, 241-2, 350.

hour passed without a major CCF break-through, was obviously succeeding, the one contingency CINCFE had not foreseen. The escape route was MacArthur's apparent first realisation with Truman's letter that he was required to stay in Korea. The charade of the Dai-Ichi's belated attempt to approve what Washington had been insisting on for three weeks must have caused bared teeth in the Pentagon as the great evacuation crisis came to its end after these largely secret exchanges. On 20 January, as the front was stabilised south of Wonju and it became quite clear that the CCF new-year offensive was over, Mac-Arthur flew to Taegu from Tokyo. In a press conference the Commander-in-Chief was adamant: 'No one,' he insisted, 'is going to drive us into the sea.' Sitting in the front row of the conference room Ridgway, who must have been fully briefed by Collins on the Washington picture five days previously, listened urbanely to MacArthur's statement. Correspondents noted that had Walker been alive he would have stood attentively to Mac-Arthur's right and rear while he spoke.

THE CCF BUBBLE BURSTS

The war of containment which was now fought in Korea until the truce talks started was a war of attrition. There were no famous cities to liberate, no historic provinces to conquer, no total victory to be won, although the effect of the war on Koreans was as terrible as any total war. Moreover, there were no clearly defined war aims. Instead, by forcing the Communist armies back, hill by hill, to the vicinity of the 38th Parallel, and by killing as many as possible of their troops, it was hoped to bring Peking and Pyongyang to the conference table to negotiate on the basis of the *status quo ante*. The Communist strategic offensive was to be opposed by a United Nations offensive-defensive.

The importance of this trial by strength between the two power blocs may be seen by the mounting intensity of the struggle by land, sea and air until the question of whether the Chinese armies could unify Korea by force of arms was finally decided in April and May. Even in January 1951 the Communist forces numbered about 486,000, and those of the UN about

365,000, figures which were to be more than doubled on each side before the truce was eventually signed. With China's entry into the war and the ensuing international ramifications, with twenty-five nations involved, with millions of men thrown into the peninsula, some from countries all over the world, the war could no longer be called a 'police action' or, the Joint Chiefs' initial favourite phrase, 'the Korean incident'. Admiral Struble's description is much more apposite, 'a major war confined to a small area'.

Ridgway had already told the Joint Chiefs before they left Korea that he intended to exploit the position in the west. Following WOLFHOUND a IX Corps reconnaissance towards Inchon on the 22nd showed that here as well as further west there were no large enemy forces close to the UN front lines. Therefore a much bigger operation, THUNDERBOLT, was planned for 25 January with both I and IX Corps each contributing one division. The objective was the Han River, but territorial gains were secondary to destruction of enemy forces. This was the beginning of the UN counter-offensive which would continue for the next three months.[1] Facing the Eighth Army on this sector as Suwon and Inchon quickly fell were the CCF 38th and 50th Armies deployed well back towards the Han. A subsidiary action of crucial tactical significance, Operation PUNCH, was the taking of the Hill 440 complex north of Suwon on 5 February by a task force of 25th Division, using completely co-ordinated artillery, infantry, armour and air. When the operation ended after eight days on 9 February over 4,200 Chinese dead were counted on the battlefield alone; UNC fatal casualties totalled 70. Not even the bottomless well could be drawn on to this extent without starting to run dry.[2] By the 10th I Corps was on the line of the Han, neutralising Seoul, having retaken Kimpo and Inchon, but both port and airfield were useless for some months so great was the destruction.

[1] I Corps consisted of the US 25th and 3rd Divisions, the Turkish Brigade, the 29th British Brigade, and the ROK 1st Division. IX Corps, US 1st Cavalry and 24th Divisions, the 27th Commonwealth Brigade, Greek and Philippine Battalions, the ROK 6th Division, and in February, 1st Marine Division; X Corps, US 2nd and 7th Divisions, three attached ROK Divisions. Between X Corps and the ROK I Corps on the east coast was the ROK III Corps.
[2] See Marshall, Hill 440, for a detailed analysis of this action.

The new tactics evolved by Ridgway to deal with the numerical superiority of the Chinese was the complete antithesis of the
long, vulnerable, mechanised columns racing towards the Yalu
in the autumn. The General constantly stressed the importance
for security and urged his corps commanders to observe three
basic principles, co-ordination, maximum punishment, and maintenance intact of major units. He summed it up as 'good foot-
work combined with firepower'. It was known at the front as
'the meatgrinder':

You began with the long-range artillery from ten miles away
enveloping the hills in tall columns of dust flung up by tons
of high explosive, followed by the quicker shell-bursts from
the more accurate lighter guns, at a shorter range. You bombarded the positions further with tank guns, while swooping
aircraft plastered them with napalm and rockets, and the
infantrymen secure in their foxholes, let loose a murderous
hail of staccato fire with rifles, machine-guns, and mortars.
This lasted for the morning. In the afternoon the infantry
crept up the slopes of the hills to find out if anyone was left
there. . . .[1]

Once the UNC infantry had displaced the remaining Communists, armour assisted by air strikes would drive into the
Chinese flanks to inflict yet more casualties before methodically
moving on to the next phase line. Any other course would only
end with infiltration into the vulnerable rear areas of Ridgway's
task forces.

The success of THUNDERBOLT meant that Eighth Army,
with its left flank anchored on the Han, could now attempt limited
offensives on the central front with the ultimate objective of
levering the Chinese out of Seoul by an outflanking move north.
The rubble heap of Wonju had been retaken by patrols as early
as 22 January and on 2 February elements of X Corps were in
Hoengsong. Ridgway now planned to use Almond's X Corps
and the ROK III Corps in Operation ROUNDUP, starting on 5
February, a limited offensive similar in execution and objectives
to that made in the west. But enemy pressure increased as
reinforcements were switched from the Han sector, and on 11-12

[1] Holles, *Now Thrive the Armourers*, p. 76-7.

February, the Chinese 40th and 66th Armies attacked three ROK divisions north of Hoengsong and broke through the UN lines using the tactics of their earlier winter offensives. Moving through the snow-covered mountains, the Chinese set up roadblocks behind the front, and Ridgway ordered a withdrawal to Wonju.

During the night of 13 February the Communist offensive switched west to the vital crossroads of Chipyong-ni, on the boundary of IX and X Corps zones. Its fall might threaten the whole west-central front. A regiment of 2nd Division and the French battalion were surrounded on the 14th by three Communist divisions, but here again Ridgway was equal to the situation. Realising that in the early stages of a Chinese offensive defence in depth was far more effective than attempting to hold linear objectives, he ordered the encircled units to dig in and be supplied by air drop. After three days, during which the Chinese infantry for the first time in Korea attacked in mass waves and so suffered untold thousands of casualties, the men were relieved. To the east around Wonju this slaughter was repeated when concentrated American artillery blasted nearly every hill and valley to the north as the Chinese and North Koreans attacked here, too, in mass infantry formations. Further east again North Korean assault troops had driven to within a few miles of Chechon, laying open X Corps' east flank, but the situation here was precariously stabilised when the whole Communist counter-offensive faded away after five or six days. The defence of Chipyong-ni and 'the Wonju shoot' showed the Chinese offensives could be stopped head on. The UN defence had triumphed—and for the remainder of the Korean War it would remain in the ascendant.

Ridgway now intended to carry on his central front limited offensive with the precisely named Operation KILLER. Scheduled for 21 February, it also had the secondary territorial aim of clearing the lateral transpeninsular road between Wonju and Kangnung. Throughout these weeks the 1st Marine Division had been fighting the guerillas in the south around Andong, for during the Communist January offensive elements of the North Korean II Corps had infiltrated through the eastern mountains to within twenty miles of Taegu—an astonishing feat. After a partial reduction by the Marines and ROK security

forces, remnants had joined up with other guerillas throughout South Korea, but when KILLER started the situation had
improved enough for the Marines to join IX Corps. With seven
US divisions now at the front, all corps' zones were moved eastwards, and on 24 February the Marines were advancing above
Hoengsong. As the first thaw came, slowing the advance, the
hills of central Korea were littered with enemy dead; by 1 March
the entire Chinese front south of the Han had collapsed and
geographical objectives of the offensive had been reached as the
UN line, free for the first time in the winter war of dangerous
salients and soft spots, stretched from Kimpo to Kangnung. The
bubble of the invincible, drug-crazed, fanatic hordes blown up
after the Chongchon had been exploded forever.

This grinding advance to within thirty miles of the Parallel,
the collapse of the Communist February offensive, and the
stability of the Eighth Army's front indicated that a line across
Korea in the vicinity of the Parallel represented a natural
strategic division of the peninsula. North and south of the
Parallel supply difficulties for an invader increased enormously.
Here the inverse equation between political control and logistic
efficiency balanced. At Wonju, about sixty miles south of the
Parallel, the Chinese were fighting with nearly 300 miles of their
supply routes south from Sinuiju open to UN air power. In
November only seventy miles of their road-rail routes had been
vulnerable to air attack. This increased distance from the Manchurian sanctuary to the front not only meant increased losses
through air attack, but many additional casualties through
frostbite, disease and starvation from which many prisoners were
suffering. Conversely an UNC advance to the Pyongyang area
would both lengthen the Eighth Army's supply lines by a 100
miles and give the air forces that much less of the Chinese
transportation system to work on. 'As our battle lines shift
north', said MacArthur in a public statement on 7 March
expressing his disgust for the war of attrition he was forced to
wage:

the supply position of the enemy will progressively improve,
just as inversely the effectiveness of our air potential will progressively diminish, thus in turn causing his numerical ground
superiority to become of increasing battlefield significance . . .

[under] existing limitations . . . the battle-lines cannot fail to reach a point of theoretical military stalemate. . . .

Read to a press conference on Suwon Airfield, this analysis was resignedly known as the 'Die for Tie' statement at the front.

Such considerations were never absent in any discussion of political and military objectives. But moreover Mao's armies were in a particularly strategically disadvantageous position in fighting well south of the Korean waist. Captured Chinese prisoners said that the CCF had only intended to move south to Hungnam, for example, *after* the destruction of the Marine Division. In the far north, before the big bug-out, the UN Command fought along 300 mile front south of the Yalu with a vast dispersion of its firepower. Below Pyongyang the conditions which favoured a protracted war of manoeuvre by the Chinese vanished as the front narrowed to about 130 miles. Here the strategic advantage rested with the sort of protracted war that the Eighth Army with its firepower had been told to fight in February and March.

Yet other factors worked against the Eighth Army. The Communist equivalent of the UN air interdiction behind the lines was their guerilla operations in South Korea. In many areas no UN supply convoy was safe. The technique was usually the same. Moving into a village on the MSR after dark the guerillas would terrorise the inhabitants into silence, build a road block and occupy the adjacent hovels, waiting for the first trucks to move through in the morning when they would be ambushed with automatic weapons and grenades. Long before the security forces arrived the Communists would have taken to the hills. Although the position was improving as spring came, the guerilla threat would continue to tie down ROK security troops for some time, as well as increasing the normal wastage rate of supplying the front line from Pusan.

Communist numerical superiority, too, over the Eighth Army was much bigger than the aggregate figures showed, as the vast amount of administrative 'tail' required to keep the highly-mechanised, high-living-standard Western forces going meant that each man in the firing line had up to four or five men behind him. It was also obvious that in the Communist armies supply and service troops were proportionately far less, not only because of the absence of the PX north of the firing line, but because the production centres for Communist food and munitions were either in Korea or near the Yalu, whereas US supplies came from factories thousands of miles away by sea.[1]

Yet the Eighth Army's come-back after January was not simply the result of the strategic disadvantages the Communists suffered as they moved south, or the development of American firepower into the lethal machinery of the meat-grinder, or the addition of X Corps. It was universally thought that the catalyst was Ridgway's personality which had initiated many changes in discipline, training and morale. When he arrived in Korea Ridgway found that attempts were being made to restore morale in some units by giving political peptalks; instead he insisted on the restoration of strict barrack-room discipline wherever possible. From that time the Eighth Army started to become a professional army, fighting not for the United Nations or against Communism but fighting because it was ordered to. A regimental commander told *Time* at the end of February, 'The boys aren't up there fighting for democracy now. They're fighting because the platoon leader is leading them, and the platoon leader is fighting because of the command, and so on up right to the top.' After speaking to Ridgway, who he found sitting beneath a Buddha at Taegu complete with the showman's grenade he invariably wore on his webbing equipment, Rene Cutforth found that he soon forgot the bug-outs, 'In five minutes I had to abandon a whole attitude.' The Eighth Army was going to hold the CCF and push them back:

> The early faith of the American troops that the whole thing could somehow be got over by machinery, without much human risk, had faded and there was a growing recognition that fabulous military expenditure of material was not perhaps a military virtue in its own right. . . . Exactly how and why the new army was transformed in a few weeks from a mob of dispirited boobs still thinking in terms of a 'press-button war' to a tough and resilient force is still a matter for

[1] It has been calculated unofficially that after the Chinese intervention, the number of Communists in uniform to those of the UNC averaged 6:5; but in fighting men the Communist superiority was no less than 5:1. Barclay, p. 196. Other figures suggest that Communist numerical superiority was usually greater than the ratio given above.

speculation and debate. I think most of the credit is due to General Ridgway, who had decided there were to be no more bug-outs. . . .[1]

What Ridgway had done was not only to give the Eighth Army a professional determination to fight without question a limited war, but, just as important, a moral ascendancy which enabled it to fight a numerically superior enemy.

ADVANCE TO LINE KANSAS

The second phase of the advance back to the 38th Parallel began in early March when Operation RIPPER pushed off on 7 March towards its objective of line IDAHO, a large salient on the central front with Chunchon at its apex. The objectives of the new limited offensive were the same as its predecessors, the destruction of enemy manpower and equipment. By keeping up the pressure on the Chinese it was also hoped to force the Communists out of Seoul by enveloping the capital from the east. About fifteen miles west of Seoul the 25th Division from IX Corps crossed the Han and struck north over the hills towards the 38th Parallel as RIPPER got under way.

The soundness of Ridgway's strategy was emphasised when Seoul fell on the 14th and the South Korean capital changed hands for the fourth time in nine months. Only 200,000 of its pre-war million and a half were left; little had changed since January and in the Chosen hotel HAPPY XMAS streamers were left from the time of the bug-out. By the 21st the Marines were in Chunchon, although now the Communists were 'rolling with the punch', and selling space for time to conserve their manpower. Once Seoul had fallen, I Corps began a movement west to the Imjin, but a drop by 187th Airborne RCT at Munsan with the objective of surrounding enemy troops fleeing to Kaesong failed. In the east the North Korean 10th Division which had rampaged around South Korea as a part of the NK II Corps had not only managed to keep its organisation intact but actually fought its way north through the ROK lines near Kangnung on 17-18 March, as amazing an achievement as its

[1] *Time*, 5 March 1951, Cutforth, p. 166-7.

original penetration and survival for two months behind the front.

But in this eastern sector there was more important news on 27 March when the ROK I Corps crossed the Parallel and took the first North Korean town of Yangyang on the last day of the month—when the first Americans in the west also moved across the Parallel after striking north from Uijongbu. Thus line IDAHO had been reached by the end of March. This time there was the greatest caution about crossing the 38th Parallel. Truman considered that the crossing should only be made on grounds of tactical security, and that that decision should be made by the responsible commander. Ridgway therefore decided to continue the advance towards the important Communist supply and communications zone bounded by the Chorwon-Kumhwa-Pyonggang 'Iron Triangle' where fresh Chinese armies were massing. At the front the decision to advance ten-

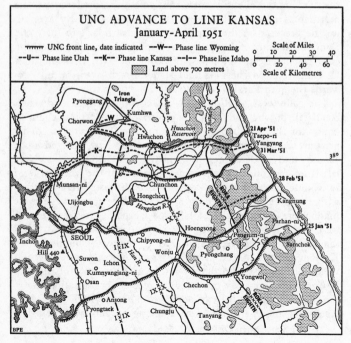

UNC ADVANCE TO LINE KANSAS
January-April 1951

▴▴▴▴▴ UNC front line, date indicated   --W-- Phase line Wyoming
--U-- Phase line Utah   --K-- Phase line Kansas   --I-- Phase line Idaho
▨ Land above 700 metres

Scale of Miles
0   10   20   30   40
Scale of Kilometres
0   20   40   60

tatively across the Parallel was stoically accepted. 'The idea of this war as an endless one,' wrote the *New Yorker* reporter, E. J. Kahn Jr., 'is almost universally accepted here. . . .'

This careful killing advance to the Parallel had not been the only military activity in Korea during the past two months. Air and naval forces had been expanding the fighting. Since 16 February Wonsan had been bombarded in a 'siege' which would go on until the last day of the war. Not only was the town an important harbour and manufacturing centre, but it was also the most southerly point where the eastern Korean rail network running down from China and the USSR could be cut by naval gunfire. In March and April Songjin and Hungnam were also placed under naval 'siege'. The threat of an amphibious landing which the offshore naval forces presented also tied down Communist forces which could have been sent to the front. Another use of the all-powerful UN navy was to support commando raids and landings on North Korean offshore islands. In March South Korean units were landed on the Wolsa peninsula south of Pyongyang, and withdrew taking prisoners with them, and on 7 April, 250 Royal Marines from the 41st Independent Commando landed on the coast just south of Chongjin in the far north-east and destroyed a section of the coastal railway. Such raids went on throughout the war. Of greater military use was the occupation of islands in Wonsan Harbour, off Songjin, Chinnampo, and the Ongjin peninsula, which could all be used as bases for air-sea rescue, radar stations and special operations although full use was only made of these islands when the stalemate war started.

Throughout these winter months, apart from close support on the battlefield, Fifth Air Force light bombers and the B-29s of FEAF Bomber Command had ranged over North Korea on interdiction targets, with the heavies concentrating on the supply centres. But as the UN ground forces advanced towards the Parallel, Intelligence reported an increasing Communist air build-up in North Korea, coinciding with preparations for the Chinese spring offensive. Dramatic evidence of this new air phase of the war was given on 12 April, the day after MacArthur's dismissal, when forty-eight B-29s escorted by seventy-five fighters went after the Antung-Sinuiju bridges. They were met by eighty MIGs from the trans-Yalu bases which shot down three Superforts and damaged seven others; nine MIGs were knocked down in what was the largest air battle of the war to date.

By now the total effect of the war had been to turn most of Korea into a desert. The cumulative result of the ground fighting, naval gunfire, the bombing and the close support strikes with the ferocious all-destroying napalm with its 2,000° F. heat, the elimination of even individual shacks which gave shelter to the Communist forces in the winter fighting all made the havoc caused before the Chinese intervention seem as nothing. Even atomic bombing could hardly have pulverised man and his property more thoroughly than this ultimate of conventional warfare. Epidemics broke out as the weather got a little warmer and thousands of corpses in ruins and on hillsides decomposed. As the Eighth Army moved north TYPHUS and SMALLPOX notices lined the MSR. 'From Taegu northwards there is practically nothing left of Korea,' René Cutforth commented, '. . . a scene of desolation as can rarely have been seen before. . . .' As spring came a layer of mauve and violet ash spread across hill and valley and paddy field and shattered town, a compound both organic and inorganic of the mutual destruction wrought by both sides.

Yet there was every evidence that the Chinese Communists still meant to conquer South Korea in spite of the holocaust of the winter fighting. Reinforcements had been flowing across the Yalu; by the middle of April there were about nineteen CCF armies in Korea. From the Dai-Ichi downwards to the front-line foxholes a massive Chinese spring offensive was expected.

Ridgway now planned to strike at the Iron Triangle, where the Chinese were already concentrating at the end of March, and from where they could switch troops to any part of the front. An UNC attack here would force the Chinese to either stand or attack and on 5 April Eighth Army began its fifth limited offensive in just over two months, RUGGED. Its objective was line KANSAS which ran across the commanding ground north of the Parallel, and four days later all units of I and IX Corps were on their phase lines. With the water barrier of the Imjin in the West, and that of the Hwachon Reservoir in the centre, this meant that the new front was only approximately 115 miles in length, so giving the UNC a chance of establishing some defence in depth to meet the coming Chinese offensive. With six US divisions now across the Parallel, the offensive continued with the intention of seizing an extension of KANSAS which ran just south of the Iron Triangle, line UTAH. By 19 April I and IX Corps were along this line, and a further advance eastwards to WYOMING was planned.

On the afternoon of 11 April Ridgway was up-front in a snowstorm supervising preparations for the reduction of the Chinese stronghold of Chorwon. The momentous news from Washington reached him slowly and not until the evening did he know that he had succeeded MacArthur. Although the former airborne general who had fought in Europe was now SCAP, and would become both SACEUR and Chief-of-Staff, his greatest achievement remains what he accomplished during his fifteen weeks in Korea commanding the Eighth Army. The Army had been transformed in morale and strength, the Communists had been pushed back from Wonju to KANSAS, and Ridgway's strategic and tactical insights when applied to the halting of the coming Chinese spring offensives would smash once and for all Communism's ambition to conquer the whole of Korea. Thus the Truman-Acheson policy of limited war was made militarily possible by that 'genuine military genius' as the *New York Times* called him when he took over in the Dai-Ichi, the second and last American pro-consul in Japan.

CHAPTER ELEVEN

THE GREAT DEBATE

> When American boys are being killed by Chinese armies, and Peking announces that they are fighting the United States and trying to destroy American forces we might as well have a declared war. . . . The commitment of a land army to Europe is a programme never approved by Congress into which we should not drift. The policy of secret executive agreements had brought us to danger and disaster. It threatens the liberties of our people. . . .
>
> ROBERT A. TAFT, in the Senate, 5 January 1951

WASHINGTON: THE SENATE V. THE PRESIDENT

As Ridgway's divisions fought to hold and drive back the Chinese in Korea, 'the Great Debate' over the past, present and future American policy raged in Washington. The new directives to the Eighth Army, MacArthur's challenging statements from Korea and Tokyo, the Hearings in the Senate Committees on the troops for Europe, and Acheson's manœuvrings at Lake Success were all closely linked aspects of the same struggle for the control of American policy.

If the Dai-Ichi had been flanked by Truman's general in Korea, then the Administration itself was simultaneously under relentless pressure from MacArthur's allies in Washington, who knew of the increasing differences between the General and his civilian and service superiors. The necessity of keeping NATO and the Allied front in the UN intact only emphasised that, while any Administration concession to the Taft-MacArthur alliance could destroy America's international coalition, too complete an alignment with the British attitude towards Peking could mean the disintegration of the Administration's precarious support in Congress.

The mid-term elections in early November had proved almost disastrous to the Democrats, although it should be remembered that Administration losses were less than in the three preceding off-year campaigns.[1] The polls, the first to be held since the Red conquest of China, the Soviet atomic bomb, and McCarthy's anti-Communist campaign had shown that large sections of the electorate had tired of the Administration's efforts and responded instead to the explanation of all their frustrations which was found in the theory of the great conspiracy. A new chapter had been added to all the crimes laid at the door of the Democrats, one that explained the Korean War, not only by Communist aggression, but by Acheson's defence perimeter speech, an expression of the near-treason and incompetency in State Department which had given Kim Il Sung the green light. Most significantly, the elections held after Inchon and before the Chongchon, had manifestly not been influenced at all by the Administration's successful handling of the Korean crisis up until November. There were other frustrations. Veterans of World War II did not relish being drafted to fight in such a remote country as Korea; the last war was only five years away. Businessmen resented the high taxation that went with the Democrats' foreign policy, and hated the idea of controls and inflation. As the commentator Samuel Lubell puts it, the Korean War was fought when it was difficult to balance 'the interests of business, farmers, and workers with one another and with those of the unorganised public.'[2]

The election results showed that in the Senate the Democratic majority was down from 12 to 2; in the House, a majority of 92 has been cut to 36. In California, Richard Nixon, elected to the Senate after his triumph in pursuing the Hiss case in the House, had defeated the Leftist Helen Douglas, attacked by even her own Democratic colleagues for opposing the Truman Doctrine and other manifestations of the containment policy. The victorious Senator Eugene Millikin in Colorado had repeatedly charged that Americans were dying in Korea because of Communist infiltration in the State Department. Taft, returned by nearly half a million majority in Ohio, the largest in his career, saw in the results a complete vindication of both his policy and of the ideas of the conservative Republicans which together could sweep him into the White House in '52. The Senate Democratic Majority Leader, Scott Lucas, and the Majority

[1] Neustadt, p. 211.
[2] Quoted in Spanier, *The Truman-MacArthur controversy*, p. 152.

Whip, Francis Meyers, had been defeated. Possibly the most significant result of all was in Maryland, where the veteran Democratic senator, Millard Tydings, the first leading Democrat to denounce McCarthy, had been defeated by a complete unknown, John M. Butler, after twenty-four years in the Senate during which he had become chairman of the important Armed Services Committee. The campaign against Tydings had been master-minded by a Chicago PR-man, Jon Jonkel, who, when later investigated by a Senate subcommittee for malpractice during the election gave a fascinating account of how mass-media electioneering relentlessly angled on Korea and the Communist issue had completely routed the boss-dominated machine-politics which had previously prevailed in Maryland. Public dissatisfaction with the Korean War had been a major factor in Tyding's defeat, as everywhere else where the Democrats had lost.[1]

Chinese entry into Korea thus meant that Taft was ready to press on with the major Congressional assault against Administration foreign policy which had been threatened even before the Chongchon. After Truman announced on 19 December that more US troops were to be sent to Europe, the first shot was fired in the debate, when next day, as noted, Herbert Hoover demanded a retreat to the 'Gibraltar of Western civilization'.

[1] Tydings was suspected of white-washing the State Department. In explaining how he merchandised doubt, Jonkel told the Privileges and Elections Subcommittee of the Senate Committee on Rules and Administration, 'I said, Let's not get into the business of proving whether or not it was whitewash, let's stay in the business that a doubt exists. . . . We had . . . the same kind of issue that the Democrats used against the Republicans in the Hoover campaign, and that was the Hoover apple, the guy selling apples in the street. . . . The Democratic Party has to resolve the issue of Communism. It is a big issue. The doubt exists. All you have to do is to go out against it.'

Butler used the Korean War as a leading issue, which Jonkel said 'was pretty hot at the time . . . he never said that Senator Tydings had held back arms from any place. You did not have to say that. All you had to say was that Senator Tydings had been chairman of the Senate Armed Services Committee. . . .' Jonkel's campaign against Tydings culminated in a saturation series of radio spots, 465 in 3½ days. One merely repeated 'B for Butler' half a dozen times in the manner of the Bromo-Seltzer ad. Listeners also heard machine-gun fire, the explosion of a mortar shell, the screech of a ricocheting bullet, then: 'DO YOU IN YOUR HEART BELIEVE THAT WE WERE READY FOR WHAT HAPPENED IN KOREA, OR COULD HAVE HAPPENED SOME PLACE ELSE? Vote for John Murray Butler, Republican candidate for the US Senate. . . .'

See S. J. Kelley, *Professional Public Relations and Political Power*, pp. 107-43.

The decision to reinforce the US garrison in Germany had been made as long ago as September 1950, and although the relevant figure of four divisions was not revealed until February 1951, any reminder at this time that the Administration's foreign policy was based fundamentally on the defence of Western Europe was anathema to the Taftite Republicans. But the debate was conducted on constitutional as well as on policy issues, for the opposition also contested the President's right to send ground troops overseas without Congressional approval. The challenge given the Administration therefore had support from many in the Senate besides orthodox Republicans, for many Democrats resented the imperious manner in which Truman and Acheson conducted policy. On 8 January Senator Wherry introduced this resolution:

> *Resolved*, That it is the sense of the Senate that no ground forces of the United States should be assigned to duty in the European area for the purposes of the North Atlantic Treaty pending the formulation of a policy with respect thereto by the Congress.

The resolution was referred from the floor for Hearings by the full Foreign Relations and Armed Services Committees on 23 January, but, before and after this date in the Senate itself and outside, Taft was to make his views well known as he became the world-famous chief domestic opponent of Truman and Acheson. His criticisms took added point from the universal feeling of national defeat after the Chongchon, the insecurity of the Eighth Army's position in January and early February, the low political prestige of the Administration, and the apparent willingness of America's chief ally to conciliate Peking, which discredited coalition warfare in the eyes of many Democrats as well as Republicans.[1]

Taft did not go so far as Herbert Hoover, who comforted himself with the reflection that even if the Soviets occupied the whole of Europe, Asiatic hordes had done the same in past ages but had disintegrated because of their internal dissensions. But

---

[1] For Taft's most comprehensive speech attacking the Administration at this time, and the succeeding debate, see the *Congressional Record*, 82nd Congress, 1st Session, pp. 54-61 ff., 5 January 1951.

underlying all the Senator's strategic premises was the assumption that the United States could be insulated from the disasters of a new *Volkerwanderung* by the use of sea and air power alone. 'It would take them at least a hundred years to build up their sea power.' As far as the present crisis was concerned Taft thought that Truman's Western European policy would be fiscally ruinous and militarily disastrous. The tremendous expense involved in arming NATO and raising new forces, even with only the planned twenty US divisions, was already at the very limit of or beyond American economic capacity. For Taft nothing could be a greater threat in any circumstances than that of a domestic overspending.

The strategy, moreover, of committing ground troops to Europe was wrong. Not only could America not afford to keep a European army, but the very existence of NATO was a provocation to the Russians to start a war in which the ports of the continent would be under nuclear attack, precluding a new Dunkirk. 'Operation Land War' thus meant that the Democrats were sending US forces into what could easily become a vast graveyard for the whole NATO army. It was hopeless to think American land forces could succeed against the Russians, when Napoleon and Hitler had failed. The US must therefore control the Atlantic and the Pacific to preserve the Western Hemisphere inviolate. Western Europe had recovered from World War II: it must now build up its own defences to hold the East. A declaration of war with China would not mean Soviet intervention in Europe: in any case a naval and air strategy against China was best.

Obviously Taft thought there was no serious external threat to America from the USSR. Yet over Korea he was willing to risk a forward policy, a characteristic contradiction of the underlying nationalism of neo-isolationism which saw in the Far East opportunity for unilateral American action unrestrained by European, 'Democratic' considerations. While Taft had reluctantly approved the initial Korean decision, the war, once China had come in, was an impossible operation. The President had usurped power unconstitutionally in sending all available forces there, an opinion which looked forward to Taft's complete reversal of his original position when in October 1951 he denounced the war as 'an unnecessary war . . . began by President Truman without the slightest authority from Congress or the people '.[1] During early 1951 he thought Korea should be abandoned altogether before buying peace with any concessions to Peking but in April he approved the MacArthur programme to win the Korean War. Here again Taft saw no contradiction in his all-or-nothing panaceas against the torment of limited war.

Those who were willing to abandon Europe were thus ready to have a showdown with China, with all its attendant risks. European fears were further increased when Joe Martin, the powerful House Republican Minority Leader and a long-time isolationist spoke in New York on 12 February. Martin accused the Administration of preventing the Chinese Nationalists from invading China, and said, 'There is good reason to believe that General MacArthur favours such an operation.' In an expression both of political demagoguery and of the liberal-puritan ethic that there should be no limitations on force once war was declared, Martin went on, 'If we are not in Korea to win, then this Administration should be indicted for the murder of thousands of American boys. . . . If we want a strategy that will save Europe and save Asia at the same time . . . we must clean out the State Department from the top to the bottom, starting with Dean Acheson.'[2]

The Administration's attempts to counter these attacks, so close in content on Korean policy to the increasing barrage of statements emerging from MacArthur, was helped by the support for NATO expressed by such Internationalist Eastern Republicans as Senator Henry Cabot Lodge, John Foster Dulles, Thomas Dewey and Harold Stassen. Here was the emerging anti-isolationist coalition that would defeat Taft for the Republican presidential nomination in 1952. Before the Senate Committees in February, leading Administration figures including Acheson, Marshall, Bradley and the Joint Chiefs, all assumed that the Taft programme was both immoral and inexpedient in abandoning allies and weakening the American global position, for the loss of Western Europe would put the second greatest industrial concentration in the world at the disposal of the

[1] *The Taft Story*, p. 165.

[2] Higgins, pp. 104-5. See Spanier, pp. 155-62 for a discussion of Taft's views at this time.

Communists. Strengthening of NATO by the four divisions — there were two US divisions already in Europe — was absolutely essential for both American and West European security. Eisenhower's testimony, after his first tour of the NATO countries as Supreme Commander, was also important as he stressed not only the importance of NATO in the world balance of power, but the moral necessity of American leadership. Although the Hearings rallied support for the White House, the increasing emergence of the Joint Chiefs in an advocatory role for the Administration showed the necessity for their prestige to support the embattled political leaders. Congress would listen to Bradley where it would not listen to Acheson, although by 1952 even Bradley's usefulness would have been exhausted as the Korean War still went on.

The Great Debate was not the only cross the Administration had to bear in these few months. Concurrently, the second Korean cease-fire resolution was presented in the UN after drafting by the British Commonwealth Prime Ministers. Acheson had thus to walk the tight-rope between Taft and Attlee. The new resolution which was passed by the Political Committee on 13 January by 50-7-1 embraced 'Five Principles',[1] which suggested a cease-fire to be followed by a four-power conference between the US, UK, USSR and Communist China to discuss the problems of Formosa and Peking's UN representation. Once again Peking replied with a demand that the cease-fire be completely contingent on the ceding of Formosa and of its 'rightful place' in the UN. As in its rejection of the December peace offer, Peking also demanded withdrawal of all foreign troops from Korea, and that Korean problems should be settled by Koreans alone. Obviously at this time the Chinese calculated — mistakenly — that if Formosa were not immediately granted them at the gun-point aimed at Wonju and Pusan, they could still conquer South Korea. Acheson described the rejection of this second resolution as a 'contemptuous disregard of a world-wide demand for peace. . . . Now, we must squarely and soberly face the fact that the Chinese Communists have no intention of ceasing their defiance of the United Nations'. The Indian Government, in its belief that the Chinese reply was not an outright rejection of the Political Committee's proposals, requested

[1] Goodrich, p. 160-4.

Peking to elucidate certain points. On 22 January Sir Benegal Rau told the Committee that the Chinese were willing to agree to a cease-fire 'for a limited time-period'; but there was no compromise on Peking's demand for Formosa and the UN seat, and no indication that the Communists were willing to accept the principle of a permanent cease-fire before negotiations. Nothing had changed.

This elucidation was quite unacceptable to the American Government, which continued to press for an UN adoption of its resolution condemning Communist China as an aggressor, and which had been tabled on 20 January. At the same time both the House and the Senate demanded by resolution that the UN should act in this manner. To preserve the grand alliance the Administration had gone along with the two cease-fire attempts despite vitriolic Republican criticism; now the Allies would have to move closer to the American position. This was made easier by the skill of the Secretary of State, for Acheson had manœuvred most shrewdly, 'accepting the form of negotiations while denying the substance of concessions'.[1] All along Acheson had calculated rightly that the Chinese would never agree to a cease-fire preceding negotiations while their armies were in a relatively favourable military situation. Speaking on 25 January in the Political Committee, the United Kingdom delegate, Sir Gladwyn Jebb, said that while his Government agreed that Communist China was guilty of aggression in Korea, it did not think that sanctions should be introduced which might extend the conflict — a genuflexion of concern at the Republican baying for tougher measures against Peking. A compromise was reached when the Allies voted for the resolution after the United States had agreed that the work of the Good Offices Committee would take priority over that of the other body created by the resolution, the Additional Measures Committee. The vital clause of the resolution, passed by the General Assembly on 1 February by 44-7-9, stated:

> that the Central People's Government of the People's Republic of China, by giving direct aid and assistance to those who were already committing aggression in Korea and by

[1] Spanier, p. 193.

engaging in hostilities against the United Nations force there, has itself engaged in aggression in Korea.[1]

At the cost of initiating any new measures against China, the front of Allied unity and collective action had been preserved once again.

But it was in the nature of the explosive political situation in Washington that any concessions to the British had to be balanced by concessions to Taft — and Chiang. During the first two months of 1951, increased funds for the US forces on Formosa were approved, and in March JCS recommended the establishment of a military assistance advisory group which the Administration approved. A military aid programme of $300 million for the island was also recommended. Soon the Pentagon announced that arms shipments to Formosa were receiving 'equal' priority to those going to Western Europe. Moreover in a few months time in the MacArthur Hearings Secretary Marshall emphasised that Formosa 'must never be allowed' to come under Communist control; while Acheson insisted that the Administration would relentlessly continue to oppose the seating of Peking in the UN and its agencies.[2] The final obsequies of Acheson's China policy took place on 18 May, tactfully assigned to Assistant Secretary of State Dean Rusk. 'We recognise the National Government of the Republic of China, even though the territory under its control is severely restricted. We believe it more authentically represents the views of the great body of the people of China, particularly the historic demand for independence from foreign control. That government will continue to receive important aid and assistance from the United States.'[3] All the Administration's lengthy and disputed good-byes to Chiang had been in vain; it was still allied to him. And there the matter rested for the remainder of the Korean War and long after.

On the original issue of sending the troops to Europe the Administration just about held its own, although not without

---

[1] Negative votes were cast by Soviet bloc, Burma and India. Afghanistan, Egypt, Indonesia, Pakistan, Saudi Arabia, Sweden, Syria, Yemen and Yugoslavia abstained.

[2] Hearings, pp. 470-1, 531, 903, 1728-9, 1934-5.

[3] Hearings, pp. 3191-2.

a sharp reminder from the Senate that it had a right to be heard on major policy. As the Hearings came to an end in March, with the Eighth Army back on the Parallel, a series of resolutions was tabled, the most important by Senators Connolly and Russell, respective chairmen of the Foreign Relations and Armed Services committees, which was offered as a substitute to the Wherry resolution. While approving the action of the President in co-operating with the NATO powers, the resolution insisted that it was the sense of the Senate that in sending troops overseas the President should consult with Congress, that the West Europeans should make contributions commensurate with their ability, and that the President should report to Congress at least every six months on the implementation of the North Atlantic Treaty. After passing the committees the resolution went to the floor of the Senate, but not before the four divisions had been excepted from its terms. By the McClellan amendment, a further Republican move, the Senate strengthened its stand: no troops apart from the four divisions should be sent to Europe without the approval of the Senate. But a move by Wherry to convert this wish into law was defeated. The presidential prerogatives had been preserved but the Executive could have no doubt of the Senate's hostility to its methods. But like the decision on the Berlin Airlift, the hydrogen bomb, the intervention in Korea, the neutralisation of Formosa, and the coming Korean armistice talks, the transfer of the four divisions to West Germany took place without the advice and consent of the Senate. The amended Connolly-Russell resolution was passed by the Senate on 4 April by sixty-nine to twenty-one votes: this was the formal end of the Great Debate. By this time a far greater political crisis for the Administration was at hand as it took on an even more formidable figure than Taft. Truman had decided to relieve MacArthur.

LAST WEEKS IN TOKYO: THE GENERAL V. THE PRESIDENT

Cutting through the rhetoric of the debate in the Senate was the indisputable fact that Ridgway was successfully implementing Truman's policy in Korea. As MacArthur's hopes faded that Washington might adopt his programme against China, he transferred his advocacy from the largely confidential messages between himself and the Joint Chiefs to the public. Hence the development of the final challenge from Tokyo to the President was geared not only to the progress of the Great Debate, but to the mounting success of the Eighth Army as it fought its way back to the 38th Parallel. Here Washington would try for a peace settlement on the *status quo ante bellum*.

As soon as Operation THUNDERBOLT smashed its way through to the Han, and with the Chinese held on the central front, Ridgway knew that he had the measure of his enemy. But to MacArthur, who instantly realised the significance of Ridgway's success, the establishment of the war of containment in Korea as a going concern meant something else—a viable alternative to his own programme. Hardly had the Han been reached when on 13 February MacArthur announced that 'the concept advanced by some that we establish a line across Korea and enter into positional warfare is wholly unrealistic and illusory'. Such a war would ensure the destruction of his forces piecemeal. In January MacArthur had used the spectre of a forced evacuation from Korea in an attempt to convert official Washington to his programme. Now, a month later, he brandished the attrition of a war of containment without end to those engaged in the Great Debate, so focusing attention on what he had publicly called 'the privileged sanctuary of Manchuria'.

At the same time he conceived an alternative to both the war Ridgway was fighting, and the war he had been so far unable to sell to the Administration. Whitney records that MacArthur had thought of a plan to defeat the Communists in Korea without crossing the Yalu. 'As at Inchon he would go for their supply lines. First . . . he would gradually regain the Seoul line for a base of future operations. Then he would clear the enemy rear, all across the top of North Korea, by massive air attacks . . . if he could not attack the massed enemy reinforcements across the Yalu, and if he could not even destroy the bridges over which they came, he would keep them back by making the south bank of the Yalu impassable. He would sow across all the major lines of enemy supply and communication a defensive field of radio-active waste, the by-products of atomic manufacture. Then, reinforced by Chiang Kai-shek's Formosan troops if he was permitted them, with simultaneous amphibious and airborne landings at the upper end of both coasts of North Korea, he would close the gigantic trap. It would be Inchon all over again, except on a far larger scale.'[1]

No mention was made of this grandiose blueprint in the Senate Hearings and possibly it was never put up to the Joint Chiefs. MacArthur himself perhaps lost interest in this compromise, and preferred to publicise his original plan of striking across the Yalu as a more decisive strategy. But in any case he could see which way events were moving in Washington. On 15 February Marshall stated that four divisions were going to Europe; there were no new divisions for CINCFE. At the same time Tokyo was told by JCS that Rashin might still not be bombed and that FEAF were to stay away from the Yalu hydro-electric complex.[2] It was all so frustrating because, as Whitney tells us, 'MacArthur believed even more deeply than before that Red Chinese aggression in Asia could not be stopped by killing Chinese, no matter how many, in Korea, so long as her power to make war remained inviolate'.[3]

As February passed slowly into March it was therefore inevitable that MacArthur decided to step up pressure against the Administration. After his attack on positional warfare on 13 February came the 'Die for Tie' statement at Suwon on 7 March, in which after outlining the mechanics of the stalemate war he insisted that there was only one way to avoid such 'savage slaughter' for the UNC:

> Vital decisions have yet to be made — decisions far beyond the scope of authority vested in me as the military commander, decisions which are neither solely political nor solely military, but which must provide on the highest international level an answer to the obscurities which now becloud the unsolved problems raised by Red China's undeclared war in Korea.[4]

Thus MacArthur informed his Command that they were fighting a completely stalemated war which could only be resolved

---

[1] Whitney, p. 461.
[2] *Hearings*, pp. 3192-93.
[3] Whitney, p. 462.
[4] The text of these two statements is printed in *Hearings*, pp. 3539-41.

if the politicians in Washington changed their minds and allowed him to strike at Red China. His military analysis of the factors which made for a stalemate was indisputable, for this is what came to pass in Korea over the next two years. The policy reasons which led Truman to choose this course rather than extend the war is a major illustration of the dilemma national leaders face when they have to adopt the only means they believe consistent with great strategic ends no matter what the internal political cost.

Ridgway's reply to the 'Die for Tie' challenge came in a press conference on 12 March when he said that the reaching of the 38th Parallel by his forces would be a 'tremendous victory'. The view was shared in Washington where new peace proposals were being hatched. Throughout February and into March, State and Defence had been conferring on terms for a Korean settlement. Illustrating the policy vacuum which had existed since the Chinese intervention, the civilians wanted to see how the military situation developed before committing themselves, while the JCS temporised on sending new directives to MacArthur until the diplomatic objectives could be precisely defined. Ridgway's success and the fall of Seoul meant that, after consultation with the Allies, a new peace approach was agreed, to be announced by Truman, and this was discussed in draft between Acheson, Marshall and the Joint Chiefs on 19 March. The proposed statement codified in effect what had been agreed between Truman and Attlee three months before. It suggested that as 'the aggressors have been driven back with heavy losses to the general vicinity from which the unlawful attack was first launched last June', the way was open for a cease-fire and 'a broader settlement for Korea'. This would open the way for the consideration of 'other problems' in the Far East by the 'processes of peaceful settlement envisaged in the Charter of the UN'. The fighting would go on meanwhile.[1]

On the 20th JCS told MacArthur the essence of the presidential peace statement in the offing, and suggested that pending negotiations there should be no major advance north of the Parallel. Did he have sufficient freedom of action to provide security for his forces? The General tartly replied that with the 'limitations' imposed on him, his current directives — still

[1] Truman, *Memoirs II*, pp. 466-7.

those issued in January — were sufficient, as it was quite imprac-
ticable for him in any case to advance into North Korea. Passing
on the message to Ridgway not to advance into North Korea
without further authority, MacArthur made an arrangement to
meet the Eighth Army Commander the end of the week, 24
March: 'Will see you at Seoul Airfield Saturday.' He was then
observed by Dean Hess, the padre-pilot, emerging from his aircraft at Yongdungpo airstrip, 'wearing dark glasses, a heavy
overcoat, and a muffler around his neck, but there was no mis-
taking that multibraided hat and the famous sharply-defined
profile. . . .'[1]

It was the last occasion Hess or anyone else was to see the profile in Korea. Before his flight MacArthur had released a statement, 'my military appraisal', he later called it in the Hearings,
which not only wrecked the new peace approach to the Communists but was his greatest challenge to Peking as well as to
Truman and the UN. It was an ultimatum to all three:

Operations continue to schedule and plan. We have now substantially cleared South Korea of organised Communist
forces. . . .
Of even greater significance than our tactical successes has
been the clear revelation that this new enemy, Red China, of
such exaggerated and vaunted military power, lacks the industrial capacity to provide adequately many critical items
necessary to the conduct of modern war. . . .
These military weaknesses have been clearly and definitely
revealed since Red China entered upon its undeclared war in
Korea. Even under the inhibitions which now restrict the activity
of the United Nations forces and the corresponding military
advantages which accrue to Red China, it has been shown its
complete inability to accomplish by force of arms the conquest of Korea. The enemy, therefore, must by now be pain-
fully aware that a decision of the United Nations to depart
from its tolerant effort to contain the war to the area of Korea,
through an expansion of our military operations to its coastal
areas and interior bases, would doom Red China to the risk
of imminent military collapse. These basic facts being established, there should be no insuperable difficulty in arriving

[1] Hess, *Battle Hymn*, p. 248.

P

at decisions on the Korean problem if the issues are resolved on their own merits, without being burdened by extraneous matters not directly related to Korea, such as Formosa, or China's seat in the United Nations.

The Korean nation and people, which have been so cruelly ravaged, must not be sacrificed. This is a paramount concern. Apart from the military area of the problem where issues are resolved in the course of combat, the fundamental questions continue to be political in nature, and must find their answer in the diplomatic sphere. Within the area of my authority as the military commander, however, it would be needless to say that I stand ready at any time to confer in the field with the commander-in-chief of the enemy forces in the earnest effort to find any military means whereby realisation of the political objectives of the United Nations in Korea, to which no nation may justly take exception, might be accomplished without further bloodshed.[1]

The precise reasons for the challenge are not known. But indication of the intended Presidential statement must have had a powerful effect on MacArthur, as here was final proof positive that Washington did not intend to adopt his programme and was 'weaseling on the original US pledge to restore Korea to the proper authorities'. Also, according to Whitney, there was another 'sinister element' in the proposals which MacArthur had so effectively torpedoed with his ultimatum. This was a scheme, concocted by the Truman-Acheson-Marshall triumvirate together with the British whereby Red China would be given Formosa and Chiang's seat in the UN, 'one of the most disgraceful plots in American history'. Whether such a plan existed is not known; but with MacArthur's challenge and the subsequent uproar over his dismissal, certainly it would have been impossible to implement.[2]

As the General may well have calculated, his offer to negotiate was indignantly rejected by Peking, 'The people of China must raise their sense of vigilance by doubling their effort for the sacred struggle.' As for the Allies, the MacArthur 'pronunciamento' as the Norwegian ambassador in Washington

[1] Truman, *Memoirs II*, p. 467-9.
[2] Whitney, p. 464-8.

called it, only magnified their distrust at the confusions of American policy. The fighting would go on, as MacArthur probably intended, for as a patriot he honestly believed that a truce in Korea, with the North still in Communist hands, and with Peking undefeated, was an immense disaster for the United States and the West. With the perfectionist belief in total solutions he had shown throughout his life he was willing to risk ending his career if he could bring home to the American public the necessity for a showdown with Red China. After all, the Presidency was about the only office MacArthur had not held of the positions open to him in his long career. There was little to lose. If the war of containment went on with all its frustrations, then perhaps public opinion, responsive after the Great Debate, would force the Government to adopt the MacArthur programme for dealing with China. His ultimatum was Mac-Arthur's supreme contribution to the Great Debate, the clearest illustration of the complex nature of the Taft-MacArthur alliance. For inside this alliance the motives of the two principals differed immensely. 'There is a great difference, in fact all the difference in the world,' Lippmann was reported as commenting in *The Times* on 11 April, the day of the General's relief, 'between Senator Taft's idea that Chiang could 'take the pressure off our boys fighting in Korea' and General MacArthur's idea that this is the time and the Far East is the place to join issues with the Communist powers and seek a military solution.'

But the General's determination was surpassed by that of the President. He correctly saw in the ultimatum the greatest threat not only to his own position but to the office of the Presidency itself. Truman decided there and then on 24 March to fire MacArthur: 'By this act MacArthur left me no choice — I could no longer tolerate his insubordination.' With the JCS Mac-Arthur's proposals had already received full consideration; 'If anything, they — and I — had leaned over backward in our respect for the man's military reputation.' While Truman did not think that MacArthur 'purposefully' challenged civilian control of the military, the result of his behaviour was that this principle was endangered. But the problem was not as simple as a threat by a man on horseback. Taft, whose views were so close to MacArthur's, was one of the most anti-militarist politicians

in the United States. It was MacArthur's immense prestige as a
soldier combined with his advocacy of a political programme
with so much appeal that had halted Truman's Korean policy
for the time being. '. . . Time and time again General Mac-
Arthur had shown that he was unwilling to accept the policies
of the Administration. By his repeated public statements he was
not only confusing our Allies as to the true course of our policies,
but, in fact, was also setting his policy against the President's. . . .
If I allowed him to defy the civil authorities in this manner, I
myself would be violating my oath to uphold and defend the
Constitution.' Truman had twice thought of relieving Mac-
Arthur before, during the VFW letter incident and again after
the Chongchon. But even before the President could work out
ways and means of firing MacArthur—no one yet knew of his
decision—another MacArthur sensation hit Washington which
precipitated immediate action.

The only apparent external manifestation of Truman's dis-
pleasure at the ultimatum was a curt message from Bradley to
Tokyo asking CINCFE to observe the order of 6 December that
all public statements by theatre commanders should be cleared
by Washington. But earlier in the month Joe Martin had
written to MacArthur enclosing his speech of 12 February, and,
trying to squeeze the last drop of political advantage accruing,
had asked MacArthur if he would comment on his suggestion
that Chiang's forces should be allowed to land on the Chinese
mainland. The letter, the immediate cause of MacArthur's downfall, stayed in the Dai-Ichi in-tray until 20 March, when Tokyo
may well have received Intelligence of the coming peace moves,
although Whitney says that the official message from JCS·did
not arrive until next day. Replying on the 20th, MacArthur
congratulated Martin on the text of his speech. 'You have certainly lost none of your old-time punch.' He went on to say that
his views, too, coincided with Martin's on Formosa: '. . . they
follow the conventional pattern of meeting force with maximum
counterforce, as we have never failed to do in the past. Your
view with respect to the utilisation of the Chinese forces on
Formosa is in conflict with neither logic nor this tradition.'
Advancing his thesis in a way that recalled his argument during
the Inchon conference in faraway August, MacArthur went on:

It seems strangely difficult for some to realise that here in
Asia is where the Communist conspirators have elected to
make their play for global conquest, and that we have joined
the issue thus raised on the battlefield; that here we fight
Europe's war with arms while the diplomats there still fight
it with words; that if we lose this war to Communism in Asia
the fall of Europe is inevitable; win it and Europe most probably would avoid war and yet preserve freedom. As you have
pointed out, we must win. There is no substitute for
victory. . . .[1]

The letter, a political time-bomb which again challenged Truman on the fundamentals of his foreign policy, was at last
dramatically read on the floor of the House on 5 April, the day
following the final vote of the Senate on the amended Connolly-
Russell resolution. This was the end. MacArthur had to go now,
immediately, no matter what the political cost. 'The time had
come to draw the line,' Truman writes, and, recording his anger
at a particular insult for such a historically-minded President,
'he was in effect saying that my policy was without logic and
violated tradition.' The same day, the conservative Republican
Freeman magazine published a statement by MacArthur that
the reason why more South Koreans were not armed was the
result of 'political decisions beyond my authority'. To Bradley
and the Pentagon here was another affront: in January, Mac-
Arthur himself had recommended building up the Japanese
National Police Reserve rather than the South Koreans.

That same afternoon Bradley was told over the telephone — in
the Hearings he could not remember who by — that the President was concerned about MacArthur's statements; he immediately told the Joint Chiefs in a meeting at 5 p.m. that they
should start looking into the 'military aspects' of the situation.
The series of angry meetings by the Administration high command which began next morning was to solve the MacArthur
problem once and for all. The biggest emotional upheaval in
American life since Appomattox was at hand.

---

[1] Truman, *Memoirs II*, pp. 472-3.

CHAPTER TWELVE

THE RECALL

> The New Year's Day *Gazette* announced . . . the dismissal of Marlborough from all his offices. . . . One can imagine the clatter of the factions, the flouts and snorts of the bewigged magnates, of their proud womenfolk, and their literary fighting cocks. They had no lack of fuel for quarrel or gossip, for taunt and rejoinder. . . .
>
> CHURCHILL, *Marlborough His Life and Times*

THE FALL OF MACARTHUR

FRIDAY morning, 6 April, in the White House. Truman asked his four closest colleagues what should be done about MacArthur. The President was careful not to say that he had already decided to dismiss the General.

Averell Harriman thought that MacArthur should have been fired two years previously over some obstruction which he had offered to Washington's occupation policy for Japan. Marshall urged caution, saying he wanted to think it over. He thought that if MacArthur were recalled, the military appropriations might encounter Congressional obstruction. Bradley looked at the question from the viewpoint of military discipline. There was a clear case of insubordination and MacArthur should be dismissed. But first he wanted to confer with the Joint Chiefs before making a final recommendation. Acheson, too, thought MacArthur would have to go, but urged caution: 'If you relieve MacArthur, you will have the biggest fight of your administration.' Wisely, Acheson urged that it was essential to have the advice of the Joint Chiefs before acting.

This meeting of the five men was broken by their attendance at a scheduled Cabinet meeting where, although the Martin letter was the subject of comment, there was no discussion of the problem uppermost in the President's mind. It was absolutely necessary to preserve secrecy over the impending relief unless the Opposition were to mobilize public opinion and thus perhaps prevent the recall. So great were the political risks in the operation that it seemed as if the king were in the Dai-Ichi and not in the White House. The deliberations of the highest civilian and military officials in the Republic, carrying out what was to be presented as an elementary defence of civilian supremacy, seemed almost a conspiracy. The morning ended with the five men returning to Truman's office when after more discussion the President asked Marshall to go over all the messages that had been exchanged between Washington and MacArthur in the last two years.

Following this prolonged discussion with Truman, the other four men met by themselves in Marshall's office on Friday afternoon; an arrangement had been made to assemble again in the White House for a conference the next morning at 9 a.m. This Saturday morning conference was brief. In it Marshall said that after reading the Pentagon files he concluded that MacArthur should have been fired two years before. Truman then asked Bradley to make the recommendation of the Joint Chiefs to him on Monday.

The later accusation of MacArthur supporters that the British — also eager to see themselves in this role — were almost instrumental in bringing about the downfall of the General is not borne out by any evidence: Truman was in any case implacably determined to go on ahead. But nevertheless, Whitehall was extremely concerned over the Martin letter. Trumbull Higgins is probably correct in suggesting that a report in *The Observer* on 8 April which stated that the British Government took 'the strongest possible exception' to the letter, was an official leak. The report in the British newspaper went on to explain that the Attlee Government interpreted this latest development 'as foreshadowing an extension of the war to the mainland of Asia'. In line with this belief, the British Embassy in Washington had already asked how MacArthur could make statements which contrasted so much with the US Government's official policy? The answer was still being worked out on the Sunday morning when Truman talked to John Snyder, his Secretary of the Treasury who, more significantly, was an old-time Missouri crony. Later, Acheson also saw Truman, but the most significant development that day was the meeting of the JCS in Bradley's office in the Pentagon at 2 p.m. Collins had been out of town earlier over the weekend, and his deputy, General Haislip, had attended the Thursday afternoon meeting. After their conference which went on for nearly two hours the Chiefs then went up to Marshall's office where they presented their unanimous recommendation that MacArthur should be relieved 'on purely military considerations' (Marshall).

The crisis would have come as no surprise to the military leaders. As Collins said in the Hearings, the question of MacArthur's removal 'had run through my mind . . . if the situation continued to develop, it might come to a point where some action might have to be taken'. But Marshall was to deny that Ridgway had been sent specially to Korea to anticipate the firing. Bradley's pragmatic reasons for the relief given in the Hearings are a useful addition to the constitutional analysis given by Truman. Apart from considerations of maintaining civilian supremacy, the Chairman of the Joint Chiefs gave two overriding reasons. Firstly, by his public statements and official messages, MacArthur had shown that he was 'not in sympathy with the decision to try to limit the conflict to Korea . . . it was necessary to have a commander more responsive to control from Washington'.

Not only had MacArthur interpreted his first Korean directive in a 'permissive' manner and ordered action above the Parallel without orders, but he had ignored two suggestions from Washington that some sort of buffer zone south of the Yalu be formed during the autumn advance. Just as he had violated policy in refusing to hold back his non-Korean forces in October, so Collins said, 'the thing might be done in some other instance of a more serious nature', 'In exercising his discretion and authority,' Acheson said on the same subject, 'I think there was worry on my part that he would exercise it in the direction of enlarging rather than confining the conflict.' The point was obvious and effective. The exchanges in January between Washington and Tokyo over staying in Korea were another example of the bad relationship between JCS and their theatre commander. If there was not disobedience there was a complete lack of *rapport*. 'The normal relationships which are desirable between one echelon of command and another had been seriously impaired', was Sherman's comment on the situation in January 1951.

The second (and more technical) reasons given by Bradley was that MacArthur had failed to comply with the presidential order of 6 December 1950 sent to all theatre commanders to clear their public statements with either the State or Defence Departments. MacArthur had been sharply reminded of this order after 24 March. In flouting the directive he had taken action which had challenged — and challenged effectively — the President's desire to make fresh Korean peace moves. He had challenged the President as the chief spokesman of the country's foreign policy. In Acheson's words, the ultimatum had aborted the peace proposals for 'the field had been occupied', and everyone was asking the question, 'who is speaking for the United States?'[1]

The recommendation of the Joint Chiefs — on which so much of the Government's case against MacArthur depended — finished the consultations on whether to get rid of MacArthur. The next consideration was how the removal could be made in the most expeditious manner. On the Monday morning, 9 April, the same five men met again with Bradley reporting the unanimous view of the JCS including himself, that the recall should take place. The other men reiterated their opinion and then Truman said that he had decided on 24 March to fire MacArthur. In 1954, when the ex-President was asked if he regretted the decision, he showed that he, too, thought like his advisers that if anything he had been too weak, and not too tough with the Arkansas Mikado. 'The only thing I repent is that I didn't do it two years sooner.'[2]

Truman then directed Bradley to draft the orders which would relieve MacArthur and appoint Ridgway to his commands, and on Tuesday afternoon at 3 p.m. the group met with the President to scrutinise the orders and the press release which would announce to the world that the Truman-MacArthur controversy had reached its climax. Truman's press secretary, Joe Short, was present to help in the drafting of the release. It was decided that Frank Pace, who had been dispatched to Tokyo to prevent any further provocations by MacArthur while his dismissal was being organised, would personally deliver the news

[1] For these comments by Administration leaders see *Hearings*, pp. 1202, 878-9, 1300, 1789, 1601, 1774-5.
[2] Whitney, p. 390.

to MacArthur at 10 a.m. on the 12th, Tokyo time, 8 p.m., 11 April in Washington. Simultaneously, General Hull, an Army General Staff officer, would tell Ridgway in Korea of his elevation. Truman then signed the order relieving MacArthur.

Right up until Tuesday afternoon all had been kept secret. The same morning the Washington *Post*, a pro-Democrat newspaper, was resigned to MacArthur getting away with it again over the Martin letter: MACARTHUR RECALL RULED OUT BY PRESIDENT 'HILL' HEARS. But now the news started to leak, and, on Tuesday evening, as Truman puts it, 'a change of plans became necessary . . . General Bradley came rushing over to Blair House'. Bradley had heard that the Chicago *Tribune*, an implacably anti-Truman paper, had wind of the news and would print it in the morning. Hoping for a clarification of a Tokyo tip that an important resignation was coming there, the *Tribune* had phoned the Pentagon for confirmation, and was keeping a line open to its Tokyo Bureau.

So great was the necessity to dismiss MacArthur before the Republicans could mobilise public support for their Marlborough that Truman immediately decided to advance the timing of the order by about twenty hours. MacArthur would be informed the usual way, through channels, of his dismissal and a radio message would be sent to Pace, at present touring the front in Korea, so that Ridgway could be informed. A race now started between the official message and the press release to carry the news to MacArthur. The order of relief went out on the Pentagon teleprinters at 0030 and was acknowledged by Tokyo at 0042; earlier Joe Short had called an emergency press conference for 1 a.m., 11 April. Truman then retired; the reporters, dragged to the White House from bed, bar and office for a 'special announcement', the first at that time since Roosevelt's death, thought that either the President had died or that war had been declared.

On arriving at the White House they were handed three releases. The first was a presidential announcement:

With deep regret I have concluded that General of the Army Douglas MacArthur is unable to give his wholehearted support to the policies of the United States government and of the United Nations in matters pertaining to his official duties.

In view of the specific responsibility imposed on me by the Constitution of the United States, and of the added responsibility which has been entrusted to me by the United Nations, I have decided that I must make a change of command in the Far East. I have, therefore, relieved General MacArthur of his commands and have designated Lt.-Gen. Matthew B. Ridgway as his successor.

Full and vigorous debate on matters of national policy is a vital element in the constitutional system of our free democracy. It is fundamental, however, that military commanders must be governed by the policies and directives issued to them in the manner provided by our laws and Constitution. In time of crisis, this consideration is particularly compelling.

General MacArthur's place in history is fully established. The Nation owes him a debt of gratitude for the distinguished and exceptional service which he has rendered his country in posts of great responsibility. For that reason I repeat my regret at the necessity for the action I feel compelled to take in his case.

The second had been sent to the General:
Order to General MacArthur from the President:

I deeply regret that it becomes my duty as President and Commander-in-Chief of the United States military forces to replace you as Supreme Commander, Allied Powers; Commander-in-Chief, United Nations Command; Commander-in-Chief, Far East; and Commanding General, US Army, Far East. You will turn over your commands, effective at once, to Lt.-Gen. Matthew B. Ridgway. You are authorised to have issued such orders as are necessary to complete desired travel to such place as you select. My reasons for your replacement will be made public concurrently with the delivery to you of the foregoing order.

The third release was the message to Ridgway of his promotion. Also released was a collection of background papers, the executive order of 6 December, the notification sent on 20 March of the President's peace plan, the text of MacArthur's statement of 24 March; the reprimand that followed it; the Martin letter; and two documents which showed that on

6 January MacArthur had responded to a message from the Joint Chiefs with a suggestion that the Japanese rather than the South Koreans be given existing arms. This last reply to MacArthur's letter in *Freeman* illustrating that the struggle between the President and the General was waged with magnificent pettiness by both whenever possible. In view of the coming political storm it was expedient, however, for the Administration now to use any ammunition available.

As reporters assembled at the White House at 1 a.m., it was 3 p.m. in Tokyo. In the American Embassy, MacArthur and his wife were finishing lunch with Senator Warren Magnuson, of Washington State, and William Sterns, a Northwest Airlines executive. Suddenly Mrs. MacArthur saw the beckoning figure of Col. Huff, the General's ADC, at the door. Huff, in tears, told her the news — he had just heard it on the radio; the press release had got to the target before the official order. Mrs. MacArthur then told the General, who reacted to the news with the superb comment, 'Jeannie, we're going home at last.' Twenty minutes later the President's order reached MacArthur; after fifty-two years he ceased to be on active service as his commands and his viceregal powers fell away. Great was the fall; he would not even have the opportunity for turning over his authority to Ridgway. Later Whitney talked to reporters: 'I have just left him. He received the news of the President's dismissal from command magnificently. He never turned a hair. His soldierly qualities were never more pronounced. This has been his finest hour.'

If surprise and resentment was the chief emotion in Tokyo, all was confusion in Korea. Ridgway, up-front in the snowstorm, accompanied by Pace, was near Chorwon on I Corps' front. Due to a breakdown of a power unit in Pusan, the relayed presidential order was unable to get through to Pace and the new CINCUNC, although Ridgway writes in his memoirs that during the afternoon a newsman said to him, 'Well, General, I guess congratulations are in order.' Later that evening, in Ridgway's temporary CP on X Corps' front, a garbled radio message reached Pace which said that Ridgway had been appointed to all US Far Eastern commands, but no reference was made of MacArthur's relief. According to Marshall in the MacArthur Hearings, the two men then 'debated the surprising nature of the message when General Almond . . . informed them it was already on the radio'. For Almond the news was sickening; he must have known that, along with the 'Bataan gang' and other MacArthur men, his career in Korea and the Far East was over. The next morning Ridgway was flown to Tokyo in Pace's Constellation for a preliminary conference with his former Commander. The MacArthur era in Japan was over.[1]

THE RETURN

Having removed the man who was simultaneously its most important field commander and its most potent political enemy, the Administration's writ at long last ran throughout its domains in Japan and Korea. With his rake-hell political courage Truman would have fired MacArthur once his mind was made up, even if all his advisers had been against the move, for of course the General, as a private citizen in the US, no matter how closely allied with Taft, could never be as great a menace to Truman's Korean policy as he was in Tokyo. But the fantastic domestic reaction to the cashiering of MacArthur, which surpassed all the calculations of the five men who had engineered the removal, made it seem at first that there was little political advantage accruing to the Government by its abrupt action.

As soon as the news broke Joe Martin was out of bed and at work on the phone with his fellow Republican politicians and his allies in Tokyo. Herbert Hoover advised MacArthur to 'fly home as quickly as possible before Truman and Marshall and their propagandists can smear you'. By 10 a.m. on the morning of the 11th — unpropitiously it was Acheson's birthday — after a conference in his office with Taft, Wherry and other Republican Congressional leaders, Martin told reporters on Capitol Hill that the conference had agreed: firstly, that there should be a massive Congressional investigation into the Administration's foreign policies, secondly, that MacArthur should be asked to address both houses of Congress — he had received reliable

---

[1] Almond was posted back to the US on 15 July. Whitney, who accompanied MacArthur back to the US, applied for retirement, as did Willoughby, before the end of April. Stratemeyer had a heart attack on 20 May and was replaced at FEAF on 10 June by Maj.-Gen. O. P. Weyland.

assurances that the General would be willing. Martin then went on, 'In addition the question of possible impeachments was discussed.' It was understood the plural indicated that Secretaries Acheson and Marshall as well as the President might be tried by the Senate for their high crimes and misdemeanors culminating in the removal of the General.

Other Congressional reaction was equally violent. On the floor of the Senate, William Jenner charged that 'this country today is in the hands of a secret inner coterie which is directed by agents of the Soviet Union. We must cut this whole cancerous conspiracy out of our Government at once. [Applause from the public gallery.] Our only course is to impeach President Truman and find out who is the secret invisible government which has so cleverly led our country down the road to destruction.' Senator Richard Nixon stated that the relief was appeasement of Communism and that the Senate should censure the President and demand the reinstatement of MacArthur. In the House, Truman's action was called 'the greatest victory for the Communists since the fall of China'. The Republican Policy Committee asked whether the Truman-Acheson-Marshall triumvirate was preparing for a 'super-Munich' in Asia. McCarthy, whose activities in recent months had been increasingly overshadowed by the ramifications of the Korean situation — he held that Truman had deliberately declared war in Korea to divert attention from his crusade against subversives in the State Department — also got into the act. In Milwaukee the Junior Senator from Wisconsin denounced Truman as 'a sonofabitch' who had decided to remove MacArthur when he was drunk on 'bourbon and benedictine'. Unless 'Operation Acheson' was called off, Asia, the Pacific and Europe would be lost to Communism, and 'Red waters may lap at all of our shores'.[1]

The attitude of the public to the firing was that of outrage and possibly a justification of the Founding Fathers, who in their wisdom and fear of the people had given the Republic a presidential and not a parliamentary form of government. From

---

[1] A few weeks later in his attack on Secretary Marshall, McCarthy had fully discovered the demagogic possibilities of Korea, '. . . a war such as never before has been seen on sea or land . . . a war without meaning except in the high personal and tragic sense in which it appears to the men who are consecrating the hills and valleys of Korea with their blood . . . a nightmare. . . .' *The History of George Catlett Marshall, passim.*

Bar Harbour to Monterey Truman and Acheson were burnt in effigy. 78,000 telegrams were sent to the White House, 20 to 1 against the recall. Congressmen were inundated with messages full of abuse against Truman, while several state legislatures passed resolutions against the dismissal. The Gallup Poll was to report that only 29% of its sample favoured the President, showing that as so often in the previous two years, dissatisfaction with the Administration cut across party lines. But many professional Democratic politicians, as well as many Republican newspapers including the *New York Times* and *Herald Tribune* supported the President on constitutional grounds. 'The people in my part of the country are almost hysterical,' one Southern senator commented, 'but there is nothing whatsoever to do in this instance except to stand with Truman. It is simply a question of whether civil government is to be maintained.'[1] On the evening of the 11th Truman's broadcast in which he said that 'by fighting a limited war in Korea, we have prevented aggression from succeeding and bringing on a general war. . . . We are trying to prevent a world war—not to start one'. But now, as later, the President was unable to project the historical necessity of his policy in political terms that would appeal to the public.[2]

MacArthur was to speak to a joint meeting of Congress on 19 April. Even before he left Tokyo there was plenty of evidence of the emotion his removal had generated, for his remote personality and the benevolent despotism of his rule had made him regarded with awe and respect, but not perhaps affection, by the Japanese. Hirohito paid him a good-bye visit in the American Embassy and broke down in tears. It was the first time in Japanese history that the Emperor had called on a foreigner holding no official capacity. On 16 April as the General drove the twenty miles from the Embassy to Haneda Airport a million people turned out to say *Sayonara* to their erstwhile conqueror and ruler, bowing low as his car passed. At Haneda he was greeted by a nineteen-gun salute, while Sabre jets and Superforts flew overhead. After thunderous applause the General stood waving for a minute before entering the aircraft. Then the Constellation, its name changed back from *SCAP* to *Bataan*, took off with Colonel Story at the controls, flew

[1] *New York Times*, 12 April 1951.
[2] See Rovere and Schlesinger, pp. 263-8, for the text of this speech.

over Fujiyama and headed over the Pacific towards Honolulu.

After a stopover at Pearl Harbour, the *Bataan* landed at San Francisco on Tuesday evening, 17 April. The crowd was so great it took MacArthur and his family, accompanied by Whitney, two hours to travel the fourteen miles to their hotel. After a reception next day in front of City Hall, the General emphasised that he was not running for President . . . 'the only politics I have is contained in a single phrase well known to you—God Save America. . . .' Such applause had not been heard on the West Coast since Roosevelt's heyday.

Next stop, Washington. When MacArthur arrived just after midnight on the 19th at the National Airport, protocol ironically demanded that he be met by Marshall, Bradley, and the Joint Chiefs; 'the very men who had supported the President's vindictive action,' complains Whitney, 'were there to blandly welcome him home.' It was an intriguing situation made even more delectable by the President's personal representative, Maj.-Gen. Harry Vaughan. As Vaughan edged away after a far from extended greeting, he was heard to comment, 'Well, that was simple.' No sooner had the Defence establishment greeted their adversary than the crowd broke through the crash barriers, mobbing MacArthur and knocking Whitney over.

The tension was unbearable in the morning as Congressmen started assembling in the House of Representatives at noon. Senior officers who had served with MacArthur sat in the line of chairs usually reserved for Cabinet officers. Then the Senators filed in, the floodlights for the television cameras were turned on. At 12.31 the General walked down the aisle to stand at the rostrum in the place usually reserved for visiting heads of State. The ovation died away. . . .

Mr. President, Mr. Speaker, distinguished members of the Congress: I stand on this rostrum with a sense of deep humility and of great pride—humility in the wake of those great American architects of our history who have stood here before me, pride in the reflection that this forum of legislative debate represents liberty in the purest form yet devised. Here are centred the hopes and aspirations and faith of the entire human race. I do not stand here for any partisan cause, for the issues are fundamental and reach quite beyond the realm of partisan consideration. They must be resolved on the highest plane of national interest if our course is to prove sound and our future protected. . . . I address you with neither rancour nor bitterness in the fading twilight of my life with but one purpose, to serve my country. . . .

After telling his listeners that the Communist challenge was a global one, MacArthur said that he would confine his speech to the problem in Asia. He emphasised that Formosa should in no circumstances be given to Communist China, a country of 'increasing dominant aggressive tendencies'. He paid tribute to the emerging democracies of Japan and the Philippines; then he came to the Korean War. 'Our victory was complete and our objectives within reach when Red China intervened with numerically superior ground forces. . . . While no man in his right mind would advocate sending our ground forces into continental China, and such was never given thought, the new situation did urgently demand a drastic revision of strategic planning if our political aim was to defeat this enemy as we had defeated the old.' He believed a new strategy was necessary:

1. The intensification of the economic blockade of China.
2. The imposition of a naval blockade against the China coast.
3. Removal of restrictions on air reconnaissance of China's coastal areas and of Manchuria.
4. Removal of restrictions on the forces of the Republic of China on Formosa with logistical support to contribute to their effective operations against the Chinese mainland.

These views, MacArthur said, 'had been fully shared in the past by practically every military leader concerned with the Korean campaign, including our Joint Chiefs of Staff'.[1]

[1] The programme advanced by MacArthur in Congress differed from that sent to JCS on 30 December. 'Air bombardment' now appeared as 'air reconnaissance', a much more politically acceptable proposition. There was now no mention of reinforcing the UN Command in Korea with Formosa Nationalist troops; that point had been replaced with the suggestion for intensified economic blockade. But he did say he had asked for permission 'to destroy the enemy-built-up bases north of the Yalu'. MacArthur continued to say in the Hearings that the sixteen-point draft contingency paper sent by JCS to the NSC on 12 January which incorporated his four points meant the Joint Chiefs agreed with him — in spite of all subsequent disavowals that this unapproved paper was predicated on a complete UN evacuation.

MacArthur's bearing, his sincerity, his delivery with its flashes of anger and emotion, the urgency of his message, all combined to make a tremendous impression. His speech which went on for thirty-four minutes was constantly interrupted by applause. His dramatic ending was both an outline of the traditional attitude which held limited war to be immoral and a personal testament.

It has been said in effect that I was a warmonger. Nothing could be further from the truth. I know war as few other men now living know it, and nothing, to me, is more revolting. I have long advocated its complete abolition, as its very destructiveness on both friend and foe has rendered it useless as a means of settling international disputes. . . .

But once war is forced upon us, there is no other alternative than to apply every available means to bring it to a swift end. . . . War's very object is victory, not prolonged indecision. In War there is no substitute for victory. There are some, who, for varying reasons would appease Red China. They are blind to history's clear lesson, for history teaches, with unmistakable emphasis, that appeasement but begets new and bloodier war. It points to no single instance where this end has justified that means, where appeasement has led to more than a sham peace. Like blackmail, it lays the basis for new and successively greater demands until, as in blackmail, violence becomes the only other alternative. Why, my soldiers asked of me, surrender military advantages to an enemy in the field? I could not answer. . . .

I am closing my fifty-two years of military service. When I joined the Army even before the turn of the century, it was the fulfilment of all my boyish hopes and dreams. The world has turned over many times since I took the oath on the Plains at West Point, and the hopes and dreams have long since vanished. But I still remember the refrain of one of the most popular barrack ballads of the day which proclaimed mostly proudly that, 'Old Soldiers never die, they just fade away.' And like the old soldier of that ballad, I now close my military career and just fade away—an old soldier who has tried to do his duty as God gave him the light to see that duty. Good-bye.

Many members of Congress, including those opposed to Mac-
Arthur's policy, were in tears. William S. White records that
'one of the most balanced and soundest men I have ever known,
a distinguished senator of great personal and political reserve
said to me as we walked back to the Senate chamber from the
House, "this is a new experience; I have never feared more for
the institutions of the country. I honestly felt that if the speech
had gone on much longer there might have been a march on the
White House." '[1] Representative Dewey Short, from Missouri,
cried later in the House: 'We heard God speak here today, God
in the flesh, the voice of God. . . .' Herbert Hoover, while not
proclaiming MacArthur's divinity, saw in him 'a reincarnation
of St. Paul into a great General of the Army who came out of
the East'. In the afternoon MacArthur drove down Pennsylvania
Avenue to be given the freedom of the City of Washington. It
was a public holiday and, as hundreds of thousands watched,
bombers and jet fighters flew overhead and artillery boomed
out over the capital.

After the ceremony MacArthur flew to New York for a parade
the next day. He moved into a suite in the Waldorf which then
became his home. The greeting given him was the greatest in
the city's history up to that time. The police estimated that seven
and a half million people turned out, compared with four
million for Eisenhower in 1945 when he returned from Europe.
Everywhere along the nineteen-mile route the crowds were out
of control. In the background factory sirens and ship's hooters
kept up the salute. The figure of the General standing up in the
back of his car dressed in trench coat and battered cap was often
invisible because of the blizzard of paper which poured down
from the skyscrapers. As he passed, men and women crossed
themselves. When the motorcade approached its destination of
City Hall the shouts rose to hysteria. . . . There he is. . . . *There
he is*. . . . THERE HE IS. . . .

It was impossible to believe that here was a dismissed senior
officer of the United States Army in uniform who was trying to
overturn the highest policies of his President, and who had only
five months before led an American Army into one of the
country's most humiliating defeats It was as if the Chongchon
had never happened. The statistics of the New York City

[1] White, *Citadel*, pp. 241 ff.

Department of Sanitation tell the story from the amount of paper collected in the streets. Previously the biggest welcome had been that given to Lindberg in 1927 after his return from Paris:

LINDBERG   1,750 tons
MACARTHUR   3,249 tons

Back in the stillness of the Waldorf, Whitney, who had ridden in the front of MacArthur's car, understandably wondered: What did it all mean? Was it a popular call to some form of duty yet undone? Was the highest office of all now open to MacArthur. . . ?

What did it all mean? MacArthur himself wisely discounted the idea that the amazing scenes with religious undertones had any direct political significance. Partly, of course, he was getting the people's gratitude for his World War II victories. Curiosity about this larger than life-size American hero who already seemed a figure out of a history book was also a powerful element in the welcome. But underlying all the hysteria was frustration with the post-war world with its background of cold war and containment, and against which all the sacrifices of Korea seemed meaningless. The recall had thus fired this emotional powder-keg, for a legendary American general had been dismissed for wanting to apply the traditional solution to the war in Korea—total effort for total victory. If in their heads the people knew there was no alternative to Truman's policy, in their hearts they responded to MacArthur in a last tumultuous outburst of the America in which limited war and the politics of coalition warfare would have been impossible.

The General's real influence on Korean strategy had ended with Collins' visit to Tokyo in January, and with the recall Mac-Arthur's influence on the Administration's Far Eastern policy in any form was over. His charismatic personality would now be completely transferred to the party political scene, an arena with values altogether more ambiguous than any in which the General had previously operated. But the Democrats could not resist the demand for an investigation into their Far Eastern policy. Eventually a compromise was agreed on the Republican proposal that open hearings, which could be exploited by all the resources of mass-media, should be held. It was agreed that closed hearings by the Joint Senate Foreign Relations and Armed Services Committees would begin on 3 May; the public of course would be excluded but censored transcripts would be issued.

To many the project was fraught with constitutional danger. On 30 April Lippmann wrote that this was an 'intolerable thing in a Republic; namely a schism within the armed forces between the generals of the Democratic Party and the generals of the Republican Party'.[1] So great were the political stakes, so great the acrimony between the President and Congress, so great the divisions between the people, that both parties would now increasingly exploit the differences between the generals.

But even before the Hearings began, events had been overtaken by the first Chinese spring offensive in Korea. Its defeat would arouse fresh peace hopes and so the political pendulum would after a while — as he had predicted — swing slowly back to Truman. In Britain too the Korean crisis of early 1951 had produced a political upheaval the effects of which would last even longer than that caused by the high carnival of Mac-Arthur's return.

[1] Spanier, p. 273.

CHAPTER THIRTEEN

BEVAN AND BRITISH REARMAMENT

> This great nation has a message for the world which is
> distinct from that of America or the Soviet Union. . . .
> There is only one hope for mankind, and that hope still
> remains in this little island.
> ANEURIN BEVAN, House of Commons, 23 April, 1951

YA'D THINK THE GUY WAS HUMAN

As the political crisis caused by the big bug-out came to a head in Washington during January, a parallel development was taking place in Britain. In the US, opinion was split between the supporters of containment and those who wanted a tougher line towards Peking. In the UK the difference was between those who supported the Truman-Attlee line, including the Conservative Opposition, and the Labour Left who thought that American policy generally was irredeemably wrong and that Britain was bound to be dragged into a disastrous war with Red China. With one group pressing for action in defiance of the Truman-Attlee understanding, and the other for withdrawal from the American alliance, both were convinced that their own country should go it alone.

Apart from the formal political terms in which the Great Debate was conducted in Britain after Attlee's return from Washington, there was much British unease about American behaviour in Korea which cut across the party lines and was not concerned with Truman's policy *per se*. Ever since Inchon, after which nothing had really gone right, the Americans had been behaving irresponsibly. Fundamentally, of course, this was a rationalisation of the old British disdain at imagined American diplomatic impetuosity, military inexperience, and personal brashness, combined with the barely disguised British envy of American dominance in the new power relationship between the two countries. All elements of the latent British anti-American syndrome were neatly illustrated in Korea, for the secondary importance of the UK troops in the campaign was emphasised by the total American direction of the war — by a flamboyant general whose rhetoric the British distrusted as much as they did his attitude towards Peking.[1]

R. W. Thompson's reactions to the Americans between Inchon and the Chongchon are characteristic. Not only did Thompson loathe the 'Great Panjandrum' but also the GIs. They chewed gum, eat their food mashed all together in a single disgusting mess, guzzled too many goodies and drank too much coke, hated marching, used up too much petrol, lacked regimental spirit, swore excessively, postured with a pseudo-Hemingway-esque toughness, and, grabbing one's arm, used such phrases as 'All Hell let loose', and 'The Marines are in there punchin', fellers!' to describe the fighting instead of the approved British understatement. The trouble was 'that lacking any kind of "classes" in their society, and all being "equal", there were in fact no accepted standards'. To someone of Thompson's self-proclaimed 'liberal views and individualist tendencies', however, MacArthur was dislikable because he assumed 'a kind of divinity'. . . . Evidently both the egalitarian habits of the GIs and the aristocratic bearing of their commander were equally intolerable.

Understandably after the Chongchon, criticism of the Americans soared in the British press, especially of the exaggerated claims of the USAF and of Willoughby's Intelligence service. American over-belligerence towards China was taken for granted along with all the other failings. But with Attlee's return from Washington, the Government and moderate opinion were convinced that Truman and Acheson could be relied on — although, really, it seemed incredible that Acheson, a sort of super-in-

[1] An important (and characteristic) reason for Tory lack of enthusiasm for the war was mentioned by Walter Elliot in the House of Commons in a speech just after the armistice: 'This has been a great war in which we have not played the major part. Such a thing is almost unknown. . . .' H. C. Deb, Vol. 518, Col. 1576. (30 July 1953). For a British view, written immediately after the Chongchon, which in general supports MacArthur's programme for dealing with Chinese intervention on strategic grounds, see G. F. Hudson, 'The Privileged Sanctuary', *Twentieth Century*, January 1951: '. . . It will probably be some time before the British public realises just what has happened or the extent of the political defeat which has been incurred . . . a defeat far more in will and purpose than in the actual contest of arms. . . .'

telligent Eden with teeth, did not really believe that an attempt should be made to buy a Korean truce with Formosa and a UN seat. Aberrations of UN policy in this direction were blamed on Congress, MacArthur, and 'the Pentagon', for the role of the Defence Department in the Truman-MacArthur controversy was usually imperfectly understood in Britain, a misunderstanding fanned to white heat whenever possible by the Labour Left. British pressure and reasoning was thought to be behind all the sound decisions of the Administration, not only in the case of Attlee restraining Truman from using the atomic bomb on North Korea and from going to war with China, but also in the relief of MacArthur, an operation for which Shinwell was later to claim partial responsibility.[1] This was not only national over-compensation for the reality of a secondary role in the alliance. During a year when the Government held office by an overall majority of only eight, it was necessary to impress on the electorate in the atmosphere of permanent electioneering which existed that the Labour leaders were the preferred party in Washington, with easy access to Truman's ear.

Thus, in spite of all criticisms, it was generally recognised that any real breach with the Americans was unthinkable. Thompson and the other correspondents were criticising the United States from the Right, for they acknowledged the necessity for the war in Korea, and saluted the abundant American self-criticism after the Chongchon. Ridgway's arrival moreover did much to improve Anglo-American relations in Korea. On the Labour Left it was a very different story, where criticism of American policy and personalities was at its most bitter since 1945. Not only were the Americans almost seen as the aggressors against the new China, but even their soldiers were presented as personally evil and sadistic. On 20 January the *New Statesman* published a short story by Alexander Baron, *The Human Kind*, with a Korean background. A Korean civilian is caught by two American soldiers watching an open-air, rear-echelon cinema show—itself another manifestation of American decadence. One of the men wants to release their captive, but the unfor-

---

[1] I felt it an honour to share some of the verbal assaults on Truman when a high official of the Pentagon, talking about Ministers responsible for Defence matters, dismissed me with the comment, " Shinwell, the guy who got Mac-Arthur kicked out. . . ."' (*Sunday Telegraph*, 6 August 1961.)

tunate Korean is then gunned down by the other, a gook-hating
sadist of a Neanderthalish sergeant: 'Whaddya know,' he gloats
as he pulls the trigger, 'ya'd think the guy was human!' Writing
for the same audience a few weeks later on 3 February, G. D. H.
Cole said that the Korean War was a civil war and that he had
wanted North Korea to win. Now, 'if Great Britain gets dragged
down into a war with China by the Americans, I shall be on the
side of China. . . .' If perhaps not all the Left were ready
to support Kim Il Sung and the Chinese People's Volunteers to
Cole's extent, the article conveyed much of the emotional content of Left-wing, anti-American feeling. At the same time
'peace' petitions, not necessarily directly connected with the
Stockholm appeal, were circulating in many British universities
and attracting a certain amount of support from the Left.

CABINET CRISIS 1951

Against this background, with both the Republicans and the
Labour Left waiting to exploit a defeat or evacuation of Ridgway's army in Korea during January, the crisis of Bevan's
resignation started to unfold. As in a C. P. Snow intrigue, the
clash of principle and power were seen in terms of personality
on both sides. This momentous British Cabinet crisis has a
further dimension in that just as Truman had to balance Taft
and the British, Attlee had to manœuvre between the Administration and his own Left. Anything that brought the governments together displeased the extremists, as the Prime Minister
and the President had seen during their stag dinner in
Washington.

The first move was a British Cabinet reshuffle announced on
17 January. Bevan — who had already missed promotion in the
previous October when Gaitskell replaced Cripps at the Treasury — was sent to the Ministry of Labour, a horizontal and not
a vertical move. The basis of a personal feud with the inner
Cabinet was thus laid. Next, on 29 January the new rearmament
figure of £4,700 million over three years was announced, amount-
ing to about 14% of the national income, the largest defence
contribution of any NATO European country, and as a frac-
tion of the national income not very much below the US figure

of about 18%.[1] Even in the previous September when introducing the earlier £3,600 million figure, Attlee had described it as the maximum possible without 'resorting to the drastic expedients of a war economy'. The Americans had in fact hoped for a £6,000 million figure, which had been supported by the UK Chiefs of Staff (Slim, Slessor, Fraser). Still, the programme was large enough for Truman and Acheson to repudiate Congressional criticism during the Great Debate which attacked the Allies for not sharing defence burdens; it was the price the British had to pay for the undoubted but not overwhelming influence which they had with the Administration. It was also the smallest possible figure if the UK was to make any serious rearmament effort.

As far as the British economic future was concerned, however, the rearmament drive could not have come at a worse time. There could be no further extension of the welfare state: 'It is no longer possible to pretend that we can rearm with one hand and build a new Jerusalem with the other,' commented the *Manchester Guardian* on 5 February. At the end of 1950, the balance of payments had been resolved in Britain's favour for the first time since 1945 and Marshall Aid had been given up. But the soaring prices of strategic commodities, combined with the fact that any increase in the national product over the next two years would now be absorbed by defence expenditures increased by 50% over the pre-Korean figure, pointed the way to the new balance of payments crisis of late 1951.[2] Unlike the booming US economy which was rising out of its 1949 doldrums with the rearmament programme, the UK economy at first just did not have the 'slack' both to rearm and to maintain a balance of payments equilibrium.

With this dilemma in the background, it was necessary to

---

[1] In mid-1950 the British Armed Forces numbered 692,000, and by April 1951 totalled 809,000; including reserve and auxiliary forces the figure was 934,000. See Cmd. 8475, and Fitzsimons *The Foreign Policy of the British Labour Government*, p. 155. It was planned to expand the regular services to 850,000 by April 1952, and provide ten regular and twelve territorial divisions.

[2] Between June and September 1950 Malayan rubber rose from 23c to 71c a pound, Malayan tin from 77c to $1.46 a pound, and Australian wool from 67c to $1.13 a pound. The initial influx of dollars was instrumental in ending Marshall Aid, but as UK rearmament and stockpiling got under way, Britain was then buying on a rising world market as well. Fitzsimons, pp. 156-7. See also Shonfield, *British Economic Policy Since the War*, pp. 56-7, 76-7, 90-5.

hard sell the rearmament programme in the debate in the Commons on 14-15 February on the Conservative motion that the Government was too incompetent to carry it out. The Government did its best and made a strong case for the new figure. Gaitskell, in supporting the necessity for massive rearmament, talked the language of containment in terms which could have come from Acheson:

> . . . our rearmament programme represents a peace policy, and a peace policy which we hope to succeed. We think that when the inherent strength of Western Europe is more effectively deployed in military terms in Europe and elsewhere it will act as a deterrent so powerful as greatly to reduce the prospect of attack upon us. . . .[1]

Also, in emphasising that production must be stepped up as much as possible, the Chancellor was careful to emphasise that *we must have the materials to do it*. Gaitskell was here hinting that the programme was completely flexible — while the Government would constantly announce its determination to stick to the full figure, if shortages of raw materials and machine tools threatened unemployment the programme would be cut.

Bevan also spoke supporting the new arms programme. But parts of his speech were obviously aimed at the Left. He warned that 'if we turn over the complicated machinery of modern industry to war preparation too quickly, or try to do it too quickly, we shall do so in a campaign of hate, in a campaign of hysteria, which may make it difficult to control that machine when it has been created'. In other places, Bevan went on, rearmament had been accomplished by a 'campaign of intolerance and hatred and witch-hunting'.[2] This was just what the Left wanted to hear, although Bevan's accusation that somehow the US rearmament drive and not the cold war itself was responsible for McCarthy's anti-Communist campaign was really quite untrue. Whatever opportunities the Korean frustration gave to McCarthy, which were considerable, the Senator's dramatic emergence with his Wheeling speech was four months before the June invasion and ten months before any drastic American rearmament was announced after the Chongchon.

[1] H. C. Deb. Vol. 484, Col. 658 (15 February 1951).
[2] Ibid., Col. 736.

Quite possibly this attempt to stake himself out as the leader of the Left in the Cabinet by confusing the Truman Administration with its enemies led to the point of no return. On 9 March Bevin, who died a month later, was replaced at the Foreign Office by Herbert Morrison. Bevan had waited for the call from No. 10 in vain; he had now been passed over three times in less than six months for senior Cabinet position. At this stage he decided to resign and look for an issue to rally Labour Party opinion against what he thought was the disastrous right-wing course the Government was taking. 'It's 1931 all over again with Gaitskell playing the part of Snowden', he was to tell Leslie Hunter, the Lobby Correspondent of the *Daily Herald*. 'He and Morrison are leading the Party to absolute disaster.'[1]

Bevan did not have to wait long to find an issue. Gaitskell's Budget was under preparation; one of his proposals to meet the increased defence charges was an impost of £13 million to be raised by a 50% charge on National Health Service dentures and spectacles, although a £50 million increase in the social services was still scheduled, mostly for the pensioners.

On 3 April, speaking in Bermondsey Town Hall, Bevan assured his audience during a round of heckling: 'I will never be a member of a Government which makes charges on the National Health Service for the patient.' The last stage of the crisis was at hand; the Budget was due in a week. When the Cabinet met to hear Gaitskell's Budget proposals, Bevan, supported by Harold Wilson, President of the Board of Trade, violently objected to the Health charges and the argument continued into an ad hoc Cabinet subcommittee composed of Gaitskell, Bevan, Tomlinson (Education) and McNeil (Scottish Secretary). There was deadlock. Depending on the differing viewpoints, either Gaitskell was stubborn and immovable, or Bevan was attempting to change previously agreed budgetary policy by using the ultimate threat of his resignation as a veto over his colleagues' decisions. But Bevan was isolated in the Cabinet. 'In the Labour movement as a whole,' writes Dalton about the crisis in his Memoirs, '. . . Bevan had a strong position, but much less strong, when it came to the crunch, than many Bevanites had imagined.'[2]

[1] Hunter, *The Road to Brighton Pier*, p. 33.
[2] Dalton, *High Tide and After*, p. 363.

Gaitskell went ahead and made his unaltered Budget speech on the afternoon of the 10th, the day before MacArthur was relieved.[1] The setting was now moved to St. Mary's Hospital, Paddington, where Attlee had been ill with a duodenal ulcer since 21 March, not to be discharged until 27 April; the strain of office was beginning to crack the Prime Minister. Bevan continued to insist that the Budget was misconceived, and receiving no sympathy from Morrison, who was now chairing Cabinet meetings, visited St. Mary's four times. He now strongly opposed the scale of military expenditure as well as the increases on the Health Service. '. . . You have extended the area of disagreement . . . a long way beyond the specific matter to which, as I understand, you have taken exception,' wrote Attlee, accepting Bevan's resignation. For as it was impossible for the Cabinet to back down, Bevan had to go. Possibly on the New Health Service alone some compromise might have been possible, but not on an issue so central to the whole foreign policy of the Government — as Bevan knew. No attempt was made by the inner Cabinet to dissuade Wilson from resigning, but Attlee authorised Dalton to offer John Freeman, Parliamentary Secretary to the Ministry of Supply and a Bevan sympathiser, either the War Office or the Board of Trade. Jobbery might succeed in minimising the crisis. Freeman turned down the offer from Dalton during a walk on Hampstead Heath. There was nothing more to be done by anyone concerned. On 21 April Bevan sent his resignation to Attlee, and it was accepted the same day by the Prime Minister. The news of Bevan's and Wilson's resignations was released early on 23 April, Freeman's the next day. Bevan would make the customary Commons personal statement on the afternoon of the 23rd.

Ever since, the resignations have been the subject of much comment as marking the dramatic beginning of a schism in the Labour Party almost as grievous as that which damned the Liberals after 1916. The Labour Left has seen Gaitskell's defence of the Korean rearmament programme as the decisive manœuvre on his road to power as Attlee's successor. The Right, *vide* the Memoirs of Attlee, Dalton and Shinwell, assume that it was

---

[1] It was noted by economists that the real kick in the Budget, suspension of the 1949 tax concession on new plant and equipment to curtail civilian consumption, was never mentioned during the Gaitskell-Bevan dispute.

personal pique and thwarted ambition alone that made Bevan resign and that if only the heavy-handed Morrison had not chaired those Cabinet meetings when Attlee was in St. Mary's some sort of compromise could have been patched up.

Yet any explanation which assumes that ideology was used solely to advance the personal interests of both sides, a means and not an end, is oversimplified. Attlee himself hints at the way in which principle and personality were inextricably mixed. Discussing Gaitskell's appointment to the Treasury he says, 'I don't think [Bevan] inspired much confidence in anyone abroad at that time. . . .'[1] If this was the case for not putting Bevan into the Treasury in October, 1950, how much stronger was the case for not putting him into the Foreign Office in March 1951 when Anglo-American relations were at their most sensitive during the Korean War. Although Bevan had supported the decision to fight in Korea, together with the need for some rearmament, his open dislike of many aspects of American policy was well known, and indeed he sometimes curiously saw the cold war not in terms of Soviet expansionism, but as a Soviet response to Western provocation.[2] Attlee must have known that both his Government's position with the Administration, and especially Acheson's with the Republican opposition would have been weakened further with Bevan as Foreign Minister. The appoint-

[1] *A Prime Minister Remembers*, p. 245. Attlee has also said much the same about his reasons for not placing Bevan in the Foreign Office. '. . . It should not be forgotten that in the time of the Labour Government he made a great number of stupid remarks about the Americans, which rather put him out of the running at the time.' London *Evening Standard*, 12 February 1962.

[2] 'Let us also remember that the Soviet revolution would not have been distorted, would not have ended in a tyranny, would not have resulted in a dictatorship, would not be threatening the peace of mankind had it not been for the behaviour of Churchill and the Tories at that time. Do not forget that in the early days when that great mass of backward people were trying to find their way to the light, were trying to lift themselves from age-long penury and oppression, they were diverted from their objectives and thrown back into the darkness, not by the malignancy of Stalin at first, but by the action and malignancy of Churchill, the City of London, New York and the rest of the capitalist world.' Bevan, *Fiftieth Annual Report of the Labour Party*, 1951, p. 12. This speech was made on 2 October 1951. The same theme was ventilated in Bevan's *In Place of Fear* (Heinemann, 1952). During the immediate post-war period, 'The dominating world position of the United States would have been much easier to accept if there had been a clear idea of what she wanted to do with it. Of that there was no clue; except, of course, that she was against Communism. . . .' See p. 125 ff.

ment would also have been heavily attacked by the Tories in Parliament at this time. If the Anglo-American understanding on Korea was to be maintained, any fundamental concession to the Bevanite Left by Attlee was as unthinkable as any major concession to the Republicans by Truman.

Whatever Bevan's personal resentments, his fundamental ideological disagreement with colleagues was shown in his resignation statement, made from the traditional place for an ex-Minister, at the end of the third bench below the gangway. The speech was a shrewd mixture which appealed simultaneously to national economic self-interest, to the attitudes of the Labour Left, which disliked rearmament and thought the Soviet threat was over-estimated, and to all those on both sides of the House who disliked Britain's junior position in relation to Washington. It was a bid for national leadership in the event of a major economic crisis or general war. His first point, ignoring the Government's intention of curtailing the rearmament programme if necessary, was that the new plan was economically and politically disastrous:

> It is now perfectly clear to anyone who examines the matter objectively that the lurchings of the American economy, the extravagant and unpredictable behaviour of the production machine, the failure on the part of the American Government to inject the arms programme into the economy slowly enough, have already caused a vast inflation of prices all over the world, have disturbed the economy of the western world to such an extent that if it goes on more damage will be done by this unrestrained behaviour than by the behaviour of the nation the arms are intended to restrain. . . . We shall have mass unemployment . . . unless something serious can be done, we shall have unemployment in many of our important industrial centres. . . .
>
> The fact is that the western world has embarked upon a campaign of arms production upon a scale, so quickly, and of such an extent that the foundations of political liberty and Parliamentary democracy will not be able to sustain the shock.

There was a sop to the Labour Left's reluctance to see the current Stalinist challenge as anything that could not be put right by aid programmes:

It has always been clear that the weapons of the totalitarian States are, first, social and economic, and only next military; and if in attempting to meet the military effects of those totalitarian machines, the economies of the western world are disrupted and the standard of living is lowered or industrial disturbances are created, then Soviet Communism establishes a whole series of Trojan horses in every nation of the western economy.

The climax of the speech was an appeal for a Third Force and an attack on Gaitskell, who with his back to Bevan listened without moving as the speaker's finger stabbed towards him. The Budget was the 'arithmetic of bedlam':

> The Budget was hailed with pleasure in the City. It was a remarkable budget. It united the City, satisfied the Opposition, and disunited the Labour Party — all this because we have allowed ourselves to be dragged too far behind the wheels of American diplomacy.
>
> This great nation has a message for the world which is distinct from that of America or that of the Soviet Union. Ever since 1945 we have been engaged in this country in the most remarkable piece of social reconstruction the world has ever seen. . . . There is only one hope for mankind, and that hope still remains in this little island. It is from here that we tell the world where to go and how to go there, but we must not follow the anarchy of American competitive capitalism which is unable to restrain itself at all, as is seen in the stockpiling that is now going on, and which denies to the economy of Great Britain even the means of carrying on our civil production. . . . There are too many economists advising the Treasury, and now we have the added misfortune of having an economist in the Chancellor of the Exchequer himself. . . . I should like to ask my right honourable and honourable friends where are they going? (Hon. Members: Where are you going?)

Bevan's statement was heard out in complete silence. He then left the Chamber with Jennie Lee and Michael Foot. On the relevant clause to authorise the New Health Charges over thirty Left Labour members abstained, and five voted against the

The frontier of liberation. Hyesanjin, 21 November 1950. Men from the 17th Regiment, U.S. 7th Division, enter the Yalu town on the Manchurian Border

The Meat grinder. British troops from the Gloucesters, U.K. 29th Brigade, I Corps, fire a Bofors gun at Chinese positions on Hill 327, near Pabalmak, south-east of Seoul. 16 February 1951

The Chinese tide turns. Whitney, Ridgway and MacArthur at the front near Suwon, 28 January 1951. Kean, CG, 2nd Division can be seen behind MacArthur

Government. On 2 May when Attlee, just out of hospital, attended the weekly meeting of the Parliamentary Labour Party there was no mention of the resignation, and the discussion was confined to road transport 'C' licences. . . . The next day the King opened the Festival of Britain and in two months the Korean armistice negotiations began. For the next few months the Cabinet Crisis was forgotten, but the divided, weakened, and exhausted Labour Party lost the October general election with the country in the throes of a foreign exchange crisis, the Government had done little to alleviate.

However, the dire economic and political consequences of rearmament predicted by Bevan failed to materialise and in the winter of 1951-52 the Truman Administration like the Churchill Government announced the first of several 'stretchouts' of the arms programme. The opening of the truce talks only emphasised that the Truman-Attlee policy of limited war had worked, and as the possibility of war with China vanished, the Bevanite critique moved away from the effects of the arms programme and US Far Eastern policy to the politically more lucrative issue of West German rearmament.

In retrospect it seems clear that Bevan's play for power in the spring of 1951 was just as much an appeal to British neutralism as Taft's campaign was to American neo-isolationism. Each believed that his country should go it alone—alone over Chinese intervention in Korea. With unconscious Platonism both men believed in the absolute supremacy of a political idea which no pragmatic necessity could ever modify. Taft was a nineteenth century *laissez-faire* liberal, Bevan a nineteenth century fundamentalist socialist. To Taft the totalitarian nightmare of Hitler and Stalin was of small concern compared with the dangers of deficit budgeting; while to Bevan, who projected his early hatred of the Tredegar Iron and Coal Company upon the whole of capitalist democracy, Chamberlain was almost indistinguishable from Hitler, Truman almost as bad as Stalin.

Both men thus thought the Soviet threat over-exaggerated by their respective governments; both men failed to see the significance of the limited war in Korea as a vast holding action which would give the West time to rearm and so to deter further Communist military adventures. Both were enemies of the Anglo-American understanding as it existed in 1951, and

after; both tried to exploit the Korean crisis for political purposes, and both were cheated by Ridgway's military success
which contained Red China in Korea and made a break between
Washington and London unnecessary. Although the Republicans were able to turn the frustrations of Korea to their electoral
advantage in 1952, it was not Taft who became president. Even
if Attlee had won the general elections of '51 or '55 it would
not have been Bevan's brand of social democracy which would
have triumphed.

Bevan's apparent reconciliation with Gaitskell after 1957 and
his premature death have meant that some strange comment
on him appeared during the last few years of his life and after.
The same commentator who in 1956 saw him as 'either a
megalomaniac or a ham' could, four years later in an obituary
article salute him as all along the reincarnation of Charles James
Fox.[1] This progression was fairly general with the non-Bevanite
public. Both evaluations were wrong. Bevan's rhetoric always
occluded his essential failure as a politician. Not only did he
miscalculate his own position in the Cabinet and country, and
also the dynamics of the East-West conflict during the greatest
crisis of his life in those early months of 1951, his failure was
even greater. His remedies for Britain's national and international problems were totally irrelevant. Moreover his insistent
belief that the military threat of Communism was always
secondary to the economic one was proved wrong even as he
made his resignation statement on Monday, 23 April 1951. In
Korea quilted masses of Chinese infantry were swarming all
over the UN positions in the moonlight. The greatest Communist offensive of the entire war, which had it succeeded might
well have brought on an even greater crisis than that of the
previous December, was beginning its second day.

[1] See Henry Fairlie in *The Spectator*, 2 March 1956, and 'Aneurin Bevan
and the art of politics', *History Today*, October 1960, p. 631 ff.

CHAPTER FOURTEEN

THE COMMUNIST SPRING OFFENSIVES

> For the Red Army . . . the basic directive is war of annihilation.
>
> MAO TSE-TUNG

> If they advance against me I shall retire before them, accepting battle if they give me favourable opportunity, for the . . . action of my lines is superior to the shock action of their columns.
>
> WELLINGTON, in the Peninsula

THE GREATEST EFFORT

RIDGWAY's successor, Lt.-Gen. James Van Fleet, arrived in Korea on 14 April. His previous career had included the command of a corps in Europe, and more recently he had supervised the reduction of the Communists in the Greek Civil War. The northwards advance of the Eighth Army continued although by burning off large areas of scrub the Chinese were concealing their movements; on IX Corps' front contact had been lost with the CCF. The advance to line UTAH went ahead, and on 19 April I and IX Corps were preparing to push ahead to WYOMING, an eastward extension of UTAH. Air observation and intelligence told of a massive Chinese build-up in the Iron Triangle area; whatever was to happen in the next few weeks could hardly come as a surprise as the Chinese made ready to launch what they termed their 'First Step, Fifth Phase Offensive', the successor to their offensives of the previous October and November, January and February. Then, during the daylight of 22 April, Communist activity suddenly increased all along the front and in the evening Chinese troops broke out of cover and, after heavy artillery preparation, started moving towards the UN lines by the light of the full moon. The first Chinese spring offensive was under way, Communism's single greatest military effort of the Korean War.

The objective of the offensive, according to Radios Pyong-yang and Peking, was the destruction of the UN Command; it was intended that Seoul would be taken as a May Day present for Stalin. Even after the defeat of their limited offensives earlier in the year and the appalling losses suffered as a result of Ridg-way's strategy, Peking was still determined to conquer the whole of Korea and to risk the consequences of retaliation carried to the mainland which might have resulted from such a victory. If Peking had been initially concerned with its Manchurian border in the autumn of 1950, it had soon calculated that the Chinese armies might accomplish what the Korean People's Army had failed to do. One attempt to conquer South Korea had failed in January. Now in April and May two massive offensives would attempt to unite Korea under Communist control, for Peking had obviously calculated that the human wave tactics of its infantry could overwhelm the seven Ameri-can divisions and two British brigades which made up the core of the Eighth Army.

The virtual disengagement of the CCF after the fall of Seoul in March and their retreat north of the Parallel were closely connected with the launching of the spring offensives. Discussing in his *Strategic Problems of China's Revolutionary War* how the Red Army meets its enemies by the judicious use of surprise and troop concentration when moving into the third and final phase of the protracted war, the strategic counter-offensive, Mao writes: '. . . To defeat the attack of an enemy who enjoys absolute superiority we rely on the new situation created out of the phase of strategic retreat. . . . However, the presence of conditions and a situation favourable to ourselves and unfavour-able to the enemy does not yet mean the defeat of an enemy . . . it is necessary for the contestants to have a decisive engage-ment. And only a decisive engagement can settle the question as to who wins and who is defeated.' Since the UNC did not possess absolute superiority anyway, a withdrawal by the Chinese armies to the Iron Triangle meant from here they could launch a counter-offensive at either western or eastern sectors of the trans-peninsular front with the objective of reaching the decision that had been lost in December with the rapid UNC withdrawal from North Korea and in January and February by Ridgway's campaign of attrition. The winter fighting had besides violated other canons of Mao doctrine. 'A "contest of attrition" is unsuited to the Chinese Red Army. . . . For the Red Army which draws upon the enemy for almost all its supplies, the basic directive is war of annihilation. . . .'[1] Highly important, too, was the fact that nowhere south of the Yalu (and especially south of the 38th Parallel) were the Chinese armies fish in the water of a war-weary and hostile Korean population.

To bring about the annihilation of the Eighth Army there were about 700,000 Communist troops deployed in North Korea, most of them Chinese. General Lin Piao, who, it seems, loosely supervised Communist operations following the Chongchon was relieved of his command of the Fourth Field Army in early March, whether from wounds, accident or illness it is still not certain, and with his disappearance from the Korean battlefield General Peng Teh-huai was placed in sole and complete charge of the CPV. Like Peng's command-post, Kim Il Sung's KPA-CPV Combined Headquarters was located in the hills near Pyongyang, but of course Peng had the last word on all operations and was the real Communist Commander-in-Chief. The Chief of Staff of the associated Supreme Headquarters of the KPA was General Nam Il, born in 1911, a former Soviet citizen of Korean parentage who had fought, like Kim Il Sung, in the Red Army in World War II, and who had returned to Korea with Kim in 1945. Over the shoulders of the North Koreans loomed the powerful cadre of Soviet advisers, headed by the Russian ambassador, until 1951 Col.-Gen. Terenty Shtykov and afterwards Lt.-Gen. Vladimir Razuvayev. All NK orders were drafted in Russian, but the Soviet officers were always careful never to give orders in public, so preserving the façade of North Korean independence.[2]

As the first spring offensive opened EUSAK intelligence calculated that of the seventy Communist divisions south of the Yalu, about thirty-six Chinese divisions were on the line between the Imjin and the Hwachon reservoir, and another twelve to

[1] See Mao, *Selected Works*, I, pp. 224 and 252.

[2] For many details of Soviet personnel in North Korea, see Monat, 'Russians in Korea' *Life International*, 21 November 1960. The writer who has since defected to the West was Polish military attaché in North Korea after September 1951. He gives the figure of 5,000 Soviet personnel in North Korea and on the Manchurian MIG bases, including jet pilots, engineers and anti-aircraft gunners.

fourteen east from the reservoir to the Sea of Japan. On the western sector, in the seventy-miles between Munsan and Hwachon, the CCF had deployed four army groups, from west to east, the XIX, III, IX, and a fourth positioned around the Hwachon reservoir. Each army group was made up of the usual three CCF armies. Chinese artillery was particularly active, but armour was not used to any extent in the spring offensives.

To meet this host, Van Fleet disposed altogether of about 420,000 ground troops; his front-line strength numbered about 230,000. Eighteen groups of FEAF were in action and each of the US divisions had now been brought up to their full strength of 18,000 men, including at least four battalions of artillery. Apart from the two corps of the ROK Army on the eastern front, other ROK divisions were sandwiched in between American divisions, for these South Korean units not only lacked

FIRST COMMUNIST SPRING OFFENSIVE
22–30 April 1951

▨▨▨▨▨▨ UNC front line, date indicated
⟶ Main CCF and NK thrusts
▨ Land above 700 metres

Scale of Miles
0   10   20   30   40

Scale of Kilometres
0   20   40   60

CCF XIX ARMY GROUP = 63, 64, 65, ARMIES
CCF III ARMY GROUP = 12, 15, 60, ARMIES
CCF IX ARMY GROUP = 20, 26, 27, ARMIES
CCF XIII ARMY GROUP = 39, 40, 42, ARMIES

organic armour and artillery, but their numerical strength was only two-thirds of an American division.[1]

The great offensive was soon under way on the night of 22 April with massed Chinese infantry assaults in echelon against the UN lines, accompanied by the familiar sound of whistles, bugles and gongs. These human-wave attacks recalled the tactics used at Chipyong-ni in February rather than those on the Chongchon when the Chinese had often attacked in line. There was an astonishing and alarming development at the very opening of the offensive, as a major enemy effort came with a Chinese thrust southwards from Kumwha, at the south-east corner of the Triangle, down the Hwachon-Chunchon axis against the ROK 6th Division of IX Corps. The South Korean division fell apart overnight, leaving a gap between IX Corps' other division, the Marines, on its right, and the 24th Infantry of I Corps on its left. Unerringly the Chinese had found the weakest part of the central front in the first few hours.

For the next two days the Marine Division was involved in fighting as heavy as anything at Inchon-Seoul or Chosin.[2] There was more Chinese artillery fire than usual, but mostly the Communists relied on mortars and automatic weapons to support the waves of their infantry. Mongolian horse cavalry was used against some American positions, but as the Marines fell back to Chunchon they refused their left flank to the west as the Chinese assault teams poured down the Pukhan valley towards Kapyong and the rear of I Corps. This manœuvre indicated that the primary objective of the offensive was a double envelopment from north and north east to isolate Seoul. The 27th Commonwealth Brigade was in action near Kapyong; by 26 April this eastern arm of the Chinese offensive had been checked, although the Seoul-Chunchon-Kansong trans-peninsular road had been crossed by the CCF near Kapyong. Further penetrations south in this area were then held along the north banks of the Han in the Kumgong-ni-Punwon-ni vicinity. Although the situation was

[1] This was partly US policy. The ROKA was built up slowly because Washington feared it might become uncontrollable. Marshall, 'Our Mistakes in Korea', *Atlantic Monthly*, September 1953.

[2] For the Marine Division in both the Chinese offensives see Montross, 'Red China on the Offensive', *Marine Corps Gazette*, July 1953. There is a survey from the Eighth Army viewpoint of both offensives in *Korea 1951-53*, pp. 102-107.

still precarious on these eastern approaches to Seoul, the Chinese had been unable to exploit their initial break-through. Attention was now focussed on the western front, for as the Chinese cut the trans-peninsular road between Seoul and Chunchon, thus weakening EUSAK's entire position, it became obvious that the main Communist effort was an all-out assault against Seoul down the Chorwon-Uijongbu corridor. On the fourth day of the offensive the fighting in Korea became a second battle for Seoul which Van Fleet was determined to hold.

On 25 April Van Fleet had thus decided to set up a new trans-peninsular line, designated NO NAME, and which ran from Seoul to Sabangu and then on to Taepo-ri on the east coast. In attempting to break off contact and fall back to a new defensive line, Van Fleet was thus ordering a retreat of up to twenty-five miles or more as he sought to preserve all his divisions intact. Simultaneously the General intended to reshuffle his forces, strengthening his western sector as IX and X Corps in the centre pulled back from the Chunchon area to the Hongchon River, and as the Marines came under Almond's command once again as part of X Corps.[1]

Since the afternoon of the 22nd Chinese pressure had mounted in three days to maximum effort as six CCF armies from the XIX and III Army groups tried to smash their way through to the ROK capital, over thirty-five miles behind the front when the offensive opened. By the evening of the 23rd, the 3rd Infantry Division which had been in action near Chorwon on the Triangle had pulled back ten miles down the MSR to the Parallel. To the west around the great peak of Kamak San which guarded two crossings of the Imjin, a Chinese army of three divisions attacked the 29th British Infantry Brigade which held a 12,000 yard front with about 6,000 men. South of the Brigade the ROK 1st Division was being driven back by another Chinese thrust down the Kaesong-Munsan route into Seoul.

Terrific Chinese pressure developed on the night of the 22nd against the British Brigade. Both the 1st Battalion, Northumber-

---

[1] The I Corps consisted of the US 1st Cavalry, 3rd Infantry and 25th Infantry Divisions, the ROK 1st Division and the UK 29th Brigade. IX Corps; US 24th Infantry and 7th Infantry Divisions, and the 27th Commonwealth Brigade (redesignated 28th Brigade after midnight 25/26 April); X Corps; US 2nd Infantry and 1st Marine Divisions, ROK 5th and 7th Divisions. To the east were the III and I Corps of the ROK Army.

land Fusiliers and an attached Belgian battalion on the right of the Brigade front were attacked together with the 1st Battalion, Gloucestershire Regiment, to the south-west. The Royal Ulster Rifles and the Centurion tanks of the 8th Hussars were in reserve on the road to Seoul behind the Brigade's position. Anthony Farrar-Hockley, then Adjutant of the Gloucesters, has described the opening of the mighty Communist offensive as the Chinese host crossed the Imjin in his sector on the night of 22 April, heading for the village of Choksong and, above it on Castle Hill, 'A' Company's position:

> The attackers enter; hundreds of Chinese soldiers clad in khaki suits; plain, cheap cotton caps; rubber-soled, canvas shoes upon their feet; their shoulders, chests and backs criss-crossed with cotton bandoliers of ammunition: upon their hips, grenades. . . . Those in the forefront of the battle wear steel helmets that are reminiscent of the Japanese. Their weapons — rifles, carbines, 'burp' guns, and Tommy guns that we supplied to Chiang-Kai-shek — are ready in their hands. Behind, on mule or pony limbers are their guns and ammunition. Between the two lines, on sweating backs, or slung between two men upon stout bamboo poles, their mortars and machine-guns travel forward. No Oxford carriers, no jeeps or trailers, no gun prime-movers here; but if they lack these aids to war, they do not lack what we do most: men. The hundreds grow to thousands on the river bank, as, padding through the night, they close with us: eight hundred Gloucesters astride the road to Seoul — the road the Chinese mean to clear at any cost.[1]

Throughout the 23rd all Chinese efforts were beaten back by the Brigade with enormous casualties to the attackers. But on the 24th with the Belgians evacuated south across the Imjin, and with the 5th Fusiliers and the Rifles hard pressed, the Chinese ground forward despite the artillery support given to the defenders, and on that evening the Gloucesters withdrew to Hill 235, 'Gloucester Hill', above the hamlet of Solma-ri, south of Choksong. The Battalion was now almost completely surrounded. During the night of the 24th, with the Chinese on

[1] Farrar-Hockley, *The Edge of the Sword*, p. 23.

Kamak-San and moving south-eastwards towards Uijongbu, a general retreat was ordered to the north of Seoul. With heavy casualties most of 29th Brigade's units got away to the south, fighting their way through Chinese ambushes. Lt.-Col. Carne, the Battalion Commander of the Gloucesters, who had twice sortied personally during the action at the head of assault groups, ordered his men to attempt a break-out at 10.30 on the 25th, but the position was hopeless. Carne himself, like most of his men, was captured after leading an unsuccessful escape party. (He was later awarded the VC for his role in this action.) Of the others, only thirty-nine men from his Battalion reached the American lines north of Uijongbu after running fights in the hills with the Chinese . . . the Brigade had suffered well over a thousand casualties.

But this stand by 29th Brigade had saved the left flank of I Corps, so making possible an orderly withdrawal down the road to Seoul. The heroic action of the Gloucesters at Solma-ri, what Van Fleet was later to describe as 'the most outstanding example of unit bravery in modern warfare', blunted the Chinese offensive, spoiling its timetable by slowing it down for a vital three days, and, moreover, a Chinese division had been destroyed by the 29th Brigade, and a CCF army badly cut up. The whole momentum of the offensive had been lost and I Corps, despite a thirty-mile withdrawal was now in a position to defend Seoul which Van Fleet intended to hold.

This time there would be no retreat south of the Han. On 27-28 April the struggle for Seoul reached its climax as Uijongbu was outflanked and the 3rd Infantry Division pulled back to positions just four miles north of the capital. To the West the South Koreans were also forced back into the outer suburbs from Munsan. But Van Fleet had no unpleasant memories of the winter fighting; he had already decided (correctly) that the Chinese armies had no mobility or logistics to exploit their advance. Yet the scenes in Seoul on the 27th indicated how close was a retreat back to Suwon and Pyongtaek again. The squares and streets of the city were jammed with artillery and tanks firing over the heads of the defenders at the Chinese less than five miles away. If CCF artillery fire fell into Seoul in return, the capital was out of the range of their mortars. *The Times* reported on the 28th that the fall of the city 'appears probable', but by the time the words were being read it was evening in Korea and the Chinese offensive was already fading away. By the next day, 29 April, the NO NAME line had been established and the Eighth Army was manning its new defensive positions all along the front.

In the east meanwhile Inje had been taken by the Communists, but further efforts to outflank Seoul through Punwon-ni by breaking across the Han above the city had been foiled. In the west, on the 29th, air strikes broke up an effort to ferry 6,000 enemy troops across the Han estuary into the Kimpo peninsula and so enter Seoul along the Inchon road. By the 30th the Chinese offensive was over and a northward movement had already begun. For this gain of up to thirty-five miles of territory the Chinese had suffered, it was estimated, at least 70,000 casualties, while UNC losses were 7,000. Once again Peking had failed to destroy the Eighth Army. Morale in the UNC was high after this great defensive victory but already the Chinese were regrouping for yet another offensive.

OFFENSIVE IN THE EAST

Even now, the Chinese were still determined to conquer South Korea. Only half their forces had been committed in the Seoul offensive and Eighth Army Intelligence knew that a major effort would soon be made to smash the NO NAME line. Van Fleet met his corps commanders on 30 April to survey defensive measures. New minefields were to be laid, artillery would be carefully registered, bands of interlocking machine-gun fire were calculated by all units. In the minefields were placed fifty-five gallon drums of napalm and petrol which could be detonated electrically. It was the same Ridgway technique of using fire-power to save UN manpower: 'We must expend steel and fire,' Van Fleet had said, 'not men. . . . I want so many artillery holes that a man can step from one to the other.' But the defence would be dynamic as well, as the General this time hoped to concentrate reserves quickly and strike back once the coming Chinese offensive was stopped by his firepower. Probing attacks were started to discover Chinese intentions, but already there was a no-man's-land of ten miles between the two sides as the Eighth

Army patrols moved north. By 7 May Uijongbu and Chunchon had been retaken by tank-infantry columns; on the east coast the ROK I Corps had jumped north nearly to Kansong.

That same day Van Fleet published a plan for a full-scale drive back to line KANSAS. But within a day or so mounting Chinese activity for a major new effort forced a postponement of the UN limited offensive. After 10 May Chinese resistance stiffened all along the front, and large supply columns were observed moving south on the central front. Enemy air activity in the north was still a problem, and on 9 May over 300 fighter-bombers attacked Sinuiju, demolishing the airbase and destroying fifteen MIGs. The Eighth Army Command had expected the Chinese to try again for a decision in the west. But now there was no doubt that the concentration of five CCF armies from the III and IX Army Groups between Chunchon and Inje opposite X Corps and the ROK III Corps meant that an offensive on the eastern front was planned. A major attempt to invade South Korea and outflank the Eighth Army through these roadless wastes of the east-central front had never been made before, although the North Koreans had infiltrated far to the south in this mountainous sector during the Communist January offensive. Although the wild broken country obviously favoured the defence, the hills and bad roads also offered some protection to the offence from air and artillery action. But to have to attempt a major offensive on this front where mobility was so restricted by the terrain showed the bankruptcy of Maoist strategy, with its emphasis on manœuvre, when faced by the Eighth Army's defensive measures. The defence had come into its own since January and had established an ascendancy over the Chinese armies which was even more conclusive than that over the North Koreans on the Naktong in the previous summer.

Van Fleet's plans for defeating the 'Second Step, Fifth Phase Offensive' were soon put to the test. It was estimated that altogether the Communist command had deployed twenty-one Chinese divisions east of Chunchon, supported by six NK divisions. On the night of 15/16 May, twelve Chinese divisions attacked along a twenty-mile front between Naepyong-ni and Nodong, with the initial blow around Hangye-ri against the ROK 5th and 7th divisions of X Corps. The South Korean divisions disintegrated, and the Communists exploited the penetration by swinging east into the rear of the ROK III Corps on the right of X Corps. NK forces were in the van of the attack. All was confusion compounded as the South Koreans on the east coast fell back to the Pangnim-ni-Kangnung section of a trans-peninsular road, a retreat along the east coast from Kansong of fifty miles. On the left of X Corps, now partly enveloped, the Marines around Chunchon were attacked on the 17th, and on their right 2nd Infantry faced a CCF-filled gap to their east while simultaneously fighting heavily along the Soyang River which flows from Inje to Chunchon.

South of Inje the maximum Chinese and North Korean penetration was now over thirty miles, but Van Fleet decided to let the enemy advance here while the 3rd Infantry Division and 187th Airborne RCT were rushed across the peninsula to the X Corps front. During redeployment to establish some coherent

SECOND COMMUNIST SPRING OFFENSIVE
16-21 May 1951

〰〰〰〰 UNC front line, date indicated
⟶ Main CCF and NK thrusts
▨ Land above 700 metres

Scale of Miles
0   10   20   30   40
Scale of Kilometres
0   20   40   60

CCF IX ARMY GROUP = 20, 26, 27 ARMIES
CCF III ARMY GROUP = 12, 15, 60 ARMIES

defence, the ROK III Corps was dissolved and its sector and forces put under X Corps and the ROK I Corps. On the 18th a partially new line was established, the modified NO NAME line, with its apex near Hangye on the Hongchon River, and which ran from there south-eastwards, so firmly narrowing the Chinese penetration to the east. The 3rd Division was sent to the southern limit of the Communist salient but complementing the redeployment was the terrific artillery support, 'the Van Fleet load', which was given the infantry. Over five times the usual ammunition allowance was fired, resulting in a minor shell shortage. While this fighting went on in the east a diversionary attack by two Chinese divisions down the Pukhan was halted at Masogu-ri, and some weak thrusts against Seoul were also checked.

What happened round Hill 800, 'Bunker Hill', on the centre of 2nd Infantry's front is typical of X Corps' reaction to the Second Step offensive, or 'The Soyang River Battle' as the Corps called it.[1] This extremely heavily bunker-fortified complex was held by the 3rd Battalion of the Division's 38th Regiment and lay north of Hangye between the Hongchon and Soyang Rivers. As to the east, 2nd Division fell back on the 18th to the modified NO NAME line, Hill 800 was the northernmost UN position in Korea. When darkness came that night there was the familiar commotion of whistles and horns as the Chinese came in for the second night. Retreating to the fastness of a bunker, after artillery fire had failed to rout the Chinese, one company asked for VT fire (variable time, proximity fuse) to be brought down directly on 800. This went on for some hours; nothing could live through it. One Artillery battalion fired more than 10,000 rounds in support of the 3rd Battalion that night. By 0400 on the 19th the Chinese had broken off; the 3rd Battalion was withdrawn to straighten the line later in the morning. It was obvious, however, before the end of the day that the Chinese offensive had collapsed, and on 20 May X Corps' front was stabilised. Next day 3rd Division moved into Soksa at the apex of the Communist penetration, and Almond was preparing to take advantage of the Chinese collapse by striking north from Hangye to Inje in an attempt to cut the neck of the

---

[1] See Gugeler, pp. 174-90, 'Hill 800'.

strategically useless salient which was the only geographical result of the offensive.

The Second Step Offensive had thus ended after four days with only a relatively narrow penetration on a secondary front. Moreover the Eighth Army as never before was ready to take advantage of this defensive victory by striking back while the Chinese were still off-balance. This third and last attempt by the CCF to conquer South Korea had ended with a carnage unparalleled before or since in the Korean War; thousands of Chinese had died in the blazing napalm detonated in front of X Corps' positions. The Communist losses were estimated to be even greater than in the first spring offensive, 90,000 in the week from 17 to 23 May.[1] There could now be no hope for the unification on Communist terms; the Chinese would have to negotiate on the basis of a divided Korea after this double failure within the space of one month. 'The Communists had proved to themselves, once and for all, that a modern army of moderate size, determined and well equipped, could withstand the assault of great masses of ill-equipped, old-fashioned infantry, no matter how courageous or fanatical they might be. The easy conquest of the civilised world by millions of expendable Asians had turned out to be a futile dream.'[2]

MILITARY OBJECTIVES, POLITICAL OBJECTIVES

Q: General, what is our goal?
Van Fleet: I don't know, the answer must come from higher authority.
Q: How may we know, General, when and if we achieve victory?
Van Fleet: I don't know, except that somebody higher up will have to tell us.

PRESS CONFERENCE, 22 April 1951

While the defeat of the spring offensives made negotiations on the basis of the permanent partition of Korea inevitable, Ridgway and Van Fleet were determined to exploit the Chinese collapse to the maximum. Not only were all possible casualties to be inflicted on the retreating Communists, but it was hoped

[1] *Hearings*, p. 1278.
[2] Cutforth, p. 188.

to advance across the Parallel, seize the Iron Triangle and establish the best possible defence line across central Korea anchored on the estuary of the Imjin in the west and resting on the transpeninsular road from Seoul to Kansong on the east coast.

The new offensive was initiated immediately with the shattering of the Second Step Offensive. In the west I Corps had started moving north as early as 18 May. Patrols advanced to Munsan, past Uijongbu to the Parallel near the 29th Brigade's battlefield on the Imjin, and towards Kumhwa on the fork road from Uijongbu. In the centre the objective of IX Corps was the western end of the Hwachon Reservoir, while in the east Van Fleet ordered X Corps to drive across the base of the Chinese salient formed by their last offensive from Hangye through Inje to Kansong. As the Marines on the left of X Corps advanced towards Yanggu, a task force of infantry from the 187th Airborne RCT led by tanks from 2nd Division struck along the Hangye-Inje road towards the Soyang River on 24 May. During the day Almond helicoptered in and urged a swift advance to exploit to the maximum the collapsing Chinese front. 'I don't care about communications,' he said, shaking his swagger stick at one of the officers, 'You get those tanks on the road and keep going until you hit a mine. I want you to keep going at twenty miles an hour.'[1] It was a visit with happier consequences than Almond's visit to his troops at Chosin; the task force reached the Soyang that afternoon after an advance of about ten miles, but bad roads and the rains, which had just started, prevented the capture of Inje until the 27th. At the end of the month the X Corps was along the Soyang, but the drive to Kansong was cancelled when the town was captured by the South Koreans moving up the east coast. For the first time the Chinese in Korea were surrendering in large numbers; 17,000 prisoners were taken during the last two weeks of May.

By the beginning of June the whole of South Korea except that part west of the Imjin and south of the 38th Parallel had been cleared of Communist troops. What were the current policy directives as the pendulum swung the UN Command back to the Parallel on the KANSAS line? Truman records that the National Security Council discussed Korean objectives on 2 and 16 May:

[1] Gugeler, p. 194.

The Joint Chiefs of Staff, 1949–53. (*Left to right*) Admiral Forrest P. Sherman, Chief of Naval Operations; General of the Army Omar N. Bradley, Chairman of the Joint Chiefs; General Hoyt S. Vanderberg, Air Chief of Staff; and General J. Lawton Collins, Army Chief of Staff. Sherman died in July 1951 and was succeeded by Admiral William F. Fechteler.

Restoration of the ROK Government to President Syngman Rhee, Capitol Building, Seoul, 29 September 1950. (*Left to right*) Doyle Hickey, Acting Chief of Staff, GHQ, FEC; Rhee, MacArthur, Ambassador Muccio, Almond, CG, X Corps; Struble, Seventh Fleet; and Walker, Eighth Army

The United Nations Command delegation to the armistice talks outside 'the United Nations house' at Kaesong, 17 July 1951. (*Left to right*) Maj. Gen. Laurence C. Craigie, USAF; Maj. Gen. Paik Sun Yup, ROKA; Vice Admiral Turner Joy, Senior Delegate and COMNAVFE 1949-52; Maj. Gen. Henry Hodes, USA; and Rear Admiral Arleigh Burke

The Communist delegation to the armistice talks at Kaesong, 16 July 1951. (*Left to right*) Maj. Gen. Hsieh Fang, Chief of Staff, CPV, Maj. Gen. Teng Hua, CPV; Gen. Nam Il, Senior Delegate and Chief of Staff, KPA; Maj. Gen. Lee Sang Cho, KPA; and Maj. Gen. Chang Pyong San, KPA

Regarding Korea, we distinguished between the political aim
— a unified, independent, democratic Korea — and the military aim of repelling the aggression and terminating the hostilities under an armistice agreement. With the fighting ended,
the purpose would be to establish the authority of the Republic
of Korea south of a northern boundary line suitable for
defence and administration and not substantially below the
38th Parallel, to provide for the withdrawal of non-Korean
armed forces from all of Korea, and to build up the ROK
forces so as to deter or repel a renewed North Korean
aggression.[1]

This restated the Administration's revisionist approach to Korea
which had been adopted during the Truman-Attlee meeting
after the Chinese intervention, and the promulgation of which
MacArthur had spoiled in March during the earlier, abortive
peace approach to Peking. Following this policy agreement,
JCS told Ridgway not to go beyond the general vicinity of
KANSAS. The fortification of this line with the object of
making it impregnable was started on 1 June, when a further
advance to WYOMING was ordered, the northward bulge of
which ran through Chorwon and Kumhwa to the Hwachon
Reservoir: Ridgway had authorised local advances to secure
better ground.

   This operation, PILEDRIVER, meant that the base only of the
Iron Triangle was now to be held, and as X Corps advanced to
the Punchbowl depression north of Inje in the east, the South
Korean forces in the ROK I Corps advancing up the east
coast pushed on towards Kosong nearly forty miles above the
Parallel. This was the northern limit of the advance. On 11
June I Corps took both Chorwon and Kumhwa, and on the 13th
two task forces, one from each town, entered the shell of Pyonggang, half-way between Seoul and Wonsan. This marked the
end of the Van Fleet counter-offensive, dictated not by the
Chinese, but by the JCS, and thus the end of major United
Nations ground action in Korea. As the hills above Pyonggang
were held by the Chinese, the Americans withdrew and the
Communists moved into the town again on the 17th. In future
neither side would hold the Iron Triangle in strength. The

[1] *Truman, Memoirs II*, p. 484.

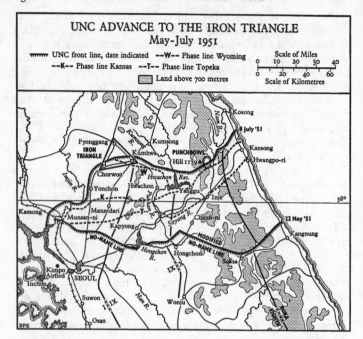

UNC ADVANCE TO THE IRON TRIANGLE
May-July 1951

〜〜 UNC front line, date indicated   --W-- Phase line Wyoming
--K-- Phase line Kansas   -T- Phase line Topeka

Land above 700 metres

Scale of Miles
0   10   20   30   40
Scale of Kilometres
0   20   40   60

fall of Pyonggang found the President paying less attention to
his Korean briefings than usual; perhaps now that MacArthur
was out of the Dai-Ichi, Truman felt that the worst was over.
'There were further advances beyond the Parallel in June,' he
writes in his *Memoirs*, 'including the temporary capture of the
North Korean capital of Pyongyang. . . .'[1]

Alas, there was to be no further occupation of Kim Il Sung's
wrecked capital, but the defeat of the spring offensives and
neutralisation of the Iron Triangle, inflicting an estimated
200,000 casualties on the Communist armies, together with the
relatively swift advance to the Munsan-Kosong line, was nevertheless a great victory for American arms. Could the Eighth
Army have carried on with its drive to the north? For Van
Fleet, the halting of the advance at the dictates of limited war
was a supreme frustration: '. . . we had the Chinese whipped.

[1] *Ibid*, loc. cit.

They were definitely gone. They were in awful shape.'[1] The opportunity would never occur again and that great military *fata morgana* which haunts analysts of the Korean War, 'the Van Fleet battle', remained unfought. But considering that the Chinese armies remained in being, and that the UNC needed another two or three divisions to engage in a war of manœuvre, it seems unlikely that even Pyongyang could have been taken. Yet the doubt remains; worth many an interesting but futile speculation as to whether mounting Chinese resistance was inevitable once KANSAS was retaken, or whether Washington's leash alone stopped Van Fleet. But in any case a serious advance to the waist (as Ridgway saw) would have completely altered the power relationship between East and West in Korea once again with incalculable consequences. Whether of course the momentum which was built up in May and June 1951 by Van Fleet's victory should have been kept up to get a swift armistice agreement is another matter.

Diplomatically, too, the Chinese had suffered by the episode of the spring offensives which convinced many UN members of Peking's utter intransigence, moving them closer to the American view. On 18 May, the same day that Dean Rusk announced that the US recognised the Republic of China as the legal government of the country and not the 'colonial Russian government' in Peking, the UN General Assembly passed a resolution demanding that members place an economic embargo on trade with Communist China. The draft had originally been presented to the Additional Measures Committee by the US representative. The resolution, passed by 47-0-8, with the neutrals abstaining, and with the Soviet bloc boycotting the proceedings, proposed a complete embargo by all states, whether in the UN or not, on the shipment to areas controlled by the Chinese Communists and North Koreans of 'arms, ammunitions and implements of war, atomic energy materials, petroleum, transportation materials of strategic value and items useful in the production of arms, ammunition and implements of war.' By October, thirty-eight UN member states and six non-members had said that they would observe the embargo.

British support of the resolution indicated in particular a

[1] Cagle and Manson, p. 309. Cf. Van Fleet, 'The Truth About Korea', *Life*, 11 & 18 May 1953.

closer alignment between London and Washington. While there had been a total US trade embargo with Communist China since 16 December 1950, and although the British Government had banned export of many strategic materials to China after the outbreak of war in Korea, rubber exports from Malaya to China had soared in the first quarter of 1951 to 46,500 tons. It was also alleged that Hongkong provided a valuable channel of strategic items to China. Speaking in the Commons on 7 May Sir Hartley Shawcross, President of the Board of Trade, announced that since 9 April the UK had restricted Malayan rubber imports into China to 2,500 tons a month. Trade with China was necessary for Hongkong's existence, but there were strategic controls, and besides, MacArthur himself had permitted some Japanese trading with China for the same reasons of economic necessity.

Other and more significant developments showed an even closer accord between the two Governments. On 5 June the British delegate to the UN Trusteeship Council supported an US resolution which deferred indefinitely consideration of Peking's admission to this body. It was also noted that in this period of mounting discussion of forthcoming armistice negotiations there was no longer any suggestion from Whitehall that the cease-fire talks should be linked with a political conference on Far East problems which would include the subjects of Formosa and China's UN seat. Almost certainly MacArthur's dismissal had cleared the way for this tougher British line towards Peking.

About the most significant British concessions of all at this time, the whole truth is not known. In February 1952 Churchill, by then Prime Minister, replying to a Labour censure motion against him for his remarks to Congress in January that if a prospective Korean armistice were broken by the Chinese, UN counter-action would be ' prompt, resolute and effective' revealed that he was only voicing policy agreed by the Attlee Government. In May 1951 the Labour Cabinet had agreed with Washington that in the event of heavy air attacks against the UNC from Chinese bases, the British Government would assent to UN counter-action ' not confined to Korea', which meant strikes against the Manchurian airfields. London in this case had insisted on the right of consultation. In September 1951 the

British had agreed that if the truce talks broke down, action 'of a more limited character' could be taken without consultation. This probably meant air strikes against those North Korean target systems such as hydro-electric plants, which had not been attacked up to that time. Churchill's parliamentary victory on this occasion was compounded from both the embarrassment of the former front bench which had not expected their pledge to be revealed, and the anger of the Labour Left that Attlee and Morrison had in effect pledged the UK to a course of action in certain circumstances which differed little from the MacArthur programme. The effect of this commitment, if publicised, in the 1951 British general election when the Conservatives had been branded as 'warmongers' would have been most interesting.[1]

With Korean military and political objectives now agreed within the Administration and with its Allies, it only needed some indication from the Communists that they were willing to talk for negotiations to begin. But how was this first move to be made? A direct approach by the West was out of the question, implying as it did a position of weakness. It was the Chinese who had twice in two months attempted unsuccessfully to conquer South Korea. Keeping up the military pressure, combined with assurances to negotiate an armistice on the basis of the *status quo*, seemed the only way. As early as 17 May, Senator Edwin Johnson had tabled in the Senate a resolution calling on all belligerents in Korea to declare an armistice along the 38th Parallel by 25 June, the first anniversary of the outbreak of war. These proposals were significantly given full coverage by the Soviet Press and radio. Johnson's resolution was followed by a radio talk on 26 May by Lester Pearson, Canadian Minister of External Affairs, sponsored by the UN, in which he said that

[1] See H. C. Deb. Vol. 496 coll. 963 ff. (26 February 1952) for Churchill's speech. Acheson has also implied that one result of the Truman-Attlee talks was a secret agreement for joint US-UK action against China in the case of complete evacuation from Korea after the Chongchon. Discussing the framing of Churchill's reply mentioned above, Acheson writes: 'Churchill's draft speech did not answer his critics, it slew them. It stated what action his critics, when in power, had agreed with us should be taken, if, after General MacArthur's defeat in North Korea, worst came to the worst. Those orders were still top secret, and perhaps, still are. At any rate it was out of the question that their specific contents should be revealed.' Acheson, *Sketches from Life*, p. 74.

the object of this 'limited United Nations war' was not 'the kind of complete capitulation of the enemy with which we have been made familiar' but the defeat of aggression against the Republic of Korea. This was again followed by Trygve Lie on 1 June, who said that a cease-fire around the Parallel would fulfil the main purpose of the Security Council's resolutions of the summer of 1950 — nothing of course was said now about the General Assembly's resolution of 7 October.

The same day, during the MacArthur Hearings, Secretary Acheson made the most authoritative statement yet of the Administration's Korean objectives. Replying to Senator Connolly he differentiated between the long-term aim of Korean unification which had been an US objective since the Cairo Declaration of 1943 and an UN objective since 1947, and the immediate aim of restoring peace and ending aggression in Korea. Referring to the immediate unification of Korea, Acheson formally and finally reversed Administration policy of the previous autumn: 'I do not understand it to be a war aim.' Some Republican senators were slow to catch on; they still thought, or wanted to think, of Korean unification. When Acheson was asked to explain it all over again next day by Senator Smith, he wearily replied: 'Well, I tried to make that clear yesterday, Senator, I am glad to go over it again.' The Secretary then said that if a cease-fire were arranged around the Parallel, 'that would accomplish the military purposes in Korea'. Acheson would attempt many times again in the next eighteen months to make it all clear, but the principle of *cuius regio, eius religio* which he had applied to the two Korean states was unacceptable to many besides Republican senators.[1]

Throughout most of June, no one really knew how the cease-fire talks would begin. Informal and secret talks between West and East began in New York. The diplomatic ambiguities were as unprecedented as the military frustrations which now passed from MacArthur to Van Fleet. At last on 23 June, Jacob Malik gave a talk on 'The Price of Peace' in the same series over the UN radio station in New York in which Pearson had spoken. His remarks on Korea were immediately taken as indicating Moscow's new policy:

[1] Acheson's important testimony is in *Hearings* pp. 1729, 1782-4.

. . . The Soviet peoples further believe that the most acute problem of the present day — the problem of the armed conflict in Korea — could be settled.

This would require the readiness of the parties to enter on the path of a peaceful settlement of the Korean question. The Soviet peoples further believe that as a first step discussions should be started between the belligerents for a cease-fire and an armistice providing for the mutual withdrawal of forces from the 38th Parallel.

Can such a step be taken? I think it can, provided there is a sincere desire to put an end to the bloody fighting in Korea.

I think that, surely, is not too great a price to pay in order to achieve peace in Korea.[1]

The Communists had withdrawn their previous demands that cease-fire talks be contingent on withdrawal of all foreign troops from the country, that Korean domestic affairs must be settled by Koreans, and that Formosa and a UN seat should be given to the People's Republic of China. They had abandoned their ambition of taking South Korea. These concessions to the Administration's demand to negotiate for a *status quo* armistice and nothing else had been made at the point of the gun held by Truman, Acheson, Ridgway and Van Fleet and for no other reason. The defeat of the spring offensives had opened the way to armistice negotiations. For different reasons both sides had decided to accept a Korean stalemate.

[1] R.I.I.A. *Documents*, 1951, p. 633.

CHAPTER FIFTEEN

THE MACARTHUR HEARINGS

> There is no policy — there is nothing, I tell you, no
> plan or anything. . .
> DOUGLAS MACARTHUR, *Military Situation in the Far East*, p. 68.

> There can be, I think, no quick and decisive solution to
> the global struggle short of resorting to another world war.
> The cost of such a conflict is beyond calculation. It is there-
> fore our policy to contain Communist aggression in different
> fashions in different areas without resorting to total war. . . .
> The application of this policy has not always been easy
> or popular. . . .
> GEORGE MARSHALL, *Ibid.*, p. 366

THE REBEL

THE MacArthur Hearings opened on 3 May when the Joint
Senate Foreign Relations and Armed Services committees
met in Room 318, the caucus room, of the Senate Office Building. Under the chairmanship of Senator Richard Russell the
committees were 'To conduct an inquiry into the military situation in the Far East and the facts surrounding the relief' of
General MacArthur. Before the hearings ended on 25 June
besides MacArthur all the leading personalities of the Administration — with the exception of course of the President — would
have testified on the ends and means of American Foreign policy.
This avalanche of talk, with its numerous digressions away from
Korea on such subjects as Yalta, the fall of the Kuomintang, the
theory of strategic air power, the prerogatives of presidential
advisers, make the massive five volume, two million word record
of *Military Situation in the Far East* a vast political case history
of America's emergence from the cocoon of a foreign policy
based on total solutions to the reality of the limited ends and
means of the cold war. The technical military and political
problems of how to end the Korean War were often obscured by
the verbiage of the politicians and their respective military

supporters; the scene was well set by Senator Russell in opening the Hearings:

> Gentlemen of the Committee on Armed Services and the Committee on Foreign Relations, today we are opening hearings on momentous questions. These questions affect not only the lives of every citizen, but they are vital to the security of our country and the maintenance of our institutions of free Government. . . . General of the Army Douglas MacArthur has consented to be the first witness at these hearings. I am sure it is unnecessary for me to attempt to recount in detail the deeds and services which have endeared General MacArthur to the American people. . . .[1]

MacArthur, who had flown down from New York with Whitney that morning, said that he had no prepared statement to make, his comments had been fully made in addressing Congress. But in his testimony which went on for three days he powerfully amplified the points he had made in his rousing address on 19 April. His often lengthy responses to the questions asked him by his Senators branched out from the Korean problem into a critique of the Administration's entire policy which gave the Republicans a most powerful case against the President.

First of all, the nature of MacArthur's revolt was only touched on in the Hearings. In never admitting that the JCS contingency paper of 12 January did *not* mean the support for his programme to end the Korean War, MacArthur was presenting his case as one shared by all responsible military men who believed in meeting force with maximum counterforce, the traditional American prescription for war. But of course MacArthur himself had seen Inchon, the drive to the Yalu and the war of containment all in political terms, and it would become clear in the Hearings once again that he was advocating a rival political policy to that of the Administration, using the absolutist doctrine to maximise

---

[1] It was not entirely a matter of principle that the transcript of the Hearings was published. The compromise agreed between the Democrats' wish for closed hearings and that of the Republicans for complete publicity was ingenious. The stenotyped transcript was, after 'takes' of a few hundred words, removed from Room 318 and the text cut on mimeograph stencils. After security deletions by State and Defence officials, the duplicated sheets were then run off for newsmen.

support for his policy. During his testimony Marshall told the Senators that while both he and Eisenhower in the past had disagreed with their civilian superiors they had not carried that difference to the public, and that MacArthur's actions as a theatre commander in doing this were 'wholly unprecedented'. It soon became clear, however, that MacArthur believed so heinous was the Administration's refusal to use maximum force against the new enemy, and so disastrous was the foreign policy which they were trying to implement by limited means, that he had found loyalty to the State and to the Administration mutually exclusive. In a speech a few weeks after the end of the Hearings to the Massachusetts legislature, he outlined his position:

> I find in existence a new and heretofore unknown and dangerous concept that the members of our armed forces owe primary allegiance or loyalty to those who temporarily exercise the authority of the executive Branch of the government, rather than to the country and its Constitution which they are sworn to defend. No proposition could be more dangerous. . . . [1]

Like the rebels of antiquity who invoked natural law to justify their revolts against tyrants who had violated traditional restraints, so MacArthur was appealing to the traditional American manner of waging war to justify his revolt against Truman. Like de Gaulle in June 1940 (and the French Algerian insurgents of 1958 onwards), or Stauffenberg and the men of 20 July 1944, he insisted that his loyalty was to his country and not to its political masters.

The Administration's way of fighting the Korean War, he told the Senators, was a disastrous innovation of policy; it was an un-American way of waging war:

> That policy . . . seems to me to introduce a new concept into military operations — the concept of appeasement, the concept that when you use force, you can limit that force . . . To me that would mean that you would have a continued and indefinite extension of bloodshed, which would have limitless

[1] Quoted in Rovere and Schlesinger, p. 315.

— a limitless end. . . . If that is the concept of a continued and indefinite campaign in Korea, with no definite purpose of stopping until the enemy gets tired or you yield to his terms, I think that introduces into the military sphere a political control such as I have never known in my life or ever studied. . . .

The general definition which for many decades has been accepted was that war was the ultimate process of politics; that when all other political means failed, you then go to force; and that when you do that, the balance of control . . . is the control of the military. . . . I do unquestionably state that when men become locked in battle, that there should be no artifice under the name of politics, which should handicap your own men. . . .[1]

There were three choices facing the Government in Korea. 'Either to pursue it to victory; to surrender to an enemy and end it on his terms; or, what I think is the worst of all choices, to go on indefinitely and indefinitely, neither to win or lose. . . .' Limited war was thus an opportunist and immoral temporising with violence, a policy of muddling along: 'There is no policy —there is nothing, I tell you, no plan or anything.' With no policy for winning in the 'normal way', the war would go on 'with no mission for the troops except to resist and fight in this accordion fashion — up and down — which means your cumulative losses are going to be staggering.'[2]

. . . I shrink — I shrink with a horror I cannot express in words at this continuous slaughter of men in Korea. The battle casualties in Korea today probably have passed the million mark. Our casualties, American casualties, have passed 65,000. . . . I cannot brush that off as a Korean skirmish. I believe that it is something of such tremendous importance that it must be solved, and it cannot be solved by the nebulous process of saying, 'Give us time, and we will be prepared; or we will be in a better shape two years from now' — which is argumentative (sic). . . .

What are you trying to protect?

[1] *Hearings*, pp. 39-40, 45.
[2] *Ibid.*, 67, 68, 30.

The war in Korea has already destroyed that nation of
20,000,000 people.

I have never seen such devastation.

I have seen, I guess, as much blood and disaster as any living
man and it just curdled my stomach the last time I was there.
After I looked at all that wreckage, and those thousands of
women and children and everything, I just vomited. . . .
What are you going to do? Once more I repeat the question,
What is the policy in Korea?[1]

ALONE IF NECESSARY

To end this purgatory of limited war, MacArthur proposed
an ultimatum to Peking, on threat of application of his programme, to 'withdraw their troops and cease their depredations
in the area of North Korea'. As if emphasising how this proposal fitted into the traditional Manichaean opposites of total
war, total peace, MacArthur mentioned his opposition to all war.
The course of action he proposed, he said, would bring the war
in Korea to a decisive end and avoid World War III:

> Now, no man in the world is more anxious to avoid the expan-
> sion of war than I am. I am just 100% a believer against war.
> I believe the enormous sacrifices that have been brought about
> by the scientific methods of killing have rendered war a
> fantastic solution of international difficulties. . . . It is a form
> of mutual suicide; and I believe that the entire effort of
> modern society should be concentrated in an endeavour to
> outlaw war as a method of the solution of problems between
> nations. . . . It is my belief that if you bring the Korean
> War to a successful conclusion, you will put off the possibility
> and diminish the possibility of a third world war.[2]

But just what was involved in the MacArthur plan for ending
the war? Was it possible to use war to end war? All along Mac-
Arthur elaborated on his strategy to cripple China's military
effort in Korea. 'They are peculiarly vulnerable to the process

[1] *Ibid.*, 82.
[2] *Ibid.*, 145.

of blockade, and the process of internal disruption by bombing. . . . All I contemplate and hope for is to disrupt the capacity of that industrially weak nation to supply the sinews of war to their armies in Korea and, therefore, make them stop this savage slaughter of our troops.' If the distribution system of China were broken up in conjunction with blockade, Peking would be unable to maintain its army of four million. Only a million men, perhaps half that, could be supplied and equipped. Anyone, however, who suggested sending US ground troops to the Chinese mainland ought to have his head examined, MacArthur had said earlier, because 'a very modest effort, military effort, on our part' would end the war.[1]

But here he had difficulties with his listeners. What would happen, Lyndon Johnson wanted to know, if the Chinese were driven back across the Yalu but still refused to sign a treaty? The United States might then have a limited war with China. 'Such a contingency,' replied the General, 'is a very hypothetical query. I can't quite see the possibility of the enemy being driven back across the Yalu and still being in a posture of offensive action.' Even more important was the possibility of whether the Russians would intervene on behalf of their Chinese allies. To Senators Wayne Morse and Brien McMahon, two of the most persistent of his interrogators, MacArthur gave this answer:

> My own belief is that what will happen in Korea and Asia will not be the deciding factor in whether the Soviet attacks us or not. If he is determined to attack us, sooner or later he will, and there is nothing that I can see that would prevent it. . . .
> . . . I believe the best way to stop any predatory surprise attack by the Soviet Union or any other potential enemy is to bring this war in Korea to a successful end, to impress upon the potential enemy that the power we possess is sufficient if he goes to war to overpower him. . . .

Considering American superiority in air-atomic striking power, the possibility of Soviet intervention should be risked, as 1951 was almost the last time when this atomic capability would have an absolute ascendancy over the USSR. For, although even at

[1] *Ibid.*, pp. 42-44, 58, 135-7, 156-7.

the time of the Hearings, MacArthur conceded, the US was 'rather inadequately prepared' to withstand a surprise one-way atomic strike by the Russians, he thought that the US should 'defend every place, and I say that we have the capacity to do so.'[1]

Underlying his whole testimony was belief that a showdown between the West and the Communists, if it had to come, should come over Korea. 'You assume of course,' he said to McMahon, 'that relatively your strength is going up much more than the enemy's. That is a doubtful assumption. . . .' When McMahon reminded MacArthur that six months before he was as sure that the Chinese would not intervene, as now he was that the Russians would not come in, the General gave an answer which neatly summed up his position on possible Soviet intervention: 'Everything that is involved in international relationships, Senator, amounts to a gamble, risk. You have to take risks.' In April 1953, in a letter to Senator Harry Byrd, MacArthur made quite explicit his belief that time was running out for the West:

Underlying the whole problem of ammunition and supply has always been the indeterminate question as to whether or not the Soviet contemplates world military conquest. If it does, the time and place will be at its initiative, and could not fail to be influenced by the fact that in the atomic area the lead of the United States is being diminished with the passage of time. So, likewise, is the great industrial potential of the United States as compared with the Communist world. In short, it has always been my own belief that any action that we might take to resolve the Far Eastern problem now could not in itself be a controlling factor in the precipitation of a world conflict.

If the Communist world was swiftly catching up with the US in nuclear-industrial technology, then it would be best to chance a showdown with the USSR over Korea in operations which anyhow would destroy Red China's 'flimsy industrial base'.[2]

Yet in stating during these exchanges that he was not an

[1] *Ibid.*, pp. 211, 69, 221, 217, 83.
[2] *Ibid.*, pp. 80, 76, *Interlocking Subversion in Government Departments*, pp. 2033-35.

authority on global defence, and did not want to be involved in anything except his 'own area', the Far East, MacArthur had weakened his case. Similarly, when McMahon read a statement which the General himself had made when he was Chief of Staff twenty years before to the effect that the national strategy of war must be decided by the head of state, and that any other course would 'not constitute delegation but abdication', MacArthur's ironic reply still gave the important point to his Democratic opponent: 'As I look back, Senator, upon my rather youthful days then, I am surprised and amazed how wise I was.'[1]

MacArthur obviously saw his proposals as going to the heart of the West-East conflict. His plan to defeat China, if successful, would liberate all of Korea, the UN war aim of the previous October. It would further change the whole strategic picture in the Far East, stopping the march of the 'new Frankenstein' which he saw as an aggressive imperialistic power in its own right, and partly reversing the great defeat that the United States had suffered with the advent of Mao Tse-tung:

It is my own personal opinion that the greatest political mistake we made in a hundred years in the Pacific was in allowing the Communists to grow in power in China. I think at one stroke we undid everything, starting from John Hay, through Leonard Wood, Woodrow Wilson, Henry Stimson, and all those great architects of our Pacific policy. I believe it was fundamental, and I believe we will pay for it for a century.

Another result of victory in Korea would be that the emerging nations of Asia might still be saved for the West. The whole economic future of the United States would be involved with raising the standard of living in the Far East. So the apocalyptic prophesy which MacArthur had given on Leyte in 1944 would come true, and, under American leadership, as the General said in Seattle in November 1951 'the human and material resources of the East would be used in compensation for the manufactures of the West'.[2]

Finally, unlike Taft and Hoover, MacArthur, despite his

[1] *Ibid.*, p. 105.
[2] *Ibid.*, p. 32, Whitney, p. 497.

Asian orientation, continually emphasised the importance of Western Europe, and the world-wide import, as he saw it, of fighting the war in Korea to a conclusive finish. The first line of defence for Western Europe, as he had so often emphasised since Inchon, was on the Yalu and not the Elbe. As for the British, their 'fundamental interest . . . is involved in this question of the Western Pacific, and I believe most sincerely that they are cutting their own throats in following the plans they have of such complete support of Red China. . . . I believe that if you do not carry this thing to a success in the Western Pacific, that it is the beginning of the downfall of Europe; that is one of the most serious arguments I make.'[1]

With its emphasis on sea and air power, on Asia as the centre of the world struggle, on the quick, total solution and above all on unilateral American action, MacArthur's testimony as a whole was the most coherent and acceptable rationalisation at the time of the revolt of the Right against Truman. 'With MacArthur,' Rovere and Schlesinger have written, 'American isolationism received its classical and mid-century formulation.' Korea was the decisive battleground between East and West. There was no substitute for victory; containment meant appeasement, defeat, death. If necessary, the Korean War would have to become the final crusade, a last crusade to destroy Communism and carried out by the United States alone:

Senator Green: Alone?
General MacArthur: Alone, if necessary. If the other nations of the world haven't got enough sense to see where appeasement leads after the appeasement which led to the second World War in Europe, if they can't see exactly the road that they are following in Asia, why then, we had better protect ourselves and go it alone.[2]

THE WRONG WAR

Following MacArthur's testimony Administration officials appeared before the Committees through the days of the second

[1] *Hearings*, p. 297-8.
[2] *Ibid.*, p. 42.

Chinese offensive and Van Fleet's advance north of the 38th Parallel. Leading the opposition to MacArthur was George Marshall, the culmination of the rivalry between the two men which had started forty years before. Now, the two senior generals of the United States Army in their final clash respectively represented the opposing political viewpoints of the Democrats and the Republicans, Western Europe-first and Asia-first, limited solutions and total solutions to the cold war. After Marshall came Truman's High Command, Bradley, Collins, Vandenberg and Sherman, followed by the Secretary of State. Other witnesses with special experience of the Far East included Maj.-Gen. Barr, whose 7th Infantry Division was the only American formation to reach the Yalu, and General Wedemeyer, Chiang's former chief of staff. Ex-Defence Secretary Louis Johnson also appeared.

The administration's two most obvious points against MacArthur which were argued time and again were simple and predictable. First, limited war in Korea gave the West time to build up its own strength. Second, MacArthur's programme might not end the war in Korea by defeating Red China; and, if applied, his offensive against the Chinese mainland might bring in the USSR and so trigger off World War III when the United States would be disastrously separated from its NATO allies. Permeating all Administration testimony in making these points was an explicit Clausewitzian rationale, a repudiation of MacArthur's absolutism, a concept which, of course, Marshall and Bradley themselves believed during World War II. 'Your objectives in a war,' Bradley told Senator Morse, 'are not entirely military. In other words, the end results of a war are a combination of military and political considerations, and you use the military to obtain your political objectives.' 'You cannot separate the military reasoning from your political background,' Collins emphasised. 'It is impossible to do it. The two are interwoven so thoroughly that I couldn't possibly consider here military factors . . . in a vacuum.' These considerations, when applied to Korea in the light of the Administration's grand strategy, meant, said Marshall, that the fighting was necessarily a 'limited war which I hope will remain limited.' Bradley defined it as a 'limited war, in that it is limited to an area'. Although Bradley. thus mentioned the geographical limitations of the war, he here

T

ignored the parallel limitations on weapons, target systems and resources ordered by the JCS, although in discussing objectives he revealed, in agreement with Acheson, that these too were limited. The Administration's Korean war aims, he said, were now 'less than' a free and United Korea.[1]

It was Bradley himself, who, emerging as the most forceful spokesman of the Administration, simultaneously outlined the Truman-Acheson grand design, its application in Korea and the futility of war with China.

> The Joint Chiefs of Staff, in view of their global responsibilities and their perspective with respect to the world-wide strategic situation, are in a better position than is any single theatre commander to assess the risk of general war. Moreover the Joint Chiefs of Staff are best able to judge our own military resources with which to meet that risk. . . .
>
> From a global viewpoint . . . our military mission is to support a policy of preventing Communism from gaining the manpower, the resources, the raw material and the industrial capacity essential to world domination. If Soviet Russia ever controls the Eurasian land mass, then the Soviet-satellite imperialism may have the broad base upon which to build the military power to rule the world. . . .
>
> Korea, in spite of the importance of the engagement, must be looked upon with proper perspective. It is just one engagement just one phase of the battle. . . . As long as we keep the conflict within its present scope, we are holding to a minimum the forces we must commit and tie down. . . . We have recommended against enlarging the war. The course of action often described as a 'limited war' with Red China would increase the risk we are taking by engaging too much of our power in an area that is not the critical strategic prize.
>
> Red China is not the powerful nation seeking to dominate the world. Frankly, in the opinion of the Joint Chiefs of Staff, this strategy would involve us in the wrong war, at the wrong place, at the wrong time, and with the wrong enemy. . . .[2]

Just how inadequate they judged MacArthur's proposals to

[1] Ibid., pp. 898-9, 1224, 610, 1065, 955.
[2] Ibid., p. 730-2.

be for defeating China was hammered home by the Joint Chiefs to the Senators. In his opinion, Bradley told Senator Connolly, to really bring China to her knees, 'you would have to do something like the Japanese did. Go in and try to get a decision. I do not believe you could get any decision by naval and air action alone.' Ground troops would be necessary. Unlike MacArthur, Collins thought that the USSR had considerable military capability in the Far East. Furthermore, any attempt to knock out China by bombing the communication and industrial centres would inevitably lead to city bombing, so consolidating the people behind a government which would by then be committed to an all-out war with the United States. Besides, the US had its own 'sanctuary' in Japan and Okinawa which was more vulnerable to enemy air action than Manchuria and China. Both China and the US were waging war under certain tacitly recognised ground rules, Bradley said.[1]

Admiral Sherman, while in favour of an UN blockade, was against an unilateral US blockade, for, without her Allies, in Marshall's words, it would 'leak like a sieve'. Port Arthur and Dairen were Soviet-controlled ports, and the act of war of an US naval blockade against these ports could precipitate a general conflict. Moreover, the effect of a naval blockade would be modified in two ways. China could still get supplies over her long land border with Russia although in the Admiral's opinion the trans-Siberian was overtaxed. Secondly, although cutting off maritime imports of machine tools, petroleum, rubber, chemicals, pharmaceutical products etc. would create great economic and military difficulties, especially if augmented by action smashing up China's railways and waterways, disruption would be a long-term process. China with its primitive subsistence economy could not be quickly reduced as could a highly industrialized country. It was best to rely on an economic blockade.[2]

Acheson had some figures on this subject to show that even before the UN economic embargo resolution, Western European nations had prohibited for export to the Communist bloc by early 1951 90% of the items which the Americans thought to be of strategic importance. The 'facts show that there already

[1] Ibid., pp. 745, 1220, 1245-6, 751, 892.
[2] Ibid., pp. 1512-25.

exists on the part of the major industrial countries of the free world an economic embargo with respect to materials of primary strategic significance'. This was the best, the safest way to hurt Peking.[1]

Undoubtedly one of the most important witnesses against MacArthur was Vandenberg, who gave the Senators a short lecture on air power which probably had more effect than Marshall's defence of containment or Acheson's enthusiasm for collective security and trade embargo. The Air Chief of Staff said that in 1951 the USAF could launch an offensive against either China or Russia, but not both countries. SAC could level the cities of China, but there was 'a possibility that it would not be conclusive', as nothing in war was certain. Most important of all the attrition on his 'shoestring air force' might be so great that the USAF's principal function as 'the sole deterrent to war . . . the single potential that has kept the balance of power in our favour' might be affected. For SAC had to be kept intact for striking at the USSR within whose borders alone lay the true strategic industrial targets of world Communism. To bomb China was to 'peck at the periphery' for there were no worthwhile strategic targets in that country, and it might invite such attrition that the United States would be left 'naked for several years to come.' The Air Force — about sixty-eight groups strong in 1951 — would have to be twice the size before the MacArthur plan could be contemplated; the aircraft industry could not replace the losses in such a campaign until 1953.[2]

Vandenberg mentioned another important consideration. If the US ever lost its Western European bases in going it alone

---

[1] *Hearings*, pp. 1726-7. In October 1951 Peking announced that there had been a complete change in the direction of China's foreign trade. In 1950 69% of Chinese exports had gone to 'capitalist states', and 78% of its imports had come from these countries. In September 1951 the ratios were respectively 22% and 29%. Even allowing for political reasons in this remarkable change, the Western embargo must have had considerable effect. See *Survey of International Affairs 1951*, p. 364-5. Although Britain and other West European countries relaxed their embargo after 1953, the US has maintained its total ban on trade with China and North Korea.

[2] For Vandenberg's testimony discussed here see *Hearings*, pp. 1378-1402. The nomenclature of the standard division of the USAF, the group, was changed to wing during the Korean War. While a heavy bomber (B-36) group numbered about thirty aircraft, and a medium bomber (B-29 or B-50) group about thirty-six planes, light bomber and fighter/fighter-bomber groups numbered about fifty and seventy-five aircraft respectively.

against China, SAC could be almost crippled if it were called upon to deal with Russia. Deprived of its NATO bases an inter-continental bomber with flight refuelling could only make two or three missions a month from North America; using the bases the same aircraft could make fifteen or twenty missions against the USSR. Without these overseas bases the USAF would have to be five or six times its present size. The bases while 'not abso-lutely essential' were 'highly desirable'. As far as Korea was concerned the main task of air power was to isolate the battle-front by interdicting enemy communications between the Yalu and the fighting.[1]

Vandenberg's point about keeping SAC intact was obliquely confirmed by Maj.-Gen. Emmett O'Donnell who had com-manded FEAF Bomber Command for the first six months of the war in Korea. O'Donnell complained that it was a 'bizarre' war, for his B-29s, as Vandenberg had earlier testified, had been used in 'blowing up haystacks'. The entire Korean peninsula, O'Donnell said, was 'just a terrible mess. Everything is des-troyed,' and thus there were no strategic targets left. In Novem-ber 1950, SAC could have hurt Communist China a great deal; if ordered to attack Manchuria, O'Donnell stated, he wouldn't have been able 'to keep the cooks on the ground'. But now, in June 1951, things were different because there was 'heavy air opposition' from the MIGs. O'Donnell acknowledged there-fore that a decision might not be possible with Red China which would still leave SAC intact to act as the deterrent: ...'Whether we can do it and still retain the Sunday punch for Russia in case they can get out of bounds is a problem out of my province.[2]

Those within whose province the problem lay had no doubts whatsoever that the Sunday punch must be preserved for the Russians. But it was easier to demolish MacArthur's case than to convince the Senators and the public that the Administration's way of ending the war was the only way, letting the war fizzle

[1] *Hearings*, p. 507. According to leaked House testimony in July 1951 there were only eighty-seven B-36 intercontinental bombers ready for action. Sixty were being modernised, and production was only two to three monthly. Rovere and Schlesinger, p. 242.

[2] *Ibid.*, pp. 3065-111. Ten years later O'Donnell, commander of the Pacific Air Forces at Pearl Harbour, was still confused and confounded by bizarre wars. Commenting on the uselessness of SAC in Laos, he was quoted as saying, 'It's like knocking an ant off a bicycle.' *Time*, 6 January 1961.

out around the 38th Parallel so that a *status quo* settlement could
be negotiated. Marshall, for example, was asked several times
how the war could end. He replied:

> . . . inflict terrific casualties on the Chinese Communist
> Forces. If we break the morale of their armies, but, more par-
> ticularly, if we destroy their best-trained armies as we have
> been in the process of doing, there, it seems to me, you
> develop the best probability of reaching a satisfactory negotia-
> tory basis. . . . If it goes on in the manner that it has for the
> last two months, and particularly in the last two weeks (9 May),
> it would appear that the trained fabric of the Chinese Com-
> munist forces will be pretty well torn to pieces. . . . We have
> apparently been encountering their best troops, and this most
> recent encounter has involved tremendous casualties for them.[1]

As Collins said, the Chinese did not have 'endless trained manpower'; and Acheson remarked that Peking would not 'pick
out its army' as the place to start eliminating its overpopulation
problem. This apparent reduction of containment to a technique
of bringing mechanised death to thousands of Asiatics through
the meatgrinder was hardly a good political point. During Vandenberg's testimony the General said that the Administration's
objective was 'to kill as many Chinese Communists as is possible
without enlarging the war at the present time in Korea'. Understandably, Senator Hickenlooper queried this whole underlying
drift of much Administration evidence:

> I understand that death and destruction is an unavoidable
> part of warfare. There is no question about that, but I empha-
> sise it because whenever we have had testimony here, at least
> so far as I know, the only concrete objective that has come out
> repeatedly is the killing of Chinese.

The war aim of a divided Korea was as dubious as the means to
bring it about, the Republican Senators would conclude.[2]

THE GRAND DESIGN: SITUATIONS OF STRENGTH

Both Acheson and Marshall attempted at length to lift the

[1] *Hearings*, pp. 365, 430.
[2] *Ibid.*, pp. 1226, 1945, 1385, 1471, 3589-90.

Administration's policy out of this context of strategic opportunism and its corollary, not completely unreal, that containment also meant limited war without end while America was converted into some sort of Lasswellian-Spartan garrison state. The aggression had been crushed, and the Communist aim of imposing their rule throughout Korea had been defeated. 'The operation in Korea has been a success', Acheson insisted. A 'powerful impetus' had been given to rearmament within and without NATO, and since June 1950 the US had doubled the number of men under arms. 'Production of matériel has been boosted to a point where it can begin to have a profound effect on the maintenance of the peace.' The idea of collective security had been put to the test and had been sustained: 'The nations who believe in collective security have shown that they can stick together and fight together.'[1] There was no question of fighting a general crusade against Communism everywhere, but Communist aggression anywhere would be met if possible. There was a plan, Acheson was saying, the plan was working, and Korea within the logics of post-1947 American foreign policy was a victory, an important victory. The defeat of the Kremlin's most powerful predatory move since 1945 would bring about a change in the enemy's behaviour, certainly as far as direct military aggression was concerned, possibly in other ways:

. . . what we must do is to create situations of strength; we must build strength; and if we create that strength, then I think the whole situation in the world begins to change so far as the potentialities of the Soviet Union being able to achieve its present purposes is concerned; and with that change there comes a difference in the negotiating position of the various parties, and out of that I should hope that there would be a willingness on the side of the Kremlin to recognise the facts which have been created by this effort of ours and to begin to solve at least some of the difficulties between east and west. . . .[2]

Similarly Bradley stated that, 'We are trying to contain aggressions', and Marshall, in the passage quoted at the head of

[1] *Ibid.*, pp. 1716-17.
[2] *Ibid.*, p. 2083.

this chapter, was even more frank in outlining the plan in which, to date, the resistance to Communist aggression in Korea had been the single most important development. The Administration's policy as explained in the Hearings was thus to keep the Western alliance intact, rearm as quickly as possible, maintain the *status quo*, and so preserve the balance of power under the umbrella of SAC by using limited war in Korea as an instrument of policy.

It should be briefly discussed here why Acheson's famous testimony quoted above emphasising how situation of strength were inseparable from the Administration's policy illustrated a subtle change of emphasis in the containment policy, one which has remained at the bottom of much Western policy towards the Communist bloc ever since. As evolved in 1947 the policy reflected Kennan's belief that resistance to Soviet expansion would result in the 'break-up or gradual mellowing' of that power. A *détente*, if it came, would be the result of domestic change in the opposing camp. Moreover, Kennan had quite consistently tended to oppose the military aspects of containment, and divergences between him and Acheson on this issue had become more frequent until he was succeeded as head of the State Department's Policy Planning Staff by Paul Nitze at the end of 1949.

On the other hand, without necessarily repudiating Kennan's ideas, as the implementation of foreign policy proceeds on many levels simultaneously, Acheson himself ever since two background briefings in February and March 1950, ironically part of the same series as the Press Club 'defence perimeter' speech, had insisted on the importance of negotiating from strength with the Communists. This was an aspiration implicit in containment from the beginning but only given a new, dramatic, significant urgency with the decision to press ahead with the crash programme on the hydrogen bomb, the North Korean invasion, and the subsequent beginning of North Atlantic rearmament in 1950. As Coral Bell had seen in her exemplary study of the whole problem, *Negotiation from Strength*, Acheson's re-casting of containment during 1950-51 with his approach that a possible settlement would come less from internal change than from diplomatic adjustment represented a revisionist rather than a *status quo* concept in the application of containment . . . 'the whole situation in the world begins to change . . .' And there can be little doubt that underlying much of the more intelligent (and pessimistic) Administration testimony in the Hearings is a concern as to whether 'negotiating from strength' would ever become a viable policy.

Unfortunately for the Administration, however well the practitioners of containment understood their own policy, and however well that policy was working, what came over to the public was the rather unexciting generalities of 'collective security', and not a dynamic presentation of a comprehensible Western strategy. The Hearings had clarified containment as much as it would ever be clarified; but the historical, military and moral necessity for this national (and Western) policy had not been projected. Probably both the Administration's reticence and the public's unreceptiveness were hangovers from the absolutist tradition which MacArthur personified. The elements of self-interest in containment were only tentatively explained; everything that had happened since 1947, reaching its climax in Korea, could not be interpreted alone in idealistic terms of upholding the UN, in defending collective security or resisting aggression. Yet some form of containment, with its mixture of idealism and *Realpolitik*, was the *only* foreign policy the United States could ever have in the nuclear age. Communicating it adequately was too much for the eroded political resources of the Truman Administration in 1951.

There were other ambiguities raised by Truman's lieutenants in the Hearings. Bradley's insistence on the 'wrong war' which MacArthur might precipitate meant that in other circumstances the Administration would certainly fight the right war, presumably over Western Europe. Bradley had no great liking for limited war *per se* and dismissed Korea as 'a poor place to fight war',[1] which showed along with other testimony that the Administration wished to liquidate its Far Eastern commitment as soon as possible — and assumed that once the *status quo* was re-established between the armies the Communists would too. That the Chinese would not oblige and that there could be another *kind* of limited war in Korea to that which had been hitherto fought only became apparent after the truce talks became bogged down. Furthermore when the Administration decided during the course of the Hearings to risk some of

[1] *Hearings*, p. 891.

MacArthur's measures (with Attlee's concurrence) in the event of heavy Communist air attacks on the Eighth Army from Manchuria, it showed that almost as important as the argument over an Atlantic versus a Pacific strategy was the question of timing—and the very closely related issue of just at whose bidding SAC was to be turned loose north of the Yalu.

But the most important question of all raised in the Hearings has still not been answered: can a democracy compete in peacetime military preparations with a totalitarian society? MacArthur tried to justify his case by implying No; the Administration, recognising that the Korean War was useful in giving an 'impetus' to building strength, assumed that time was on their side. Yet the transcript shows that Administration spokesmen always qualified their remarks that time was on the side of the West. Although this preoccupation with the timing was muted, it has an even greater, painful, interest a decade later in the heyday of Khrushchev's missile diplomacy. Thus Admiral Sherman, while acknowledging the value of Korean rearmament, commented, '. . . definitely, in the short term, time is on our side'. Acheson similarly hedged: 'The basic premise of our foreign policy is that time is on our side, if we make good use of it.' While Vandenberg, who had told the Committees that he had been alarmed at the extent of Soviet technical progress during the second war, was rather more explicit. When he was asked by Lyndon Johnson if time was on the side of the West: 'Well, if war were a science instead of an art, Senator Johnson, I would answer unequivocally that time is not in our favour. . . . I would say that the general indications would be that it is questionable whether time is on our side. . . .'[1]

The significance of these qualifications, as of MacArthur's underlying preoccupation that the early 1950s was the last period when the United States could have risked with impunity total war with the USSR, was barely recognised at the time. It became clear during the Hearings that public opinion did not want MacArthur's 'victory' in Korea, and that to end the war as soon as possible was the national objective. For the remainder of the Administration's life its control over Korean policy was unchallenged, but the vast discontent with the Democrats which had started with the China White Paper and reached its climax

[1] *Ibid.*, pp. 1613, 1720, 1440.

with MacArthur's recall was perpetuated by the Hearings, and continued to permeate all political life. If Truman's grand strategy, however inadequately presented and however inadequate to force the coming stalemate war to an end, was probably the right one, he could never become a popular war leader in the turmoil created by the tensions of limited war. Eventually the Democrats would be toppled in November 1952, and the chief beneficiary of MacArthur's revolt would be another five-star general; while the programme of limitless objectives which MacArthur had outlined in the Hearings would eventually, after subtle transmutations, become best known to the world through that supporter of containment until 1950, John Foster Dulles.

As for MacArthur's personal position, the Senate inquiry had pricked the huge bubble of emotion generated by the recall. The problem was now how to get peace in Korea, but MacArthur was not now involved in it. Other forces besides political ones were working for the president against his erstwhile arch-opponent. In the first year of the Korean War the national employment figure reached the all-time high of sixty-two million jobs. MacArthur with his Taftite domestic ideology of the 'simple but immutable pattern etched by our forefathers' belonged to an earlier, inner-directed America that could have no place in the affluent society created by limited war. After the Hearings the General returned to New York following a speech-making tour, and went to the ball game. A tape recording of a seventeen-gun salute was played, and as the General left the stand the strains of *Old Soldiers Never Die* started ringing out. Suddenly a wag in the crowd shouted, 'Hey Mac, how's Harry Truman?' The roars of laughter against the General was solid evidence that the great April binge was at last over. Demos had decided that even MacArthur was human, and would have to fade away.

KOREA—LIAISON OFFICERS MEET

The MacArthur Hearings ended on 25 June, one year after the North Korean invasion, with O'Donnell's testimony; the Senators issued their varying statements in the next few days. A joint statement said that, 'The issues that might divide our

people are far transcended by the things which unite them. . . .'
Malik's speech in New York on 23 June had seemed to indicate
that the path to peace charted by the Administration in the
Hearings was the right one. On the 27th Gromyko told Admiral
Kirk, the US ambassador in Moscow, that the USSR had in
mind discussions on purely military questions between the
commanders, and that political questions would not be discussed.
The next day Trygve Lie stated his opinion that the US had the
right to conclude a cease-fire without any further authorisation
by the Security Council or the General Assembly, but that
political negotiations on the future of Korea must be left to these
UN bodies. Lie also considered at this time that the 'Committee
of sixteen', set up as a consultative body in Washington after
the Chongchon by the Allies who had forces in Korea, did not
have the status of an UN body. Day by day decisions would be
therefore made outside the direct surveillance of the UN,
allowing greater flexibility.

The only dissenting voice from the arrangements being made
to initiate truce talks came from President Rhee, understandably aggrieved that the unified Korea he had spent his life working for was about to be made impossible as a result of the proposed military settlement between the two blocs. Rhee stated
on 30 June that he would refuse to recognise any situation
that 'conflicts with national sovereignty or territorial integrity
of the Republic of Korea'. For him, he emphasised, a cease-fire
at the 38th Parallel would not be acceptable. But this problem
seemed — at the time — the least of all worrying Washington. Its
Korean satellite would just have to go along with the truce talks.
Preliminary arrangements were now initiated within a week of
Malik's offer. On 29 June a directive was sent to Ridgway which
ordered him to broadcast the following message to the Communist Commander-in-Chief:

As Commander-in-Chief of the United Nations Command I
have been instructed to communicate to you the following:
'I am informed that you may wish a meeting to discuss an
armistice providing for the cessation of hostilities and all acts
of armed force in Korea, with adequate guarantees for the
maintenance of such armistice.
Upon the receipt of word from you that such a meeting is

desired I shall be prepared to name my representative. I propose that such a meeting could take place aboard a Danish hospital ship in Wonsan Harbour.'

Following this message sent on 30 June, a reply came from Pyongyang on 2 July signed by Kim Il Sung as Supreme Commander of the KPA and General Peng Teh-huai — this radiogram revealed for the first time the identity of the commander of the CPV. They proposed that instead of meeting on the *Jutlandia* at Wonsan, negotiations be opened at Kaesong, in the no-man's-land west of the Imjin and about three miles south of the 38th Parallel. Ridgway agreed, answering with a suggestion that representatives from the two commands meet on 10 July, and liaison officers on the 5th; and after another radio exchange an initial meeting for 8 July was set. The three UN liaison officers would travel to Kaesong by helicopter leaving Kimpo at 0900, while the Communist officers would jeep down from Pyongyang the previous evening.

On the morning of the 8th, the UN helicopter carrying the three UNC officers, Col. Jack Kinney, USAF, Col. James Murray, USMC, and Col. Soo Young Lee, ROKA, crossed the Imjin. Circling the bombed ruins of Kaesong, the machine descended on a marked landing field outside the town. After an ominous silence the three men were approached by an escort officer and two interpreters, and taken to a former tea house which subsequently became the site of the armistice negotiations. Present were Col. Chang, KPA, Lt.-Col. Kim, KPA, and Lt.-Col. Tsai, CPV. Arrangements were then made for the main delegations to meet on 10 July in the same place.

In Washington, the Joint Chiefs[1] thought the talks would last about three weeks, but being military men they also had to be realistic. It might take as long as six weeks to get an armistice. After all, four Communist attempts and one United Nations attempt, all unsuccessful, to unify Korea in a single year had led to an obvious military stalemate. The Communists were now unable, and the West unwilling, to seek 'victory' in Korea.

---

[1] Sherman died suddenly in Naples on 22 July and was replaced as CNO on 1 August by Admiral William F. Fechteler.

PART III

WAR FOR PEACE

8 July 1951 – 27 July 1953

CHAPTER SIXTEEN

RELAXING THE PRESSURE

> Under the slogan of safeguarding the revolutionary base
> areas and safeguarding China, we can rally the greatest
> majority of the people to fight single-mindedly, because
> we are the victims of oppression and aggression. . . .
> Defensive battles in a just war can not only exercise a
> lulling influence on the politically alien elements, but
> mobilise the backward sections of the masses to join in the
> war. . . .
>
> MAO TSE-TUNG

MEETING AT THE KAESONG TEAHOUSE

FOLLOWING the safe return of Kinney and his liaison team
from Kaesong on the afternoon of 8 July the official UNC
communique concluded that 'The meeting was harmonious
throughout.' This rash hint of optimism showed that, understandably perhaps, no one on the Western side had any idea
whatsoever that the military armistice negotiations which had
begun that day would go on for over two years before a cease-
fire was signed. On the morning of 10 July the helicopter carrying the senior UN delegate, Vice-Admiral Turner Joy, Commander Naval Forces Far East, and four other delegates, flew
from Munsan across the Imjin to Kaesong. In a jeep ride from
the landing site they were taken to the building assigned to the
delegation, 'the United Nations house', and from there to the
conference site, the tea house on the outskirts of Kaesong at
Kwangmum Dong. Throughout, the UNC delegates were surrounded by North Korean guards brandishing burp guns; the
staff officers who had travelled to Kaesong by truck from Munsan with the previously agreed white flags on their vehicles had
been photographed by Communist newsmen to provide evidence that the UNC was coming to Kaesong to surrender. Western journalists were not present. Thus from the very beginning
it became clear that although Kaesong was thought to be

in no-man's land, it was really controlled by the Communists.

Entering the teahouse at 1100 hours, the UNC delegation was escorted into a room where the five-man Communist delegation was standing. One of them said, 'I am Nam Il,' to which the reply was given, 'I am Admiral Joy.' The North Korean delegates were clad in grey, formal, Soviet-style uniforms, while the Chinese were dressed in their characteristic cotton khaki uniforms with no rank insignia of any kind: the UN personnel wore khaki drills and shirts.

After a few minutes delegates with their staffs and interpreters, who had waited outside, convened in an adjacent conference room facing each other across a green felt-covered table to discuss the first item, the agenda. Besides Joy, the UNC delegation consisted of Rear-Admiral Arleigh Burke, who had earlier in the war been Joy's Deputy Chief of Staff and who later was to become Chief of Naval Operations, Maj.-Gen. Henry Hodes, Eighth Army Deputy Chief of Staff, Maj.-Gen. Lawrence Craigie, USAF, and Maj.-Gen. Paik Sun Yup, CG, ROK I Corps. General Nam Il, the senior Communist delegate, as noted above, was Chief of Staff of the KPA, but the real leader of the delegation, to whom all its members deferred, was Maj.-Gen. Hsieh Fang, Chief of Staff of the CPV. Most of the talking was done by these two men together with Maj.-Gen. Lee Sang Cho, Chief of Staff, Front Headquarters, KPA, for the two other Communist delegates, Lt.-Gen. Teng Hua, CPV, and Maj.-Gen. Chang Pyong San, Chief of Staff of the KPA I Corps, rarely spoke. Two staff officers of the KPA-CPV delegation, Colonels Tsai and Chang, who had met Kinney on 8 July, did more of the actual negotiating than any of their superiors; while the personnel of the UNC delegation changed frequently, there were fewer changes with the Communist team.

No sooner had the talks started than they were broken off by Joy on the 12th over the Communist refusal to admit newsmen as part of the UNC delegation. Ridgway asked for a reassurance on this and other matters relating to the neutrality of the site before the talks could be resumed, and after a favourable reply from Kim Il Sung and Peng Teh-huai on 14 July, the delegations met again the next day. It was agreed that Kaesong should be the centre of a neutral zone, five miles in radius, which only military police with small arms could enter, and that within half-a-mile radius from the conference site there should be no armed men.

The road leading to Kaesong from Munsan was to be unrestricted to members of the UNC delegation's party; it was also agreed that the personnel of each delegation's party should not exceed 150, and that the composition of each party was the sole responsibility of each side. Thus the way was open for newsmen to visit the conference site.

Even before the talks had been broken off it was clear that there were great differences between the two sides in their negotiating positions. The general objectives of the UNC delegation were to get a cease-fire along the militarily defensible line of contact between the armies, a joint commission to supervise the truce, and the exclusion of all political questions from the negotiations which were regarded as purely military discussions to stop the fighting. Nam Il had insisted that the agenda itself should make specific reference to the establishment of the 38th Parallel as the demarcation line, and to the withdrawal of foreign troops from Korea. Both troop withdrawal and re-establishment of the Parallel were regarded as political questions by Ridgway and Joy. The Parallel carried with it a recognition of the pre-war political division of Korea, and, besides, the firing line in July 1951 was defensible, unlike the Parallel.

Joy in his book on the armistice negotiations, *How Communists Negotiate*, amusingly illustrates the differing attitudes on the fight for the agenda. Americans meeting to discuss, for example, arrangements for a baseball game might submit an agenda as follows (1) Place of game, (2) Time of game, (3) Selection of umpires. The Communists were asking for an agenda which ran: (1) Agreement that the game is to be played at Shanghai, (2) Agreement that the game is to be played at night, (3) Agreement that the umpires be Chinese. The agenda as agreed on 26 July resembled that proposed by the UNC; but while refusing to budge on the content of the agenda, Joy had also made a concession by not insisting on immediate International Red Cross visits to the Communist POW camps. The order of the items on the agenda reflected the importance of the demarcation line to both sides; its real significance only came to be seen later:

(1) Adoption of agenda.
(2) Fixing a military demarcation line between both sides so as to establish a demilitarised zone as a basic condition for a cessation of hostilities in Korea.
(3) Concrete arrangements for the realisation of a cease-fire and an armistice in Korea, including the composition, authority and functions of a supervising organisation for carrying out the terms of a cease-fire and armistice.
(4) Arrangements relating to prisoners of war.
(5) Recommendations to the governments of the countries concerned.

When the talks on Item 2 began on 27 July, the two sides seemed as far apart as ever on the demarcation line, with the Communists insisting on the Parallel, and the UNC suggesting a line slightly to the north of the firing line to compensate for the cessation with the proposed truce of their air and naval action which ranged to the Yalu. This was a bargaining manœuvre to underline the UN objective of a demarcation line based on the front line. Soon the dispute over the admittance of the newsmen was seen as only the first of many incidents which were presumably planned by the Communists for the purpose of attempting to strengthen their negotiating position, or for propaganda reasons, or both. On 4 August heavily armed Chinese soldiers marched across the path of the UNC delegation as they approached the teahouse. Ridgway then broke off the talks for six days, but after resumption on 10 August, following reassurances that such incidents would not happen again, the talks were still deadlocked. If the 'incidents' which eventually culminated in the abandonment of Kaesong by the armistice delegations were intended as an attempt to put pressure on the UNC delegation, the angry abuse and recrimination between the delegates which became a formalised pattern of charge, counter-charge, accusation, counter-accusation, faithfully reflected not only the military stalemate in Korea — the thunder of the opposing artillery in the hills to the east of Kaesong could be heard by the delegations as they argued — but West-East relations generally.

There were different manifestations of acrimony. At the first meeting in Kaesong, Joy had been provided with a chair so low that he almost sank out of sight of Nam Il towering above him on the other side of the table; and the miniature North Korean flag which stood on the green felt between the delegates was carefully constructed so it topped that of the UN by six inches. While the Communists reasonably insisted on being addressed as 'the delegation of the KPA and the CPV', they referred to the ROK and Chiang Kai-shek as 'the murderer Rhee' and 'your puppet on Formosa'. Again, the ROK delegate objected to the North Korean use of the term *Chosen* to mean Korea; this had been used by the Japanese and *Hankuk* was the name always used by the South Koreans. The following excerpt from the transcript of 11 August is characteristic; the previous day there had been a silence of two hours eleven minutes in the conference room following Joy's reiteration of the UNC position on the demarcation line:

General Nam Il: With regard to your statement yesterday that your side is through with discussing our proposal of the 38th Parallel, I cannot but consider it as a rude and improper declaration that you are not willing to reach a settlement. . . . I have pointed out that your insistence on placing the military demarcation line to the north of the 38th Parallel and within our positions proves that it is you who have malicious political intentions . . . we contend that the arguments supporting your proposal are untenable and, therefore, your proposal is unreasonable, unfair and indeed absurd. . . .

Admiral Joy: . . . Yesterday you used the word 'arrogant' in connection with a proposal the United Nations Command delegation now has before this conference. The United Nations Command delegation has been in search of an expression which conveys the haughty intransigence, the arbitrary inflexibility, and the unreasoning stubbornness of your attitude. Arrogance is indeed the word for it. From the very first day of these conferences your arguments have reflected the very essence of arrogance. . . . In adhering to your futile fixation on an effort to divide Korea by cloaking political manœuvres under the guise of a military armistice, you have blocked every effort of the United Nations Command delegation to make progress towards a cessation of bloodshed and suffering. . . . Your arrogance and bad faith stain through every attempted deception. The immutable facts hold you guilty of having delayed, and of continuing to delay, the end of hostilities in Korea. . . . Today we have again made no progress. . . .[1]

This daily exchange of *tu quoques* at Kaesong which had been transferred on 17 August to a joint subdelegation created to discuss Item 2 came to an end when the talks were again broken off 23 August. This followed another 'incident' when the UNC was charged by the Communist liaison officers of dropping a napalm bomb during the night of 22/23 August in the neutral conference area. This was an inversion of the earlier technique of threatening the UNC delegation, for they now could be presented as representatives of a Command which opposed peace in Korea. The evidence presented was ludicrous according to the UNC liaison officers who examined the site of the 'attack', and when they refused to accept UNC responsibility, the talks were immediately recessed by the Communist liaison officers — hardly possible without previous high-level arrangements. In the next two months there were thirteen alleged major violations of the Kaesong neutral zone charged by the Communists, but all except three of these were either fabricated or the work of irregular Korean partisans who opposed the negotiations. However much these incidents succeeded as a propaganda ploy for internal Communist consumption, as a device for delaying the talks and improving the Communist position at the negotiating table they failed, for in late August an Eighth Army limited objective offensive was initiated, partially restoring the military pressure which had been relaxed since June.

PANMUNJOM: PERMANENT CONFERENCE SITE

Ridgway was determined to remove the conference site from Kaesong and, after denouncing Communist charges of violations of the neutral zone as 'baseless and intentionally false' in a broadcast on 6 September, he suggested that the site of the talks be moved to a more suitable place. After several meetings by liaison officers at the hamlet of Panmunjom, on the main road

[1] See Joy, pp. 40-53. A set of the Kaesong-Panmunjom transcript is available at the Hoover Institute, Stanford University, California.

five miles east of Kaesong and about fifteen miles west of Munsan, and where the officers had met regularly since the beginning of the truce talks, the Communists proposed on 7 October
that the armistice negotiations be transferred to this tiny cluster
of deserted huts. Ridgway agreed and after meeting a dozen
times between 10 and 22 October, the liaison officers worked out
an eight-point agreement, ratified by the delegations, with five
associated 'mutual understandings', which henceforward controlled arrangements at the conference site until the end of the
war. Panmunjom was designated as the centre of the circular
neutral zone of a 1,000 yard radius, and a three-mile radius
around Munsan and Kaesong was also neutralised, as well as
two hundred metres on either side of the Kaesong-Munsan road.
Reducing the size of the neutral area and relocating the site
more exactly in no-man's-land both helped to preclude incidents
and Communist exploitation of their position as 'hosts' at Kaesong. The Communists built the delegates' and conference tents,
the UNC provided light and heat and also four captive balloons
floating at 1,000 ft. altitude to mark the periphery of the neutral
zone.

With these administrative arrangements completed, the talking got under way again on 25 October when the plenary session

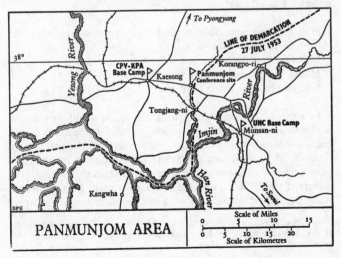

PANMUNJOM AREA

once again referred Item 2 to a subdelegation. The opening exchanges in this subcommittee at Panmunjom is an excellent illustration of the long, indecisive, suspicious palaverings which were as characteristic of the negotiations as the exchanges of abuse:

Maj.-Gen. Lee Sang Cho, KPA: Now we will open the meeting.
Maj.-Gen. Henry Hodes, USA: Okay.
 Lee: Do you have any ideas about the military demarcation line?
 Hodes: We ended the last conference before the suspension by asking for your proposal. Do you have one?
 Lee: We should like your opinion first.
 Hodes: We gave our opinion many times, and asked for your proposal based on our proposal. As it was your proposal to have the subdelegation meeting, we expected you to have a proposal. Let's have it.
 Lee: You said you had made a new proposal, but we have heard nothing new which would break the deadlock.
 Hodes: That's right. You haven't.

(After fifty minutes discussing the subject, a recess of fifteen minutes was taken.)

 Hodes: Were you able to find some proposal to solve the problem while you were out?
 Lee: Did you?
 Hodes: Is the answer that you didn't?
 Lee: We haven't thought of one.[1]

In spite of this nonsense, with the building of permanent facilities at Panmunjom the procedure of the conference soon became institutionalised. Initial contact between the two delegations could be made on a radio telephone circuit between the liaison officers at Kaesong and Munsan. After each meeting, staff officers at the UNC Apple Orchard base camp at Munsan would study the transcript and prepare a number of contingency papers

[1] Vatcher, *Panmunjom*, pp. 80-81. This definitive survey of the whole course of the Korean military armistice negotiations is written by a former staff member of the UNC delegation.

for the next day, so that their delegates could counter immediately any number of possible ploys by the Communists. During their discussions the delegates attempted, as far as possible, to get some sort of agreement on broad principles on the agenda item being discussed, before it was turned over to subdelegation. When the subdelegation deadlocked, the item was taken up by the staff officers, and most of the wording of the final armistice agreement was the result of staff officer and liaison officer meetings. Each morning the respective delegations would leave Kaesong and Munsan for Panmunjom. The Communists travelled in a black Imperial Chrysler captured in Seoul during the summer of 1950, escorted by Soviet and captured US jeeps, while from Munsan the UNC delegation continued to fly to the talks by helicopter. Then,

> Sharply at the agreed hour delegates filed into the conference tent, the Communists entering at one end, the UNC at the other. After everyone was seated, the Senior Delegate who had not opened the previous meeting would speak. Each side took turns in opening the meetings. The Senior Delegate, sitting in the centre of the other delegates along a long green-felt-covered table, would read one sentence, stop, and the interpreters would stand up and translate, first into Korean, then Chinese in the case of the UNC, or into English and Chinese in the case of the Communists. Afterwards the Senior Delegate would speak another sentence, and so on until he had completed what he had to say. . . . After each side had elaborated on its stand to the extent that it was able and willing, one would exclaim, 'If you have nothing more to say, I suggest that we recess until tomorrow, at this time.' To this the other would usually reply, 'I agree.' Both sides would then file out. . . . Outside the tent at Panmunjom correspondents always gathered anxiously. . . .[1]

It was against this background that the talks by the subdelegation on the demarcation line went on. The two months hiatus in the negotiations with Van Fleet's limited offensive had not been without effect, for the Communists were now no longer insisting on the 38th Parallel, and agreed (on 31 October) to a

[1] Vatcher, p. 78.

demarcation line based on the firing line. Disagreement now centred around the UNC claim to Kaesong and the Communist insistence on a contact line which would have meant a twenty-mile UNC retreat from the actual firing line between the armies. Joy records that the Communist 'line of contact' was actually behind some Eighth Army divisional headquarters. On another occasion, to emphasise that a position near Panmunjom asked for by the Communists was well behind the front, a helicopter was offered their staff officers to fly over a battle that was being fought five miles north of this point. The offer was declined.

The arguments on Item 2 moved into their final phase on 5 November when the UNC made a new proposal. Abandoning any claim to Kaesong they proposed a demarcation line based completely on the contact line which would be the centre of a four-kilometre wide demilitarised zone. But by assuming that fighting would continue while the agenda items were discussed, the proposal stipulated that, subject to agreement by staff officers, the demarcation line must be the 'actual line of contact at the time of the signing of the armistice'. This meant, of course, that the Eighth Army would still be able to keep up the pressure on the enemy, and understandably the Communists refused to accept this proposal. They demanded that either agreement on Item 2 should mean an immediate cease-fire while discussion on the other items proceeded, or that the UNC delegation should formally propose that the agenda be revised so that Item 2 become Item 5. But the time was past for this, which would have put the onus for temporising on the cease-fire on the UNC. Once again there was an impasse.

The question of whether the military pressure was to be relaxed or not was of crucial significance to the negotiations at this stage. Besides the naval blockade of North Korea and the associated 'siege' of Wonsan, Hungnam and Songjin which tied down numbers of troops deployed against a possible amphibious operation, a large-scale tactical air interdiction effort, Operation STRANGLE was under way, designed to isolate the battlefront from the Yalu.[1] Even if this primary objective was unattainable, considerable attrition was being inflicted on the Communist armies and their supply lines. Most important of all there was the increasing power of the Eighth Army. By August 1951 Van

[1] See Chapter 20.

Fleet had over 586,000 men under him, and although only 229,000 were in the Eighth Army proper and the rest under his control in the various UN contingents and the ROK army, EUSAK, its headquarters transferred from Taegu to Seoul, was by now the hardest-hitting army the US had ever put into the field up to this time. After a pause in operations during mid-summer, Van Fleet had decided on a limited offensive with three objectives. First, he wanted to keep the Communist armies away from the Hwachon reservoir, the source of Seoul's water and electric power. Second, to protect the road and railway which ran north from the ROK capital to Chorwon, at the base of the Triangle, and the pivot of the central and western fronts. Thirdly, as always, he wanted to inflict as many casualties as possible on the Communists with his firepower.

Between August and October there was heavy fighting on the eastern front as X Corps and ROK I Corps improved their positions north and east of Hwachon Reservoir in the Punchbowl area. West of this depression, where the key peak of Taeusan or Hill 1179 had been taken in July, 2nd Infantry Division after two months of heavy fighting for the aptly named Bloody Ridge-Heartbreak Ridge complex had reached its final objectives by 14 October. A few weeks before, by 18 September, the Marines had consolidated north of the Punchbowl, so firmly anchoring their line on the northwest leg of the Soyang. From here the front ran north-eastwards below the Nam River valley to the coast south of Kosong. Between the Punchbowl and Kumhwa, further west in IX Corps sector, 24th Division had taken the heights above Kumsong by 21 October, the limit of the advance here, and over twenty miles north of the Parallel. On the western front, too, the pressure had been kept on by I Corps, when five divisions, ROK 1st, Commonwealth, US 1st Cavalry, 3rd and 25th Infantry, advanced northeast and west of the Imjin to establish a new line, JAMESTOWN, by 12th October which cushioned the MSR to Chorwon.[1] It was during the fighting on the heights of JAMESTOWN that Private William Speakeman, attached to the KOSB, won the VC on the night of 4/5 November when the Chinese attacked and eventually captured Hills 217

---

[1] 1st Commonwealth Division was formed on 28 July 1951 from 28th Commonwealth Brigade, 29th British Brigade, 25th Canadian Brigade and other units. See Barclay pp. 83-93.

and 317 about two miles west of the Imjin. An indication of the future course of the war was that during these operations unprecedented Communist artillery concentrations had been used. The possession of so much commanding ground all along the front had now given Van Fleet his strongest possible defensive line in the area north of the Parallel, and the casualties inflicted during this limited objective offensive must have contributed to the Communist concessions in proposing Panmunjom as the conference site and in tentatively agreeing to abandon their demand for a demarcation line based on the 38th Parallel.

The end of this limited offensive and the beginning of final agreement on the demarcation line came on 12 November when Ridgway ordered Van Fleet to cease offensive action and to begin an active defence of the front line, the Main Line of Resistance. From now on Van Fleet could not make an attack involving over a battalion (about 1,000 men) without CIN-CUNC's permission. Operations were limited to strengthening the MLR, resisting enemy attacks, and establishing an outpost line up to 5,000 yards ahead of the main positions. Ridgway's order to cease operations preceded a new UN proposal on Item 2 at Panmunjom on 17 November which had previously been discussed by the Committee of sixteen. This was an ingenious compromise with the Communist demand for a cease-fire once agreement on Item 2 was reached: it also showed the urgency that Washington felt about ending the war. The proposal suggested that the current contact line should constitute the demarcation line in the centre of the demilitarised zone *provided the armistice was signed within 30 days of agreement on the proposal*. If the armistice were not signed within this period, the demarcation line would be the contact line when the armistice was eventually signed.

Whilst the new proposal apparently gave every incentive to reach an agreement quickly, it also stabilised the front for a month, for obviously neither side, and especially the UNC, would undertake offensive operations during the thirty-day period if territorial gains would have to be relinquished when an armistice was signed. The Communists had thus gained a thirty-day *de facto* cease-fire on the ground, for after the sub-delegation agreed to a slightly modified version of the UNC pro-

posal on the 23rd, followed by a swift survey of the front line by
the staff officers, the plenary session, meeting for the first time
since 25 October, ratified the agreement on 27 November.
According to Joy, the proposal had been decided on over the
strenuous protests of his delegation at Panmunjon and Ridgway.
'This concession to the Communists was the turning point of
the armistice conference. Thereafter, because the fighting slack-
ened, we lacked the essential military pressure with which to
enforce a reasonable attitude towards the negotiations.'[1] Opening the way to this concession, Joy thought, was the failure to
realise the use the Communists would make of the order of the
agenda, with the subject of the demarcation line at its head. This
meant that Nam Il and Hsieh Fang could reasonably insist that
agreement on a cease-fire should be reached prior to the other
substantive items. No general agreement was signed at Panmunjon by 27 December: in attempting to trade a temporary
cease-fire for a quick armistice the Administration had lost its
gamble.

THE POLITICAL WAR

From this breathing space given the Chinese in November-
December 1951 dated the construction of the vast fourteen-mile
deep defensive network which protected the Communist armies
for the remainder of the Korean War. It was deeper than anything on the Western Front in the World War I, and was even
engineered for defence against nuclear attack. The Eighth
Army's MLR, on the contrary, consisted of a bunkered trench
system slashed across the Korean hill-tops from sea to sea, with
an occasional half-organised secondary line. Both sides were
really immobilised under the conditions they had chosen to
fight. The Communist artillery, heavily reinforced by the end
of 1951 was dug in so deeply that it could not be moved out and
up to support an advance of their infantry. Relying on its firepower to offset the prodigal use of Chinese manpower, the United
Nations Command had almost no mobile reserves to exploit
enemy weaknesses and initiate advances — even if the high command had so desired.

[1] Joy, p. 129.

Thus, during the twenty months to the armistice, ground fighting consisted mostly of skirmishing in between the two stalemated main lines. From the rival outposts, which sometimes jostled each other, patrols fought to probe enemy defences, take prisoners, gather intelligence, and generally cushion the Main Lines of Resistance. Sometimes large attacks were launched up to divisional strength by the Communists and which then resulted in counter-commitment up to regimental strength by the Eighth Army. Thus, from this time on to the end of the war, most battles bear the names of outposts and vital positions on the MLR . . . The Hook, White Horse Hill, Sniper's Ridge, Triangle Hill, Capitol Hill, Luke the Gook's Castle. Ridgway's successor, Mark Clark, has written of this strange fighting, 'the enemy was able at any time to mass enough men to dent our line wherever and whenever he desired. No defence-line can be so strong that it cannot be dented by an enemy who is ready to expend the lives necessary to make the dent. When the enemy made these pushes we would roll with the punch rather than stand our ground stubbornly and be overrun. Then if the Communists had taken terrain features important to our line of defence we had to counterattack to capture them. That is where we suffered our heaviest casualties. . . .'[1]

Would there have been any way to avoid this costly positional war, where not only defensive networks behind the 155-mile front were comparable to those of World War I, but UNC strategic force/distance ratios, with divisions occupying 5/10 miles, were approaching those of Flanders? Could the Eighth Army again have driven towards the Yalu, or defeated decisively the Communist armies *inside* Korea, something different from that advocated by MacArthur? Van Fleet fervently thought this, and believed that as Japan, apart from the UK, was an un-equalled overseas base for the US, the best strategy would have been to attempt an advance to the 'waist', with supporting amphibious landings.[2] However initially plausible this idea of amphibious landings at Wonsan, Haeju, Chinnampo or Kojo appears, there seem no real grounds for thinking that it could

---

[1] Clark, *From the Danube to the Yalu*, p. 101.
[2] See Cagle & Manson, pp. 308-9 and *Interlocking Subversion in Government Departments*, pp. 2030-31 for Van Fleet's advocacy of the waist as the best defence line.

have succeeded without reinforcements. Ridgway, the best judge of military reality in Korea during 1951, thought himself that the Munsan-Kosong line was the best, and his opinion may be taken as authoritative: 'If we had been ordered to fight to the Yalu, we could have done it — if our government had been prepared to pay the price in dead and wounded that action would have cost. From the purely military standpoint the effort, to my mind, would not have been worth the cost. . . . We stopped instead on what I believe to be the strongest line. . . .'[1] And Mark Clark has written that, while he submitted a 'broad plan' to win the war, this could not have been accomplished without bombing the trans-Yalu bases, for, with limited forces, 'and without widening the scope of the conflict' he would have incurred 'overwhelming losses . . . staggering casualties'.[2]

Yet in the two years of the 'talking' war, US casualties alone, which numbered just under 80,000 for the first year of the war, ran to about 30,000 each year. There can be no doubt that there was an excellent chance that a truce might have been forced from the Communists by the end of 1951 if the pressure had been kept up, not by using either the MacArthur or Van Fleet plans, but by fighting a different kind of limited war to that which the Administration found itself committed once the truce talks started. Kissinger has commented that the 'decision to stop military operations, except those of a purely defensive nature, at the *very beginning* of the armistice negotiations reflected our conviction that the process of negotiation operated on its own inherent logic independently of the military pressures brought to bear. But by stopping military operations we removed the only Chinese incentive for a settlement; we produced the frustration of two years of inconclusive negotiations.'[3] And Bernard Brodie, a senior member of the RAND Corporation, has correctly seen the long-term political disadvantages that followed from this failure to force the war to its end:

No doubt the cardinal error as we see it today was the halting of our offensive at the moment when the Communists first indicated an interest in opening armistice negotiations. This

[1] Ridgway, *Soldier*, p. 219-20.
[2] Clark, pp. 72, 12-13.
[3] Kissinger, *Nuclear Weapons and Foreign Policy*, pp. 50-51.

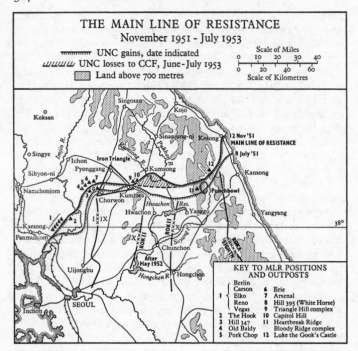

THE MAIN LINE OF RESISTANCE
November 1951 - July 1953

〰〰〰 UNC gains, date indicated
〰〰〰 UNC losses to CCF, June-July 1953
▨ Land above 700 metres

Scale of Miles
0   10   20   30   40
0   20   40   60
Scale of Kilometres

KEY TO MLR POSITIONS AND OUTPOSTS

1	Berlin	6	Erie
	Carson	7	Arsenal
	Elko	8	Hill 395 (White Horse)
	Reno	9	Triangle Hill complex
	Vegas	10	Capitol Hill
2	The Hook	11	Heartbreak Ridge
3	Hill 347		Bloody Ridge complex
4	Old Baldy	12	Luke the Gook's Castle
5	Pork Chop		

error, attributable to our political rather than our military leadership, had nothing to do with our desire to keep the war limited. Interrogation of prisoners revealed that the Communist Chinese army facing us had been in a truly desperate condition undergoing large scale defections, when a few words by Jacob Malik . . . caused us to relax the pressure. Although, there were some limited UN offensives afterwards, the pressure was never fully reapplied. We paid bitterly for that error in the great prolongation of negotiations, in the unsatisfactory terms of the settlement, and above all in the disillusionment and distaste which the American people developed as the main emotional residue of their experience with limited war.[4]

[1] Brodie, *Strategy in the Missile Age*, p. 318.

Possibly Brodie is overkind to the military in his comments. The implications of Bradley's remark in the Hearings that Korea was a 'poor place' to fight a war indicated that the JCS, too, had failed to realise that once the Communists were brought to the conference table by the smashing of their mass offensives, they might on the contrary think that Korea was a very good place to wage their sort of limited war against the West if their opponent's negotiating position was not backed by powerful military pressure. The reasons for this miscalculation are complex. Understandably impatience and optimism reigned in Washington once the truce talks opened. In the MacArthur Hearings the Administration had staked its prestige on its ability (and eagerness) to bring peace to Korea once the Communists cried enough; the political difficulties at home and with the Allies in getting support to carry on the offensive would have been enormous, possibly insuperable. Yet the domestic political problems posed by the prolongation of the war were enormous too and, for the Democrats, quite disastrous. The President had unfortunately sacrificed in dealing with MacArthur any leeway he might have had in Korean policy to force a quick truce, and the last opportunity to get a 1951 armistice went on 12 November and with the succeeding offer of a thirty-day *de facto* cease-fire.[1]

There are also more intangible reasons why American policy became paralysed by the Communist manœuvreing at Panmunjom. Containment, in spite of its realistic assessment of mutual strengths, did not allow sufficiently for the totally integrated military-political strategy which the Communists would now use so cleverly in Korea. Acheson had himself hoped in the Hearings that, once situations of strength had been created, satisfactory negotiations might soon follow. But even after the undeniable situation of strength created in Korea by Ridgway and Van Fleet there was no compelling reason why satisfactory negotiations should follow, possessing their 'own inherent logic', unless force was also used, which, while it would not have resulted in 'victory' would at least have precluded stalemate without end. Moreover, if Acheson tended to think in terms of

---

[1] Private information to the author suggests that during the debates on Korean policy inside the Administration in late 1951, it was Truman who advocated that ground pressure should be kept up. Bradley's opposing view prevailed.

fighting *or* negotiation, many less intellectually alert and less conditioned to think in terms of limited means and limited objectives would be frustrated and angered by the military situation in Korea at the end of 1951 when it became obvious that the only way left to the UNC to end the war was by attempting to beat the Communists into a truce with their sea and air power. In the long saga of attempted 'Negotiation from Strength' the story of the Korean truce talks therefore remains a peculiarly disquieting one.

Indeed it was easier for those in command, both politically and militarily, to think that the stalled truce talks were a prelude to another Chinese offensive using their shiny new air force built up so carefully during 1951 in the Antung complex of bases. At least this course of action could be fitted into a war/peace category. Eden's memoirs, *Full Circle*, are thus interesting as much for what they omit as for what they briefly mention about the renewal by the Churchill Government of Attlee's understanding with Truman to bomb the Manchurian bases should a Communist air offensive be launched from them against the Eighth Army.[1] Eden also discusses in some detail the framing of the proposed public warning with the Americans and other UN countries involved in Korea during January 1952 that probably action would not be confined 'within the frontiers of Korea' in the event of a major truce violation. This was a safeguard suggested by the Unified Command when it was realised that there could be no foolproof guarantees against a post-armistice build-up written into the truce and the warning to the Communists was eventually published in August 1953. But nowhere in his passages on the Korean problem does Eden suggest that the chief problem with the Chinese was to get a truce in the first place. Probably Peking realised only too well by now that it would be impossible to restrain the US if an agreed truce were broken — Vandenberg had said as much in a radio interview during November 1951 — and was thus quite content to let the war simmer while the talks went on.

It therefore seems obvious that Peking — it would be assuming a great deal to say that Kim Il Sung and friends had much influence at all on anything happening in Korea by this time

[1] See Eden, pp. 13-19. The British favoured a bombing programme but not a blockade. 'No general air attack on Chinese towns was contemplated.'

— saw in the talks at Panmunjom a profitable means of prolonging the war while simultaneously subjecting the United States in particular and the West in general to ceaseless charges of imperialism, warmongering, conspiring against peace, massacring Communist prisoners and, above all, the major plank in the Communist Korean War propaganda programme, waging bacteriological warfare against the Chinese and Korean peoples. These blackmailing accusations, the price of their cessation a truce on Communist terms, would not only tend to weaken the political purpose of the Western countries involved in Korea, but might also affect both the military efficiency of the UN effort and the resolution shown by the UNC delegates at Panmunjom. The effect of such repeated charges in responsive neutralist countries could also be converted into anti-Western propaganda in the forum of the UN.

Probably the most important Chinese objective of all once the Communist aim of conquering the entire peninsula had been relinquished was to rally the Chinese masses behind Peking by manipulating the spectre of Western imperialism in Korea. This is a point explicitly made in Mao's *Strategic Problems of China's Revolutionary War* when he asserts that a strategic defensive war waged by a Communist country paralyses 'politically alien elements' as the people are shown to be victims of aggression, with the implication that a Communist society can always outlast a democratic society in such a protracted war. The thought-reform programme and its associated terror which came to a climax in China during the Korean War could also simultaneously be applied to Western POWs in Korea. This would be a particularly sophisticated tactic in the political war against the West, for converted prisoners could always influence their domestic opinion through the mails and suitable visitors, and there were other possibilities of long-term espionage through converts. To achieve all these ends the Chinese could — and did — sacrifice their coolie troops in tens of thousands. Merely to end a war they hardly understood, the United Nations Command had to trade inevitably some of its most precious commodity, manpower. One of the most terrible remarks by an American on the war is the comment by a young Marine Corps sergeant, Martin Russ, in his journal after the funeral of some of his comrades killed on the western front in early 1953: 'The

most disturbing thing of all is that not one of them knew why
they were dying. . . .'[1]

S. L. A. Marshall and others have tantalisingly but inaccurately
compared the Communist techniques for frustrating the armistice negotiations at Kaesong and Panmunjom with Trotsky's
'No war, no peace' manœuvre at Brest-Litovsk. Trotsky would
have enjoyed Panmunjom more than Brest for the very good
reason that Hsieh Fang and Nam Il were in a much stronger
position than the People's Commissar for Foreign Affairs who
was opposed by Lenin for taking his unprecedented stand when
the survival of the infant Soviet regime was at stake. Hsieh Fang
was in a much better position than Trotsky as his armies had
fought their enemy to a strategic, if not to a tactical, stalemate.
Thus while Hoffman, the operations genius of 'HLH', was able
to puncture Trotsky's dialectics in a few days merely by ordering
the feldgrau to advance deep into Russia, no such drastic orders
were given by Ridgway and COMNAVFE at Panmunjom.
Hence Joy's unhappy reflection after his experiences 'that in
debating with the Communists there is no substitute for the
imperative logic of military pressure. . . . Patience and logic
are essential, but they can never be decisive. In the end might
is essential to right, not because you or I would have it that way,
but because, unless we have armed might and unless we are
willing to use that armed might in dealing with the Communists,
we cannot win our point and, in fact, we may not survive to
argue our point. . . .'[2]

Joy's personal deductions from the palaverings at Kaesong and
Panmunjom underline the failure of American (and Allied)
strategy to deal with this last phase of the war. The original

[1] Russ, *The Last Parallel*, p. 293. Cf. with a New China News Agency comment on the war in October 1958: 'The Volunteers applied Chairman Mao's
military ideas during the war as the guide to their operations. At the outset,
in accordance with the situation on the Korean battlefield, the Volunteers
decided on the correct strategic line of "concentrating on mobile warfare
combined with positional warfare in places, and guerilla warfare," and wiped
out the enemy effectives and repulsed the enemy offensives. After the five
great campaigns they switched over in good time to the strategic line of
"engaging in protracted warfare while conducting positive defence" and
strictly subordinated the military struggle to the political struggle. As a result,
they won one battle after another! Hsieh, *Communist China's Strategy in the
Nuclear Era*, p. 140.

[2] *Interlocking Subversion in Government Departments*, p. 2146.

North Korean challenge had been met successfully by co-ordinated diplomacy and force; the divorce of these two means in the drive to the Yalu had helped to bring about the Chinese incursion. The many problems of this second phase of the war, in turn, had been solved after much expenditure of blood, treasure and political skill. For this last phase of the war that had begun with truce talks and which foreshadowed Sino-Soviet strategy in the post-Stalin era, there remained no Western answer. Power lacked purpose as it had been divorced from diplomacy — assuming it is possible to call the tri-lingual charade in the tent at Panmunjom diplomacy. The Communists were therefore able for two years to wage their war for 'peace'. Yet war it was, nevertheless. 'This was not "war" as most Americans had been taught to think of it. It was the use of military action as an instrument of politics and propaganda — an instrument of "policy" in a sense which Clausewitz could scarcely have envisaged.'[1]

[1] Millis, p. 368.

CHAPTER SEVENTEEN

DEADLOCK AT PANMUNJOM

> . . . in a legitimate order, a conference represents a struggle to find formulas to achieve agreement; in a revolutionary order, it is a struggle to capture the symbols which move humanity.
>
> HENRY KISSINGER

MILITARY ARMISTICE COMMISSION AGREED

THE first snow of the Korean winter fell on the western sector during the night of 23 November, and on the 25th, the first anniversary of the Chongchon, it snowed all day. For the next few months ground activity along the MLR was down to a minimum, consisting of patrols, raiding and artillery duels which increased in intensity as both sides went on reinforcing their armies. Two US National Guard divisions, the 45th and 40th arrived in Korea during December and January and replaced the 1st Cavalry and 24th Infantry in I and IX Corps respectively. Van Fleet was constantly juggling his divisions both along the front and between the front and reserve areas to maintain combat efficiency; corps boundaries remained static until the spring when the ROK II Corps was placed on the Kumsong sector, between the IX and X Corps.

The Western sector was the most important, and therefore on 1 May 1952 I Corps consisted of the Marine, Commonwealth, and 45th Infantry Divisions, as well as the ROK 1st Division. Further east IX Corps included the US 7th and 40th Divisions and an ROK division, while X Corps was made up of the US 25th Division and two South Korean divisions. Altogether Van Fleet controlled eight Western divisions — 2nd and 3rd Divisions were in reserve — and some nine ROK divisions on the front line.

Across the United Nations MLR the Communist high command had moved the NK I Corps from the west to the eastern Nam River front in December, which was held to the south by the ROK I Corps, so that along the whole central and western front the Eighth Army was now facing the CCF. Throughout the winter UN naval and air operations had continued against Communist Korea. In north-west Korea, in 'MIG Alley' between the Chongchon and the Yalu, Sabrejets from Kimpo and MIG-15s from the Antung bases fought their weird stratospheric war eight miles up as FEAF sought to maintain control of the air and so deny the North Korean airfields to the Communist Air Forces.

It was against this backdrop of war that the truce talks at Panmunjom moved slowly forward through the winter into the spring until all items on the agenda were dealt with except one, that dealing with the prisoners of war, on which no agreement could be reached on whether there should be voluntary repatriation or not. This deadlock was to prolong the war for fifteen months. Yet at first it had seemed difficult enough to get agreement on Item 3 — concrete arrangements for the realisation of a cease-fire and armistice, although there was no mutually unacceptable principle to divide the two sides as there had been at first over the demarcation line and would be when it came to agreeing over the prisoner issue.

The debate on Item 3 started immediately after the agreement on the demarcation line in the plenary session on 27 November. The UNC proposed that, in general, there should be no build-up of forces after the armistice, and that a commission should be appointed with an associated supervisory organ to see that the cease-fire was being observed, and which would have 'free access to all parts of Korea'. The Communist proposals also suggested a military armistice commission, but, in disagreement with Joy and his colleagues, called for the withdrawal of all armed forces from rear and coastal islands of the other side, which would of course affect the UN military position but not that of the Communists. Nam Il soon made it clear that his side in also asking for a complete withdrawal of all foreign troops from Korea after an armistice dismissed the principle of rotation and replacement favoured by the UNC, and as for the proposal for inspection by a supervisory organ regarded it as 'a brazen interference in the internal affairs' of North Korea. An additional UNC suggestion — which was regarded as vital in preventing major truce violations — asked for the prohibition of airfield construction or improvement throughout Korea after the armistice, and this too was rejected by the Communists.

On 3 December Nam Il suggested that the supervisory organ should be composed of neutral nations, also that neither side should introduce forces into Korea after the truce 'under any pretext', indicating a strong Communist stand against troop rotation. At this stage of the manœuvring, a subdelegation on Item 3 was formed which met on 4 December; and a further subdelegation to discuss Item 4 (POWs) met on 11 December. After a series of proposals and counter-proposals a new UNC memorandum was submitted on 12 December. It abandoned the earlier claim to coastal islands after the truce, and accepted the idea of neutral nation inspection teams outside the demilitarised zone; inside the zone the UNC indicated a preference for joint observer teams responsible to the military armistice commission 'which shall be responsible for supervising the execution of and adherence to the whole armistice agreement'. There was no UNC withdrawal of its demand for restrictions on airfield construction, and the UNC memo of 12 December also suggested that the neutral observer teams should now have the right of aerial observation and photo reconnaissance over all Korea; the UNC had proposed a few days earlier that the armistice commission itself should organise these flights. The Communists did, however, respond with the concession that troop rotation not to exceed 5,000 monthly should be permitted. Thus while the principle of a MAC and neutral nation supervisory commission was jointly accepted there was still major disagreement on the function (and effectiveness) of these bodies.

Almost deadlocked in subdelegation, the debate on Item 3 was transferred to the staff officers on 21 December, and by the end of the year, when the UNC dropped its demand for photo-reconnaissance there were three matters outstanding:

(1) Restrictions on airfield construction.
(2) Adequate ground inspection by neutral teams.
(3) The limits on rotation of personnel to be allowed.

On the question of airfield construction both sides refused to budge, so the haggling was concentrated on the limits of troop rotation. The UNC asked for a limit of 75,000 men per month, as with a rotation agreement of only 5,000 its army of 600,000 would be tied down indefinitely in Korea, a contingency which could not possibly be tolerated by the US Government. At the end of January there was still no agreement, but by 23 February, after whittling away each other's demands, a monthly figure for troop rotation of 35,000 had been agreed. Concurrently, discussions on the limits of ground inspection by the Neutral Nations Supervisory Commission (NNSC) were being held and the UNC had reduced its demands for complete inspection of all Korea to inspection of certain ports of entry. Here the UNC were asking for twelve ports open to inspection, and the Communists offering three. On 14 February the Communists had injected a bargaining demand into this aspect of the talks when they had asked that the inspection teams of the NNSC should see every detail of military equipment entering Korea, including that on the secret list. This was patently unacceptable to the UNC as Communist members on the inspection teams could see such US equipment as electronic gun-sights and radar, while Communist special equipment was based in Manchuria. Finally the UNC agreed to cut down its demand for ports of entry to five, and the Communists abandoned their claim for 'secret weapon' inspection. As the North Koreans did not want Pyongyang on the list, the ten ports as agreed on 20 March were, in the north, Sinuiju, Sinanju, Manpojin, Hungnam, and Chongjin; in the south, Pusan, Inchon, Kangnung, Kunsan and Taegu.

There had also been disagreement on the procedure and composition of the NNSC as well as its effectiveness. At first the Communists had asked that the voting on the NNSC and its organisations should be unanimous — so that even one of the proposed Communist members of the commission could veto its work. But here they eventually agreed that its voting need not be unanimous — in the unlikely event of the Communist members of the NNSC disagreeing, the Communists had already imposed their most effective veto on the NNSC by successfully fighting the UNC proposal for photo-reconnaissance. In any case, it soon became obvious after the signing of the Armistice that the NNSC, in the absence of a chairman, was invariably deadlocked on all matters of importance so that the Communists had a veto without insisting on a formal unanimity. Much more significant was the Communist demand for the inclusion of the

USSR, along with Poland, Czechoslovakia, Norway, Sweden and Switzerland on the NNSC. The delegates had previously agreed that the 'neutral' nations should be 'acceptable to both sides' and the UNC refused to consider (and thus recognise) the prime mover of the Korean War as a neutral. The injection of the USSR was seen as another bargaining point to force a withdrawal of the UN position on airfield construction which up until March was unchanged. Similarly the Communists refused the UN suggestion that the number of neutral nations to be nominated by each side be reduced from three to two, so eliminating the USSR. By the beginning of April the discussions on Item 3 were deadlocked on these two matters, while the staff officers conducted lengthy debates on the proper translations for *Korea* and *United Nations* in the draft armistice agreement.

However, on Item 5, Recommendations to the governments of countries concerned, there had been surprisingly quick agreement. Discussion had cautiously started on 6 February in plenary sessions, when Nam Il had proposed a draft which had excluded the ROK from the proposed peace conference, and to which Joy had objected. After some discussion the Communists had submitted a revised draft on 16 February:

> In order to insure the peaceful settlement of the Korean question, the military commanders of both sides hereby recommend to the governments of the countries concerned on both sides that, within three months after the armistice agreement is signed and becomes effective, a political conference of a higher level of both sides be held by representatives appointed respectively to settle through negotiations the questions of the withdrawal of all foreign forces from Korea, the peaceful settlement of the Korean question etc.

The next day Joy accepted this draft subject to three reservations: (1) That the recommendation would be made by CINCUNC to the UN as well as to the Republic of Korea, (2) That in accepting the term 'foreign forces' the UNC delegate did so on the basis of the Communists' own statement that it meant 'non-Korean forces', (3) That the words 'et cetera' should not be taken as relating to matters outside of Korea. This last reservation, of course, referred to Formosa and China's UN seat. The

Communists were amazed by this swift acceptance — had they made a mistake? — and demanded a recess which went on until 19 February when the draft article, which as Paragraph 60 of the Armistice Agreement led eventually to the Geneva Conference of 1954, was turned over by Joy to the staff officers 'to complete any necessary mechanical details'. No further plenary meetings were held on Item 5. As Joy has written, his acceptance was based on the word *recommend* in the draft, which meant that the governments concerned could always turn down any suggestion which reached them from Panmunjom. . . .

But the swift agreement on this peripheral point was a massive exception to the usual rules of Panmunjom. By 25 April, after over sixty subdelegate and seventy-two staff officer meetings, Item 3 was referred back to the plenary session. On 28 April in executive plenary session Joy stated what was the UNC's final attempt to resolve the deadlock on airfield construction, Soviet membership of the NNSC, and prisoner repatriation. He proposed a package deal in which the UNC would drop its insistence on prohibiting airfield construction if the Communists would accept the omission of Norway and the USSR from the NNSC, and also, the single issue that would prolong the war into the summer of 1953, the principle of non-forcible repatriation. This issue had already proved the most intractable in the entire armistice discussions.

UNC STAND: VOLUNTARY PRISONER REPATRIATION

The first subdelegation meeting on Item 4, Arrangements relating to prisoners of war, took place on 11 December and the armistice conference did not really dispose of this subject until the truce was signed nearly twenty months later. More than any other item on the armistice agenda the disagreement on prisoner repatriation revealed the differing moral and political attitudes between the two sides fighting in Korea and which were summed up in the respective answers given to the question: should force be used to repatriate these Communist prisoners of war who did not wish to return home? By the end of 1951 it had become clear that a large number of these prisoners were strongly anti-Communist. At first the question of principle involved in forcible repatriation was obscured by the great difficulty of finding out the exact number of UNC prisoners held in the north. The Communists refused to produce lists until the United Nations agreed to release all prisoners immediately on the signing of an armistice, with the implication that all captives would be thus exchanged. They also refused to allow the International Committee of the Red Cross to visit their camps.

After the UNC members on the subdelegation had refused to discuss any substantive matter on Item 4 until they had the necessary information, a provisional list of prisoners were exchanged by the two sides. For the UNC it was a tremendous shock. The Communist list contained the names of over 7,000 South Koreans, nearly 3,200 Americans which, with the prisoners of other UN contingents included 919 Britons, made up a total of 11,559. Yet as early as March 1951 they had announced over their radio that they held 65,000 United Nations prisoners. Altogether there were 100,000 UNC missing at this time, mostly South Koreans; and Washington's figure of Americans missing was no less than 11,224. Even on the Communists' own figures of March and December there was a discrepancy of 53,000; it looked as if about 8,000 US prisoners had either died or been killed after capture.[1] These figures, released within a week of Christmas, meant that there was not going to be a quick armistice; the domestic reaction in the United States to this new horror from Korea started the final surge of public opinion which would within just over a year put Eisenhower in the White House.

General Lee Sang Cho, apparently at this stage accepting the principle of voluntary repatriation, explained to the subdelegation that the discrepancy of 53,000 in the Communist figures

[1] This figure came unpleasantly near the truth. The official casualty lists of the war show that a total of 7,140 Americans were captured of whom 2,701 died in captivity. Another 5,127 died while missing. The Korea War Crimes Division of the US Army compiled a report which was extensively quoted by Ambassador Cabot Lodge to the UN General Assembly on 30 November 1953. He stated that 17,000 civilian Koreans had been murdered by the Communists for political reasons, 1,940 UN prisoners had been force-marched to death, 7,300 had died in enemy POW camps through cruelty and neglect, and 11,600 UN soldiers had been killed on capture. A resolution condemning such atrocities was passed by the Assembly. This was opposed by the Soviet bloc. See US Army, Korean Communications Zone: *Extract of Interim Historical Report, Korea War Crimes Division, cumulative to 30 June 1953.*

arose from the fact that thousands of their prisoners had been allowed to go home, and that other foreign (Western) prisoners had been 'released at the front' because they did not wish 'to join the war against people who fight for their real independence. . . . I tell you that the righteous people of the world praise this revolutionary policy of ours. . . .' Lee was almost unable to finish this part of the statement as he was choking with laughter. Other UN prisoners, he went on, had been killed by UN air raids, escaped, or died 'because they didn't like work and exercise in their daily life'.

The UNC replied by producing lists on which a total of 132,000 Communist prisoners were shown. There were 96,000 North Koreans, 20,000 Chinese, and another 16,000 ROK citizens captured fighting with the North Koreans who retained Communist sympathies. The balance of the figure of 176,000 prisoners which had been earlier reported to Geneva by the ICRC as the UNC total was made up of 6,000 who had died or escaped, and 38,000 South Koreans, taken after impressment into the KPA and the Communist guerillas, or just the human flotsam of war, and all now reclassified as civilian internees. They were all against removal to North Korea. The United Nations Command claimed that most of the missing South Koreans had been impressed into the People's Army; the Communists that the civilian internees and those POWs refusing repatriation had been kidnapped by the United Nations for return, as General Lee put it, 'to a certain friend of yours in South Korea . . . a certain friend of yours in Formosa'.

After these figures had been digested by the two delegations and a new series of vituperative contingency papers drawn up, negotiations centred around proposals put by Rear-Admiral Libby for the UNC at the beginning of 1952 on 2 January. The admiral suggested a one-for-one exchange of prisoners, both soldiers and civilians, until one side had released all it held. Those remaining, who all then would have been in UNC hands, could opt for repatriation. Delegates of the ICRC would interview all POWs 'in order to insure that the choice regarding repatriation is made without duress', for as Libby told the Communists the UNC proposals expressly provided that 'all repatriation will be voluntary'. A slightly reworded version of this plan, which was rejected by the Communists, also met no success on 8 January and thus it became clear within a month of the beginning of talks on Item 4 that the positions of the two sides were mutually irreconcilable.

The principle of voluntary repatriation had not been adopted by the Allies without some unease. It meant that the UN prisoners in North Korea would remain in Communist hands under particularly unpleasant conditions until agreement was reached at Panmunjom. Yet humanitarian considerations made it impossible to write into the truce agreement a fugitive slave act which would have resulted in the many thousands of anti-Communist prisoners being delivered to the fate of Vlasov's pathetic rabble in 1945. Moreover — and this too was an important consideration — if it could be shown conclusively that large numbers of Communist troops preferred to stay in the imperialist camp instead of returning to the camp of peace, then a major propaganda defeat would have been inflicted on the Communists. Conversely, if the North Koreans and the Chinese could force their opponents to repatriate large numbers of their defected prisoners to death and imprisonment, then that would be a tremendous victory for Peking and Pyongyang. Possible future defectors from the Communist world would be deterred. The Communists might well have thought, too, that as the United Nations had yielded on their demand for photo reconnaissance and prohibition of airfield construction after the armistice they might be forced out of their stand on voluntary prisoner repatriation.

Both sides could unilaterally interpret the Geneva Convention to support their position. Article 118 of the 1949 Convention states that 'prisoners of war shall be released and repatriated without delay' after the cessation of hostilities. Thus the Communists could emphasise *repatriation* while the United Nations pointed to the word *release*, and went on to make their case in the following way. Neither the US or UK Governments had ratified at this time the Convention, although of course the UNC observed its provisions in Korea, and the position of the Allies was that nothing in the Convention qualified the right of a prisoner to seek political asylum after release. Yet during the debates on the drafting of the Convention in 1949 the US and the USSR had taken opposite stands to those taken by the respective West-East delegates at Panmunjom. The US had argued for total repatriation because then the West was seeking the return of over a million repatriated German POWs in Russia, while the Soviet had defended the right of voluntary return. This was an unmentionable at Panmunjom by either side, although reference was made both in the truce tent and by Acheson in the General Assembly on 24 October 1952 to the fact that the Red Army proclamations to the besieged garrisons of Stalingrad and Budapest in the second war had promised voluntary repatriation. Indeed, Acheson showed that a series of treaties signed by the Soviet since (and including) Brest-Litovsk accepted the principle of voluntary repatriation.

These legalisms had little influence on the course of the negotiations, although they were useful in the propaganda war. Throughout January and February the subdelegation and the staff officers attempted to find some sort of compromise, but no semantic formula could be found to close this chasm. The UNC reworded its description of its position from 'voluntary repatriation' to 'no forced repatriation' and agreed that joint Red Cross teams might visit the POW camps instead of ICRC teams alone. By 5 March the Communists were proposing that repatriation should be settled on the basis of the lists exchanged on 18 December, which meant that if the UNC ceased its demand for an explanation of the whereabouts of the 53,000 UN prisoners 'sent home' and 'released at the front' the Communists would drop their demands for the return of 38,000 civilian internees. This proposal was tacitly accepted by the UNC. Then, in a move which led directly to the complete deadlock of the talks, on 2 April, Colonel Tsai suggested that in order to discover how many prisoners were willing to accept repatriation, new lists should be prepared, a process which both sides realised involved screening of prisoners. Apparently it appeared likely that any figure of over 100,000 POWs to be repatriated by the UNC would mean an armistice, as not too much face would have been lost by the Communists. However, most of the prisoners held by the United Nations were interned at Koje-do, off the south coast of Korea, where violence had been simmering for almost nine months between the prisoners and their guards and between themselves. During the screening, which was accompanied by a Joint Sino-North Korean amnesty statement read over the camp loudspeaker system, riots started, followed by an attempted breakout which was only stopped by shooting: it was found impossible to screen many prisoners. A provisional list showed that only 70,000 prisoners out of the 132,000 wanted to return. The announcement of these figures opened a new phase of acrimony at Panmunjom. Writes Joy, 'On hearing these results the Communist delegation went through the overhead of the tent at Panmunjom. They charged the United Nations Command with every manner of crime relative to the prisoners. They contended that the screening was done under conditions forcing the prisoners to reject Communism. Admiral Libby remarked to me, 'We have passed the point of no return. . . .'[1]

With this reaction from Nam Il, Joy and his colleagues realised that it was impossible to solve Item 4 by itself, and hoped to break the deadlock by combining their proposals on Item 4 with those on Item 3. The package deal of 28 April was the consequence when Joy abandoned the UNC demand for restriction on airfield building if the Communists would drop the name of the USSR (and Norway) from the NNSC and also accept the principle of non-forcible repatriation. Following this UNC initiative, there were a series of executive plenary sessions in which Nam Il agreed to drop the USSR from the NNSC in exchange for the abandoning of airfield rehabilitation. But on the single issue of prisoner repatriation there was no agreement—the one difference that now prevented an armistice. The news was made public on 7 May. On this principle the United Nations could not and would not yield. Yet within a few hours of the announcement of total impasse at Panmunjom over repatriation there was a revolt of Communist prisoners at Koje which completely obscured the essential rectitude of the stand taken by Joy, as well as of the significant fact that large numbers of Communist POWs repudiated their governments.

THE KOJE STORY

Koje Island! Again the gloomy shadow of Maidanek has come upon the world, again the stench of corpses . . . again the groans of the tormented. . . . We have learnt that 'civi-

[1] Joy, p. 153·4.

lised' Americans can be yet more inhuman, yet more infamous than the bloody Hitlerites. Dachau was a death camp, Maidanek was a death factory. Koje is a whole island of death . . .
Pravda

On this large island about thirty miles south-east of Pusan the majority of the Communist prisoners had been interned since the spring of 1951. Most of the North Koreans had been taken after Inchon, most of the Chinese captured in the summer of 1951. By that time there were 163,000 prisoners in UN POW Camp 1, which included the hospital at Pusan as well as Koje: the camp was divided into compounds which held up to 6,000 prisoners. Unlike the Communist POW camps, there were visits by the ICRC. In the late summer of 1951 two delegates from Geneva after visiting Koje and Pusan reported that the compounds 'have reached almost the maximum state of perfection in layout, decorations and cleanliness . . . heavy workers now receive supplemental food . . . hospital patients less than 2% of camp strength. . . . The delegate was present at a perfectly organised athletic meeting . . . from the splendid physique of the contestants, the ration scale would appear to be adequate. . . .'[1]

Yet already by this time the first incidents between the inmates and their guards had occurred, and on Korean Independence Day (15 August) a break-out attempt at Pusan had resulted in the death of nine prisoners. Another three had been killed at the same time on Koje after a clash between guards and prisoners. The Geneva delegates had noted that the spokesmen elected by the prisoners were not interested in prisoners' rights under the Convention, but rather in serving the respective pro- and anti-Communist factions they represented. Koje was already polarised into two groups, a microcosm of the Korean War in all aspects of its civil and ideological strife, as the two factions, often existing within the same compound, fought out their differences, terrorizing the minority.

By November 1951 the ICRC was hinting that screening would have to be carried out, as so many prisoners were anxious not to be repatriated. As truce discussions on Item 4 started, affairs went from bad to worse. On 18 February when guards

[1] White, *The Captives of Korea*, p. 135-6.

entered Compound 62 to find out which of the prisoners there were ROK civilians impressed into the KPA, they were attacked by 1,500 Communist prisoners armed with iron bars, clubs, barbed wire and other home-made weapons. The guards opened fire and seventy-five inmates were killed and over a hundred wounded. A month later on 13 March there was more violence when twelve North Koreans were killed, and on 10 April there was another riot coinciding with the screening agreed at Panmunjom; three prisoners and four guards were killed. By now many compounds were completely controlled by the Communist prisoners, thus preventing the screening from being completed. Even before the screening, the ICRC had suggested that the unmanageable compounds be broken up into smaller units, but nothing was done due to shortage of men and material. In any case Tokyo had played down the situation on the island as it was afraid if the facts were known it might give the Communists another excuse to delay the truce.

But Nam Il and Lee Sang Cho, who was also head of the KPA's Military Intelligence Section, had known all along what was happening on Koje; they had planned it. After the suppression of the Communist compounds in June 1952 Tokyo at last discovered the full extent to which the prisoners on Koje were controlled by the North Korean Army, which still regarded their prisoners as having combatant status. Not only were the prisoners inside the Communist compounds controlled by military organisations, but branches of the Korean CP, the Korean Labour Party, were also in action. Radio receivers ensured that Pyongyang was able to contact its men on Koje; while a network of civilian agents who lived on the island outside the camp meant that messages passed by work-details could be sent back to the KPA's Guerilla Guidance Bureau and its Espionage Department, the two agencies which supervised activities on Koje.

In overall control of the Koje Communists was 'General Leading Headquarters', a political committee divided into four sections: Political Security, which carried out the functions of the NK Security Police inside Koje; Organisation and Planning, which kept communications flowing both ways between the island and Pyongyang; Agitprop, which conducted indoctrination; and fourthly, the Guard Section which was also the execution squad which carried out the sentences of the People's Courts which ruled the Communist compounds. Until Pyongyang realised that this situation was best exploited by increasing the pressure of the rioting in direct proportion to the delicacy of the truce talks on prisoner repatriation, it had been planned that the Communist cadres would attempt a simultaneous breakout, cross over to the mainland only a few miles away, and then disperse and link up with the North Korean guerillas still operating on the Chiri San hills northwest of Chinju.

The plans of the KPA's Military Intelligence Section now came to a head on 7 May; the announcement of the deadlock in the truce talks also coincided with General Mark Clark's arrival in Tokyo to take over from Ridgway who was off to SHAPE.[1] That same day Communist rioters in Compound 76 captured the commandant of Koje, Brig.-Gen. Dodd, who had been asked by compound spokesmen if he would speak to them regarding grievances. The unfortunate Dodd, who had foolishly walked down to the compound entry, had been dragged inside, as planned, by a returning latrine detail. The initial demands for Dodd's release included permission to form a vast Communist POW organisation, complete with intercompound telephones, office equipment down to mimeograph machines, and a couple of trucks. As Koje's communications with the mainland were precarious, and no one wanted to be the first with the bad tidings, the news was slow in reaching Tokyo. The first Clark heard about the seizure of Dodd was from Ridgway: 'Wayne, we've got a little situation over in Korea. . . .' The new Commander-in-Chief — he was due to take over formally on the 12th — felt as if he had walked into 'a swinging door'. 'I hadn't bothered to ask anyone in Washington about the POWs, because my experience had been with old-fashioned wars. . . . Never had I experienced a situation in which prisoners remained combatants and carried out orders smuggled out to them from the enemy High Command.'[2]

[1] With the coming into force of the Japanese Peace Treaty on 28 April 1952 the office of SCAP ended. Clark therefore inherited only three commands from Ridgway. He shortly left the Dai-Ichi for the compound outside Tokyo that had been Tojo's GHQ. 'Often as I sat at my desk I thought I had better not make the mistake of losing a war. . . .' Clark, *From the Danube to the Yalu*, p. 130.

[2] Clark, p. 39.

On 10 May, with Dodd still held in Compound 76, came a demand that the acting commandant, Brig.-Gen. Colson, sign a statement undertaking that there be no *more* forced screening, no inhumane treatment of prisoners *in the future*. The pressure on Colson to sign was heightened by Dodd being allowed to talk over the compound telephone; his life was at stake. Eventually he gave the prisoners the undertaking, and Dodd was released. As a result of this forced admission the truce tent became incandescent with Nam Il's accusations which radiated outwards through the world-wide network of Communist propaganda outlets. On taking over command, Clark repudiated Colson's statement as it was extorted by violence, and later both Dodd and Colson were demoted to colonel.[1] A new commandant was appointed, and the 187th Airborne RCT was sent to Koje, together with British and Canadian reinforcements. At last on 10 June resistance in Compound 76 was smashed by the paratroops using tear gas and concussion grenades and, although no firearms were used, yet thirty-one Communists and an American were killed. Following this reassertion of control on Koje the Chinese prisoners were sent to Cheju-do, and many pro-Communist South Koreans shipped to nearby Pongam island. The large compounds were split up. Yet the problem had not really been solved. There were still smaller riots on Koje, an uprising among the Chinese on Cheju on 1 October and on 14 December after an attempted six-compound break-out on Pongam Island eighty-two prisoners were killed — on the very day when Peking rejected the Indian resolution then before the General Assembly which called for a solution to the armistice deadlock on the basis of no forcible repatriation.

Proceedings at Panmunjom with any hope of progress in reaching an agreement had thus ended with the package proposal of 28 April and the Koje uprising. On 12 May, according to William Vatcher, the Communists 'launched their most vicious propaganda tirade of the entire armistice proceedings'. Ten days later Joy replied with a farewell broadside during his last appearance at Panmunjom before leaving for the US. He

[1] As a result of the Koje riots, responsibility for controlling the POW camps, supplies, rehabilitation of Korean roads and railways and co-ordination of all relief work was taken away from EUSAK and given in August 1952 to the new Korean Communications Command, responsible to GHQ, Tokyo.

charged the Communists with 'a constant succession of delays, fraudulent arguments, and artificial attitudes' to obstruct an armistice so as to rebuild their armies shattered in the summer of 1951. The Admiral characterised as 'colossal impertinence' their references to the Geneva Convention to maintain their 'inhuman proposition' of forcible repatriation on which 'no amount of argument and invective will move us'. Joy's successor at Panmunjom was Maj.-Gen. (later Lt.-Gen.) William K. Harrison.[1]

No noteworthy developments took place until July when the Communists announced that if the UNC would forcibly repatriate all the Chinese POWs, an armistice could be arranged. There was no response. Five days later on 13 July the United Nations announced the result of their full screening of the Communist prisoners. From the combined total of 112,000 North Korean prisoners and pro-Communist ROK civilian internees, 76,600 demanded repatriation. From over 20,000 CPV personnel, 6,400 opted for return to Communist China. Total: 83,000 out of 132,000, just over 60%. Concurrently, after careful screening, the release of the 38,000 anti-Communist ROK civilian internees was begun. If the grand total of 170,000 prisoners held by the UNC was taken, just over half had refused repatriation to North Korea or China. One last face-saving suggestion was made by Harrison when he told the Communists that if the figure of 83,000 were added to that of the 38,000 internees 'released directly', it could be announced that 121,000 Communist POWs had been released. This proposal, too, as expected, was rejected, and in August when a typhoon blew down the conference tents, the United Nation team resignedly accepted a Communist offer to erect a permanent wooden building for their deliberations. The feeling that Panmunjom was now quite unrelated to the problem of ending the war, and had become the fourth, propaganda, front of the fighting was evident in the exchanges, completely divorced, unlike the earlier talks, from any thought of solving substantive problems. Moreover, if the Admiral had tended to regard the Communist delegation as infinitely dangerous totalitarians who might yet encompass the downfall of the West, the aristocratic Harrison, a descendant both of the

---

[1] Joy was leaving to become superintendent of the US Naval Academy, Annapolis.

ninth and of the twenty-third presidents of the United States, regarded his adversaries as criminals:

General Nam Il: It is solely in the interest of a handful of munition merchants and warmongers of your side that the soldiers of seventeen nations have been driven by your side to come far from their native countries and carry out inhuman destruction and murder against the innocent people of Korea at the cost of their own lives, although people throughout the world who uphold peace and justice unanimously condemn your side for launching and carrying on this unjust war. . . . When your outrageous proposition of forceful retention of war prisoners has gone bankrupt and you can no longer use it as a camouflage to play deceit, your side cannot but resort to vituperation and distortion in these conferences. This only shows how desperate and disreputable. . . .

General W. K. Harrison: . . . Some of your language this morning is what we civilised countries associate with common criminals or persons who through ignorance or stupidity are unable to speak logically or convincingly. In their frustration they resort to efforts to insult . . . (20 September 1952).[1]

At last, to round off proceedings for the rest of the year, Harrison, after consultations between the governments concerned on the United Nations side, presented three alternative proposals on the repatriation problem on 28 September, 'any one of which will lead to an armistice if you truly desire one'. (1) All non-repatriated prisoners, after identification in the demilitarised zone, should have the right to return to their captors. (2) All non-repatriates would be interviewed by neutral representatives in the zone, and would be free to go to the side of their own choice. (3) All non-repatriates would be placed in the zone and without any screening would be free to go to the side of their own choice. Harrison then suggested that after a recess of ten days the delegations meet again on 8 October. After their last journey across the Imjin to Panmunjom in 1952 the UNC delegates heard Nam Il insist that all Chinese prisoners must be returned to Communist control. Harrison, reading from a

[1] Vatcher, pp. 151-3.

contingency paper, then unilaterally recessed the plenary meeting as the UNC had no further proposals to offer; liaison officers would continue to meet. Thereupon the United Nations and Communist delegations left Panmunjom for the winter, the UN staff to Munsan, Seoul and Tokyo, the Communist staff to Pyongyang and Peking.

A week later, on 14 October, the General Assembly met in New York where it was hoped some sort of solution to the prisoners deadlock could be worked out. Acheson soon told the General Assembly that the United States would fight on for a just armistice in Korea; he considered that the UN now faced a test of its staying power.

On 24 October, the American delegation submitted to the Political Committee a resolution supported by twenty other countries, including the UK. It called upon Peking and Pyongyang to recognise the right of the UNC POWs to non-forcible repatriation. The resolution was backed by Acheson in the powerful speech mentioned above which discussed the entire history of prisoner repatriation in the twentieth century. Just over a week later the American presidential election proved to be the first in a series of events that eventually ended the war. But for the UNC prisoners in North Korea the deadlock at Panmunjom meant another winter of captivity — and indoctrination.

CHAPTER EIGHTEEN

THE CAULDRON OF REBIRTH

We must be engineers of the human soul.

V. I. LENIN

You think it is important that I have kept the Japanese from expanding. . . . I tell you it is more important that I have kept the Communists from spreading. The Japanese are a disease of the skin; the Communists are a disease of the heart.

CHIANG KAI-SHEK, in 1941

WINTER ON THE YALU

FROM early 1951 to the end of the war the UNC prisoners in North Korea were subjected to a systematic attempt at mass conversion to Communism, unprecedented in previous British and American military history, although of course the Russians had used an indoctrination programme similar in many ways with their German prisoners in World War II. Like the Koje disturbances and the bacteriological warfare campaign, the propaganda exploitation of the indoctrinated Western prisoners in Korea fitted easily into the general framework of the peace campaign aimed at ending the war on Communist terms. But the indoctrination programme also had a significance slightly apart from the immediate issues and propaganda demands raised by the Korean War. It was a practical demonstration to a captive Western audience that the war was just another example of the historical process that would not end until the final inevitable victory of Communism; and that the prisoners should be converted to the 'truth' about history for their own good.

The years since the end of the war have shown that it is much easier to understand *how* the UNC prisoners in North Korea were conditioned than *why* they succumbed to indoctrination. Certainly the question of motive has been occluded by the spate of films, plays and novels and reports written ever since the extraordinary scenes at Panmunjom after the armistice when returning 'progressive' United Nations prisoners sang the *Internationale* and chanted 'Communism is peace'. These men showed that something almost beyond comprehension at first had happened to many Western prisoners during their captivity. And so, from *Time Limit* and *The Rack* to *The Manchurian Candidate* and the mighty speculations of why George Blake was won to Communism, interest moves from the ritual of indoctrination and confession to the possibility of the 'sleeping agent' — by 1959, seventy-five agents had been found among the repatriated US prisoners, many of them, of course, never suspected of being 'progressive' prisoners.

Much that has been written about the North Korean prison camps has either wittingly or unwittingly fostered both the idea of brainwashing[1] as a mysterious and almost irresistible process and the really contradictory assertion of the irremediable decadence of Western society in general and that of the United States in particular. Perhaps the best-known report of all on the captives of North Korea is Eugene Kinkead's *Why They Collaborated*, published originally in the US under the title of *In Every War But One*. Kinkead has written of the 'wholesale collaboration' of almost one-third of the American prisoners, that even '. . . the majority had yielded in some degree to Communist pressure'. Yet his misleading interpretation fails to take full account of the initial physical conditioning in the prison camps against which the whole indoctrination programme must be considered.

The camps were divided into two clusters. The first, around Pyongyang, consisted of a group of transit or penal compounds, such as 'the Beancamp', at Suan, alone of this group a CCF camp and named after the prevailing diet; 'The Caves', Camp 9, at Kangdong; 'Pak's Palace', run by a deranged major of the KPA; and Camp 12, 'the Peace Fighters' Camp', which held indoctrinated British and American troops recruited from 'the Caves' and other camps where the living conditions were unspeakable. But it was the second cluster of eight permanent

[1] The term was first used by the American journalist Edward Hunter, *Brainwashing in Red China* (1951), and is a translation of the Chinese colloquialism *hsi nao* ('wash brain'). If at all possible it should be avoided as the various processes known loosely by the term are called in official Chinese Communist terminology, *szu-hsiang kai-tsao* — 'ideological reform' or 'thought reform'.

camps run by the CCF and established north-east of Sinuiju along the seventy-five mile stretch of the Suiho Reservoir, that was the heart of the Communist POW organisation. The first permanent camp was set up at Pyoktong in January 1951 (Camp 5); this was the GHQ of the prison-camp system. Although some American prisoners were taken in the summer of 1950, it was not until the late autumn that large numbers of prisoners from both 1st Cavalry's action at Unsan and of course 2nd Division's disaster at Kunuri meant the creation of a permanent prison-camp system.

Many prisoners were force-marched to the Yalu, often in their summer fatigues through the Korean winter, and there was no attempt to give them any special clothing or food; the basic diet was boiled corn or millet. Philip Deane has recorded how, along with US Army prisoners, missionaries, nuns, journalists and diplomats, he was force-marched north-eastwards along the Yalu from Manpojin during early November 1950, supervised by a sadistic North Korean major, 'The Tiger'. Scores of GIs fell out and died. Deane stayed near their destination, Chunggangjin, until February 1951 when he was moved back to Manpo. By then of the 777 Americans in his party in September 1950, 60% were dead from starvation and privation.

At the infamous Pyoktong, conditions were even worse, although it seems generally agreed that if the Chinese during the winter of 1950-51 killed their prisoners by deliberate neglect, the North Koreans who had handled the captives before they became primarily a Chinese responsibility killed them by calculated brutality. At the beginning of the new year there were over 2,000 prisoners in the newly-formed Camp 5 housed in native huts, with others constantly arriving from the south; the battle line was now, it will be remembered, below Suwon and Wonju. At first, the American doctors were allowed to make rounds to the sick, but as the Chinese started to break up the prisoners' command structure, not only were officers separated from enlisted men, but sergeants and corporals also, and so the sick were forced to the special doctors' compound; most of them were so ill that this they found impossible to do. These enlisted men were the conscripts, aged usually between eighteen and twenty-one who had been sent to Korea from Japan; these were yet the men who had saved the Naktong line and Pusan six

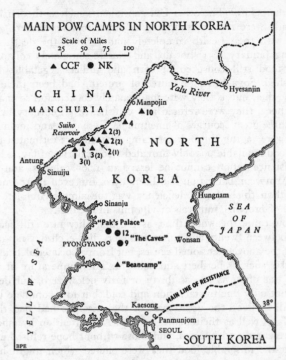

MAIN POW CAMPS IN NORTH KOREA

Scale of Miles
0   25   50   75   100

▲ CCF   ● NK

CHINA

MANCHURIA

Yalu River   ○ Hyesanjin

● Manpojin
▲ 10

Suiho Reservoir
▲ 5 ▲ 2(3)
▲ ▲ 2(2)
1 3(1) 3(2) 2(1)

○ Antung
○ Sinuiju

NORTH

KOREA

○ Sinanju   ○ Hungnam

"Pak's Palace"
● ● 12   "The Caves"
PYONGYANG ○ ● 9

SEA
OF
JAPAN

○ Wonsan

▲ "Beancamp"

MAIN LINE OF RESISTANCE

YELLOW SEA

○ Kaesong   38°

○ Panmunjom
○ SEOUL   SOUTH KOREA

BPE

Camp 1 Chongsong. About 50 miles north-east of Sinuiju. Established March 1951.

Camp 2 (Branch 1) Pin Chon-ni. About 70 miles north-east of Sinuiju. Officers' camp established in October 1951.

Camp 2 (Branch 2) Ogye-dong, ten miles east of above. Penal camp established August 1952.

Camp 2 (Branch 3) Chang-ni. On the Yalu ten miles north of above. Officers and aircrew, established March 1952.

Camp 3 (Branch 1) Changsong. Near the Yalu north of Camp 1. Established August 1951. Enlisted men/other ranks.

Camp 3 (Branch 2) Songsa-dong. Established August 1952 for new prisoners.

Camp 4 Kuup-tong. About 110 miles north-east of Sinuiju. Sergeants.

Camp 5 Pyoktong. About 70 miles north-east of Sinuiju. Established January 1951; enlisted men/other ranks after October 1951.

Camp 9 Kangdong. Known as 'The Caves', consisting of tunnels in the hillside.

Camp 10 Kanggye. Indoctrination centre established in October 1950 for UNC troops captured in north-east Korea.

Camp 12, near Pyongyang. Established in May 1951 for six months, prisoners then transferred to Pyoktong.

Pak's Palace, also known as *Pak's Death House*, north of Pyongyang.

The Beancamp, Suan.

months before. (The other UN contingents such as the Turkish Brigade were mostly composed of older, regular soldiers.) But now with their health completely undermined, the death rate during January 1951 shot up, and morale completely collapsed. The food still consisted of corn and millet, vegetables had vanished. Soya beans, a source of protein, had been included in the diet, but as they were inadequately cooked and so caused diarrhoea, they were refused and vanished. By February, when the three great scourges of pneumonia, dysentery and malnutrition were raging through the camp, the doctors estimated that the food available possibly provided 1,200 calories a day; a bare subsistence ration cannot be less than 1,600 calories, and the US Army combat ration had been 3,500. But even more important than this calorific deficiency was the almost complete absence of proteins, minerals or vitamins in the diet.

Now came the worst time, as the mortality rate still soared and between twenty and thirty prisoners died each day not only from the above mentioned causes, but from associated deficiency diseases such as beriberi and pellagra. The temperature at this time was often as low as thirty or forty below zero, but death was not only due to starvation and cold, but to a complete lack of will to live: the great mass of the prisoners had had their minds as well as their bodies broken. Any attention by officers was resented and rejected, and those without hope refused even to eat the miserable food they were offered which might have helped save them. Often they collapsed in despondency, put a blanket over their heads and died untended in a pool of their own fæces. Of those still living, often the strong bullied the weak for their food, and threw them out from their cramped huts into the snow when they could no longer look after themselves. More nursed their friends and went to look for food and water when allowed. By the end of February the death rate had reached twenty-eight a day, and now the Chinese allowed small amounts of penicillin and sulphonamides to be used; but without food and proper shelter the drugs could do little good. Even as late as June the Briton Derek Kinne noted that thirty-nine prisoners died at Camp 1 at Chongsong in one day.

With the spring and the substitution of kaoliang — coarse barley which contains Vitamin B—for cracked corn, the death rate started coming down. But not all who had survived the winter lived. Some died with the first warm days as the last grains of salt were forced from their bodies by the climbing sun. Others died in their sleep from exhaustion. But as the enlisted men stopped dying, now the officers started expiring in scores. Why? The doctors eventually decided that being older and having a slower metabolic rate they had taken longer to burn up their reserves. But now death claimed them too, and in August, when the last West Point graduate died, their percentage of deaths exactly equalled that of the enlisted men.

Although the exact figure is not known, about 1,500 Americans died at Camp 5 alone during the first quarter of 1951. The significance of these figures in relation to the Chinese indoctrination programme can be quickly seen. For of all the 7,190 US personnel in Communist captivity, 2,730, or 38% died — this figure in the US Department of Defence's report on the Korean prisoners, *POW — The Fight Continues After the Battle* differs slightly from the official casualty list. The prisoner death rate in the hulks where the British kept their prisoners during the Revolutionary War is estimated at 33%, that of the US prisoners in Axis captivity in World War II, about 11%. Furthermore, over 99% of all the Army prisoners who died did so in that first year of war; only nineteen died in the last two years of the war. With this terrible winter in mind, for those who wished to escape the mass graves on the Yalu, the lesson was obvious. Compulsory lectures on Communist theory started at Pyoktong in March 1951 when prisoner morale was at its nadir, significantly coinciding with the slightly improved diet. In April, Commandant Ding had lined up an audience of prisoners: 'Study hard, Comrades, with open minds, and you will get home soon. But if you don't we'll dig a ditch for you so deep that even your bourgeois bodies won't stink.'[1] At the same time, casting a cold professional eye around, the doctors in

[1] White, *The Captives of Korea*, p. 105. Contains an account of the winter, 1950-51 at Pyoktong, compiled from statements of returned prisoners. His story of the UN prisoners is cross-cut to that of the Communist prisoners in UNC hands. Useful figures provided on differences of feeding arrangements between Pyoktong and Koje. Unlike Kinkead, White emphasises environment rather than 'lack of discipline' in causing high death among US prisoners in the Yalu camps. See *Interlocking Subversion in Government Departments* pp. 1830-48 for detailed testimony by an US Army doctor imprisoned at Pyoktong of the co-relation between nutrition and the success of the indoctrination programme.

Camp 5 noticed that some prisoners were just noticeably less starved than others. . . .

TO MAKE YOU A BETTER MAN

In many cases, indoctrination had started long before prisoners reached the prison camps. From the highest to the lowest no one was exempt. No sooner had General Dean, the highest-ranking UNC prisoner, been captured after the fall of Taejon, than the treatment started. He was told by his interrogator, 'General, you're a brave man, but you're very ignorant politically.' Three years of intense Marxist-Leninist indoctrination followed, during which Dean never weakened, although he was kept for much of this time in a small house near Pyongyang, hidden by the North Koreans from the Chinese. When at last this prize captive was released he wrote, 'I'm an authority now on the history of the Communist Party and much of its doctrine.' Similarly Anthony Farrar-Hockley, captured at Solma-Ri with most of the British prisoners held by the Communists, was harangued during the very early stages of his march to the north by a CCF education officer, Chen, who told him that now he had the good fortune to be liberated he was in the hands of a truly democratic and humanitarian government.[1] Fusilier Derek Kinne, captured with the Fifth Fusiliers just west of Solma-Ri, and who was to win the GC for his conduct during captivity, was at first exposed to a North Korean officer, 'Capitalist! Imperialist aggressor! Tool of Wall Street! Raper of Korean national aspirations!', before he too was taken under the wing of the more urbane Chen. '. . . We understand your position. That is why, providing you show yourself to be sorry for fighting for those criminals, the American generals and big business men, we shall help you to rehabilitate yourself; make you a

---

[1] Nearly all the Commonwealth prisoners were either captured at Chunghung Dong, outside Seoul, during the opening of the Chinese new year offensive on 3 January, when the RURs suffered, or at Solma-ri when fortunately weather conditions at least had improved. Of a total of 1,188 Commonwealth missing in Korea, 1,036 were repatriated. UK figures are 1,102 and 978 respectively. One Briton refused repatriation. There are slight variations in the different casualty tables. See Barclay, 223.

better man. . . . I'm sure your conscience will help you to understand.'

Yet these remarks were an accurate foretaste of many *leit-motifs* of thought-reform in Korea, as for example the insistence on the cause of the war as the crisis of overproduction in the West which had caused the United Nations to launch an aggressive war against North Korea in the search for new markets, and consequently the need for each prisoner to undergo ideological repentance and resurrection. The official Chinese designation of their attitude towards their prisoners, probably the ultimate Orwellian touch about international Communism's myriad Korean activities, was 'the Lenient Policy', which they claimed was superior to canons of the Geneva Convention as a code for prisoner treatment. The Chinese stated that as the war was the product of imperialist aggression against a peace-loving country, *all* UNC soldiers were *ipso facto* war criminals. But as most UN soldiers were also working men who had been misled by their capitalist rulers, therefore they would not be shot if they admitted their mistakes, and showed themselves to be progressive. Reactionary prisoners who refused to see the truth were not entitled to the benefits of the Lenient Policy; whatever treatment a prisoner received, whether he proved progressive or reactionary, it was better than what he deserved: death. The legal basis of the Lenient Policy in Communist eyes lay in the reservation the USSR had entered against Article 85 of the 1949 Geneva Convention, which protected the rights of POWs, claiming that 'in accordance with the principles of the Nuremberg trial', the Soviet Union insisted on its right to try prisoners for war crimes and crimes against humanity. And it was precisely this reservation that Chou En-lai made when Peking recognised the Convention in July 1952. (The North Korean government as early as July 1950 had announced that it was 'strictly abiding' by the Convention which in practice it repudiated even more than the Chinese.)

At first, the Lenient Policy in action meant compulsory lectures and discussions which went on until 10 o'clock at night, and which often were delivered in the open air. Typical subjects were 'The Democratic Reformation and Democratic structure in North Korea and the Peaceful Unification Policy of the North Korean Government', or 'The aggressive war brought on by the

American imperialists and Rhee and his traitors will end in their defeat'. S. J. Davies, the captured chaplain to the Gloucesters, has mentioned some of the lecture subjects presented to his officer group in a transit camp between Pyongyang and Sunchon:

Corruption of the UN by the American warmongers.
The Chinese people's right to Formosa.
The Stockholm Peace Appeal.
Progress in People's China.
Churchill, tool of the Truman-MacArthur-Dulles fascist clique.
The Soviet Union heads the World Peace Camp.

These indoctrination efforts were complemented by complete Chinese control of every detail of the prisoners' living conditions. Each camp was divided into prisoner companies varying in number from three to seven, and each company held between 60 and 350 men. An average company numbered about 200 men. The company was then subdivided into platoons and ultimately squads of six to fifteen prisoners which were the most important unit. Chinese-appointed squad leaders, whose authority cut across the normal chain of command, were given the task of keeping order and reporting to the authorities on the opinions of the men in their group. In the same way progressives were put in control of the camp committees which were supposed to administer details of welfare. Thus by neutralising and separating their prisoners' former leaders the Chinese were helping to create the moral chaos on which they built their indoctrination successes — and by using converted progressives to do much of their policing they further helped to undermine the other prisoners' morale. Parallel with the progress of the indoctrination lectures went this systematic attempt to isolate every man under Communist authority from his fellow men, using the pressures of hunger, fear, anxiety and guilt.

By mid-1952 the compulsory lectures were considered a failure and the emphasis switched to 'voluntary' study groups led by progressives. Personal interrogation and indoctrination had proved it could have a more powerful effect. At frequent intervals prisoners were asked to write elaborate self-criticisms of their political attitudes and class backgrounds, 'cognitions', and these personal details were often used to effect by the interrogators, fluent English speakers of great intelligence, in their sessions; the interrogation rooms were usually equipped with recording devices, and sometimes with one-way mirrors. Threats of coercion and non-repatriation alternated with chats about home, cigarettes, some good food and walks around the camp with the interrogator. The intellectual approach in both the compulsory lectures and the personal indoctrination sessions was the same. From analysing the Korean War as imperialist aggression, the critique moved on to a detailed criticism of the shortcomings of Western countries in terms of Southern lynchings and colonialism, and so to the idyllic life of socialism in the people's democracies. Together with the emotional pressures involved this dramatic presentation of Marxism-Leninism to prisoners who often not only failed to comprehend why they had fought in Korea, but even the rudiments of democracy itself, was bound to have some sort of effect. Away from lectures and interrogation, news of the outside world reached prisoners through Radios Peking and Pyongyang piped through a public-address system; the camp library was well stocked with objectively progressive literature which showed up the evils of the West — Dickens, Dreiser, Howard Fast and Ehrenburg . . . all human activity since the creation was shown as leading to the peace of Communism.

Kinkead has characterised the psychological techniques of indoctrination as 'repetition, harassment and humiliation', and Philip Deane, who could cap every quotation thrown at him from the sacred Communist texts, writes that for him 'it was not indoctrination by an interlocutor who irritates you and whose arguments you're goaded to refute. It was endless repetition — a monotonous and single-minded repetition which . . . began to make an impression. . . .' To others their indoctrinator became a therapist in a transference situation to whom they confided their personal problems and plans for life after repatriation. Others studied the writings of Lenin and Stalin so assiduously that on return home they could expound the theory and practice of Communism and its superiority to democracy with some of the most skilful of the specially trained US Army interrogators. Yet, on many, indoctrination had little effect.

Obviously the Lenient Policy with its emphasis on confession and repentance, and its propaganda exploitation in the context of the Korean War closely resembled the prisoner indoctrination programme developed by the Russians with their German prisoners a decade before. Indoctrination techniques are an adaptation of the well-known methods initiated in the USSR to get apparent co-operation and confession from important political prisoners, techniques described in *Darkness at Noon* and by Weissberg, Stypulkowski and others, and used not only in the Moscow Trials of the mid-1930s but against Mindszenty, Rajk, Slansky and various Westerners such as Robert Voegeler and Edgar Saunders. In these cases extreme pressure over a prolonged period applied to an isolated individual had resulted in at least a temporary change of character, and it is this process, also used extensively by the Chinese, which is generally known as 'brainwashing', as opposed to the milder military 'indoctrination'. In Korea, the only Westerners given the full brainwashing treatment were the USAF personnel from whom bacteriological warfare confessions were demanded. But the Korean indoctrination programme was more thorough than the Russian experiments with their German captives, and must be briefly examined in relation to its more powerful and comprehensive parent, the thought-reform programme in Red China, 'one of the most powerful efforts at human manipulation ever undertaken'.[1]

Perhaps the greatest difference between Russian and Chinese treatment of 'enemies of the state' is that while in the USSR the authorities do not worry too much about future attitudes of the prisoner during his punishment, in China punishment is seen as a stage in regeneration. The Russians believe in the deterrent of punishment, the Chinese in bringing about a permanent change of attitude. Hence, while the NKVD-MVD has eliminated whole classes, such as anti-*Kholkoz* peasants and *kulaks*, deported entire nationalities as in the case of the Volga Germans and half a dozen other national groups, or liquidated large sections of the CPSU itself and of the high command of

[1] Lifton, *Thought Reform*, p. 4-5. This is the most valuable book on Chinese conversion techniques yet published. It does not concern itself with the military application of thought-reform in Korea, but gives (p. 485) a list of references in medical journals to the Korean indoctrination programme. See especially Hinkle and Wolff, 'Communist Interrogation and Indoctrination of "Enemies of the State"', *Archives of Neurology and Psychiatry*, August 1956, Vol. 76, No. 2.

the Red Army, the Chinese decided that as *all* outside the Chinese Communist Party are suspect, the entire nation were potential converts.[1] This attitude, and the evolution of thought-reform, owes much to the nature of the Chinese civil war, for the Communists had to find some way of ensuring the maintenance of popular support in areas temporarily lost by them as the guerilla fighting ebbed and flowed year after year over huge distances. Within this context, of course, intellectuals and bourgeois Chinese have been especially suspect, and, following methods evolved to convert defectors from the KMT during the 1930s, thought-reform processes for converting intellectuals were perfected in Yenan in the early 1940s. By these trial-and-error methods, paralleled by Mao's own political development, Communism in China had been effectively Sinified. Robert Lifton has shown that thought-reform is no mere Pavlovian conditioning, but an extremely subtle assault on the identity, eclectic in source, yet owing most to the applied principles of both Soviet Communism and Chinese culture.

Thus, thought-reform's chief psychic opponent has been Chinese traditional filialism, the respect for family which had formed the basis of Chinese society for millennia. The attack on the image of filial piety was begun under the influences of the early revolutionary Kuomintang, helped by the imported ideals of western liberalism. By subsequently destroying all three influences, the thought-reform programme has effectively removed any rival to its own doctrines in the minds of most Chinese. The assault on the old identities in the vast communal thought reform sessions that ravaged China in the years following the Communist victory of 1949 meant many millions were forced to confess their class guilt and to discover the necessity for a new progressive identity on the hard journey towards Maoist harmony. If the emphasis in thought-reform, on sin, guilt and confession, is a residue from Russia's Christian-Byzantine past incorporated into Communism, the importance of 'harmony' and 'sincerity' derives from Confucian ideals. Combining these influences, thought-reform has thus become a far more formidable

---

[1] This in no way means that the CCP eschews less subtle methods to maintain its rule when necessary. In September 1952 Peking's Finance Minister, Po Yi-po announced that two million Chinese had been liquidated since the establishment of the regime.

weapon of mass coercion than the Soviet show trial. If Soviet crime and punishment is still best illustrated in the drama of Rubashov and Gletkin, then thought-reform's power is seen in the spectacle of the Western progressives holding 'Fight-For-Peace' parades on the banks of the Yalu, or those Chinese liberals who have apparently embraced Communism.

Even if the indoctrination programme in Korea lacked the success its manipulators had achieved in China, there were many in the Yalu camps, who, while not completely converted to Communism, were affected not only by physical pressures but by the inculcation of the fear of total annihilation and total abandonment that lies at the heart of thought-reform and indoctrination. Thus for some, their old personalities were eroded away and a new one born under the stress of those piti-less months. For them indoctrination means rebirth. Lifton records a French doctor arriving in Hong Kong after over three years exposure to thought-reform:

> From the imperialistic side we are not criminals; from the people's side we are criminals. If we look at this from the im-perialists' side, re-education is a kind of compulsion. But if we look at it from the people's side it is to die and be born again.[1]

PROGRESSIVES AND REACTIONARIES

In considering the effects of the prisoner indoctrination pro-gramme in Korea, it is important to distinguish between the short-term and long-term results. Following a reasonably wide-spread break-down in morale, many UNC prisoners assisted the Communist peace campaign. But the long-term objective of the programme, the conversion of prisoners, failed, and many prisoners even in spite of the coercive efforts of the Chinese resisted all attempts to enlist them in the fight for peace.

These efforts to conscript prisoners into the propaganda battle were impressive. In the spring and summer of 1951 not only were peace committees organised in many prison camps to sign the Stockholm Peace Appeal and other peace declarations to the

[1] Lifton, p. 20.

General Assembly, the Security Council, and the Communist-front World Peace Council, but a central co-ordinating committee for the entire prison-camp system was created, the 'Central Committee of the United States-British War Prisoners Peace Organisation'. This central committee produced the news sheet, *Peace Fighter's Chronicle*, but, as the Chinese elaborated their informer network of progressives, the peace committees and the co-ordinating committee lapsed. Nevertheless many local peace-aligned news-sheets published by the progressives appeared in the camps, and from 1952 onwards a fortnightly newspaper, *Towards Truth and Peace* was published at Pyoktong ('the Progressives' Camp') which circulated to all the prison camps.

This dragooning of the prisoners to add greater weight to peace appeals was only part of the campaign to give the outside world the impression that the UNC's own POWs repudiated Western policy in Korea. The Chinese made great use of incoming and outgoing mail. The families of reactionary prisoners received very few if any letters, for without the approved phrases included it was unlikely that letters would reach their destination. On other occasions, prisoners undergoing interrogation were told that some mail would be a reward for information, while reactionaries were informed that as a punishment mail was being withheld.

Until the first exchange of prisoner lists at Panmunjom in December 1951 prisoners had not been allowed to write home, and thus not only relatives but even the UNC were dependent on Communist channels such as the London *Daily Worker* for news about prisoners. In Britain relatives were subjected to constant pressure by Communist-front organisations to attend rallies 'to get the boys home from Korea'. Particularly active in this campaign was the National Assembly of Women which forwarded letters brought back from North Korea by its chairman, Mrs. Monica Felton. These activities of pro-Communist Westerners who visited the Yalu camps were an important part of the campaign to undermine morale among prisoners. There was Jack Gaster, a London solicitor who visited North Korea in March 1952 as a member of the delegation of the International Association of Democratic Lawyers investigating UN atrocities and bacteriological warfare. On his return, Gaster reported in the *Worker* that prisoners received more meat, fats and sugar to eat 'than anyone in Britain receives from a ration book'. A year before Gaster's visit in February, 1951 a correspondent of the *Daily Worker*, Michael Shapiro, had harangued a group of Americans as 'warmongering dogs' who deserved to die like dogs, and when he was verbally attacked by a sergeant of the RURs suffering from the beri-beri which eventually killed him, had the man marched out with the comment, 'I'll have you shot.'

Monica Felton herself visited North Korea in both 1951 and 1952, but the two chief 'visitors' were Alan Winnington of the London *Worker* and the Australian Wilfred Burchett who reported for the Paris *Ce Soir* and *L'Humanité*. Besides general propaganda activities helpful to the Chinese such as the drafting of bacteriological warfare statements for brainwashed US airmen, both Winnington and Burchett visited Camps 1 (Chongsong) and 5. Welcomed at the latter, they had a warm reception at Camp 1, a stronghold of unreduced British and American reactionaries. Derek Kinne records that during a talk at Chongsong, Burchett was greeted by a row of reactionaries waving nooses of old rope at him: 'You'll hang, you bastard'. But although these people were giving aid and comfort to the enemy they could not be charged with treason as in Korea there was no state of war. Nevertheless, Hartley Shawcross once stated that it seemed likely that from a legal point of view such aid and comfort could be brought within the definition of treason; the British courts were never asked to decide.

Such resistance that greeted Burchett and Winnington indicated the strength of feeling against the authorities in the camps, a fact which has been overlooked in many reports. By 1952, in their efforts to break down active and passive resistance from the reactionaries, the Chinese had completely atomised such groups. Not only were officers separated from the sergeants and placed in camps of their own, such as Camp 2, Branch 1, at Pin Chon-ni, which contained Farrar-Hockley and Chaplain Davies, but separate penal camps for hard core reactionaries from both officers and men were formed. The penalties for 'hostile attitude', escapes and refusal to acquiesce in indoctrination were enormous, including extreme physical brutality such as beating, solitary confinement in wooden boxes, suspension by hands and feet from a beam and marching over the frozen Yalu in mid-winter in bare feet. Derek Kinne has catalogued such physical pressures used by the Chinese, for after a time at Camp 1 he was sent to the penal compound of Camp 2, Branch 2, at Ogyedong where were imprisoned, says the British Defence Ministry report, *Treatment of British Prisoners of War in Korea*, 'men who had distinguished themselves by their heroic resistance to all Chinese brutality'. Kinne himself tells a story which shows that on occasion even the progressives forgot their indoctrination. During a camp concert at Chongsong a British sergeant recited a bit of doggerel:

> They seek him here, they seek him there,
> They seek for Mao everywhere.
> Should he be shot — or should he be hung?
> That damned elusive, elusive Mao Tse-tung.

In the uproar that followed before it was suppressed by the guards, all joined in:

> All the veneer of antagonism the Chinese had wrought between us nation by nation, colour by colour, age by age, was forgotten in that undeniable reminder that we were all one, men who sprang from the same understanding of the word 'freedom'. However maltreated it might be at times in our own lands, it was a word which held a vital meaning for us, although it clearly meant nothing for these products of a vast Asiatic backwater. . . .[1]

Why then did the Chinese not obtain more successes in indoctrination and conversion? An important reason was of course that the shadow of the armistice lay over their programme, and that full coercive measures leading to the death of their reactionary prisoners could not be applied once a preliminary exchange of prisoner lists had been made. Even in a Chinese Communist framework indoctrination and conversion had to pro-

---

[1] Kinne, *The Wooden Boxes*, p. 107-8. See also *No Rice for Rebels* for an account of resistance to Chinese brutality at Chongsong and Ogye-dong by a reactionary from the Gloucesters, L./Cpl. R. F. Mathews (as told to Francis S. Jones).

ceed in ways which could not open the Chinese to counter-charges by the West that they had deliberately liquidated their captives. Then again, resistance was made easier by the vast cultural-linguistic gap between the Anglo-Americans and the Chinese, reinforced by the guilt that inevitably accompanied any concession by a Western prisoner to those whose armies were in fact, if not in law, at war with the forces of his own country in Korea. For whereas in China thought-reform was able to mobilise a whole series of intellectual, emotional and physical pressures around a patriotic appeal to the potential resister, this was not possible with the Korean prisoners. As we know now, many of those who seemed to collaborate or who 'played it cool' did so from motives of self-preservation rather than of sympathy to Communism. Pyoktong was hardly a good advertisement for the benevolence of Marxism-Leninism.

Various reports and autobiographies dealing with life in the Yalu camps all tend to make this point, that while real collaborators and real resisters formed a relatively small proportion of the prisoners, those who played it cool made up the largest group. In Camp 1, Derek Kinne remarks, referring to both British and US personnel, those who collaborated were either Communist sympathisers, opportunists, or the frightened. The majority group was that 'whose policy was "Stay clear of trouble."' The British Defence Ministry report considers the Chinese indoctrination success 'comparatively small', yielding to the national complacency just as US writers characteristically over-emphasise the moral collapse of American troops. The British report says that officers and senior NCOs who made up 12% of the total British troops in captivity were 'almost completely unaffected' by indoctrination, but of the remaining junior NCOs and other ranks 'some two-thirds remained virtually unaffected. Of the remainder, most absorbed sufficient indoctrination to be classed as Communist sympathisers. . . . A small minority — about forty altogether — returned home convinced Communists.' Thus while it concedes that there was a significant collapse of British morale, the report emphasises that the Chinese — apparently — failed to make many converts.

With the Americans, of course, it is a more complex story. The heart-searching produced by their prisoners' collapse produced the Defence Department report mentioned above which contains a new prisoner code of conduct, differing hardly at all from the traditional principles of military conduct in captivity, and which was promulgated by President Eisenhower in 1955. The report ends with the sentence: 'The Korean story must never be permitted to happen again.' The Korean POW story was also responsible for the creation by the US Army of the vast task force of psychiatrists, lawyers and intelligence experts who examined all the POWs, and on which Kinkead bases his commentary: 'This tremendous and detailed study, of a scope and complexity never before attempted by the armed services of this country, made an effort to obtain all pertinent facts about the background and prison experiences of every American soldier taken captive. . . .'

This report obviously carries the implication that the collapse of morale in the prison camps was due to inadequately tough training methods and has been convincingly attacked as representing the views of a reactionary, scape-goating clique of disciplinarians in the Pentagon.[1] Nevertheless, it gives the figure of outright collaborators as 13% equally split between the weak, the opportunists, and the genuine converts, this last approximating the British figure, and confirming the low effectiveness of indoctrination as a means of conversion in Korea. The resisters were equally made up of those neurotics who always resented authority, and those well-integrated individuals, the bravest of the brave, who made no concessions whatsoever to their enemy. The largest group of all were those who 'played it cool', numbering about 75%. 'They co-operated in indoctrination and interrogation sessions in a passive sort of way, although there was a tendency to refuse to do anything obviously traitorous,' writes Kinkead, certainly qualifying in this remark (p. 130) his earlier assertions (pp. 16, 49) that almost a third, or a 'majority' of the US prisoners had either collaborated or 'yielded in some

[1] Peters, 'When the Army debunks the Army', *Encounter*, July 1960. Peters alleges that Kinkead himself has been indoctrinated by 'a small group of Army officials'. 'Why this self-critical national insistence, at the expense of logic, fact and even decency, on a GI burden of guilt?' He also attacks the methodology of the report: cf. Biderman, *The March to Calumny*, a recent study by a sociologist which claims that the collapse in the prison camps has been over-emphasised for the wrong reasons. Biderman demonstrates that most 'collaboration' was either inconsequential or co-operation of the sort which no prisoner can ever avoid. The overwhelming number of American prisoners, he insists, became extremely anti-Communist.

degree' to the Chinese. Indeed, only fourteen US Army officers and men were court-martialled for misbehaviour in the prison camps, and eleven found guilty of offences ranging from informing to murder; in addition eight others were relieved or dishonourably discharged from the Army. One Marine was dismissed from the Service and four USAF personnel were discharged.

Thus the story which must never be permitted to happen again fizzled out in a series of obscure courts martial years after the end of the war. But the imprint of indoctrination remains, with the humiliation that in the battle for the mind in North Korea, many temporarily weakened — yet in circumstances which could be again repeated for there can be no conclusive answer to thought reform and indoctrination so long as man is weak and fallible. Yet for all their efforts, the Chinese only succeeded in converting one in twenty-five of their Anglo-American prisoners. But twenty-one Americans and one Briton, Marine Andrew Condron, went through the full ritual of ideological death and rebirth on the Yalu, for after the armistice they lived in Peking. Eventually three of the Americans and the Briton returned home. When Condron arrived back in the UK during October 1962 he was quoted as saying:

We called our camp — Pyoktong Camp No. 5 — Pyoktong University. I can only talk about my camp. I have heard that other fellows who were prisoners were beaten up. I cannot say this was untrue, I just don't know. Personally, I never saw anyone being ill-treated by Chinese. . . .

There was no reason at all to assume that Condron did not believe what he was saying.

CHAPTER NINETEEN

PEKING: BACTERIA FOR PEACE

A conqueror is always a lover of peace . . . he would
like to make his entry into our state unopposed.
VON CLAUSEWITZ

In der groesse der luege liegt immer ein faktor des
geglaubtwerdens. (The bigger the lie, the more easily it is
believed.)
ADOLF HITLER

RALLY FOR PEACE

We demand the unconditional prohibition of the atomic
weapon as an instrument of aggression and mass extermina-
tion of people, and the establishment of strict international
control over the fulfilment of this decision.

We will regard as a war criminal that government which
first uses the atomic weapon against any country. We call
upon all people of goodwill all over the world to sign this
call.

(Stockholm, 19 March 1950)

ALMOST the entire output of Communist political and psychological warfare against the Western cause in Korea was
linked in one way or another with the petition issued by the
World Peace Committee in March 1950 which called for the
unconditional prohibition of all atomic weapons. The Stockholm petition was followed by many other peace appeals which
echoed the objectives of this first and most famous appeal and
which formed the central creed of the Communist-sponsored
international peace movement. Many millions inside the Communist countries signed the Stockholm appeal and its successors,
but the use of the peace movement as a device for consolidating
the masses behind Communist governments was only one of its
functions.

Primarily, in demanding Western abandonment of its one
sure deterrent against the outbreak of a general Soviet war of

conquest, the peace movement was designed to exploit what Lenin once called 'the pitiful pacifism of the bourgeoisie', the inhibitions the West possesses about the use of atomic weapons, the Western liberal confusion about the part that force plays in all international relations. Moreover the launching of the Stockholm appeal so close to the Communist invasion of South Korea indicates that Moscow might well have calculated that some new, powerful, all-embracing blow in its peace offensive was needed as a precautionary move just in case the US was provoked into contemplating the use of atomic weapons against the Communist bloc as a result of the North Korean advance over the 38th Parallel. And once it was obvious that nuclear weapons would not be used in the Korean War, the peace movement was geared to ending the fighting on Communist terms, aligned to the demands of the Chinese and North Korean negotiators at Panmunjom.

Yet the Stockholm petition was only the culmination of the peace movement which had originated as part of Stalin's pre-Korean offensive against Western Europe; it had started with the Wroclaw (Breslau) conference of 'intellectuals' held just after the beginning of the Berlin blockade in August 1948. It was during this conference that Alexander Fadeyev made his famous denunciation of Eliot, Eugene O'Neill, Dos Passos, Malraux (and Sartre) as intellectual jackals and hyenas. These literary pleasantries apart, the chief result of the conference was the creation of a central co-ordinating committee (eventually known as the World Peace Council) to organise the international peace movement which had been floated at Wroclaw. Next, the committee, then known as the International Liaison Committee of Intellectuals For Peace, called a World Congress of the Partisans for Peace in Paris during April 1949—just a few weeks after signing of the North Atlantic Treaty. From the Paris Congress emerged a re-designed World Committee for Peace, to which ultimately all national, regional, local and 'professional' peace committees throughout the world were affiliated in ascending order. Its chairman was Professor Joliot-Curie, the former chairman of the French Atomic Energy Commission.

Two more meetings of the WPC were held in Rome and Paris before Stockholm. Other peace conferences were organised during 1949 in New York, Bucharest, Prague, Tokyo, Budapest,

Mexico City and Moscow, so that by the spring of 1950 the peace movement was well organised on a global basis. With the world congresses, and the more frequent meetings of the WPC went a thorough exploitation through all available mass-media of the need for peace which was projected in a completely anti-American context. It was clear from the beginning of the movement that, in attempting to rally the Western middle classes to its support, it was trying to recreate the emotional pattern of the Popular Front. In the 1930s many non-Marxists had completely identified Communism with democracy; the task of the peace movement in the 1950s was to convince all progressive people of goodwill that Communism was peace. To carry this message and to translate the directives of the WPC into action there were, besides the resources of the CP itself, the old established front organisations for friendship and cultural relations with the USSR and its satellites, and also the international fronts formed at the end of the war such as the World Federation of Trade Unions, the Women's International Democratic Federation, and the International Association of Democratic Lawyers. And now of course there were the brand new peace committees and the professional fronts for peace — 'the peace organisations of the professions'. These included in the UK such bodies as Artists for Peace, the Medical Association for the Prevention of War, Teachers for Peace, and the Author's World Peace Appeal, which became a permanent organisation after launching its petition in April 1951.

This organisational superstructure of the movement emphasised that many not overtly pro-Communist could support the demand for peace and especially the Stockholm appeal and the various peace petitions with their stress on the horrors of the atomic bomb. Yet the peace petitions in no way condemned aggression as such, and ignored also the various Communist paramilitary techniques, such as subversion, insurrection, and revolutionary strikes, which, culminating in the North Korean invasion, had created and cemented the North Atlantic alliance armed with the atomic bomb as the only way of preventing a Soviet occupation of Western Europe. It also seemed possible at this time (as later) that any inspection system for nuclear weapons could easily be circumvented in a totalitarian state. To sign any Communist-sponsored peace petition was, therefore, to sign an invitation to the Red Army to march to the Atlantic.

Inevitably the activities of the peace movement came to a climax during 1950-51 when the North Korean invasion and especially the Chinese incursion across the Yalu made general war seem more likely than at any time since 1945. By August 1950, according to its sponsors, one-eighth of the human race had signed the Stockholm petition, including the entire population of the USSR; eventually it was claimed that more than 500 million people had signed. In Britain, where the petition had met with no great success, it was presented to the House of Commons with over a million signatures by Sidney Silverman, MP, during December 1950. The activities of the WPC in the UK had reached their peak during the previous month, for plans had been made in the summer to hold a second world peace congress in London. The Government refused visas to about 200 foreign applicants who wanted to attend the congress after its venue had been changed to Sheffield, and as a result the meeting was held instead in Warsaw, electing there a new World Peace Council of over 200 people. Henceforward the direction of the movement lay in the control of the Council's executive committee of about two dozen members.

Already the WPC, which Attlee had frankly denounced on 1 November 1950 as 'an instrument of the Politbureau', had been mentioned as a possible alternative to the UN as a forum for the peace-loving peoples. Long, too, before the momentum of the Stockholm petition had been exhausted a new appeal had been launched, following a meeting of the WPC in Berlin in February 1951, demanding a five-power peace pact. The WPC considered that a refusal to sign by one of the big five which included Communist China, was an indication of aggressive purposes. By April 1952 it was claimed by the WPC's executive that over 600 million people had signed the five-power peace pact petition. . . .

While the activities of the peace movement owed much of their limited success to Western subjective inhibitions about the use of force, Kissinger has shown how inside the Communist bloc the leaders have systematically minimised the effect of nuclear weapons ever since 1945, not only to retain freedom of action and to maintain internal morale during the cold war, but also to assert that capitalist technology had not developed a weapon that might stalemate the class war.[1] Soviet military doctrine in the immediate post-war period perpetuated Stalin's ukase of 1942 that 'constantly operating factors' such as man-power, morale and the stability of the home front won wars. The bomb, while it was condemned as a weapon of mass destruction, was not the ultimate weapon. In keeping with this doctrine, as late as January 1950 *Pravda* was asserting that only 8,400 people were affected at Hiroshima; no mention was made of the first US explosion of a thermo-nuclear device at Eniwetok in November 1952, and only in 1954 was the first picture of the atomic mushroom published in the USSR.

Once, however, nuclear parity had been reached with the explosion of the Soviet hydrogen bomb in August 1953 — just a few days after the end of the Korean War — Soviet psychological warfare and diplomacy has alternated peace propaganda and disarmament proposals with direct threats of nuclear war. Now the attack is aimed at the fears of the West as well as at its inhibitions. The Soviet rocket threat to Britain at the time of Suez is a development in this strand of policy, as is Khrushchev's explosion of a fifty-seven-megaton bomb in the autumn of 1961, and the subsequent threat to use a weapon even larger than a 100-megatons.

It is against this background of gradually increasing Soviet nuclear strength that the peace movement as an adjunct of Communist policy in Korea must be seen. Yet indigenous neutralist movements in Western countries since Korea, appealing to the same emotions exploited by the Stockholm petition, have achieved even greater success than the Communist peace movement through not being linked to Soviet policy. Similarly, the official Communist view of nuclear weapons still tends to minimise their absolute nature. Soviet military doctrine envisages operations continuing by land, sea and air *after* an exchange of nuclear strikes by the two super-powers; only in 1959-60 did Krushchev admit that a new war would not spare any participant.

In Korea the West had not used nuclear weapons. But in order to prevent any consideration of a bombing programme against China to break the ground stalemate, and to perpetuate the political pressures raised and manipulated by the peace movement, it was necessary to prove that after all the US had used

[1] See Kissinger, Chap. 11. 'The Soviet Union and the Atom'.

weapons of mass destruction against the Korean people . . . bacteriological warfare.

A CRIME AGAINST THE PEOPLE: BACTERIOLOGICAL WARFARE

> (the UNC) . . . these bandits in generals' uniforms, the butchers in white gloves, the bloody bigots and traders in death who have unleashed the most inhuman carnage in history, warfare with the assistance of microbes, fleas, lice and spiders. . . . *Pravda*

The big lie, as its father well knew, must always in its appeal to human credulity and irrationality, contain an element not too far removed from reality. The first big lie of the Communist propaganda offensive against the United Nations cause in the Korean War claimed that the ROK and the United States had attacked North Korea. Behind this mendacity lay the reality of the alliances built up by the US and its allies to contain Communist expansion. The second bacteriological warfare big lie was more subtle. Its appeal lay in the 'scientific' image of the West in Asia, and in the fact that United Nations air power was the single most powerful weapon its Command possessed in its attempt to force the truce talks to an end on reasonable terms. Moreover, both the charges of aggression and germ warfare were framed so that they would rally the Chinese and North Korean home fronts, and, exploited inside the framework of the peace movement, create the maximum confusion amongst liberal opinion in the West.

That the evolution of the bacteriological warfare campaign can be traced in rather more detail than most Communist psychological warfare campaigns is due solely to the return of many of the American airmen who had been coerced into giving 'confessions' of waging germ warfare. But even before the opening of the campaign in February 1952 there were indications that Peking and Pyongyang were attempting to create a climate of opinion where accusations of germ warfare would be favourably received. As early as 8 May 1951, Pak Hen Yen, the North Korean Foreign Minister, alleged that the Americans were spreading smallpox germs in North Korea; and a month later the Chinese vice-president of the WIDF, speaking in Sofia, demanded that the US stop using bacterial warfare in Korea. But nothing was heard of the charges until 18 February 1952 when Moscow Radio broadcast the following statement during a Korean-language commentary entitled 'Alertness as a weapon for the Korean people':

In order to dissolve the solidarity of the Korean home front, the American interventionists are sending spies and disruptive elements into North Korea for the purpose of obtaining military secrets, poisoning wells, and spreading smallpox and typhus bacteria in various places. One of the more villainous methods practised by the American interventionists is the sending of lepers secretly into North Korea.[1]

These accusations were taken up by Pak Hen Yen on 22 February, repeated by Chou En-lai two days later, and on 25 February the activities of the WPC were brought into the campaign when the Chinese sent a protest about US germ warfare to Joliot-Curie. By 8 March, Chou was claiming that American aircraft had dropped insects, rats, shell-fish and chicken feathers impregnated with disease germs on Chinese as well as North Korean territory. The Far East Command in Tokyo denied the charges on 27 February, followed by Acheson on 4 March, who also, a week later, asked the ICRC to investigate the facts alleged by the Communists. No reply was received from Peking and Pyongyang to the subsequent ICRC offer on 12 March to examine the facts of germ warfare, and the offices of the World Health Organisations were also turned down by the Communist governments: as expected, Washington immediately accepted the ICRC offer. With an investigation by an impartial body blocked from the very beginning of the campaign, the Communists were also able to take the initiative through a 'fact-finding' commission of the IADL which had arrived in North Korea at the beginning of March to investigate Anglo-American atrocities alleged by Monica Felton during the previous summer. Not only was Mrs. Felton the president of the British NAW, but she was also vice-president of one of the more important international fronts — the WIDF.

Inevitably the IADL commission, even before leaving Korea on

[1] Pelling, *The Third World War*, p. 136.

19 March, confirmed that bacteriological warfare had been used by the USAF: 'We are horrified beyond measure at the facts we have ascertained.' The Democratic Lawyers issued a report in Peking on 2 April and then returned to Europe where they held a congress in mid-April, giving more publicity to the charges of American bacteriological warfare. Jack Gaster, a British member of the commission, who, it will be recalled, had visited the Yalu POW camps, continued the campaign in London following the Vienna congress of the IADL. During a press conference on 23 April, Gaster said the commission had substantiated not only germ warfare but the atrocity allegations, and demanded an international tribunal on the Nuremberg example to try the guilty. . . . Yet the confirmation of germ warfare by the IADL was based on nothing more than statements made to the commission in Korea; as such its report was suspect even to many who wanted to believe the charges.

This problem of finding acceptable 'scientific proof' was already in hand even before the Vienna Congress of the Democratic Lawyers, when the high command of the peace movement, the executive of the WPC, met at Oslo at the end of March. Rejecting the services of ICRC and the WHO, the executive, after hearing the evidence of germ warfare, decided to appoint an independent and impartial group of scientists to find out the truth about the bacteria. The 'International Scientific Commission' when formed consisted of six scientists whose professional qualifications were well known. It included as Soviet member, Dr. Zhukov-Verezhnikov, the chief medico-legal expert at the Khabarovsk bacteriological war crimes trial in 1949 when Japanese officers had been sentenced for waging germ warfare against China; and a British representative, the Cambridge biochemist, Dr Joseph Needham, FRS, who like the other members of the Commission was active in the fight for peace — he was President of the British-China Friendship Association. Preparations were soon being made for the ISC to go to China and North Korea as quickly as possible.

Why did the Communists choose bacteriological warfare as the subject of their campaign to give the peace movement a fillip in 1952? Interestingly enough, germ warfare, with its evil associations of mass death and civilian suffering, had long been a favourite with Stalinist propagandists. In the 1930s the *kulaks* had been accused of using anthrax to kill their cattle as a protest against collectivisation — germ warfare on the home front by enemies of the people. Moreover, as recently as the summer of 1950, the Americans had been accused of dropping Colorado beetles in Poland, East Germany and Czechoslovakia. But besides the horror easily aroused by germ warfare, there were other, more pragmatic reasons for this choice.

Just as anthrax and the Colorado beetle could be easily used to explain away the breakdown of an agricultural system wrecked by the excesses of collectivisation in the USSR and Eastern Europe, so bacteriological warfare could be utilised to excuse the typhus, smallpox, influenza and other epidemics known to be raging in China during the winter of 1951-52, and partly caused, no doubt, as in North Korea, by the breakdown of health services as a result of the war.[1] Thus the Peking and Pyongyang regimes could transfer the blame for such epidemics from themselves to the Americans. Moreover, the three-anti campaign (corruption, waste and bureaucracy) and the five-anti campaign (bribery, tax evasion, fraud, theft of state assets and leakage of state economic secrets) were in top gear in China throughout 1952, with other propaganda and thought reform stimuli to cement the masses behind the Peking regime. The first alert on germ warfare which Pak had sounded in May 1951 had been quickly recognised by the authorities as coming at too dangerous a time of the year, for the 'planted' evidence needed in the campaign might start real epidemics in the summer, but not of course in the safer winter time.

These technical problems having been dealt with during 1951 there still remained the necessity of making it quite clear that the Americans were using germ warfare. The ISC had to be presented with apparently irrefutable proof of the USAF's diabolical activities. Even the finds of 'evidence' throughout Manchuria and North Korea was not conclusive . . . how did the bacteria get there? The final link in the chain of proof and the beginning of the climax of the campaign came on 4 May in a broadcast from Radio Pyongyang . . . two USAF fliers, Lieutenants Quinn and Enoch, had confessed that they had dropped

---

[1] The *Times* on 21 April 1952 quoting the *People's World* of 21 February 1952 said that the big epidemics in China were caused by an unusually dry winter and the inefficiency of the medical services.

explosive germ bombs on North Korea during January 1952 after special bacteriological warfare briefings starting in August 1951 in Japan and later at Kunsan in south-west Korea.

The story of Quinn and Enoch and the other airmen who were interrogated for germ warfare confessions is only in some ways similar to the indoctrination story in the POW camps. For as the germ warfare confessions were highly important to the Communists, so the pressures were far greater than in the indoctrination programme and some airmen may truly be said to have been brainwashed. The ordeal of Quinn and Enoch is typical. Their B-26 was shot down on 13 January during a raid on Anju, on the Chongchon. Preliminary interrogation about their background, briefing and training methods gave no indication of the ordeal to come. Then came Pak's accusation of germ warfare on 22 February: confessions were absolutely necessary if the story was to stand up. Soon relays of interrogators were demanding germ warfare confessions from the two airmen, held in solitary confinement. They were told they were war criminals and would never see America again. But that if they confessed they would be a 'people's hero' entitled to the Lenient Policy. Explained Enoch afterwards, 'insanity, death or these absurd confessions were the alternatives'.[1]

At last, at the beginning of May, while other captured airmen such as Lieutenants O'Neal and Kniss were also being interrogated, Quinn and Enoch capitulated. Soon after agreeing to write a germ warfare confession, Enoch met Wilfred Burchett, who, with Alan Winnington, had been given the task of editing the confessions into a propaganda film script. Delighted to see a Western face, Enoch told Burchett that his confession was rubbish. 'Are you trying to tell me,' asked Burchett angrily, 'that this isn't so?'[2] The unfortunate Enoch was discovering that in North Korea in the early 1950s not even a Caucasian could be trusted. Other airmen gave elaborate confessions thinking they were playing a practical joke on the Chinese. But there was little humour in the testimony which Quinn, Enoch, O'Neil and Kniss read out to the ISC later in the summer; and which was filmed and given world-wide distribution by Communist propaganda outlets including the peace committees.

[1] White, *The Captives of Korea*, p. 168.
[2] *Ibid.*, loc. cit.

. . . The use of bacteriological warfare is one of the detriments to world peace. Its use threatens our very civilisation. This type of warfare is against all known humanitarian principles. The peace-loving peoples of every country condemn this type of warfare and the people who gave orders to use it. . . . The people of America must realise the seriousness of these terrible weapons and rise up together and stop this germ warfare. Only then can all mankind have peace. . . .(O'Neal)

. . . I want it to be known by whoever reads this statement that it is my own sense of justice, my own ability to tell right from wrong has forced me to let everyone know the facts. . . . This inhuman warfare must be stopped. I offer these facts to the world that an inhuman weapon is being used in Korea by the US forces. . . . (Kniss)

. . . It is very clear from these facts that the capitalistic Wall Street warmongers in their greed, their ruthless greed, have caused this horrible crime of bacteriological warfare in order to get more money for themselves in the hope of spreading the war. . . . I was forced to be a tool of these warmongers, made to drop germ bombs and do this awful crime against the people of Korea and the Chinese Volunteers. . . . They explained the lenient policy towards POWs which I brought up as I was on the propaganda of the Wall Street imperialists, found very difficult to understand. But the Chinese Volunteers were very patient. They issued me with warm clothing against the cold, gave me excellent food, bedding and a warm place to sleep. I am eternally grateful for their kind treatment. At last after much patience on the part of the Volunteers I realised my crime. My own conscience bothered me a great deal and it is very good to be rid of this burden and to confess and repent. I have realised my terrible crime against the people. . . . (Quinn)[1]

The follow-up to this intensification of the germ warfare cam-

---

[1] The confessions of Quinn, Enoch, O'Neal and Kniss are found between pp. 491-608 of the *Report of the International Scientific Commission for the Investigation of the Fact concerning Bacterial Warfare in Korea and China* (Peking, 1952).

paign in the summer of 1952 was world-wide. Riots against germ
warfare were started by Communist supporters in many countries. Peking Radio asserted that on Koje Chinese and Korean
prisoners were being used in human experiments to improve the
efficiency of the bacterial attacks. The Soviet Navy magazine
Red Fleet reminded its readers that during the Crimean War
the Anglo-French forces had used cannon balls containing pois-
onous substances. Everywhere in North Korea and North China
germ-hunting squads were on the look-out for US aircraft and
their deadly cargo. By June, when the campaign reached its
climax, Mark Clark thought that it was a prelude to the Communists' own use of germ warfare in Korea.

The next development in the campaign was the emergence
from China in early July of Dr Hewlett Johnson, the Dean of
Canterbury, and who many in the Communist bloc thought to
be head of the English state church. 'No one can have any
doubt of the reality of this deed', the Dean told reporters in
Hong Kong on 3 July. Back in London the Dean went on to tell
a meeting of the British-China Friendship Association that the
'facts about germ warfare are conclusive and irrefutable'. In
Mukden, the Dean had seen in a test tube insects found on an
ice rink and which his hosts told him were infected with disease
germs. Demands in Parliament to have the Dean's letters patent
revoked, or to have him examined by psychiatrists or an investigating tribunal were turned down. It was explained, not for the
first time, that as Dr. Johnson had not committed the felony of
treason, or heresy — it was not a violation of the thirty-nine
articles to believe in US bacteriological warfare — he could not
be defrocked under the Church Discipline Act (1840). Almost
simultaneously with the Dean's appearance in London after his
journey to China — he had not crossed the Yalu into Korea —
the WPC was carrying on the offensive in East Berlin. From
here *The Times* reported on 7 July that the meeting of the Council had been almost monopolised by the subject of Korea; the
impression was given that not only were infected organisms
raining down from the Korean sky but that the Americans had
even succeeded in poisoning the fishing waters just off the coast.

Then in September came what was intended as the final
all-revealing proof of bacteriological warfare, the publication in
Peking of the ISC report, a 330,000-word, 665-page document.

The Commission had arrived in the Chinese capital at the end of June, visited Manchuria in mid-July and North Korea at the end of July. The report confirmed that the USAF was using germ warfare. Of thirteen incidents detailed in North Korea, and thirty-seven in China, the report discussed four Korean and fifteen Chinese incidents in great detail. For example, at Hoi-Yang in North Korea, thousands of flies had been observed in April 1952 following the visit of a circling US aircraft: 'the conclusion was that these flies could only have been disseminated by the American plane'. At Kang-Sou, also in Korea, fleas had been found in a jam jar; a peasant who had washed his face in the water died of plague, *Pasteurella pestis*. At Kuantien, a Manchurian town near the Korean border, a cylinder had been dropped by a US aircraft . . . after a search, flies, spiders and feathers infected with *Bacillus anthracis* had been found near the fragments. At Dai-dong in North Korea, two people had died of cholera after eating raw clams found on a hillside. The USAF had knocked out the purification plant of the nearby reservoir and then contaminated the water with the cholera-impregnated clams. Not only did the report include an examination of such incidents and the full transcript of the four American airmen's confessions of waging germ warfare, but Dr. Zhukov-Verezhnikov confirmed that the Americans were using the same sort of germ warfare methods that the Japanese had used in China. Thus the US imperialists were the true successors to the Japanese fascists.

An analyst of the ISC report, John Clews, has written that 'None of the evidence produced in the Report proves the charges: but there is no doubt that, in general, the "evidence" was found as stated'.[1] Clews has shown that the evidence on which the commission reported was found either in North Korea where the Russians had a great measure of internal control, or near the railway leading down from the Siberian railhead at Blagoveshchensk through Manchuria to Harbin and Soviet-leased Port Arthur and Dairen. Ever since 1946 Soviet anti-epidemic teams had been working in Manchuria and North Korea, and these special teams using the Soviet communication lines could easily have planted this BW evidence; the Chinese did not at that time have the facilities for such an elaborate hoax.

[1] Clews, *The Communists' New Weapon — Germ Warfare*, p. 14.

Indeed, that the ISC's conclusions were based not on scientific evidence at all but on an acceptance of their hosts' veracity was admitted by members of the commission on their return to Europe. When the Swedish member Dr. Andrea Andreen returned to Stockholm in September she was quoted as saying that, 'We felt so sure of the integrity of our Chinese hosts that we entirely trusted statements which they made regarding the American use of germ warfare. The scientific foundation of the Commission's work consisted of the fact that the delegates implicitly believed the Chinese and North Korean accusations and evidence.' Needham had very much the same to say in a press conference in London on 26 September: '. . . We accepted the word of the Chinese scientists. It is possible to maintain that the whole thing was a kind of patriotic conspiracy. I prefer to believe that the Chinese were not acting parts.'[1] Thus the whole weight of the ISC report was shown to rest on no more than its members' credulous belief in the human infallibility of their Chinese and Korean guides — to put it at its most charitable.

This non-existent basis for the 'scientific' proof of germ warfare in no way inhibited the campaign which was sustained in a monster Congress of Peoples for Peace held in Vienna during December 1952. This third world congress was attended by the biggest galaxy of intellectuals that the peace movement had been able to rally. Besides Joliot-Curie, the platform included Brecht, Aragon, Léger, Sartre, Ehrenberg, Fadeyev, Bernal, the Dean of Canterbury and Mrs. Sun Yat-sen. The Congress held a rousing special session on bacteriological warfare which was addressed amongst others by Dr. Zhukov-Vereznhikov and Dr. Lu Chen Hen, North Korean Vice-Minister of Health. The congress called for an immediate end to hostilities in Korea (on the basis of an UNC capitulation on the prisoner repatriation issue) and condemned American germ warfare: '. . . we categorically demand the immediate prohibition of biological warfare. . . .'

Then, in the late winter of 1952-53, came another burst of confessions from Pyongyang on 22 February 1953, the anniversary of the first charges from North Korea. Two Marine Corps officers, Colonel Schwable, Chief of Staff of the 1st Marine Air Wing, and Major Bley had admitted that a JCS directive of October 1951 had ordered the laying down of a disease belt

[1] Pelling, pp. 143-4.

across North Korea using cholera, yellow fever and typhus. The confessions were circulated during the next month in the UN by the Soviet delegation, as it was known the US was pressing for the creation of a UN Commission to investigate germ warfare. Yet even Schwable and Bley were not the highest ranking airmen from whom the Communist were able to extract BW confessions. Colonel Walker Mahurin, a famous World War II ace in Europe, and who had been executive assistant to Thomas Finletter, the US Air Force Secretary at the beginning of the Korean War confessed, as did Colonel Andrew Evans, a former member of the Pentagon staff of General Vandenberg. Who could know better than these men that the USAF was deeply implicated in germ warfare? At last on 23 April 1953, the General Assembly voted by 52-5-3 to set up a five-power commission to investigate the germ warfare accusations. Few expected, and rightly, that Peking and Pyongyang would even acknowledge the new commission, ineffective from its birth. Three months later on 27 July the armistice was signed at Panmunjom and prisoner repatriation began.

The last act of the drama of the bacteriological warfare campaign was played out with a speech given by Dr. Charles Mayo, of the famous Minnesota clinic, to the United Nations Political Committee on 26 October 1953.[1] Dr. Mayo submitted to the Committee sworn statements by many airmen who had confessed to waging germ warfare, including Quinn, Enoch, O'Neal, Kniss, Schwable and Bley, which testified that the confessions had been extracted after the application in many cases of what Mayo called 'extreme and prolonged physical and mental torture'. Altogether, Mayo said, 107 USAF personnel had been accused of waging germ warfare. Of these thirty-six had signed confessions — this figure was later amended to thirty-eight — and forty, in spite of all pressures, had refused to sign. The remainder were either dead or missing. There had been no playing it cool on the issue of germ warfare confessions. The treatment given the airmen, as Mayo described it, resembled that given in Communist countries to those from whom important political confessions are wanted. It was later calculated that statements from twenty-three prisoners had been used in the campaign.

[1] The text of Mayo's speech is in the *State Department Bulletin*, 9 November 1953.

The airmen had been interrogated at great length while being kept in solitary confinement and with great alteration, depending on their co-operation, in food and general treatment. The pressures used according to Dr. Mayo were 'calculated to disintegrate the mind of an intelligent victim, to distort his sense of values to a point where he will not simply cry out, "I did it!" but will become a seemingly willing accomplice to the complete destruction of his integrity'. In the interrogation centre at Pak's Palace near Pyongyang, the Sino-North Korea staff were directed by Soviet personnel. There was another special interrogation camp at Mukden, across the Yalu in Manchuria. Colonel Mahurin had at one time no less than fifteen interrogators working on him and only broke after eight months of extreme duress. One USAF lieutenant was interrogated for over 1,800 hours in North Korea and Manchuria and yet another was confronted by his inquisitors for over eight hours a day for sixty days and four hours daily for fifty-four days, never writing a confession. Lieutenant James Stanley was interrogated and tortured for four months, confined in a hole in the ground, stood to attention for long periods and then interrogated again with a spotlight six inches away from his face. When he still refused to confess to germ warfare the Chinese gave him up as an impossible reactionary.

These stories show that there was a 'vast organisation' (Mayo) working on the bacteriological warfare campaign. As the campaign went on, so the sophistication of the interrogators increased. Forty different fabricated stories were scrapped and all confessions fitted into one master story into which all differing details could be reconciled. Moreover, the role of the germ warfare campaign as it became a major plank in Communist global propaganda evolved into something more than a psychological warfare offensive inside the context of the Korean War. Only the death of Stalin in March 1953, after which policy changed, playing down the confessions, prevented a mass show trial of the airmen on the pattern of the Moscow trials and the great assize of the Titoist leaders, Stalin's final indictment of the whole structure and history of American imperialism. Yet unlike the accusations of 'the Doctor's Plot', the germ warfare campaign had never been repudiated by the Communists. No doubt, many Asians to this day believe the US instigated bacteriological warfare in Korea; and the charges may easily be revived if and when policy so demands. The ultimate significance of the campaign is in what it reveals of Communist ethics with their relativist conception of truth and the consequent dismissal of objective 'bourgeois' justice as a historical anomaly. When Colonel Mahurin was writing and rewriting his confession, his interrogators easily admitted to him that it had no factual basis. Whatever opportunist calculations attended the launching of the bacteriological warfare campaign, by the end this inspired fabrication had become a dogma of official policy. Another big lie had become an objective truth of the Party, forever.

CHAPTER TWENTY

TOKYO: BLOCKADE AND INTERDICTION

> In spite of the general opinion to the contrary, the Korean War has been a very complex one . . . a laboratory study of limited military action in the support of a very difficult political situation.
>
> GEN. O. P. WEYLAND, USAF

> The failure of air power, through interdiction, to stop the fighting in Korea follows a historic pattern. Except in a few isolated instances during World War II (such as the Normandy landings), there is much evidence to show that an air effort to interrupt an enemy's supply system *has never been wholly successful.* . . .
>
> CAGLE and MANSON, *The Sea War in Korea*

KOREA IS A PENINSULA

JUST as the world-wide Communist propaganda offensive was supported by endless Chinese probing attacks along the Korea MLR during 1951-53, so the UN and US insistence that there could be no capitulation to Nam Il's demands at Panmunjom was backed by relentless pressure against North Korea by naval and air forces. This new war of attrition between UN firepower and Communist manpower in the last two years of the war emphasised how the objectives of both sides in Korea were now identical. During the first phase of the war, up to Inchon, the UN had wished to restore the 38th Parallel, while the North Koreans wanted to unify Korea militarily. During the next phase, until the Chongchon, it was the UN's turn to attempt unification, an objective which yielded after the Chinese intervention to the aim of the first phase of the war — defence of the ROK. Then, of course, it was the Chinese who were attempting to unite Korea, and the abandonment of this ambition in the summer of 1951 with the beginning of the truce talks meant that both sides in this fourth and last phase of the war had an identical political-military objective. That objective was the attainment of a favourable armistice based on the continued partition of Korea, with the corollary that whereas all sorts of political benefits apparently accrued to the Chinese in perpetuating the war, exactly the opposite was the case with the Truman Administration. Therefore during the last phase of the war the great strategic question was this: could the war be brought to an end by UNC air and naval action alone?

During these long months it only came to be slowly understood by many naval and air commanders that while (as always) air and sea power could prevent the defeat of the UNC, ultimately military success or failure in Korea would still be evaluated by the amount of territory controlled by the respective ground forces. The naval war in particular demonstrated the interdependence of the three services, but it also showed how Korean geography helped to redress the balance caused by Chinese manpower resources and Manchurian sanctuary protection. The point is well made in an anecdote about Van Fleet. When the General was in Greece in 1947 commanding the US military mission there, his colleague Rear-Adm. Dyer once stressed to him that, because Greece was a peninsula, geography made the application of sea power particularly appropriate as, if necessary, naval bombardments and amphibious landings could easily be used. Four years passed and Dyer, then the newly-appointed commander of the UN blockading force in Korea waters, was ushered into Van Fleet's office in Seoul. As the admiral entered, Van Fleet jumped to his feet, threw his arms into the air and exclaimed, 'Korea is a peninsula!'

The amphibious landings at Pohang, Inchon and Wonsan and the Hungnam evacuation had spectacularly illustrated the value of sea power around the peninsula during the first three phases of the war, and GHQ planners were constantly intrigued by the possibility of using the amphibious weapon again. Vice-Adm. Briscoe, Joy's successor as COMAVFE, seriously considered a landing near Haeju, but another two or three divisions from the US would have been required, a neat illustration of the arguments against a forward strategy once the truce talks started. Another possible site for a landing was Kojo, between Wonsan and Kosong, where the invaders could drive south to the rear of the Chinese in the Iron Triangle area. The plan had been approved by Ridgway but when Bradley turned up in Korea during October 1951 he cancelled the landing, saying, 'We want no more of the enemy's real estate.'[1]

With amphibious landings thus precluded by high policy, lack of resources and the enemy's growing beach defences, the Navy's chief task in the last phase of the war was blockade, followed by support to the interdiction programme discussed below. Other duties, often little publicised, including minesweeping, escort work, anti-submarine patrols, and the control of coastal fishing. But the blockade was vital, and moreover complemented the interdiction effort, for, by eliminating all coastal and deep-water traffic to North Korea from Soviet and Chinese ports, supplies which would have been moved in this way were forced on to the road and rail system under attack by bombing and naval bombardment. The blockade had been established at the beginning of the war, but, as with the air campaign, limits had been set on the sensitive borders of Korea with the USSR and China. In the north-east the line was at 41° 51′ N., just above Chongjin, and in the north-west it was 39° 35′ N. to keep ships away from the mouth of the Yalu. Since the destruction of the North Korean gunboats in July 1950 there was no opposition from Communist surface forces, but there was always a serious Communist coastal mine-laying effort. After all, mines had closed Wonsan, Hungnam and Chinnampo for some weeks in the autumn of 1950 as effectively as any action by surface forces. The blockade ships, too, were opposed by cleverly sited shore batteries in North Korea which scored many hits on the smaller vessels, for to maintain the blockade of North Korea under international law, every part of the blockaded coast had to be under surveillance by ship every twenty-four hours.

The blockade force had been created in the early days of the war from British and American ships in Japanese waters, and on 12 September it was designated Task Force 95, 'United Nations Blockading and Escort Force.' TF 95 was split into two, Task Group 95.1 patrolling the west coast, under the command of a British Rear-Adm. for the duration of the war, and TG 95.2, responsible for the east coast from the bomb-line to Chongjin. During the spring of 1951, when the front was becoming stabil-

[1] Cagle and Manson, p. 391.

ised, the chain of command of the blockade force was integrated with that of the other naval forces under COMNAVFE. In overall command of TF 95 was the Commander of the Seventh Fleet, who exercised operational control through the senior cruiser division commander of Task Force 77, the fast carrier force which usually operated in the Sea of Japan with four flattops. When TF 95 came under control of Seventh Fleet on 3 April 1951 it meant that the Air Force and the Eighth Army could contact any naval unit by dealing with the Fleet commander rather than by calling task group commanders on an individual basis.

The organisation of the blockading force reflected the different conditions on east and west coasts. In the west there was a light carrier element, and a surface blockade element of light cruisers, destroyers, frigates and minesweepers, while on the east coast TG 95.2 was split into four elements each of which patrolled a section of the long coastline from Kosong to above Chongjin. Both the task groups included an island defence element to guard the North Korean offshore islands held by the UNC.[1] Bombardment duties of the blockade force not only included attacks on the exposed road and rail routes which ran along the coast from Songjin to Hungnam, but support of the ground forces at each end of the front, often involving deep naval gunfire support by some of the largest ships afloat — altogether four battleships, *Missouri, Iowa, New Jersey* and *Wisconsin* served in Korean waters. A typical example of this sort of gunfire support was the help given by the *Wisconsin* to the Marine Division on the eastern sector of X Corps' front in January 1952. The battleship's huge sixteen-inch shells were fired over the entire ROKA front to land sixteen miles inland. Prisoners reported that on seeing the size of unexploded shells they felt it was high time to surrender.

Apart from the pressure brought on the Communists by blockade and bombardment, there were two other closely related naval operations which provided an important part of the UNC campaign against North Korea while the armistice negotiations dragged on at Panmunjon. These were, firstly, the naval 'siege' of the important ports of Wonsan, Hungnam and

[1] See Cagle and Manson, pp. 281-373 for details of the command structure and operation of the blockade.

Songjin and secondly, the occupation of over a dozen important off-shore islands all around the North Korean coast and on which were erected radio and radar stations, air-sea rescue bases and even airstrips from which raids were launched on Communist coastal communications and agents sent into North Korea.

The siege of the north-eastern Korean ports grew out of a plan to occupy the offshore islands evolved quite empirically in the winter of 1950-51. Many senior officers still thought that as the Eighth Army would fight its way north again after the Chinese advance past the Parallel, possession of North Korean offshore islands would give a valuable springboard to the UNC for offensive operations when the time came. In particular it was thought of landing ROK Marines on Cho-do, off Chinnampo, the Paengyong-do group off the Ongjin peninsula, and the island group in Wonsan harbour. As Wonsan was the chief port of North Korea it was further decided to attempt the continual bombardment of the port from its inner harbour, which would completely close the town to all shipping, tie down large numbers of Communist troops with the amphibious threat, and help to dislocate an important transportation centre.

The 'siege' started on 16 February, and went on for 861 days until the very last day of the war. On 24 February Sin-do in Wonsan harbour was occupied by ROK Marines, and on 8 March the 'siege' was extended to Songjin and on 26 April to Hungnam although these ports were only bombarded from their outer harbours and with less frequency than Wonsan. Altogether seven islands in Wonsan harbour were occupied, and the fire-control party on Hwangto-do was only 3,000 yards offshore. On Yo-do, the base island four miles from the Communist shore batteries, and occupied at different times by units of Drysdale's Royal Marine Commandos, US Marines, and ROK Marines, an emergency airstrip was constructed in June 1952 on which later aircraft force-landed. Pilots who ditched in Wonsan harbour were rescued by helicopter from an LST patrolling nearby.

According to Cagle and Manson, the USN commander of the special task element which guarded these islands in Wonsan harbour was awarded the title of 'Mayor of Wonsan'—'a non-political office', whose successive incumbents held as token of the honour a large gilded wooden key. Photo interpretation experts

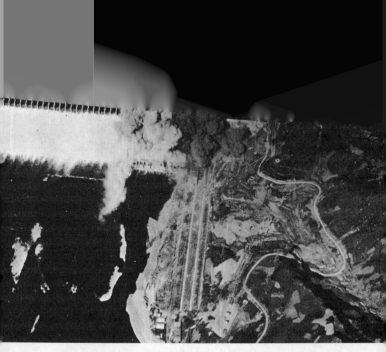

The power house at the Supung Dam, Suiho Reservoir, under heavy and effective air attack. 23 June 1952. Note Chinese territory across the Yalu on the extreme left of the photograph

'-86 Sabrejets over Korea.

The hunters: MIG-15s

The bridges at Sinanju, linking Pyongyang with Sinuiju and Manchuria, the most important chokepoint in the North Korean transportation system. When this picture was taken in May 1952 all five bridges over the Chongchon were knocked out, but complete interdiction was never achieved. Later a sixth bridge was built here.
See Chapter 20

Low Level attack. An F-80 Shooting Star jet of the Fifth Air Force deposits a tank of napalm on the Communist supply centre at Suan, south-east of Pyongyang. Anti-aircraft fire from a sandbagged position at the side of the road leaves a trail. 8 May 1952

estimated that eventually half the air and coastal defences of North Korea were concentrated at Wonsan, besides many thousands of troops, a spectacular illustration of a small investment of naval power tying down large Communist resources which might have been used at the MLR to greater effect.

Other islands occupied by South Korean Marines on the east coast included Nan-do, near Kojo, and the Yang-do group near Songjin. There was a parallel operation on the west coast. Not only were Paengyong-do held and the associated islands of Taechon-do, Sochong-do, Yonpyong-do, and U-do ten miles off the Ongjin peninsula, but also Cho-do and Sok-to in the Taedong estuary. Even more daringly, Taewha-do, almost in the Yalu mouth, was occupied in early November 1951, but the island was re-taken by the Chinese after a month. These island radar stations and air-sea rescue bases were particularly useful in saving fighter pilots who ditched on their way back from the dog-fighting in the north-west. From South Korea agents were ferried to the islands, and then despatched into North Korea, not only on special operations, but to contact the anti-Communist partisans who pinned down many enemy troops. Some of these partisans were not under the control of the UNC and these freelance operators — bandits — fought as ferociously against the Communists as they had previously against UN troops. Often air strikes were launched on information passed on by the partisans. In October 1951, for example, the guerillas radioed that a high-level conference of Communist Party members from the CPV and KPA was to be held at Kapsan, about sixty miles north of Songjin in mountainous country. Only fifteen minutes after the conference began in a special Security Police Compound, a strike from TF 77 levelled the area; the guerillas who had watched the attack reported that over 500 Communist officials had been killed, and all the records of the Korean CP destroyed. As the truce approached, thousands of the guerillas were evacuated via the offshore islands, although others stayed behind and the story of the underground war in North Korea still remains largely secret as some of the clandestine networks and groups are still in existence.[1]

---

[1] See *Banner over Pusan* by Ellery Anderson for details of special operations in N. Korea, including Cho-do and Taewha-do, by a British officer. Also Clark, pp. 200-2.

These activities all ensured that the blockade of North Korea was both effective and successful. The larger success of the naval war may be seen in the fact that six out of seven UN personnel who went to Korea went by sea, and sea power kept the UNC supplied, in action and ultimately on the peninsula itself. The interdiction efforts of the naval forces were less successful than the blockade, but here they were geared to a campaign initiated by the USAF. The relative success of the US Navy's activities in Korea, pragmatically designed to make the best of circumstances in a limited war, reflected its official doctrine which rejected the total solutions of total war. The attempt to prove that one service by itself could force the war to an end was left to the airpower specialists.

AIRPOWER, THE INDECISIVE FACTOR?

Even more dramatically than the naval war with its shifting emphasis from amphibious operations to blockade and bombardment the different phases of the air war were contingent upon the political decisions taken by both sides. In phase one, as noted above when discussing the problems of the defence of the Pusan perimeter, the emphasis of all air operations was on close support to help the ground troops. As soon as the defence of the perimeter hardened, an increasing amount of resources were diverted to interdiction attacks on the North Korean supply lines stretching back for hundreds of miles from the Naktong, and which, together with close support, were vital in halting the KPA advance towards Pusan. During the advance to the Yalu, with the bombline almost on the Manchurian border, there was a complete strategic reversal, and the Chinese were able to prepare for their winter offensive, almost immune from air attack. By the end of September 1950 O'Donnell's FEAF Bomber Command had eliminated the eighteen JCS-chosen strategic targets in North Korea such as the chemical manufacturing complex at Hungnam and the Wonsan oil refineries.

Already the vast differences between the use of air power in Korea and its classic application against the Axis had become apparent. The first task of air power, that of establishing control over friendly areas had been accomplished by the UN air forces

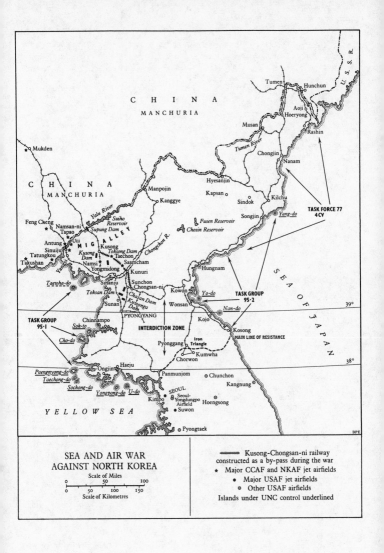

SEA AND AIR WAR
AGAINST NORTH KOREA

Scale of Miles

0   50   100

0   50   100   150

Scale of Kilometres

┼┼┼┼┼┼ Kusong-Chongsan-ni railway
constructed as a by-pass during the war
★ Major CCAF and NKAF jet airfields
● Major USAF jet airfields
◉ Other USAF airfields
Islands under UNC control underlined

in the first month of the war. The second task, a continuation of the first, that of conducting operations over enemy territory and destroying not only his aircraft in the air and on the ground, but also hostile air bases and supporting facilities, had only been partly carried out. With the fateful appearance of the first MIG-15 over North Korea on 1 November 1950, it was instantly realised that the main air resources of the new enemy were now located beyond reach of FEAF in Manchuria where a huge Chinese Communist Air Force — the Chinese People's Armed Forces Air Force — was being created with the assistance of Soviet resources and concentrated in the Antung bases. While at least the MIGs could be drawn into North Korean skies, the third task of airpower, strategic destruction of enemy sources of raw material, factories, and the associated transportation system was precluded by the very nature of the war. Only a few second-rate 'strategic' targets in North Korea, together with that part of the Communist transportation system between the Yalu and the MLR, were open to attack.

During the early weeks of phase three of the war following the Chongchon, the main emphasis of the Fifth Air Force and of Bomber Command reverted to the close support role as in the early days of the war. Once again these efforts, coupled with mounting interdiction attacks as Chinese supply-lines lengthened, helped to stop the CCF on the Pyongtaek-Samchok line in January 1951. The strategic objective of this phase of the fighting, to halt the Communist advance and to force the beginning of armistice talks, was brought about by the halting of the Chinese spring offensives, when the CCF were on the move in great numbers from the Yalu southwards and extremely vulnerable to all varieties of air attack. However, with the beginning of the fourth phase of the war with the delegations meeting at Kaesong, the necessity for close support manifestly declined with the gradual arrival of the stalemate war on the ground. Often substituted for artillery, even after July 1951 close support still accounted for about 30% of all Air Force sorties, as compared to about 10% in the European war. But with the stalemate close support operations, according to O. P. Weyland, had reached 'a point of diminishing returns',[1] and in accordance with its belief throughout the war that the place to destroy

[1] Stewart, *Airpower*, p. 22.

enemy firepower was not at the MLR but on its way to the front, the Air Force initiated in June 1951 what had for long tantalised the Tokyo planners — an all-out strategic air interdiction campaign with the object of isolating and paralysing the Communist armies in the field and so forcing an early end to the truce talks.

Concurrently, and closely related to the interdiction effort in its objective, a determined attack was launched at the Communist airfield-building programme in North Korea. So rapid had been the build-up of the CCAF during 1951 that if the Chinese could stage their aircraft on to North Korean fields UNC air supremacy might be lost and a new phase of the ground fighting begin. Peking well understood that an air offensive from Manchuria would be answered by retaliatory action at the trans-Yalu bases, so the first objective of the airfield building programme was to establish some measure of Communist air control in north-west Korea between the Yalu and the Chongchon — 'MIG Alley'. It was thus in the air-to-air fighting that the new strength of the CCF began to be felt.

The MIG, flying at near sonic speeds and armed with one 37-mm. and two 20-mm. cannons, was a formidable machine and had first clashed with the F-86 Sabre jet, armed with six .50 machine-guns, and the only UN interceptor that could match it, over Sinuiju on 17 December 1950.[1] Gradually operations from beyond the Yalu were stepped up. During February 1951 several

---

[1] For an outline of this phase of the air war see also Stewart, *Airpower*, pp. 32-50. The F-86 and the MIG-15 had first been test-flown within a few months of each other at the end of 1947. The MIG was marginally faster than the F-86 above 35,000 feet, with a substantially better service ceiling, a 20% greater climb rate and a 15% smaller turning circle. It suffered from severe directional snaking and compressibility effects above Mach .86 which reduced its effectiveness as a gun platform. It also tended to go into a spin after too tight a turn. Unlike the F-86, it could not be flown transonically and another drawback was the slow fire-rate of its large calibre cannon and inadequate ammunition capacity. Green and Fricker, *The Air Forces of the World*, pp. 256-7. The extent of the huge Soviet air defence effort against the threat of SAC during the Korean War and of which the Manchurian build-up formed such an important part, is shown by the fact that in 1951 the Americans calculated that between 5,500 and 6,200 MIGs were produced. Production of the already obsolescent F-84 was in the middle hundreds, the F-86 in the low hundreds for the same year, while only fifty of the jet B-47s which replaced the B-29 and B-50 were made. About 300 of these new bombers which tipped the scales back towards SAC came off the assembly lines in 1952. Alsop, *The Reporter's Trade*, pp. 176-7.

B-29 strikes in the Sunchon area had been met by the Soviet swept-wing fighters, but this initial sparring ended on 12 April when forty-eight B-29s escorted by seventy-two fighters struck at the Antung-Sinuiju bridges to be met by a swarm of eighty MIGs. Three of the Superforts were shot down for nine MIGs, which were operating not only from Antung but from nearby bases at Tapao, Tatungkou, and Takushan. Hundreds of MIGs were also based in the Mukden area. It was during the next few weeks that agreement was reached between Washington and London to strike at these bases if they were used to attack the Eighth Army. Throughout the summer increasing numbers of MIGs, vectored by their GCI radar towards the approaching UNC formations, appeared over North Korea. During the late spring, monthly sighting of MIGs had numbered between 300 and 400, by September, the figure had risen to 1,400, and in October it was 3,000. From Antung the MIGs would fly across the Yalu in mass formations, sending scouting elements to the Wonsan and Chinnampo areas, while individual MIGs would reach south of Seoul. Gradually the F-80, the F-84, and the Gloster Meteors flown by 77th Australian Squadron were withdrawn south of the Chongchon on patrol and escort duties leaving the control of the air in north-west Korea to be disputed between MIG and Sabre jet.[1]

Then, during September 1951 photo reconnaissance indicated that a major Communist jet airfield construction effort was under way south of Sinuiju at Saamcham, Taechon and Namsi, part of a much larger programme involving the building of thirty-four fields throughout North Korea. Taechon and Saamcham fields were knocked out in mid-October for the loss of one B-29, but when eight of the medium bombers attacked Namsi on 23 October with fighter escort they were met by about 150 MIGs. Three B-29s were shot down and the other five all damaged. For a week after the 'Battle of Namsi' large MIG formations crossed the Yalu daily and the momentous decision was taken to stop daylight bombing missions by B-29s. Using radar and shoran (electronic beam navigation) the Superforts went on to wage a successful night campaign against the airfields, and at the war's end only a few MIGs were staged across

[1] See Odgers, *Across the Parallel*, pp. 196-229. This is the story of the Australian Squadron in Korea.

the Yalu. Moreover by the end of 1951 another F-86 group was formed at Suwon to aid the hard-pressed US 4th Fighter Interceptor Group based on Kimpo. But as Vandenberg told a Pentagon press conference on 21 November 1951, 'Almost overnight China has become one of the major air powers of the world.' The massive investment of Soviet aircraft in the CCAF meant that since the outbreak of the Korean War China had become the world's third air power, a position it still keeps. And although Peking did not risk its brand-new air force to strike at the MLR, or at Kimpo, or even seriously to dispute UNC air supremacy south of the Chongchon, the CCAF had done something in the Korean context which the Luftwaffe had been unable to do. It had stopped precision daylight bombing by the USAF over an important part of enemy territory.

While this air war in the north-west was coming to its climax in autumn 1951, a few score miles south the interdiction campaign was also reaching its maximum effort from its tentative beginnings at the end of 1950. The best definition of the aims of the interdiction campaign—the JCS *Dictionary of Military Terms* translates 'interdict' as 'to prevent or hinder by any means, enemy use of an area or route'—is by Cagle and Manson:

> In effect the task of air power — both land-based and sea-based — during these twenty months was to sever the Korean peninsula at the Yalu and Tumen rivers, to undercut the peninsula, and to float the entire land mass out into mid-ocean where interdiction, in concert with naval blockade, could strangle the supply lines of the Communists and thereby force their retreat and defeat.[1]

The conception was similar to that which in 1944 had isolated the Normandy front from the rest of France by the cutting of the Loire and Seine bridges and the elimination of railway junctions in north-east France. The successes of air power in

---

[1] There is an interesting account of the interdiction campaign in Cagle and Manson, Chap. 8, '*The Struggle to Strangle*'. General Weyland has also written a survey of the USAF's problems in the war in Stewart, *Airpower*, pp. 5-30; for a general history of the air war see Futrell, *The USAF in Korea, 1950-53*. An extremely detailed survey, partly written by the same author and produced by the USAF's historical division, also exists and is mentioned in the Bibliography.

crippling the earlier Communist offensives in Korea also influenced the planners. As early as November 1950 aircraft from
TF 77 and the Fifth Air Force had destroyed six of the most
important bridges over the Yalu between Sinuiju and Hyesanjin,
but the river had soon frozen over. During the following months,
in the first phase of the interdiction campaign the chief target
was the Korean railway system, with the air forces concentrating on the western, and the navy on the eastern network, a
division which had tentatively originated the previous summer
when Stratemeyer had told the Navy to keep their activities east
of longitude 127°, a division that was, with small variations,
adhered to for the rest of the war.

On the west coast three lines crossing the Yalu between Sinuiju
and Manpojin ran down through Sinanju and Kunuri to Pyongyang where once across the Chongchon and the Taedong supplies fanned out through a web of subsidiary routes to the
MLR; on the east coast three lines from the USSR and Manchuria met at Kilchu, and ran down the east coast to a junction
at Kowon, where a lateral line ran westwards to Pyongyang,
and the main line continued south to Wonsan and the front.
The pre-war daily capacity of the western net was estimated at
6-9,000 tons, cut down to 1,000-1,500 tons by air attack. The
eastern net could handle 5,000 tons daily before the war, but
the aircraft from TF 77 had reduced this to 500 tons, so perhaps the Communists were receiving about 2,000 tons daily by
rail in early 1951. This seemed immensely successful until the
demands of Chinese logistics were calculated. Each UN soldier
in Korea required at least sixty pounds of supplies a day: but
the Communist soldier needed only ten pounds, so that a CCF
division of 10,000 men consumed fifty short tons daily.

During 1951-52 there were about ninety Communist divisions
in Korea, and about sixty of these were at the front so only about
3,000 tons daily were needed by the Communist forces facing
the Eighth Army. Over half this requirement could still be
supplied by the railways, and the balance was easily made up by
road transport and human bearers each of whom could carry
about forty-five pounds for twelve miles overnight. Hundreds
of thousands of North Koreans were recruited for this purpose.
Emphasising the increasing importance of the road network,
the count of Communist vehicles jumped from 7,300 in January

1951 to 54,000 in June. This was the development which led to the second and crucial phase of the interdiction campaign, Operation STRANGLE, which rather unwisely announced in its code name its intention of cutting off the MLR from the rest of North Korea. Starting in June 1951 a strip of territory stretching across North Korea for a depth of one degree of latitude above 38° 15' was divided between the Fifth Air Force, naval aircraft, and the 1st Marine Air Wing. The road system was broken down into eight main routes and all bridges, embankments, choke points, defiles and tunnels designated as targets. Night intruders and B-29s took up the task when the fighter-bombers left off. The result: pilots reported that the number of Communist trucks moving on the roads remained unchanged. The Communists were able to repair the roads faster than STRANGLE could destroy them; and as a transport system the road network had greater flexibility than the rail network.

In August Operation STRANGLE moved to its climax as the planners decided to destroy both rail and road targets. Rail experts advised as well as bridge-busting the elimination of isolated rail areas at about one mile intervals in order to force the dispersal of repair gangs and to reduce the concentration of

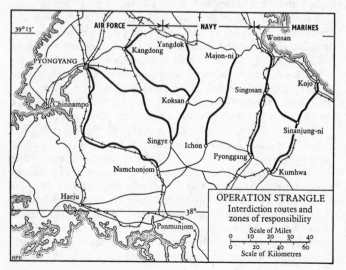

OPERATION STRANGLE
Interdiction routes and
zones of responsibility

Scale of Miles
0   10   20   30   40

Scale of Kilometres
0   20   40   60

the ever-growing flak defences of North Korea. By the end of 1951 there was no Communist reaction either at Panmunjom or on the MLR, and a new technique was adopted, the destruction of entire stretches of the road and rail network. Sometimes crater overlapped crater for distances of up to two miles, but there was still no isolation of the front and flak was forcing the fighter-bombers up to higher altitudes. By the spring of 1952, it was becoming obvious that interdiction, without offensive action by the Eighth Army, was unable to stop the Communists from supplying their forces in spite of the use of almost 100% of the offensive air potential of TF 77, 70% of the potential of TF 95, the Fifth Air Force and Bomber Command, and 60% of the Marine Air Wing on Operation STRANGLE. By June 1952 it was obvious with the POW deadlock at Panmunjom that peace was no nearer. Accordingly the decision was taken in that month to de-emphasise interdiction and to seek new target systems for the air forces to destroy in their attempt to end the war.

Much discussion has surrounded the failure of the campaign, which incredibly enough was never closely co-ordinated between the USAF and the USN at GHQ level in Tokyo, but merely supervised by the Fifth Air Force through the Joint Operations Centre at Seoul. The following seem to be the outstanding reasons why the Communist MLR was never isolated:

(1) The raw materials and factories supplying the Communist forces could not be touched.

(2) Of the Communist distribution system in North Korea, only supply routes and the rolling stock could be attacked. The personnel which kept the roads and railways open were immune to attack, as were the stockpiles of supplies secreted in many caves and tunnels in the mountains.

(3) The astonishing ingenuity of the NK Military Highway Administration and the Railroad Recovery Bureau which, by highly-organised bridging, track and road-laying techniques, and construction of elaborate by-passes, were able to keep supplies moving. The skill with which Communist supply convoys moved at night, undetected, was also of supreme importance.

(4) Above all interdiction failed because it was not co-ordinated with offensive action by the UNC ground forces. Even

if the USAF claim that 90% of Communist supplies were stopped by interdiction is true, the remaining 10% gave the CCF sufficient supplies to carry on the war *while the front was static* — and even to stockpile a certain amount, as the Chinese limited offensives in June-July 1953 showed. On the other hand, but for the interdiction campaign Chinese ground activity might have been much heavier during the stalemate war.

There would be no Normandy in Korea, and, in this case-history of limited war at any rate, it had been shown that air-power by itself was unable to force the war to an end. The only way to halt completely Communist supplies rolling to the front would have been occupation of North Korean lines of communications by armed men. . . .

WANTED: A TARGET SYSTEM

With the abandonment of the interdiction campaign, the emphasis of the air offensive, its objective unchanged from that of forcing the Communists to sign a truce at Panmunjon, switched to those 'strategic' target systems in North Korea which had either been hitherto untouched or repaired since Bomber Command's offensive in the first few months of the war. This new phase of the air war opened on 23 June 1952 with a spectacular daylight combined strike by over 500 Air Force, Navy and Marine aircraft against the Japanese-built North Korean hydro-electric system, the single biggest UNC air attack of the war to date. Not only did the target system supply most of North Korea's electricity, but also 10% of the current used by the Manchurian industrial complex. As the largest plant, Suiho, was on the Yalu, political sensitivity to the border had precluded earlier attacks, as well as that fact that it had been easier to destroy North Korean factories than the hydro-electric power-source. But by 1952 certain Communist war industries had been dispersed and constructed underground. The best way to hit these plants was by destroying their power source, supplied not only by Suiho, the fourth biggest generating station in the world, with a capacity of 400,000 kw, but also by the associated plants in the integrated North Korean grid system of Chosin, Fusen, and Kyosen in north-east Korea.

Half the attacking force had knocked out the Suiho power-plant and transformers by the afternoon of the 23rd; the huge 350-ft. high, 3,000-ft. long Supung dam which linked North Korea to Manchuria was untouched. The three other plants were also severely damaged, and the lights went out all over North Korea. The attacking fighter-bomber pilots over Suiho had seen several hundred MIGS lined up at Antung, but the Chinese jets did not attempt to oppose the UNC strike and took off instead, heading into Manchuria, presumably as a result of the Chinese High Command's belief that the raid was the first stage of an air offensive across the Yalu by the United Nations. Operations continued against the north-eastern plants for a few more days, and in September there was a B-29 strike against Suiho. The big plant was again bombed in February 1953, when some power had been restored, although the total reconstruction of the industry must have taken some years with a consequent strain on Chinese and North Korean resources. There had been no inter-Allied consultation before the June attack and this omission was understandably criticised in West-minister. Yet the destruction of the hydro-electric plants had probably taken place a year too late, as the operation might have had some effect on Communist willingness to negotiate if it had been synchronised with the defeat of the Chinese armies the previous summer.

The next major daylight strike in the new campaign was against Pyongyang on 11 July, another joint effort, when over 1,200 fighter-bombers and dive-bombers roamed over the city for eleven hours destroying factories, barracks and airfields, depositing over 1,400 tons of bombs and 23,000 gallons of napalm on the North Korean capital. Radio Pyongyang went off the air for a couple of days, but there was no reaction at Pan-munjom. By the time the capital's installations had been patched up, it was time for another strike and on 29 August 1952, 1,403 sorties by land- and carrier-based aircraft from every country with air units based in Korea and Japan hit Pyongyang in what was cheerfully known as the 'All United Nations Air Effort', the single biggest strike of the war.

These attacks on Pyongyang were supported by further raids

on manufacturing areas and transportation centres. In June, Bomber Command's B-29s took out the light metals plant at Yangsi, near Sinuiju, and a series of strikes by naval aircraft from TF 77 finally eliminated nearly all important industrial plants in north-east Korea, no matter how remote. The Sindok lead and zinc mills were bombed out on 27 July, followed by a strike against the Kilchu magnesite plant the next day. On 1 September the Aoji synthetic oil refinery, only eight miles from Soviet territory, was gutted; and after operating against remaining industrial targets in Chongjin, Kowon and Hoeryong, a city on the Tumen, during the next few months dive-bombers from the carriers raided Rashin on 10 December. This was the town's first raid since 25 August 1951, when, following the lifting of the restriction on air attacks by JCS, Navy fighters had escorted B-29s to the port into which so much equipment came from the USSR.

By January 1953 there was no indication that the Communists were abandoning their stand on voluntary prisoner repatriation, and it appeared that the wrecking of the remaining North Korean industries and supply centres had no more effect on the truce talks than the interdiction campaign. In Tokyo and Taegu the USAF planners came up with a new target system, chosen with some of the lessons of the interdiction effort in mind. At Sinanju and Yongmidong there was a major choke-point on the west Korean road and rail networks where these routes funnelled across the Taeryong and Chongchon rivers within a few miles of each other. The four pre-war road and rail bridges had already been increased to eleven because of the attention of the fighter-bombers. Now the planners proposed a concentrated air attack over a period of days which would completely neutralise the crossings, and thus dislocate the entire transport system between Pyongyang and the Yalu by blocking up all the associated marshalling yards which would then be attacked in turn.

During the night of 9 January B-29s bombed the bridges, and next day hundreds of fighter-bombers took up the attack. After five days all the bridges and their approaches were destroyed. Altogether 2,292 combat sorties had been mounted, 54% of all FEAF sorties during this time, a disproportionately large effort even for the relative success of the operation, which had caused chaos in the north-western Korean rail net. This scale of attack could not be sustained with existing FEAF resources, and on 21 January, six days after the end of the operation, limited supply across the rivers by night was once again under way after an eleven-day break. Moreover, thousands of Communist labourers were building a new rail link between Kusong and Kunuri which would completely by-pass Sinanju-Yongmidong in case of further assault on this sensitive spot. Even interdiction on this scale was hardly decisive.

The last special target system attacked during the war seems in retrospect to have been the most vulnerable as regards the possibilities of bringing out a change in the Communist negotiating position. Twenty irrigation dams near important transportation routes supplied 75% of the water for North Korean rice production, and their destruction had been planned since October 1952. But there were complex considerations before this new campaign could be initiated. The best time for attacking the dams in order to obtain maximum results was either in May or August when the rice crop could be almost completely destroyed. Tactically, breaking the dams could influence the truce talks because the floods caused could wash away roads and railways and supply dumps. Strategically, the dam-busters could cause famine in North Korea among both civilians and the Communist armies and so force the Chinese to export rice across the Yalu from their own country whose economy in 1952-53 was already strained to its limit. It was also considered that gradual destruction of the dams would be best from psychological warfare considerations, so that the Korean farmers would tend to blame the Communists for prolonging the war, rather than the UNC for initiating an all-out attack against food supplies.

Accordingly in early May 1953, when once again the talks at Panmunjom seemed bogged down, although the Communists had apparently conceded the principle of no forcible prisoner repatriation, a series of strikes was initiated against five of the twenty dams. Between 13 and 16 May the Toksan and Chasan dams north of Pyongyang were broken by F-84s; the strikes achieved spectacular tactical success since the main road and rail communications running north from the capital were cut by the floods. In the next few weeks Kuwonga, near Chasan, and Kusong and Toksang, north of the Chongchon, were attacked, but the water level was lowered by enemy emergency action, preserving the dams—but still accomplishing part of the pur-purpose of the attack in that the efficiency of these irrigation systems was impaired. Yet pilots noticed also the furious activity of repair teams. By the time of the Kusong-Toksang strikes in mid-June agreement had been signed at last on prisoner repatria-tion at Panmunjom, an agreement probably brought about by the American threat of general war against China. Yet this final demonstration of another threat hanging over the North Korean and Chinese economy may well have been a subsidiary motive in persuading Peking at last to write off the war. After all, the fifteen remaining irrigation dams could have been destroyed in as many days. Much too late, the USAF had at last found a pos-sibly decisive target system.

During these last few months of the war, the air war seemed to be ending where it began. The Navy was waging a campaign of 'Cherokee' strikes against enemy supply dumps up to twenty miles behind the MLR. Although technically not close support these strikes reflected the Navy's tenacious belief that destruc-tion of enemy material close to the front was far more damag-ing to him than destruction and interdiction in the rear. And on the last day of the war B-29s bombed once again Saamcham and Taechon airfields in an attempt to prevent a post-war air build-up in North Korea, a fear proved correct when less than two months after the cease-fire a defected MIG pilot who landed at Kimpo announced that he had flown from Pyongyang air-field where Communist forces were once again staged in strength.

Yet if D-Day for the USAF had not come in 1950-51 Korea was still far from being a police action. Even if over 850 MIGs had been downed in the Alley for only fifty-eight Sabre jets, with never less than seventeen or eighteen groups (wings) in-volved in Korea, including seven fighter and fighter-bomber groups, the USAF had lost some 2,000 aircraft through all causes during the war. In addition the Navy and Marines lost about 1,200 planes. Only half of these were lost in combat, the rest through accident and mechanical failure. The total USAF losses then amounted to about twenty groups over the three years of the war—equivalent to between one-third and one-quarter of the Air Force's strength in June 1950. . . . The cost to the Communists was also high. About 1,000 of their aircraft were shot down, and the USAF estimates that they lost another 1,800 aircraft through crashing en route to their home bases, accidents, training, and mechanical failure. In June 1950 the Chinese were not operating any MIG-15s in squadron service, but by July 1953 they were using about 2,000 jet fighters, nearly all of them in Manchuria. Of the total Communist losses of 2,800 aircraft, about 2,000 jets were estimated lost from all causes, making a grand total of about 4,000 MIGs invested in the CCAF by the USSR during the Korean War. For this investment the Communists never once had air control over North Korea.[1]

The air war in Korea had shown that not only interdiction was indecisive, but that the ingenuity of the search by the USAF for a decisive target system was surpassed only by the ingenuity of the Communist repair organisation. Like the furious apostles of Douhet at British Bomber Command HQ at High Wycombe during the World War II, the USAF planners in Tokyo had learnt that in limited war too, air power by itself could not end the fighting. The Korean War would be ended, as it began, by political decisions taken outside the peninsula. The fall of the Democrats in the presidential elections of November 1952 showed that the American people were ready to take any steps to end the war in the wasteland that Korea had become by the spring of 1953.

Most Korean War novels reflect in their documentary realism, often indistinguishable in style from the many reportage chronicles of the war, the confusions and frustrations of what Norman Mailer's hero in *The Deer Park* calls 'that Asiatic war which had gone its intermittent way'. One novel above all others emerges from the war which translates its writer's experience of the war in the air into a work of art comparable with anything written by V. M. Yeates, Richard Hillary or Saint-Exupéry. Like Cleve Saville, the fallen hero of his novel *The Hunters*, James Salter flew in a Sabre jet group based on Kimpo. Half an hour away from the concrete runways on the banks of the Han, across the infinitely cold, blue, hostile skies of North Korea, where the horizon lies hundreds of miles into China, is

[1] See Stewart, *Airpower*, pp. 286-8 for a summing up of the cost of the air war.

the Yalu, 'the river', and Antung. On the enemy airfields, the Sabre pilots see from afar the dust storms as the MIG bandit trains take off to meet them, the beautiful Soviet-built aircraft scissoring across the river in their scores between Sinuiju and Suiho, 'the dam'. Eight miles up in the contrails these magnificent champions of the two halves of the world meet in furious combat at sonic speed. Back at Kimpo, the American pilots are obsessed by 'Casey Jones', the legendary Russian ace who flies a black-striped MIG from Antung. Frenetic rivalries break out as they themselves try to become aces before the war is talked to its end at Panmunjom. These rivalries and the strain of combat combine to destroy Saville. He eventually shoots down Casey Jones. The kill cannot be confirmed because Saville's wingman crashes, and so the supreme victory eludes him. Soon, quite inevitably, Saville himself is downed by the relentless MIGs, the hunters. . . .

Panmunjom, looking towards the north-west. White tent on the right is the Communist delegates'; nearby are the two conference tents. The two dark tents are those assigned to the UNC delegates and the press. The armistice hall where the truce was signed was constructed immediately adjacent to the site shown here. April 1952

Pork Chop Hill, as seen from the Main Line of Resistance at Hill 347. The picture was taken the day Pork Chop was evacuated by 7th Division—11 July 1953

Panmunjom, 27 July 1953. The two senior delegates to the truce talks, Lt. General W. K. Harrison and General Nam Il, sign the armistice agreement

As Commander-in-Chief of the United Nations Command, General Mark Clark signs the armistice agreement at the UNC base camp at Munsan, Korea. General Weyland and Admiral Briscoe look on.
27 July 1953

CHAPTER TWENTY-ONE

THE FALL OF THE DEMOCRATS

(those who wear the Democratic label) '. . . wear it with
the stain of a historic betrayal; wear it with the blood of
dying men who crawled up the hills of Korea while the
politicians in the Democratic Party wrote invitations to the
Communists to join them at the United Nations.'
                                    Senator JOE McCARTHY

'The Democrats seemed to be saying prosperity was
more important than the life of my boy.'
            Texas housewife during the 1952 election.

'I shall go to Korea.'
            DWIGHT EISENHOWER, 24 October 1952

A GIGANTIC SACRIFICIAL EFFORT

As the truce talks at Panmunjom were recessed for winter on
8 October 1952, the heaviest fighting since Heartbreak Ridge
a year before broke out on the central front. To the west of the
Iron Triangle, on the boundary between I and IX Corps, the
Chinese launched massed infantry attacks on 6 October against
Hill 395, White Horse Hill, which threatened the MSR into
Chorwon. The next day 93,000 rounds of artillery and mortar
fire fell on the Eighth Army, the heaviest Communist daily
barrage since the beginning of the war. Probably the Chinese
were now attempting to put pressure on American public
opinion at the height of the presidential campaign; after ten
days of bitter fighting in which the ROK 9th Division, assisted
by artillery and air strikes, held its positions, the Communists
broke off the action. An entire division of the CCF 38th Army
had been destroyed.

As a diversion, and to strengthen IX Corps' position on the
opposite corner of the Triangle near Kumhwa, four UNC battalions, two from the U.S. 7th Infantry Division and two from
the ROK 2nd Division, started a limited attack on 14 October

to seize the Triangle Hill complex. From here Chinese observation teams overlooked the supply route into Kumhwa. But despite the usual air and artillery support Operation SHOWDOWN did not go according to plan, as the Chinese, well dug in, resisted effectively and as both sides increased their manpower ante for what soon became a prestige as well as a military objective. After two weeks of fighting when the action at last tailed off, IX Corps held one corner of Triangle Hill, half Sniper's Ridge and most of the mamiliform Jane Russell Hill. But to gain these peaks of dubious military value the UNC had suffered over 8,000 casualties, most of them South Korean; the Chinese had lost half as many again. At the climax of the action a battalion a day of US troops from 7th Infantry had gone through the CCF meatgrinder. There was no wonder Mark Clark thought the operation 'unsuccessful'.

With the election campaign in its last few weeks, there could hardly have been a more inconvenient illustration for the Democrats of the cost and nature of the war than SHOWDOWN, for by October Korea had become the chief issue in one of the most bitterly fought of all presidential campaigns. Long before the beginning of the campaign it was obvious that the outgoing Administration was hard-pressed. Earlier in 1952 the President's Gallup rating had sunk to 26%, and during the campaign, according to the commentator Samuel Lubell 'many people burst into profanity at the mere mention of Truman's name'. Acheson, after the unprecedented criticisms of him by the Republican Right, had now become more of a liability than an asset to his party, while Marshall, whose political usefulness as a non-partisan member of the Administration had been destroyed by McCarthy's defamatory attack of June 1951, had been replaced three months later by Robert Lovett. But the new Defence Secretary, an independent Republican, a man of the personal stamp of Acheson or Forrestal, was inevitably distrusted by both New Dealing Democrats and most Republicans. As for Bradley, whose castigations of Taftite neo-isolationism had increased in sharpness and frequency since the MacArthur Hearings, even many Democrats felt by 1952 that his advocacy of the Administration's foreign policy was an untoward intrusion of the military into foreign affairs, no matter how valuable had been the services of the general during the previous two years in selling containment to the public as the political stock of his civilian colleagues fell. Furthermore, Adlai Stevenson himself, chosen as the Democratic candidate on 26 July, was far less well known than Dwight Eisenhower, triumphally adopted after Taft's defeat in the Republican convention on 11 July.

This political fragility of the leading figures of the Truman regime only reflected the vast discontent with containment and Korea. Paradoxically, the only participants in the national dilemma over Korea who were relatively indifferent to its outcome were the troops. Wherever possible, hot meals, frequent mail and showers were available, as the Administration used both material and psychological means to combat the depressing effect of the ground stalemate. 'No means were spared to incorporate as much of the American civilian standard of living as possible into the Main Line of Resistance. By the end of the conflict American troops were fighting on a level of physical luxury and comfort unique in world history.'[1] But as the casualty lists showed, death could not be abolished on the MLR. More important than creature comforts, such as they were, was a rotation policy which meant that after nine to twelve months at the front each soldier was sent home — altogether 565,000 Army personnel were rotated through Korea in three years. Unlike World War II when troops were in for the duration, the political stresses of limited war demanded rotation which, as Samuel Huntington puts it, 'divorced the personal goals of the troops from the political goals of the government'. As a result, whatever the frustrations of the generals and the public, who yearned for a traditional World War II ending to Korea, the attitude of the troops themselves was completely professional in its indifference to the Administration's policy — an attitude of course which had its beginnings with Ridgway's tenure of command over the Eighth Army.

If morale was tolerably good on the MLR, at home it was bad, exploding in resentment not only with the Korean stalemate, but against containment and all its ramifications which were criticised for tolerating the existence of Communism and not attempting to destroy it. Since mid-1951 the emerging ideologist of the Republican Opposition to containment was John Foster Dulles, special consultant with the rank of ambassador to

[1] *Huntington*, p. 388.

the State Department until March 1952. More than anyone else, Dulles had seen the intervention in Korea in terms of American liberal idealism. As the men from Task Force Smith were taking up their positions at Osan in July 1950 he had made an Independence Day speech at the base of the Washington monument in the nation's capital: 'What we are doing today is in keeping with the tradition of our past. We can say with pride that our spirit today is the spirit of '76 and that our living today is faithful to the principles on which our nation was founded. . . .'[1] Almost two years later when Dulles's enthusiasm for the Korean War had long since evaporated he still approved of Truman's decision. During May 1952 in his famous *Life* article *A Policy of Boldness*, which was filled with the rhetoric of the Republican answer to the 'treadmill policies' of containment, 'liberation', he could still write that Truman's defence of the ROK was 'courageous, righteous and in the national interest'.[2]

But in Dulles' view the Korean aspects of containment, while laudable, were part of a policy that did not go far enough. Long before the presidential campaign, Dulles, although still in the service of the state, had come to doubt the whole moral basis of containment which the Republican platform of 1952 — drafted largely by him — called 'negative, futile and immoral'. While implementing Truman-Acheson policies Dulles had undergone a conversion from containment to liberation, just as after America's entry into the second war he was converted from isolationalism to internationalism. The Korean experience was crucial in this second conversion. Dulles' view that containment was wrong was publicly uttered in an address given on 30 May 1951:

Heretofore, we have had either peace or we have had war. When we have had peace we have had a large degree of individual freedom and an absence of regimentation and militarism. When we have had war there has been an enemy to conquer, by all possible violence, and a considerable surrender of individual choice in order better to marshal our strength for a victory which would restore peace and freedom. There was an end that was in sight and a sure knowledge of

[1] Rovere, *The Eisenhower Years*, p. 60.
[2] *Life*, 19 May 1952.

how to reach that end ... [now] we are engaged in a gigantic sacrificial effort. of a kind which, in the past, we have made only in the face of obvious and dire peril and only to force an early decision which would end the necessity for such sacrifices. Today the peril to our homeland seems to many to be somewhat speculative, while continuance of our present measures could impair the very foundations of our American way of life without forcing an abandonment of Soviet strategy.[1]

Manifestly Dulles believed that the US could not base its foreign policy on the acceptance of such gigantic sacrificial efforts as Korea. Moreover, Dulles as a practising Christian had written two books since the later 1930s — *War, Peace, and Change* (*1939*) and *War or Peace* (*1950*) — in which he explored the ways in which he thought the moral force of Christianity could be applied to foreign affairs. He believed that in all international relations, as in all human activity, 'dynamic' spiritual forces prevailed over 'static' material ones. Communism at present represented a dynamic world force, but this was a role that could be reversed if the free world seized the spiritual offensive from the Communists by conforming its policies to the natural or moral law of what was right. Only thus could America recapture its traditional role in world affairs, Dulles insisted in February 1952:

Our nation was dedicated, at birth, to serve not only its own welfare but the welfare of mankind. . . . If we get back into that mood, then we would not tremble before the menace of Soviet despotism. It would be the despots that would do the trembling. There comes a time in the life of any great people when their work of creation ends. They lose their sense of purpose and of mission in the world, seeking only to conserve what they have. Material things begin to seem more important than spiritual things and security seems more a matter of military defence than of a spiritual offence. Surely that hour has not struck for us. . . .[2]

Only by a Republican-led crusade could the spirit of '76 be

[1] Quoted in Osgood, *Limited War*, pp. 190-91.
[2] *Ibid*, p.. 202.

rekindled, a crusade that meant the rejection of containment, that put in its place an American foreign policy aimed at liberating those millions living in the Communist empire.

Liberation was supposed to work by exercising unrelenting political, economic and moral pressure on the Communist bloc from outside, and by attempting to initiate the same pressures inside the Iron Curtain. The strategy outlined by Dulles and Eisenhower throughout the campaign, and found in *A Policy of Boldness*, owed much besides Dulles' ideas in its tangled intellectual roots to traditional liberal attitudes on foreign affairs and to the political-military ideas expressed by MacArthur after his recall. Certainly this syncretistic Republican alternative to containment with its strategic corollary of using the threat of atomic retaliation to prevent local Communist aggression was a most sophisticated projection of neo-isolationist ideas, for nowhere did it deny the necessity for America's allies. Its vitality may be seen in the fact that American foreign policy for the rest of the decade was permeated by the assumptions of the liberation policy as advocated during the campaign of 1952. As the defender of freedom on earth, Dulles had written in *A Policy of Boldness*, the United States wanted and expected liberation to occur. 'We do not want a series of bloody uprising and reprisals', he went on, insisting that there could be peaceful separation from Moscow as Tito had shown. And the non-military nature of the proposed liberation was emphasised by Eisenhower speaking on 13 August 1952. Criticising 'mere containment', the General went on to say that a true peace programme 'must include as one of its peaceful aims the restorations of the captive nations. . . .'

But emphasis was also put during the campaign on the strategy that came to be known as 'Massive Retaliation' after Dulles later outlined the policy in its most comprehensive form in a speech on 12 January 1954. During the campaign, references to atomic retaliation had been excluded from the Republican platform on Eisenhower's insistence, but it was Massive Retaliation rather than liberation which eventually came to be the most publicised alternative to containment. Both Eisenhower and Dulles believed strongly that, if the Communists had been warned that North Korean aggression would be met by American forces, the war in the Far East would never have occurred, and from this sprang the central creed of the Retaliation thesis, as expressed by Dulles in a speech in Pittsburg on 15 May 1952. 'The only effective way to stop prospective aggressors is to convince them in advance that if they commit aggression, they will be subjected to retaliatory blows so costly that their aggression will not be a profitable operation.' China, in particular, Dulles thought, was particularly vulnerable to a bombing programme in the case of further aggression. Predictably, therefore, the new policy promised a forward policy in Asia while playing down the importance of Western Europe.

If liberation and retaliatory bombing, combined with pledges to end the war in Korea, represented the foreign and military aspects of new policy, there was another series of promises in the Republican platform that reflected the domestic and pacifist strands in the party's ideology. Repeatedly Republican spokesmen used the bogey of militarism and bankruptcy in their attacks on the Democrats, but these Taftite elements only dramatised the contradictions of liberation when seriously presented as a viable alternative to containment.[1] This emphasis on fiscal retrenchment, combined with the promised reliance on air-atomic power, was but a return to the pre-1950 defence policy of the Democrats, ignoring the problems raised by Korea, and thus a political fugue from the unpleasant dilemmas of limited war. As the result of this escapism Dulles later in the decade often found himself, as Robert Osgood has written, speaking loudly and carrying a small stick. 'Yet, to the end, [Dulles] stubbornly refused to abandon his rollback hopes. He clung to them as a moral, libertarian objective after they proved unattainable during his Secretaryship. He was constitutionally incapable of reconciling himself to any other course.'[2]

[1] Between 1950 and 1953, US annual defence expenditure rose by $32 billion, while the Gross National Product increased by $57 billion (adjusted to the purchasing power of the dollar in 1952). Thus the increase in production was nearly double the increase in the military programme, while overall manufacturing capacity increased by 25% during the same period. Defence expenditure during the period of the war averaged about 14% of the GNP, compared with 40% during World War II. On whatever grounds the Administration could be attacked for the prosecution of the war, it was hardly true to say that the war strained the economy. Brodie, pp. 374-5.

[2] Drummond and Coblentz, *Duel at the Brink*, pp. 71-2. See also Goold-Adams, *The Time of Power*, Chaps. 5 and 6 for a sympathetic discussion of Dulles' role in ending the Korean War.

In the summer of 1952 the national realisation that there was
no alternative to containment lay in the future. Instead, in a
mounting torrent of carefully directed oratory, the Democrats
were accused of malfeasance, ineptitude, treason and of waging
war without end in Korea, the alleged ultimate crime of containment. All the frustrations and wrong-doing of the twenty
years of treason were to be swept away in Eisenhower's campaign,
in what the five-star General himself called, 'a great crusade—
for freedom in America and freedom in the world'.

K₁C₂: MERCHANDISING THE CRUSADE

Organisation, strategy and tactics of the Republican crusade
were all influenced by the Party's mass-media triumphs in the
trial run of the mid-term elections of 1950. The strategy board
which served Eisenhower and his Vice-Presidential candidate,
Senator Richard Nixon of California, was composed of representatives of the four important groups in the campaign. These
were the Republican National Committee, the Congressional
Campaign Committee, the Citizens for Eisenhower-Nixon and
the personal entourages of the two candidates which included
such figures as Governor Sherman Adams of New Hampshire
and the Californian PR-man, Murray Chotiner, Nixon's campaign manager. Working in almost an executive capacity with
the public relations division of the National Committee were
the Kudner Agency and Batten, Barton, Durstine and Osborn.
Both advertising agencies had previously worked with Taft,
Dewey and Dulles in their Congressional and White House campaigns. Kudner handled space media, posters, press and campaign literature, while both agencies worked together on the all-
important radio and television schemes.

As opposed to this highly-integrated apparatus the parallel
groups on Stevenson's strategy board were more autonomous.
And while the Democratic candidate had public relations men
in his entourage, and the publicity division of the Democratic
National Committee was active throughout the campaign with
press releases, literature and liaising with the radio-TV networks, Stevenson relied far less than his opponents on the use of
advertising agencies. The two agencies used by the Democrats

were the Joseph Katz Company of Baltimore and the Chicago office of Erwin Wasey. Other publicity men helping Stevenson were journalists and seconded government information officers rather than the genuine Madison Avenue product in the Republican Camp. Moreover, while Stevenson himself often decided campaign strategy with the advertising men employed as tacticians, the Republican campaign used its mass-media men as strategists. They played a major part in producing the comprehensive 'Campaign Plan', produced in standard agency format, which was presented to Eisenhower at Denver in August 1952. This charted in tremendous detail the entire strategy, tactics, literature, speeches, and the relative importance of the different media of the Republican campaign . . . 'the most complete blueprint ever drawn up in advance of a presidential campaign'.[1]

The basis of Democratic strategy during the campaign was a fighting defence of the social security given by their successive administrations in the previous twenty years, coupled with hair-raising prophesies of the coming depression if the Republicans were returned. This defensive strategy was summed up in their campaign slogan: *You never had it so good*. There was no place for Korea in this incantation. The Democrats also calculated that a large turn-out on election day could mean success. But the Republicans in 1952 also expected that a large vote would mean success for them. Abandoning their previous 'me-too' approach which brought defeat in the three previous presidential campaigns, the 'Campaign Plan' assumed that whereas the independent floating voters, at which the GOP campaigns in the 1940s had been aimed, numbered about four million people, the stay-at-homes, who had been ignored in the Wilkie-Dewey days, numbered about forty million. If the emotions of these indifferent voters could be aroused against the Democrats a Republican victory was certain. The corollary of this assumption was that as the stay-at-homes would not bother to go to election meetings or could not be moved to vote by traditional precinct politicking, they would have to be brought to the polls by a mass-media assault, using all the propaganda themes the Repub-

[1] Kelley, p. 1. See pp. 144-201 in *Professional Public Relations and Political Power* for a detailed survey of the mass media techniques used in the 1952 campaign.

licans could muster. An offensive strategy was imperative, for then the Opposition would be choosing its own battleground. Concluded this section of the 'Campaign Plan': '. . . the recommended strategy is: *Attack! Attack!* and *Attack!*'

If the Republican strategy was an offensive one, there were three excellent weapons which had been used time and time again since 1950, and which now in 1952 Senator Karl Mundt, co-chairman, Republican Speaker's Bureau, referred to as K_1C_2— Korea, Communism, Corruption. Bernard C. Duffy, president of BBD & O, summed up the personal aspect of the campaign as one of 'merchandising Eisenhower's frankness, honesty, and integrity, his sincere and wholesome approach'. And if Ike was to be a white-collar FDR, Dulles as the ideas man and Nixon as the hatchet man made up the Republican triptych, surrounded by such other figures as Taft, Knowland and McCarthy to help them in the assault on Stevenson, his Vice-Presidential candidate, Senator John Sparkman and of course, Harry Truman.

As the campaign got under way in the late summer, a battle slowly developed between the image of the Hoover apple with its associated soup kitchens and K_1C_2. An important part of the Republican campaign was the use of visual aids as used by advertising agencies. A series of film strips with recorded synchronised narration was produced with such titles as 'Korea— The Price of Appeasement' or 'America's Creeping Socialism' and which were shown before gatherings which would not have been reached by formal campaign oratory such as service clubs, church groups and employee organisations. The strips could be presented by anyone, not necessarily a political speaker, and by lending projectors many firms made a campaign contribution to the GOP. Another genre were political comic books. A favourite issue was the spine-chilling story of *From Yalta to Korea* which explained the 'Tragedy that has cost over 100,000 American casualties and countless billions of dollars'. The *dramatis personae* of the great betrayal were Hiss, Owen Lattimore and Acheson. The reasons for Korea lay 'in seven years of little-noticed events . . . Stalin met Roosevelt and Churchill at Yalta. Representing the United States were Roosevelt, Byrnes, Stettinius, and a man named Alger Hiss. . . . When President Truman later checked Roosevelt's personal files, he discovered a startling document that would eventually wreck the peace. . . .' Through such means many of the 'stay-at-homes' were given the Republican case against the Democrats.

Then quite suddenly in mid-September the campaign moved into its final phase. On 18 September James Wechsler's *New York Post* ran a front-page story about an $18,000 fund that wealthy Californians had set up for Nixon to use as 'expenses'. Eisenhower at first refused to commit himself to Nixon's support, much to his anger, and even many Republicans asked that he stood down from the campaign. When challenged by newsmen who alleged that preparations were under way to whitewash Nixon, Eisenhower pounded his fist into his palm: 'Nixon has got to be as clean as a hound's tooth'. On 23 September the Senator explained in a nation-wide television address that 'not one cent of the $18,000 or any other money of that type ever went to my personal use'. The money had all been used to fight Communism and corruption in the Administration. After describing his financial struggle to establish a home, Nixon told his audience of a gift which a supporter had sent his two children:

Do you know what it was? It was a little cocker spaniel dog in a crate which he'd sent all the way from Texas, black and white, spotted, and our little girl, Trisha, the six-year-old, named it Checkers. And you know the kids, like all kids, love the dog, and I just want to say this right now that regardless of what they say about it, we're going to keep it. . . .

Pat and I have the satisfaction that every dime we've got is honestly ours. I should say this—that Pat doesn't have a mink coat, but she does have a respectable Republican cloth coat, and I always tell her that she'd look good in anything. . . .

There was a less uxorious ending to the address:

. . . let me say this last word — regardless of what happens, I'm going to continue this fight. I'm going to campaign up and down America until we drive the crooks and the Communists and those that defend them out of Washington. And remember, folks, Eisenhower is a great man. Believe me. He's a great man. And a vote for Eisenhower is a vote for what's good for America.

Eisenhower was watching in the manager's office of the Cleveland public auditorium. Soon Mamie was in tears, and according to the ever-present Sherman Adams in *Firsthand Report* Eisenhower was 'visibly moved and deeply impressed' by the performance. He said Nixon was a completely honest man. Downstairs there was wild shouting and cheering from 13,000 people: 'We want Nixon! We want Nixon!'

Although the Democrats dismissed Nixon's comeback speech as corn, PR-men pointed out that the episode had been a disaster for Stevenson's image because just as he was beginning to be known nationally he had been driven from the news for five whole days. Other observers, less interested in Madison Avenue's auguries, saw in the surge of sympathy for Nixon proof that millions of people who knew that Eisenhower and Taft were not their sort identified themselves with the Nixon's difficulties in keeping up payments on the mortgage and the car (a 1950 Oldsmobile). After twenty years of Democratic rule the common man had moved up in the social scale and an alliance of traditional Republicans and their new white-collar allies was being created through the Power of K_1C_2.

THE PLEDGE

By the last few weeks of the campaign it was obvious that Korea had become the leading issue. Roper polls indicated that in January 1952 one quarter of those interviewed thought the war was a major national problem: by October over half of those asked raised the issue. Eisenhower's concentration on the problem was obvious as early as 21 August when although he supported Truman's decision not to bomb across the Yalu he said that the Republicans could and should call attention to 'the really terrible blunders that led up to the Korean War'. In a speech at Philadelphia on 4 September he elaborated:

. . . there was a failure to build up adequate strength in Korea's own defence forces. We are in that war because this Administration abandoned China to the Communists. We are in that war because the Administration announced to all the world that it had written off most of the Far East as beyond our direct concern.

A month later on 2 October in an expression of his aversion to using American ground troops in Asian wars, the General proposed that only ROK soldiers man the front line: 'If there must be a war there, let it be Asians against Asians, with our support on the side of freedom.'

By this stage of the campaign, Truman, who had left Washington on 27 September on a whistle-stop tour, was supporting Stevenson in his best 'Give-'em-hell' style. The President was also a believer in the theory of the offensive. On 4 October he denounced the entire Republican strategy:

> In recent years this country has been deluged with the greatest outpouring of falsehoods about our foreign policy that was ever cooked up by a group of irresponsible politicians. . . . This wave of filth has had one purpose . . . and only one. That is to win the election for the Republicans. . . .

On 17 October the President blasted Eisenhower's 'Asians against Asians' proposal:

> And now in recent days, he is apparently suggesting that we pull our troops out of Korea and let the South Koreans do all the fighting. . . . Now I have never seen anything cheaper in politics. We cannot do what he suggested — without appeasing Communism in Korea — and he knows it. There are about 50% more South Korean troops in the battle lines today than there are Americans.

Stevenson also attempted to cope with the Korean issue by emphasising that there were no easy solutions to it — like the cold war:

> We are living in a cruel and dangerous world — a world in which the wise man keeps his rifle clean, his guard up, and tries to think as straight as he can shoot. . . . There are no short-cuts to national security. There are only short-cuts to defeat.

But as so often with the Administration's defence of its foreign policy, Stevenson's essentially rational approach to Korea aroused little enthusiasm in the country. Samuel Lubell, who travelled throughout the United States during the election, has written that 'the frustrations over Korea were the most important single propellant behind Eisenhower's sweep,[1] and that Eisenhower's popularity stood behind the anger raised by Korea and higher prices and taxes in the list of forces helping the Republicans. Most observers agree with this judgement. Everywhere the most important card the Democrats were playing was the prosperity of recent years and the possibility of another slump under the Republicans. But countering these fears, Lubell found, was the anguish raised by the war in Korea. 'To anyone interested in human psychology it was fascinating to watch how these two sets of emotions—the dread of another economic depression and the frustrations over the seemingly endless stalemate in Korea —came to grips with one another.' The theme of 'You never had it so good' with its materialistic appeal provoked guilty reflections for many voters as they realised that prosperity since 1950 had been paid for by the death and suffering in Korea.

Lubell records one conversation in which a Democratic supporter argued, 'If the Republicans win, they'll cut your pension, you'll all be selling apples again,' to which the response was, 'Maybe so, but at least it won't be bloody apples.' The phrase 'blood money' referring to the current prosperity was used right across the country, Lubell discovered. Many voters with husbands or sons in the armed forces—two million men had either been conscripted or called up as reservists between the outbreak of war and election day—felt they were being tested before God by the Democrats slogan as to which they valued more highly: dollars or lives. A Texas farm wife told Lubell that she remembered the depression, 'but my nineteen-year-old boy is going into the Army soon. The Democrats seemed to be saying prosperity was more important than the life of my boy'. Again, although many voters supported Eisenhower because they thought he would end the war, on the larger question of West-East conflict Lubell found that the enunciations of the absolutist tradition by MacArthur and Dulles were shared by many. No one credited Russia with any desire for peace; and

---

[1] Lubell, *Revolt of the Moderates*, p. 265. See especially pp. 37-43 for a summary of the clash between fear of depression and fear of war during the election.

if peace in Korea was the first choice of all those he spoke to, then all-out war was the next choice in preference to indefinitely trading hills on the MLR.

As the campaign came to its climax Eisenhower was scheduled to speak at the Detroit Masonic Temple on 24 October. One of his speechwriters, Emmet Hughes, a senior editor of *Life*, was struck by the 'dramatic possibilities' (Sherman Adams) of having Eisenhower pledge that he would make a personal trip to Korea. 'We knew it was right long before Eisenhower delivered it,' writes Adams, who goes on to say in *Firsthand Report* that when copies of the speech were shown to reporters on the campaign train they exclaimed, 'That does it — Ike is in. . . .':

> The first task of a new Administration will be to review and re-examine every course of action open to us with one goal in view: to bring the Korean War to an early and honourable end. That is my pledge to the American people. For this task a wholly new Administration is necessary. The reason for this is simple. The old Administration cannot be expected to repair what it failed to prevent. Where will a new Administration begin?
>
> . . . That job requires a personal trip to Korea. I shall make that trip. Only in that way could I learn how best to serve the American people in the cause of peace. I shall go to Korea. That is my second pledge to the American people. . . .

The pledge was repeated on the 27 and 29 October as the $1.5 million saturation radio-TV spot campaign featured in the Campaign Plan reached its height in forty-nine vital counties in twelve states. (The time-buyers: BBD&O, production: Ted Bates and Company.) As the most effective way of combating 'You Never had it so Good', the blitz-spot campaign had been timed late enough in the campaign to preclude Democratic rebuttal:

> *Voice:* It was extra tough paying my income-tax when I read about the internal revenue tax collectors being fired for dishonesty.
>
> *Eisenhower:* Well — how many tax payers were shaken down, I don't know. How many crooks escaped, I don't know. But I'll find out after next January.

Voice: General, the Democrats are telling me I never had it so good.

Eisenhower: Can that be true when America is billions in debt, when prices have doubled, when taxes break our backs, and when we still are fighting in Korea? It is tragic. It is time for a change.

Still another prong of the final Republican assault against the Democrats involved the Communism-in-Government issue. Nixon had already called Stevenson an 'appeaser' and a 'dupe of Hiss', but this theme demanded an even greater expert on subversion than the Californian Senator. A speech given by the grand inquisitor himself from Chicago was televised and broadcast nationally on 27 October. The subject of McCarthy's address: Stevenson's 'aid to the Communist cause and the extent — the extent to which he is part and parcel of the Acheson-Hiss-Lattimore group'. Mentioning several of Stevenson's staff as having subversive connections, the Senator twice referred to Stevenson as 'Alger' during his speech:

. . . he and his whole camp, as well as every crook and Communist in Washington knows that if I am chairman of that committee (Permanent Sub-committee on Investigations of the Government Operations Committee) and Republicans control the other committees, then we will have the power to help Dwight Eisenhower scrub and flush and wash clean the foul mess of corruption and communism in Washington. . . .

On election eve, 3 November, the Democrats presented national radio-TV speeches by Truman, Stevenson, Vice-President Barkley and Sparkman. The Republicans followed with an hour-long progress-report to Eisenhower on the crusade produced by BBDO and incorporating scenes from all over the country. Fast cross-cutting sequences followed each other, of cash-registers ringing up higher prices, of Alger Hiss, of the Rosenbergs, of Korea, of Eisenhower's Abilene home, of the General with Churchill. A girl from San Francisco, a foreign-born labourer, Louis Bromfield, a Negro, all told of their support for Eisenhower, as well as a Korean War veteran. . . . 'Well, all the guys I knew out in Korea figure there's only one man for the job, General, and that's you. We've been getting kind of tired of politicians. . . .'

Stevenson conceded late on 5 November. Eisenhower had received thirty-three million votes, the largest ever recorded by a presidential candidate, to Stevenson's twenty-seven million. The victor's electoral vote was 442, and thirty-nine states had voted Republican. The Democrats' hold on the solid South had been broken for the first time since 1928, and other large groups which had previously supported them had also swung — workers, Catholics, immigrants and young voters. Suburbia especially had declared for Eisenhower-Nixon. The new Congress would be Taftite Republican. After twenty years the rule of the Democrats, which Edmund Wilson had seen ushered in with Roosevelt's first inaugural under the cold, grey skies of Washington in March 1933, 'There is a suggestion, itself rather vague, of a possible dictatorship,' was at last over.

CHAPTER TWENTY-TWO

THE ATOMIC THREAT

> We told them we could not hold it to a limited war any longer. . . . They didn't want a full-scale war or an atomic attack. . . .
>
> DWIGHT EISENHOWER

> (The Armistice) was no free-will gift of peace by the Communists. . . . It came only after the Communists realised that, unless there was a quick armistice, the battle area would be enlarged so as to endanger the sources of aggression in Manchuria. . . .
>
> JOHN FOSTER DULLES

THE CRUISE OF THE *HELENA*

THE President-elect was in Korea from 2–5 December, his every movement in inspecting forward units of the Eighth Army cocooned by strict censorship which nevertheless could do nothing to protect him from the intense cold of the third winter of the war. With Eisenhower was an impressive collection of civilian and military brass — Defence Secretary-designate Charles E. Wilson, Omar Bradley, Admiral Arthur Radford, CINCPAC, Press Secretary James Hagerty and others. At a high-level conference at Eighth Army HQ Eisenhower met every senior commander in the theatre. Although Mark Clark had prepared a detailed estimate of the forces required to implement his 'broad plan' for victory in Korea, 'the most significant thing about the visit of the President-elect was that I never had the opportunity to present this estimate for his consideration. The question of how much it would take to win the war was never raised. It soon became apparent, in our many conversations, that he would seek an honourable truce.'[1]

Thus the Korean visit was most significant in influencing the future defence policies of the new Administration for 'The view

[1] Clark, p. 221.

Eisenhower got of the dour life of the American combat soldiers and the dissipation of American resources in a remote, indecisive struggle intensified his determination to obtain a settlement one way or another.'[1] From Korea Eisenhower flew to Guam and boarded the cruiser *Helena*, which sailed on to Wake Island, where most of the newly-appointed Cabinet joined him for a series of conferences as they sailed towards Honolulu. Over two years had passed since the Truman-MacArthur meeting on the atoll and the end of the war was still not in sight.

Only on 24 November Vyshinsky, speaking in the UN for the Chinese and North Koreans as well as the USSR, had rejected the Indian compromise resolution on prisoner repatriation which Acheson had accepted. This, while asserting the relevant provision of the Geneva Convention, stated that 'force shall not be used against prisoners of war to prevent or effect their return to their homelands', and proposed the creation of a neutral nations repatriation commission to return home all POWs. If, at the end of ninety days following the armistice, there remained any non-repatriated prisoners their status would be determined by the post-war political conference already agreed in the draft Armistice Agreement. In the last resort those who refused to go home would become wards of the United Nations. This Indian resolution was approved by the General Assembly on 3 December by fifty-four to five. Although the Chinese on 28 November had indicated their approval for the alternative Soviet resolution which involved forcible repatriation it was learnt in New Delhi that when the Indian proposals had been submitted to Peking on 16 November, the Chinese had not expressed any decisive objection to the plan apart from stating their disapproval of voluntary repatriation. If this indicated a split between Moscow and Peking over ending the war, the differences were soon resolved, for on 14 December Chou denounced the General Assembly's resolution as void, illegal, unfair and unreasonable in a masterpiece of invective which was in all probability timed to coincide with the bloody riots on Pongam Island. Pak Hen Yen followed with a similar repudiation from Pyongyang on

---

[1] Donovan, *Eisenhower, The Inside Story*, p. 17. This account of the first Eisenhower Administration draws on Cabinet papers and interviews with Cabinet officers.

17 December. The problem of prisoner repatriation remained outstanding and Stalin's war was still a going concern.

Together with colleagues on the *Helena*, Eisenhower outlined his belief that fiscal retrenchment was absolutely necessary in the coming years unless the country's strength was to be sapped by overspending, and of course this immovably mercantile outlook was to dominate both the General's Administrations. Once again Dulles expounded his idea that wars were caused by miscalculation, citing his favourite example of Acheson's Press Club speech misleading the Russians and North Koreans. To Dulles' advocacy of using the threat of atomic retaliation to prevent local communist aggression was added the powerful voice of Radford. The Admiral also believed that the US should concentrate a strategic reserve in North America and that local defence on the Eurasian periphery should be left to indigenous levies, and both he and Charles Wilson agreed that Asia was the future pivot of the cold war. But Eisenhower himself apparently believed that once Western Europe was strong enough to defend itself, the Asian problem would become manageable. However, the future President had been very impressed by Radford's presentation of the new strategy and from now on he was marked out as Bradley's successor when the Chairman of the JCS retired the following August. The Admiral had all the right political as well as military ingredients, for whereas Bradley represented containment, Western Europe and limited war, Radford antithetically personified atomic retaliation, Asia, sea-air power and thus the much advertised new dynamic approach of the incoming Administration.

At any rate, six weeks before the inaugural Eisenhower and Dulles had agreed on the *Helena* that the Korean stalemate could not be tolerated, and therefore they 'had determined to make it clear to the Communists that to delay the truce indefinitely would be to invite the United States to enlarge the war and to strike at China not only in Korea but on two or three other fronts of its own choosing'.[1] The incantation that henceforth it would be the United States and not the Communists who would choose offensive opportunities was heard in Eisenhower's statement at La Guardia Field on 14 December after flying home from Honolulu. Henceforward, he announced, the enemy would

[1] Donovan, p. 115.

be impressed by deeds, 'executed under circumstances of our own choosing', a phrase with only slight alterations prominent in Dulles' formal pronouncement of the new strategy in January 1954. Moreover, as if emphasising that the new approach owed much to MacArthur, who had announced on 5 December that he had 'a clear and definite solution' to the war which would not start a general conflict, Eisenhower and Dulles conferred with him shortly after their return from the Pacific. According to Sherman Adams' memoirs, the MacArthur solution was a 'precisely stated intention to drop an atom bomb after full notification to the North Koreans of our purposes'.[1] MacArthur was convinced that this threat would be enough to end the war, and indeed it was the threat of eventual atomic attack which played a major part in ending the war.

Soon after the inaugural on 20 January, when Truman and Eisenhower, forever estranged because of the bitterness of the election campaign, rode in almost complete silence from the White House to the Capitol, came the first hint of the new policy. On 2 February 1953 Eisenhower said in his first State of the Union speech that the Seventh Fleet would no longer screen the Chinese mainland from Chinese attacks. The new instructions implied no aggressive intent, the President emphasised, and in fact long before the 'de-neutralisation' order, ever since the Chinese intervention in Korea, raids by Chiang's forces from the offshore islands had been carried out without interference from the US Navy, as well as some operations from Formosa itself with the same objective of contacting mainland anti-Communist guerillas. But here was a first warning to Peking that Taiwan might yet be used for larger operations against the mainland unless a truce were coming in Korea.

By the beginning of March there was still no indication of any break in the Panmunjom deadlock. Yet although the bacteriological warfare charges were rekindled in February by the confessions of Schwable and Bley, the peace campaign had by now reached a point of diminishing returns, and with the truce talks recessed Panmunjom was no longer an effective propaganda forum. Moreover, the effects of the air and naval campaign against North Korea which would soon culminate in the

1 Adams, *Firsthand Report*, p. 48.

attack against the irrigation dams, combined with the strain of the war on the Chinese economy, meant there were pressing reasons why Peking should end the war. By the end of 1952 there were over a million Chinese troops in North Korea, with a total of 1.2 million men altogether under Peng's command, according to Mark Clark. The Eighth Army's own strength at the beginning of 1953 had reached the huge figure of 768,000, including supply and service troops.

Then, some time between March and May the Chinese decided to write off the war. Besides the important but incalculable effects of the war on their economy two factors above all seem to have influenced Peking. The first was the death of Stalin on 5 March and the consequent political thaw in the Communist world; the second was the threat by the United States Government to carry atomic war to the Chinese mainland unless a truce were signed. The night following Stalin's death the Communists sent up flares and star clusters all along the MLR, and each soldier fired off his weapon into the air at about the same time in a sundown farewell salute to the dead dictator. Yet with the end of Stalin's life there came indications within the month that his war, too, would end. The first sign was a reply to a letter sent by Clark to Kim Il Sung and Peng Teh-huai on 22 February suggesting that an exchange of sick and wounded be organised between the two commands. In the Communist reply on 28 March which agreed to the exchange there was a suggestion that this first move could 'lead to the smooth settlement of the entire question of prisoners of war. . . .' When Clark suggested a meeting of liaison groups the Communists agreed on 2 April. With their letter they enclosed the full text of a statement made by Chou En-lai on 30 March following his return from Stalin's funeral in Moscow, and endorsed by Kim Il Sung, which assented to a neutral nation repatriation scheme for the POWs. While indicating that he did not approve of the principle of voluntary repatriation Chou said that the two Communist governments concerned

> propose that both parties to the negotiations should undertake to repatriate immediately after the cessation of hostilities all those prisoners of war in their custody who insist upon repatriation and to hand over the remaining prisoners of war to a

neutral state so as to ensure a just solution to the question of their repatriation.[1]

At last the deadlock on Item 4 had been broken by what was virtually a Communist capitulation in accepting a scheme which resembled the Indian plan which Peking had rejected the previous December. Liaison groups met as scheduled on 6 April, agreement was reached on all technical details on the 11th, and on 20 April, 'Little Switch' began when the first 6,670 Communist and 684 UNC personnel were exchanged at Panmunjom. Already on 9 April, Philip Deane, George Blake and their colleagues had crossed the Yalu at Sinuiju for their journey back to Britain via Manchuria and the Trans-Siberian railway to Moscow. Their long journey had begun when at Antung the party had entered a *wagon-lit*. . . .

Then, in a preliminary letter exchange at Panmunjom, Harrison had suggested to Nam Il on 17 April that Switzerland be appointed the neutral custodian nation within Korea for the POWs, and that sixty days be allowed to determine their attitudes to repatriation. Consequently on 26 April the first plenary session at Panmunjom since the previous October met in the truce hut. But peace, ever elusive, was not yet destined to come to Korea.

OUTPOST PORK CHOP: A NATIONAL ISSUE

At the beginning of 1953 ground activity along the MLR had simmered down to routine patrolling, and small-scale attacks after the autumn fighting. To the north of the front between the two armies, numbering nearly two million men, the general Communist dispositions remained unchanged from the previous year with the Chinese holding the front westwards from the Punchbowl. South of the line the Eighth Army Corps boundaries remained unaltered although Van Fleet and Lt.-Gen. Maxwell D. Taylor, who took over the Eighth Army on 11 February, continued to switch divisions between front and reserve and between corps. While the total (and title) of the eight Western divisions on Korea remained unchanged, due to

[1] Vatcher, pp. 181-2.

the expansion of the ROK Army EUSAK now controlled altogether twenty divisions. By the time of the armistice in July
the South Koreans, who had been holding about two-thirds of
the line, were contributing sixteen divisions, most of them with
their own organic artillery.

But with the spring, even though the war at last looked like
ending, came a mounting series of Communist assaults on the
Eighth Army. While initially concentrated on I Corps, these
culminated in a limited offensive against the ROK II Corps sector
around Kumsong in June and July which produced the heaviest
fighting since the 1951 spring offensives. These last offensives
were exceptional. It was the fighting for White Horse and the
Triangle Hill complex, over the Hook in the Commonwealth
divisional sector, and at the Reno-Vegas-Elko-Berlin outpost complex on the far western front, held by the Marines since March
1952, which were the characteristic engagements of the stalemate
war. Beyond the fortified bunkers and trenches of the Main
Line of Resistance extended the strangely code-named outposts,
up to 5,000 yards ahead of the main positions, and yet again in
front of the outposts were the outguard listening posts, the
northernmost antennae of the UNC and of the Western world
in Korea.

The eerie waste between the two defensive systems was a
psychological warfare as well as an infantry battleground. UNC
psywar, directed from GHQ, Tokyo, made great use of such
themes as Russian manipulation of Chinese and Korean forces
for their own ends, the generous treatment accorded UN
prisoners, and the lethal properties of UN firepower. As many as
a third of the Communist prisoners said that they had surrendered because of UNC psywar; but the strategic limitations imposed on the military in the war precluded any full-scale effort.[1]

In *The Last Parallel* by Martin Russ, probably the best chronicle of the stalemate war, the author records not only the tedium
and danger of the fighting, but the infinite variety of Chinese
psychological warfare tactics. Loudspeaker announcements that
the CPV were only defending Manchuria, that the US was waging germ warfare in Korea, and that Ike was a big-money boy
who was not interested in that precious Communist commodity,

[1] Storey, 'Psywar in Korea', *Army Combat Forces Journal*, July 1952, gives
a brief survey of these activities.

peace, alternated with Western songs, ballads and pop tunes frequently played in arrangements by Chinese bands. Jazz Age numbers from the roaring twenties were a favourite of Chinese psywar experts, and often featured live female vocalists. While peering into the gloom of North Korea and the Communist world from the parapets of the MLR United Nations soldiers could listen to numbers made famous by Paul Whiteman, Bix Beiderbecke or Crosby, or such tunes as *Autumn in New York*, *The Last Rose of Summer* or, an especial favourite by the Chinese, *There's No Place Like Home*.

Such sweet music, relayed by courtesy of the CPV, drifted first of all over the UNC outposts which bore the main brunt of Communist attacks against the MLR and which marked the high-tide of Van Fleet's autumn 1951 offensive. While US Army manuals indicated that outposts should not be used to initiate close combat, as soon as static warfare developed in Korea it was recognised that any defence of the MLR would entail holding outposts as a buffer, for otherwise no-man's-land, the main battlefield between the opposing armies during the stalemate war, would be handed over to the enemy. Besides this strategic consideration, outposts were tactically valuable because they drew out the Communists infantry from their caves and tunnels into the open where they could be destroyed by UNC artillery. And as the truce talks dragged on, outposts unfortunately came to have an increasing political value as both sides insisted to each other at Panmunjom that they were militarily in the ascendant.

All three reasons entered into the decision to defend outpost Pork Chop when it was attacked by the Chinese in April 1953 as the truce talks approached their climax. The outpost was on an important part of I Corps' sector of the MLR near the boundary with IX Corps, and stood about twelve miles west of the rubble-pile of Chorwon and not far from White Horse. Less than a mile south of Pork Chop was Hill 347, an important bastion of the MLR, with outposts Snook, Erie and Arsenal to the east, and Old Baldy to the west, which the Chinese had taken in March 1953. The Communists thus overlooked the access road to Pork Chop from Hill 347 as well as holding the ridges of Hasakkol and Pokkae to the north. The peak inside the 200-metre contour which gave this precariously-held piece of real estate its name was only 234 metres above sea level. The entire surface of 'The Chop' had been engineered with a convoluted rifleman's trench running around the perimeter. Sandbagged, heavily timbered and fire-slotted bunkers had then been built into the trench system at thirty-yard intervals, and all the technical lessons learnt in nearly two years of Korean trench fighting were incorporated in the fortifications of the outpost.

On the night of 16 April two under-strength platoons of Easy Company, 31st Regiment, 7th Infantry Division (Maj.-Gen. Arthur Trudeau) had just taken over Pork Chop. Divisional G-2 knew that a Chinese attack in the area was scheduled, but most of Pork Chop's defenders did not know this. Altogether there were ninety-six men on the hill, including engineers, artillery-men and medics, and of these twenty were on outguard duty in the listening posts on the forward slopes of The Chop. The scene for the fight had been set by the sounds of dirge-like Chinese music which had drifted over from Hasakkol in the early evening, and which an interpreter had said was prayer music as the Communists prepared to die. For the next few hours all was silence as the outguards settled down in their fox-holes and a small patrol probed the valley floor below Pork Chop.

Then between 2200 and 2300 two full assault companies of Chinese infantry left Hasakkol, jogged across the valley, and reached the ramparts of Pork Chop without anyone there knowing of their arrival in the confusion of battle, as both the patrol and the outguards had clashed with the attackers. In Easy Company's CP at the rear of the Hill, Lt. Thomas Harrold lost contact with his First Platoon on the left of his position as the Chinese barrage came in about 2300, and his line to Battalion also went dead. The Lieutenant then fired a red rocket towards the MLR asking for a 'flash' curtain barrage of VT proximity fuse and high-explosive shells which in theory should stop the Chinese follow-up, leaving the Communist infantry on the hill to be dealt with by the defenders. For twenty minutes the combined fire from both sides pinned down the infantry but when as soon as it lifted, about 2325, the Chinese were all over the First Platoon's sector of 'The Chop' grenading and burp-gunning the defenders in their bunkers. Harrold, together with some other officers and NCOs, turned his CP into a blockhouse barring the rear of the hill, but most of his First Platoon had been killed, and Second Platoon were pinned down in their bunkers. By 0200 hours the attack had stalled as the Chinese began to reorganise.

Now started the second phase of the battle. Regiment decided to relieve Pork Chop and a preliminary sortie was launched by a platoon of Love Company moving up from the vicinity of Hill 200, between the MLR and The Chop. This first attempt was easily repelled by the Chinese because the relief column thought that the hill was mostly still held by Americans, but at 0430 a much more serious attempt was made by the whole of King Company to clear the Chinese from Pork Chop. It was planned that, while King moved up the rear of the Hill, the two remaining platoons of Love would strike from the East along the finger that led from Hill 200. But by now the Communists had been given enough time to consolidate their gains and there were heavy casualties taken by both sides before the remnants of King and Love reached the summit of The Chop. While these American casualties were not numerous enough at first to abandon the relief expedition, they were still sufficient to preclude the clearing of the Chinese from Pork Chop. By noon the total active strength of the three companies committed to The Chop numbered only about fifty-five men and the Chinese still infested most of the trench line. Moreover as King Company's movement petered out, fresh Chinese reinforcements reached The Chop, coming in from the north-west over the approaches to Brinson Finger.

While the deadlock on the hilltop continued, the higher echelons all the way back to GHQ in Tokyo were brooding over the problem of whether to continue the fight. If The Chop fell, the Chinese could next hit the MLR and with the truce talks about to start again any weakening of the front could not be risked. 'The fight was local but the issue was national.'[1] The atomic threat to Red China and Stalin's death had no relevance to the problem of Pork Chop; it was the infantry who have to fight and die, for GHQ and Army realised that a decision to go ahead might result in another battalion-a-day fracas like Triangle Hill. At last the question, Do you want to hold Pork

[1] Marshall, *Pork Chop Hill*, p. 163. See also Kintner, 'Pork Chop, Battle for a Korean Outpost', *Army Combat Forces Journal*, March 1955. This article covers the July fighting for the Chop in great detail.

Chop? was answered, late in the afternoon. Trudeau was given authority to hold the hill if he could and to use if necessary the Second Battalion, 17th Regiment. As George Company from that Regiment had already been through the meatgrinder on The Chop while this decision was being made on the command level, that meant that 31st Regiment had been given two companies. The First Battalion of the 17th Regiment was moved to the Pork Chop area but not yet committed. Only two groups of Americans on the highest knob of Pork Chop and in the CP blockhouse were now still fighting.

Fox Company fought their way to the top of the hill by 2130: to meet them the Chinese dropped on Pork Chop the heaviest barrage of the fight so far. Following the disintegration of Fox, the second available company of the 17th Regiment was thrown in; Easy reached the hill by marching north into enemy-held no-man's-land and going up the face of The Chop, their backs to Pokkae, and so achieving the surprise which for the first time challenged the Chinese hold decisively. Everywhere the Communists fought back with grenades and machine-guns but by 0250 on the 18th the MLR was told — prematurely — that Pork Chop was under American control. Soon more Chinese came in from Hasakkol and Pokkae, and as the second dawn of the battle

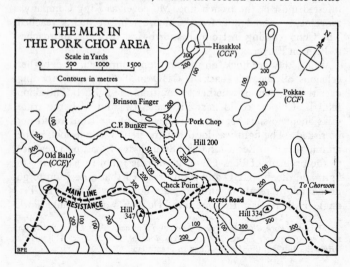

THE MLR IN
THE PORK CHOP AREA

Scale in Yards
0   500   1000   1500

Contours in metres

Hasakkol
(CCF)

Pokkae
(CCF)

Brinson Finger

C.P. Bunker   234   Pork Chop

Hill 200

Old Baldy
(CCF)

Stream

Check Point

To Chorwon

MAIN LINE OF RESISTANCE

Access Road

Hill 347   Hill 334

came up Able Company from the reserve battalion was committed. The outcome of the fight was still in question, and as it went on throughout the day Fox, Easy and Able took the same punishment that the other companies had suffered. Then, at last, the Chinese cried enough, and by the end of the 18th April, 7th Division once again held the Chop as the smoke blew away. The battle had set up a new record. On the second day the Eighth Army's supporting guns had fired over 77,000 rounds in support of the men on the Chop, an effort which when measured against the narrow front involved was an all-time record. The intensity of the Chinese shoot could not have been less. There was little wonder that Pork Chop had been picked clean by the opposing guns.

But the Chinese were determined to have the hill. Throughout the summer as 7th Division laboriously rebuilt the shattered bunkers and trenches, more mortar and artillery fire fell on these few acres than on the rest of the division. Two hours before midnight on 6 July a huge Chinese barrage thundered down on 7th Division, concentrating on Pork Chop, now held by First Battalion, 17th Regiment. Saturation infantry attacks against The Chop followed the barrage, far heavier than anything in the April fighting. A single bunker with two or three Americans would be besieged by up to ten times that number of Chinese. A succession of companies, battalions, and ultimately regiments then fought to save Pork Chop. Throughout the 7th the situation was chaotic as both sides went on reinforcing and as hand-to-hand fighting for the bunkers and trenches continued throughout the day. Trudeau visited the outpost and decided on a night counter-attack by a company of 32nd Regiment, because Chinese interdiction of all routes from Hills 347 and 200 — directed from their OPs on Old Baldy — made a daylight assault impractical. By dawn on the 8th the position was still inconclusive with sporadic small-arms and automatic weapons fighting continuing on the outpost.

At a conference at 0800 on 8 July in 17th Regiment's CP attended by Trudeau, Maj.-Gen. Clarke, I Corps, Maxwell Taylor, and others, the brass decided to launch a two-company daylight attack in mid-afternoon. The weather was overcast, there were no air strikes, but the attack was stalled only when elements of Second Battalion, 17th Regiment, had almost carried their objectives. The Chinese were able to match each American company with a battalion; artillery barraging by both sides was terrific. The see-saw went on during the 9th, and next day the position on The Chop was chaotic with elements of four US battalions on the hill from 17th and 32nd Regiments, and with control becoming increasingly difficult. By the morning of the 11th, five US battalions had been thrown in to hold a company-size outpost, and the Chinese were using at least an entire division. A second command conference was held, this time in 7th Division's CP. The armistice was near, the ante could not possibly be raised any more, and Taylor reluctantly made the decision to withdraw. All the sacrifices to hold Pork Chop had been for nothing. During the long day of the 11th July all Americans were withdrawn to the MLR by the armoured personnel carriers that had been used throughout this second phase of the fight. Engineers sowed demolition charges, and artillery fire and air strikes completed the work of making the outpost uninhabitable for the Chinese. Sixteen days later the armistice was signed. To-day The Chop lies partly in the demilitarised zone and partly in Communist territory.

NEW WAYS OF WAR?

As the fighting flared and spurted in these clashes all along the MLR, there were still high hopes that peace would soon be signed at Panmunjom when the plenary delegations met on 26 April. But before the war ended in three months time there were two great crises to be surmounted, the first to get the Communists finally to agree to the armistice, the second when Syngman Rhee threatened to wreck this laboriously reached agreement which would perpetuate indefinitely the division of his country.

During this first plenary meeting of 1953 Nam Il presented a six-point Communist proposal which, briefly, called for an agreement to send all non-repatriated prisoners to a neutral state outside Korea within three months of the signing of the truce. During the next six months agents of their Governments would have facilities to persuade the prisoners to come home. After the expiry of this time, all remaining non-repatriates would be kept in the custody of the neutral state until the post-war political conference envisaged by the armistice provided for their disposal. Nam Il also objected to the choice of Switzerland as the neutral custodian. As these proposals meant that the non-repatriates might be incarcerated indefinitely if — as seemed only too likely — the conference failed to agree, Harrison rejected the Communist plan. The provision which required the movement of the non-repatriates outside Korea was also unacceptable to Harrison as it would mean practical difficulties of transportation. He insisted that sixty days was sufficient to determine the attitudes of the prisoners.

With this immediate impasse all hopes of an early truce vanished and the proceedings at Panmunjom reverted to normal with angry, abusive exchanges of recriminatory charges and counter-charges. The condition of the UNC repatriates in 'Little Switch' added to the tension for many sick and wounded had been left behind on the Yalu in favour of indoctrinated progressives sent home early as a gambit in the peace campaign. Argument continued on the place of custody for non-repatriates, duration of custody and which neutral state should look after the prisoners. To increase the pressure on the Communists after their unacceptable plan of 26 April, Clark's psychological warfare staff put into operation a long-cherished scheme for disaffecting the Communist Air Forces. On 27 April the UNC offered $100,000 and political asylum to the first Communist pilot to deliver them an undamaged MIG, and $50,000 for each succeeding machine. The message was broadcast in Russian, Chinese and Korean and when the wind was blowing in the right direction B-29s dumped thousands of leaflets announcing the offer over Sinuiju and the Yalu mouth so that they were blown over Manchuria as well as North Korea. There was no immediate response but two months after the armistice a North Korean pilot from Pyongyang touched down at Kimpo — and the USAF had its first combat model of the Soviet fighter to test-fly at its leisure.

After further sterile exchanges at Panmunjom in which the Communists refused to accept Pakistan as the custodian nation on the grounds that agreement should first be reached on moving the prisoners out of Korea, and Harrison unsuccessfully proposed — as a concession to Rhee — that all non-repatriates should be released with the armistice, Nam Il turned up with a completely recast plan for prisoner repatriation on 7 May. The Communists now proposed that a neutral nations repatriation commission (NNRC) be formed of the four nations already chosen to form the supervisory commission, Czechoslovakia, Poland, Sweden and Switzerland, together with India, and this commission take custody of the non-repatriates in Korea. The period assigned for persuasion by the agents of the non-repatriates' Government was cut to four months (120 days), and the prisoners' ultimate fate was still to be decided by the political conference. As the UNC thought that a five-power custodial force was too cumbersome and because there was still no guarantee of civilian status and eventual political asylum for the repatriates, Nam Il's proposals were rejected.

By this time Harrison, Clark and Washington had, in effect, to manœuvre between the Communists and Rhee, who was in a powerful position to oppose the armistice for with his ultimate authority over the ROK Army he could, in Clark's words, 'take the major part of the war right out from under my command'. Accordingly on 13 May UNC counter-proposals suggested that all Korean prisoners should be released to civilian status on the signing of the armistice, but that the Chinese non-repatriates should be turned over to a NNSC whose custodial forces and chairman should be Indian. After sixty days all non-repatriates would be granted civilian status and therefore freedom. Inevitably these proposals were rejected by Nam Il the next day. Both sides by now agreed on the supervisory commission but there were major differences still on its composition and on the fate of remaining non-repatriates. Deadlock, as so often before, seemed certain.

But Washington had now come to the end of the line with the Panmunjom story. While the talks were recessed, and after consultations with the Administration and between the Allies on the highest level, final proposals for presentation at Panmunjom were sent to Clark on 23 May. They provided for the transfer of all prisoners to the NNRC, which would be constituted with an Indian chairman and Indian custodial forces alone. After a sixty-day period for repatriation of those who wished to return home, a period of 90 or 120 days for 'explaining' would be allowed after which non-repatriates would either be released as civilians or else their disposition would be referred to the General Assembly. Writes Mark Clark, 'If, however, the Communists rejected this final offer and made no constructive proposals of their own, I was authorised to *break off* the truce talks rather than to recess them, and to carry on the war in new ways never yet tried in Korea.'[1] This warning, it has been said, was conveyed to Peking by the Indian Government after Dulles had told Nehru in New Delhi during a visit which began on 22 May that unless an armistice was forthcoming in Korea the US would broaden the war. Although Nehru has reportedly denied that he personally knew anything about the atomic threat to Peking, there can be no doubt at all that Indian officials Dulles met passed the message on to Peking.

Simultaneously at Panmunjom the delegations met in executive session on 25 May when these US proposals were tabled. The next plenary session was on 4 June when the Communists accepted, with minor changes, the final UNC plan for the prisoners. There was a small amount of haggling over the number of 'explainers', and the Communists refused to accept the General Assembly as a possible custodian because the UN were belligerents in Korea. But the longer wardship proposed for the repatriates in the plan of 25 May was an UNC concession, as was Washington's agreement to turn over all prisoners to the NNRC, no matter what Rhee said. Thus it was agreed between the two sides that after two months for repatriation, remaining prisoners would be open to persuasion by their respective Governments for a further ninety-day period. If, after a further thirty-day period, the post-war conference had been unable to agree on their disposition, the non-repatriates would revert to civilian status. Within a further thirty days the prisoners who so desired would be sent to a neutral country by the Indian Red Cross or the NNRC, which would then dissolve itself. It was carefully written into the 'Terms of Reference for Neutral Nations Repatriation Commission' that after 120 days in its custody all repatriates would become civilians and thus no prisoner would be held for more than six months after the truce. On 8 June, after eighteen months negotiation over Item 4 of the Armistice agenda, the 'Terms of Reference' were

Clark, p. 252.

2E

signed by Nam Il and Harrison.[1] The armistice agreement, but for the drawing of the final demarcation line, was complete.

While at the time this agreement which preserved the principle of voluntary repatriation was ascribed to the post-Stalin thaw or Chinese and North Korea war weariness, there was little immediate appreciation of how much the threat of 'new ways' of war had forced the Chinese to end the war. As there are no Chinese sources available, the evidence is necessarily circumstantial, but the fact remains that within a couple of months of the atomic threat Peking called it quits in Korea. But there is plenty of evidence that Eisenhower and Dulles were in earnest about fighting if necessary a no-holds-barred war to unite Korea, using atomic weapons and in which the trans-Yalu bases would have been attacked.

Admiral Joy, for example, has written that in the spring of 1953 the US began giving serious consideration 'to extending United Nations Command military operations into Red China The threat of atomic bombs was posed; defeat for Red China became a possibility. . . . In understandable prudence they took the only step open to them to remove the growing threat of a holocaust. . . . It was as simple as that. It had always been as simple as that.'[2]

'As a warning of what might come if the Communists did not end the stalemate, the United States in the spring moved atomic missiles to Okinawa,' Donovan writes, also stating that in early 1953 the Administration authorised appropriations for raising additional ROK divisions, continued to re-equip the USAF in Korea with Sabrejets, and in July sent another Marine division to the Far East.[3]

Dulles himself was convinced that the threat to China brought about the armistice. Speaking to the Geneva conference on Korea in April 1954 he said that the truce came 'only after the Communists realised that, unless there was a quick armistice, the battle area would be enlarged so as to endanger the sources of aggression in Manchuria. Then and only then did the Communist rulers judge that it would be expedient to sign the Armistice.' Furthermore, in his famous 'brinkmanship' interview in

[1] See Appendix D.
[2] Joy, p. 161-2.
[3] Donovan, p. 116.

January 1956, Dulles indicated what targets would have been attacked in China to win in Korea. 'They were specific targets reasonably related to the area. They did not involve massive destruction of great population centres like Shanghai, Peking or Canton. . . .'[1]

As for the man who would have ordered the strikes across the Yalu, Donovan writes, 'At no time, however, did the President make a formal decision to enlarge the war. Some of those who were closest to him at the time are convinced that he would certainly have done so if the stalemate had dragged on. But his fervent hope was for a truce, and he would have regarded war against China as a dread step to be taken only as a last resort.'[2] But at the time of writing (1963) the most revealing details of the threat to Peking have come from Sherman Adams, who had a unique access to the secrets of the Eisenhower regime before his fall. An interesting morsel retailed by Adams is that the Churchill Government in early 1953 again pledged support to the US in extending operations against Communist China if necessary: 'As negotiations with the Communists proceeded, Eisenhower made ready to launch a counter-attack on the Chinese, this time with atomic weapons, if they started to fight again. Dulles also secured a promise from the British at the NATO foreign ministers' meeting that they would come back into a broadened war with us in Korea if the truce broke down. . . .'[3]

'In May, during talks with Nehru in India, Dulles said that the United States could not be held responsible for failing to use atomic weapons if a truce could not be arranged. This message was planted deliberately in India so that it would get to the Chinese Communists, as it did.'

[1] *The Korean Problems at the Geneva Conference*, p. 48. 'How Dulles Averted War', *Life*, 16 January 1956, p. 78.

[2] Donovan, p. 119.

[3] The NATO foreign ministers met in Paris 23-25 April, and again from 10-14 July, Bidault and Salisbury, deputising for Eden, conferred with Dulles in Washington. The communiqué after this meeting stated that if Communist aggression were renewed in Korea, the UN would again support 'the restoration of peace and security'. There was no specific reference to Korea in the April communiqué. The Declaration of Sixteen, its terms agreed in January 1952, which threatened action against China if the Korean aggressions were renewed, was not formally signed until 27 July 1953.

Long afterwards (Adams goes on), talking one day with Eisenhower about the events that led up finally to the truce in Korea, I asked him what it was that brought the Communists into line. 'Danger of an atomic war,' he said, without hesitation. 'We told them we could not hold it to a limited war any longer if the Communists welched on a treaty of truce. They didn't want a full-scale war or an atomic attack. That kept them under some control.[1]

Ending the Korean War thus seems to have been the first vindication of the Massive Retaliation theory. In this duel at the brink with the Communists Dulles won and so fulfilled the Republican election pledge that they would end the Korean War — the greatest achievement of the Eisenhower years. Yet the war was still not finally ended with the tortuous agreement over prisoner repatriation. Within ten days a huge new crisis was precipitated by Rhee's release of over half the non-repatriates, and it seemed as if the Communists might repudiate as a result the laboriously reached Armistice Agreement. In the last few weeks of the war the world was reminded that, even if the fighting in Korea was an epitome of the larger world struggle, the war would end as it had begun three years before with the focus on the frustrations of a divided Korea. However much their country had been devastated by the war most Koreans still passionately demanded the unification promised at Cairo ten years before and which now was impossible as long as the cold war went on.

[1] See Adams, *Firsthand Report*, pp. 102, 48-9.

CHAPTER TWENTY-THREE

THE TRUCE OF THE BEAR

When he stands up like a tired man, tottering near and near;
When he stands up pleading, in wavering man-brute guise,
When he veils the hate and cunning of his little swinish eyes;
When he shows as seeking quarter, with paws like hands in prayer,
That is the time of the peril — the time of the truce of the Bear!

RUDYARD KIPLING

RHEE'S ANTI-ARMISTICE CAMPAIGN

FROM the very beginning of the resumption of talks at Panmunjom over prisoner repatriation the ROK Government had indicated that it would oppose an armistice which left Korea divided. As early as 3 April the South Korean Foreign Minister, Pyun Yung Tai, had told the American ambassador, Ellis Briggs, that the ROK would demand a price for co-operating with the truce. It soon appeared that this remark by Pyun was an understatement. On 24 April, two days before the senior delegates met, the ROK ambassador in Washington told Eisenhower that President Rhee was prepared to withdraw ROK forces from the United Nations Command if any armistice were signed which permitted the Chinese to remain south of the Yalu. As a result, on 27 April Clark flew to Seoul from Tokyo for the first of a series of meetings with Rhee which were to prove as nerve-cracking for CINCUNC as were the negotiations with the Communists for his delegates at Panmunjom.

Rhee was concerned over the fate of the Korean non-repatriates, as well as being completely unresponsive to Clark's point that, as neither side had 'won' in Korea, there could be no question of insisting on a CCF withdrawal. Rhee did say, however, that the threat to withdraw his forces from the UNC was only an eventuality for the future; he would discuss any such extreme action with Clark personally, he promised. The ROK anti-truce campaign now moved into top gear, and South Korean pressure was insistent enough for the UNC again to propose unsuccessfully at Panmunjom that the non-repatriates should be released with the armistice. Following the Communist proposals of 7 May suggesting a NNRC, Clark again flew to Seoul on 12 May and found Rhee even more strongly against a truce. Rather than have Indian and other troops guarding the Communist repatriation mission on ROK soil he would unilaterally release all the non-repatriates, who were often guarded by rear-echelon South Korean troops. This objection to the Communist repatriation agents was not in itself unreasonable as potential spies and saboteurs would have freedom of roam all over the ROK.

Ten days later Washington made its final offer over the prisoners which of course was presented to the Communists in executive session at Panmunjom on 25 May. Clark was to inform Rhee of the offer at the same time. In return for ROK agreement to observe the armistice and to leave their forces under UNC control, Rhee was offered an overflowing cornucopia by Washington. First, an early sixteen-nation announcement that all the countries who had fought against Communism in Korea would again resist aggression there and that retaliatory efforts in future might not be confined to Korea. Second, the US promised to build up the ROK Army to twenty divisions, with appropriate increases in air and naval strength. Third, there would be generous provision for post-war economic rehabilitation to augment aid programmes already in operation by UN Civil Assistance Command, organised by the Eighth Army to concentrate on emergency short-term relief, and the UN Korean Rehabilitation Agency, set up in December 1950 and which administered long-term projects. A $1,000 million programme at least was envisaged.[1] Clark thought immediately that the emotional effect on Rhee of his statement that the US Government was determined to get a truce if possible with the Communists 'was profound. I had never seen him so disturbed'. The armistice meant that the South Korean President, who was now

[1] According to the *Handbook of Korea*, pp. 383-4, total US aid to the ROK from 1945-57 totalled over $2.3 billion. Most post-war aid was siphoned through the International Co-operation Administration. When UNKRA ceased operations in June 1958, it had administered $148 million worth of aid. The emergency relief programme had distributed, mostly during the war, $474 million worth. Over thirty UN countries contributed to these programmes.

seventy-eight, would never realise his tenaciously-held ambition of ruling a united Korea. Indeed, Dr. Rhee so disapproved of the negotiations with the Communists that it is said he had ordained that the word Panmunjom was never to be mentioned in his presence. He was convinced that if UN troops ever withdrew from Korea, the aggression would be renewed.

It was hardly surprising therefore that from 25 May onwards the ROK boycotted the armistice talks, and the delegate, Maj.-Gen. Choi Duk Shin, was not present at Panmunjom when the final US offer was made that day — word somehow having reached him of its contents. But there were other and far more serious ways in which the South Koreans could obstruct an armistice. Not only could they release the non-repatriates, organise riots and demonstrations against the armistice and refuse to have the NNRC on their territory, all of which they did. Worst of all, they could attack the Communist armies unilaterally along the two-thirds of the front held by their troops. Even if Clark and Taylor cut off ROK supplies and equipment, the Communists might still counter-attack and perhaps overwhelm the Western UNC troops as well as the South Koreans, so bringing on the atomic holocaust.

Rhee's powerful bargaining position with Washington did not arise simply as a result of his control of the South Korean Army. In spite of all his unpopularity outside South Korea where he was often and absurdly seen as a greater menace than Stalin, he commanded a great deal of support inside his own country. Besides the Army and the sinister Japanese-trained police force, the ramshackle bureaucracy and the highly-disciplined nationalist organisations supported him. His patriotism and his relentless ambition of unifying Korea gave him popular sanction for his suppression of political opponents in the faction-ridden atmosphere of the wartime capital of Pusan. (When Rhee, during late 1952, was denied authority by Clark, on grounds of military inconvenience, to move his government back to Seoul, thirty-five miles from the MLR, he insisted on setting up his personal headquarters in the city, which meant that most ministries returned there willy-nilly.)

On the whole Rhee seems to have thought that the Korean people were not worthy of him, a conviction which partly led to his final downfall seven years after the armistice, but during the wartime years his wrath was chiefly directed at the politicians rather than the people. Having been elected by the Assembly as the President for a four-year term in 1948, he had proposed in August 1951 an amendment to the constitution whereby he would be in future elected by direct popular vote, so dishing his many enemies in the Chamber. In the spring of 1952, after the amendment had been rejected by the Assembly, executive pressure was increased on the Opposition and martial law was declared in Pusan and district during May, ostensibly as an answer to Communist guerilla activities. Immediately fifty members of the Assembly were arrested and some charged with conspiring with the Communists. Although Parliament voted to abrogate martial law, Rhee ignored this injunction and the amendment was soon pushed through the railroaded Assembly. In August, Rhee, who had survived an assassination attempt in June, was returned triumphantly to office by over five million votes of the seven million cast. The arrested Assembly members were then released.[1]

Despite Rhee's methods, many millions of North Koreans as well had voted for him, by foot. The in-fighting of ROK politics and the bribes that were paid to South Korean officials were infinitely preferable to the draconian taxes, confiscations and repression of the North. Even before the war over two million people had moved south across the Parallel, and during the advances and retreats of 1950-51 many hundreds of thousands more fled from the North. When the stalemate war began the refugees continued to move south by making their way to the offshore islands from where they could be ferried to the ROK and eventually the South Korean Government calculated that since 1945 four million people had left the North for the South.

In addition to these considerations of a strong army and his popular support, Rhee also had a powerful moral hold over the Administration. Behind all US-ROK differences lay Rhee's knowledge that after three years of bloody fighting, South Korea could hardly be abandoned by its most powerful ally. After all, the US had far less justification for deferring to Rhee's unpopularity with the Allies than to the ROK whose national survival had been at stake in the war and which had suffered

[1] A full acount of Rhee's purge of his opponents may be found in the 1952 UNCURK report to the General Assembly, A/2187.

far more casualties than all the other UN contingents put together. Nevertheless, Washington's offer on 25 May was its last concession to Rhee as well as to the Communists in the Administration's drive to get an armistice.

The crisis with the South Koreans came to a head within days of the Communist acceptance of the prisoner proposals on 4 June. Rhee was now not only offered a bilateral security pact with the US in a letter from Eisenhower on 6 June if he promised to be good, but in 'a supreme effort to bring Rhee round before he did something drastic, President Eisenhower formally, but secretly, invited him to the White House to talk things over' (Clark). The offer was declined; it was too late to do anything. During the small hours of 18 June, in Clark's words, 'All Hell broke loose' and a new major crisis was at hand when ROK guards on Rhee's orders started releasing 25,000 anti-Communist Korean POWs from camps all over South Korea. During the following few nights another 2,000 were let loose. There were now only about 22,000 prisoners left for handing over to the NNSC as possible victims for the Communists. All except nearly 8,000 of the Koreans had been released, and Rhee's popularity was at an all-time high in the ROK.

There was consternation and anger in Tokyo and Washington where, after an understandable delay while the bearers of bad news waited to see just how bad the damage was, Dulles was awakened at 2 a.m. on the 18th by the State Department duty officer on the phone with the news just received by radio from Korea. The Secretary of State immediately called the President and both men decided there and then that if Rhee's action meant that the projected truce was wrecked and heavy fighting broke out on the MLR as the Communists repudiated their agreement, the US would go ahead and take the war to mainland China. The targets beyond the Yalu had already been chosen.

For the next few days the question of war with Peking hung in the balance. Resentment ran high against Rhee in Washington and Eisenhower had to remind Republican Congressional leaders that the enemy was not Rhee but the Communists. The warhawks of the previous November now wanted a truce, and Nixon in his new role as an Administration moderate had been busy softening up Congressional resistance to an agreement with the Communists which was less advantageous to the US than that originally demanded by the Truman Administration at Panmunjom. Even Knowland, who was about to succeed Taft on his death in July as the Republican Senate Leader, had appealed to Rhee not to wreck the truce, although the Californian Senator thought it was not an honourable peace.

According to Sherman Adams, in the Cabinet meeting the morning following Dulles' telephone call, the President had said that, 'I can't remember when there was ever a forty-eight hours when I felt more in need of help from someone more intelligent than I am.' Eisenhower had asked the ROK ambassador what would happen if US support were withdrawn from his country and the Korean had replied, 'We would die.' While the discussion was going on, a message from Clark was passed to Dulles. CINCUNC was reporting that Rhee was willing for the US to walk out of Korea. Henry Cabot Lodge said that Mac-Arthur had told him a few days previously in an airliner that Rhee would shortly be liquidated by the Opposition. A few moments later another message from Clark was on the table, saying that Rhee was threatening again to withdraw his troops from the UNC. The meeting ended on a note of complete helplessness with Eisenhower saying, 'We're coming to a point where it's completely impossible. There's one thing I learned in the five years I served in the Army out there — we can never figure out the workings of the Oriental mind. You just can't tell how they will react.' Looking around the table the President went on, 'If anyone has any ideas, for God's sake, don't hold them back.' No one said anything.

This frightening situation was resolved with the despatch to Seoul of Walter Robertson, Assistant Secretary of State for Far Eastern Affairs, in one last attempt to talk sense to Rhee. But before Robertson arrived in Seoul on 25 June, Clark had sent (and published) a letter to Rhee in which he stated that not only was the release of the POWs a violation of the Taejon Agreement of 1950 but that he was 'profoundly shocked' by the abrogation of the personal understanding between the two men that no drastic ROK action would be taken without consultation. This was the strongest official public criticism of Rhee ever made by an American. Clark followed up the letter with another visit to Seoul. Rhee now promised not to release the remaining repatriates, and Clark also managed to extract an understanding from him that while the ROK would not sign the Armistice Agreement, it would support it. This was sufficient in the circumstances as the truce was a purely military arrangement between the opposing commanders. Clark also suggested that Rhee's objection to having custodial forces on his territory could be met by placing the NNRC in the demilitarised zone, but no definite arrangement was made yet.

By the time Robertson and party arrived in Tokyo on the 24th it was clear that the Communists were not going to repudiate the agreement, although they were accusing the UNC of conniving in the kidnapping of the prisoners. Peking now needed an armistice too much to risk general war. Understandably, the Communists wanted assurances that the UNC would support the armistice whatever the ROK did. To gain time while Rhee was brought under control, Harrison recessed the talks at Panmunjom on 20 June — Clark had originally hoped that the truce could have been signed on the very day the prisoners were released. When Robertson arrived in Seoul on the third anniversary of the outbreak of war he was met by wild anti-truce demonstrations before he began his talks with Rhee. Dulles' emissary managed to calm down the South Korean by listening to him day after day as he poured out his complaints and frustrations. Leaving Seoul on 12 July Robertson carried with him a letter from Rhee to Eisenhower promising that he would not obstruct the armistice, and giving up his demand that the Chinese should be asked to withdraw from North Korea. It was also agreed that the remaining Korean non-repatriates should be handed over to the NNRC in the demilitarised zone.

The price paid for Rhee's assent to the armistice was heavy. The promise of the mutual security pact was confirmed, as was the agreement to build up the ROK Army to twenty divisions. A first instalment of $200 million in economic aid was to be delivered in the near future, and there was to be a high-level meeting between the ROK and the US on joint objectives in the post-armistice political conference. Dulles himself arrived in Seoul in August to carry out this part of the agreement. The US was now able to go ahead with signing the armistice and Rhee had shown the world that he was not an American puppet, but a powerful force in his own right. Yet probably from the concessions which Washington had to make on this occasion sprang Rhee's conviction that he was indispensable to the US, a belief which, together with the increasing intolerance of his own people noted above, led directly to his fall in 1960 when the Administration at last refused to go along with him after yet another rigged election.

If American policy in its eagerness to get an armistice was inevitably one of placating Rhee, the Communists now also necessarily proceeded to cut him down to size as they showed they could smash the ROK divisions on the MLR at will. As early as 10 June, after the Terms of Reference had been signed, the Chinese had launched a particularly heavy attack against the lines of the ROK II Corps which formed a shallow salient pointing towards Kumsong on the east-central front. Striking down the valley of the Pukhan the Chinese forced back the II Corps in confusion as the heaviest fighting since the spring offensives of 1951 flared up. After a week in which Maxwell Taylor moved up divisions to the threatened sector from reserve and from X Corps on the right, the Chinese were halted. But only after pushing back the South Koreans nearly three miles on an eight-mile front.

Within a few weeks Pork Chop was overrun as a warning to the Americans, but Peng Teh-huai was keeping his final, spectacular effort in Korea for the ROK Army. Although the plenary meetings at Panmunjom were resumed on 10 July, now it was the turn of the Communists to stall as they completed their preparations. The blow fell on the night of 13 July when the Chinese broke through the ROK-held right flank of IX Corps. The crack ROK Capitol division was badly hit and collapsed, and three other South Korean divisions were mauled as the fighting spilled over into the ROK II Corps sector once again. The Chinese effort was an even more unpleasant reminder of their 1951 offensives than the fighting the previous month.

Maxwell Taylor ordered the IX Corps and the II Corps to hold a new line on the Kumsong River, moved the US 3rd Infantry Division over from Chorwon to the right of IX Corps, and brought up the 187th Airborne RCT and part of the US 24th Infantry Division which Clark had already sent over from Japan to Korea in case of trouble. Other ROK units were switched again from reserve and from X Corps to II Corps. After a counter-attack on 17 July some lost ground above the Kumsong was regained, and by the 20th the CCF limited offensive in which at least seven divisions had been committed was over.[1] Once again UNC firepower had inflicted appalling casualties on the Communists, but the Chinese artillery fire itself had been of an almost unbelievably high concentration and Eighth Army commanders thought that their opponents had been using up in June and July all the shells stockpiled near the front during the stalemate war. Altogether there were over 14,000 UNC casualties, most of them South Korean.

The military results of the offensive, the strengthening of the Chinese MLR on the central front and the Eighth Army's loss of the Kumsong salient, although important, were secondary to the political implications. The CCF had quite clearly shown that it would mean engulfment and suicide for Rhee's divisions to go it alone in moving north. Moreover the demarcation line which was drawn immediately after this last offensive by the Communists manifestly now presented a true balance of politico-military power in Korea. It only now remained for the truce to be signed.

ARMISTICE, 27 JULY 1953

With this last — and unnecessary — bloodbath now over, the Communists indicated on 19 July they were prepared to conclude an armistice. That same day they were told by Harrison that the UNC would maintain the armistice if it were broken by the ROK, and that it would not support in any way unilateral action by the South Koreans. But it was also made clear to them that the Command would not use force against the South Koreans if they infringed the agreement. Clark had already arranged with his commanders that if in spite of everything the worst happened and Rhee went north, the UNC would relinquish the entire front to the ROK Army and attempt 'to get out of the way'. What really emerged in the unspoken agreement between the two sides on 19 July was that if Rhee's Army was foolish enough to attack the Communists, the war need not be expanded if the Chinese merely pulverised the

[1] For Taylor's detailed dispositions in meeting the June-July CCF limited offensives, see *Korea 1951-53*, pp. 281-3.

South Korean forces without involving the UNC's Western divisions.

By 23 July the liaison and staff officers meeting in executive session had agreed that the non-repatriates would be delivered to the custody of the NNRC in the demilitarised zone near Panmunjom. All that now remained was for the staff officers to draw the final demarcation line from which each side would withdraw two kilometres, review the wording of the agreement, arrange the date of signing which was fixed for 27 July, and to make the necessary arrangements for the signing ceremony in the large wooden Armistice Hall which the Communists had built just behind the truce hut at Panmunjom. These last-minute arrangements provoked one last squabble, which epitomised the latent tensions on the armistice site during the last hours of the war, when the Communists painted two six-foot high reproductions of Picasso's *Dove*, the trade mark of the peace campaign, over the entrance to the Hall. They were not erased until their liaison officers were told that unless the offending birds were removed the UNC would not sign and the war would go on.

Further disagreement broke out over the participants in the signing ceremony. It had been originally agreed that Clark, Kim and Peng would face each other across a table at Panmunjom and sign the truce. At the last minute the Communists insisted that their leaders would make the journey south from Pyongyang on the condition that no South Korean would attend the armistice ceremony in any capacity, and that no Nationalist Chinese newsmen would be allowed in the neutral zone on armistice day. The Communists wanted only official photographers from each side to record the ceremony. As these proposals were unacceptable to the UNC, it was agreed that Harrison and Nam Il would sign at Panmunjom, after which the copies of the agreement would be countersigned by the commanders-in-chief in their respective headquarters.

Every syllable of the Armistice Agreement had been written and rewritten many times, and represented the power balance in Korea just as much as did the tortuous and microscopically-surveyed demarcation line. At its most northerly point the line was forty miles north of the Parallel on the Sea of Japan below Kosong, from where it curved sharply south to above the Punchbowl before running in an east-west direction to the south of

Kumsong and north of Kumhwa and Chorwon. From the western side of the Iron Triangle the boundary then dipped sharply south-westwards, slicing across the Imjin to Panmunjom and so to the Han estuary which was neutralised by the Agreement. To the west of the Han the five groups of offshore islands south of the 38th Parallel and in sight of the Communist mainland remained in South Korean hands, but of course all other UNC-held islands were abandoned. Three years of war had meant that North Korea had gained 850 square miles of territory south of the Parallel while the ROK had gained 2,350 square miles north of the June 1950 boundary. (This is the only Communist-held territory ever to have been formally abandoned.) For both sides the fighting had proved an unprecedentedly expensive way of purchasing (or losing) real estate, yet the demarcation line represented a much stronger defence position than the 38th Parallel as it possessed a geographical basis all along its approximately 155-mile length. Thus by its insistence on this line the UNC had won a point in the armistice negotiations.

On the other hand, the absence of any prohibition on airfield construction and of any foolproof inspection system to detect the build-up of war material after the armistice which was prohibited by sub-paragraph 13d, represented a Communist victory, soon demonstrated after the signing. Within days of the truce this provision was violated as the MIGs started staging from Manchuria on to the hastily reconstructed airfields all over North Korea. On the POW issue the United Nations at much cost had both stuck to their principles in refusing to repatriate prisoners forcibly, and won a considerable propaganda victory.

As for the final outcome of the fighting, Paragraph 60 envisaged the political conference meeting within three months of the Armistice Agreement to establish a final 'peaceful settlement' of the Korean question. Only then, technically, would a state of peace come to Korea. This touches on one of the most ironic aspects of the war, its status. Quite rightly the Preamble to the Armistice Agreement nowhere referred to a state of war as, of course, formal belligerency never existed between the major contenders in Korea. Only North Korea was ever believed to have declared war on South Korea, and the ROK did not sign the truce. The million Chinese in Korea were all there as individual volunteers, and the sixteen countries of the UN were fighting on a recommendation of the Security Council to repel armed attack and to restore peace and security in the area. The war had not been a war, and the Preamble referred merely to stopping 'the Korean conflict', an ambiguous phrase which has often been invoked by Western politicians and publicists. Communist commentators usually refer to the victorious struggle of Korean liberation.

Then, at last, the very final arrangements were completed for the truce to be signed by the two senior delegates at 1000 hours at Panmunjon on 27 July. Members of the future Military Armistice Commission, the Neutral Nations Repatriation Commission and the Neutral Nations Supervisory Commission were all at hand. In the Armistice Hall three hundred people were ready to watch the signing, including representatives from all the countries fighting in Korea. Promptly at the agreed time Harrison and Nam Il entered the Hall through separate entrances for what was the 159th and final plenary session of the Korean military armistice conference and sat down at separate tables. The American was tieless and jacketless, the North Korean in full uniform complete with gold medals. There were nine copies each of the Armistice Agreement and of the Supplementary Agreement on transferring the non-repatriates to the demilitarised zone;[1] each agreement was prepared in English, Chinese and Korean in triplicate. The two men took twelve minutes to sign the eighteen documents and then left the Hall without speaking or looking at each other, as at the end of all their previous meetings.

The documents were taken to the UNC Advance HQ at Munsan, where Clark signed eighteen times in the Camp theatre at 1300 hours. All copies were returned to Panmunjom and sent to Pyongyang for signature by Kim and Peng. Eventually the six English copies were returned to the UNC: the original of the final map of the demarcation line now lies in the United Nations library in New York. For Harrison the signing had been 'a necessary but unpleasant task',[2] and after Clark had completed the sparse ceremonies which so befitted the ending of the war which no one had won, he read an extremely brief statement which began, 'I cannot find in me to exult at this

[1] See Appendix D.
[2] Letter to the author.

General James Van Fleet, CG,
EUSAK, 1951-53

Vice Admiral R. P. Briscoe,
COMNAVFE, 1952-54

General O. P. Weyland, CG,
FEAF, 1951-54

Lt. Gen. George E. Stratemeyer,
CG, FEAF, 1949-51

Lt. General Maxwell D. Taylor, CG, EUSAK, 1953-54, with Mark Clark and Col. Coumanakous, CO, Greek Battalion, United Nations Command, 6 March 1953

General Peng Teh-huai, Commander of the CPV in Korea

Kim Il Sung

hour. . . .' Later Clark wrote in his memoirs that by signing he had gained the 'unenviable distinction' of being the first US Commander in history to sign an armistice without victory.

As the two men started to sign the truce at Panmunjom it was 9 p.m. EDT, 26 July in Washington. The news was immediately flashed to Eisenhower, who was waiting to go on the air. Sitting at a desk presented to the White House by Queen Victoria, the President spoke at 10 p.m.:

> For this nation the cost of repelling aggression has been high. In thousands of homes it has been incalculable. It has been paid in terms of tragedy. . . . Soldiers, sailors and airmen of sixteen different countries have stood as partners beside us throughout these long and bitter months, America's thanks go to each. In this struggle we have seen the United Nations meet the challenge of aggression — not with pathetic words of protest, but with deeds of decisive purpose. . . . We have won an armistice on a single battleground — not peace in the world. We may not now relax our guard nor cease our quest.

Moscow also noted the end of the war in a message from Malenkov to the Chinese Communist and North Korean leaders which congratulated them on winning 'a great victory in the cause of defending peace in the Far East and throughout the world'. There were no celebrations on Broadway.

In Korea the fighting was still not over, for the armistice did not come into operation until 2200 hours. UNC aircraft still flew over North Korea, the blockade forces carried on desultory shelling of the coastline, and shots rattled out on the MLR. Then the guns were stilled and the hills from sea to sea were illuminated by thousands of flares. A full moon hung low in the sky. The fighting had ended within a few miles of where it had begun over three years before. Everywhere UNC troops saw the Chinese and North Koreans looking for souvenirs between the lines. On Old Baldy, just across the valley from Pork Chop, North Korean girls were singing and dancing, while Communist soldiers waved *papier maché* Picasso doves and psywar loudspeakers blared an invitation to 'come on over and talk'. On outpost Arsenal UNC soldiers were invited to join the loudspeaker announcer in a rendering of 'My Old Kentucky Home'.

Over on the western sector of the MLR the UN troops were singing the Marine Corps hymn. The first men from Outpost Ava straggled back to the MLR and later at night some Chinese strolled over and left some candy and handkerchiefs on the base of the outpost while the Marines stared at them in silence.

After thirty-seven months and at least four million casualties, the Korean phase of the struggle between the North Atlantic powers and the Sino-Soviet bloc was over.

POSTSCRIPT: IS TIME ON OUR SIDE?

> We will bury you. . . . If it is a question of fighting
> against imperialism we can state with conviction that we
> are all Stalinists.
>
> N. S. KHRUSHCHEV

> Those who wish to live and to survive in a world
> different from the one Stalin created and which still
> exists and is still as strong as ever, must fight for their
> lives. . . .
>
> MILOVAN DJILAS

THE story of Korea since the war is quickly told. The promised initial grant of $200 million was quickly approved by the Senate after the signing of the truce; and by 30 July both sides had completed their withdrawal from the demarcation line to the borders of the demilitarised zone, the front-line positions which the armies hold today. Dulles arrived in Seoul on 4 August and four days later the mutual security treaty between the US and the ROK was initialled. It was understood that the ROK forces would remain under the Unified Command until the formal signing of the treaty, which eventually took place in Washington in October. In fact the arrangement first entered into by the Taejon Agreement has remained in force and the UNC still exercises ultimate operational authority over the South Korean armed forces. In Moscow on 8 August Chairman Malenkov in a speech to the Supreme Soviet hailed the truce as 'a victory for the peace-loving forces' and stated that 1,000 million roubles had been assigned for (North) Korean rehabilitation. Malenkov also announced that the USSR now possessed the secret of the hydrogen bomb, a claim that was soon confirmed on 12 August by Western monitoring devices which recorded a thermo-nuclear explosion inside the Soviet Union. The period of absolute American nuclear superiority was virtually over.

Other diplomatic measures were taken by the Allies to guard against a renewal of the fighting. On 7 August in a report to the Security Council Mark Clark revealed that the sixteen UN members with armed forces in Korea had signed a declaration in Washington on 27 July, the terms of which had been agreed in January 1952. The 'Declaration of Sixteen' stated that the nations concerned would faithfully support the Armistice and do everything possible to bring about a united, independent and democratic Korea. The Declaration concluded:

We affirm, in the interests of world peace, that if there is a renewal of the armed attack, challenging again the principles of the United Nations, we should again be united and prompt to resist. The consequences of such a breach of the armistice would be so grave that, in all probability, it would not be possible to confine hostilities within the frontiers of Korea. . . .

The Declaration has never been withdrawn and even if it had never been issued, both sides had increasingly come to realise since the summer of 1951 that any major renewal of the aggression would indeed have resulted in action not confined 'within the frontiers of Korea'.

At Panmunjom the exchange of those prisoners who wished to be repatriated started on 5 August in 'Big Switch'. Altogether 75,799 prisoners were returned to the Communists including only 5,640 of the twenty thousand Chinese in UNC hands. The balance of the Communist sick and wounded had already been repatriated in 'Little Switch'. At the same time 12,760 UNC prisoners were returned from the North, including nearly 3,600 Americans and 946 Britons and the full story of the Yalu camps and the extent of the indoctrination programme at last became known.

Soon after the end of Big Switch on 6 September the UNC completed on 23 September the operation of transferring to the NNRC and the Indian Custodial Force over 22,000 Chinese and North Korean non-repatriates, while the Communists delivered 359 former UNC personnel who did not wish to return home, including twenty-three Americans and one Briton. Explanations by the repatriation missions proceeded in a spirit of violence as the anti-Communist prisoners often attacked the emissaries from Peking and Pyongyang.

While the problem of the disposal of the non-repatriates was at last being solved at Panmunjom, the long-term problem of

Korea and of the composition of the political conference was being discussed by the General Assembly. The US saw the conference as one between the two sides, and it could point to the wording of Paragraph 60 of the Armistice Agreement to support its stand. Unlike Britain and the Commonwealth countries, Washington did not want India to attend the conference, as New Delhi had refused to send combat troops to Korea, and thus the US rejected a round-table meeting. The US was also only willing to have the USSR in the conference as a belligerent and not as a neutral. After a vote in the Political Committee on 27 August when it became obvious that a resolution inviting India could not command a two-thirds majority, Krishna Menon announced that he would not press for a vote on Indian admission in the General Assembly. The next day the fifteen-Power resolution on Korea — South Africa did not join with the other Allies in sponsoring the resolution or in attending the Geneva Conference — was passed by the Assembly. It approved the armistice and provided that all nations which had contributed armed forces to the Unified Command could participate in the conference, and that USSR could participate 'provided the other side desires it'. The resolution also reaffirmed that 'the objectives of the United Nations remain the achievement by peaceful means of a unified, independent and democratic Korea'.

During the debates on the composition of the conference, the USSR had steadfastly insisted not only on the inclusion of India but of half a dozen other neutrals and now the Chinese Communists and the North Koreans took up the refrain. However, after a series of exchanges through the Swedish Government Washington agreed with Peking and Pyongyang that their representatives should meet at Panmunjom in October to discuss arrangements for the Korean political conference, although the Americans nervously insisted that they did not think that Panmunjom would be a suitable site for the full conference. On 26 October Ambassador Arthur Dean, who later headed the US delegation to the nuclear-test ban negotiations at Geneva, met Mr. Ki Sok-Bok and Mr. Huang Hua at Panmunjom and immediately an angry dispute broke out over the agenda . . . with the American delegate insisting that the time and place of the conference should be settled first while the Communists wanted to discuss initially the question of admitting neutral nations, one of which they insisted should be the USSR. In the plaintive words of the State Department White Paper on the Geneva Conference, 'The Communists, instead of seriously negotiating for the conference, directed constant vituperation, week after week, at the American negotiator, while insisting on unacceptable arrangements for the conference which would depart from the terms of the Armistice Agreement.' Then, on 12 December, the Communists suddenly accused the US of conspiring perfidiously with Syngman Rhee the previous June in releasing the Korean non-repatriates. Dean broke off the talks, and retired to Washington, leaving behind a deputy at Panmunjom.

Other developments at Panmunjom may have contributed to the Communists in effect forcing these talks to their end. The great majority of the non-repatriates had indicated that they did not wish to return to Communist control. As soon as this became obvious the Communist repatriation missions attempted to filibuster the NNRC by dragging out their interviews to inordinate lengths so that it could be claimed later that as most of the prisoners had not been interviewed they had been intimidated and later kidnapped by agents of Rhee and Chiang in connivance with the UNC.

Under the Armistice Agreement the explanations supervised by the NNRC came to an end on 23 December and the Indian Chairman of the Commission, Brig.-Gen. K. S. Thimayya, decided that as the political conference had not met he would formally return all non-repatriates to their previous custodians on 20 January. But the Chairman also thought that in the absence of a conference non-repatriates should retain POW status. In reply to this inspired piece of fence-sitting, the UNC replied that in accordance with the truce agreement all prisoners had been promised civilian status 180 days after the signing and that therefore they would release all their non-repatriates at midnight on 22 January 1954. Thus, despite Communist protests, on 20 January, 21,809 prisoners, 14,227 Chinese and 7,582 Korean, marched out of the demilitarised zone and across 'Freedom Bridge' over the Imjin into the UNC lines. At one minute after midnight on 23 January the non-repatriates became civilians; the Chinese prepared to sail to Formosa from Inchon, and the Koreans reported to the ROK authorities. A few days later

347 Communist non-repatriates including twenty-one Americans and Marine Andrew Condron were handed over by the NNSC to Communist Red Cross officials; and eighty-eight Chinese and Koreans, having suffered enough from the East-West conflict in Korea, applied to go to India. On 1 February the NNRC voted to dissolve itself. The tortuous story of the captives of Korea was at last over.

Events now moved towards the setting up of the conference. The deadlock was broken by the Foreign Ministers' conference on Germany and Austria in Berlin during February 1954. The four powers agreed to call a conference of the Korean belligerents in Geneva in April to reach a peaceful settlement on Korea, while the problem of restoring peace in Indo-China would be discussed in another phase of the meeting. The neutrals were not to be invited. When the conference opened on 26 April in the Palais des Nations, it was evident that, as far as the Korean phase was concerned, the spirit of Panmunjom ruled over the tranquil waters of Lake Leman.

From the very beginning, it was clear there was a complete impasse between the two sides. The Allies wanted all-Korean elections supervised by the UN; the Communists insisted that first a Joint Commission with equal numbers from North and South Korea should be formed to arrange the elections. Moreover, Chou En-lai also suggested a neutral nations supervisory commission on the lines of the body already operating in Korea to supervise the truce, which, like the proposed Joint Electoral Commission it was supposed to assist, would make its decisions unanimously, so giving the Communists a double veto on all arrangements. Predictably, too, the Communists refused to consider the UN in any way responsible for Korean reunification.[1]

When at last the deadlocked Korean phase of the conference ended on 15 June a 'Declaration by the Sixteen' signed by the Allies and the ROK reaffirmed their objectives of UN-supervised free elections throughout Korea. As no understanding between the two sides was reached, the Armistice Agreement remained in force and the responsibility for uniting Korea reverted to the UN, where it has now rested since 1947. An exchange of notes between Peking and Pyongyang, and the countries which contributed forces to the Unified Command, during 1958-9 was as

[1] For these details see *The Korean Problem at the Geneva Conference.*

abortive as the Geneva Conference. The Communists demanded complete UN withdrawal from the ROK as they claimed that by November 1958 the CPV had entirely withdrawn across the Yalu; any agreement on the means of reunification was contingent on such United Nations evacuation from Korea. Moreover, the Communists refused to recognise, as always, the competency of the UN to deal with Korea. The Western reply was to transmit to Peking a copy of the latest UN resolution on Korea, for ever since the Armistice every session of the General Assembly has resolved in discussing the annual UNCURK report that its objective is still a unified, independent and democratic Korea brought about by UN-supervised elections.[1] As far as the UN is concerned, there the matter rests. Since that time an 'Austrian' solution for Korea has been canvassed in the United Nations and elsewhere, although most experts agree that there is no direct analogy between these countries as now two governments have been established in Korea for half a generation. There thus seems no prospect of Korea being reunited in the foreseeable future. As long as the cold war goes on and probably even afterwards, the Land of the Morning Calm will remain divided. . . .

For Korea itself, chosen as the bloodiest battlefield yet between the two dominant philosophies of our age, the results of the war were so catastrophic that the country has never really recovered. Apart from the ravages of the armies in the field, which extended from the Naktong to the Yalu, there were the effects of the sea and air campaigns against North Korea. By 1953 the KPA, which in 1950 had virtually destroyed the ROK Army and almost pushed the Eighth Army into the sea at Pusan, was only operating at Corps strength on a relatively narrow sector of the battlefront. North Korea's military casualties were at least half a million and another million civilians are believed to have vanished in addition to the four millions who have fled south since 1945 when the population of the country totalled about nine million. Thus in the early 1960s the population of the country was estimated to be still only 10 million.

By the time the shooting stopped, therefore, there can be no

[1] *The Record on Korean Unification*, pp. 194-241 *passim*.

doubt that the Democratic People's Republic of Korea with all its cities and industries rubble heaps, and with normal life at an end, only existed as a state in so far as it was held together by the military operations of Communist China. For North Korea aggression had not paid off. Recently Pyongyang has claimed that pre-war production levels have been restored and surpassed. Most of the coal, electric power and heavy industry of Korea are in the North and there seems little doubt that by the usual totalitarian means capital accumulation can indeed be increased so that North Korea will eventually became an economically viable member of the Communist bloc.

For South Korea the effects of the war were only little less disastrous. To the South Korean military casualty list of about 300,000 must be added at least a million civilians lost, and when the war ended there were 2.5 million refugees in the South and another 5 million people living on relief: the total number of civilian Korean dead has never been accurately calculated. Divorced from the natural resources of the North, with a population of well over twenty million, and with a large standing army of nearly twenty divisions, there has never been any real measure of recovery in the South despite post-war US economic aid averaging about $200 million a year. Without economic prosperity it has never been able to build democratic political institutions. It seems hardly surprising therefore that after Syngman Rhee was at last overthrown in April 1960 and succeeded by the John Chang Administration, the new regime was unable to solve the ROK's problems and was itself toppled by a military *coup* in May 1961 inspired by General Chung Hee Park.

So political division, the destruction of the war, economic stagnation, and the continuing threat from the North have all combined to give South Korea a puritan military dictatorship which resembles so many others in Africa and Asia where democracy has been unable to solve the problems of independence. The leaders of the junta have promised that as soon as their revolutionary mission has succeeded, full democracy will be restored to the ROK, a promise all the more ironical because of the sacrifices of the UN members which fought to defend South Korea from Communist domination. Conquest from the north and subsequent totalitarian rule would have been infinitely worse than any excesses or abuses committed by Rhee and his successors. Yet, in spite of the war, South Korea remains a country where government by consent has still to emerge. On the other hand South Korean foreign policy remains undeviatingly pro-Western.

A major result of the war with consequences that are still incalculable was the consolidation and emergence of Communist China as one of the world's great powers. If Peking had been unable to conquer South Korea as almost seemed possible in early 1951, it had still inflicted a major defeat on a Western army and prevented the unification of Korea under UN auspices. Even after the defeat of the 1951 spring offensives Peking managed to perpetuate the War for another two years and thus by the judicious manipulation of the Hate-America, Peace, and Bacteriological Warfare themes in the thought-reform programme cemented the masses and the intellectuals all the more thoroughly behind the regime. Abroad, the eviction of UNC forces from North Korea showed that the new China was fully able to defend its own interests against the most powerful nation in the world and Peking became quickly respected and feared as a force to be reckoned with in Asian and world affairs. Communist parties all over Asia took new strength from Peking's successes in Korea and all neutral states were impressed by these successes in varying degrees. Moreover, the build-up of Communist China's Armed Forces between 1950 and 1953 meant that Peking ended the war with a far more powerful military posture than when the Chinese armies crossed the Yalu. Ever since China has maintained and developed the huge army and air force perfected as a result of the war in Korea.

But given that on balance the regime gained by crossing the Yalu and winning a politico-military victory almost as great as crushing the KMT, these triumphs were won at a heavy cost which has probably influenced Chinese policy ever since. It was North Korea, progressively levelled by UNC sea and air power during the stalemate war, which paid the greater part of the bill for Communist China's emergence as a great power. But the vast Chinese casualties in the war, estimated between one and one-and-a-half million and consisting of highly-trained manpower, together with the destruction of so much equipment, must surely have had some effect on later economic growth in

China. Added to the mountains of Chinese dead in Korea was the drain of part-purchasing supplies and equipment, including thousands of MIGs, from the USSR, and also the diversion of resources to North Korea both during the war and for rehabilitation there after the truce.

Lastly, and most humiliating of all for Peking, so great was the US response to Chinese participation in Korea that Formosa, which but for the Korean War would inevitably have fallen to the Communists in 1950-51, was never taken; even the capture of the offshore islands of Quemoy-Matsu has been frustrated ever since by the US. Thus not all of Peking's objectives in the summer of 1950 were achieved by intervention in Korea. Moreover, further Chinese Communist adventures in South East Asia have been deterred by the implacable enmity of the United States. Indeed, in retrospect it can be seen that the Korean armistice and the Geneva settlement on Indo-China a year later mark the end for the time being of the attempt by the Sino-Soviet bloc to expand by force. United States policy in Korea clearly warned the Communists that if they continued in the 1950s to pursue their end of world domination by armed attack, total war would result. Thus since 1953-54 the emphasis of the Communist offensive has switched to the economic and political fields, with the emerging ex-colonial states the chief battleground. This does not mean of course that the West should relax its military posture for a moment: the threat of Communist guerilla warfare as practised in Laos and South Vietnam is almost as potentially dangerous as direct armed attack on the Korean pattern.

If both Korean states were pulverised by the war and Communist China emerged with power and prestige enhanced at heavy cost, the significance of the War as far as the United States and its allies were concerned is still uncertain, as the conflict which gave rise to Korea is still raging in all its manifestations. It seems fair to say that two mutually exclusive viewpoints exist. On the significance of the war, and which are directly related to the respective attitudes taken by Truman and MacArthur in 1951. Both sides agree only that the decisions taken by the Administration in 1951 have a central relevance to the whole drama of West-East relations as they have since developed. Richard Rovere has noted that following the truce, official Washington including Congress was cast into gloom, shame and disillusion over what Rovere himself calls 'the unmentionable victory'. As an exception Dulles himself, and presumably Eisenhower, expressed satisfaction with the settlement for reasons which were essentially those advanced by Truman and Acheson for their policy: aggression had been repelled and collective security upheld. Thus in a contemporary comment Rovere wrote of the war in terms which have been used in one way or another by all defenders of keeping the war limited:

> History will cite Korea as the proving ground of collective security, up to this time no more than a plausible theory. It will cite it as the turning point of the world struggle against Communism and as the scene of a great victory for American arms, one the future will celebrate even though the present does not.[1]

As always this view tends to overlook the fact that as the Korean decision was meant to uphold NATO as well as to enforce collective security, it was an act in strategic terms of defending North Atlantic *selective* security, as there were parts of the world in 1950 where Communist aggression would not have been contained — as Rovere and Schlesinger have remarked in *The General and the President.* Thus the idealistic components of collective security in the Korean decision should always be disentangled from the underlying basis of containment which lay in *Realpolitik.* Just as important is it to recognise that while two great victories were indeed won by American arms in September 1950 and in April-May 1951, greater political and military preparation for limited war might have altered decisively the outcome of the war. The stalemate might have been avoided and a much more satisfactory politico-military settlement reached if risks and objectives in the drive to the Yalu had been more carefully calculated, or if an armistice could have been forced on the Communists a year later when the truce talks began. In both cases a settlement might have been reached which while not freeing the whole of Korea and still keeping the war limited, would have meant a demarcation line further north than that eventually agreed, or a more favourable armistice

[1] Rovere, *The Eisenhower Years,* p. 145.

agreement. In either case a decisive political defeat would have been forced on the Communists and later UNC casualties avoided.

Nevertheless, having made these reservations it must be recognised that the Truman Administration did wage war within the demands of a coalition in such a way that the whole fabric of Western defence was immeasurably strengthened. In spite of strong domestic opposition both Truman and Eisenhower frequently took notice of Allied and UN opinion. In this way American policy in Korea gathered much more support than if it had been unilateral action by the United States. And if the position of the US was reinforced by its identification with the UN, so the machinery and self-confidence of the UN in responding to the North Korean challenge was immensely strengthened. If the aggression had gone unchallenged there is no doubt at all that the drift to general war at the end of the 1940s would have been greatly accelerated and that the next predatory Communist move would have precipitated World War III. The USSR did take note with Truman's Korean decision that any further military adventures would lead to general war. The principles of the United Nations as far as military aggression is concerned were upheld. South Korea was saved from totalitarian conquest. The US and the UN in the 1950s behaved better than Britain and the League of Nations in the 1930s.

Of supreme importance in the development of later Western strategy was the effective creation of the NATO armed alliance in response to Korea. Although NATO antedated the war, the West was virtually disarmed, apart from SAC, in June 1950. Even if all the divisions planned by SHAPE, which was formally activated in April 1951, never arrived, there was no disarmament after 1953 and NATO budgets ever since have reflected the force levels of the Korean War years. Whatever NATO's inadequacies in conventional forces and the imperfections of such associated pacts as SEATO and CENTO, the Western rearmament of the 1950s made increasingly unlikely the possibility of a surprise Communist invasion of Western Europe succeeding. And whatever the later development in Soviet missile and nuclear technology, the shifting of the Communist offensive to the underdeveloped countries and the replacement of the

American atomic ascendancy by a balance of terror, nothing can alter the existence of the powerful NATO defence structure and economic revival of Western Europe which came about as a result of the Korean challenge.

Thus in sticking to a Clausewitzian policy of waging limited war as an instrument of policy, the Truman Administration did keep the coalition intact, repelled the Communist aggression and strengthened Western defences so that other Eastern bloc advances were deterred and prevented. In retrospect this is the major Western political achievement since 1945. The tragedy of the fall of the Democrats was that, in displaying greater strategic insight than Roosevelt, Truman was unable to appear as a war leader so great were the absolutist confusions of American public opinion. Yet American involvement in Korea, the greatest and noblest act of recent American history, and which cost the country over 142,000 casualties and perhaps $20 billion, more than any other action gives the United States the moral right to Western leadership. The irony of the great limited war of the 1930s in Spain and of the total war of the 1940s was that democrats were forced into alliance with one monster in fighting to defeat another. This did not happen in Korea. While the Korean decision was deeply rooted in Western self-interest as well as idealism, and in spite of the ambiguities of defending a regime not completely democratic, in Korea there was as good a cause to fight for as the West will ever find, for no completely untainted crusade has ever existed.

There can be no conclusive assumption yet that history will judge the decision to keep the war limited a right one. If one judges that Truman behaved rightly it must always be borne in mind that the UN war aim of a united Korea, promulgated after Inchon, never came to pass and that a general Korean settlement in our time is unlikely. Much more important is the recognition that the role of the United Nations in the Korean War was essentially peripheral. Only the absence of the USSR from the Security Council in June and July 1950 enabled the UN to identify itself so completely with the Western intervention. Otherwise the Soviet veto, while it would not have altered the rightness or the necessity of Truman's action, would have deprived US action of UN endorsement. Thus the Security Council decisions in June 1950 were the exception which proved the rule that the United Nations cannot be used to compose differences between East and West.

At the time it was thought that by reasserting the residual power of the General Assembly in the 'Uniting for Peace' resolution of November 1950 a deadlocked Security Council could be by-passed. But in recent years the emergence of the powerful neutral bloc in the United Nations has made it at least conceivable that in some future crisis not only would the West be unable to get a decision from the Security Council but that the Assembly itself might not condemn an act of aggression by the Eastern bloc in certain circumstances. This only emphasises that Western action in Korea was right and just on its own merits and not alone because it was sanctioned by the UN; and that the US might not be so lucky in future as it was in June 1950.

From the failure to unite Korea and to inflict a decisive defeat on Communist China springs an opposite view of the Korean War which sees it as a defeat and not as a victory, a turning point on the way down and not on the way up. All the senior military commanders in Korea with the exception of Ridgway and Maxwell Taylor believe that it was a disaster for the US not to have forced the issue with Peking after the CCF intervention. The gradual waning of the liberal absolutist tradition in the United States so that its defenders now increasingly appear self-consciously 'conservative' or even more extreme has in no way invalidated MacArthur's urgent concern with the relative growth of the two blocs and the question of whether time is on the side of the West. As Kissinger has written, 'Because of our obsession with building strength, we overlooked the fact that our relative military position would never be better than it was at the very beginning of the containment policy. We were so aware of the vulnerability of our allies that we underestimated the bargaining power inherent in our industrial potential and our nuclear superiority.'[1]

The rapid growth of Communist nuclear and industrial technology in the last decade has thus emphasised that the positions taken by the President and the General in 1951 have still great relevance to the West-East conflict. Those who insist that time is not on our side point to the great Soviet technological advances

[1] *The Necessity for Choice*, p. 178.

which they see as an erosion of the Western position so grave that eventually the US will be left with the alternatives of submission or fighting a nuclear war of despair far more terrible than one fought in 1951. Thus the end of the road for the West will indeed bring peace, what James Gavin has called 'the peace of Carthage'. In this view the failure to unite Korea, to defeat Communist China and to have a showdown with the USSR if necessary was the beginning of the decline of the West, and thus the Chongchon appears as not merely the repulse of a hubristic attempt to break the ground rules of containment but a catastrophic failure to respond to the decisive Sino-Soviet challenge. It is analogous, as the Alsop Brothers see it, to the Athenian repulse at Syracuse in the Peloponnesian War, the moment from which ever after, the road ran downwards, although it was not seen at the time.

As the possibility of total war still exists in the early 1960s, it appears in any case that the Truman-MacArthur controversy, shorn of its more personal and party political minutiae, however fascinating, has still not been resolved. If some sort of armed truce with the Eastern bloc can be achieved through the latter-day variations of containment, including the emergence of some sort of Atlantic union, President Kennedy's 'true course of history', then Truman will have been justified for ever in buying time in Korea to rearm the West. For after all, MacArthur in 1951 failed to see the possibility of the resurgence of Western Europe. But if the mushroom, submission, or a Carthaginian fate remain for us then MacArthur will have been vindicated to those few survivors who wish to salute his historical insight. Certainly the General's uncomfortable premise that time is not necessarily on the side of the West has by no means been disproved. For after all, to assume that the West is sooner or later bound to reach a favourable settlement in the cold war is not justifiable. This belief reflects a historicist delusion as great as that preached by the Communists and their external allies in the ranks of the Western neutralists, appeasers and neo-Marxists.

In this perspective the Eisenhower years appear as a barren period when the passions of the absolutists and the neo-isolationists were abated. By a great irony born of the revulsion against Korea, the lessons of that war were largely ignored. It has been left to another Democratic Administration to apply the lessons of the Truman-Acheson era and with pragmatic approach and limited goals to practise openly once again the techniques of a new containment policy against the Communist bloc. Over the years Acheson's remark in the MacArthur hearings seems less a political self-justification than a sibylline utterance, the vastly expensive twelve-word lesson of Korea, the greatest of all the limited wars:

. . . time is on our side if we make good use of it.

Today Harry Truman lives at his home in Independence, Missouri, where he first heard the news of the outbreak of war in Korea on that Saturday evening in June 1950. Still active in Democratic politics he occasionally journeys to New York and gives reporters his views on national and world affairs during brisk, early-morning walks in Central Park. Sometimes he refers scathingly to his differences with MacArthur. Nearby the General, the aged eagle of the Waldorf, lives in seclusion in a suite decorated with Chinese and Japanese tapestries, a reminder of his many years spent in the Far East. In his last major speech on his seventy-fifth birthday in 1955 he expressed his belief that war could now no longer solve anything: 'Whatever betides the ultimate fate of the Far East — and indeed of the world — will not be settled by force of arms. We may all be practically annihilated — but war can no longer be an arbiter of survival.' In 1961 MacArthur made one last trip to the Far East, receiving a rapturous welcome in the Philippines. In Tokyo, Haneda Airfield was deserted when his aircraft landed; he did not go on to Korea, where a large statue of him stands in Seoul.

General Marshall is dead and, of the Truman Joint Chiefs at the time of the recall, Vandenberg and Sherman are also dead. Collins is in retirement, and Bradley himself, as the only other five-star general of the US Army besides Eisenhower and MacArthur, cannot ever be retired. Of the wartime commanders of the Eighth Army, Walton Walker, the victor of the Naktong and the loser of the Chongchon lies in the Arlington National Cemetery, Virginia. Ridgway, who retired in 1955 as Army Chief-of-Staff after a bitter quarrel with Eisenhower over defence appropriations, lives in a suburb of Pittsburg. Van Fleet has made his home in Florida; recently he was given a hero's welcome in Seoul where he is known as 'the father of the ROK Army'. Maxwell Taylor is now President Kennedy's Chairman of the JCS, and as such alone of the senior Korean War commanders to have major influence on the making of present-day United States policy. As a self-professed Clausewitzian, Taylor is a strong advocate of developing limited war capability; the strategy of flexible response which he has expounded in his book *The Uncertain Trumpet* has become President Kennedy's version of containment. And as if to emphasise the continuity between the Truman and Kennedy years, Dean Acheson is now also a senior adviser to the White House. Mark Clark who signed the armistice for the United Nations retired shortly afterwards to become the president of a military college in South Carolina. And of the two senior UNC delegates at Panmunjom, Admiral Joy is dead while General Harrison has retired to a place in the sun in Florida. Exiled from the country for which he fought so long and so hard, Dr. Syngman Rhee lives in complete obscurtiy in Hawaii.

In Pyongyang Kim Il Sung is still Prime Minister, and no sooner was the war over than General Nam Il was appointed Foreign Minister, a post which he still keeps. Fortune however has not been kind to the other members of the North Korean Government. Shortly after the armistice, in August 1953, Radio Pyongyang announced that ten senior officials had been condemned to death for passing state secrets to the US and ROK Intelligence Services and for plotting to overthrow the regime. Among those unmasked for these crimes against the state and party was the ringleader of the plot, a former Minister of Justice, the former deputy Minister of Culture and Propaganda, the former head of the Korean Society for Cultural Relations with the USSR and Pak Hen Yen, Nam Il's predecessor as Foreign Minister and onlie begetter of the bacteriological warfare campaign. A North Korean Vice-Premier committed suicide to escape arrest. Further victims included the Pyongyang's former ambassadors to Peking and Moscow. The reasons for this purge of truly Stalinist proportions remain a matter of conjecture; it has been suggested that the liquidated constituted a Beria-aligned anti-party group which was prepared to come to an accommodation with Rhee as a manœuvre in the power struggle which racked the Communist world after Stalin's death.

Moreover, following this purge of what was known as the 'domestic faction' of the Korean Labour Party, Kim and Nam Il carried out another ritual blood-letting during 1956-57 when the Chinese-oriented 'Yenan faction' was eliminated, the climax of course of an intra-mural feud in Pyongyang which had simmered since 1945. Even so, in an agile display of political acrobatics, by the time of the great Sino-Soviet feud in the early 1960s, Kim was by now tentatively backing Mao against Khrushchev.

Time has also dealt unevenly with the Chinese leaders. Chou En-lai is still the Prime Minister of the Central People's Government. The men who commanded the two CCF Army Groups which crossed the Yalu in autumn 1950, Chen Yi and Lin Piao, are now respectively Peking's Foreign Minister and Defence Minister. The most spectacular change of fortune has come to Peng Teh-huai who was in fact if not in name the Communist Commander-in-Chief in Korea and was promoted Marshal in 1955. In August 1959, during a meeting of the Central Committee of the CCP, Peng, then Defence Minister, attacked the entire policy of the Communes, the Great Leap Forward, and the organisation of the Army with particular reference to nuclear strategy. An even more heinous offence, Peng had previously told N. S. Khrushchev of his criticism. He was thus arrested, degraded and his supporters denounced by the CCP's ideocrats as an anti-party group of 'right-opportunists'. Peng himself was subjected to an intensive course of reindoctrination and has since been relegated to a state farm in North China as superintendent. Thus the man who was responsible for the indoctrination of the UNC prisoners in North Korea has himself become the victim of the theory and practice of thought reform in having to be ideologically reborn. By mid-1962 it was even rumoured in Communist China that Peng had secretly fled to Taiwan. . . .

Korea itself, of course, is still in a state of neither war nor peace. Besides the two American divisions on the new MLR, United Nations troops include a company of Turks, a company of Thai troops and small liaison groups from other countries. The Commander of the Eighth Army, who is also head of the US forces in Korea as well as CINCUNC, is now responsible to the Commander-in-Chief Pacific after the abolishing of the Far East Command in 1957. During May and June 1956 the UNC, after inter-Allied consultation, announced that because of Communist violation of the truce safeguards relating to the build-up of war equipment, it was suspending those provisions of the Armistice governing the operations of the NNSC in South Korea. The inspection teams of the Commission then withdrew to the demilitarised zone at Panmunjom; they had never been able to function properly. Without the power of inspection the reduced NNSC is now welcomed by the ROK; the Swiss and Swedish members are regarded as valuable representatives of the neutral presence in the DMZ who may still report on truce infractions should they occur outside the zone.

A year following the withdrawal of the inspection teams, in June 1957, the UNC at last told the Communist side in the Military Armistice Commission that it was entitled to be relieved, because of the continuing Communist build-up, of observing the provisions of sub-paragraph 13d of the Armistice Agreement which prohibited the renewal and reinforcement of equipment. Since that date old equipment and weapons have been replaced and renewed by both sides without any inhibitions whatsoever. To the north Kim Il Sung's reconstituted Air Force is particularly powerful with its many hundreds of MIGs, while to the south, Honest John tactical guided missiles with atomic warheads guard all the invasion routes south between Kaesong and the Sea of Japan.

But perhaps it is at Panmunjom itself rather than on the new MLR where each side relentlessly observes its enemy through binoculars that the spirit of East-West relations in Korea is best savoured. Here the war manifestly has never ended and the ritual of enmity is as carefully and enthusiastically observed between the two sides as it was during those first meetings at this once remote place in the summer of 1951. Yet the Armistice that was supposed to last ninety days has now endured for a decade. The Neutral Nations Supervisory Commission still meets weekly to consider violations of truce provisions which neither side observes. About once a month the full Military Armistice Commission meets to engage in formal and fruitless recrimination over violations of the Armistice. The denunciations by the Chinese Communists and the North Koreans of US imperialism and its South Korean puppets, and by the United Nations Command members of Communist perfidy and dishonesty, rarely vary. Whatever the state of the cold war on other fronts, here it is always blowing hot. Here the spirit of Camp David never penetrated. Every day except Sundays and holidays the liaison officers meet to report on the increase or decrease in personnel strengths and on the expenditure of ammunition. The UNC duty officer speaks first on Tuesdays, Thursdays and Saturdays, the Communist officer on the other days. There is never a flicker of personal recognition.

There is also another side to Panmunjom. Now that they are relieved of their duties, the NNSC members have moved into permanent buildings. Many parties are given and for them life is one long search for distraction. Panmunjom has also become a tourist trap where visitors peer at the meetings of the MAC as its members abuse each other and sometimes the exchanges are relayed to the crowds through loudspeakers. A new town, almost a new industry, has grown up. From a grandstand, visitors may look over the paddy fields and the hillocks to Kaesong where after all the Armistice was never signed, and nearby is 'the bridge of no return' at the north of the DMZ, so-called because once past here, the repatriated POWs could never return to the south. Beyond, above the desolation and the proliferating wild life of the demilitarised zone as it stretches away to the Sea of Japan, loom the blue hills of North Korea.

APPENDICES

A—Contributions to the United Nations Command by members of
United Nations.

B—Senior Commanders in the Korean War, 25 June 1950-27 July
1953.

C—Selected casualty list.

D—Text of the Military Armistice Agreement and the supplementary agreement on prisoners of war. (Source: FO Cmd. 8938,
pp. 14-35, UN doc. S/3079.)

E—Bibliography.

APPENDIX A

Contributions to the UNC by the members of the UN.

Australia: Two infantry battalions, part of the British Commonwealth 1st Division, some naval forces, and a fighter squadron (77th Squadron, RAAF).

Belgium: One infantry battalion.

Canada: A reinforced infantry brigade, including tank and artillery forces, part of the Commonwealth Division, some naval forces, and a squadron of transport aircraft.

Colombia: One infantry battalion and a naval frigate.

Ethiopia: One infantry battalion.

France: One reinforced infantry battalion.

Greece: One infantry battalion and transport aircraft.

Luxembourg: One infantry company.

Netherlands: One infantry battalion and naval forces.

New Zealand: One regiment of artillery, part of the Commonwealth Division.

Philippines: One infantry battalion and one company of tanks.

Thailand: One infantry battalion, naval forces, air and naval transports.

Turkey: One infantry brigade.

Union of South Africa: One fighter squadron (No. 2 Squadron, SAAF).

United Kingdom: Two infantry brigades, one armoured regiment, one and a half artillery regiments, one and a half combat engineer regiments and supporting ground forces, all part of the Commonwealth division; the Far Eastern fleet; and two Sunderland squadrons of the RAF.

Medical Units: Denmark, Italy, India, Norway and Sweden.

APPENDIX B

Senior Commanders in the Korean War, 25 June 1950-27 July 1953

Commander-in-Chief, United Nations Command

General of the Army, Douglas MacArthur	8 July 1950
Lt.-Gen. Matthew B. Ridgway	11 April 1951
(promoted Gen., 11 May 1951)	
General Mark Clark	12 May 1952

Commanding General, Eighth US Army in Korea (EUSAK)

Lt.-Gen. Walton H. Walker	13 July 1950
Lt.-Gen. Matthew B. Ridgway	26 December 1950
Lt.-Gen. James Van Fleet	14 April 1951
(promoted Gen. 1 August 1951)	
Lt.-Gen. Maxwell D. Taylor	11 February 1953
(Gen. 23 June 1953)	

Commanding General, US I Corps

Maj.-Gen. John B. Coulter	2 August 1950
Maj.-Gen. Frank W. Milburn[1]	11 September 1950
Maj.-Gen. John W. O'Daniel	19 July 1951
Maj.-Gen. Paul W. Kendall	29 June 1952
(Lt.-Gen. 16 September 1952)	
Maj.-Gen. Bruce C. Clarke	11 April 1953

Commanding General, IX Corps

Maj.-Gen. Frank W. Milburn	10 August 1950
Maj.-Gen. John B. Coulter	12 September 1950
Maj.-Gen. Bryant E. Moore	31 January 1950
(Moore died following a helicopter accident on 23 February).	
Maj.-Gen. Oliver P. Smith, USMC	24 February 1951
Maj.-Gen. William F. Hoge	5 March 1951
(Lt.-Gen. 3 June 1951)	
Maj.-Gen. Willard G. Wyman	24 December 1951

[1] Milburn was acting CG, EUSAK, 23-26 December 1950 following Walker's death. The Corps was then commanded by Maj.-Gen. William B. Kean.

Maj.-Gen. Joseph P. Cleland	31 July 1952
Maj.-Gen. Reuben E. Jenkins	9 August 1952
(Lt.-Gen. 8 November 1952)	

Commanding General, X Corps

Maj.-Gen. Edward M. Almond	26 August 1950
Maj.-Gen. Clovis E. Byers	15 July 1951
Maj.-Gen. Williston B. Palmer	5 December 1951
Maj.-Gen. I. D. White[1]	15 August 1952
(Lt.-Gen. 7 November 1952)	

Commanding General, Far East Air Forces (FEAF)

Lt.-Gen. George E. Stratemeyer	26 April 1949
Lt.-Gen. Earle E. Partridge (acting)	21 May 1951
Maj.-Gen. O. P. Weyland	10 June 1951
(Lt.-Gen., 28 July 1951; Gen., 5 July 1952)	

Commanding General, Fifth Air Force (FAF)

Lt.-Gen. Earle E. Partridge	6 October 1948
Maj.-Gen. Edward J. Timberlake	21 May 1951
Maj.-Gen. Frank F. Everest	1 June 1951
Lt.-Gen. Glenn O. Barcus	30 May 1952
Lt.-Gen. Samuel E. Anderson	31 May 1953

Commander, Naval Forces Far East (COMNAVFE)

Vice-Adm. Turner Joy	26 August 1949
Vice-Adm. R. P. Briscoe	4 June 1952

Commander, Seventh Fleet, Task Force 70

Vice-Adm. A. D. Struble	6 May 1950
Vice-Adm. H. H. Martin	28 March 1951
Vice-Adm. R. P. Briscoe	3 March 1952
Vice-Adm. J. J. Clark	20 May 1952

Chief of Staff, ROK Army

Maj.-Gen. Chae Pyongdok	10 April 1950
Lt.-Gen. Chung Il Kwon	30 June 1950
Maj.-Gen. Yi Chongchan	23 June 1951
Lt.-Gen. Paik Sun Yup	23 July 1952- 5 May 1953

[1] Maj.-Gen. I. P. Smith was acting CG, X Corps, 10-12 July 1952; Maj.-Gen. David L. Ruffner, acting CG, 12-14 August 1952; and Maj.-Gen. Joseph P. Cleland, acting CG, 1-7 April 1953.

APPENDIX C

Battle casualties of the Korean War

ROK

According to an UN release of 23 October 1953, ROK casualties in the Korean War totalled 1,313,836, including about a million civilians. No definitive breakdown of the ROK military casualties has ever been reached, but the following figures are approximately correct: Killed, 47,000; wounded, 183,000; Missing and POW, 70,000; Total: 300,000.

United Nations

Apart from the US losses, the battle casualties of the other UN contingents of the UNC are calculated to have been as follows:

Dead: 3,194
Wounded: 11,297
Missing and POW: 2,769
Total: 17,260
(Source: UN release, 23 October 1953.)

Of this total the Commonwealth casualties killed, wounded and missing were 7,268:

	Killed	Wounded	Missing/POW	Total
Australia	261	1,034	37	1,332
Canada	294	1,202	47	1,543
India		4		4
New Zealand	22	79	1	102
South Africa			1	1
UK	686	2,498	1,102	4,286
Totals	1,263	4,817	1,188	7,268

(Source: Barclay, *The First Commonwealth Division*. 1,036 prisoners were repatriated by the Communists.)

Communist China-North Korea

There is no Defence Department estimate of Communist casualties, nor is there any known Communist casualty list.

In the UN release referred to above it was estimated that the CCF had lost 900,000 men, the North Koreans 520,000. A special report to the UN Secretary General by the UNC on the armistice (S/3079), dated 7 August 1953, states that 'enemy casualties are estimated at between one and a half and two million'. NK civilian casualties are estimated unofficially at about one million.

United States

	Total	Army	Navy	USMC	Air Force
Total casualties	142,091	109,958	2,087	28,205	1,841
Deaths	33,629	27,704	458	4,267	1,200
Killed in Action	23,300	19,334	279	3,308	379
Wounded in Action	105,785	79,526	1,599	24,281	379
Died	2,501	1,930	23	537	11
Other	103,284	77,596	1,576	23,744	368
Missing in Action	5,866	4,442	174	391	859
Died	5,127	3,778	152	391	806
Returned	715	664	13	0	38
Current Missing	24	0	9	0	15
Captured or interned	7,140	6,656	35	225	224
Died	2,701	2,662	4	31	4
Returned	4,418	3,973	31	194	220
Refused repatriation	21	21	0	0	0

(Source: Office of the Secretary of Defence.)

APPENDIX D

AGREEMENT BETWEEN THE COMMANDER-IN-CHIEF, UNITED NATIONS COMMAND, ON THE ONE HAND, AND THE SUPREME COMMANDER OF THE KOREAN PEOPLE'S ARMY AND THE COMMANDER OF THE CHINESE PEOPLE'S VOLUNTEERS, ON THE OTHER HAND, CONCERNING A MILITARY ARMISTICE IN KOREA

Panmunjom, July 27, 1953

PREAMBLE

The undersigned, the Commander-in-Chief, United Nations Command, on the one hand, and the Supreme Commander of the Korean People's Army and the Commander of the Chinese People's Volunteers, on the other hand, in the interest of stopping the Korean conflict, with its great toll of suffering and bloodshed on both sides, and with the objective of establishing an armistice which will ensure a complete cessation of hostilities and of all acts of armed force in Korea until a final peaceful settlement is achieved, do individually, collectively, and mutually agree to accept and to be bound and governed by the conditions and terms of armistice set forth in the following Articles and Paragraphs, which said conditions and terms are intended to be purely military in character and to pertain solely to the belligerents in Korea.

ARTICLE I

Military Demarcation Line and Demilitarised Zone

1. A Military Demarcation Line shall be fixed and both sides shall withdraw two (2) kilometres from this line so as to establish a Demilitarised Zone between the opposing forces. A Demilitarised Zone shall be established as a buffer zone to prevent the occurrence of incidents which might lead to a resumption of hostilities.
2. The Military Demarcation Line is located as indicated on the attached map (Map 1)[1].
3. The Demilitarised Zone is defined by a northern and a southern boundary as indicated on the attached map (Map 1)[1].

[1] Not printed.

4. The Military Demarcation Line shall be plainly marked as directed by the Military Armistice Commission hereinafter established. The Commanders of the opposing sides shall have suitable markers erected along the boundary between the Demilitarised Zone and their respective areas. The Military Armistice Commission shall supervise the erection of all markers placed along the Military Demarcation Line and along the boundaries of the Demilitarised Zone.

5. The waters of the Han River Estuary shall be open to civil shipping of both sides wherever one bank is controlled by one side and the other bank is controlled by the other side. The Military Armistice Commission shall prescribe rules for the shipping in that part of the Han River Estuary indicated on the attached map (Map 2)[1]. Civil shipping of each side shall have unrestricted access to the land under the military control of that side.

6. Neither side shall execute any hostile act within, from, or against the Demilitarised Zone.

7. No person, military or civilian, shall be permitted to cross the Military Demarcation Line unless specifically authorised to do so by the Military Armistice Commission.

8. No person, military or civilian, in the Demilitarised Zone shall be permitted to enter the territory under the military control of either side unless specifically authorised to do so by the Commander into whose territory entry is sought.

9. No person, military or civilian, shall be permitted to enter the Demilitarised Zone except persons concerned with the conduct of civil administration and relief and persons specifically authorised to enter by the Military Armistice Commission.

10. Civil administration and relief in that part of the Demilitarised Zone which is south of the Military Demarcation Line shall be the responsibility of the Commander-in-Chief, United Nations Command; and civil administration and relief in that part of the Demilitarised Zone which is north of the Military Demarcation Line shall be the joint responsibility of the Supreme Commander of the Korean People's Army and the Commander of the Chinese People's Volunteers. The number of persons, military or civilian, from each side who are permitted to enter the Demilitarised Zone for the conduct of civil administration and relief shall be as determined by the respective Commanders, but in no case shall the total number authorised by either side exceed one thousand (1,000) persons at any one time. The number of civil police and the arms to be carried by them shall be as prescribed by the Military Armis-

[1] Not printed.

tice Commission. Other personnel shall not carry arms unless specifically authorised to do so by the Military Armistice Commission.

11. Nothing contained in this Article shall be construed to prevent the complete freedom of movement to, from, and within the Demilitarised Zone by the Military Armistice Commission, its assistants, its Joint Observer Teams with their assistants, the Neutral Nations Supervisory Commission hereinafter established, its assistants, its Neutral Persons Inspection Teams with their assistants, and of any other persons, materials and equipment specifically authorised to enter the Demilitarised Zone by the Military Armistice Commission. Convenience of movement shall be permitted through the territory under the military control of either side over any route necessary to move between points within the Demilitarised Zone where such points are not connected by roads lying completely within the Demilitarised Zone.

Article II

Concrete Arrangements for Cease-Fire and Armistice

A.—General

12. The commanders of the opposing sides shall order and enforce a complete cessation of all hostilities in Korea by all armed forces under their control, including all units and personnel of the ground, naval, and air forces, effective twelve (12) hours after this Armistice Agreement is signed. (See paragraph 63 hereof for effective date and hour of the remaining provisions of this Armistice Agreement.)

13. In order to ensure the stability of the Military Armistice so as to facilitate the attainment of a peaceful settlement through the holding by both sides of a political conference of a higher level, the Commanders of the opposing sides shall—

(a) Within seventy-two (72) hours after this Armistice Agreement becomes effective, withdraw all of their military forces, supplies, and equipment from the Demilitarised Zone except as otherwise provided herein. All demolitions, minefields, wire entanglements and other hazards to the safe movement of personnel of the Military Armistice Commission or its Joint Observer Teams, known to exist within the Demilitarised Zone after the withdrawal of military forces therefrom, together with lanes known to be free of all such hazards, shall be reported to the Military Armistice Commission by the Commander of the side whose forces emplaced such hazards. Subsequently, additional safe lanes shall be cleared; and eventually, within forty-five (45) days after the termination of the seventy-two (72) hour period, all such hazards shall be removed from the De-militarised Zone as directed by and under the supervision of the Military Armistice Commission. At the termination of the seventy-two (72) hour period, except for unarmed troops authorised a forty-five (45) day period to complete salvage operations under Military Armistice Commission supervision, such units of a police nature as may be specifically requested by the Military Armistice Commission and agreed to by the Commanders of the opposing sides, and personnel authorised under paragraphs 10 and 11 hereof, no per-sonnel of either side shall be permitted to enter the Demilitarised Zone.

(b) Within ten (10) days after this Armistice Agreement becomes effective, withdraw all of their military forces, supplies and equip-ment from the rear and the coastal islands and waters of Korea of the other side. If such military forces are not withdrawn within the stated time limit, and there is no mutually agreed and valid reason for the delay, the other side shall have the right to take any action which it deems necessary for the maintenance of security and order. The term 'coastal islands', as used above, refers to those islands which, though occupied by one side at the time when this Armis-tice Agreement becomes effective, were controlled by the other side on June 24, 1950; provided, however that all the islands lying to the north and west of the provincial boundary line between Hwanghae-Do and Kyonggi-Do shall be under the military control of the Supreme Commander of the Korean People's Army and the Com-mander of the Chinese People's Volunteers, except the island groups of Paengyong-Do (37°58'N, 124°40'E), Taechong-Do (37°50'N, 124°-42'E), Sochong-Do (37°46'N, 124°46'E), Yonpyong-Do 37°38'N, 125°40'E), and U-Do (37°36'N, 125°58'E), which shall remain under the military control of the Commander-in-Chief, United Nations Command. All the islands on the west coast of Korea lying south of the above-mentioned boundary line shall remain under the military control of the Commander-in-Chief, United Nations Com-mand. (See Map 3.)[1]

(c) Cease the introduction into Korea of reinforcing military per-sonnel; provided, however, that the rotation of units and personnel, the arrival in Korea of personnel on a temporary duty basis, and the return to Korea of personnel after short periods of leave or tem-porary duty outside of Korea shall be permitted within the scope prescribed below. 'Rotation' is defined as the replacement of units or personnel by other units or personnel who are commencing a

[1] Not printed.

tour of duty in Korea. Rotation personnel shall be introduced into and evacuated from Korea only through the ports of entry enumerated in paragraph 43 hereof. Rotation shall be conducted on a man-for-man basis; provided, however, that no more than thirty-five thousand (35,000) persons in the military service shall be admitted into Korea by either side in any calendar month under the rotation policy. No military personnel of either side shall be introduced into Korea if the introduction of such personnel will cause the aggregate of the military personnel of that side admitted into Korea since the effective date of this Armistice Agreement to exceed the cumulative total of the military personnel of that side who have departed from Korea since that date. Reports concerning arrivals in and departures from Korea of military personnel shall be made daily to the Military Armistice Commission and the Neutral Nations Supervisory Commission; such reports shall include places of arrival and departure and the number of persons arriving at or departing from each such place. The Neutral Nations Supervisory Commission, through its Neutral Nations Inspection Teams, shall conduct supervision and inspection of the rotation of units and personnel authorised above, at the ports of entry enumerated in paragraph 43 hereof.

(d) Cease the introduction into Korea of reinforcing combat aircraft, armoured vehicles, weapons and ammunition; provided, however, that combat aircraft, armoured vehicles, weapons, and ammunition which are destroyed, damaged, worn-out, or used up during the period of the armistice may be replaced on the basis of piece-for-piece of the same effectiveness and the same type. Such combat aircraft, armoured vehicles, weapons, and ammunition shall be introduced into Korea only through the ports of entry enumerated in paragraph 43 hereof. In order to justify the requirement for combat aircraft, armoured vehicles, weapons, and ammunition to be introduced into Korea for replacement purposes, reports concerning every incoming shipment of these items shall be made to the Military Armistice Commission and the Neutral Nations Supervisory Commission; such reports shall include statements regarding the disposition of the items being replaced. Items to be replaced which are removed from Korea shall be removed only through the ports of entry enumerated in paragraph 43 hereof. The Neutral Nations Supervisory Commission, through its Neutral Nations Inspection Teams, shall conduct supervision and inspection of the replacement of combat aircraft, armoured vehicles, weapons, and ammunition authorised above, at the ports of entry enumerated in paragraph 43 hereof.

(e) Ensure that personnel of their respective commands who violate any of the provisions of this Armistice Agreement are adequately punished.

(*f*) In those cases where places of burial are a matter of record and graves are actually found to exist, permit graves registration personnel of the other side to enter, within a definite time limit after this Armistice Agreement becomes effective, the territory of Korea under their military control, for the purpose of proceeding to such graves to recover and evacuate the bodies of the deceased military personnel of that side, including deceased prisoners of war. The specific procedures and the time limit for the performance of the above task shall be determined by the Military Armistice Commission. The Commanders of the opposing sides shall furnish to the other side all available information pertaining to the places of burial of the deceased military personnel of the other side.

(*g*) Afford full protection and all possible assistance and co-operation to the Military Armistice Commission, its Joint Observer Teams, the Neutral Nations Supervisory Commission, and its Neutral Nations Inspection Teams, in the carrying out of their functions and responsibilities hereinafter assigned; and accord to the Neutral Nations Supervisory Commission, and to its Neutral Nations Inspection Teams, full convenience of movement between the headquarters of the Neutral Nations Supervisory Commission and the ports of entry enumerated in paragraph 43 hereof over main lines of communication agreed upon by both sides (See Map 4),[1] and between the headquarters of the Neutral Nations Supervisory Commission and the places where violations of this Armistice Agreement have been reported to have occurred. In order to prevent unnecessary delays, the use of alternate routes and means of transportation will be permitted whenever the main lines of communication are closed or impassable.

(*h*) Provide such logistic support, including communications and transportation facilities, as may be required by the Military Armistice Commission and the Neutral Nations Supervisory Commission and their Teams.

(*i*) Each construct, operate, and maintain a suitable airfield in their respective parts of the Demilitarised Zone in the vicinity of the headquarters of the Military Armistice Commission, for such uses as the Commission may determine.

(*j*) Ensure that all members and other personnel of the Neutral Nations Supervisory Commission and of the Neutral Nations Repatriation Commission hereinafter established shall enjoy the freedom and facilities necessary for the proper exercise of their functions, including privileges, treatment, and immunities equivalent to those

[1] Not printed.

ordinarily enjoyed by accredited diplomatic personnel under international usage.

14. This Armistice Agreement shall apply to all opposing ground forces under the military control of either side, which ground forces shall respect the Demilitarised Zone and the area of Korea under the military control of the opposing side.

15. This Armistice Agreement shall apply to all opposing naval forces, which naval forces shall respect the waters contiguous to the Demilitarised Zone and to the land area of Korea under the military control of the opposing side, and shall not engage in blockade of any kind of Korea.

16. This Armistice Agreement shall apply to all opposing air forces, which air forces shall respect the air space over the Demilitarised Zone and over the area of Korea under the military control of the opposing side, and over the waters contiguous to both.

17. Responsibility for compliance with and enforcement of the terms and provisions of this Armistice Agreement is that of the signatories hereto and their successors in command. The Commanders of the opposing sides shall establish within their respective commands all measures and procedures necessary to ensure complete compliance with all of the provisions hereof by all elements of their commands. They shall actively co-operate with one another and with the Military Armistice Commission and the Neutral Nations Supervisory Commission in requiring observance of both the letter and the spirit of all of the provisions of this Armistice Agreement.

18. The costs of the operations of the Military Armistice Commission and of the Neutral Nations Supervisory Commission and of their Teams shall be shared equally by the two opposing sides.

B.—Military Armistice Commission

1. Composition

19. A Military Armistice Commission is hereby established.

20. The Military Armistice Commission shall be composed of ten (10) senior officers, five (5) of whom shall be appointed by the Commander-in-Chief, United Nations Command, and five (5) of whom shall be appointed jointly by the Supreme Commander of the Korean People's Army and the Commander of the Chinese People's Volunteers. Of the ten members, three (3) from each side shall be of general or flag rank. The two (2) remaining members on each side shall be major-generals, brigadier-generals, colonels, or their equivalents.

21. Members of the Military Armistice Commission shall be permitted to use staff assistants as required.

22. The Military Armistice Commission shall be provided with the necessary administrative personnel to establish a Secretariat charged with assisting the Commission by performing record-keeping, secretarial, interpreting, and such other functions as the Commission may assign to it. Each side shall appoint to the Secretariat a Secretary and an Assistant Secretary and such clerical and specialised personnel as required by the Secretariat. Records shall be kept in English, Korean, and Chinese, all of which shall be equally authentic.

23.—(a) The Military Armistice Commission shall be initially provided with and assisted by ten (10) Joint Observer Teams, which number may be reduced by agreement of the senior members of both sides on the Military Armistice Commission.

(b) Each Joint Observer Team shall be composed of not less than four (4) nor more than six (6) officers of field grade, half of whom shall be appointed by the Commander-in-Chief, United Nations Command, and half of whom shall be appointed jointly by the Supreme Commander of the Korean People's Army and the Commander of the Chinese People's Volunteers. Additional personnel such as drivers, clerks, and interpreters shall be furnished by each side as required for the functioning of the Joint Observer Teams.

2. Functions and Authority

24. The general mission of the Military Armistice Commission shall be to supervise the implementation of this Armistice Agreement and to settle through negotiations any violations of this Armistice Agreement.

25. The Military Armistice Commission shall: —

(a) Locate its headquarters in the vicinity of Panmunjom (37° 57′ 29″ N., 126° 40′ 00″ E.). The Military Armistice Commission may re-locate its headquarters at another point within the Demilitarised Zone by agreement of the senior members of both sides on the Commission.

(b) Operate as a joint organisation without a chairman.

(c) Adopt such rules of procedure as it may, from time to time, deem necessary.

(d) Supervise the carrying out of the provisions of this Armistice Agreement pertaining to the Demilitarised Zone and to the Han River Estuary.

(e) Direct the operations of the Joint Observer Teams.

(*f*) Settle through negotiations any violations of this Armistice Agreement.

(*g*) Transmit immediately to the Commanders of the opposing sides all reports of investigations of violations of this Armistice Agreement and all other reports and records of proceedings received from the Neutral Nations Supervisory Commission.

(*h*) Give general supervision and direction to the activities of the Committee for Repatriation of Prisoners of War and the Committee for Assisting the Return of Displaced Civilians, hereinafter established.

(*i*) Act as an intermediary in transmitting communications between the Commanders of the opposing sides; provided, however, that the foregoing shall not be construed to preclude the Commanders of both sides from communicating with each other by any means which they may desire to employ.

(*j*) Provide credentials and distinctive insignia for its staff and its Joint Observer Teams, and a distinctive marking for all vehicles, aircraft, and vessels, used in the performance of its mission.

26. The mission of the Joint Observer Teams shall be to assist the Military Armistice Commission in supervising the carrying out of the provisions of this Armistice Agreement pertaining to the Demilitarised Zone and to the Han River Estuary.

27. The Military Armistice Commission, or the senior member of either side thereof, is authorised to despatch Joint Observer Teams to investigate violation of this Armistice Agreement reported to have occurred in the Demilitarised Zone or in the Han River Estuary; provided, however, that not more than one half of the Joint Observer Teams which have not been despatched by the Military Armistice Commission may be despatched at any one time by the senior member of either side on the Commission.

28. The Military Armistice Commission, or the senior member of either side thereof, is authorised to request the Neutral Nations Supervisory Commission to conduct special observations and inspections at places outside the Demilitarised Zone where violations of this Armistice Agreement have been reported to have occurred.

29. When the Military Armistice Commission determines that a violation of this Armistice Agreement has occurred, it shall immediately report such violation to the Commanders of the opposing sides.

30. When the Military Armistice Commission determines that a violation of this Armistice Agreement has been corrected to its satisfaction, it shall so report to the Commanders of the opposing sides.

3. *General*

31. The Military Armistice Commission shall meet daily. Recesses of not to exceed seven (7) days may be agreed upon by the senior members of both sides; provided, that such recesses may be terminated on twenty-four (24) hour notice by the senior member of either side.

32. Copies of the record of the proceedings of all meetings of the Military Armistice Commission shall be forwarded to the Commanders of the opposing sides as soon as possible after each meeting.

33. The Joint Observer Teams shall make periodic report to the Military Armistice Commission as required by the Commission and, in addition, shall make such special report as may be deemed necessary by them, or as may be required by the Commission.

34. The Military Armistice Commission shall maintain files of the reports and records of proceedings required by this Armistice Agreement. The Commission is authorised to maintain duplicate files of such other reports, records, &c., as may be necessary in the conduct of its business. Upon eventual dissolution of the Commission, one set of the above files shall be turned over to each side.

35. The Military Armistice Commission may make recommendations to the Commanders of the opposing sides with respect to amendments or additions to this Armistice Agreement. Such recommended changes should generally be those designed to ensure a more effective armistice.

C.—*Neutral Nations Supervisory Commission*

1. *Composition*

36. A Neutral Nations Supervisory Commission is hereby established.

37. The Neutral Nations Supervisory Commission shall be composed of four (4) senior officers, two (2) of whom shall be appointed by neutral nations nominated by the Commander-in-Chief, United Nations Command, namely, Sweden and Switzerland, and two (2) of whom shall be appointed by neutral nations nominated jointly by the Supreme Commander of the Korean People's Army and the Commander of the Chinese People's Volunteers, namely, Poland and Czechoslovakia. The term 'neutral nations' as herein used is defined as those nations whose combatant forces have not participated in the hostilities in Korea. Members appointed to the Commission may be from the armed forces of the appointing nations. Each member shall designate an alternate member to attend those

meetings which for any reason the principal member is unable to attend. Such alternate members shall be of the same nationality as their principals. The Neutral Nations Supervisory Commission may take action whenever the number of members present from the neutral nations nominated by one side is equal to the number of members present from the neutral nations nominated by the other side.

38. Members of the Neutral Nations Supervisory Commission shall be permitted to use staff assistants furnished by the neutral nations as required. These staff assistants may be appointed as alternate members of the Commission.

39. The neutral nations shall be requested to furnish the Neutral Nations Supervisory Commission with the necessary administrative personnel to establish a Secretariat charged with assisting the Commission by performing necessary record-keeping, secretarial, interpreting, and such other functions as the Commission may assign to it.

40.—(a) The Neutral Nations Supervisory Commission shall be initially provided with, and assisted by, twenty (20) Neutral Nations Inspection Teams, which number may be reduced by agreement of the senior members of both sides on the Military Armistice Commission. The Neutral Nations Inspection Teams shall be responsible to, shall report to, and shall be subject to the direction of, the Neutral Nations Supervisory Commission only.

(b) Each Neutral Nations Inspection Team shall be composed of not less than four (4) officers, preferably of field grade, half of whom shall be from the neutral nations nominated by the Commander-in-Chief, United Nations Command, and half of whom shall be from the neutral nations nominated jointly by the Supreme Commander of the Korean People's Army and the Commander of the Chinese People's Volunteers. Members appointed to the Neutral Nations Inspection Teams may be from the armed forces of the appointing nations. In order to facilitate the functioning of the Teams, subteams composed of not less than two (2) members, one of whom shall be from a neutral nation nominated by the Commander-in-Chief, United Nations Command, and one of whom shall be from a neutral nation nominated jointly by the Supreme Commander of the Korean People's Army and the Commander of the Chinese People's Volunteers, may be formed as circumstances require. Additional personnel such as drivers, clerks, interpreters, and communications personnel, and such equipment as may be required by the Teams to perform their missions, shall be furnished by the Commander of each side, as required, in the Demilitarised Zone and in the territory under his military control. The Neutral Nations Supervisory Commission may provide itself and the Neutral Nations Inspection Teams with such of the above personnel and equipment of its own as it may desire; provided, however, that such personnel shall be personnel of the same neutral nations of which the Neutral Nations Supervisory Commission is composed.

2. *Functions and Authority*

41. The mission of the Neutral Nations Supervisory Commission shall be to carry out the functions of supervision, observation, inspection, and investigation, as stipulated in sub-paragraphs 13(c) and 13(d) and paragraph 28 hereof, and to report the results of such supervision, observation, inspection and investigation to the Military Armistice Commission.

42. The Neutral Nations Supervisory Commission shall:—

(a) Locate its headquarters in proximity to the headquarters of the Military Armistice Commission.

(b) Adopt such rules of procedure as it may, from time to time, deem necessary.

(c) Conduct, through its members and its Neutral Nations Inspection Teams, the supervision and inspection provided for in sub-paragraphs 13 (c) and 13 (d) of this Armistice Agreement at the ports of entry enumerated in paragraph 43 hereof, and the special observations and inspections provided for in paragraph 28 hereof at those places where violations of this Armistice Agreement have been reported to have occurred. The inspection of combat aircraft, armoured vehicles, weapons, and ammunition by the Neutral Nations Inspection Teams shall be such as to enable them to properly ensure that reinforcing combat aircraft, armoured vehicles, weapons, and ammunition are not being introduced into Korea; but this shall not be construed as authorising inspections or examinations of any secret designs or characteristics of any combat aircraft, armoured vehicle, weapon, or ammunition.

(d) Direct and supervise the operations of the Neutral Nations Inspection Teams.

(e) Station five (5) Neutral Nations Inspection Teams at the ports of entry enumerated in paragraph 43 hereof located in the territory under the military control of the Commander-in-Chief, United Nations Command; and five (5) Neutral Nations Inspection Teams at the ports of entry enumerated in paragraph 43 hereof located in the territory under the military control of the Supreme Commander of the Korean People's Army and the Commander of the Chinese People's Volunteers; and establish initially ten (10) mobile Neutral Nations Inspection Teams in reserve, stationed in the general vicinity of the headquarters of the Neutral Nations Supervisory Commission, which number may be reduced by agreement of the senior members of both sides on the Military Armistice Commision. Not more than half of the mobile Neutral Nations Inspection Teams shall be despatched at any one time in accordance with requests of the senior member of either side on the Military Armistice Commission.

(f) Subject to the provisions of the preceding sub-paragraph, conduct without delay investigations of reported violations of this Armistice Agreement, including such investigations of reported violations of this Armistice Agreement as may be requested by the Military Armistice Commission or by the senior member of either side on the Commission.

(g) Provide credentials and distinctive insignia for its staff and its Neutral Nations Inspection Teams, and a distinctive marking for all vehicles, aircraft, and vessels, used in the performance of its mission.

43. Neutral Nations Inspection Teams shall be stationed at the following ports of entry:—

Territory under the military control of the United Nations Command		Territory under the military control of the Korean People's Army and the Chinese People's Volunteers	
Inchon	(37°28'N, 126°38'E)	Sinuiju	(40°06'N, 124°24'E)
Taegu	(35°52'N, 128°36'E)	Chongjin	(41°46'N, 129°49'E)
Pusan	(35°06'N, 129°02'E)	Hungnam	(39°50'N, 127°37'E)
Kangnung	(37°45'N, 128°54'E)	Manpo	(41°09'N, 126°18'E)
Kunsan	(35°59'N, 126°43'E)	Sinanju	(39°36'N, 125°36'E)

These Neutral Nations Inspection Teams shall be accorded full convenience of movement within the areas and over the routes of communication set forth on the attached map (Map 5).[1]

3. General

44. The Neutral Nations Supervisory Commission shall meet daily. Recesses of not to exceed seven (7) days must be agreed upon by the members of the Neutral Nations Supervisory Commission; provided, that such recesses may be terminated on twenty-four (24) hour notice by any member.

45. Copies of the record of the proceedings of all meetings of the Neutral Nations Supervisory Commission shall be forwarded to the Military Armistice Commission as soon as possible after each meeting. Records shall be kept in English, Korean, and Chinese.

[1] Not printed.

46. The Neutral Nations Inspection Teams shall make periodic reports concerning the results of their supervision, observations, inspections and investigations to the Neutral Nations Supervisory Commission as required by the Commission and, in addition, shall make such special reports as may be deemed necessary by them, or as may be required by the Commission. Reports shall be submitted by a Team as a whole, but may also be submitted by one or more individual members thereof; provided, that the reports submitted by one or more individual members thereof shall be considered as informational only.

47. Copies of the reports made by the Neutral Nations Inspection Teams shall be forwarded to the Military Armistice Commission by the Neutral Nations Supervisory Commission without delay and in the language in which received. They shall not be delayed by the process of translation or evaluation. The Neutral Nations Supervisory Commission shall evaluate such reports at the earliest practicable time and shall forward their findings to the Military Armistice Commission as a matter of priority. The Military Armistice Commission shall not take final action with regard to any such report until the evaluation thereof has been received from the Neutral Nations Supervisory Commission. Members of the Neutral Nations Supervisory Commission and of its Teams shall be subject to appearance before the Military Armistice Commission, at the request of the senior member of either side on the Military Armistice Commission, for clarification of any report submitted.

48. The Neutral Nations Supervisory Commission shall maintain duplicate files of the reports and records of proceedings required by this Armistice Agreement. The Commission is authorised to maintain duplicate files of such other reports, records, &c., as may be necessary in the conduct of its business. Upon eventual dissolution of the Commission, one set of the above files shall be turned over to each side.

49. The Neutral Nations Supervisory Commission may make recommendations to the Military Armistice Commission with respect to amendments or additions to this Armistice Agreement. Such recommended changes should generally be those designed to ensure a more effective armistice.

50. The Neutral Nations Supervisory Commission, or any member thereof, shall be authorised to communicate with any member of the Military Armistice Commission.

ARTICLE III

Arrangements relating to Prisoners of War

51. The release and repatriation of all prisoners of war held in the custody of each side at the time this Armistice Agreement becomes effective shall be effected in conformity with the following provisions agreed upon by both sides prior to the signing of this Armistice Agreement.

(*a*) Within sixty (60) days after this Armistice Agreement becomes effective, each side shall, without offering any hindrance, directly repatriate and hand over in groups all those prisoners of war in its custody who insist on repatriation to the side to which they belong at the time of capture. Repatriation shall be accomplished in accordance with the related provisions of this Article. In order to expedite the repatriation process of such personnel, each side shall, prior to the signing of the Armistice Agreement, exchange the total numbers, by nationalities, of personnel to be directly repatriated. Each group of prisoners of war delivered to the other side shall be accompanied by rosters, prepared by nationality, to include name, rank (if any) and internment or military serial number.

(*b*) Each side shall release all those remaining prisoners of war, who are not directly repatriated, from its military control and from its custody and hand them over to the Neutral Nations Repatriation Commission for disposition in accordance with the provisions in the Annex hereto: 'Terms of Reference for Neutral Nations Repatriation Commission.'

(*c*) So that there may be no misunderstanding owing to the equal use of three languages, the act of delivery of a prisoner of war by one side to the other side shall, for the purposes of this Armistice, be called 'repatriation' in English, ' 송환 ' (song hwan) in Korean, and ' 遣返 ' (ch'ien fan) in Chinese, notwithstanding the nationality or place of residence of such prisoner of war.

52. Each side ensures that it will not employ in acts of war in the Korean conflict any prisoner of war released and repatriated incident to the coming into effect of this Armistice Agreement.

53. All the sick and injured prisoners of war who insist upon repatriation shall be repatriated with priority. In so far as possible, there shall be captured medical personnel repatriated concurrently with the sick and injured prisoners of war, so as to provide medical care and attendance *en route*.

54. The repatriation of all of the prisoners of war required by sub-paragraph 51 (*a*) hereof shall be completed within a time limit

of sixty (60) days after this Armistice Agreement becomes effective. Within this time limit each side undertakes to complete the repatriation of the above-mentioned prisoners of war in its custody at the earliest practicable time.

55. Panmunjom is designated as the place where prisoners of war will be delivered and received by both sides. Additional place(s) of delivery and reception of prisoners of war in the Demilitarised Zone may be designated, if necessary, by the Committee for Repatriation of Prisoners of War.

56.—(a) A Committee for Repatriation of Prisoners of War is hereby established. It shall be composed of six (6) officers of field grade, three (3) of whom shall be appointed by the Commander-in-Chief, United Nations Command, and three (3) of whom shall be appointed jointly by the Supreme Commander of the Korean People's Army and the Commander of the Chinese People's Volunteers. This Committee shall, under the general supervision and direction of the Military Armistice Commission, be responsible for co-ordinating the specific plans of both sides for the repatriation of prisoners of war and for supervising the execution by both sides of all of the provisions of this Armistice Agreement relating to the repatriation of prisoners of war. It shall be the duty of this Committee to co-ordinate the timing of the arrival of prisoners of war at the place(s) of delivery and reception of prisoners of war from the prisoner of war camps of both sides; to make, when necessary, such special arrangements as may be required with regard to the transportation and welfare of sick and injured prisoners of war; to co-ordinate the work of the joint Red Cross teams, established in paragraph 57 hereof, in assisting in the repatriation of prisoners of war; to supervise the implementation of the arrangements for the actual repatriation of prisoners of war stipulated in paragraphs 53 and 54 hereof; to select, when necessary, additional place(s) of delivery and reception of prisoners of war; to arrange for security at the place(s) of delivery and reception of prisoners of war; and to carry out such other related functions as are required for the repatriation of prisoners of war.

(b) When unable to reach agreement on any matter relating to its responsibilities, the Committee for Repatriation of Prisoners of War shall immediately refer such matter to the Military Armistice Commission for decision. The Committee for Repatriation of Prisoners of War shall maintain its headquarters in proximity to the headquarters of the Military Armistice Commission.

(c) The Committee for Repatriation of Prisoners of War shall be dissolved by the Military Armistice Commission upon completion of the programme of repatriation of prisoners of war.

57.—(a) Immediately after this Armistice Agreement becomes effective, joint Red Cross teams composed of representatives of the national Red Cross Societies of the countries contributing forces to the United Nations Command on the one hand, and representatives of the Red Cross Society of the Democratic People's Republic of Korea and representatives of the Red Cross Society of the People's Republic of China on the other hand, shall be established. The joint Red Cross teams shall assist in the execution of both sides of those provisions of this Armistice Agreement relating to the repatriation of all the prisoners of war specified in sub-paragraph 51 (a) hereof, who insist upon repatriation, by the performance of such humanitarian services as are necessary and desirable for the welfare of the prisoners of war. To accomplish this task, the joint Red Cross teams shall provide assistance in the delivering and receiving of prisoners of war by both sides at the place(s) of delivery and reception of prisoners of war, and shall visit the prisoner of war camps of both sides to comfort the prisoners of war and to bring in and distribute gift articles for the comfort and welfare of the prisoners of war. The joint Red Cross teams may provide services to prisoners of war while *en route* from prisoner of war camps to the place(s) of delivery and reception of prisoners of war.

(b) The joint Red Cross teams shall be organised as set forth below:—

(1) One team shall be composed of twenty (20) members, namely, ten (10) representatives from the national Red Cross Societies of each side, to assist in the delivering and receiving of prisoners of war by both sides at the place(s) of delivery and reception of prisoners of war. The chairmanship of this team shall alternate daily between representatives from the Red Cross Societies of the two sides. The work and services of this team shall be co-ordinated by the Committee for Repatriation of Prisoners of War.

(2) One team shall be composed of sixty (60) members, namely, thirty (30) representatives from the national Red Cross Societies of each side, to visit the prisoner of war camps under the administration of the Korean People's Army and the Chinese People's Volunteers. This team may provide services to prisoners of war while *en route* from the prisoner of war camps to the place(s) of delivery and reception of prisoners of war. A representative of the Red Cross Society of the Democratic People's Republic of Korea or of the Red Cross Society of the People's Republic of China shall serve as chairman of this team.

(3) One team shall be composed of sixty (60) members, namely, thirty (30) representatives from the national Red Cross Societies of each side, to visit the prisoner of war camps under the administration of the United Nations Command. This team may provide services to prisoners of war while *en route* from the prisoner of war camps to the place(s) of delivery and reception of prisoners of war. A representative of a Red Cross Society of a nation contributing forces to the United Nations Command shall serve as chairman of this team.

(4) In order to facilitate the functioning of each joint Red Cross team, sub-teams composed of not less than two (2) members from the team, with an equal number of representatives from each side, may be formed as circumstances require.

(5) Additional personnel such as drivers, clerks, and interpreters, and such equipment as may be required by the joint Red Cross teams to perform their missions, shall be furnished by the Commander of each side to the team operating in the territory under his military control.

(6) Whenever jointly agreed upon by the representatives of both sides on any joint Red Cross team, the size of such team may be increased or decreased, subject to confirmation by the Committee for Repatriation of Prisoners of War.

(c) The Commander of each side shall co-operate fully with the joint Red Cross teams in the performance of their functions, and undertakes to ensure the security of the personnel of the joint Red Cross team in the area under his military control. The Commander of each side shall provide such logistic, administrative and communications facilities as may be required by the team operating in the territory under his military control.

(d) The joint Red Cross teams shall be dissolved upon completion of the programme of repatriation of all the prisoners of war specified in sub-paragraph 51 (a) hereof, who insist upon repatriation.

58.—(a) The Commander of each side shall furnish to the Commander of the other side as soon as practicable, but not later than ten (10) days after this Armistice Agreement becomes effective, the following information concerning prisoners of war:—

(1) Complete data pertaining to the prisoners of war who escaped since the effective date of the data last exchanged.

(2) In so far as practicable, information regarding name, nationality, rank, and other identification data, date and cause of death, and place of burial, of those prisoners of war who died while in his custody.

(b) If any prisoners of war escape or die after the effective date of the supplementary information specified above, the detaining side shall furnish to the other side, through the Committee for Repatriation of Prisoners of War, the data pertaining thereto in accordance with the provisions of sub-paragraph 58 (a) hereof. Such data shall be furnished at ten-day intervals until the completion of the programme of delivery and reception of prisoners of war.

(c) Any escaped prisoner of war who returns to the custody of the detaining side after the completion of the progamme of delivery and reception of prisoners of war shall be delivered to the Military Armistice Commission for disposition.

59.—(a) All civilians who, at the time this Armistice Agreement becomes effective, are in territory under the military control of the Commander-in-Chief, United Nations Command, and who, on June 24, 1950, resided north of the Military Demarcation Line established in this Armistice Agreement shall, if they desire to return home, be permitted and assisted by the Commander-in-Chief, United Nations Command, to return to the area north of the Military Demarcation Line; and all civilians who, at the time this Armistice Agreement becomes effective, are in territory under the military control of the Supreme Commander of the Korean People's Army and the Commander of the Chinese People's Volunteers, and who, on June 24, 1950, resided south of the Military Demarcation Line established in this Armistice Agreement shall, if they desire to return home, be permitted and assisted by the Supreme Commander of the Korean People's Army and the Commander of the Chinese People's Volunteers to return to the area south of the Military Demarcation Line. The Commander of each side shall be responsible for publicising widely throughout the territory under his military control the contents of the provisions of this sub-paragraph, and for calling upon the appropriate civil authorities to give necessary guidance and assistance to all such civilians who desire to return home.

(b) All civilians of foreign nationality who, at the time this Armistice Agreement becomes effective, are in territory under the military control of the Supreme Commander of the Korean People's Army and the Commander of the Chinese People's Volunteers shall, if they desire to proceed to territory under the military control of the Commander-in-Chief, United Nations Command, be permitted and assisted to do so; all civilians of foreign nationality who, at the time this Armistice Agreement becomes effective, are in territory under the military control of the Commander-in-Chief, United Nations Command, shall, if they desire to proceed to territory under the military control of the Supreme Commander of the Korean People's

Army and the Commander of the Chinese People's Volunteers, be permitted and assisted to do so. The Commander of each side shall be responsible for publicising widely throughout the territory under his military control the contents of the provisions of this sub-paragraph, and for calling upon the appropriate civil authorities to give necessary guidance and assistance to all such civilians of foreign nationality who desire to proceed to territory under the military control of the Commander of the other side.

(*c*) Measures to assist in the return of civilians provided for in sub-paragraph 59 (*a*) hereof and the movement of civilians provided for in sub-paragraph 59 (*b*) hereof shall be commenced by both sides as soon as possible after this Armistice Agreement becomes effective.

> (*d*)—(1) A Committee for Assisting the Return of Displaced Civilians is hereby established. It shall be composed of four (4) officers of field grade, two (2) of whom shall be appointed by the Commander-in-Chief, United Nations Command, and two (2) of whom shall be appointed jointly by the Supreme Commander of the Korean People's Army and the Commander of the Chinese People's Volunteers. This Committee shall, under the general supervision and direction of the Military Armistice Commission, be responsible for co-ordinating the specific plans of both sides for assistance to the return of the above-mentioned civilians, and for supervising the execution by both sides of all of the provisions of this Armistice Agreement relating to the return of the above-mentioned civilians. It shall be the duty of this Committee to make necessary arrangements, including those of transportation, for expediting and co-ordinating the movement of the above-mentioned civilians; to select the crossing point(s) through which the above-mentioned civilians will cross the Military Demarcation Line; to arrange for security at the crossing point(s); and to carry out such other functions as are required to accomplish the return of the above-mentioned civilians.
>
> (2) When unable to reach agreement on any matter relating to its responsibilities, the Committee for Assisting the Return of Displaced Civilians shall immediately refer such matter to the Military Armistice Commission for decision. The Committee for Assisting the Return of Displaced Civilians shall maintain its headquarters in proximity to the headquarters of the Military Armistice Commission.
>
> (3) The Committee for Assisting the Return of Displaced Civilians shall be dissolved by the Military Armistice Commission upon fulfilment of its mission.

ARTICLE IV

Recommendation to the Governments concerned on both Sides

60. In order to ensure the peaceful settlement of the Korean question, the military Commanders of both sides hereby recommend to the Governments of the countries concerned on both sides that, within three (3) months after the Armistice Agreement is signed and becomes effective, a political conference of a higher level of both sides be held by representatives appointed respectively to settle through negotiation the questions of the withdrawal of all foreign forces from Korea, the peaceful settlement of the Korean question, &c.

ARTICLE V

Miscellaneous

61. Amendments and additions to this Armistice Agreement must be mutually agreed to by the Commanders of the opposing sides.

62. The Articles and Paragraphs of this Armistice Agreement shall remain in effect until expressly superseded either by mutually acceptable amendments and additions or by provision in an appropriate agreement for a peaceful settlement at a political level between both sides.

63. All of the provisions of this Armistice Agreement, other than paragraph 12, shall become effective at 2200 hours on July 27 1953.

Done at Panmunjom, Korea, at 1000 hours on the 27th day of July, 1953, in English, Korean, and Chinese, all texts being equally authentic.

KIM IL SUNG
Marshal, Democratic People's Republic of Korea.
Supreme Commander Korean People's Army.

PENG TEH-HUAI
Commander, Chinese People's Volunteers.

MARK W. CLARK
General, United States Army.
Commander-in-Chief, United Nations Command.

Present:

M̸W̸,   *W K Harrison*

NAM IL   WILLIAM K. HARRISON, Jr.
General, Korean People's Army.   Lt.-Gen., United States Army.
Senior Delegate.   Senior Delegate,
Delegation of the Korean   United Nations Command
People's Army and the Chinese   Delegation.
People's Volunteers.

ANNEX

TERMS OF REFERENCE FOR NEUTRAL NATIONS REPATRIATION
COMMISION

(See Sub-paragraph 51 (*b*))

I.—*General*

1. In order to ensure that all prisoners of war have the opportunity to exercise their rights to be repatriated following an armistice, Sweden, Switzerland, Poland, Czechoslovakia and India shall each be requested by both sides to appoint a member of a Neutral Nations Repatriation Commission which shall be established to take custody in Korea of those prisoners of war who, while in the custody of the detaining Powers, have not exercised their right to be repatriated. The Neutral Nations Repatriation Commission shall establish its headquarters within the Demilitarised Zone in the vicinity of Panmunjom, and shall station subordinate bodies of the same composition as the Neutral Nations Repatriation Commission at those locations at which the Repatriation Commission assumes custody of prisoners of war. Representatives of both sides shall be permitted to observe the operations of the Repatriation Commission and its subordinate bodies to include explanations and interviews.

2. Sufficient armed forces and any other operating personnel required to assist the Neutral Nations Repatriation Commission in carrying out its functions and responsibilities shall be provided exclusively by India, whose representative shall be the umpire in accordance with the provisions of Article 132 of the Geneva Convention, and shall also be chairman and executive agent of the Neutral Nations Repatriation Commission. Representatives from each of

the other four Powers shall be allowed staff assistants in equal number not to exceed fifty (50) each. When any of the representatives of the neutral nations is absent for some reason, that representative shall designate an alternate representative of his own nationality to exercise his functions and authority. The arms of all personnel provided for in this paragraph shall be limited to military police type small arms.

3. No force or threat of force shall be used against the prisoners of war specified in paragraph 1 above to prevent or effect their repatriation, and no violence to their persons or affront to their dignity or self-respect shall be permitted in any manner for any purpose whatsoever (but see paragraph 7 below). This duty is enjoined on and entrusted to the Neutral Nations Repatriation Commission. This Commission shall ensure that prisoners of war shall at all times be treated humanely in accordance with the specific provisions of the Geneva Convention, and with the general spirit of that Convention.

II.—Custody of Prisoners of War

4. All prisoners of war who have not exercised their right of repatriation following the effective date of the Armistice Agreement shall be released from the military control and from the custody of the detaining side as soon as practicable, and, in all cases, within sixty (60) days subsequent to the effective date of the Armistice Agreement to the Neutral Nations Repatriation Commission at locations in Korea to be designated by the detaining side.

5. At the time the Neutral Nations Repatriation Commission assumes control of the prisoner-of-war installations, the military forces of the detaining side shall be withdrawn therefrom, so that the locations specified in the preceding paragraph shall be taken over completely by the armed forces of India.

6. Notwithstanding the provisions of paragraph 5 above, the detaining side shall have the responsibility for maintaining and ensuring security and order in the areas around the locations where the prisoners of war are in custody and for preventing and restraining any armed forces (including irregular armed forces) in the area under its control from any acts of disturbance and intrusion against the locations where the prisoners of war are in custody.

7. Notwithstanding the provisions of paragraph 3 above, nothing in this agreement shall be construed as derogating from the authority of the Neutral Nations Repatriation Commission to exercise its legitimate functions and responsibilities for the control of the prisoners of war under its temporary jurisdiction.

III.—*Explanation*

8. The Neutral Nations Repatriation Commission, after having received and taken into custody all those prisoners of war who have not exercised their right to be repatriated, shall immediately make arrangements so that, within ninety (90) days after the Neutral Nations Repatriation Commission takes over the custody, the nations to which the prisoners of war belong shall have freedom and facilities to send representatives to the locations where such prisoners of war are in custody to explain to all the prisoners of war depending upon these nations their rights and to inform them of any matters relating to their return to their homelands, particularly of their full freedom to return home to lead a peaceful life, under the following provisions:—

(*a*) The number of such explaining representatives shall not exceed seven (7) per thousand prisoners of war held in custody by the Neutral Nations Repatriation Commission; and the minimum authorised shall not be less than a total of five (5);

(*b*) The hours during which the explaining representatives shall have access to the prisoners shall be as determined by the Neutral Nations Repatriation Commission, and generally in accord with Article 53 of the Geneva Convention Relative to the Treatment of Prisoners of War;

(*c*) All explanations and interviews shall be conducted in the presence of a representative of each member nation of the Neutral Nations Repatriation Commission and a representative from the detaining side;

(*d*) Additional provisions governing the explanation work shall be prescribed by the Neutral Nations Repatriation Commission, and will be designed to employ the principles enumerated in paragraph 3 above and in this paragraph;

(*e*) The explaining representatives, while engaging in their work, shall be allowed to bring with them necessary facilities and personnel for wireless communications. The number of communications personnel shall be limited to one team per location at which explaining representatives are in residence, except in the event all prisoners of war are concentrated in one location, in which case, two (2) teams shall be permitted. Each team shall consist of not more than six (6) communications personnel.

9. Prisoners of war in its custody shall have freedom and facilities to make representations and communications to the Neutral Nations Repatriation Commission and to representatives and subordinate bodies of the Neutral Nations Repatriation Commission and to inform them of their desires on any matter concerning the prisoners

of war themselves, in accordance with arrangements made for the purpose by the Neutral Nations Repatriation Commission.

IV.—*Disposition of Prisoners of War*

10. Any prisoner of war who, while in the custody of the Neutral Nations Repatriation Commission, decides to exercise the right of repatriation, shall make an application requesting repatriation to a body consisting of a representative of each member nation of the Neutral Nations Repatriation Commission. Once such an application is made, it shall be considered immediately by the Neutral Nations Repatriation Commission or one of its subordinate bodies so as to determine immediately by majority vote the validity of such application. Once such an application is made to and validated by the Commission or one of its subordinate bodies, the prisoner of war concerned shall immediately be transferred to and accommodated in the tents set up for those who are ready to be repatriated. Thereafter, he shall, while still in the custody of the Neutral Nations Repatriation Commission, be delivered forthwith to the prisoner of war exchange point at Panmunjom for repatriation under the procedure prescribed in the Armistice Agreement.

11. At the expiration of ninety (90) days after the transfer of custody of the prisoners of war to the Neutral Nations Repatriation Commission, access of representatives to captured personnel as provided for in paragraph 8 above, shall terminate, and the question of disposition of the prisoners of war who have not exercised their right to be repatriated shall be submitted to the Political Conference recommended to be convened in paragraph 60, Draft Armistice Agreement, which shall endeavour to settle this question within thirty (30) days, during which period the Neutral Nations Repatriation Commission shall continue to retain custody of those prisoners of war. The Neutral Nations Repatriation Commission shall declare the relief from the prisoner of war status to civilian status of any prisoners of war who have not exercised their right to be repatriated and for whom no other disposition has been agreed to by the Political Conference within one hundred and twenty (120) days after the Neutral Nations Repatriation Commission has assumed their custody. Thereafter, according to the application of each individual, those who choose to go to neutral nations shall be assisted by the Neutral Nations Repatriation Commission and the Red Cross Society of India. This operation shall be completed within thirty (30) days, and upon its completion, the Neutral Nations Repatriation Commission shall immediately cease its functions and declare its dissolution. After the dissolution of the Neutral Nations Repatriation

Commission, whenever and wherever any of those above-mentioned civilians who have been relieved from the prisoner of war status desire to return to their fatherlands, the authorities of the localities where they are shall be responsible for assisting them in returning to their fatherlands.

V.—*Red Cross Visitation*

12. Essential Red Cross service for prisoners of war in custody of the Neutral Nations Repatriation Commission shall be provided by India in accordance with regulations issued by the Neutral Nations Repatriation Commission.

VI.—*Press Coverage*

13. The Neutral Nations Repatriation Commission shall ensure freedom of the press and other news media in observing the entire operation as enumerated herein, in accordance with procedures to be established by the Neutral Nations Repatriation Commission.

VII.—*Logistical Support for Prisoners of War*

14. Each side shall provide logistical support for the prisoners of war in the area under its military control, delivering required support to the Neutral Nations Repatriation Commissions at an agreed delivery point in the vicinity of each prisoner of war installation.

15. The cost of repatriating prisoners of war to the exchange point at Panmunjom shall be borne by the detaining side and the cost from the exchange point by the side on which said prisoners depend, in accordance with Article 118 of the Geneva Convention.

16. The Red Cross Society of India shall be responsible for providing such general service personnel in the prisoner of war installations as required by the Neutral Nations Repatriation Commission.

17. The Neutral Nations Repatriation Commission shall provide medical support for the prisoners of war as may be practicable. The detaining side shall provide medical support as practicable upon the request of the Neutral Nations Repatriation Commission and specifically for those cases requiring extensive treatment or hospitalisation. The Neutral Nations Repatriation Commission shall maintain custody of prisoners of war during such hospitalisation. The detaining side shall facilitate such custody. Upon completion of treatment, prisoners of war shall be returned to a prisoner of war installation as specified in paragraph 4 above.

18. The Neutral Nations Repatriation Commission is entitled to

obtain from both sides such legitimate assistance as it may require in carrying out its duties and tasks, but both sides shall not under any name and in any form interfere or exert influence.

VIII.—*Logistical Support for the Neutral Nations Repatriation Commission*

19. Each side shall be responsible for providing logistical support for the personnel of the Neutral Nations Repatriation Commission stationed in the area under its military control, and both sides shall contribute on an equal basis to such support within the Demilitarised Zone. The precise arrangements shall be subject to determination between the Neutral Nations Repatriation Commission and the detaining side in each case.

20. Each of the detaining sides shall be responsible for protecting the explaining representatives from the other side while in transit over lines of communication within its area, as set forth in paragraph 23 for the Neutral Nations Repatriation Commission, to a place of residence and while in residence in the vicinity of, but not within each of, the locations where the prisoners of war are in custody. The Neutral Nations Repatriation Commission shall be responsible for the security of such representatives within the actual limits of the locations where the prisoners of war are in custody.

21. Each of the detaining sides shall provide transportation, housing, communication, and other agreed logistical support to the explaining representatives of the other side while they are in the area under its military control. Such services shall be provided on a reimbursable basis.

IX.—*Publication*

22. After the Armistice Agreement becomes effective, the terms of this agreement shall be made known to all prisoners of war who, while in the custody of the detaining side, have not exercised their right to be repatriated.

X.—*Movement*

23. The movement of the personnel of the Neutral Nations Repatriation Commission and repatriated prisoners of war shall be over lines of communication as determined by the command(s) of the opposing side and the Neutral Nations Repatriation Commission. A map showing these lines of communication shall be furnished by the command of the opposing side and the Neutral

Nations Repatriation Commission. Movement of such personnel, except within locations as designated in paragraph 4 above, shall be under the control of, and escorted by, personnel of the side in whose area the travel is being undertaken; however, such movement shall not be subject to any obstruction and coercion.

XI.—*Procedural Matters*

24. The interpretation of this agreement shall rest with the Neutral Nations Repatriation Commission. The Neutral Nations Repatriation Commission, and/or any subordinate bodies to which functions are delegated or assigned by the Neutral Nations Repatriation Commission, shall operate on the basis of majority vote.

25. The Neutral Nations Repatriation Commission shall submit a weekly report to the opposing Commanders on the status of prisoners of war in its custody, indicating the numbers repatriated and remaining at the end of each week.

26. When this agreement has been acceded to by both sides and by the five Powers named herein, it shall become effective upon the date the Armistice becomes effective.

Done at Panmunjom, Korea, at 1400 hours on the 8th day of June, 1953, in English, Korean, and Chinese, all texts being equally authentic.

NAM IL
General, Korean People's Army.
Senior Delegate,
Delegation of the Korean
    People's Army and the
    Chinese People's Volunteers.

WILLIAM K. HARRISON, Jr.
Lieutenant-General, United
    States Army.
Senior Delegate,
United Nations Command
    Delegation.

TEMPORARY AGREEMENT SUPPLEMENTARY TO THE ARMISTICE
AGREEMENT

In order to meet the requirements of the disposition of the prisoners of war not for direct repatriation in accordance with the provisions of the Terms of Reference for Neutral Nations Repatriation Commission, the Commander-in-Chief, United Nations Command, on the one hand, and the Supreme Commander of the Korean

People's Army and the Commander of the Chinese People's Volunteers on the other hand, in pursuance of the provisions in paragraph 61, Article V, of the Agreement concerning a military armistice in Korea, agree to conclude the following Temporary Agreement supplementary to the Armistice Agreement:—

1. Under the provisions of paragraphs 4 and 5, Article II, of the Terms of Reference for Neutral Nations Repatriation Commission, the United Nations Command has the right to designate the area between the Military Demarcation Line and the eastern and southern boundaries of the Demilitarised Zone between the Imjin River on the south and the road leading south from Okum-ni on the north-east (the main road leading south-east from Panmunjom not included), as the area within which the United Nations Command will turn over the prisoners of war, who are not directly repatriated and whom the United Nations Command has the responsibility for keeping under its custody, to the Neutral Nations Repatriation Commission and the armed forces of India for custody. The United Nations Command shall, prior to the signing of the Armistice Agreement, inform the side of the Korean People's Army and the Chinese People's Volunteers of the approximate figures by nationality of such prisoners of war held in its custody.

2. If there are prisoners of war under their custody who request not to be directly repatriated, the Korean People's Army and the Chinese People's Volunteers have the right to designate the area in the vicinity of Panmunjom between the Military Demarcation Line and the western and northern boundaries of the Demilitarised Zone, as the area within which such prisoners of war will be turned over to the Neutral Nations Repatriation Commission and the armed forces of India for custody. After knowing that there are prisoners of war under their custody who request not to be directly repatriated, the Korean People's Army and the Chinese People's Volunteers shall inform the United Nations Command side of the approximate figures by nationality of such prisoners of war.

3. In accordance with paragraphs 8, 9 and 10, Article I, of the Armistice Agreement, the following paragraphs are hereby provided:—

(a) After the cease-fire comes into effect, unarmed personnel of each side shall be specfically authorised by the Military Armistice Commission to enter the above-mentioned area designated by their own side to perform necessary construction operations. None of such personnel shall remain in the above-mentioned areas upon the completion of the construction operations.

(b) A definite number of prisoners of war as decided upon by both sides, who are in the respective custody of both sides and who are not directly repatriated, shall be specifically authorised by the Military Armistice Commission to be escorted respectively by a certain number of armed forces of the detaining sides to the above-mentioned areas of custody designated respectively by both sides to be turned over to the Neutral Nations Repatriation Commission and the armed forces of India for custody. After the prisoners of war have been taken over, the armed forces of the detaining sides shall be withdrawn immediately from the areas of custody to the areas under the control of their own side.

(c) The personnel of the Neutral Nations Repatriation Commission and its subordinate bodies, the armed forces of India, the Red Cross Society of India, the explaining representatives and observation representatives of both sides, as well as the required material and equipment, for exercising the functions provided for in the Terms of Reference for Neutral Nations Repatriation Commission shall be specifically authorised by the Military Armistice Commission to have the complete freedom of movement to, from, and within the above-mentioned areas designated respectively by both sides for the custody of prisoners of war.

4. The provisions of sub-paragraph 3 (c) of this agreement shall not be construed as derogating from the privileges enjoyed by those personnel mentioned above under paragraph 11, Article I, of the Armistice Agreement.

5. This Agreement shall be abrogated upon the completion of the mission provided for in the Terms of Reference for Neutral Nations Repatriation Commission.

Done at Panmunjom, Korea, at 1000 hours on the 27th day of July, 1953, in English, Korean and Chinese, all texts being equally authentic.

KIM IL SUNG
Marshal, Democratic People's Republic of Korea.
Supreme Commander, Korean People's Army.

PENG TEH-HUAI
Commander, Chinese People's Volunteers

MARK W. CLARK
General, United States Army.
Commander-in-Chief, United Nations Command.

Present:

NAM IL
General, Korean People's Army.
Senior Delegate,
Delegation of the Korean
People's Army and the Chinese
People's Volunteers.

WILLIAM K. HARRISON, Jr.
Lieutenant-General, United
  States Army.
Senior Delegate,
United Nations Command
Delegation.

APPENDIX E

BIBLIOGRAPHY

1: OFFICIAL AND SEMI-OFFICIAL DOCUMENTS AND SOURCES

Appleman, Roy E., *South to the Naktong, North to the Yalu*, Office of the Chief of Military History, Department of the Army, United States Government Printing Office, Washington, 1961. A volume in the series 'United States Army in the Korean War'.

Barclay, C. N., *The First Commonwealth Division, The Story of British Commonwealth Land Forces in Korea, 1950-53*, Gale and Polden, Aldershot, 1954.

Bartlett, Norman (editor), *With the Australians in Korea*, Australian War Memorial, Canberra, 1954.

Cagle, Cmdr. M. C. and Manson, Cmdr. F. A., *The Sea War in Korea*, United States Naval Institute, Annapolis, 1957.

Congressional Record, 1950-54:

——, *Military Situation in the Far East*, Hearings before the Joint Senate Committee on Armed Services and Foreign Relations, 82nd Congress, 1st Session, USGPO, Washington, 1951. Cited as *Hearings* or 'MacArthur Hearings'. Indispensable reading for the basic issues of the war.

——, *Institute of Pacific Relations*, Hearings before the Sub-committee to investigate the Administration of the Internal Security Act of the Senate Judiciary Committee, 82nd Congress, 1st Session, USPGO, Washington, 1951-52.

——, *Interlocking Subversion in Government Departments*, Hearings before the same Sub-committee, 83rd Congress, 2nd Session, US-GPO, Washington, 1954-55. Hearings on the Korean War and Related Matters: Parts 21 (Mark Clark), 22 (Stratemeyer), 24 (Van Fleet), 25 (Almond), 26 (Joy). Known as the Jenner Sub-committee Hearings.

——, *The Korean War and Related Matters*, Report of the above Sub-committee hearings on the Korean War, 84th Congress, 1st Session, USGPO, Washington, 1955.

——, *Substance of Statements made at Wake Island Conference*, compiled by General Bradley. Prepared for the Senate Armed Services and Foreign Relations Committees, USGPO, Washington, 1951.

Congressional Record, 1950-54:

——, *The United States and the Korean Problem: Documents 1943-53*, Senate Document No. 74, Committee on Foreign Relations, USGPO, Washington, 1953.

Department of State:

——, *United States Relations with China, 1944-49*, USGPO, Washington, 1949. The 'China White Paper'.

——, *United States Policy in the Korean Crisis, 1950*, USGPO, Washington, 1950.

——, *United States Policy in the Korean Conflict, July 1950-February 1951*, USGPO, Washington, 1951.

——, *The Korean Problem at the Geneva Conference, April 26-June 15 1954*, USGPO, Washington, 1954.

——, *The Record on Korean Unification 1943-60.* Narrative Summary with Documents. USGPO, Washington, 1960.

Documents on International Affairs: 1949-50, 1951, 1952, 1953, Royal Institute of International Affairs, London, 1953-56.

Extract of Interim Historical Report, Korean War Crimes Division, cumulative to 30 June 1953, US Army, Korean Communications Zone, USGPO, Washington, 1953.

Foreign Office:

——, *Korea: a summary of developments in the Armistice negotiations and the prisoner of war camps.* Command 8596. HMSO, London, 1952.

——, *Korea: a summary of further developments in the military situation, armistice negotiations and prisoner of war camps up to January 1953.* Command 8793. HMSO, 1953.

——, *Special Report of the Unified Command on the Korean Agreement signed at Panmunjom, July 27 1953.* Command 8938. HMSO, 1953. (S/3079.)

Futrell, Robert F., *The United States Air Force in Korea, 1950-53*, Duell, Sloan & Pearce, New York, 1961.

Gugeler, Russell A., *Combat Actions in Korea*, Combat Forces Press, Washington, 1955.

Handbook of Korea by Chae Kyung Oh, Director, Office of Public Information, Republic of Korea. Pageant Press, New York, 1958.

House of Commons Debates, 1950-53.

Karig, Capt. W., Cagle, Cmdr. M. C., and Manson, Lt-Cmdr., *Battle Report, The War in Korea*, Farrar and Rinehart, New York, 1952.

Linklater, Eric, *Our Men in Korea*, HMSO, London, 1952.

Marshall, S. L. A., *Operation Punch and the Capture of Hill 440. Suwon, Korea, February 1951*, Operations Research Office, Johns Hopkins University, Baltimore, 1952.

——, *Commentary on Infantry Operations and Weapons Usage in Korea, Winter 1950-51*. Publishers as above, 1953.

Miller, J., Carroll, O. J., and Tackley, M. E., *Korea 1950*, a pictorial volume with commentary, OCMH, USGPO, Washington, 1952.

——, *Korea 1951-53*, companion volume to above, OCMH, USGPO, 1956.

Montross, Lynn, and Canzona, Capt. Nicholas, *US Marine Corps Operations in Korea*, Historical Branch, USMC HQ, USGPO, Washington, 1954-57. Vol. I, *The Pusan Perimeter*, Vol. II, *The Inchon-Seoul Operation*, Vol. III, *The Chosin Reservoir Campaign*. Vol. IV, *The East-Central Front*, (Montross, Lynn, Kuokka, Major Hubard, D., and Hicks, Major Norman, W.), 1962. This last volume describes USMC operations up until March 1952.

Odgers, G., *Across the Parallel*, The Australian 77th Squadron with the USAF in the Korean War, Heinemann, London, 1953.

Operations in Korea, US Military Academy, West Point, 1954.

POW—The Fight Continues After the Battle, Department of Defence, Washington, 1955. The report on the US prisoners in North Korea.

Report of The International Scientific Commission for the Investigation of the Facts concerning Bacterial Warfare in Korea and China, N. P., Peking, 1952.

Stewart, Col. James F. (Editor), *Airpower, The Decisive Force in Korea*, Van Nastrand, Princeton, 1957.

Survey of International Affairs, 1949-50, 1951, 1952, 1953, R.I.I.A., London, 1953-56.

Treatment of British Prisoners of War in Korea, Ministry of Defence, HMSO, 1955.

United States Air Force Operations in the Korean Conflict: Vol. I, 25 June-1 November 1950; Vol. II, 1 November 1950-30 June 1952; Vol. III, 1 July 1952-27 July 1953. Historical Division, USAF.

Westover, John G., *Combat Support in Korea*, Combat Forces Press, Washington, 1955.

2 : Memoirs, autobiographies, biographies, and personal records

Acheson, Dean, *Sketches from Life*, Hamish Hamilton, London, 1961.

Adams, Sherman, *Firsthand Report*, Harper, New York, 1961.

Anderson, Ellery, *Banner over Pusan*, Evans Brothers, London, 1960.

Attlee, Lord, *A Prime Minister Remembers*, Heinemann, London, 1961.

Baillie, Hugh, *High Tension*, Harper, New York, 1959.

Bevan, Aneurin, *In Place of Fear*, Heinemann, London, 1952.

Blair, Clay, *Beyond Courage*, Jarrolds, London, 1955.

Bryant, Sir Arthur and Field Marshal Lord Alanbrooke, *Triumph in the West, 1943-46*, Collins, London, 1959.

Clark, Gen. Mark, *From the Danube to the Yalu*, Harrap, London, 1954.

Crosby, Philip, *Three Winters Long*, Brown and Nolan, Dublin, 1955.

Cutforth, René, *Korean Reporter*, Allan Wingate, London, 1955.

Dalton, Lord, *High Tide and After*, Muller, London, 1962.

Davies, S. J., *In Spite of Dungeons*, Hodder and Stoughton, London, 1954.

Dean, Gen. William, *General Dean's Story*, as told to William Worden, Viking, New York, 1954.

Deane, Philip, *Captive in Korea*, Hamish Hamilton, London, 1953.

Donovan, Robert J., *Eisenhower: The Inside Story*, Harper, New York, 1956.

Drummond, Roscoe, and Coblentz, Gaston, *Duel at the Brink*, Weidenfeld and Nicolson, London, 1961.

Eden, Sir Anthony, *Full Circle*, Cassell, London, 1960.

Farrar-Hockley, A., *The Edge of the Sword*, Muller, London, 1954.

Forrestal, James, *The Forrestal Diaries*, edited by Walter Millis and E. S. Duffield, Viking, New York, 1951.

Goold-Adams, Richard, *The Time of Power*, Weidenfeld and Nicolson, London, 1962.

Gunther, John, *The Riddle of MacArthur*, Harper, New York, 1951.

Hess, Dean, *Battle Hymn*, Peter Davies, London, 1957.

Higgins, Marguerite, *War in Korea*, Lion Books, New York, 1952.

Holles, R. O., *Now Thrive the Armourers*, Harrap, London, 1952.

Hunt, Frazier, *The Untold Story of Douglas MacArthur*, Devon-Adair, New York, 1954.

Hunter, Leslie, *The Road to Brighton Pier*, Barker, London, 1959.

Jones, E. S., *No Rice for Rebels*, as told by R. F. Mathews, Bodley Head, London, 1956.

Joy, Adm. Turner, *How Communists Negotiate*, Macmillan, New York, 1955.

Kahn, E. J. Junior, *The Peculiar War*, Harper, New York, 1951.

Kenney, Gen. George, *The MacArthur I Know*, Duell, Sloan and Pierce, New York, 1951.

Kinne, Derek, *The Wooden Boxes*, Muller, London, 1955.

Lubell, Samuel, *The Revolt of the Moderates*, Harper, New York, 1956.

Panikkar, K. M., *In Two Chinas*, Allen and Unwin, London, 1955.

Ridgway, Gen. Matthew, B., *Soldier*, Harper, New York, 1956.

Rovere, Richard, *Senator Joe McCarthy*, Methuen, London, 1960.

Russ, Martin, *The Last Parallel*, Rinehart, New York, 1957.

Thompson, R. W., *Cry Korea*, Macdonald, London, 1951.

The Private Papers of Senator Vandenberg, edited by Arthur Vandenberg, Jr., with V. A. Morris, Gollancz, London, 1953.

Vatcher, William, *Panmunjom*, Praeger, New York, 1958.

Voorhees, M. B., *Korean Tales*, Simon and Schuster, New York, 1952.

White, William S., *The Taft Story*, Harper, New York, 1954.

Whitney, Maj.-Gen. Courtney, *MacArthur, His Rendezvous with History*, Knopf, New York, 1956.

Willoughby, Maj.-Gen. Charles, and John Chamberlain, *MacArthur 1941-1951*, Heinemann, London, 1956.

Truman, Harry S., *Memoirs*, Vol. II, *Years of Trial and Hope*, Hodder and Stoughton, London, 1956. *The extracts are used by permission of the publishers and International Co-operation Press Service Inc.*

3: SECONDARY SOURCES

Alsop, Joseph and Stewart, *The Reporter's Trade*, Reynal, New York, 1958.

Bell, Coral, *Negotiation From Strength*, Chatto & Windus, London, 1962.

Berger, Carl, *The Korean Knot, A Military-Political History*, University of Pennsylvania Press, Philadelphia, 1957.

Biderman, Albert D., *The March to Calumny*, Macmillan, New York, 1962.

Brodie, Bernard, *Strategy in the Missile Age*, The Rand Corporation, Princeton University Press, Princeton, 1959.

Von Clausewitz, *On War*, Modern Library ed., Random House, New York, 1943. Translated by O. J. Matthijis Jolles.

Clews, John, *The Communists' New Weapon — Germ Warfare*, Lincolns Praeger, London, 1952.

Dille, John, *Substitute for Victory*, Doubleday, New York, 1954.

Dupuy, R. E. and T. N., *Military Heritage of America*, McGraw Hill, New York, 1956.

Epstein, Leon D., *Britain — Uneasy Ally*, Chicago University Press, Chicago, 1954.

Fitzsimons, M. A., *The Foreign Policy of the Labour Government, 1945-51*, Notre Dame University Press, Notre Dame, 1953.

Gavin, Lt.-Gen. James, *War and Peace in the Space Age*, Hutchinson, London, 1959.

Goldman, Eric, *The Crucial Decade*, Harper, New York, 1956.

Goodrich, L. M., *Korea: A Study of US Policy in the UN*, Council on Foreign Relations, New York, 1956.

Graebner, Norman, *The New Isolationism*, Ronald, New York, 1956.

Green, W., and Fricker, J., *The Air Forces of the World*, Macdonald, London, 1958.

Gurney, Gene, *Five Down and Out*, Putnam, New York, 1958.

Hart, B. H. Liddell, *Deterrent of Defence*, Stevens, London, 1960.

Higgins, Trumbull, *Korea and the Fall of MacArthur*, O.U.P., New York, 1960.

Howard, Michael (editor), *Soldiers and Governments, Nine Studies in Civil and Military Relationships*, Eyre and Spottiswoode, London, 1957.

Hsieh, Alice Langley, *Communist China's Strategy in the Nuclear Era*, Prentice-Hall, Englewood Cliffs, N.J., 1962.

Hunter, Edward, *Brainwashing in Red China*, Vanguard Press, New York, 1951.

Huntingdon, Samuel, *The Soldier and the State*, Harvard University Press, Cambridge, 1957.

Kelley, S. J., *Professional Public Relations and Political Power*, Johns Hopkins Press, Baltimore, 1956.

Kennan, George, *American Diplomacy, 1900-1950*, Chicago University Press, Chicago, 1951.

——, *The Realities of American Foreign Policy*, Princeton University Press, Princeton, 1954.

Kinkaid, Eugene, *Why they Collaborated* (US Title: *In Every War But One*), Longmans, London, 1960.

Kissinger, Henry, *Nuclear Weapons and Foreign Policy*, Council on Foreign Relations, Harper, New York, 1957.

——, *The Necessity for Choice*, Chatto & Windus, London, 1960.

Leckie, Robert, *The March to Glory*, World Publishing Co., Ohio, 1960.

——, *Conflict: The History of the Korean War, 1950-53*, Putnam, New York, 1962.

Levi, Werner, *Modern China's Foreign Policy*, University of Minnesota Press, Minneapolis, 1953.

Lifton, Robert J., *Thought Reform*, Gollancz, London, 1960.

Mao Tse-tung, *Selected Works*, Vols. I-IV, Lawrence and Wishart, London, 1954-56.

Marshall, S. L. A., *The River and the Gauntlet*, Morrow, New York, 1953.

——, *Pork Chop Hill*, Morrow, New York, 1956.

McCune, George M., *Korea Today*, Harvard University Press, Cambridge, 1950.

Millis, Walter, with Harvey Mansfield and Harold Stein, *Arms and the State*, Twentieth Century Fund, New York, 1958.

Neustadt, Richard, *Presidential Power*, Wiley, New York-London, 1960.

Osgood, Robert E., *Limited War*, Chicago University Press, Chicago, 1957.

Poats, Rutherford Poats, *Decision in Korea*, MacBride, New York, 1954.

Rovere, Richard, *Affairs of State, The Eisenhower Years*, Farrar, Straus, New York, 1956.

——, with Schlesinger, Arthur, Jr., *The General and the President*, Farrar, Straus, New York, 1951.

Shonfield, Andrew, *British Economic Policy Since the War*, Penguin Books, London, 1959.

Spanier, John W., *The Truman-MacArthur Controversy and the Korean War*, Harvard University Press, Cambridge, 1959.

Stone, I. F., *The Hidden History of the Korean War*, Turnstile Press, London, 1952.

Thomas, R. C. W., *The War in Korea, 1950-53*, Gale and Polden, Aldershot, 1954.

White, William L., *The Captives of Korea*, Scribner, New York, 1956.

White, William S., *The Citadel*, Harper, New York, 1957.

Whiting, Allen S., *China Crosses the Yalu*, Macmillan, New York, 1960.

Willoughby, Maj.-Gen. Charles, *Aid and Comfort to the Enemy*, N.P., New York (?), 1953 (?).

4: Press and Periodical Articles

Air University Quarterly Review, Maxwell Air Force Base, Alabama.
——, 'Korea — An Opportunity Lost', Spring 1957.

Army, Washington, D.C.
——, 'MacArthur's Divided Command', Capt. Martin Blumenson, November 1956.
——, 'The Inchon Landing — Perilous Gamble or Exemplary Boldness?', Lt.-Col. James F. Schnabel, May 1959.
——, 'Korea Ten Years After', June 1960. Special number devoted to the war with many valuable articles and a feature, 'Korea on Maps'.

A.M.A. Archives of Neurology and Psychiatry, 'Communist Interrogation and Indoctrination of "Enemies of the State"', Hinkle and Wolf, August 1956.

Army Combat Forces Journal, Washington, D.C., 'Pork Chop,

Battle for a Korean Outpost', Col. William R. Kintner, March, 1955.

——, 'Psywar in Korea', Dale Storey, July 1952.

Atlantic Monthly, Boston, 'Our Mistakes in Korea', S. L. A. Marshall, September 1953.

Encounter, London, 'When the Army debunks the Army', William Peters, July 1960.

Foreign Affairs, New York, 'The 38th Parallel', Arthur L. Grey, April 1951.

(US) *Journal of Nervous and Mental Diseases*, 'The Germ Warfare Statements', G. Winokur, Vol 122, 1955.

Journal of the Royal United Services Institution, London, 'The Land Campaign in Korea', Maj.-Gen. B. A. Coad, No. 585, February 1952.

Life, New York.

——, 'A Policy of Boldness', John Foster Dulles, 19 May 1952.

——, 'The Truth About Korea, Gen. James Van Fleet, 11, 18 May 1953.

——, 'How Dulles Averted War', James Shepley, 16 January 1956.

——, 'Russians in Korea', Pawel Monat, 21 November 1960 (*Life International*).

Marine Corps Gazette, Quantico, Va., 'Red China on the Offensive,' Lynn Montross, July 1953.

Military Review, Fort Leavenworth, Kan., 'The Lost Corps', R. C. Cameron, Vol. 33, No. 2.

Orbis, Philadelphia.

——, 'The Lessons of Korea: War and the Power of Man', Alvin J. Cottrell and James E. Dougherty, Spring 1958.

——, 'Strategic Surprise in the Korean War', James E. Dougherty, Fall 1962.

Saturday Evening Post, Philadelphia, 'Why We Went to War in Korea', Beverly Smith, 10 November 1950.

Twentieth Century, London, 'The Privileged Sanctuary', G. F. Hudson, January 1951.

United States Naval Institute Proceedings, Annapolis, Maryland.

——, 'Inchon — The Analysis of a Gamble', M. C. Cagle, January 1954.

——, 'Errors of the Korean War', M. C. Cagle, March 1958.

ACKNOWLEDGEMENTS

The writer would like to express his thanks to the following who have helped him, and without whose assistance, in one way or another, this book could not have been written in its present form: Miss B. L. Coombs and Mr V. Rigby, Imperial War Museum Library; Miss N. Cresswell, Public Information Office, US Naval Forces Europe; Mr C. E. Dornbusch, New York Public Library; Miss L. Finch and Mr S. Yonge, Swansea Public Library; Lt.-Gen. W. K. Harrison; Mr R. W. Harvey, Office of the Assistant Secretary of Defence; Capt. Frank Manson, USN; Brig.-Gen. S. L. A. Marshall, USAR; Mr Tong Jin Park, former Chargé d'Affaires, Republic of Korea Embassy, London; Miss N. Philips, USIS Library, London; Miss P. Russell, Kensington Public Library; Gen. Matthew B. Ridgway; Brig. J. Stephenson, Royal United Services Institution Library; Maj.-Gen. Courtney Whitney; the China Quarterly; the Division of Naval History, USN; the Historical Division, USAF; the Historical Services Division, Office of the Chief of Military History, US Army; Industrial Research and Information Services Ltd; the War Office Library; the Library of the Royal Institution of International Affairs.

I should also like to thank Mr Alan Maclean of Macmillan & Co Ltd for his interest in the book since its inception, and Mr H. C. Waddhams and Mr B. P. Elkins for their care and patience during the drawing of the maps. My especial thanks to Mr Anthony Hartley for reading the manuscript.

Grateful acknowledgement is also made to the following publishers and individuals to quote from their publications: Roy E. Appleman, *South to the Naktong, North to the Yalu*, Office of the Chief of Military History, Department of the Army (Wash. DC); Bernard Brodie, *Strategy in the Missile Age*, The Rand Corporation, Princeton University Press; M. C. Cagle and F. A. Manson, *The Sea War in Korea*, US Naval Institute, Annapolis; Mark Clark, *From the Danube to the Yalu*, Harrap; Anthony Farrar Hockley, *The Edge of the Sword*, Muller; George Kennan, *American Diplomacy 1900-1950*, Chicago University Press; *Selected Works of Mao Tse-tung*, Laurence and Wishart; Walter Millis, *Arms and the State*, The Twentieth Century Fund, New York; Robert Neustadt, *Presidential Power*, Wiley, New York-London; Harry S. Truman, *Years of Trial and Hope*, Hodder and Stoughton; Allen S. Whiting, *China Crosses the Yalu*, The Macmillan Co. New York; Courtney Whitney, *MacArthur, His Rendezvous with Destiny*, Knopf.

Kensington, Sept. 1963.

GLOSSARY

CCF	Chinese Communist Forces
CINCFE	Commander in Chief, Far East
CINCUNC	Commander in Chief, United Nations Command
CINCPAC	Commander in Chief, Pacific
COMNAVFE	Commander Naval Forces Far East
CPV	Chinese People's Volunteers
CV	Aircraft Carrier
DPRK	Democratic People's Republic of Korea
DMZ	Demilitarised Zone
EUSAK	Eighth US Army in Korea
FAF	Fifth Air Force
FEAF	Far East Air Forces
GCI	Ground Control Intercept
IADL	International Association of Democratic Lawyers
ICRC	International Committee of the Red Cross
ISC	International Scientific Commission
JCS	Joint Chiefs of Staff
KMAG	Korean Military Advisory Group
KMT	Kuomintang
KPA	Korean People's Army
LCVP	Landing Craft, Vehicle and Personnel
LST	Landing Ship Tank
LVT	Landing Vehicle Tracked
MAC	Military Armistice Commission
MLR	Main Line of Resistance
MSR	Main Supply Route
NAW	National Assembly of Women
NK	North Korean
NNRC	Neutral Nations Repatriation Commission
NNSC	Neutral Nations Supervisory Commission
PRC	People's Republic of China
RCT	Regimental Combat Team
ROK (A)	Republic of Korea (Army)
TF	Task Force
TG	Task Group
UNC	United Nations Command
WIDF	Women's International Democratic Federation
WPC	World Peace Council

INDEX

Acheson, Dean; negotiation from strength, xiii, 280-1, 305-6; ' defence perimeter ' speech, 18, 64, 280; reaction to Korean invasion, 21-2; policy, 56, 59; chief target of Republican Opposition, 60-1, 173, 201; miscalculates Peking's intentions, 64-5, 111-12, 114; reaction to Chinese intervention, 132, 151, 166-167, 168-9, 202-4; on Korean unification, 100-1, 262; on Taft proposals, 201-2; opposes UN seat for China, 204; on MacArthur's recall, 214, 216-17; at MacArthur Hearings, 275-6, 279-80, 282; liability to Democrats in 1952 campaign, 386; Kennedy adviser, 450

Adams, Governor Sherman, 392, 399, 419-20

Air warfare: USAF's role in US strategy, 14-15; carpet bombing ineffective on Naktong front, 46, 48; interdiction v. close support, 49-51; North Korean Air Force (NKAF), 37; FEAF Bomber Command, 49; FAF, 49, 51; FEAF Joint Operations Centre at Taegu, 50; Sinuiju strike, Nov. 1950, 130-1, April 1951, 193-4; USAF nomenclature, 276n; ' MIG Alley ', 311, 372; interdiction campaign, 372-8; Chinese Communist Air Force (CCAF), 371, 374; F-86 and MIG-15, 372 and n; Daylight bombing of NK airfields stopped, 373-4; Operation STRANGLE, 376-7; strategic targets, 378-82; aircraft losses, 382-3

Alanbrooke, see Brooke, Sir Alan

Almond, Maj.-Gen. Edward, 72, 79, 91, 125, 127, 130; sanguine outlook, 160, 163, 165; after MacArthur's recall, 220-1, 248, 256

Anderson, Vernice, 119

Andreen, Dr Andrea, 360

Aragon, Louis, 360

Armistice Agreement, 430-1, 462 ff; Military Armistice Commission (MAC), 311, 452-3

Atomic bombs: USSR detonates atomic weapon, 56; and thermonuclear weapon, 435; Mao Tse-tung on, 141; possible threat by Truman, 166-7, 170; and Stockholm petition, 347-52; Eisenhower considers use to end war, 402

Attlee, C. R., 33-5, 121n, 143, 144-5; Truman-Attlee talks, 168-71; and Bevan's resignation, 233 ff; attacks WPC, 350; assents to air attacks on Manchuria in certain circumstances, 260-1

Austin, Warren, 99, 103-4

Australian troops, 109, 128, 457

Avon, see Eden, Sir Anthony

Bacteriological warfare, 307, 338, 352 ff; International Scientific Commission (ISC), 354 ff; confessions, 355 ff; how extracted, 361-2

Baron, Alexander, 232-3

Barr, Maj.-Gen. David G., 79, 273

Belgian troops, 457

Bell, Coral, 280

Bernal, J. D., 360

Bevan, Aneurin, 170, 171; resignation, 235 ff

Bevin, Ernest, 102, 121n, 133, 146-7, 236

Blake, George, 110, 329, 407

Bley, Maj., 360-1

Bradley, Gen. of the Army, Omar, 22-3, 118-20; reaction to Chinese intervention, 131-2, 137, 151; on Taft proposals, 201-2; on recalling MacArthur, 214, 216-17; at MacArthur Hearings, 273-5, 281; in Korea, Oct. 1951, 366; and 1952

Bradley—*Cont.*
elections, 386-7, 402; retirement, 404

Brainwashing, *see* Indoctrination

Brecht, Bertold, 360

Bridges, Senator Styles, 57

Briscoe, Vice-Admiral R. P., 365

British-China Friendship Association, 354, 358

Brodie, Bernard, 112, 303-4

Brogan, D. W., 58

Brooke, F. M., Sir Allan, CIGS (Viscount Alanbrooke), 71

Bunker, Col. ' Larry ', 71, 118

Burchett, Wilfred, 342, 356

Burke, Rear-Admiral Arleigh, 290

Butler, Senator Hugh, 61

Butler, R. A., 168

Cagle, Cmdr. M.C., 96, 176

Cain, Senator, 101

Canadian troops, 457

Capps, Lt.-Cmdr. Arlie, 80

Carne, Lt.-Col., V.C., 250

Chang, Col., 285, 290

Chang, John, 21, 441

Chang Pyong San, Maj.-Gen., 290

Chen Yi, Gen., 109, 139, 451

Chiang Kai-shek, Generalissimo: offers troops, 27; collapse of KMT, 61-3; and US politics, 56-8, 63-4, 66; flees to Formosa, 62; talks with MacArthur, 73; *and see* Formosa

China, Nationalist, i.e. *see* Chiang Kai-shek *and* Formosa

China, People's Republic of (PRC): motives for supporting Russian moves in Korea, 18-19; proclaimed, 62; *k'ang yi* and *fan tuei*, 105-6, 141; ' Hate America ' campaign, 105-6; reaction to invasion of N. Korea, 106-9; attitude to US policy, 112-14; strategic doctrines, 139-40; ' Resist America, Aid Korea ' campaign, 141-2; demands Formosa and withdrawal from Korea, 171-2, 202-203; thought reform in, 338-40; ends deadlock, 406; emerges as a great power, 442-3; *and see* Chinese Communist Forces

Chinese Communist Forces (CCF); 4th Field Army, 20, 104, 109; cross Yalu, 110; in action, 129; CPV, 131; strength of, 133-4, 136, 190*n*, 245-6,

Chinese Communist Forces—*Cont.*
406; tactics, 138, 156; organisation and doctrine, 138-41; at the Chongchon, 155 *ff*; take Seoul, 177; strategy, 188-90; Spring 1951 offensives, 243 *ff*; politico-military strategy, 1951-3, 301 *ff*; casualties, 251, 255, 258, 442-3, 461; prisoners, 317; post-war state, 442

Chinese People's Volunteers (CPV), 131; *and see* Chinese Communist Forces

Choi Duk Shin, Maj.-Gen., 423

Chongchon, River, 129, 155-60, 174

Chotiner, Murray, 392

Chou En-lai, 76, 107; aims to unify Korea, 171-2; motives to end war, 406-7

Chung Hee Park, 441

Chung Il Kwon, Lt.-Gen., 39

Church, Maj.-Gen., John H., 42

Churchill, Sir Winston, 145, 146, 168, 260-1; and plans to end war, 306, 419

Chu Teh, Gen., 138-9

Clark, Lt. Eugene, 84, 86

Clark, Gen. Mark, 302-3; takes over SCAP, 323-4, 402, 421-2; rebukes Rhee, 426-7; signs Armistice, 432-3; in retirement, 450

Clausewitz, Karl von, xi, xiii-xiv

Clews, John, 359

Coad, Brig. B. A., 128

Cole, G. D. H., 233

Collins, Gen., US Army Chief of Staff, 22-3, 81, 99; visits Tokyo, 161, and the front, 179, 183; on MacArthur's dismissal, 216; at MacArthur Hearings, 273, 275

Colombian troops, 457

Colson, Brig.-Gen., 324

Commonwealth Brigade, 109, 128, 129, 249-50

Commonwealth Division, 299*n*

Communist bloc: claim US and UN action illegal, 33; US attitude to, 55 *ff*; Sino-Soviet policy on Korea, 76, 104, 107; possibility of intervention by, 99-100, 103, 108

Condron, Andrew, 346

Connolly, Senator, 205, 262

Containment policy, xii *ff*, 29-30, 55-6, 59, 100, 169-70; and negotiation

Containment policy—*Cont.*
  from strength, 280-1; in retrospect, 443 *ff*; President Kennedy's version, 450
Coulter, Maj.-Gen. John B., 53
Craigie, Maj.-Gen. Lawrence, 290
Cuba, xvi
Cutforth, Rene, 177, 190-1, 194

Dalton, Hugh: and Bevan's resignation, 236
Davies, Ernest, 146
Davies, Chaplain S. J., 336, 342
Dean, Arthur, 437-8
Dean, Maj.-Gen. William F., 37, 38; and fall of Taejon, 40-1; in captivity, 334
Deane, Philip, 36, 39-41, 110, 330, 337, 407
Dewey, Thomas, 24, 201
Diller, Brig.-Gen. Le Grande, 70
Dodd, Brig.-Gen., 323-4
Doyle, Rear-Admiral James H., 79, 81, 127, 166
Dulles, John Foster, 23, 56; on containment policy, 100; and evolution of liberation policy, 283, 387-391; supports NATO, 201; 'Massive Retaliation', 390-1, 404-5, 417-20; and the 1952 elections, 394; 'brinkmanship', 418-19; and Rhee, 425
Dupuy, T. N. and R. E., 174

Eberle, Maj.-Gen. George, 125
Eden, Sir Anthony (Earl of Avon), 98, 306
Ehrenberg, Ilya, 360
Eisenhower, Gen. Dwight W., 14; as Supreme Commander, NATO, 172, 202; and 1952 elections, 387, 390, 392 *ff*; and Nixon, 395-6; visits Korea, 399, 402-3; first Eisenhower Administration, 404-5, 417 *ff*, 425
Enoch, Lt., 355-6, 361
Ethiopian troops, 457
EUSAK (Eighth US Army in Korea), 38; morale, 39-40, 176-7, 181; role in advance to the Yalu, 103; at end of war, 408
Evans, Col. Andrew, 361

Fadeyev, Alexander, 348, 360

Farrar-Hockley, Anthony: on the Imjin, 249; in captivity, 334, 342
Fechteler, Admiral William F., 285*n*
Felton, Monica, 341-2, 353
Finletter, Thomas, 22; Finletter Commission, 15, 56
Formosa: neutralised, 23-5, 31; MacArthur and, 63, 66, 179-81; British attitude to, 144; Communist China demands, 171-2, 202-3; US military aid for, 204; 'de-neutralised', 405, 443; *and see* Chiang Kai-shek *and* Martin, Joe
Forrestal, James, 67, 70
Freedman, Max, 110
Freeman, John, 237
French troops, 187, 457

Gaitskell, Hugh: and British rearmament, 233 *ff*
Gaster, Jack, 341-2, 354
Gavin, James, 448
Gay, Maj.-Gen. Hobart R., 39
Geneva Conference of 1954, 315, 437, 439
Germany, West, 172
Gloucestershire Regiment, 1st Battn., 249-50
Greek troops, 185*n*, 457
Gromyko, A. A., 284

Hagerty, James, 402
Hamblen, Col., 118-19
Harriman, Averell, 26, 74, 118, 167, 214
Harrison, Lt.-Gen. William K., 325-7, 415; signs Armistice, 432; in retirement, 450
Hickenlooper, Senator, 278
Hickey, Maj.-Gen. Doyle, 79*n*, 125
Higgins, Marguerite, 40
Hirohito, Emperor of Japan, 223
Hiss, Alger, 56, 64
Hodes, Maj.-Gen. Henry, 290, 296
Hoover, Herbert: 'Gibraltar of Western civilisation' speech, 173, 198, 199; after MacArthur's recall, 221, 227
Hopkinson, Henry, 98
Hsieh Fang, Maj.-Gen., 290
Huang Hua, 437
Huff, Col. Sid, 71-2, 220
Hughes, Emmet, 399

Huntington, Samuel, 116, 387

Inchon landing, 53, 77 ff; capture of Inchon, 88, Kimpo airport, 89, and Seoul, 92; assessment of, 95-7; 'Operation Common Knowledge', 96; ultimate effects, 97
Indoctrination, 307-8, 328-9, 334 ff; 'The Lenient Policy', 335-6; brainwashing, 329n, 337-8; and thought reform, in China, 338-40; results, 344-6
International Association of Democratic Lawyers (IADL), 341, 349, 353-4

Japan, 31, 223
Jebb, Sir Gladwyn, 203
Jenner, Senator William, 222
Jessup, Philip, 22, 63, 65, 118-19
Johnson, Dr Hewlett, 358, 360
Johnson, Louis, 18, 22, 73, 76
Johnson, Senator Lyndon, 269
Joint Strategic Plans and Operations Group, 79
Joliot-Curie, Prof. J.-F.: and Soviet 'peace', offensive, 348, 353, 360
Jonkel, Jon, 198
Joy, Vice-Admiral Turner, COM-NAVFE, 72, 80, 125, 289 ff, 324-5, 418; death, 450

Kaesong talks, 289 ff; agenda, 292; and see Panmunjom
Kang Kon, Lt.-Gen., 43
Kean, Maj.-Gen. William B., 39, 51
Keiser, Maj.-Gen. L. B., 155, 157-9
Kennan, George, 29, 100, 280
Kennedy, President J. F., xvi, 450
Kenney, George, 70
Kim, Lt.-Col., 285
Kim Il Sung, 4, 6, 10-11; becomes Premier of North Korea, 13; as C.-in-C., 43, 245, 285, 306; later history, 450-1
Kinkead, Eugene, 329, 337, 345-6
Kinne, Derek, 332, 334, 342-4
Kinney, Col. Jack, 285
Ki Sok-Bok, 437
Kissinger, Henry, xvi, 303, 350, 447

Kniss, Lt., 356-7, 361
Knowland, Senator, 57; on Formosa,

Knowland, Senator—Cont.
63; on advance into N. Korea, 100; in 1952 elections, 394; appeals to Rhee, 426
Korea: general description, 7-8; history, 8-9; 38th Parallel, 9-10; US-Soviet Joint Commission on Trusteeship, 11, 12; UN unification proposals, Oct. 1950, 98 ff; devastation of, 194, 440-1; demarcation line, 430-1; reunification proposals, 439-440; present situation, 451-2
Korea, Democratic People's Republic of (North Korea, DPRK): invades S. Korea, 3-7; motives, 18-20; Korean National Democratic Front, 11-12; proclamation of, 13; Korean Communist parties, 17; navy, 17; air force, 17, 37; Security Police, 42-3; 94; atrocities in S. Korea, 93-4; partisans and agents in, 369; post-war recovery, 441; post-war purges, 450-451; and see Korean People's Army
Korea, Republic of (South Korea, ROK): Interim Government, 11; republic proclaimed, 13; Communist subversion, 15-16; state of army, 16; army placed under UNC, 38-9; Rhee regime, 93; US and UN aid to, 422n, 441; post-war conditions, 441-2; casualties, 441, 460
Korean Liaison Office, 133
Korean Military Advisory Group (KMAG), 16, 22, 25
Korean People's Army (KPA), 16-17; first clash with US troops at Osan, 37-8; tactics used, 40; casualties, 43-4, 440, 461; virtual destruction of, 94-5; ground strength, 48; joint KPA-CPV HQ, 139, 245
Korean Volunteer Corps (KVC), 11, 17, 19, 106
Korean War, main events: invasion begins, 3-7; US troops land, 36-7; Battle of the Kum, 39-40; Taejon, 40; Pusan Perimeter, 43 ff; Naktong Bulge, 1st Battle, 45-6, 2nd, 52; Inchon landing, 85-8; UN capture Seoul, 92, cross 38th Parallel, 104, and take Pyongyang, 123; Wonsan landing, 127; Yalu reached, 129; Chinese at Unsan, 129; 'General Winter', 135; Chongchon, 155-60,

Korean War—*Cont.*
174; Chosin, retreat from, 161-6; Ridgway takes over, 176; Chinese take Seoul, 177; counter-offensive begins, 185; Chipyong-ni crossroads and the 'Wonju shoot', 187; UN retake Seoul, 191, and re-cross Parallel, 192; Chinese first Spring offensive (1951), 243; Solma-ri, 250; second Spring offensive, 252; counter-offensive, 256; truce talks begin, 284, Heartbreak Ridge, 299; psychological warfare, 408-9, 415; Outpost Pork Chop, 409-14; Kumsong salient, 428-9; Armistice, 433-4; Treaty signed, 435

Laos crisis (1961), 110
Lattimore, Owen, 63, 65
Lee Sang Cho, Maj.-Gen., 290, 296, 316-17, 322
Léger, Fernand, 360
Leviero, Anthony, 121-2
Libby, Rear-Admiral, 317, 320
Liddell Hart, B. H., 53
Lie, Trygve, 262, 284
Lifton, Robert, 338n, 339
Lin Piao, Gen., 109, 139, 245, 451
Lippmann, Walter, 229
Lodge, Senator Henry Cabot, 201
Lovett, Robert, 386
Lu Chen Hen, Dr, 360
Luxembourg troops, 457

MacArthur, Gen. Douglas, 15, 22, 23; bombs N. Korean targets, 25; appointed CINCUNC, 35; decides on Inchon landing, 53, 77 ff; and the 'great conspiracy', 58; attacks US Formosa policy, 63, 66; 'the MacArthur problem', 66 ff; early career, 68-9; on world affairs, 69-70; anti-Navy feeling, 70; SCAP years, 71; the MacArthur cult, 71; defence talks with Chiang, 73; VFW letter, 74-5, 116, 118; defends CHROMITE, 82-3; takes Seoul and restores Rhee there, 91-3; gambles at Inchon, 95-6; directives on crossing the Parallel, 99-100, 102-3, 108; demands KPA's surrender, 104, 108-9; underestimates Truman, 116-17; discounts Communist intervention, 118-20;

MacArthur—*cont.*
plans amphibious landing at Wonsan, 124; retains direct command of X Corps, 124-5, 127, 160, 165; disregards directives by advance to the Yalu, 127-8; bombs frontier bridges, 130-1; continues to the Yalu despite Chinese intervention, 134-7, 147 ff; 'Home by Christmas' message, 148, 150; why not halted from Washington, 150-2; 'an entirely new war', 157; forced to retreat, 160; blames directives, 160-1, 174-5; criticism of, 173-4; *hubris*, 175-6; demands Formosan troops, bombing and blockade of China, 179-81; annihilation bogey, 181-2; by-passed by Truman, 183; accepts the inevitable, 183-4; 'Die for Tie' statement, 188-9, 207-8; radio-active waste plan, 206-7; issues 'my military appraisal', 209-11; the Taft-MacArthur alliance, 211; supports Joe Martin, 212-13; decision to dismiss, 214 ff; returns to USA, 223-4; addresses Congress, 224-7; MacArthur Hearings, 264 ff; and USSR, 269-70; consulted by President Eisenhower, 405; in retirement, 449; *and see* Wake Island Conference

McCarthy, Senator Joe, 59, 65, 222, 235, 386, 394, 400
McMahon, Senator, Brien, 114, 269-71
Mahurin, Col. Walker, 361-3
Malenkov, Georgi, 433, 435
Malik, Jacob, 21, 76, 101; cease-fire proposal, 106, 262-3
Mao Tse-tung, 30, 62-3; discounts Western goodwill, 113n; on strategy, 138 ff, 244 ff, 307 ff; on the atomic bomb, 141
Marquat, Maj.-Gen., 71-2
Marshall, Gen. George, 62, 76, 103; reaction to Chinese intervention, 151, 166; on Taft proposals, 201-2; 'Formosa must never come under Communists', 204; on recalling MacArthur, 214-16; at MacArthur Hearings, 273, 278-80; replaced 386
Marshall, S. L. A., 133-4, 159, 174
Martin, Joe, 201, 212-13, 215, 221-2
Matthews, Francis, 22, 75, 76

Mayo, Dr Charles, 361-2
Milburn, Maj.-Gen. Frank W., 53
Military Armistice Council (MAC), 311, 452-3
Millikin, Senator Eugene, 197
Morrison, Herbert, 236-8
Morse, Senator Wayne, 269
Muccio, John, 4, 118
Mundt, Senator Karl, 394
Murray, Col. James, 285

Nam Il, Gen., 245, 290-1, 293, 322, 326; signs Armistice, 432; NK Foreign Minister, 450-1
Napalm, 194
National Assembly of Women (NAW), 341, 353
National Security Council: directive on N. Korea, 99-100; and JCS 16-point contingency paper on war with China, 182, 225n, 265
Naval war, 17, 37, 79, 84-6, 193; blockade, 366-70; siege of Wonsan, Hungnam and Sagjim, 367 ff
Needham, Dr Joseph, 354, 360
Nehru, Jawaharlal, 417, 419
Netherlands troops, 457
Neutral Nations Supervisory Commission (NNSC), 312-15, 452-3
New Statesman, 143-4, 232-3
New Zealand troops, 457
Nieh Jung-chen, Gen., 106-7
Nitze, Paul, 280
Nixon, Senator Richard, 197, 222, 392, 394, 400; 'expenses' fund, 395-6; 425
North Atlantic Treaty Organisation (NATO), 30-1; and German rearmament, 172; Eisenhower as Supreme Commander, 172; the 'Great Debate', 172-3, 196 ff; European bases and USAF, 276-7; effect of Korean war on, 445-6

O'Donnell, Maj.-Gen. Emmett, 277, 370
O'Neal, Lt., 356-7, 361
Operations: BLUEHEARTS, 78; CHROMITE, 79 ff; TAILBOARD, 124 ff; WOLFHOUND, 183, 185; THUNDERBOLT, 185-6; PUNCH, 185; ROUNDUP, 186; KILLER, 187-8; RIPPER, 191; RUGGED, 194; PILEDRIVER, 257; STRANGLE,

Operations—Cont.
298, 376-7; SHOWDOWN, 386

Pace, Frank, 22, 118-19, 217-18
Paik Sun Yup, Maj.-Gen., 290
Pak Hen Yen, 352-3, 355, 450
Panikkar, K. M., 106-7, 110-11, 113
Panmunjom talks, 294 ff; demarcation line, 297-8, 300-1; 30-day cease-fire, 300-1, 305; agreement reached, 406; present-day tourist attraction, 452-53; and see Armistice agreement; Neutral Nations Supervisory Commission; Repatriation, voluntary
Pearson, Lester, 261-2
Peng Teh-huai, Gen., 139, 245, 285, 451
Philippine troops, 185n, 457
Pusan: defence of, 26; Perimeter, 43-53
Pyongyang, 123

Quinn, Lt., 355-7, 361

Radford, Admiral Arthur, 118, 402, 404
Rau, Sir Benegal, 203
Razuvayev, Lt.-Gen. Vladimir, 245
Refugee problem, 42, 177, 424
Repatriation, voluntary, 311, 315 ff; screening proposal, 319, 321, and results, 325; Koje revolt, 320-4; Indian compromise plan, 403, 406-7; Nam Il's proposals, 414-16; Neutral Nations Repatriation Commission (NNRC), 416-17, 438-9; agreement reached, 417; Rhee and Korean non-repatriates, 420, 421-3, 425, 427; 'Big Switch', 436; final release of non-repatriates, 438-9
Rhee, Dr Syngman, 4, 6-7, 10; becomes President, 13; restored to Seoul, 93; anti-Armistice campaign, 284, 416, 420, 421 ff; releases non-repatriates, 425; overthrown, 441; in Hawaii, 450
Ridgway, Lt.-Gen. Matthew, 176-7; cures 'bug-out fever', 183-4, 190-1, 387; new tactics of, 186, 206, 208; succeeds MacArthur, 195, 217-21; and Kaesong talks, 290 ff; and Panmunjom, 300-1; against further advance, 303; to SHAPE, 323; retirement, 449

Robertson, Walter, 426-7

Rusk, Dean, 21, 22, 118-19, 204

Russ, Sgt. Martin, 307-8, 408

Russell, Senator Richard, 205, 264-5

Salisbury, 5th Marquess of, 145-6

Salter, James, 383-4

Sartre, Jean-Paul, 348, 360

Schnabel, Lt.-Col., 95

Schwable, Col., 360-1

Seoul, 4, 7, 92, 93, 177, 191

Service, John Stewart, 63

Shapiro, Michael, 342

Shawcross, Sir Hartley, 260, 342

Shepherd, Lt.-Gen., 78, 83

Sherman, Admiral, 22-3, 81, 82, 83, 99; on MacArthur's dismissal, 216; at MacArthur Hearings, 275, 282; death, 285n

Shinwell, Emmanuel, 232

Short, Dewey, 227

Short, Joe, 217-18

Shtykov, Col.-Gen. Terenty, 245

Silverman, Sidney, 350

Smith, Gen. Bedell, 132, 183

Smith, Lt.-Col. Charles B., 37; Task Force Smith, 37-8

Smith, Maj.-Gen. O. P. 78, 81, 84, 91, 135, 162, 164

Snyder, John, 215

Soo Young Lee, Col., 285

South African troops, 457, 460

Spanier, John, 121

Sparkman, Senator John, 394

Speakeman, Pte. William, V.C., 299

Stassen, Henry, 201

Stevenson, Adlai, 387, 392 ff

Stone, I. F., 121

Story, Lt.-Col., 72, 118, 223

Stratemeyer, Lt.-Gen. G. E., 25, 46, 72, 221

Struble, Vice-Admiral A. D., 79-80, 84, 127

Sun Yat-sen, Mrs, 360

Supreme Commander for the Allied Powers (SCAP), 67-8

Supreme HQ Allied Powers in Europe (SHAPE), 30

Taejon Agreement, 38-9, 435

Taft, Senator Robert A., 57-8, 61; on Formosa, 63, and Korea, 65-6; and the 'Great Debate', 198 ff; after MacArthur's dismissal, 221; and

Taft—Cont.
Bevan compared, 241-2; defeat in Republican convention, 387; in 1952 election, 394; death, 426

Taylor, Gen. Maxwell D., 407, 413-414, 428, 450

Teng Hua, Lt.-Gen., 290

Thai troops, 451, 457

Thimayya, Brig.-Gen. K. S., 438

Thompson, R. W., 90, 231

Tokchon gap, 157

Trudeau, Maj.-Gen. Arthur, 410, 412-413

Truman, Harry S., 21, 22; orders intervention in South Korea, 23, and action in North Korea, 26-7; neutralises Formosa, 24-5; 'police action', 26; commits ground troops to action, 27-8; his assessment of Korea's significance, 30-1; opposition to his foreign policy, 30, 56, 59-61; refuses aid to Chiang, 63, 73; relations with MacArthur, 74-5, 115-116, 150-2; miscalculates Peking's intentions, 112, 132; atomic bomb threat, 166-7, 170; on extreme Republicans, 170; on 'rectifying aggression', 182-3; on recrossing Parallel, 192; decides to fire MacArthur, 211, 214 ff; revises Korean objectives, 257-8; and Truce talks, 305; and 1952 elections, 386-7, 397; policy in retrospect, 446 ff, in retirement, 449; and see Wake Island Conference

Tsai, Lt.-Col., 285, 290

Turkish troops, 157, 331, 451, 457

Tydings, Millard, 198

Union of Soviet Socialist Republics (USSR): and Korean war, 19-20, 245n; promise non-intervention, 26; first atomic bomb test by, 56; US and, 99-100, 103, 116, 119-20, 121; indoctrination techniques, 338-9; and bacteriological warfare, 359-60; Stalin's death, 406; detonates hydrogen bomb, 435; and see Communist bloc

United Kingdom: places warships under MacArthur, 24-5; supports UN resolution, 33; troops from, 44, 49, 51, 53, 128, 249-50, 457; reaction to Chinese intervention, 143 ff, 167-

United Kingdom—*Cont.*
168; attitude to Formosa, 144; against war on China, 203; anti-Americanism, 230-3; defence expenditure, 233-4; Armed Forces, 234*n*; moves closer to USA, 260-1; casualties, 460

United Nations Assembly: resolution on Korean unification, 101-2, 108; cease-fire proposal, 202; condemns Chinese aggression, 203-4; embargo on trade with China, 259-60

United Nations Command (UNC): contributions by members to, 32-3, 457; set up, 35; role of navy, 37, 84-86, 193; strength, 43-4, 48-9, 148, 184-5, 246, 298-9, 406; firepower *v.* manpower, 53, 90; lack of military intelligence, 133-4; casualties, 176, 460-1; prisoners, 316; begins counter-offensive, 185; Geneva 'Declaration by the Sixteen', 1954, 436, 439; present organisation, 451-2

United Nations Commissions: on Korea (UNCOK), 6, 13; Temporary, on Korea (UNTCOK), 12; for the Unification and Rehabilitation of Korea (UNCURK), 109; Korean Rehabilitation Agency (UNKRA), 422

United Nations Security Council: calls for cease-fire, 21-2; resolves to use force, 24; discusses cease-fire, 171; effect of Russia's absence, 446-447

United States of America: attitude to war, x *ff*; forces withdrawn from Korea, 13-15; economic aid, 16; decision to intervene, 23; statistics of forces in Korea, 32-3; first landing in Korea, 36-7; bi-partisan foreign policy, 56; policy towards China, 56; 'great conspiracy' myth, 57-8; opposition to Truman-Acheson policies, 59-61; China Lobby demonology, 63-4; McCarthyism, 65; directives on possible Sino-Soviet intervention, 99-100, 103, 108; miscalculate Chinese position, 110-14, 120-1; Republican gains (1950), 132, 196-8; from liberation to containment, 169-170; expects world war, 172; impact of retreat on, 173; reaction to MacArthur's dismissal, 221-3,

United States of America—*cont.*
227-9; presidential election (1952), 327 386 *ff*; defence expenditure, 391*n*; effect of war on, 443-5; official casualty list, 461; *and see* National Security Council

United States Army Forces in Korea (USAFIK), 32-3, 37

Vandenberg, Gen., 22-3; visits the front, 179, 183; at MacArthur Hearings, 276-8, 282; death, 449

Vandenberg, Senator Arthur, 56-7

Van Fleet, Lt.-Gen. James, 243, 248, 250, 251, 258-9; restricts operations to battalion strength, 300-2; in retirement, 450

Vaughan, Maj.-Gen. Harry, 118, 224

Vincent, John Carter, 63

Vyshinsky, A. Ya., 104, 107, 403

Wake Island Conference (1950), 115-122; those present, 118; 'stenographic eavesdropping', 119; MacArthur discounts Communist intervention, 118-20

Walker, Lt.-Gen. Walton H., 38-9, 41-48, 72, 84, 124-5, 184; rivalry with Almond, 125; in advance to Yalu, 128-9; on Chinese offensive, 157-9; killed, 176, 449

Wedermeyer, Gen. Albert, 14, 273

Weyland, Maj.-Gen. O. P., 95, 221*n*

Wherry, Senator, 57, 61, 173, 199, 205

White, Williams S., 60, 65

Whitney, Maj.-Gen. Courtney, 25, 72, 118, 122, 174-5, 220, 221*n*

Willoughby, Maj.-Gen. Charles, 71-2, 174, 175, 221*n*

Wilson, Charles E., 402, 404

Wilson, Harold, 236-7

Winnington, Alan, 342, 356

Women's International Democratic Federation (WIDF), 349, 353

World Peace Council (WPC): Stockholm Peace Appeal, 340-1, 347-51; and bacteriological warfare, 353-4, 358

Wright, Maj.-Gen. Edwin, 125

Wu Hsui-chan, Gen., 171

Younger, Kenneth, 107-8

Zhukov-Verezhnikov, Dr, 354, 359-60